# ANNUAL REVIEW OF IRISH LAW 1992

# Annual Review of Irish Law 1992

Raymond Byrne
B.C.L., LL.M., Barrister-at-Law
Lecturer in Law, Dublin City University

William Binchy
B.A., B.C.L., LL.M., Barrister-at-Law
Regius Professor of Laws, Trinity College Dublin
Formerly, Research Counsellor, The Law Reform Commission

THE ROUND HALL PRESS
DUBLIN

The typesetting for this book was produced by
Gilbert Gough Typesetting, Dublin for
THE ROUND HALL PRESS
Kill Lane, Blackrock, Co. Dublin
*and in North America by*
THE ROUND HALL PRESS
c/o International Specialized Book Services,
5804 NE Hassalo Street, Portland, OR 97213.



A catalogue record for this book
is available from the British Library.

ISBN1-85800-001-7

ISSN 0791-1084

Printed by
Betaprint, Dublin

# Contents

# Preface

In this sixth volume in the Annual Review series, our purpose continues to be to provide a review of legal developments, judicial and statutory, that occurred in 1992. In terms of case law, this includes those judgments which were delivered in 1992, regardless of whether they have been (or will be) reported and which were circulated up to the date of the preface. Once again, it is a pleasure to thank those who made the task of completing this volume less onerous. Mr Justice Brian Walsh (who, as we have mentioned in previous volumes, was the originator of the concept of an Annual Review of Irish Law) continues to be most supportive and we remain very grateful for this. Once again, we are in the debt of a number of people for providing access to library facilities. In particular, Ms Peggy McQuinn, of the Office of the Supreme Court, Ms Margaret Byrne and Ms Mary Gaynor, of the Library of the Incorporated Law Society of Ireland, and Mr Jonathan Armstrong and Ms Therese Broy, of the King's Inns Library, were as helpful as ever with a number of difficult queries from the authors. And once again, Ms Jennifer Aston, Librarian in the Law Library, Four Courts, was also especially helpful in facilitating access to statutory material which is otherwise very difficult to source. We would also like to express our heartfelt thanks to the staffs of the Dublin City University and Trinity College libraries for their assistance in the research for this volume. This sixth volume in the Annual Review series also marks a departure from previous years. The authors are delighted to have had the benefit of specialist contributions on Company Law and Revenue Law included in the volume. The authors continue to take final responsibility for the overall text as in the past, but are especially grateful for the contributions of David Tomkin and Alan Dignam in Company Law and of Dermot Kelly, Barrister-at-Law, in Revenue Law. The authors would hope that these specialist contributions will become a feature of future Reviews. William Binchy would also like to thank his many colleagues at Trinity College Law School for their help in relation to several of the matters discussed in this Review. Particular thanks are due to Hilary Delany, who read the Equitable Remedies chapter and made a number of very useful suggestions for improvement, to Eoin O'Dell, whose comments relating to the decisions on Contract Law were most incisive, to Paul Coughlan, who gave considerable assistance in regard to Land Law, and to Anthony Whelan, who was similarly helpful in relation to the complexities of the law on abortion. William Binchy also wishes to thank Mr Kenneth Bredin and Ms

Mary Donnelly for their helpful comments on medical negligence and Ms Maureen Ryan for her assistance on aspects of the private international law of tort.

As with the previous two Annual Reviews, we are also very grateful to the Incorporated Law Society of Ireland, as Trustees of the Arthur Cox Foundation, for their generous financial research assistance in connection with the preparation of this volume. Finally, we are ever grateful to the Round Hall Press, and in particular Michael Adams, Gilbert Gough and Martin Healy, whose professionalism ensures the continued production of this series.

Raymond Byrne and William Binchy,
Dublin

September 1994

# Table of Cases

# Other Tables

## TABLE OF CONSTITUTIONAL ARTICLES

## TABLE OF IRISH STATUTES

# ANNUAL REVIEW OF IRISH LAW 1992

# Administrative Law

## GOVERNMENT FUNCTIONS

**Appropriation** The Appropriation Act 1992 provided as follows. For the year ended 31 December 1992, the amount for supply grants was £7,925,107,000 and for appropriations-in-aid was £964,177,401. A shortfall for the year 1990, comprising a sum of £95,753 for supply grants and of £315,401 for appropriations-in-aid was also included.

**Borrowing power of State bodies** The Financial Transactions of Certain Companies and Other Bodies Act 1992 is a retrospective Act authorising State bodies to enter into currency and other swap transactions as part of their debt management. Many State bodies had, in recent years, entered into such swap transactions, but their validity had been questioned after the House of Lords ruled in *Hazell v Hammersmith and Fulham LBC* [1991] 2 AC that such swap transactions, being speculative in nature, were *ultra vires* the powers of English local authorities. It was felt that clarifying legislation was required in order to avoid any similar problems in relation to Irish State bodies. Hence the retrospective nature of the 1992 Act, s. 2 of which provides that State bodies 'shall have and be deemed always to have had' the power to enter into swap transactions. For details on the Minister for Finance's powers in the 1992 Act to prevent overtly speculative swap transactions, see Robert Clark's Annotation, *Irish Current Law Statutes Annotated.*

**Diplomatic functions**

*Fees* The Diplomatic and Consular Fees (Amendment) Regulations 1992 (SI No. 8) and the Diplomatic and Consular Fees (Amendment) (No. 2) Regulations 1992 (SI No. 268) amended the 1982 Regulations of the same title.

*Immunity* The Convention on Assistance in the Case of a Nuclear Accident or Radiological Emergency (Privileges and Immunities) Order 1992 (SI No. 144) confers immunity from claims or taxes on foreign rescue workers who might come to Ireland under the terms of the 1986 Convention on Assistance in the Case of a Nuclear Accident or Radiological Emergency. The 1986 Assistance Convention was incorporated into Irish law by the Radiological Protection Act 1991: see the 1991 Review, 372-5.

Similarly, the International Convention on the Establishment of an International Fund for Compensation for Oil Pollution Damage (Privileges and Immunities) Order 1992 (SI No. 186) confers immunity in respect of activities arising from the enforcement of the 1971 International Convention on the Establishment of an International Fund for Compensation for Oil Pollution Damage. The 1971 Convention was, in effect, incorporated into Irish law by the Oil Pollution of the Sea (Civil Liability and Compensation) Act 1988: see the 1988 Review, 437-9 and the Safety and Health chapter, 535, below.

The 1992 Orders were made under the Diplomatic Relations and Immunity Act 1967.

**Marine**

The Dun Laoghaire Harbour Rates Order 1992 (SI No. 108) lays down the charges for use of Dun Laoghaire harbour. The Order was made under the Dun Laoghaire Harbour Act 1990: see the 1990 Review, 4.

**Semi-State bodies**

*ACC Bank* The ACC Bank Act 1992 provided for a number of substantive changes concerning what was formerly the Agricultural Credit Corporation plc, as part of the government strategy to allow the State banking sector to broaden its base and provide the same range of services as their private sector counterparts. The Act came into force on 24 April 1992: ACC Bank Act 1992 (Commencement) Order 1992 (SI No. 170). S. 2 of the 1992 Act provides that the Agricultural Credit Corporation plc is henceforth ACC Bank plc. This was intended to facilitate a widening of ACC's base, as well as paving the way for possible partial or full privatisation. S. 5 of the 1992 Act permits ACC Bank to engage in a full range of banking activities, no longer limited to the agricultural sector in any way (see the 1988 Review, 38). S. 4 authorised the Minister for Finance to provide by Regulation for Central Bank supervision of ACC Bank's activities, subject to any relevant modifications or adaptations, in order to bring ACC into line with other high street banking institutions in the State: see now ACC Bank Act 1992 (Section 4) Regulations 1992 (SI No. 373). S. 6 increases the total possible number of directors to nine. S. 7 of the Act provided for an increase in ACC's authorised share capital from £35 million to £50 million. S. 8 provided for an increase in ACC's borrowings from £800 million to £1,000 million (see the 1988 Review, 38). Finally, ss. 10 and 11 of the Act provide that ACC Bank can avail of the benefit of the provisions of the Bankers' Books Evidence Act 1879 and of the Bills of Exchange Act 1882 in the same manner as banks in the private sector. See also the discussion of the ICC Bank Act 1992, below.

*B & I Line* The B & I Line Act 1991 (discussed in the 1991 Review, 4) came into effect on 31 January 1992: B & I Line Act 1991 (Section 7) (Commencement) Order 1992 (SI No. 25 of 1992) and B & I Line Act 1991 (Section 8) (Commencement) Order 1992 (SI No. 26 of 1992).

*ICC Bank* The ICC Bank Act 1992 provided for a number of substantive changes concerning what was formerly the Industrial Credit Corporation plc. The Act came into force on 23 July 1992 on its signature by the President. The ICC Act should be seen in conjunction with the ACC Bank Act 1992, disucssed above, and as part of the government strategy to streamline the State banking sector so that it is entitled to provide the same services as the private banking entities. S. 2 of the 1992 Act provides that the Industrial Credit Corporation plc is henceforth ICC Bank plc. This was intended to facilitate a widening of ICC's base as well as pave the way for partial or complete privatisation if required. S. 4 of the 1992 Act permits ACC Bank to engage in a full range of banking activities, no longer limited to the industrial lending sphere. S. 3 authorised the Minister for Finance to provide by Regulation for Central Bank supervision of ICC Bank's activities, subject to any relevant modifications or adaptations, in order to bring ICC into line with other high street banking institutions in the State: see now ICC Bank Act 1992 (Section 3) Regulations 1993 (SI No. 24 of 1993). S. 5 provided for an increase in ICC's borrowings from £1,000 million to £1,300 million (see the 1990 Review, 5). Finally, s. 7 of the Act provides that ICC Bank can avail of the benefit of the provisions of the Bankers' Books Evidence Act 1879 and of the Bills of Exchange Act 1882 in the same manner as banks in the private sector.

*Irish Land Commission* The dissolution of the Land Commission under the Irish Land Commission (Dissolution) Act 1992 is discussed in the Agriculture chapter, 16, below.

*Marine Institute* The Marine Institute, which is intended to undertake, co-ordinate, promote and assist in marine research and development, was established on 30 October 1992 under the Marine Institute Act 1991 (Establishment Day) Order 1992 (SI No. 316). On the 1991 Act, see the 1991 Review, 5.

**State in litigation** The status of the Office of Public Works as occupier of national monuments to which the public has access was considered by the Supreme Court in *Clancy v Commissioners of Public Works* [1991] ILRM 567.

**Tribunals of Inquiry** In May 1991, the Minister for Agriculture and Food decided to establish a Tribunal of Inquiry into the Beef Industry, arising from certain allegations made in an ITV 'World in Action' programme and other allegations made in Dáil Éireann. The subsequent resolutions of both Houses of the Oireachtas concerning the Tribunal had the effect of conferring on it the powers contained in the Tribunals of Inquiry (Evidence) Acts 1921 and 1979. The Tribunal's sole member and Chairman was Mr Justice Hamilton, President of the High Court. In the 1991 Review, we referred to a number of decisions in which various aspects of the Tribunal's activities were reviewed. In 1992 and 1993, there was further case law arising from the Tribunal's continued deliberations. Given the wide-ranging nature of the issues raised in these decisions, they appear in various parts of the Reviews in which they are discussed. It may, therefore be of some help to list these decisions here for ease of reference.

In *Boyhan v Tribunal of Inquiry Into the Beef Industry* [1992] ILRM 545; [1993] 1 IR 217, Denham J dealt with the question of representation before the Tribunal: see the 1991 Review, 11-12.

In *Goodman International v Mr Justice Hamilton* [1992] ILRM 145; [1992] 2 IR 542, the High Court and Supreme Court rejected the argument that the Tribunal was invalidly exercising the judicial power, in other words that it was, in effect, a court of law. In rejecting this claim, the courts decided that the Tribunal could address matters which had in the past or which might in the future become justiciable disputes in the courts: see the 1991 Review, 109-11. For a perceptive analysis of the issues in that case, see Úna Ní Raifeartaigh's article in (1992) 2 Irish Criminal Law Journal 141.

In *Attorney General v Mr Justice Hamilton* [1993] ILRM 81; [1993] 2 IR 250, the Supreme Court (reversing O'Hanlon J in the High Court) held that the Tribunal was excluded from hearing evidence concerning Cabinet deliberations, deciding that such deliberations are absolutely confidential pursuant to Article 28.4 of the Constitution: see the Constitutional Law chapter, 212-17, below.

In 1993, in *Attorney General v Mr Justice Hamilton (No. 2)* [1993] ILRM 821, the Supreme Court (reversing in part Geoghegan J in the High Court) held that the Tribunal was precluded by Article 15.13 of the Constitution from examining a TD or Senator concerning any utterances made by them in the Oireachtas or indeed from examining them as to the source of information on which such utterances in either House was made. In *Goodman International v Mr Justice Hamilton (No. 2)* [1993] 3 IR 307 and *Goodman International v Mr Justice Hamilton (No. 3)* [1993] 3 IR 320, Geoghegan J went further in holding that, although TDs and Senators had no constitutional privilege to refuse disclosure of the sources of information which had been revealed to them in respect of statements and utterances made outside the

Houses of the Oireachtas, a common law privilege independent of the Constittuion existed in their favour. These three decisions will be discussed in the 1993 Review.

By contrast, in *Kiberd v Mr Justice Hamilton* [1992] ILRM 574; [1992] 2 IR 257 the High Court affirmed existing Irish case law to the effect that a journalist has no constitutional or common law right to claim privilege in respect of confidential sources of information. Unlike TDs or Senators, therefore, the journalist remains in the same position as any other witness. This case will also be discussed in the 1993 Review.

## JUDICIAL REVIEW

**Availability** In *MacPharthalain and Ors v Commissioners of Public Works and Ors* [1992] 1 IR 111, Blayney J held that the designation of lands by the Wildlife Service of the Office of Public Works as an area of scientific interest was amenable to judicial review: see the discussion in the Agriculture chapter, 18-19, below.

In *Chestvale Properties Ltd and Hoddle Investments Ltd v Glackin* [1992] ILRM 221; [1993] 3 IR 35, Murphy J indicated that an inspector appointed under s. 14 of the Companies Act 1990 might in some instances act in a quasi-judicial capacity, thus giving rise to possible judicial review of any decisions made by the inspector: see further the Company Law chapter, 68-73, below.

In *TV 3 Television Co Ltd and Ors v Independent Radio and Television Commission*, High Court, 4 May 1992; Supreme Court, 26 October 1993, Blayney J held that judicial review lay where fair procedures were not observed in the context of the award of a TV franchise: see the Communications chapter, 49-50, below.

In *Gutrani v Minister for Justice* [1993] 2 IR 427, the Supreme Court held that a decision of the Minister for Justice in a refugee application was subject to judicial review: see the discussion in the Aliens and Immigration chapter, 22-23, below.

By way of contrast, in *Roche v Waller and Ors*, High Court, 23 July 1992, the plaintiff, a professional jockey, instituted plenary summons proceedings seeking to quash a decision of the respondents, the Turf Club. While the plaintiff's case (rejected by Costello J at the interlocutory injunction stage) was based on the failure of the Turf Club to comply with the rules of natural justice, judicial review was not sought, presumably on the ground that the Turf Club derives its authority from contract, in line with the views expressed by Barr J in *Murphy v Turf Club* [1989] IR 172 (1989 Review, 14). However, on the failure by the Supreme Court to deal authoritatively with this issue, see the discussion in the 1990 Review, 12-14, and the 1991 Review, 14.

**Jurisdictional error** In *Sweeney v Brophy and DPP* [1993] ILRM 449; [1993] 2 IR 202, the Supreme Court addressed the question of what constitutes a jurisdictional error in a criminal trial. In this context, the Court considered the scope of its decision in *The State (Holland) v Kennedy* [1977] IR 193. The case is discussed in the Criminal Law chapter, 268-70, below. See also *Lennon v Clifford* [1993] ILRM 77, discussed in the Criminal Law chapter, 270, and the Revenue Law chapter, 519.

**Fair procedures/natural justice**

*Audi alteram partem* In *Gutrani v Minister for Justice* [1993] 2 IR 427, the Supreme Court considered whether fair procedures had been observed in the context of an application for refugee status: see the discussion in the Aliens and Immigration chapter, 22-3, below.

In *TV 3 Television Co Ltd and Ors v Independent Radio and Television Commission*, High Court, 4 May 1992; Supreme Court, 26 October 1993, Blayney J considered the requirements of fair procedures in the context of the award of a TV franchise: see the Communications chapter, 49-50, below.

See also *Madden and Ors v Minister for the Marine* [1993] ILRM 436; [1993] 1 IR 567 in the Fisheries chapter, 377-9, below.

Finally, in *Roche v Waller and Ors*, High Court, 23 July 1992, referred to above, 7, Costello J declined to grant an interlocutory injunction to the plaintiff, a professional jockey, in respect of a suspension imposed by the respondents, the Turf Club. Costello J held that the Turf Club had correctly applied the rules of natural justice in connection with the hearing it had conducted into allegations of improper riding methods employed by the plaintiff in the course of a horse race.

*Bias* In *Chestvale Properties Ltd and Hoddle Investments Ltd v Glackin* [1992] ILRM 221; [1993] 3 IR 35, Murphy J discussed, though ultimately did not reach, an allegation of bias against an inspector appointed under s. 14 of the Companies Act 1990: see further the Company Law chapter, 68-73, below.

**Legitimate expectation** In *Wiley v Revenue Commissioners* [1993] ILRM 482, the Supreme Court held that the applicant failed to meet the requirements of the legitimate expectation doctrine. In so doing, the Court upheld the approach taken by Blayney J in the High Court ([1989] IR 350), discussed in the 1989 Review, 9-11.

The background to the case was as follows. The applicant had certain physical disabilities which prevented him from driving an ordinary motor vehicle. He had no use in one leg for driving purposes and his left ankle was damaged as a result of extra stress placed on it. In 1983 and 1985, he purchased new motor vehicles for which he obtained from his local authority certificates of exemption from road tax under s. 43(1) of the Finance Act 1968, which applies only where the driver 'is wholly, or almost wholly, without the use of each of his legs.' Under the Imposition of Duties (No. 236) (Excise Duties on Motor Vehicles, Televisions and Gramophone Records) Order 1979, the Revenue Commissioners operated a refund scheme on the excise payable on motor vehicles. This scheme was based on the same criteria as for the road tax refund, and until 1986 the Revenue accepted a certificate of exemption from road tax as proof of entitlment to the excise duty refund. Thus, in 1983 and 1985, the applicant obtained the excise duty refund on presentation of the road tax exemption certificates. However, in 1986 the Revenue altered their policy and required a copy of the medical certificate on which the road tax exemption was granted.

In 1987, when the applicant applied for a refund under the 1979 Order, he was refused on the ground that the medical certificate did not indicate that he was without the use of each of his legs. The applicant then sought judicial review of this refusal on the ground that, as he had received the refunds in 1983 and 1985, he had a legitimate expectation that he would receive the refund in 1987, and that the Revenue Commissioners had not been entitled to change its policy without notice to him. As already noted, in the High Court, Blayney J dismissed his claim and the Supreme Court (Finlay CJ, Hederman, McCarthy, O'Flaherty and Egan JJ) upheld this conclusion.

Delivering the leading judgment, the Chief Justice stated that since the applicant knew or ought to have known that his physical condition did not entitle him to any refund under the 1979 Order, he could argue only that he had an expectation to a refund based on the fact that he had been given such a refund in the past, but this could not be described as a legitimate expectation. This analysis was in line with that adopted by Blayney J in the High Court. In addition, Finlay CJ concluded that to accede to the applicant's arguments would involve the Court ordering a statutory body to act *ultra vires* the powers conferred on it by statute, and he considered that the Court should not extend the boundaries of legitimate expectation in this way.

In a concurring judgment, O'Flaherty J opined that the boundaries of legitimate expectation in Irish case law were similar to those established in the jurisprudence of other courts. He referred in this context to the decision of the Court of Justice of the European Communities in *Commission v Council* [1973] ECR 575 and to the decision of the Privy Council in *Attorney-General of Hong Kong v Ng Yuen Shiu* [1983] 2 AC 629. It is notable that a similar comparision between Irish and EC principles of judicial review had been made by Costello J in *Emerald Meats Ltd v Minister for Agriculture,* High Court, 9 July 1991 (see the 1991 Review, 199-200).

The *Wiley* decision illustrates the developing trend that, while legitimate expectation remains an important head of relief in Irish administrative law, its limits are equally clear.

It may also be noted that, in *Gutrani v Minister for Justice* [1993] 2 IR 427, the Court was reluctant to stretch the legitimate expectation doctrine: see the discussion in the Aliens and Immigration chapter, 20f, below.

Another case in which a legitimate expectation was not, on the facts, established was *Donohue v Revenue Commissioners* [1993] 1 IR 172.

**Practice and procedure**

*1 Delay* In *Eurocontainer Shipping plc v Minister for the Marine,* High Court, 11 December 1992, Barr J rejected an argument that relief should be refused on the ground of delay, applying the test laid down by McCarthy J in *The State (Furey) v Minister for Justice* [1988] ILRM 89: see the Transport chapter, 625, below.

*2 No useful purpose* The refusal of judicial review on the ground that it would be of no avail to the applicant was discussed in *MacPharthalain and Ors v Commissioners of Public Works and Ors* [1992] 1 IR 111 (see the Agriculture chapter, 17-18, below) and in *Heavey v Pilotage Committee of the Dublin Pilotage Authority*, High Court, 7 May 1992 (see the Transport chapter, 621-3, below).

*3 Remittal* In *Sheehan v Reilly* [1993] ILRM 427; [1993] 2 IR 81 and *Sweeney v Brophy* [1993] ILRM 449; [1993] 2 IR 202, the Supreme Court dealt with the question of remittal under O.84, r.26(4) of the Rules of the Superior Courts 1986: see respectively the Constitutional Law chapter, 152-4, and the Criminal Law chapter, 268-70, below.

**Reasonableness** In *Matthews v Irish Coursing Club* [1993] 1 IR 346, O'Hanlon J quashed a decision of the respondent Coursing Club for unreasonableness. The case arose in the following way.

The applicant had entered two greyhounds for the 1990 JP McManus Irish Cup, the premier event in the Irish coursing calendar which was organised by the Irish Coursing Club, a statutory body governed by the Greyhound Industry Act 1956. The application fee was £100 per dog. One of the applicant's dogs, Needham's Bar, reached the final of the competition, but was beaten by another dog, Flashing Crystal. The prize for the winner was £8,000. Subsequently, drug testing on the winning dog indicated that prohibited stimulants had been administered to it prior to the race. At a meeting of the Coursing Club's general purposes sub-committee in March 1990, attended by the owner of Flashing Crystal and her solicitor, it was decided that the prize money for the race would be forfeited, a fine of £500 imposed and the greyhound be suspended from racing, coursing and stud duties until 1 January 1991. An appeal by the owner of Flashing Crystal to the executive committee of the Coursing Club was heard in June 1990 and this resulted in a fine being imposed of 50% of the prize money won by Flashing Crystal, subject to a minimum fine of £1,000 and that no penalties be imposed on the greyhound. There was no reference as to who was regarded as the winner of the 1990 JP McManus Irish Cup.

Prior to the June meeting, the applicant had written to the secretary of the Coursing Club indicating that, if the matter was not resolved in accordance with Coursing Club rules, he reserved the right to issue proceedings. He then instituted the instant proceedings. The main complaint of the applicant was that the Coursing Club had acted unreasonably in failing to disqualify Flashing Crystal from being regarded as the winner of the 1990 JP McManus Irish Cup, as provided for in Rule 88 of the Coursing Club. The respondent argued that, since Rule 88 provided that it 'may' order disqualification where prohibited drugs are used on greyhounds, this was a matter for the Club's discretion.

O'Hanlon J quoted with approval the judgment of Henchy J in *The State (Keegan) v Stardust Victims Compensation Tribunal* [1987] ILRM 202; [1986] IR 642 that an unreasonable decision is one that 'plainly and unambiguously flies in the face of fundamental reason and common sense'. O'Hanlon J also relied on a phrase used by Lord Reid in *Demetriades v Glasgow Corporation* [1951] 1 All ER 457: 'so unreasonable as to be perverse.'

Applying these principles to the instant case, O'Hanlon J agreed that the Coursing Club should be allowed a large amount of discretion in connection with the penalties it may impose in cases such as the present. However, he considered that, while the Court might not have interfered if the interests of the owner of Flashing Crystal only were being taken into account, it had failed to take account of the applicant's interests. He considered that, since the applicant had paid a fee to enter the competititon he was entitled to expect that the competition would be run in accordance with the Coursing Club's rules and that other competitors would not use unfair means to gain victory. In this context, he considered that the Coursing Club's decision was 'inexplicable' in view of the evidence of doping which had not been challenged in substantive terms by the owner of Flashing Crystal. O'Hanlon J also concluded that the applicant was entitled to have his interest in having a decision made by the Coursing Club as to who was the true winner of the 1990 JP McManus Irish Cup, and not left in abeyance as had appeared from the decision of the executive committee in June 1990. The case thus fell within those exceptional circumstances referred to by Henchy J in the *Keegan* case which justified interference by the courts with a decision-making body.

This was particularly so in light of the fact that the Coursing Club was the statutory body responsible for the coursing industry under the Greyhoud Industry Act 1958. He therefore ordered the Coursing Club to reconsider the matter in the light of his findings. The allusion to third party rights by O'Hanlon J finds echoes in the later judgment of Johnson J in *Madden and Ors v Minister for the Marine* [1993] ILRM 436; [1993] 1 IR 567 (see the Fisheries chapter, 377-9, below).

The judgment of O'Hanlon J is unexceptional in the sense that it is in line with the recent case law on reasonableness arising from the Keegan case (see the 1987 Review, 13-15, the 1989 Review, 15-16, the 1990 Review, 14-20 and the 1991 Review, 16-19). However, one slight quibble might be raised in connection with his allusion to the phrase 'so unreasonable as to be perverse' from the speech of Lord Reid in *Demetriades v Glasgow Corporation* [1951] 1 All ER 457. O'Hanlon J noted that this expression 'is familiar to courts of appeal when it is sought to upset the findings of a jury on an issue of fact in one of the lower courts'. Doubtless this was an *obiter* comment by O'Hanlon J on Lord Reid's phrase, but it raises the perenniel issue of the distinction between judicial review and an appeal on a point of law. Academics might argue that, in recent years, the distinction between the two might seem to be more rhetorical than real, but certainly the courts have been zealous to ensure that, time and again, the distinction between the two is maintained. Indeed, O'Hanlon J's overall approach in *Matthews* eschews any departure from the mainstream in this respect, but nonetheless his use of Lord Reid's phrase may stimulate some further debate on the distinction between errors of law within jurisdiction, which cannot be corrected on judicial review, and *ultra vires* errors, which of course are susceptible to judicial review.

# Agriculture

## ABATTOIRS

**Abattoirs inspection** The Abattoirs Act 1988 (Commencement) Order 1992 (SI No. 88) brought Parts IV and V of the 1988 Act into force as from 1 June 1992. Parts IV and V of the Act concern veterinary control and hygiene as well as the levying of fees by local authorities for meat and animal inspection. This Order paved the way for SI Nos. 89 and 90, discussed below. On the 1988 Act, see the 1988 Review, 37-8.

**Meat inspection** The Abattoirs Act 1988 (Veterinary Examination) Regulations 1992 (SI No. 89) lay down the general procedure for meat inspection to ensure that it is fit for human consumption. The Abattoirs (Health Mark) Regulations 1992 (SI No. 90) provides for the placing of a Health Mark on meat to indicate that it is fit for human consumption, as envisaged by s. 40 of the 1988 Act. Finally, the European Communities (Fees for Health Inspections and Controls of Fresh Meat) Regulations 1992 (SI No. 177) introduced further changes in the regime for meat inspection. The Regulations, which came into effect on 6 July 1992, implemented Directive 85/73/EEC, Decision 88/408/EEC and Directive 88/409/EEC. To do so, the Regulations amended a number of previous Regulations concerning meat inspection as well as affected provisions of the Abattoirs Act 1988. They should be read in conjunction with the other Regulations discussed above.

## ANIMAL DISEASE ERADICATION

During 1992, a number of Regulations and Orders were made to introduce further measures to protect against the spread of diseases in animals. Notable here were Regulations connected with the implementation of powers contained in the Diseases of Animals Act 1966: see below.

**BSE** The Diseases of Animals (Bovine Spongiform Encephalopothy) (Amendment) Order 1992 (SI No. 289) further amends the 1989 Order of the same title (1989 Review, 17) to provide that compensation for slaughter of herds infected with BSE may be refused where reasonable precautions have not been taken by the owner of the herd in question. See also the

Importation of Carcases and Animal Products (Prohibition) (Amendment) Order 1992 (SI No. 283), below.

**Carcase import** The Importation of Carcases and Animal Products (Prohibition) (Amendment) Order 1992 (SI No. 283) is aimed at restrictong importation of matter which could contribute to the spread of animal disease.

**Export of livestock generally** The European Communities (General Authorisations for Exports of Agricultural Products) Regulations 1992 (SI No. 266) impose restrictions on the export of certain agricultural products. The Livestock (Regulation of Export) (Amendment) Order 1992 (SI No. 418), made pursuant to s.29 of the Diseases of Animals Act 1966, requires a licence for the export of any livestock.

**Horse exports** The Horses (Regulation of Export) (Amendment) Order 1992 (SI No. 297) amends the 1960 Order of the same title to provide that licences for the export of horses are now required for exports to Great Britain, Northern Ireland and the Isle of Man.

**Notifiable diseases** The Diseases of Animals Act 1966 (Commencement) Order 1992 (SI No. 249) brought the following provisions of the 1966 Act into effect on 7 September 1992: ss. 16, 21, 31, 34, 42-45, 55 and 57. These sections relate primarily to the extension of powers by which animal diseases are controlled by the Department of Agriculture and Food. The Diseases of Animals (Notification of Infectious Diseases) Order 1975 (Amendment) Order 1992 (SI No. 250) extended the number of equine diseases notifiable under the 1966 Act. The Diseases of Animals (Notification of Infectious Diseases) Order 1992 (SI No. 251) specified the other animal diseases regarded as notifiable under the 1966 Act. The Diseases of Animals Act 1966 (First Schedule) (Amendment) Order 1992 (SI No. 252) extended the definition of 'disease' contained in the 1966 Act and also extends the enforcement powers contained in the 1966 Act.

## GROWTH PROMOTERS

The European Communities (Control of Oestrogenic, Androgenic, Gestagenic and Thyrostatic Substances) (Amendment) Regulations 1992 (SI No. 427) introduced further powers for the Gardai to seize and detain growth promoters pursuant to the 1988 Regulations of the same title. In the 1993 Review, we will discuss how these Regulations now come under the aegis of the Animal Remedies Act 1993.

# PLANT HEALTH

**Cereal crops** The European Communities (Cereal Seed) (Amendment) Regulations 1992 (SI No. 29) and the European Communities (Cereal Seed) (Amendment) (No. 2) Regulations 1992 (SI No. 382) amend the Regulations of 1981 to 1990 by revising the fees for cereal crop inspection and certification of cereal seed required under the Regulations.

**Feedingstuffs** The European Communities (Marketing of Feedingstuffs) (Amendment) Regulations 1992 (SI No. 143) amended the 1984 Regulations of the same title to implement a signifciant number of Directives on the standards associated with placing feedingstuffs on the market.

**Fodder plants** The European Communities (Seed of Fodder Plants) (Amendment) Regulations 1992 (SI No. 199) and the European Communities (Seed of Fodder Plants) (Amendment) (No. 3) Regulations 1992 (SI No. 370) amended the Regulations of 1981 to 1991 of the same title in order to implement Directives 89/100/EEC and 91/376/EEC. The European Communities (Seed of Fodder Plants) (Amendment) (No. 2) Regulations 1992 (SI No. 234) revised the relevant fees under the Regulations.

**Oil plants and fibre plants** The European Communities (Seed of Oil Plants and Fibre Plants) (Amendment) Regulations 1992 (SI No. 301) amended the Regulations of 1981 to 1991 of the same title to implement Directive 92/9/EEC.

**Organisms harmful to plants or plant products** The European Communities (Introduction of Organisms Harmful to Plants or Plant Products) (Prohibition) (Amendment) Regulations 1992 (SI No. 214) amended the Regulations of 1980 to 1990 to implement the following Directives: 90/506/EEC, 90/80/EEC, 90/113/EEC, 91/27/EEC, 91/102/EEC, 91/103/EEC, 91/660/EEC, 91/661/EEC and 92/10/EEC.

**Pesticide use** The European Communities (Classificationn, Packaging and Labelling of Pesticides) (Amendment) Regulations 1992 (SI No. 416) are referred to in the Safety and Health chapter, 528, below.

**Pesticide residues** The European Communities (Pesticide Residues) (Feedingstuffs) Regulations 1992 (SI No. 40) implement Directive 91/132/EEC. They prohibit placing on the market feedingstuffs to which the Regulations apply if they contain certain pesticide residues, such as DDT, in a quantity greater than that specified in the Regulations.

## PROPRIETARY PLANT RIGHTS

The Plant Varieties (Proprietary Rights) (Amendment) Regulations 1992 (SI No. 35) and the Plant Varieties (Proprietary Rights) (Amendment) (No. 2) Regulations 1992 (SI No. 369) extended the plant varieties over which copyright-like rights exist under the Plant Varieties (Proprietary Rights) Act 1980.

## POULTRY

**Egg Products** The European Communities (Egg Products) Regulations 1992 (SI No. 419) implemented Directive 91/684/EEC and amended the 1991 Regulations concerning egg products.

**Live poultry** The European Communities (Live Poultry and Hatching Eggs) Regulations 1992 (SI No. 362) implement Directive 90/539/EEC on the standards to be applied to poultry husbandry.

**Marketing standards for eggs** The European Communities (Marketing Standards for Eggs) Regulations 1992 (SI No. 254) consolidated with amendments previous Regulations concerning the marketing of eggs in order to implement the requirements of Council Regulations 1907/90, 1274/91, 3540/91 and 2221/92. The 1992 Regulations revoked Regulations of 1973, 1977 and 1987 of the same title.

## REPEAL OF LAND BONDS AND LAND COMMISSION LEGISLATION

The controversial land bond scheme, whereby the Irish Land Commission paid for land it compulsorily acquired by issuing land bonds which were then redeemable on foot of annual draws, was brought to a close by the Land Bond Act 1992. The principal mechanisms associated with the scheme were the Guarantee Fund and the Land Bond Fund. The government had already decided to redeem remaining land bonds, so that both Funds had become largely redundant. The Land Bond Act 1992, apart from ss. 4, 5 and 6, came into force on its signature by the President on 18 March 1992. Ss. 4, 5 and 6, which concerned the transfer of any remaining sums in the Funds to the Exchequer, came into effect on 29 May 1992: Land Bond Act 1992 (Sections 4 and 5) (Commencement) Order 1992 (SI No. 135). It may be noted that the land bond scheme had survived a constitutional challenge: see *Dreher v Irish Land Commission* [1984] ILRM 94.

The Land Bond Act 1992 in effect recognises that the process of enfranchising tenant farmers in Ireland is now complete. The process began in 1881 with the establishment of the Irish Land Commission in the wake of the enormous political battle in Ireland, initiated by Michael Davitt's Land League, for agrarian reform and leasehold enfranchisement.

Clearly associated with the Land Bond Act 1992, therefore, is the Irish Land Commission (Dissolution) Act 1992, which provides for the formal dissolution of the Irish Land Commission itself. This Act requires a Commencement Order to come into effect, but at the time of writing, no Commencement Order has been made. For an analysis of the enormous social impact of the Land Commission, see Richard Humphreys' Annotation, *Irish Current Law Statutes Annotated.*

## RETIREMENT OF FARMERS

The European Communities (Retirement of Farmers) Regulations 1992 (SI No. 148) provided for an increase in the annuity payable to retiring farmers under the terms of the 1974 Regulations of the same title.

## VETERINARY MEDICINE

The European Communities (Recognition of Qualifications in Veterinary Medicine) (Amendment) Regulations 1992 (SI No. 253) amended the 1980 to 1987 Regulations of the same title to give effect to Directives 89/594/EEC and 90/658/EEC.

## WILDLIFE

**Area of scientific interest** In *MacPharthalain and Ors v Commissioners of Public Works and Ors* [1992] 1 IR 111, Blayney J held that the designation of lands by the Wildlife Service of the Office of Public Works as an area of scientific interest was amenable to judicial review. The case arose in the following way.

The first two applicants had agreed to sell land they owned near Roundstone, County Galway, to the third applicant who proposed to develop the land as a landing strip. The third applicant's application for planning permission to develop the land in this way was rejected in 1989 by Galway County Council on a number of grounds. One of these grounds was that the land in question formed part of an area which had been designated in 1987 by the Wildlife Service of the Office of Public Works as an area of international scientific interest.

The applicants had been unaware that their land had been designated as one of international scientific interest and they instituted the instant proceedings seeking to have this determination quashed. It emerged in the proceedings that such determinations are made form time to time by the Wildlife Service after surveys conducted of various locations. Notification of such designations would then be forwarded to county councils and other planning authorities and to the Departments of Agriculture and Forestry. However, no notice would be given to members of the public. The applicants' lands adjoined an area known as the Roundstone Bog, which had been designated as an area of international scientific interest in 1982; the applicants' lands were included in the designated area after a further survey in 1987.

Evidence was given to the effect that, where such a designation was given, the land in question would not be granted an afforestation grant under s. 9 of the Forestry Act 1946, and that this would make such an area uneconomic for afforestation purposes and would then be very difficult to sell. This proved to be an important factor in the applicants' case.

Blayney J held that the designation of land of being of scientific interest was more than the mere conveying of information to interested parties. In view of the effect of such designation on the availability of grants under the Forestry Act 1946, the designation amounted to a decision that affected the rights of the applicants in the instant case. It thus fell within the category of decisions designated by May CJ as 'judicial' (and thus amenable to review) in the well-known decision *R. (McEvoy) v Dublin Corporation* (1878) 2 LR Ir 371, which Blayney J noted had been approved by Palles CB in *R. (Wexford Co Co) v Local Government Board* [1902] 2 IR 349 and by Walsh J in *The State (Stephen's Green Club) v Labour Court* [1961] IR 85. See also Blayney J's own judgment in *Gallagher v Corrigan*, High Court 1 February 1988 (1988 Review, 10-12) and of Barr J in *Egan v Minister for Defence*, High Court, 24 November 1988 (1988 Review, 28-9). Since the designation had affected the applicants' interests and they had been no opportunity to object to it, Blayney J concluded that *certiorari* lay to quash it on the grounds that it had been done contrary to the requirements of natural justice. He recognised that this might not affect the planning application concerning the lands in question, as the refusal had been made on a number of grounds other than the designation issue. Nonetheless, he concluded, with some hesitation, that the case did not come within the category of cases in which the granting of judicial review would be of absolutely no benefit to the applicants. On this area, see the 1988 Review, 35-6 and the 1990 Review, 12. He thus declined in exercise of his discretion to refuse to grant judicial review in the instant case.

**Wildbirds** The European Communities (Wildbirds) (Greenland Whitefronted Goose, Shovelar and Curlew) Regulations 1992 (SI No. 228) gave effect to the protections for the wildbirds named in the Regulations as required by Directive 79/409.

# Aliens and Immigration

## CITIZENSHIP

In *Gomaa v Minister for Foreign Affairs and Ors*, High Court, 24 July 1992, the applicant had been born in Dublin in 1990 in unusual circumstances. His father, Mr Gomaa, was an Egyptian national who had been employed as a chef in the Egyptian embassy in Ireland between September 1989 and September 1990. The Department of Justice issued Mr Gomaa with a permit under the Aliens Act 1935 entitling Mr Gomaa to remain in the State during his employment with the embassy. Mr Gomaa's wife joined him in Dublin in October 1989, and she received a permit under the 1935 Act allowing her to remain in Ireland until October 1990.

By virtue of his position as a member of the service staff of the embassy, Mr Gomaa was entitled to certain diplomatic immunities and exemptions under the Vienna Convention on Diplomatic Relations, as implemented in Irish law by the Diplomatic Relations and Immunities Act 1967. Article 39(2) of the Vienna Convention provides that:

> When the functions of a person enjoying privileges and immunities have come to an end, such privileges and immunities shall normally cease at the moment when he leaves the country, or on the expiry of a reasonable period in which to do so, but shall subsist until that time. . . .

On 4 September 1990, the Department of Foreign Affairs was informed by the Egyptian Embassy that Mr Gomaa's employment at the embassy had been terminated and that he and his wife would be departing by plane for London en route to Cairo on 8 September. The Department of Justice endorsed a permit on Mr Gomaa's passport entitling him to stay in Ireland, provided he did not enter into employment, until 11 September 1990. In September 1990, the applicant's mother, Mrs Gomaa, was in about the final month of her pregnancy. She had been attending the National Maternity Hospital in Dublin, and had been strongly advised not to travel by air before giving birth. However, Mr and Mrs Gomaa flew to London on 8 September 1990, where Mrs Gomaa was unwell and required medical attention. Rather than going to a London hospital, the couple stated that they decided to return to Dublin by train and boat journey since Mrs Gomaa was known as a patient in the National Maternity Hospital.

It was in those circumstaces that the applicant was born in Dublin. Mr Gomaa applied for an Irish passport on his behalf and this was granted. Subsequently, however, the Department of Foreign Affairs took the view that the applicant was not entitled to an Irish passport and sought to have it impounded. This was based on the terms of s.6 of the Irish Nationality and Citizenship Act 1956. S. 6(1) of the 1956 Act provides that every person born in Ireland is an Irish citizen from birth. However, s.6(5) of the 1956 Act provides:

> Subsection (1) shall not confer Irish citizenship on the child of an alien who, at the time of the child's birth, is entitled to diplomatic immunity in the State.

The applicant's case was that, at the time of his birth, his father's diplomatic immunity under Article 39(2) of the Vienna Convention, quoted above, had ended and that s.6(5) of the 1956 Act did not therefore apply. As a consequence, the applicant's parents claimed that the applicant was entitled to remain in Ireland and to be cared for by his parents.

However, in his *ex tempore* judgment in the case, Barr J rejected the applicant's claim that his father's diplomatic immunity had ended. This turned on his interpretation of Article 39(2) of the Vienna Convention, and in particular the provision in that Article that diplomatic immunity 'normally' ceased when the person functions ended and after they left the State, 'or on the expiry of a reasonable period in which to do so.' Barr J held that the word 'normally' indicated that special circumstances, such as the medical emergency which occurred in the instant case, could occur so that immunity continued even after a person left the State and after the functions connected with their immunity had also come to an end. Thus, in the instant case, the departure of Mr and Mrs Gomaa from the State did not automatically bring Mr Gomaa's immunity to an end. In addition, Barr J noted that Article 39(2) expressly provided for 'a reasonable period' during which immunity could be extended. It was accepted that, if Mr Gomaa had applied for an extension to remain in Ireland for the birth of the applicant, this would have been granted by the authorities. In this light, Barr J interpreted Mr Gomaa's re-entry by boat into Ireland with his wife as 'a graft on his original quasi-diplomatic status and enabled them to remain in Ireland for such further period which might be regarded as reasonable in all the cirumstances.' Indeed, Barr J noted that the authorities had granted Mr and Mrs Gomaa a permit to remain in Ireland on their return in the same terms as the permit issued immediately before their departure for London. This supported his conclusion that the diplomatic immunity remained in force at the time of the applicant's birth. Barr J thus concluded that the applicant was not an Irish citizen and therefore not entitled to an Irish passport under the 1956 Act.

## PROCEDURE

In *Fakih v Minister for Justice* [1993] ILRM 274; [1993] 2 IR 406, O'Hanlon J dealt with the procedures applicable where the Minister for Justice considers an application for refugee status. Without diminishing the importance of O'Hanlon J's judgment in that case, we will not deal with that judgment in detail here because many similar issues were addressed by the Supreme Court in its later decision in 1992 in *Gutrani v Minister for Justice* [1993] 2 IR 427.

The *Gutrani* case arose in the following way. The applicant, a Libyan national, came to Ireland on a student visa in 1983. The visa expired in 1984, but the applicant did not leave the State and went into hiding. He was found in September 1989 working in a restaurant without a work permit. The Minister for Justice subsequently ordered the applicant to leave the State, in default of which he was liable to deportation. The applicant did not leave the State but applied for permission to remain on as a refugee.

He relied on the terms of the 1951 UN Convention on Refugees and the 1967 Protocol to that Convention. Ireland was a signatory of both the Convention and the Protocol, but neither had been ratified by the State and thus neither had been incorporated into domestic law. Under relevant Irish case law, such as *In re Ó Laighléis* [1960] IR 93 and *Norris v Attorney General* [1984] IR 36, therefore, it seemed at first sight that the applicant had little basis on which to claim the benefit of the Convention and Protocol on a domestic court. However, by a letter dated 15 December 1985, the Minister for Justice had undertaken to the UN High Commissioner for Refugees (UNHCR) to apply the principles of the Convention and Protocol in deciding applications for refugee status. The letter also stated that the application of the Convention principles would not preclude consideration of humanitarian grounds for leave to remain in the State. The terms of the letter were the basis for the applicant's claim.

The Minister had, in the instant case, refused the applicant's claim for refugee status after a hearing at which the applicant's legal advisers were present and after the papers in the matter had been transmitted to the UNHCR whose representative did not consider that the applicant had made out a case. The applicant sought judicial review of the Minister's refusal, in the course of which he sought to introduce additional evidence. In the High Court, O'Hanlon J refused to admit the additional evidence and dismissed each of the grounds on which relief was sought. On appeal, the Supreme Court (Hederman, McCarthy and O'Flaherty JJ) affirmed this decision. It is important to note, however, that although the applicant's claim was dismissed, the leading judgment of McCarthy J contains some significant comments on the procedures to be applied in refugee applications.

Speaking for the Court, McCarthy J pointed out that the Minister had not contested that he was required to deal with the application under the 1951 UN Convention in accordance with the letter to the UNHCR of 15 December 1985. Having established such a scheme, he stated that the Minister was bound to apply it. The Court rejected the suggestion that this was due to the operation of the doctrine of legitiamte expectation; rather it was because it was the procedure which the Minister had undertaken to enforce, and thus, the Minister's decision was subject to judicial review to ensure compliance with the scheme entered into. This approach to the 1985 letter echoes the view taken in relation to non-statutory schemes such as the Criminal Injuries Compensation Scheme and the Civil Legal Aid Scheme: see *The State (Creedon) v Criminal Injuries Compensation Tribunal* [1989] ILRM 104; [1988] IR 51 (1988 Review, 17-18) and *Cosgrove v Legal Aid Board* [1991] 2 IR 43 (1990 Review, 144-7).

However, in *Gutrani*, the Court then went on to hold that in the High Court O'Hanlon J had correctly refused to admit additional evidence on judicial review since to do so would be to challenge the findings of fact made by the Minister. Nor did the Court consider that judicial review could be a vehicle for reopening the question of the applicant's status, since this issue had been determined in the procedures adopted by the Minister. Finally, the Court concluded that there was no basis for the assertion that the Minister had failed to take account of any relevant factor, including any humanitarian factor in the applicant's case. In a concurring judgment, O'Flaherty J went even further and suggested that it was doubtful if any humanitarian factor was relevant in the instant case. This was because he felt that this would concern matters such as illness, family commitment or personal considerations not related to political relationships and none of these had been raised by the applicant.

It may be noted, however, that in subsequent proceedings in 1993, *Gutrani v Governor of Training Unit Mountjoy Prison*, High Court, 19 February 1993, the applicant was released from custody and granted permission to remain in Ireland: see the discussion in Editorial (1993) 11 ILT 69. It appears at the time of writing that, arising from the Gutrani case and others of a similar nature, the terms of the 1951 UN Convention on Refugees and the 1967 Protocol to that Convention may be incorporated into Irish domestic law. We will discuss any such development in a future Review.

## VISA REQUIREMENTS

The Aliens (Amendment) Order 1992 (SI No. 326) amended the Principal Order of 1946 by specifying that citizens of former Yugoslavia require a visa to enter the State. The Aliens (Amendment) (No. 2) Order 1992 (SI No. 348) specifies the visa requirement for citizens of Poland. Finally, the Aliens (Amendment) (No. 3) Order 1992 (SI No. 442) removed the visa requirement for citizens of the Czech Republic or of the Slovak Republic.

# Commercial Law

## ARBITRATION

In *Sweeney v Mulcahy* [1993] ILRM 289, O'Hanlon J considered whether the parties had incorporated into their arrangement the RIAI conditions of engagement and scale of minimum charges. In holding that they had, he also concluded that the RIAI conditions concerning arbitration in the event of a dispute was also part of the contract between the parties. On this basis, he granted a stay on proceedings in accordance with s. 5 of the Arbitration Act 1980.

## CASUAL TRADING

*Crosby v Delap and Dublin County Council* [1992] ILRM 564 involved an evidential point in a prosecution brought by Dublin County Council against the applicant under s. 3 of the Casual Trading Act 1980. Johnson J's judgment in the case also established that he was prepared to take judicial notice of the meaning of the words 'fast food' and 'chuck-wagon'.

The summons against the applicant alleged that he engaged in casual trading outside the Council's designated casual trading area. The particulars alleged that the applicant had sold cooked foods which were cooked at the place of sale. At the trial in the District Court, evidence was given for the Council that the applicant had been seen trading in 'fast food' from a 'chuck-wagon' at the location specified in the summons, that the applicant had been approached and had stated he was the owner of the chuck-wagon, and that the location in the summons was outside the Council's designated casual trading area. At the end of the Council's case, the applicant applied for a dismissal on the ground that the Council had not demonstrated that the applicant had been in breach of the 1980 Act by selling goods that were cooked at the place of sale. The respondent Judge of the District Court refused this application to dismiss and indicated that the applicant was required to reply to the Council's case. The applicant then sought judicial review of this decision.

The case centred on s. 2 of the 1980 Act. S. 2(1) of the 1980 Act provides that, subject to s. 2(2), casual trading means selling goods by retail at a place that is a casual trading area. S. 2(2) of the 1980 Act then sets out a number of situations that do not amount to casual trading. The applicant referred to two of these. S. 2(2)(d) of the 1980 Act provides that casual trading 'does not include . . . selling of . . . cooked foods (other than those cooked at the place of sale). . .', while s. (2)(g) of the 1980 Act provides that casual trading 'does not include . . . selling in respect of which it is shown by the seller — (i) that any profits therefrom are for use for charitable purposes' or for certain other stated purposes in resoect of which no profit will accrue to the seller. The applicant sought to draw a distinction between s. 2(2)(d) and s. 2(2)(g), arguing that in the first situation the onus was on the prosecution to establish that the accused person was involved in selling cooked foods that has been cooked at the place of sale, whereas under s. 2(2)(g) of the Act, the onus wouod be on the accused to establish that he fell within the exemptions provided for there.

Johnson J agreed with the interpretation suggested by the applicant, but this was to no avail. He accepted that the onus of proof was on the Council to establish that the food was cooked at the location and that the location was not a designated casual trading area, but he found that this onus had been discharged by the Council. This required Johnson J to interpret the evidence form the Council that the applicant had been seen selling 'fast food' from a 'chuck-wagon'.

Johnson J did not find any difficulty in explaining these words, and in doing so it might be said that traditional views as to what a judge can or cannot take judicial notice of may have to be revised. He stated:

> In my view the plain and ordinary meaning of fast food and chuck-wagon as utilised in the present day by normal and ordinary people is well known. Fast food is accepted to be hamburgers, cheese burgers and other forms of junk food which are sold hot, either in premises or from wagons or vans at the roadside. A chuck-wagon is a name which should be known to anyone who has either (a) attended a moving cinema palace or (b) read any western books in the course of their lives. It was originally the cooking wagon which accompanied cattle trains when the cowboys were bringing cattle from the West to the railheads. In the period of the last 25 to 30 years the name has grown up in Ireland and is well known and to be seen in the form of vans and caravans which appear in many parts of the country at functions, or merely at the roadside in which fast food is cooked[,] prepared and sold to passers-by. And indeed *Chambers 20th Century Dictionary* reinforces my view.

On the basis of this understanding of the evidence given in the District Court concerning 'fast food' and 'chuck-wagon', Johnson J was prepared to conclude that the Council had discharged the onus of it under s.2(2)(d) of the

1980 Act and that there was 'clear, ample and cogent evidence' that food cooked at the location specified in the summons was being sold by the applicant. On this basis, he held that the respondent Judge was correct in holding that the applicant had a case to answer.

## COMPETITION

**Anti-competitive agreements and abuse of dominant position** In *Masterfoods Ltd (t/a Mars Ireland) v HB Ice Cream Ltd* [1993] ILRM 145, Keane J, in an extremely detailed judgment, rejected claims that certain agreements were in breach of EC or Irish competition law. The case concerned whether HB could insist that freezer cabinets owned by it and then supplied to retailers in Ireland should exclusively contain HB products.

The plaintiff claimed that such and 'exclusive use' condition breached Articles 85 and 86 of the EC Treaty or the terms of the Restrictive Practices (Groceries) Order 1987, which had been continued in force under a Commencement Order made under the Competition Act 1991. It also claimed, in effect, that it was entitled to use such HB freezer cabinets for its products, principally Mars ice cream bars, which it was introducing to the market in Ireland. After an exhaustive review of the authorities, Keane J rejected the plaintiff's argument and found that the 'exclusive use' condition laid down by HB for its freezer cabinets was not in breach of EC or Irish competition law. Keane J's judgment also accepted the claim by HB that the Mars company refrain from using the HB cabinets for Mars products and that it refrain from attempting to procure breaches of the 'exclusive use' condition. It will be recalled that HB had, in 1990, obtained an interlocutory injunction prohibiting breach of the 'exclusive use' condition: see *HB Ice Cream Ltd v Masterfoods Ltd* [1990] 2 IR 463 (see the 1990 Review, 272-3). In effect, the grounds on which the interlocutory relief was obtained were those on which the substantive action were successfully fought by HB.'

In his judgment, Keane J dealt first with the standard of proof required in a case such as the present. He accepted that, in certain instances, breach of Articles 85 or 86 of the EC Treaty could lead to criminal sanctions through the imposition of fines by the European Commission under Regulation 17/62/EEC. However, Keane J concluded that, in line with the Supreme Court decision in *Banco Ambosiano Spa v Ansbacher & Co. Ltd* [1987] ILRM 669, the standard of proof in a case such as the present remained that of the balance of probability.

As to whether HB were in breach of Article 85 of the EC Treaty, Keane J accepted that the relevant 'market' for the purposes of the instant case was was the 'impulse purchasing' markets in ice-cream. The issue thus arose as to whether the 'exclusive use' condition constituted an agreement or practice in breach of Article 85. In rejecting the arguments put forward by Mars on this point, Keane J paid particular attention to the fact that such conditions were well-established in the ice-cream market for many years, and that HB had not employed that condition with the object of distorting competition in the market. Although he accepted that, in some respects, the effect of he condition was to impact on competition, this was not in itself sufficient to breach the terms of Article 85. He noted that one element of the 'exclusive use' condition was that retailers were free to terminate their agreement with HB and thus move to another ice-cream supplier.

As to whether HB were in breach of Article 86 of the EC Treaty, Keane J accepted that HB had a dominant position in that market. However, he rejected the claim that there had been 'abuse' of that position under Article 86. He noted that, in this context, there had been a difference of opinion expressed by the many expert witnesses called by the parties as to whether the 'exclusive use' condition was an unacceptable barrier to entry into the market.

Of some interest on this aspect of the case, Keane J reviewed not only the case law of the Court of Justice under Article 86 of the EC Treaty but also of the United States Supreme Court in connection with US anti-trust competition law. Keane J noted that there were many differences in the overall economic context between the US market, where there was an established single market, and the EC market, which was developing towards a single market. This made acceptance of some of the US anti-trust principles difficult to apply in the European context. However, Keane J noted that the 'rule of reason' approach developed by the US Supreme Court, in which trade restraints which were not clearly invalid would be subjected to a test of compatibility with the overall purpose of anti-trust law, had been applied by the Court of Justice to Article 86 of the Treaty of Rome. This was especially so where intellectual property rights were involved, as in the leading franchising case *Pronuptia de Paris GmbH v Pronuptia de Paris Irmgard Schillgalis* (Case 161/84) [1986] ECR 353.

As to whether the 'exclusive use' condition in the instant case breached Article 86, Keane J reviewed the authorities in great detail. In concluding that no breach of Article 86 had been established, he relied in particular on the summary of the Court of Justice's jurisprudence given by Advocate General Kirschner in *Tetra Pak Rausing SA v Commission* (Case 27/76) [1978] ECR 207 to the effect that an undertaking may act in a profit-oriented way, strive to improve its market position and pursue legitimate interests but not in a way that, foreseeably, will limit competition more than is necessary. In that context, Keane J concluded that, given the history of the 'exclusive use' condition, HB had not acted in breach of Article 86. He considered that no evidence had been presented that HB's undoubted dominance in the market had produced serious adverse effects for Irish consumers of ice cream products.

Keane J also considered the connection between Article 222 of the EC Treaty and Articles 85 and 86. Article 222 provides that the EC Treaty shall not prejudice the operation of the domestic rules governing property ownership. However, as Keane J pointed out in his judgment, the Court of Justice has indicated that the use of property rights may in some instances amount to a breach of Articles 85 and 86, citing the decision in *AB Volvo v Erik Veng (UK) Ltd* (Case 238/87) [1988] ECR 6211 in this respect. Mars argued that, in the instant case, HB should be compelled to allow Mars to use the HB freezer cabinets. But Keane J concluded that this would involve such a radical interference with HB's property rights that it would in fact be in breach of Article 222.

Turning finally to domestic law, Keane J was asked to decide whether the 'exclusive use' condiiton breached the Restrictive Practices (Groceries) Order 1987. Article 9 of the 1987 Order prohibited agreements 'which has or is likely to have the effect of limiting or restricting entry to trade in any grocery goods.' Keane J did not consider that the condition in the instant case was the kind of agreement intended to be captured by Article 9 of the 1987 Order. Indeed, he was reluctant to find that an arrangement that met the detailed requirements of Articles 85 and 86 of the EC teraty could be declared invlaid by reference to what he described as the 'somewhat laconic and uninformative nature' of Article 9 of the 1987 Order. In this context, he considered that the 'rule of reason' approach referred to earlier might be relevant in the interpretation of the 1987 Order.

On the 1987 Order itself, it may be noted that the Competition Act 1991 envisaged the repeal of the Restrictive Practices Acts 1972 and 1987 under which it had been made. However, as we noted in the 1991 Review, 24, while the 1972 and 1987 Acts were repealed by the Competition Act 1991 (Commencement) Order 1991 (SI No. 249 of 1991), the Order also left intact the 1987 Order. It was argued in the *Masterfoods* case that this aspect of the Commencement Order was *ultra vires* the Minister for Industry and Commerce. However, Keane J rejected this on the ground that the Order-making power conferred on the Minister by s. 2(1) of the 1991 Act was drafted in sufficiently broad terms to allow the Minister to repeal the 1972 and 1987 Acts except in so far as this involved the 1987 Order. This aspect of his judgment in of general interest in that the Order-making power in s. 2(1) of the 1991 Act is of a type to be found in many Acts of recent years.

In summary, then, Keane J found that HB was not in breach of any aspect of competition law, whether Community or purely domestic. On HB's claim that it had suffered damages as a result of the attempts by Mars to use its freezer cabinets for Mars ice-cream, he did not consider that any evidence had been adduced to substantiate a claim for damages. However, he did grant a permanent injunction against Mars prohibiting it from using the HB freezer cabinets for Mars products. In that sense, the HB case was entirely successful.

**Enforcement procedure in Circuit Court** S. 6 of the Competition Act 1991 (see the 1991 Review, 23-5) provided for the enforcement of the terms of the 1991 Act by an aggrieved person in either the Circuit Court or High Court. The power to do so in the High Court was brought into force in 1991: Competition Act 1991 (Commencement) Order 1991 (SI No. 249 of 1991). The power to do so in the Circuit Court was brought into effect on 2 November 1992 by the Competition Act 1991 (Section 6(2)(b)) (Commencement) Order 1992 (SI No. 299).

**Groceries order** The repeal of Restrictive Practices Acts 1972 and 1987 by the Competition Act 1991 (Commencement) Order 1991 (SI No. 249 of 1991), subject to the retention of the Restrictive Practices (Groceries) Order 1987, was upheld by Keane J in *Masterfoods Ltd (t/a Mars Ireland) v HB Ice Cream Ltd* [1993] ILRM 145, above.

**Mergers and take-overs** The Proposed Merger or Take-over Prohibition Order 1992 (SI No. 56) prohibited the proposed increase from 29.9% to 53.09% of Independent Newspapers plc's holding in the Tribune Group (publishers of the Sunday Tribune newspaper). The Order was made by the Minister for Industry and Commerce under the Mergers, Take-Overs and Monopolies (Control) Act 1978 after the Competition Authority had reported to the Minister that the proposed increase would be in breach of competition law.

**Undertakings** In the 1991 Review, 23-5, we discussed the overall effect of the Competition Act 1991, which introduced into Irish law the competition rules contained in Articles 85 and 86 of the Treaty of Rome. It will be recalled that s. 4 of the 1991 Act prohibits and declares void, subject to certain important exceptions, any agreements, decisions and concerted practices between 'undertakings' which have the effect of preventing, restricting or disorting trade in any part of the State — this provision is comparable with Article 85 of the Treaty of Rome. S. 5 of the 1991 Act prohibits the abuse by any 'undertakings' of a dominant position in trade in the State, or a substantial part of the State — this provision draws on Article 86.

In *Deane and Ors v Voluntary Health Insurance Board* [1992] 2 IR 319, the Supreme Court addressed the issue as to what constitutes an 'undertaking' for the purposes of the 1991 Act. The background to the case was a dispute over fees to be paid by a hospital (represented by the plaintiffs) to the defendant Board. A number of issues arose in the case, and the application of the 1991 Act to the defendant arose as a preliminary question of law.

S. 3 of the 1991 Act defines an 'undertaking' as, *inter alia*, any person 'engaged for gain in the production, supply or distribution of goods or the provision of a service'. The Board argued, *inter alia*, that it was not an undertaking within s. 3 of the 1991 Act. It referred in particular to s. 4 of the Voluntary Health Insurance Act 1957 by which it was required to fix subscriptions for health insurance cover so that its revenue for any year is sufficient, but only sufficient, to meet the charges properly chargeable to revenue.

In the High Court, Costello J held that the Board was not an undertaking within the meaning of s. 3 of the 1991 Act, but on appeal by the plaintiffs, the Supreme Court (Finlay CJ, Hederman and Egan JJ) reversed this finding and concluded that the 1991 Act did apply to the Board.

The argument turned on the meaning of the word 'gain' in s.3 of the Act. Delivering the Court's leading judgment, Finlay CJ quoted with approval the definition of 'gain' given by Jessel MR in *Re Arthur Average Association* (1875) LR 10 Ch App 542. From this, the Chief Justice concluded that 'gain' connoted something obtained or acquired, and was not limited to pecuniary gain. He rejected the Board's contention that it be equated with the word 'profit', and he commented that if the Oireachtas had intended to refer only to undertakings engaged in making profits it would unambiguously have so stated.

The Court also rejected the contention that the word 'gain' was ambiguous. However, even if it had been persuaded on this point, Finlay CJ noted that in those circumstances the Court would have been entitled to have had regard to the Long Title of the 1991 Act. And having regard to its stated object of adopting by analogy Articles 85 and 86 of the EC Treaty, the Board's argument would have severely restricted the application and extent of the 1991 Act in a manner unintended by the Oireachtas.

It remains to discuss the range of application of the 1991 Act in the light of the *Deane* case. Aside from dealing with the circumstances of the instant case, Finlay CJ indicated that the true meaning of s. 3 was that it related to activities carried on or a service supplied in return for a charge or payment. This would exclude, he said, a charitable association which spent money without any charge or payment. It is of interest to note that, during the Oireachtas debate on the 1991 Act, the question of the Act's application to local authorities was raised, since they were not specifically excluded from the terms of the Act. Ultimately, it was considered that the Act would apply where, for example, local authorities were engaged in providing services where they are paid for such services. It was suggetsed, however, that they would not be acting for gain where they imposed service charges: 409 *Dáil Debates* col. 966, quoted by Cregan, Annotation to 1991 Act, *ICLSA*. On wonders whether this view continues to be correct in the light of *Deane*. The reference by the Chief Justice to a charitable association as an example of an organisation falling outside the terms of the 1991 Act would appear to be extremely limited in its scope. In addition, the general thrust of *Deane* appears to be to extend rather than restrict the potential sweep of the 1991 Act. It might be argued in that light that not only would all local authority activities be covered by the 1991 Act but also many of the activities of central government Department and agencies.

Finally, it may be noted that, when the substantive action in the *Deane* case was dealt with in the High Court, it was held that the resolution of the case did not require consideration of the 1991 Act: see *Callinan and Ors v Voluntary Health Insurance Board*, High Court, 22 April 1993. This decision will be discussed in the 1993 Review.

## FINANCIAL SERVICES

**Banking confidentiality** In *Glackin v Trustee Savings Bank and Anor* [1993] 3 IR 55, Costello J held that the common law confidentiality between banker and customer must be regarded as overridden by the powers conferred on a person appointed by the Minister for Industry and Commerce as an inspector pursuant to s. 14 of the Companies Act 1990. The decision is discussed more fully in the Company Law chapter, 182-3, below.

**Banking: State sector** The amendments effected by the ACC Bank Act 1992 and the ICC Bank Act 1992 are discussed in the Administrative Law chapter, 000, above. Arising from the ICC Bank Act 1992, the Central Bank Act 1971 (Section 7(4)) Order 1992 (SI No. 328) adds the ICC Investment Bank Ltd to the list of banks specified in s.7(4) of the 1971 Act, inserted by s. 30 of the Central Bank Act 1989. The effect is that ICC Investment Bank Ltd does not require a licence from the Central Bank for carrying on a banking licence.

**Building society as insurance intermediary** S. 30 of the Housing (Miscellaneous Provisions) Act 1992 (discussed in the Local Government chapter, 441, below) amended s. 29 of the Building Societies Act 1989 to remove any doubt that a building society could act as an insurance intermediary, i.e. an insurance agent, under the Insurance Act 1989. This was done to put building societies in the same position as banks in this respect.

**Credit institutions** The following Regulations on credit institutions apply to licensed banks and also ACC Bank and ICC Bank. As to ACC and ICC, see the Administrative Law chapter, 4-5, above. They do not apply to credit unions or friendly societies, which continue to be regulated under different legislative regimes. The European Communities (Credit Institutions: Accounts) Regulations 1992 (SI No. 294) implement Directives 86/635/EEC and 89/117/EEC and require the preparation of accounts in accordance with the format specified in the Directives. The European Communities (Licensing and Supervision of Credit Institutions) Regulations 1992 (SI No. 395), implementing Directive 89/646/EEC, authorise credit institutions registered in any EC Member State to operate in Ireland without a Central Bank licence. Supervision of such institutions will be effected in their 'home' State. The Central Bank Act 1971 was amended accordingly by SI No. 395. Finally, the European Communities (Consolidated Supervision of Credit Institutions) Regulations 1992 (SI No. 396) implemented Directive 92/30/EEC and revoke 1985 Regulations of the same title. These require that Central Bank supervision of credit institutions be effected on a consolidated basis, that is on a group, not a company, basis. This was, in fact, already in place as a matter of practice, but the Regulations enhance the formal powers of the Central Bank under the Central Bank Acts 1971 and 1979.

**Friendly societies** The Friendly Societies Regulations 1992 (SI No. 59) amend the 1988 Regulations of the same title in respect of supervisory committees and increases in the limit of funds to be held.

**Moneylenders** The Moneylenders Act 1900 (Section 6) (Exemption) Order 1992 (SI No. 378), made under ss.6 and 6A of the 1900 Act, as amended by s. 136 of the Central Bank Act 1989 exempts certain financial transactions and institutions from the provisions of the 1990 Act. See on this point the 1989 Review, 38.

**Trustee Savings Banks** The Trustee Savings Banks Act 1989 (Removal of Difficulty) Regulations 1992 (SI No. 133) amended s. 23 of the 1989 Act to take account of the amalgamation of the Cork, Limerick and Dublin Trustee Savings Banks to form the TSB Bank. The Regulations were made under s. 5 of the 1989 Act.

## FINANCIAL TRANSFERS (EXCHANGE CONTROL)

**General** The Financial Transfers Act 1992 is a short, but highly significant, Act which replaces the Exchange Control Act 1954 in light of the establishment of the EC Internal Market on 1 January 1993. The Exchange Control (Continuance) Act 1990 had continued the 1954 Act in operation until 31 December 1992 pending complete liberalisation of this area: see the 1990 Review, 31. For a comprehensive analysis of the Irish regime prior to the 1992 Act and of the relevant provisions of Community law which led to the 1992 Act, see McMahon and Murphy, *European Community Law in Ireland* (Butterworths, 1989), Chapter 19.

The core provision of the 1992 Act is s. 4(1), which provides that the Minister for Finance 'may by Order make provision for the restriction of financial transfers between the State and other countries.' The phrase 'financial transfers' is defined in s. 3 of the Act as including:

> all transfers which would be movements of capital or payments within the meaning of the treaties governing the European Communities if made between Member States of the Communities.

S. 4(2) of the 1992 Act further emphasises the EC dimension by stating that any Order under the Act 'shall be made in conformity with the treaties governing the European Communities.' Thus, any Order under the 1992 Act must be in line with EC Treaty principles as well as developing policy, for example, on UN economic sanctions, rather than being based on Irish exchange control policy. S. 7 provides for a negative resolution procedure in the Oireachtas in respect of any Orders made under s. 4.

S. 5 of the 1992 Act provides that it is an offence to contravene any provision of an Order made under s. 4 of the Act, while s. 6 of the 1992 Act provides for penalties for non-compliance. Where a summary prosecution is brought, penalties of up to £1,000 and up to one years' imporisonment are provided for. However, on indictment, fines of up to £10 million and imprisonment for up to 10 years are possible, thus indicating the serious international dimension to the 1992 Act.

The 1992 Act came into operation on 18 December 1992 on being signed by the President. Within three days, two Statutory Instruments had been signed by the Minister for Finance, purportedly under s. 4, in order to continue financial sanctions previously put in place under the Exchange Control Act 1954. The Financial Transfers (Iraq) Regulations 1992 (SI No. 414) replaced the Exchange Control Regulations 1991: see the 1991 Review, 26. The Financial Transfers (Federal Republic of Yugoslavia (Serbia and Montenegro)) Regulations 1992 (SI No. 415) replaced the Exchange Control Regulations 1992 (SI No. 134). Both these SIs, requiring Central Bank permission to make any financial transfers to the States in question, in accordance with UN Security Council sanctions, were stated to come into effect on 1 January 1993.

One brief comment may be made on these. Since both SI No. 414 and SI No. 415 replace Statutory Instruments which were titled 'Regulations' it is, perhaps, understandable that both are described as 'Regulations' made under the power conferred by s. 4 of the 1992 Act. However, s. 4, of course, authorises the Minister to make 'Orders' only, and on this basis there may be some difficulty in enforcing both SIs were that to become necessary. This is of some importance in view of the international significance of the requirements imposed by both SIs and also the enforceability of the penalties provided for in s.6 of the 1992 Act.

**Role of Central Bank** In *Desmond and Dedeir v Glackin, Minister for Industry and Commerce and Ors (No. 2)* [1993] 3 IR 67 (discussed more fully in the Company Law chapter, 74-81, below), an inspector had been appointed to investigate a transaction involving a number of companies under the Companies Act 1990. The inspector requested the Minister for Industry and Commerce to obtain certain exchange control information concerning the transaction. The Minister requested the Minister for Finance to obtain this information from the Central Bank to whom it had been given in the first place under the exchange control legislation.

The High Court and Supreme Court held that the Minister for Finance had been entitled to seek the exchange control information from the Central Bank under s. 19 of the Central Bank Act 1989, since the Central Bank acted as agent for the Minister in the collection of exchange control information under s. 28 of the Exchange Control Act 1954 (now replaced by the Financial Transfers Act 1992: see above). The courts also held the Minister was, in turn, entitled to pass on such information to another Minister and did not act in breach of s. 4 of the Official Secrets Act 1963.

In the High Court, O'Hanlon J had stated that no right to privacy, whether common law or constitutional in nature, had been breached in the instant case through the communication of the exchange control information from the Central Bank to the inspector. He noted that the communication related entirely to the better performance of public functions by public bodies and that the protection of a free society would not be better served by the operation of affairs of State in water-tight compartments. The Supreme Court (Finlay CJ, Hederman, McCarthy, O'Flaherty and Egan JJ) affirmed this general approach.

## FREEDOM TO PROVIDE SERVICES

**Hairdressing** The European Communities (Right of Establishment and Freedom to Provide Services in Hairdressing) Regulations 1992 (SI No. 315) implemented Directive 82/489/EEC.

**Veterinary medicine** The European Communities (Recognition of Qualifications in Veterinary Medicine) (Amendment) Regulations 1992 (SI No. 253) amended the 1980 to 1987 Regulations of the same title to give effect to Directives 89/594/EEC and 90/658/EEC.

## GUARANTEE

In *Hong Kong and Shanghai Banking Corp v Icarom plc (Meadows Indemnity Co. Ltd, Third Party)*, Supreme Court, 31 July 1992 the Court affirmed a decision of Blayney J that a contractual arrangement made between the defendant and the third party amounted to a guarantee.

The somewhat complex background to this decision may be described as follows. A Greek businessman, operating through a Swiss company called Amaxa SA, wished to finance the purchase of an interest in a hotel in Corfu involving a sum in the region of IR£6 million. Amaxa had been refused a loan by a number of banks on the basis that inadequate security was available. Amaxa was told that a Credit Guarantee Insurance Agreement (CGI Agreement) might be regarded as sufficient security for the loan. The defendant company's general manager in London (the defendant then bearing the title Insurance Corporation of Ireland plc) was approached with a view to entering into such a CGI Agreement. He brought the proposal to the third party, Meadows, to which he acted as consultant, with a view to re-insuring the CGI Agreement. Meadows agreed to this, on condition that the loan to Amaxa itself be properly secured. The plaintiff bank (the bank) was then approached to effect the loan to Amaxa, the bank requiring the defendant to 'front' the CGI Agreement, that is act as principal since it was not satisfied that Meadows had sufficient capital to take on the Agreement.

The loan agreement and the CGI Agreement were effected. Shares in the Greek hotel were purportedly transferred to the defendant to secure the loan to Amaxa. The defendant later discovered that it was not lawful under Greek law to transfer shares in the hotel to a non-Greek national. Amaxa defaulted on the loan agreement, and the bank sought payment from the defendant under the CGI Agreement. The defendant repudiated liability on the basis that the CGI Agreement was a contract of insurance and that there had been non-disclosure of material information by the bank, namely that the bank had been aware that the transfer of shares in the hotel to a non-Greek national was not lawful under Greek law. The defendant also argued that it was entitled to an indemnity from Meadows, but Meadows submitted that since the defendant had not effected security for the loan to Amaxa, no indemnity arose. In the High Court, Blayney J found for the plaintiff and also held that the defendant was not entitled to claim an indemnity against *Meadows: sub nom. International Commercial Bank plc v Insurance Corporation of Ireland plc*, High Court, 19 October 1990 (see the 1990 Review, 32-4). The defendant appealed this decision solely on the question of claiming an indemnity from Meadows. The Supreme Court (Finlay CJ, McCarthy and O'Flaherty JJ) dismissed the appeal, affirming Blayney J's decision.

Delivering the Court's decision, McCarthy J stated that it was probably accurate to describe the agreement between the defendant and Meadows as one in which Meadows agreed to insure the defendant in respect of a loss that might be sustained under the CGI Agreement. He concluded that this was, in essence, a contract of guarantee. He went on to note, however, that, whether the contract between the defendant and Meadows was one of guarantee or of insurance, the reality of it was that the agreement to indemnify arose if, and only if, the loan to Amaxa was secured in the manner intended by the parties. Since the loan had not been so secured, he concluded that there was nothing on which the contract to insure could operate, and thus the trial judge had been correct in holding that the Meadows agreement to insure was inoperative.

## INSURANCE

**Insurance intermediary: building society** S. 30 of the Housing (Miscellaneous Provisions) Act 1992 (discussed in the Local Government chapter, 441, below) amended s.29 of the Building Societies Act 1989 to remove any doubt that a building society could act as an insurance intermediary, i.e. an insurance agent, under the Insurance Act 1989. This was done to put building societies in the same position as banks in this respect.

**Motor insurance** The European Communities (Non-Life Insurance) (Amendment) Regulations 1992 (SI No. 244) gave effect to the Motor Insurance Directive, 90/618/EEC. For other Regulations in this area, see the Transport chapter, 628, below.

## INTELLECTUAL PROPERTY

**Copyright dispute** *Phonographic Performance (Irl) Ltd v Controller of Industrial and Commercial Property and Ors* [1993] 1 IR 267 is an important decision on the effect of referring a copyright dispute to the Controller of Industrial and Commercial Property.

The applicant company, PPI, was incorporated by Irish recording companies in order to protect the copyright in connection with the public performance and broadcasting of the recording companies' records, tapes and CDs. S. 17 of the Copyright Act 1963 provides that the playing in public of any recording constitutes a copyright infringement where this is done without the payment of 'equitable remuneration' to the copyright owner. In accordance with s. 29 of the 1963 Act, PPI had published a 'licence scheme' setting down a schedule of payments for various types of public broadcast of Irish recordings. A number of parties, including Radio Telefís Éireann (RTE) and various disco operators (the respondents in the instant proceedings) were in dispute with PPI as to the rate of 'equitable remuneration' properly payable under s. 17 of the 1963 Act. They referred the dispute to the Controller of Industrial and Commercial Property pursuant to s. 31 of the 1963 Act. The Controller had decided that he had jurisdiction to hear the references under s. 31 of the 1963 Act, and PPI then sought judicial review of this decision. PPI argued that only a reference under s. 32 of the 1963 Act could be made, since s. 31 was limited to disputes concerning 'published' material, whereas RTE and the disco operators also sought to dispute the rate of equitable remuneration on future recordings.

The crucial point in this is that, where a dispute is referred to the Controller under s. 31, persons broadcasting or otherwise using the copyright material will not be deemed to infringe the copyright provided they give an undertaking to pay the amount determined by the Controller. Such an undertaking had been given by the respondents. Therefore, if the the respondents were correct in their contention, then they would not be required to make payments under the licence scheme pending the outcome of the referral to the Controller. Barr J concluded that the respondents were incorrect in their view of the 1963 Act and that, therefore, PPI was entitled to the relief sought.

Crucially he concluded that, having regard to the wording of ss. 17 and 31 of the 1963 Act, it was evident that a dispute referred to the Controller under s. 31 could not include the broadcasting or public user of a published recording in the future. Therefore the right to continue to broadcast material which was in dispute, subject to an undertaking, could not include future use or broadcasting.

Then he dealt with the question as to whether RTE stood in a different position from the other parties in dispute. He concluded that it did not. Although RTE had argued that, since it was a statutory broadcasting body, it was not required to seek a licence from PPI in the way that the disco operators were, Barr J held that this was irrelevant since the crucial queston was whether a licence scheme existed. Citing with approval the decision in *Performing Rights Society Ltd v Workingmen's Club and Institute Union Ltd* [1988] FSR 586, he considered that s. 32 of the 1963 Act envisaged that a licence scheme was in the nature of a standing invitation to treat and that a reference under s.32 was not dependent on the existence of a licensor-licensee relationship.

Barr J concluded that the tenor of the 1963 Act was that, where a licensing scheme was in existence, the matter should be referred to the Controller under s. 32 whose decision would be binding on all members of the class of persons affected by the decision. Pending the decision of the Controller, he stated that the requirement to pay the amount set in the licence scheme continued to apply to all persons covered by the scheme. Accordingly, in the instant case the Controller only had jurisdiction to hear a dispute under s. 32 of the 1963 Act.

It is of interest to note that essentially the same view had been taken by Keane J in connected interlocutory proceedings in an ex tempore judgment delivered less than two weeks before the judgment of Barr J: see *Phonographic Performance (Irl) Ltd v Chariot Inns Ltd*, High Court, 7 October 1992 (discussed in the Equitable Remedies chapter, 315, below).

**Copyright rules** The Copyright (Proceedings before the Controller) Rules 1964 (Amendment) Rules 1992 (SI No. 149) revised the fees payable under the 1964 Rules.

**Passing off** In *Muckross Park Hotel Ltd v Randles and Dromhall Hotel Co. Ltd*, High Court, 10 November 1992 Barron J found passing off had occurred through the defendants' use of the name 'Muckross Court Hotel' as well as the use of of certain stationery which would have led to confusion with the 'Muckross Park Hotel' owned by the plaintiff company.

In *An Bord Trachtála v Waterford Foods plc*, High Court, 25 November 1992, Keane J dealt, inter alia, with the questions whether the existence of goodwill in connection with a logo had been established as well as whether confusion was likely to arise from the two logos involved in the case.

Another interesting case in this area was the *ex tempore* judgment of Carroll J in *Gabicci Plc v Dunnes Stores Ltd*, High Court, 31 July 1991. The case reached only the interlocutory stage but is of general interest because of the issues raised. The plaintiff, the well-known Italian clothes company, applied for an interlocutory injunction seeking to restrain the defendant company from selling a range of men's sweaters.

The plaintiff claimed that the sweaters for sale in the defendant's outlets were, for all intents and purposes identical to Gabicci's own 'M Range' of men's sweaters. The plaintiff averred on affidavit that the defendant had purchased the sweaters in question from the Italian company (also called

Gabicci) which manufactured the 'M Range' of sweaters for Gabicci. There was a direct conflict of evidence on the plaintiff's contention that the defendant company had requested the Italian supplier to copy the Gabicci design; the defendant strenuously denied this and averred that, on the contrary, it had requested the supplier for a design unique to Dunnes. Carroll J pointed out that it was not appropriate to attempt to resolve this evidential dispute at the interlocutory stage, but concentrated on the issue of comparison.

On this point, she found in favour of the plaintiff's contention that the Dunnes' sweaters were, in effect, the same as the Gabicci sweaters, even if not identical. She accepted the dictum of O'Higgins CJ in *Adidas KA v Charles O'Neill & Co. Ltd* [1983] ILRM 112 that the mere copying of a design is not, of itself, sufficient to ground an action for passing off. However, she was content to conclude that there was a fair issue to be tried on the basis that the affixing of the Dunnes Stores own label 'St Bernard' to the sweaters did not sufficiently distinguish the goods so as to avoid confusion. She commented that this was not a matter of Dunnes following a fashion trend and giving good value but concerned the sale of sweaters which were, in effect, the plaintiff's.

Carroll J also considered that, because of what she described as 'the undoubted resulting damage to the plaintiff's goodwill', damages would not be an adequate remedy for the plaintiff and that the balance of convenience favoured the granting of an injunction. She also rejected an argument by the defendant that, if an injunction were granted then Dunnes could face a 'snowball effect' as other plaintiffs sued them for passing off. Carroll J commented that this seemed 'far fetched' but that the answer to it was that each case would turn on its merits, and that an injunction would, or would not, be granted depending on whether the circumstances were exactly the same as or different from the instant case.

**Patents** Because of its breadth, the Patents Act 1992 is discussed under a separate heading below, 41.

**Proprietary plant rights** Two sets of Regulations made in 1992 extended the plant varieties over which copyright-like rights exist under the Plant Varieties (Proprietary Rights) Act 1980: see the Agriculture chapter, 16, above.

**Trade marks rules** The Trade Marks Rules 1963 (Amendment) Rules 1992 (SI No. 313) revise the fees payable in respect of applications for trade marks and also deal with the procedures concerning applications for non-exclusive licences under the Trade Marks Act 1964.

## INTERNATIONAL TRADE

**Exports to Serbia and Montenegro** The European Communities (Prohibition of Trade with the Republics of Serbia and Montenegro) Regulations 1992 (SI No. 157) gave effect to Council Regulation 1432/92, while the European Communities (Prohibition of Trade with the Republics of Serbia and Montenegro) (No.2) Regulations 1992 (SI No. 203) gave effect to Decisions 92/285/ECSC and 92/314/ECSC. Both concern the sanctions imposed in relation to the conflict in former Yugoslavia.

**Exports to Libya** The European Communities (Prevention of Supply of Certain Goods and Services to Libya) Regulations 1992 (SI No. 146) gave effect to Council Regulation 945/92.

**Import of iron and steel products** The Restriction of Imports (Iron and Steel Products from the Republic of South Africa) (Revocation) Order 1992 (SI No. 54) revoked the 1989 Order, and thus eased the severe restrictions in this area arising from the partial lifting of international sanctions against South Africa. The 1992 Order was made under the Restriction of Imports Act 1962. The European Communities (Surveillance of Imports of Certain Iron and Steel Products) Regulations (SI No. 105) concern the regime to be applied in respect of imports of the specified iron and steel products from third countries other than EFTA States.

**Import of textile products** The European Communities (Surveillance of Certain Textile Products Imports) Regulations 1992 (SI No. 34) lays down restrictions, in accordance with EC requirements, on imports of textiles from third countries.

## PATENTS ACT 1992

**Commencement and repeals** The Patents Act 1992 involves a substantial updating of domestic patents legislation. We will not provide here a comprehensive account of the 1992 Act, but rather concentrate on some of its more significant elements. For a detailed analysis, see Shane Smyth's Annotation, Irish Current Law Statutes Annotated.

The 1992 Act came into force on 1 August 1992: Patents Act 1992

(Commencement) Order 1992 (SI No. 181). The effect was to repeal the Patents Act 1964 and the Patents (Amendment) Act 1966 from that date, subject to the transitional provisions which are helpfully relegated to the First Schedule to the 1992 Act.

**European and international context** Through the incorporation of many new provisions on patentability, which we discusss below, the 1992 Act has harmonised Irish law with international developments. Thus, the 1992 Act provides for the implementation of the European Patent Convention, 1973 (EPC) and the Washington Patent Co-Operation Treaty, 1970 (PCT). Both of these were intended to provide for some uniformity in the area of patentability, and many of the provisions of the 1992 Act reflect those in the EPC. The UK Patents Act 1977 also to a large extent incorporated the EPC into UK law, though there are also some differences in points of detail.

In 1989 the EC Member States signed an Agreement Relating to Community Patents, which committed them to ratification of EPC as part of the EC Internal Market programme. It was accepted that certain elements of EPC and of the 1989 Agreement, particularly the creation of a centralised litigation procedure for Community patents granted by the European Patent Office (discussed below, 45), were outside the scope of the obligations 'necessitated' by EC membership as envisaged in Article 29.4.3 of the Constitution, and that a further constitutional amendment was required to ratify it. This was achieved by including ratification of the 1989 Agreement relating to Community Patents in the referendum on the Maastricht Treaty on European Union (on Maastricht, see the European Community chapter, 326, below). The patents element of the referendum was contained in what is now Article 29.4.6 of the Constitution. EPC entered into force in this State on 1 August 1992 with the commencement of the 1992 Act.

**Patents Office and Controller** Ss. 6 and 7 of the 1992 Act retain the regime which existed under the 1964 Act by which patents are granted by the Controller of Patents, Designs and Trade Marks who continues as head of the Patents Office. S. 79 of the Act provides that the Controller is appointed by the government and that future Controllers must be appointed from within the civil service. S. 80 provides for the appointment by the Minister for Industry and Commerce (now the Minister for Enterprise and Employment) of officers of the Controller. Ss. 84 to 89 of the Act concern the keeping of the Register of Patents in the Patents Office, and ss. 90 to 96 concern the procedure in proceedings before the Controller. The details are contained in the Patents Rules 1992 (SI No. 179). S. 99 of the 1992 Act provides that fees are to prescribed from time to time. Again, the current fees are laid down in the Patent Rules 1992. S. 100 of the 1992 Act provides for the publication by the Controller of the Patents Office Journal, which is the new title for the Oficial Journal of Industrial and Commercial Property. S. 103 requires the Controller to prepare an Annual Report, which must be laid before the Houses of the Oireachtas within six months following the year to which it relates. This time limit was not included in the Patents Act 1964. For a similar time constraint, see s. 26 of the Safety, Health and Welfare at Work Act 1989.

**Patentable inventions** S. 9(1) of the 1992 Act contains the general definition of patentable inventions. It provides that an invention is patentable 'if it is susceptible of industrial application, is new and involves an inventive step'. 'Industrial application' is further defined in s.14 of the Act, 'novelty' is defined in s.11 and 'inventive step' is defined in s.13. These sections reflect the requirements of EPC, and their meaning has been elucidated in the case law on patents.

The remainder of s. 9 of the Act provides for a number of exceptions to patentability, many of which repeat similar exceptions contained in the 1964 Act. These include: a discovery, a scientific theory or a mathematical method; an aesthetic creation; the presentation of information; a scheme, rule or method for performing a mental act, playing a game or doing business; or methods of treatment of the human or animal body by surgery.

S. 9(2)(c) explicity excludes for the first time from patentability 'a program for a computer'. The protection of computer programs is now dealt with in the European Communities (Legal Protection of Computer Programs) Regulations 1993 (SI No. 26 of 1993), which link such protection to the Copyright Act 1963. Indeed, a number of the other matters excluded from patentability under s. 9 of the 1992 Act can attract copyright protection under the 1963 Act.

S.10 of the 1992 also excludes from patentability inventions which are contrary to public order and morality. S. 10 also excludes plant or animal varieties, but these are protected by virtue of the sui generis provisions of the Plant Varieties (Proprietary Rights) Act 1980. S. 10 also excludes from patentability essentially biological processes for the production of plants or animals, but does not exclude from patentability a microbiological process or the products thereof. As Shane Smyth's Annotation, *ICLSA*, points out this means that certain microbiological fermentation processes continue to be patentable under s. 10 of the 1992 Act, as under the 1964 Act (on the environmental aspects to genetically modified organisms (GMOs), see s. 111 of the Environmental Protection Agency Act 1992, discussed in the Safety and Health chapter, 529, below).

Finally, s. 9(5) authorises the Minister for Industry and Commerce (now the Minister for Enterprise and Employment) to modify by Order the provisions of ss. 9, 10 and 11 to give effect to EPC or amendments to it to which the State becomes a party. While this would appear to be an extraordinarily wide-ranging provision, it may be thought that Article 29.4.6 of the Constitution will be used to protect it from challenges to its validity.

**Patent ownership** S. 16 of the 1992 Act provides that the right to a patent belongs to its inventor or successor in title, but that if the inventor is an employee, the right to a patent is to be determined by the law of the State in which the employee is wholly or mainly employed. As Shane Smyth points out in his Annotation, *ICLSA*, the position of an employee in Irish law is governed by common law. In the absence of express terms to the contrary, it will be implied into a contract of employment that patent rights belong to the employer. A similar position applies in the copyright context. As far as many reserach institutions are concerned, of course, the matter will be dealt with by an express policy or conditions under which there is, to some extent, a sharing of patent rights and, ultimately, royalties.

**Patent application and revocation** Ss. 18 to 35 of the 1992 Act concern the procedure for applying for a patent from the Patent Office up to the date of its grant or refusal, while ss. 57 to 62 deal with revocation of a patent. The detailed provisions are contained in the Patent Rules 1992 (SI No. 179).

**Term of patent** S. 36 of the 1992 Act provides for an increase in the term of a patent life from the term of 16 years provided for in the 1964 Act to one of 20 years. Again, this reflects the position in the EPC, and also takes account of continuous representations, from the pharmaceutical industry in particular, to bring Irish law into line with international norms. It may be noted, however, that the 20 year term provided for in the 1992 Act cannot be extended in any way, unlike the 10 year extension period possible in certain circumstances under the 1964 Act. For an example of such extension, see *Application of Technobiotic Ltd*, High Court, 14 December 1989 (1989 Review, 47-8). However, as with s. 9(5) of the 1992 Act, the Minister is empowered by s. 36(4) to alter by Order the period for which a patent may continue in force to take account of any international treaty to which the State become party. It would appear that as this provision is not linked to EPC, as s. 9(5) is, it may be subject to some attack for being an invalid delegation, in breach of the principles contained in *Cityview Press Ltd v An Chomhairle Oiliúna* [1980] IR 381: see the discussion of *McDaid v Sheehy* [1989] ILRM 250; [1991] ILRM 342; [1991] 1 IR 1 in the 1989 Review, 111-4 and the 1990 Review, 464-5.

**Effect of patent** Ss. 40 to 46 of the 1992 Act describe the detailed rights conferred on the proprietor of a patent during the term of a patent. S. 40

empowers the proprietor to prohibit what is generally described as direct infringement, such as placing on the market a product which is the subject-matter of a patent. In general, lack of knowledge is not regarded as a defence in a case of direct infringement. S. 41 of the 1992 Act empowers the patent proprietor to prohibit indirect infringement, where one person provides a third party with the means, relating to an essential element of the patented invention, for putting into effect the invention to which the patent relates. Here, it must be shown that it would be obvious to a reasonable person that the means involved are suitable and intended for putting the invention into effect.

**Action for infringement** S. 47 provides that civil claims for infringement of patent rights, including injunctive relief, must be brought in the High Court. Ss. 48 to 56 deal with ancillary matters related to such actions, many of which are similar to the provisions contained in the (now repealed) Patents Act 1964.

**Short-term patents** Ss. 63 to 67 of the 1992 Act introduce the novel concept of a short-term patent, whose term is 10 years. While s. 63(4) of the 1992 Act require novelty and industrial application as with an invention to which the 20 year term applies, the third requirement of inventive step becomes, for the short-term patent, a requirement that 'it is not clearly lacking an inventive step.' The procedures for applying for a short-term patent are much less onerous than for a full patent, but on the other hand, the proprietor of a short-term patent has somewhat less extensive rights concerning infringement than the proprietor of a full patent. It remains to be seen whether the short-term patent will prove attractive to inventors.

**Patent agents** Ss. 105 to 109 deal with patent agents. Of particular interest is s. 107, which concerns the registration of patent agents. The relevant qualifications for registered patent agents are laid down in the Register of Patent Agents Rules 1992 (SI No. 180)

**EPC and recognition** Ss. 119 to 131 of the 1992 Act concern the recognition and effect of international patent Conventions, in particular the European Patent Convention (EPC), referred to earlier, 42. Of especial importance in this context is that s. 119 provides that a patent granted by the European Patent Office under EPC has the same status as a patent granted by the Irish Patents Office. S. 123 gives the High Court jurisdiction to determine disputes concerning a patent granted under EPC. S. 124 also provides that a decision given by a court of competent jurisdiction in another contracting State to EPC must be recognised in this State, that it such a decision has the same status as if made by the High Court. Both ss. 123 and 124 were required by the EPC Protocol on Recognition so that there could be a centralised litigation system for EPC.

**International patent applications** S. 127 of the 1992 Act allows Ireland to be designated in an international patent application and that it is deemed to be an application for a European patent under EPC. This complies with the requirements of the Washington Patent Co-Operation Treaty, 1970.

## PUBLIC SUPPLY AND WORKS CONTRACTS

The initial steps in implementing the EC-based requirement that public supply and public works contracts be open to bids from commercial undertakings in all Member States was given effect in 1992. The European Communities (Award of Public Works Contracts) Regulations 1992 (SI No. 36) gave effect to Directives 77/72/EEC, 80/767/EEC and 88/295/EEC on the award of public works contracts, while the European Communities (Award of Public Supply Contracts) Regulations 1992 (SI No. 37) gave effect to Directives 71/304/EEC, 71/305/EEC and 89/440/EEC concerning the award of public supply contracts. The European Communities (Review Procedures for the Award of Public Supply and Public Works Contracts) Regulations 1992 (SI No. 38) provide for a significant enforcement mechanism for the relevant Directives. The High Court is designated as the review body in respect of these contracts and may quash any contract which has been awarded in breach of the terms of the Directives concerned.

## WEIGHTS AND MEASURES

**Certification procedure** The European Communities (Non-Automatic Weighing Instruments) Regulations 1992 (SI No. 424) implemented Directive 90/384/EEC on the free movement in the EC of non-automatic weighing instruments (that is, those requiring human operation) and also the certification and checking procedure under the control of weights and measures inspectors.

**Metric units of measurement** The European Communities (Units of Measurement) Regulations (SI No. 255) is a highly significant piece of legislation. It implements the 1989 Directive on Units of Measurement, 89/617/EEC, and provides for the phased implementation, over a time period laid down in the Regulations, of the use of metric measurements in virtually all commercial transactions. The 1989 Directive does not make mandatory the sole use of metric units. For discussion of the earlier 1979 Directive on Units of Measurement, 80/181/EEC, see *The People v Ferris* (1986) 3 Frewen 114.

**Winter and summer time** The Winter Time Order 1992 (SI No. 371) gives effect to Directive 92/90/EEC on the setting of Winter Time (and thus also Summer Time) for 1993 and 1994.

# Communications

## BROADCASTING

**Broadcasting Complaints Commission** The Radio and Television (Complaints by Members of the Public) Regulations 1992 (SI No. 329) provide that the Broadcasting Complaints Commission is empowered to hear complaints concerning broadcasts licensed under the Radio and Television Act 1988.

**Ministerial announcement** *McCann v An Taoiseach and Ors (No. 2)*, High Court, 5 October 1992 was an unsuccessful attempt to injunct a Ministerial announcement by An Taoiseach concerning government policy in the referendum campaign on the Maastricht Treaty on European Union: see the discussion in the Constitutional Law chapter, 219-20, above.

**Radio licence: business** The Wireless Telegraphy (Business Radio Licence) (Amendment) Regulations 1992 (SI No. 114) revised the fees for obtaining a business radio licence and amended the Wireless Telegraphy (Business Radio Licence) Regulations 1949 to 1986 for that purpose.

**Radio licence: radio 'hams'** The Wireless Telegraphy (Experimenter's Licence) (Amendment) Regulations 1992 (SI No. 132) reduced the age at which a person may obtain an experimenter's licence (more commonly known as a radio 'ham's' licence) from 16 to 14 years. The 1992 Regulations also increased the licence and examination fees and amended the Wireless Telegraphy (Experimenter's Licence) Regulations 1937 to 1986 for these purposes.

**Radio links** The Wireless Telegraphy (Radio Link Licence) Regulations 1992 (SI No. 319) provide for the fees for radio links.

**Restrictions on broadcasting** Under the Broadcasting Authority Act 1960 (Section 31) Order 1992 (SI No. 4), effective until 19 January 1993, spokespersons for certain named and proscribed organisations were prohibited from broadcasting any material, including party political broadcasts, on Radio Telefís Éireann or stations licenced under the Radio and Television Act 1988. The Broadcasting Authority Act 1960 (Section 31) (No.2) Order 1992 (SI

No. 42) prohibits any broadcast of spokespersons for organisations proscribed under the Act of the British Parliament entitled the Northern Ireland (Emergency Provisions) Act 1991.

The extent of the restrictions imposed by Orders under s. 31 was considered by the Supreme Court in *The State (Lynch) v Cooney* [1983] ILRM 89; [1982] IR 337. In 1992, the issue was further addressed by O'Hanlon J in *O'Toole v Radio Telefís Éireann*, High Court, 31 July and 18 December 1992; [1993] ILRM 458 (SC). In the *O'Toole* case, it was held that the s. 31 Orders did not prohibit all forms of interviews with members of Sinn Féin, but only with spokespersons. Since this issue was addressed by the Supreme Court in its judgment in the *O'Toole* case in July 1993 and since 1993 saw further discussion of Orders under s.31 (in *Brandon Book Publishers Ltd v Radio Telefís Éireann* [1993] ILRM 806 and *Brandon Book Publishers Ltd v Independent Radio and Television Commission*, High Court, 29 October 1993) we will return to discuss this issue in more detail in the 1993 Review.

**Television franchise withdrawal** In *TV 3 Television Co Ltd and Ors v Independent Radio and Television Commission*, High Court, 4 May 1992; Supreme Court, 26 October 1993, Blayney J held invalid the withdrawal by the respondent, the Independent Radio and Television Commission (IRTC), of a television franchise which it had granted to the applicants. The background to the case was as follows.

The IRTC had been established by the Radio and Television Act 1988 with a view, *inter alia*, to entering into a contract with some person or persons for the provision of a television programme service. Having examined a number of proposals, the IRTC decided in April 1989 to award the franchise to operate an independent national TV channel to what was known as the Windwill consortium, represented by the applicants. This decision was stated in the IRTC's minutes to be 'subject to suitable contracts being negotiated.' After this decision, the consortium found that technical transmisison problems and the extent of the revenue earning capacity of Radio Telefís Éireann (RTE) placed serious impediments in establishing an effective national TV channel. These were addressed by the Broadcasting Act 1990, which permitted the operators of the independent TV channel to use independent transmission equipment and also placed new advertising limits on RTE. In consequence, the consortium submitted a revised business plan to the IRTC in April 1991.

In June 1991, at a meeting between the consortium and the IRTC, it was agreed that the consortium provide the IRTC by the end of August 1991 with precise information on the identity and extent of the investors in the consortium, whose membership had altered since 1989. After this meeting the consortium became aware that the Department of Communications was undertaking a review of the Broadcasting Act 1990, and that the advertising limits on RTE might be removed. The consortium was unable to obtain precise information from the Department, and informed the IRTC that arising from this it was unable to provide the financial information requested in the June meeting. The IRTC deferred any decision on the effect of this, but in October 1991, it communicated to the consortium its decision to withdraw, with immediate effect, what it described as the conditional offer of the TV franchise. The applicants sought judicial review of this decision, and as we already indicated, Blayney J granted certiorari quashing the withdrawal of the franchise.

Blayney J held that s.6 of the 1988 Act required the IRTC to award the contract for a television programme service to the most suitable applicant, having regard to the criteria set out in s. 6; and that, once it had done so, all that remained was for the actual terms of the contract to be negotiated with the applicant and to enter into that contract forthwith under s. 4 of the 1988 Act. He held that there was no obligation on the IRTC to make any further investigations into the applicant since, in the event that misleading information was provided to it, it could withdraw a contract under s.14 of the Act.

While he found it difficult to categorise the relationship between the IRTC and the consortium in the period between April 1989 and October 1991, Blayney J considered that it probably fell short of a contractual relationship. However, when viewed against the background of the 1988 Act, he felt that the decision in April 1989 undoubtedly constituted a promise by the IRTC to enter into a contract with the consortium, and the decision in October 1991 amounted to a unliateral cancellation of the April 1989 promise. Applying the principles contained in the leading Supreme Court decisions *East Donegal Co-Op Ltd v Attorney General* [1970] IR 317 and *O'Brien v Bord na Mona* [1983] ILRM 314; [1983] IR 255, Blayney J held that in making these decisions, the IRTC was exercising an administrative function created by statute and was thus obliged to act in accordance with the principles of constitutional justice. Since the IRTC had not given notice of its intention to cancel its April 1989 decision or any prior notice of its reasons, or given the applicants an opportunity to be heard, he concluded that the decision to withdraw the franchise should be quashed.

In a judgment delivered on 26 October 1993, the Supreme Court upheld the decision of Blayney J. We will return to that decision in the 1993 Review.

## FILMS

S. 2 of the Censorship of Films (Amendment) Act 1992, which provides for the appointment of Assistant Censors to the Film Censor, derives largely from the obligation on the Censor in the Video Recordings Act 1989 to classify all video films. While classification of films had taken place since 1923 under the Censorship of Films Acts 1923 to 1970, the enactment of the Video Recordings Act 1989 placed a much greater burden on the Censor, which required additional staff to classify video films. The 1992 Act is a response to the needs identified by the 1989 Act, and provided for the implementation in practice of the certification provisions of the 1989 Act which had already been brought into force in 1991: see the 1991 Review, 383-4.

Ss.3 and 4 of the 1992 Act also amend, respectively, s. 11 of the Censorship of Films Act 1923 and s. 10 of the Video Recordings Act 1989 by providing that, in the event of a successful appeal from the decision of the Censor to the Censorship of Films Appeals Board, the fee paid in advance for such appeal shall be returned to the appellant. Until the 1992 Act, the 1923 and 1989 Acts merely provided for forfeiture of the fee in the event of an unsuccessful appeal.

The 1992 Act came into force on 5 August 1993: Censorship of Films (Amendment) Act 1992 (Commencement) Order 1993 (SI No. 237 of 1993).

## TELECOMMUNICATIONS SERVICES

**Access to public telecommunication networks** The European Communities (Telecommunications Services) Regulations 1992 (SI No. 45) implemented the EC Framework Directive on Access to Public Telecommunications Networks (90/387/EEC), which provided for a liberalisation in the value added and data transmission areas. The Regulations also amend ss. 87 and 111 of the Postal and Telecommunications Services Act 1983 to take account of this liberalisation and, consequently, limited Bord Telecom's previous exclusive rights in this area.

**Schemes** The Telecommunications Scheme 1992 (SI No. 19) consolidates with amendments all previous Telecommunications Schemes.

## VIDEO RECORDINGS

**Assistant censors** The connection between the Video Recordings Act 1989 and the Censorship of Films (Amendment) Act 1992 is discussed above.

# Company Law

David Tomkin and Alan Dignam
of Dublin City University

## DEBENTURES

**Fixed charge** In *Jackson and AIB Capital Markets plc v Lombard & Ulster Banking Ltd* [1992] 1 IR 94, Costello J determined whether certain refunds belonged to the first debenture holder, or to another bank, which had lent money subsequently.

The plaintiff bank, AIB Capital Markets plc (Capital) loaned money to Mahon & McPhillips Ltd (the company) and its associated companies, secured by a mortgage debenture. This contained a fixed charge over all the 'book debts and other debts' of the company then and from time to time owing to it. In 1989, the company borrowed from Lombard & Ulster Banking Ltd (Lombard) to pay a number of insurance premiums. The company ran into financial difficulties. Capital appointed a receiver under the terms of its debenture. Brokers acting for the company obtained a cancellation of the insurance policies and a partial refund of the premiums. The refund was paid to Lombard who claimed that their loan agreement with the company gave them priority over Capital. Capital disputed this. Capital argued that the refund was a debt covered by clause 2.7 of the mortgage debenture granted to it charging:

> as a first fixed charge all book debts and other debts now and from time to time due or owing to the plaintiff bank, together with all rights and powers of recovery in respect thereof.

Lombard argued that the refund was not covered by this clause. The refund did not constitute a debt in favour of the company, but was a refund of monies owned by Lombard. Lombard pointed to the terms and conditions contained in the application form for the loan. Included there, was a provision that if a receiver was appointed, then Lombard would be entitled to immediate payment of the balance of the loan outstanding and, as paragraph 2 (e) stated, would be:

> entitled to terminate or procure the termination of the insurance cover provided under the policy/policies for which purpose the loan was

> advanced and take possession of such part of the premium as may be refunded by the insurance company.

As well as this, paragraph 4 of the application stated:

> [t]he applicant hereby assigns to the bank the benefit of all monies assured by the policy/policies or to be payable thereunder or by virtue thereof and all parts of the premiums which may be refunded to hold the same unto the bank absolutely as security for the obligations of the applicant on foot of this agreement.

On the basis of these two paragraphs, Lombard argued that the money had been paid to the brokers specifically to pay the insurance premiums, that although the bank had lost all right to the monies once they were paid it had not lost the right to any part of the premiums which might be refunded.

Costello J held the premium repaid did not constitute a 'book debt' to Mahon and McPhillips, but did constitute 'other debts'. Referring to *In re Keenan Bros Ltd* [1985] ILRM 641; [1985] IR 401, he held that once it was decided that the plaintiff bank had obtained a fixed charge on the company's future debts, then the agreement to refund the premiums created debts which were immediately captured by the charge. The fixed charge of the plaintiff bank therefore took priority, and it was entitled to the refunded premiums in priority to the defendant bank.

From the judgment, and in particular from analysis of *In re Keenan Bros Ltd*, the refunds were captured by the clause in the first debenture, which dealt with 'book debts and other debts now and from time to time owing'. Why was the defendant bank driven to argue that the refunds were not so charged? There was an omission to search the Companies Register for antecedent charges registered under s. 99 of the Companies Act 1963.

Where a system of registration under s. 99 obtains, it is commercially dangerous to lend money without making full searches against the borrower. This is despite the judgment of the Supreme Court in *Welch v Bowmaker (Ireland) Ltd* [1980] IR 251 in which a second bank was successful in claiming priority as against an earlier lender, despite the existence of a 'negative pledge' clause, as the second bank's inquiries had not revealed either the existence, or more plausibly, the extent of the first bank's charge.

**Fixed or floating charge** Denham J in *In re Wogan's (Drogheda) Ltd (No. 1)* [1993] 1 IR 157 had to decide whether the debenture created a fixed charge over the company's book debts.

In 1985 Wogan's (Drogheda) Ltd, building suppliers, initially had a turnover of £1.84 million with a workforce of 20. From 1 April 1989 to 31 December 1990 Wogan's sustained a substantial loss of £454,000. It continued trading in 1991, but the losses continued. The company became insolvent. On 19 December 1991 a petition was presented to appoint an examiner, under s. 2 of the Companies (Amendment) Act 1990. The examiner applied for directions under s. 7(6). The net question was whether Hill Samuel had an effective fixed charge over book debts. The examiner proposed a scheme of arrangements that would have meant that Hill Samuel would have received only a portion of the debt due to it if the charge was only a floating one.

Denham J held that even though the charge was described as a 'fixed' charge, this was not of itself conclusive: *In re Armagh Shoes Ltd* [1982] NI 59; *In re Keenan Brothers Ltd* [1985] ILRM 641; [1985] IR 401. Her judgment concentrates on the criteria laid down for a fixed charge in *In re Keenan Brothers Ltd.* She appears to have considered as a key requirement the one emphasised by McCarthy J [1985] IR 423:

> [i]n my view it is because it was described as a specific or fixed charge and was intended to be such,that the requirements of a special bank account was necessary; if it were a floating charge payment into such an account would be entirely inappropriate.

Thus Denham J held the presence of a 'special bank account' was critical. Clause 5(b) of the Wogan's debenture provided . . .' [t]he Company hereby covenants to pay into such banking account or accounts as may be designated for such purpose by the lender . . . all monies which it may receive in respect of book debts and other debts or securities'.

Denham J stated that as the company had not in fact opened a specific account and did not operate the account in conformity with the powers accorded to them in the debenture, the deed operated to create a floating charge and not a fixed charge. From the judgment it appears as if the floating charge could have been converted into a fixed charge on the designation by the lender/respondent of a specific bank account, and its consequent operation in conformity with this. Denham J also held that in view of the terms of the deed, it was appropriate to receive evidence that the lender did not designate any such specific account, in support of her finding whether the floating charge had now become fixed.

Her decision was appealed to the Supreme Court. Finlay CJ (with him, Hederman J, McCarthy J, O'Flaherty and Egan JJ) considered the submission that the fundamental principle applicable in the construction of the debenture in question was common to the construction of all contracts, that the intention of the parties is evidenced only by the terms of the contract. Evidence of the parties' conduct subsequent to formation was inadmissible. Denham J was mistaken in allowing evidence that a specified account had not been designated.

It was also submitted that Denham J was incorrect in her interpretation of *Keenan*: it was not necessary that there be should be evidence of the actual designation of a bank account into which book debts were to be paid, which would be monitored and controlled by the lender, in order that the charge be a fixed one. All that was necessary, was that the terms of the debenture include a term with regard to the designation of accounts into which the book debts were to be paid. Then a fixed charge arose.

The respondents argued that the High Court decision was correct: it was critical to inquire whether there was a specified or designated account into which book debts were to be paid. They also submitted that clause 5(b) must be construed as imposing an obligation to lodge the monies received in respect of book debts into such account which was entirely conditional upon the specification or designation of the account concerned. The condition arising from the provision did not operate and was not an element in the construction of the debenture until such designation had occurred. Thus if *Keenan* were followed, only a floating charge would be created.

Finlay CJ (referring to Keane J's judgment in *Keenan*) rejected the subsequent conduct of the parties as an admissible guide to the construction of the contract. In none of the subsequent Supreme Court Judgements is there any expression of dissent from Keane J's opinion. Finlay CJ went on to quote Lord Reid in *Whitworth Street Estates Ltd v Miller* [1970] AC 583 at 603 where he said:

> I must say that I had thought that it is now well settled that it is not legitimate to use as an aid in the construction of a contract anything which the parties said or did after it was made. Otherwise, one might have the result that a contract meant one thing the day it was signed, but by reason of subsequent events meant something different a month or a year later.

Finlay CJ found that Denham J's decision could not be supported on the basis that it was correct to admit evidence of the failure to designate an account as evidence to assist in the interpretation of the contract. Such a decision could only be supported if the clause was construed as conditional only, becoming effective between the parties if and when an account was designated. Thus it would be construed as a floating charge until the designation of an account.

Finlay CJ held the clauses in the debenture had the precise characteristics which were set out in the judgment of McCarthy J in *Keenan*. The charge was what it said: a fixed charge. He thus allowed the appeal, set aside the Order made in the High Court and refused the declaration that the charge over the book debts was not a fixed charge.

The Supreme Court held that the High Court was clearly in error in allowing the parties' subsequent conduct to aid in the interpretation of the contract. There are however reasonable practical objections to the application of this rule in all situations. For example, is it wrong for a judge to investigate whether or not the contract was varied by subsequent writing or words? If not, would it be wrong to see if the written contract was varied by later unilateral action accepted by the other party?

Once the Supreme Court held that Denham J was wrong in her approach, it was just a matter of deciding if the clauses of the debenture in question fitted the requirements set out in *Keenan*. The debenture in question did fit the requirements and so it created a fixed charge over the book debts. It now seems clear that to fulfil the requirements of *Keenan* there must be a clause similar to 5(b); i.e. one which states the company granting the debenture will pay into a banking account or accounts as may be designated by the lender, all monies it may receive in respect of book debts. Whether the account or accounts are subsequently designated or not has no effect on the validity of the charge as a fixed charge.

The Supreme Court decision has been criticised by Michael Fealy 'Fixed Charges Over Bookdebts: A Loosening of the Reins' (1993) 12 ILT 133-135.

In this article Fealey argues forcefully that Denham J's interpretation of clause 5(b) is correct. He concludes his criticism of the Supreme Court decision on policy grounds, by stating, at p. 135:

> [i]t now seems possible for a creditor to allow his debtor the flexibility of continuing to trade in the ordinary course of business, and yet retain all the advantages of fixed security over him by the simple expedient of providing for such separate and controlled accounts as may be designated. This seems unfair to other creditors who may deal with the debtor to their prejudice assuming that the debtor is trading normally with his own assets.

Fealy suggests that this case goes towards the consummation of every banker's dream — the creation of a fixed security over the stock in trade of a debtor.

This point is argued even more forcibly by Dr M. Forde, *Company Law*, p. 503, who states 'it now appears that one can also have a fixed charge on a company's other current assets, such as stock in trade, raw materials and the like'. He continues to suggest how a document could be drawn up, which, while describing itself as creating a fixed charge, permits the company to continue dealing with those items in the ordinary course of business. He suggests that the floating charge will now become 'practically defunct and changes in the Companies Acts, to deal with preferential debts, can be anticipated'. To date, the Irish legislature has not yet dealt with this alarming possibility.

# MINORITY PROTECTION

**Amendment of pleadings to claim under *Foss v Harbottle*** In *Balkanbank Ltd v Taher and Ors*, High Court, 12 February 1992, the High Court considered the nature of minority proceedings under *Foss v Harbottle*.

In 1989 Balkanbank (a semi-state bank incorporated under Bulgarian law) agreed with Via Holdings Ltd (then Taher Investments Ltd (TIL)) to take part in a joint business venture. The vehicle for this joint venture was Balkan International Ltd (BIL), incorporated in Ireland on the 19th of February 1990. Balkanbank and TIL were equal shareholders. The Board of Directors consisted of two nominees from Balkanbank, Ivan Mironov, the President of Balkanbank and Assen Ochanov, and two nominees from TIL, Naser Taher, who was Chairman of the Board and Kevin McGrath.

In June 1990 Balkanbank made a block deposit of $7 million in the American Express Bank (AEB) in Vienna. The purpose was to provide a security against which BIL could obtain loans to finance proposed projects. Soon after the deposit was made, Mr Taher and Mr McGrath, acting in their capacity as directors of BIL, obtained a loan of $7 million dollars from AEB in Vienna and transferred the entire sum to a bank account owned by BIL in the Banque Nationale de Paris in Dublin. Various disbursements were made from that account and a balance of $4,150,000 remained on deposit in the name of the solicitors for the defendants.

Balkanbank claimed that in obtaining the loan of $7 million Mr Taher and Mr McGrath acted wrongfully, fraudulently and in breach of their duty to BIL; that the Board resolution on foot of which the loan was obtained was invalid; that Balkanbank had no knowledge of the resolution, or of the fact that the loan was being obtained; and that the payments made out of the moneys borrowed constituted a wrongful disposal of assets of BIL. Balkanbank sought damages for fraud and breach of trust as well as a number of injunctions against Mr Taher, Mr McGrath and TIL. Balkanbank required an account of moneys received by the fourth defendant, a company managed by Mr Taher, and concomitant injunctive relief.

The defendants contended that the resolution which authorised the loan was valid, and that the Balkanbank Directors had full knowledge of the transaction. BIL also counterclaimed against Balkanbank for breach of a contract to transfer shares owned by Balkanbank in a Bulgarian company called Air Via Ltd.

Most of this judgment deals with conflicting evidence about whether the Bulgarian Directors were aware of the resolutions of the board, and whether they were aware of the loan and assented to it. In dealing with the issue of fraud and breach of duty, Blayney J found that Balkanbank did know of the loan and that it had assented to it and as such there was no fraud or breach of duty on the part of Messrs Taher and McGrath. Balkanbank claimed for damage and loss due to disbursements from the $7 million loan, which were not approved by the Balkanbank directors. It submitted that the case came within one of the exceptions to the rule in *Foss v Harbottle* (1843) 2 Hare 461, enabling a shareholder to sue where damage to the company is caused by conduct on the part of the majority in control of the company amounting to a fraud on the minority.

Blayney J, as the defendants did not object, made adjustment to the statement of claim, and dealt with the case as a derivative action brought by Balkanbank on behalf of BIL. The reason Blayney J did this was because Balkanbank and TIL were equal shareholders and so there was no question of any disbursements from the $7 million loan being approved by the majority shareholders. Mr Taher's casting vote as chairman put TIL in control. Balkanbank were in the same position as a minority shareholder.

Blayney J found that the majority of the disbursements made were irregular, as they were not made pursuant to a resolution of the Board of Directors but rather were made by Mr Taher or both Mr Taher and Mr McGrath. Even though these disbursements were irregular, Mr Taher and Mr McGrath only had to account for $1,271,494 which was an amount used to pay the start up expenses of BIL. The rest of the disbursements from the $7 million although irregular were amounts which had been used for projects approved by Balkanbank.

Dealing with the counterclaim by the defendants Blayney J was of the opinion that he had not sufficient evidence before him to assess any damages. He was also of the opinion that he would have no jurisdiction to deal with the internal affairs of a foreign company. Nonetheless he was asked by council for the defendant to grant an order for specific performance or to make a declaration that Balkanbank was to do all in its power to procure the registration of BIL as owner of 49% of the shares in Air Via Ltd. Blayney J dismissed any order for specific performance as it would be unenforceable on a company not amenable to the jurisdiction of the Court. Dealing with the issue of a declaration, he found that it also would have no reality as any agreement there may have been between Balkanbank and BIL for the transfer of shares to BIL was always conditional on BIL being accepted by all the shareholders in Air Via Ltd as a member of the company. As it was clear that the shareholders of Air Via Ltd would not accept BIL as a member such a declaration was pointless.

Some criticism can be levelled at Blayney J's re-articulation of the rule in *Foss v Harbottle*, which he adopted verbatim from Gower. But the rule in Ireland is subject to some particular exceptions. For example a general exception subsists in Ireland (but no longer apparently in the U.K.) 'when the justice of the case requires it': *Moylan v Irish Whiting Manufacturers Ltd*, High Court, 14 April 1980.

There appears to be some confusion in Blayney J's judgment as to the difference between a derivative action and a representative or class action. The judge said:

> I have treated this as being a derivative action brought on behalf of Balkan International but in any such action it is necessary for the plaintiff to plead that the action is brought on behalf of himself and all the other shareholders of the company.

This is with respect incorrect: the procedure is surely for the oppressed shareholder to bring an action on behalf of himself and the other oppressed shareholders in the name of the company against the company and the oppressors. Where there are only two shareholders, it seems peculiar to require the oppressed shareholder to claim on behalf of himself and his oppressor. The action is properly a derivative rather than a representative action.

One wonders why Blayney J, having expressed himself prepared to amend the pleadings to encompass an action under *Foss v Harbottle*, did not amend the pleadings to deal with the case on the basis of oppression as defined in s. 205 of the Companies Act 1963? This route permits maximum judicial flexibility, allows an order to be framed as the judge thinks fit, and, moreover, does not invoke the complicated and ambiguous jurisprudence devolving from *Foss v Harbottle* in the context of Irish law. The agreement between Balkanbank and BIL did not conform to Bulgarian law, and the judgment evidences the risk of failure to obtain proper advice about foreign law, or perhaps, failure to implement that advice.

## LIFTING THE VEIL

Barron J in *H. Albert de Baby & Co. N.V. v O'Mullane & Ors*, High Court, 2 June 1992, had to consider whether the situation which arose in this case was one which justified the lifting of the veil of incorporation.

In 1979 De Bary, a Dutch bank, commenced lending substantial sums of money to a group of companies, in which a Mr O'Mullane was the controlling light. This group purported to have bought and sold vast quantities of butter and sterling. These were the underlying security for the loans. Difficulties ensued, and the bank could not get satisfactory financial information despite its prolonged negotiations with Mr O'Mullane. Eventually it did get information; but this was somewhat disquieting, as none of the butter appeared to actually exist. The Bank considered that a serious breach of the contract with them had occurred. The Bank attempted to resolve the situation but considered that the defendants proposals were inadequate. This, combined with the alarming absence of butter, prompted the Bank to call in its loan. The present proceedings were then instituted. The Bank submitted that there had been serious default, deceit and lack of good faith. The defendants denied this and submitted that there had been no default, no notice of default had been given, and even if it had been given there should have been time for the defendants to arrange their affairs. It was germane to De Bary's case that the veil of incorporation should be lifted.

It was agreed that the legal relationship between the parties was subject to Dutch law. Barron J then decided that the account was being operated by the defendants in a manner which breached the agreement with the Bank. Under Dutch law, the Bank was not entitled to call in the loan on demand. Further, the defendant was entitled to be given time to come up with a reasonable solution to the problem. But having regard to the seriousness of the breach and the Bank's attempts to remedy the situation, the termination was valid. Apart from the Bank's remedy for breach of contract, the Bank made two further submissions. First that it be able to go behind the veil of incorporation of the several companies and to recover against the assets of any of them. Second that the Bank recover damages for deceit from Mr O'Mullane, and the several companies, in deceit and in conspiracy.

Barron J decided from the evidence and from the lack of credibility he attributed to the defendants who appeared as witnesses there was only one organisation at all times relevant to the proceedings and only one business. He then turned to consider whether fraud had occurred:

> [f]raud consists of the making of a representation of present fact which is untrue knowing it to be untrue or being reckless as to whether or not it is untrue for the purpose of inducing particular conduct on the part of the person to whom the representation is made and which does induce that conduct and as a result of which that person is damnified. In the present case it is quite clear that the bank has been damnified. It is equally clear that the Bank relied upon what it was told by the defendants. The question to be determined is whether the bank was given false information known to be false or not caring whether it was true or false for the purpose of inducing the Bank to continue making advances to the defendants in accordance with the facility agreed.

He held a number of misrepresentations were made by the defendants, knowing that they were false and with the intention of inducing the Bank to advance money. Those representations were made with the authority of Mr O'Mullane and so he was responsible for them. Thus the tort of deceit had been established and so Mr O'Mullane was responsible for the losses which the Bank had sustained. Barron J therefore held that in the instant case it would be unconscionable not to lift the veil of incorporation.

It is suggested that the area of lifting the veil requires some judicial analysis. This case does not develop or re-interpret the existing case law satisfactorily. Instead, it merely suggests that where it would be unconscionable not to do so, this will be done.

## INSPECTION

Inspections under the Companies Act 1990 can be initiated either by court order or by warrant of the Minister. Under the first, the Court can appoint an inspector under s. 7 of the Act, on the application of a shareholder, a creditor, the company itself or a director. When an order is made under s. 7 the Court specifies the matters to be investigated. The Court can also appoint an inspector under s. 8 of the Act, on the application of the Minister for Industry and Commerce. When an Order is made under s. 8 the matters to be investigated are not required to be specified in the Order and so the investigation may encompass a wider scope. Under the second method, that is under s. 14, the Minister for Enterprise and Employment (formerly the Minister for Industry and Commerce) can appoint an inspector by warrant. A s. 14 warrant states that the inspector is appointed to investigate and report on the membership of the company to determine the true persons who are or have been financially interested in the company or are able to control or materially influence the policy of the company.

In 1992, both types of investigations gave rise to discussion. In the Siúicre Éireann cases, there were two investigations, one under s. 8, the other under s. 14. In the Telecom cases, the investigation was initiated by warrant under s. 14.

**Liability for costs in a s. 8 inspection** In *Minister for Justice v Siúicre Éireann cpt* [1992] 2 IR 215 Lynch J considered whether the Minister should be reimbursed for his expenses in connection with the inspection.

Siúicre Éireann (Siúicre) was established in 1933. The Minister for Finance on behalf of the State held all the share capital of Siúicre, and exercised a dominant position in relation to the Board of Directors of Siúicre. About June 1990, it was decided that the Minister for Finance should dispose of approximately 55% of the state's holding in Siúicre, by means of privatisation. A holding company called Greencore was formed in 1991. The Minister exchanged the ordinary shares owned by him in Siúicre for shares in Greencore amounting at that time to 100% of the equity of Greencore. This exchange took place on the 20th of March 1991.

On 18 April 1991 the Minister for Finance sold 27,400,000 of his shares in Greencore and Greencore issued 12,056,544 new shares to the public, all at the price of 230p per share except for 6,500,426 shares which were offered for sale at 184p each, to certain employees and beet growers. The Minister for Finance had thus reduced the State's holding in Greencore and its various subsidiary companies from 100% to 45%.

In September 1991, the Minister for Industry and Commerce applied to the High Court to have inspectors appointed to Siúicre, and related companies. In support of this application, civil servants within the Department of Industry and Commerce deposed to the possibility of serious irregularities. Accordingly an appropriate order was made.

On 25 February 1992, the inspectors reported to the High Court. This report found various irregularities (possible and probable) in the conduct of the enterprise (Siúicre, Greencore and their subsidiaries). These irregularities all occurred between 1988 and the privatisation. In the report, the only criticism of the Board of Directors of Greencore since privatisation was that they ought to have dismissed Mr Comerford forthwith, instead of agreeing to his resignation on terms. That was not a matter that gave rise to the investigation of the enterprise.

The Minister for Justice, pursuant to s. 13(1)(a) of the Companies Act 1990, applied to Court for the reimbursement to him of expenses incurred (about £1,150,000).

The Minister for Justice contended that the scheme of Part II of the 1990 Act imposes the liability for the expenses of investigation whether under s. 7 or s. 8, on the Minister for Justice in the first instance. S. 13 intends that the Minister should be reimbursed by the company or one of the companies dealt with in the report as soon as possible.

The Minister contended that Talmino, although not a related company, and therefore not formally investigated, was dealt with extensively in the report, was at the root of much of the controversy, and was therefore liable to reimburse the Minister.

Siúicre and the other respondents who formed part of the enterprise submitted that the matters under investigation occurred at a time when the enterprise was owned and controlled by the State and thus the State should bear the cost of such any investigation. They further contended that it would be unfair to pass on the costs to the 70% of public which now owned shares in the enterprise and who had nothing to do with the alleged irregularities.

Talmino contended that it was not the subject of the investigation and that adverse comment was not a proper criterion for fixing liability. Furthermore Talmino was not incorporated in the State, had never carried on business in the state and thus did not satisfy the requirements of s. 17 and therefore s. 13 does not apply to it.

Lynch J held that the general rule must be that the Minister should be reimbursed for his expenses in such an investigation. Such investigations are in the public interest. S. 13 intended that it is *prima facie* right that a company or companies dealt with in the report should reimburse the State its costs and expenses. In this particular instance, he held, there were very special facts which have to be taken into account. Those facts were:

1. The alleged wrongdoing took place when the State controlled the enterprise. Since then the State had sold on 55% of its share in the enterprise without any knowledge of the irregularities.

2. Since then, the State had further sold another 15% (in February 1992) knowing of the likelihood of irregularities being uncovered by the Inspectors' report. Those who bought the 15% shareholding also knew of an ongoing investigation.

3. The State had thus divested itself of 70% of its shareholding in the enterprise and was seeking to impose liability for the irregularities on this 70% shareholding. Most had nothing whatsoever to do with the enterprise when the irregularities occurred.

4. The enterprise had already incurred very substantial costs and expenses in meeting various financial and other inquiries.

Lynch J concluded it would be more equitable in the light of these facts, that those in ultimate control at the time of the wrongdoing should bear the costs of the investigation rather than the successors. Thus he refused the Minister's application as against the first nine respondents.

In considering Talmino and its liability, Lynch J dealt specifically with three issues. Firstly, was Talmino a body corporate dealt with in the report within the meaning of s. 13 (1) (a)? No definition was given in the Companies Acts 1963 to 1990 and so the ordinary meaning of the words should be given. After considering the final report of the Inspectors and its references to Talmino he decided that it was a company 'dealt with in the report'.

Secondly, did the legislature in enacting paragraph (a) of s. 13(1) of the 1990 Act, intend to widen the scope of companies liable to repay the expenses of the Minister for Justice, to include companies dealt with in the report yet not under investigation? Here Lynch J decided that if the Court had power to order a company dealt with in the report, but not under investigation, to pay these expenses it could lead to strange results. The company might never have had a proper chance to put its case to the Inspectors. Thus he decided he was limited to ordering the repayment of the expenses by only such bodies corporate as were under investigation and are dealt with in the report. The power did not extend to bodies corporate which were dealt with in the report but were not under investigation such as Talmino.

Third, though Talmino was not liable anyway, Lynch J considered whether Talmino carried on business in the state within the meaning of s. 17

of the 1990 Act. There is no definition of the expression 'to carry on a business' in the Companies Acts 1963 to 1990 and therefore the phrase should be given its ordinary meaning. He decided that as the only activity Talmino had engaged in the state was to acquire 2,425 shares in Gladebrook Company Ltd in 1989 and to sell and transfer those shares to Siúcre in 1990 this did not constitute 'carrying on a business'. Therefore s. 17 of the 1990 Act did not operate to apply s. 13 to Talmino and the Court did not have any power to order any part of the expenses of the investigation to be repaid by Talmino to the Minister for Justice.

Thus he held that:

> [t]he application of the Minister for Justice for repayment of such expenses by Talmino must therefore be refused for the foregoing two reasons namely that Talmino was not under investigation by the Inspectors and that it is a foreign company not carrying on business in the State.

Lynch J stresses the facts are unusual. The matters under investigation took place while the State was in control of the enterprise. The provisions of s. 13 of the 1990 Act did not apply. This will not be the normal situation in an investigation. The intention of the legislature in enacting the provisions of s. 13 was essentially to make the wrongdoer financially culpable for the expenses of the Inspectors. In order to ensure that this was an equitable solution to the problem of who should pay for the investigation, any order under s. 13 is at the discretion of the Court. Here it would have been inequitable for the Court to have passed the liability for the expenses of the investigation on to largely innocent shareholders.

The second part of the judgment dealing with Talmino points out certain inadequacies in both the investigative process and in the provisions of s. 13. Lynch J was clear that Talmino was not under investigation and was therefore not liable for the expenses of the investigation. He also held that Talmino was not a company carrying on business in the State.

The basis of the Minister for Justice's claim that Talmino should contribute to the expenses, was that Talmino featured in the report and was at the root of the controversy. Lynch J rejected this as Talmino was not under investigation. If, as the Minister contended, Talmino was at the root of the controversy then why was it not joined to the investigation? This may have been due to the second point raised by Lynch J above, that Talmino was not carrying on a business in the State and so the provisions of s. 17 of the 1990 Act did not apply to it.

Future investigations under the 1990 Act will have to contend with similar problems with regard to companies incorporated outside the State and not carrying on a business in the State. S. 17 serves to restrict the scope of any investigation where such a company is involved and protects that company from liability for the expenses of such investigation. This was surely not the intention of the legislature and needs to be changed.

On the whole this judgment may have brought financial considerations to the fore of any future investigations of companies where there has been state control or semi-state involvement. In is unlikely that any Minister will (unless public interest has been aroused) instigate a costly investigation into such companies when his Department may eventually have to foot the bill.

**Investigation under s. 14 and who may be investigated** In *Lyons v Curran* [1993] ILRM 375, Blayney J had to determine whether the inspector's warrant permitted him to investigate and report on Talmino Ltd.

In December 1988 Gladebrook Ltd purchased 49% of the shares in Sugar Distributors Holdings Ltd and subsequently resold them to Siúicre Éireann CPT in February 1990 at a very substantial profit. The resale price was £8,680,000 payable in loan notes. Gladebrook was owned thus: C. Lyons, T.G. Keleghan, C.Garavan and Talmino Ltd, 22% each; M. Tully, 12%. On the resale of the Sugar Distributors Holdings Ltd shares to Siúicre Éireann, Talmino became entitled to a loan note for £2,104,900.

On 12 September 1991, the Minister for Industry and Commerce Maurice Curran, to investigate and report on certain companies including Gladebrook. Mr Curran's final report to the Minister stated that it was probable that:

> [Chris Comerford] is the beneficial owner of Talmino, the owner of the Talmino loan note, and Messrs Kelegan, Lyons and Murphy (the applicants) have no beneficial interest in that Company or that loan note.

The applicants claimed that they and not Mr Comerford were the true beneficial owners of Talmino and that this issue was the subject of proceedings between Mr Comerford and the applicants. S. 22 of the Companies Act 1990 provides that the Inspector's report would be admissible in those proceedings as evidence:

> (a) of the facts set out therein without further proof unless the contrary is shown, and
> (b) of the opinion of the Inspector in relation to any matter contained in the report.

The applicants opined that this would be prejudicial to their case in the proceedings with Mr Comerford. These proceedings were instituted, claiming Mr Curran's report (or such parts of it as refer to Talmino) be quashed. It was argued that the warrant by which he was appointed gave no power to investigate Talmino, since Talmino was not mentioned therein; furthermore it was a company registered outside Ireland, and it was argued, as such, outside the scope of the investigation.

Blayney J held that the case turned on a single issue 'whether the respondent's warrant gave him the power to investigate and report on Talmino'. To address this, Blayney J gave his opinion on the correct construction of s. 14(1) of the Companies Act under which the Inspector was appointed. He stated:

> where an Inspector finds a Company as shareholder in the Company he is investigating, he must go further and seek to determine the persons who are the beneficial owners of that company. If he does determine who such persons are, then clearly he has the duty and the power to include that determination in his report. And if he is unable to make a positive determination, but is able to form an opinion as to who the persons probably are, I consider that he still has a duty to include his findings in his report as it would be relevant to include and, furthermore, s. 22 clearly envisages an Inspector expressing opinions as his report is admissible in civil proceedings as evidence 'of the opinion of the Inspector in relation to any matter contained in the report'.

The applicants had submitted that if Mr Curran was entitled to investigate Talmino, then this meant that s. 9 as adapted by s. 14, which give powers to investigate related or subsidiary companies, after Ministerial approval, would be unnecessary.

The purpose of s. 9, held Blayney J, was where the inspector 'thinks it necessary for the purposes of his investigation to investigate also the membership' of another body corporate. The Inspector in such situations does not know for certain that it is necessary to investigate the body corporate, and may not be correct in his view; that is why the approval of the Minister is needed. But in the instant case, the inspector knew that it was necessary for the purposes of his investigation of the companies named in the warrant, to investigate Talmino. The inspection of Talmino was therefore within the powers already granted to him by the Minister. Talmino was not a 'related' company and so s. 9 could not have applied to it.

This case should be seen in the light of the Telecom litigation which is dealt with elsewhere in this chapter.

Blayney J referred to the Telecom litigation in his judgment, specifically *Glackin v Trustee Savings Bank* [1993] 3 IR 55 and *Probets and Freezone Investments Ltd v Glackin and Ors* [1993] 3 IR 134.

The Inspector's powers to investigate companies not mentioned in his warrant of appointment are twofold. First, if the Inspector is certain that the investigation of that company is necessary for the purposes of the overall investigation, he may investigate and report on that company. This power is inherent in the powers granted to the Inspector under s. 14. Secondly, if the company is a related company within the definition of s. 9 and the Inspector 'thinks' but does not know that an investigation is necessary for the purposes of the overall investigation then he can apply to the Minister to have the investigation extended to that company. In future, the only challenge that a company in the position of Talmino may bring to an inspection initiated under s. 14, must be based on the inspector's belief that it is necessary for the overall investigation is held *mala fide* or unreasonably.

## THE TELECOM INQUIRY

On 19 June 1990, Telecom Éireann purchased the Johnston Mooney & O'Brien site at Ballsbridge, Dublin 4. The purchase price of the site was £9.4 million. It subsequently emerged that the site had changed hands the previous year for £4 million. The purchase of the site at Ballsbridge and the dealings leading up to it became a subject of considerable public controversy. Who had benefitted, and had they done so at the public expense?

On 14 September 1991 the Minister for Tourism, Transport and Communications established a formal inquiry into various dealings leading to the purchase of the Ballsbridge site in June 1990. The Committee of Inquiry met persons and representatives of the parties involved in both the earlier sale of the site for £4 million and the later sale to Telecom Éireann for £9 million.

In October 1991, the Committee of Inquiry produced a comprehensive interim report. The report revealed that the site was purchased in 1989 from the Liquidator of Johnston Mooney & O'Brien by United Property Holdings Ltd (UPH), a company in which Mr Dermot Desmond, a well-known Dublin financier, had a substantial interest. In January 1990, UPH vested the site in Chestvale Properties Ltd (Chestvale), a wholly owned subsidiary of UPH. Mr Desmond was heavily involved in negotiating the purchase of the site to UPH and in the subsequent re-sale to Telecom Éireann in June 1990. In April 1990, the UPH subsidiary, Chestvale, was sold to Delion Investment Dealings Ltd (Delion), a Cypriot registered company, for a consideration of £2.75 million in Ansbacher Bank guaranteed loan notes due on the 16 August 1994. Delion also agreed to take on the existing debts of Chestvale which were of an indeterminable amount. On the same day, Delion sold the site on to Hoddle Investments Ltd (Hoddle) for £9.3 million and on 29 June 1990, Hoddle sold the site to Telecom Éireann for £9.4 million.

The report contained a large amount of detailed background information, but failed to come to any concrete conclusions as to who benefitted from the transactions. The Inquiry requested the immediate appointment of an inspector under s. 14 Companies Act 1990.

On 9 October 1991 the Minister for Industry and Commerce, opining that there were circumstances suggesting that it was necessary in the public interest so to do, appointed John A. Glackin as inspector to investigate and report on:

> [t]he membership of Chestvale Properties Ltd and Hoddle Investment Ltd and otherwise with respect to these companies for the purposes of determining the true persons who are or have been financially interested in the success or failure (real or apparent) of these companies or able to control or materially to influence the policy of these companies.

Following his appointment, Mr Glackin sought information from various parties concerning the subject-matter of his investigation. The following is a summary of the 1992 judgments in the company law-related litigation which arose during the course of Mr Glackin's investigation.

**Extent of Inspector's powers, retrospective nature of legislation and bias**
In *Chestvale Properties Ltd and Hoddle Investments Ltd v Glackin* [1992] ILRM 221; [1993] 3 IR 35, Murphy J considered the extent of the Inspector's powers under s. 14, whether the legislation was retrospective or not and the allegation that the Inspector was biassed, and thus disqualified from acting.

Mr Glackin (the inspector) wrote to Noel P. Smyth of Noel P. Smyth and Partners Solicitors (Chestvale and Hoddle were their clients) stating:

> [i]t has come to my attention that you are a person within the meaning of S. 10(1) of the Companies Act 1990 who may now or in the past had in your possession books and documents of or relating to the companies [Chestvale and Hoddle] and I should be obliged if you would produce these to me in the immediate future. I look forward to hearing from you within the next 24 hours.

A similar letter was sent to Ansbacher Bankers requiring information on Chestvale, Hoddle and Delion. Mr Glackin requested specific information on,

> relevant bank statements, copy bank drafts and cheques, loan applications with supporting documentation, security documents including guarantees and indemnities and copies of all relevant correspondence.

By affidavit, Mr Smyth claimed that he could not comply with the inspector's demands. To do so would infringe professional legal privilege. Also, the 1990 legislation could not be used to authorise the production of documents which came into existence prior to the commencement of the relevant sections of the 1990 Act, without infringing the constitutional presumption against retrospectivity of legislation. Ansbacher Bank Ltd agreed to disclose information regarding Chestvale, but, on the advice of their solicitors and counsel, expressed doubts as to the rights of the inspector to documents regarding Delion.

A week after his original letter, the inspector instigated proceedings against the Bank and the solicitor seeking an order directing the defendants to produce the documents requested by the inspector. The inspector also applied *ex-parte* for, and was granted an order directing the defendants to preserve within the jurisdiction all relevant documents.

Chestvale and Hoddle applied for judicial review. The grounds were:

1. Part II of the Companies Act 1990 (ss. 10 and 14) is not retrospective in effect, and thus did not empower the inspector to compel production of documents which came into existence prior to the commencement of the Act. Were the Act to be construed as being retrospective in effect then it would be unconstitutional.

2. The inspector's firm had at one time in the past acted as solicitors for Patrick Doherty who claimed to be the beneficial owner of the issued share capital in the applicant companies. The inspector was disqualified from acting in that capacity, as he could not be seen to be or would not be seen to be impartial.

3. The demand made for documents relating to Delion was unsustainable; the examiner was not appointed to investigate or report on the membership of that company. The company was not a 'related company' within the meaning of s. 9 of the 1990 Act as adapted by s. 14(5). The demand for documents as a whole is a single demand and if the part relating to Delion was invalid, then the whole demand was invalid.

4. The inspector's demand was so wide and oppressive in both its terms and time limits that it was an unreasonable and invalid use of the statutory powers which the Act purported to confer on the inspector.

Murphy J, addressing the retrospectivity argument, outlined the accepted definition set out in *Hamilton v Hamilton* [1982] ILRM 290; [1982] IR 466. There legislation is said to be retrospective if it:

> takes away or impairs any vested right acquired under existing laws or creates a new obligation, or imposes a new duty, or attaches a new disability in respect to transactions or considerations already passed.

He then considered the common law presumption that parliament intended the legislation to be prospective. The basis of this presumption was that retrospective operation would cause injustice. The issue here was whether an inspector could exercise the powers under the 1990 Act to procure documents or obtain information which pre-dated the coming into operation of the Act. Murphy J was in no doubt that although the Act did not expressly say so, the intention of the legislature was that it should so operate. He states that:

> Part II thereof was intended to be available to him [the inspector] to enable him to explore matters which are of their nature historic in their origins and which would entail, at least in the years immediately following the enactment of the 1990 Act, a review of facts and documents pre-dating the coming into operation of the Act.

Turning to the question of the constitutionality of this effect, was Article 40.3, which protected property rights infringed? The Attorney General contended that this right was a personal one: a corporate body could not avail of it. Murphy J agreeing, held that 'the absence of an individual Irish citizen asserting his own constitutional rights is fatal to the argument'.

Murphy J said the limited intrusion on the applicants' contractual rights consequent on the 1990 Act could not be seen as an unjust attack on the applicants' property rights or a failure to vindicate them as far as practicable. The minimal interference was fully justified as a means of reconciling the exercise of property rights with the exigencies of the common good as provided by Article 43.2.1 of the Constitution.

In concluding this first ground he stated:

> [i]t is my view, therefore, that notwithstanding the presumption against retrospectivity in all legislation enacted by the Oireachtas, Part II of the Companies Act 1990 operates retrospectively to the extent that any inspector appointed by the Minister under s. 14 of that Act is entitled to compel the production of documents from persons having the custody thereof notwithstanding the fact that the contract under which such custody was obtained was made before the relevant sections of the legislation came into operation and this is so whether the person having such custody is a bank or a solicitor though subject in the case of a solicitor to the preservation by s. 23 of the Act to the full legal professional privilege of the client.

Secondly, was Mr Glackin disqualified on the grounds of bias? Blayney J held Mr Glackin would be necessarily disqualified from exercising a quasi-judicial function in any matter in which Mr Doherty was involved. Were Mr

Glackin an arbitrator in a dispute involving Mr Doherty, a 'right minded person' viewing the situation from the arbitral opponent's side, would be bound to conclude that there was 'a real likelihood of bias'. Mr Glackin or any other person in such a position might act with absolute integrity and independence — this was immaterial. *O'Donoghue v Veterinary Council* [1975] IR 398 holds that 'the reasonable suspicion of bias would invalidate the purported exercise of a judicial function'. This established, Blaney J questioned whether an inspector appointed under s. 14 has a function of a judicial nature. After considering parallel situations under previous legislation, he held that there could indeed be a judicial nature to the function of a s. 14 appointed inspector.

Here Murphy J concluded that the very preliminary stage of the inquiry meant that no proceedings were currently in place, analogous to a judicial hearing. 'It may well be that a position will be reached where Mr Glackin is exercising a quasi-judicial function but until that stage is reached the present application is premature'.

Had the applicant companies *locus standi* to question the impartiality of the inspector? No, since this involved questions of the relationship between Messrs Glackin and Doherty. Murphy J held that what had passed between Mr Glackin and Mr Doherty or his associates and Messrs. Gerrard Scallan and O'Brien did not affect Mr Glackin's appointment as a s. 14 inspector.

Regarding the inspector's demands for the Delion documents, Murphy J held that Delion was not a related company within the meaning of s. 9 of the Companies Act 1990 as applied by s. 14(5)(c). Even if Delion were so related, the required Ministerial approval was not obtained for the investigation of that company. But the demand for the Delion documents did not invalidate or impugn in any way the validity of the appointment of the inspector. Nor would it excuse the addressee from producing documents relating to Delion if they also related to either Chestvale or Hoddle.

Was the demand made by the inspector for books and documents expressed in such terms and with such time limits as to amount to an abuse of the inspector's statutory powers and therefore invalid? Neither the bank nor the solicitors raised any objection based on administrative difficulty. The only concern expressed by both was that they ensure they did not breach the duty owed to clients and former clients. Hence Murphy J held that the answer must be negative.

The restrospectivity argument is of interest. Murphy J dealt with this in great detail, concluding that though the Act was retrospective in effect, the legislature had so intended this. Regarding the constitutionality aspect, a corporate body could not avail of a personal right contained in the constitution. Murphy J held, considering the legislation in the light of Article 40.3, that any interference with property rights was justified in the common good.

The judgment leaves unanswered some issues about corporations and constitutional rights. *Quinn's Supermarket Ltd v Attorney General* [1972] IR 1 excludes a company from constitutional claim to equality of treatment. *PMPS Ltd and Moore v Attorney General* [1983] IR 339 holds that the inclusion in Article 43.1 of the Constitution of the terms 'natural right', 'by virtue of his rational being' in Article 43.1 prevents a company from claiming a right of private property. The instant case afforded an opportunity for a principled articulation of the reason for the distinction between human and corporate personality, which was not taken up.

A corporate body by virtue of its separate legal identity can enter into contracts with other personalities both legal and human. The act of forming the contract creates property rights for the parties involved. For a human personality these property rights are protected by Article 43.1 but for a corporate body there is no protection.

The problem has arisen from the use in certain articles of the Constitution of words applicable only to human personalities. There is a difference between an article such as Article 40.4 which guarantees *habeas corpus* and Article 43.1 which contains the right to protection of property. That difference lies in the need for the protection of the property of the human personalities involved in any contractual relationship with a corporate body.

In the *P.M.P.S.* case it was held that the shareholder of a corporate body could take an action on the grounds that if the corporation suffered then his property rights inherent in his membership would also suffer. Thus the shareholder is the proper plaintiff in all such situations. But this gives no scope to creditors or others whose legal interests are enmeshed in the corporate structure, but who have suffered grievances which would attract Constitutional remedy if they were claiming as citizens.

Patrick Ussher, *Company Law in Ireland* (Sweet & Maxwell, London 1986) points out there is the potential danger of double indemnity. The plaintiff shareholder could be awarded personal compensation and the corporation obtain compensation on other non-constitutional grounds for the same loss. The shareholder as proper plaintiff fails to address the issue of the constitutional rights of the creditor who has a legal relationship with corporate body. Who is the proper plaintiff in a liquidation? Clearly the shareholder is inappropriate and the creditors may all have differing priorities.

Murphy J gave no precise reason why, although documents specific to Delion were outside the scope of the Inspector's power to demand, documents which related to Delion and also related to either Chestvale or Hoddle were obtainable.

It appears that the answer lies in the wording of s. 14, repeated in the warrant appointing Mr Glackin as an inspector, to investigate and report on:

> [t]he membership of Chestvale Properties Ltd and Hoddle Investments Ltd and otherwise with respect to these companies for the purposes of determining the true persons who are or have been financially interested in the success or failure (real or apparent) of these companies or able to control or materially to influence the policy of these companies.

The wording 'and otherwise' seems to give the inspector wide powers to investigate anything to do with these companies as long as it is to determine those interested or in control of the company. Thus the inspector can require documents which relate to Delion as long as they also relate to either Chestvale or Hoddle.

But the judgment does not determine whether the inspector must justify the grounds for requesting documents relating to Chestfield and Hoddle from Delion. It possibly does not even determine whether the inspector could have requested all documents relating to Chestfield and Hoddle. Nor does it explain whether, if the inspector requested documents relating to Chestfield and Hoddle, Delion could challenge the request on the grounds that some or all the documents were not relevant to determining 'the true persons financially interested' or 'in control' of the companies named in the warrant.

S. 14(4) (which was expressly referred to in the warrant) gives powers to the inspector to extend his investigation to other 'circumstances'. This subs. provides:

> [s]ubject to the terms of an inspector's appointment, his powers shall extend to the investigation of any circumstances suggesting the existence of an arrangement or understanding which, though not legally binding, is or was observed or likely to be observed in practice and which is relevant to the purposes of the investigation.

Assuming that such circumstances might, in the opinion of the inspector, reasonably be presumed to exist between companies in the warrant on one side and Delion on the other, does this section give extra authority to the request for documents from Delion? The wording of subs. (4) is not apt, we believe, to extend the scope of the inspection to companies not named in the warrant, except where there are non-binding arrangements.

Consequently, we do not believe that the judgment deals adequately with Delion's objection to disclosure of information about Chestvale and Hoddle. We note that the phrase '[s]ubject to the terms of an inspector's appointment' is ambiguous. May the powers under s. 14(4) only be invoked if the warrant permits this, or is it sufficient that their use be not specifically precluded by the warrant?

**Extent of Inspector's powers, nature of public interest in appointment, use of information obtained from Central Bank, and constitutionality of s. 10(5) of the Companies Act 1990** In *Desmond and Dedeir v Glackin & Ors (No. 2)* [1993] 3 IR 67, O'Hanlon J questioned whether (a) the inspector's powers extended to companies not under investigation; (b) the information obtained by the inspector from the Central Bank could be used by him without limit; (c) whether the Minister had to state in the Warrant the nature of the public interest involved in the Inspectors appointment and (d) the sanction for non-compliance with the inspector's request for information was constitutional. (Refusal carried the same penalty as contempt of court.)

The inspector sought information concerning the subject matter of the investigation from Mr Desmond. Desmond met the inspector on four occasions in November and December 1991 and answered some questions. Other questions arose from information the inspector had obtained from the Central Bank about movement of funds in and out of the country in the time leading up to the Telecom transaction. Yet others addressed the role of Freezone Investments Ltd (Freezone) an Isle of Man registered company, in the financing of Chestvale's purchase of the site in Ballsbridge. Mr Desmond did not answer these. He challenged Mr Glackin's right to put these queries. He applied to the High Court for leave to apply for judicial review.

The relief Mr Desmond sought included: (1) an order of *certiorari* quashing the warrant of appointment of the inspector for failure to disclose on its face the nature of the public interest justifying the appointment or, alternatively; (2) *mandamus* directing the Minister to state the public interest involved in making the appointment; (3) prohibition preventing the Inspector from continuing his inquiries while seeking information into the personal business affairs of the applicants or the business affairs of Freezone and/or Mr Colin Probets (owner of Freezone), or the business transactions between Dedeir (an unlimited company of which Mr Desmond is Chairman and owner of approximately 80% of the equity through a holding company) and Freezone and/or Colin Probets; (4) prohibition, stopping the Inspector from continuing his investigations while making use of information obtained from the Central Bank in breach — as alleged by the applicants — of the Central Bank Acts, 1942 to 1989; (5) a declaration that the Inspector had exceeded his powers under the s. 14 of the Companies Act 1990, how he questioned and sought assistance from Mr Desmond; (6) a declaration that s. 10(5) of the Companies Act 1990 (the provision that refusal to answer the Inspector or produce the information he requires is punishable in the same manner as contempt of court) is invalid under the Constitution and in particular Articles 38 and 40 thereof; (7) a declaration that the Inspector and the Minister breached the Central Bank Acts 1942 to 1989 in obtaining information for use by the Inspector and an injunction compelling them to return all such materials to the Central Bank.

O'Hanlon J addressed four questions which he saw as essential in determining the present proceedings. The first of these questions was:

(1)(a) Is the warrant of appointment of Mr Glackin as Inspector invalid by reason of the failure to state therein the nature of the public interest upon which the Minister relied in making the appointment?

(b) Alternatively, is it appropriate to grant an order of *mandamus* to compel the Minister to disclose the nature of the public interest which motivated him in making the appointment under the Act?

In answering both the above questions, O'Hanlon J found that s. 14 of the Companies Act 1990 under which Mr Glackin was appointed, did not impose an obligation on the Minister to define in express terms the nature of the public interest upon which he relied as justifying the appointment. However he also referred to the Supreme Court's decision in *The State (Lynch) v Cooney* [1982] IR 337 which decided that an appointment by the Minister such as this could be challenged, if the opinion of the Minister relied upon as justifying the appointment was not *bona fide* held or not factually sustainable or unreasonable. In dealing with this point O'Hanlon J found that no such grounds had been relied upon in the present case, he stated:

> I have no doubt that it was quite clear at that stage [when Mr Glackin was appointed] to all interested parties what was the nature of the public interest involved in the appointment of the Inspector, and that it arose by reason of the very substantial price paid by a semi-state body for the Ballsbridge property within a short period after it had changed hands at a price which was some millions of pounds less than that paid by Telecom Éireann. There is also the circumstance that the Chairman of Telecom Éireann had an indirect interest in UPH which had sold the property a short time previously for a price far below that paid by Telecom Éireann.

O'Hanlon J also pointed out that Mr Desmond did not raise the failure to specify the nature of the public interest during the questioning, or request information about the public interest from the Minister prior to the start of these proceedings. O'Hanlon J answered questions 1(a) and (b) in the negative.

The second question was: Whether an order of prohibition be granted to restrain the inspector from continuing his investigation while at the same time seeking information from the applicants concerning— (a) their personal business affairs, (b) the business affairs of Freezone Investments Ltd and/or Colin Probets, (c) the business transactions between the second named applicant and Freezone Investments Ltd and/or Colin Probets.

O'Hanlon J referred to Mr Desmond's grounding affidavit. Mr Desmond denied that he obtained any financial reward for his services in the sale of the Ballsbridge property. He said the inspector was not satisfied with his assurances that he was not financially interested in the provision of finance for the purchase of the site by Freezone and Colin Probets even though Mr Colin Probets bore out Mr Desmond's contention. The Inspector had continued his inquiries into Freezone, UPH, Dedeir, and R. & J. Emmet plc (of which Mr Desmond was a director and shareholder and of which Freezone was a shareholder) even though they were not 'related companies'. Mr Desmond complained that the inspector had been prying into his personal affairs which were unrelated to the matters under investigation.

O'Hanlon J also addressed the inspector's affidavit in reply. The lengthy affidavit based on information from Mr Desmond and others placed Mr Desmond at the centre of all the transactions under investigation. Based on this information the inspector was not satisfied that Mr Desmond was a person who was not financially interested in the success or failure of Chestvale and/or Hoddle. The inspector also contended that Mr Colin Probets had not a sole beneficial interest in Freezone and that as Freezone was a person interested in the financial success or otherwise of Chestvale he was entitled to inquire into the true identity of the persons on whose behalf Freezone acquired or held its interest in the success or failure of Chestvale. He stated:

> [u]ntil explained otherwise, the matters and the information available to me at present in relation thereto, raise the implication of an arrangement or understanding such as is mentioned in my warrant and which I believe I am entitled and indeed obliged to investigate.

O'Hanlon J concluded the interrogation of Mr Desmond had not been excessive and unreasonable, finding:

1. That Mr Desmond was involved with the Ballsbridge site from the first relevant transaction up until the sale to Telecom Éireann.

2. The inspector was told that the only beneficiaries from the transaction on the vendors' side were Mr Doherty and companies owned and controlled by him as vendors and Freezone and Mr Probets who were paid £1.3 million interest on a short-term loan which enabled Mr Doherty to purchase the site from UPH.

3. Mr Desmond put a very considerable amount of time and commercial expertise into bringing about the original sale by UPH to Mr Doherty and by Mr Doherty and Chestvale to Telecom, in a situation where UPH (in which Mr Desmond had a beneficial interest) had to stand by and watch the property change hands at a greater price than that obtained for it by UPH a short time previously.

4. Mr Glackin by virtue of the evidence made available to him believes that Mr Desmond master-minded all the relevant transactions to the extent that Mr Smyth (solicitor for Mr Doherty, Chestvale and Hoddle) said he was in the dark as to the identity of the clients for whom he was acting until the entire transaction was completed. Ansbacher Bank who provided part of the finance needed to purchase the property from UPH said it was in the dark too.

5. The inspector was fully justified in addressing questions to Mr Desmond as to his involvement with all parties including Irish companies and off-shore companies who were involved in the transactions through which the property became vested in UPH and then by devious routes involving at different times the intervention of Chestvale, Hoddle, Delion, Mr Doherty, Mr Probets and Freezone, became vested in Telecom Éireann.

6. None of the companies were related companies within the meaning of s. 9 of the Companies Act 1990 and there had been no Ministerial approval for the extension of the investigation to such companies. This, though, did not prevent the Inspector from addressing questions and seeking information from Mr Desmond as to the true persons financially interested in the success or failure of Chestvale and Hoddle, or able to control or materially influence the policy of the companies. O'Hanlon J agreed with Murphy J's judgment in *Chestvale Properties Ltd and Hoddle Investments Ltd v Glackin* [1992] ILRM 221; [1993] 3 IR 35 on the same point: see pp. 68-73, above.

The third question addressed by O'Hanlon J was as follows: Should an order of prohibition be granted to restrain the inspector from continuing his investigation while making use of information obtained from the Central Bank, having regard to the provisions of the Central Bank Acts 1942 to 1989, the Official Secrets Act 1963, and/or rights of privacy and confidentiality arising at Common Law or under the Constitution?

The exchange control information in question had been provided by the Central Bank to the Minister for Finance who passed the information to the Minister for Industry and Commerce who in turn passed it to the Inspector. The first issue dealt with by O'Hanlon J was that of the passing on of the information by the Central Bank to the Minister for Finance. Here he held that the Central Bank in its exchange control function was only exercising powers delegated to it by the Minister for Finance under the Exchange Control Act 1954. Thus the Central Bank was duty bound to provide the information to the Minister for Finance when it was requested.

The applicants' contention that the Central Bank and the Minister owed a duty of confidentiality to them was dismissed for the same reason, as the Minister had delegated his powers to the Central Bank and they were bound to comply with his request, and no mention of the Minister had been made in the Central Bank Acts as regards confidentiality. The duty of confidentiality in the Acts applied only to the Governor, directors, officials and other servants of the Central Bank. Thus once the information came into the Minister's possession he held it untrammelled by the provisions of the Central Bank Acts.

The claim under the Official Secrets Act 1963 was dismissed, as the communication of the information had been authorised by a Minister at each stage, as is allowed under s. 4(4) of the Act.

O'Hanlon J then discussed the right to privacy and confidentiality at common law and under the Constitution. He concluded that while there was a Common law and Constitutional right to privacy and confidentiality, there was a clear public interest in having all the information needed by the Inspector for the purposes of his investigation made available. Significantly, O'Hanlon J did not see any clear public interest of equal or near-equal weight in denying the Inspector access to the information. Thus the obtaining of the information from the Central Bank and making it available to the Inspector was permissible and did not involve a breach of a duty of confidentiality. The third question had thus been dealt with.

Finally, O'Hanlon J considered whether s. 10(5) of the Companies Act 1990 was invalid having regard to the provisions of the Constitution, and whether the applicants or either of them had *locus standi* to assert such a claim.

Ss. 10(5) reads:

> [i]f any officer or agent of the company or other body corporate or any such person as is mentioned in subs. (2) refuses to produce to the inspectors any book or document which it is his duty under this s. so to produce, refuses to attend before the inspectors when required so to do or refuses to answer any question which is put to him by the inspectors with respect to the affairs of the company or other body corporate as the case may be, the inspectors may certify the refusal under their hand to the court, and the court may thereupon enquire into the case and, after hearing any witnesses who may be produced against or on behalf of the alleged offender and any statement which may be offered in defence, punish the offender in like manner as if he had been guilty of contempt of court.

O'Hanlon J held that the above subsection contravened Article 38 of the Constitution (dealing with trial of offences), citing *In re Haughey* [1971] IR 217. There the Supreme Court found that similar legislative provisions could be construed in three possible ways, all unconstitutional. Here the power given to the High Court to '. . . punish the offender in like manner as if he had been guilty of contempt of court' was unconstitutional for the reasons stated in *Haughey*.

Since the inspector had not invoked the provisions of s. 10(5), it was argued that the applicants had no *locus standi* to raise the issue of unconstitutionality. But it emerged that the inspector had invoked the provisions of the subsections. and that the matter had been adjourned in the High Court. O'Hanlon J, noting this, also opined that the applicants had *locus standi* to raise the issue once and impasse had been reached in the questioning of Mr Desmond. There was a clear possibility or probability of the inspector resorting to the remedy under s. 10(5) of the Act. The *locus standi* objection was rejected. It was agreed that ss. (5) and (6) (provision for the Court to make such order as it sees fit) of s. 10 of the Companies Act 1990 could remain intact, deleting only the power given the High Court under subs. (5) to punish for an offence. The remaining provisions specify a clear procedure for dealing with differences of opinion between the inspector and persons he seeks to question.

While the bulk of O'Hanlon J's judgment was taken up with the Constitutional issues, there were some items of interest to company law practitioners. The scope of the power to investigate given to the Inspector under s. 14 of the Companies Act 1990 is very wide. O'Hanlon J comes to the same conclusion as Murphy J in his decision in *Chestvale Properties Ltd and Hoddle Investments Ltd v Glackin* [1992] ILRM 221; [1993] 3 IR 35 with regard to the scope of the inspector's power to investigate. O'Hanlon J's judgment is fuller. He stated:

> [t]his may well involve asking about the association of the applicants or either of them with other companies, and as to the conduct of the affairs of those companies so far as this is known to the applicants, if these matters in the reasonable opinion of the Inspector appear to him to impinge on the involvement of Chestvale and Hoddle with the Ballsbridge property.

Thus the only possible challenge to the scope of the Inspector's power to investigate would be on the grounds that he did not hold a 'reasonable opinion'. While it is important that the Inspector should be enabled to carry out a full and proper investigation (and the wideness of scope of s. 14 is helpful), there is one worrying aspect of such a wide power. What would happen if the Inspector discovers matters unrelated to the investigation but which would be of interest to the Revenue Commissioners or the Director of Public Prosecutions? Mr Glackin recognised this possibility himself in his affidavit in reply to Mr Desmond where he states:

> I accept that if in the course of so doing I discover matters which I consider not to be relevant to the investigation I am carrying out, these

> matters will not form part of my report for the Minister for Industry and Commerce.

While the inspector's hypothetical solution appears commendable, is also implausible. Would any inspector be in a position to withhold any information he judges 'unrelated' from the Minister? How would he decide? Once the Minister obtained the information he could pass it on to interested parties. A constitutional challenge to the passing of the information would be difficult, as there is a clear public interest in passing the information, which is likely to outweigh the public interest in it remaining confidential.

O'Hanlon J said the present procedure for questioning the inspectors request for information by way of judicial review was inappropriate. The correct procedure is an application by the Inspector based on s. 10(5) and (6), requesting the High Court to arbitrate in the matter. The Court can then make such order as it sees fit.

On appeal to the Supreme Court, Finlay CJ (Hederman, McCarthy and Egan JJ concurring) held that the applicants had *locus standi*; that s. 10(5) was repugnant to Article 38.1. of the Constitution; that the words 'punish in like manner as if he had been guilty of contempt of Court' were to be severed from subs. (5) as well as the words '[w]ithout prejudice to its power under subs. (5) the Court may after a hearing under that subsection' in subs. (6). Both subsections could stand, with deletions.

The same day, McCarthy J delivered the Supreme Court judgment on the non-constitutional issues in the appeal, upholding the High Court's decision.

In *Probets and Freezone Investments Ltd v Glackin and Ors* [1993] 3 IR 134, O'Hanlon J was faced with a similar challenge to that posed in *Desmond and Dedier v Glackin* above.

This application for judicial review was substantially the same as the claim for relief in *Desmond and Dedeir v Glackin (No. 2)* above. The trial judge, O'Hanlon J, who was judge in the *Desmond* case stated:

> I regard the issues that arise for consideration in the present case as having been in large measure decided by the judgment in the previous case and I do not consider it necessary to cover again much of the ground covered in that decision.

O'Hanlon J held that no objection could be taken to the way in which the Central Bank information was obtained or used. The Minister's failure to recite the nature of the public interest in the inspectors warrant was unobjectionable.

Had the inspector exceeded his powers in inquiring into the relationship between Colin Probets and/or Freezone and Dermot Desmond and/or Dedeir and should he be restrained from such inquiries?

The previous judgment related the Inspector's view of Mr Desmond's involvement in the events leading up to and including the Telecom transaction. It detailed Freezone's and Colin Probets' part. Mr Desmond was heavily involved in all relevant transactions: but claimed he had no financial interest, save through his beneficial interest in UPH.

O'Hanlon J stated:

> [a]s a result — to a very large extent — of this period of intense activity on the part of Mr Desmond, profits amounting to some millions of pounds appear to have accrued over a period of less than two years to Mr Doherty and his companies, and to Freezone and Mr probets. The inspector would not be unreasonable in assuming, until the contrary was established to his satisfaction, that Mr Desmond had been, or was to be, rewarded in some tangible manner for his contribution to the success of these ventures and further grounds for such assumption would have emerged when he learned that Mr Desmond was closely associated with Mr Probets and Freezone, that he had a Power of Attorney to act for Mr Probets, and had acted as guarantor for some of the liabilities of Freezone.

The Inspector had reasonable grounds to inquire into all links between Mr Desmond on the one hand and Mr Probets and Freezone on the other. It was part of ascertaining who benefitted by the dealings involving Chestvale, Hoddle and the Ballsbridge property. The inspector could ask Mr Desmond and Mr Probets about financial transactions involving UPH, Chestvale, Hoddle, Delion and Freezone as well as transactions involving Mr Desmond and Mr Probets in their personal capacity. Judicial review relief was refused.

The facts are the same as in the *Desmond and Dedeir* case, above. O'Hanlon J emphasized the connection between Mr Desmond and Freezone and/or Mr Colin Probets. Though he could easily have referred to his judgment of the previous day in order to dismiss the application, he emphasized the reasonableness of the inspector's inquiry into any connection between Mr Desmond Freezone and/or Mr Colin Probets. Perhaps this application was just procrastinative. That both Mr Desmond and Mr Colin Probets should bring identical applications was unnecessary. Some judicial annoyance is discernible.

Yet the decision was appealed to the Supreme Court. McCarthy J's judgment (Egan J, Finlay CJ and Hederman JJ concurring), emphatically approved that of the lower Court.

> [i]n my view, the logic of the learned trial Judge is irrefutable. The applicants, like any other person or party affected by the scope of an

> inquiry under s. 14 [of the Companies Act 1990], are entitled to invoke the assistance of the courts if their rights are being infringed, but the Courts will not come to their aid in the obstruction of legitimate inquiry. I would dismiss the appeal.

This appeal was more tactically expeditious than forensically justifiable.

**Extent of Inspector's power to investigate, refusal to comply with an Inspector's demand for information** In *Glackin v Trustees Savings Bank* [1993] 3 IR 55, Costello J, had to decide whether or not the TSB could be forced to give information about funds held by them.

Mr Desmond, on behalf of Delion told Ansbacher to pay the sum of £1.3 million and another sum of £1.131 million into a numbered account in the Trustee Savings Bank Ltd (TSB). Mr Glackin asked TSB for information about this. It was refused: hence the present proceedings. Prior to the hearing, it became clear that the money in the account belonged to Freezone. Freezone then applied to be joined as party to the proceedings. Costello J referred to O'Hanlon J's judgment (26 February) where he held that s. 10(5) (the committal for contempt provision) was unconstitutional, but did not affect the Court's powers under subs. 6.

Costello J treated the present application before him as an ex- parte application to hold an inquiry. Thus Freezone were not added to the proceedings, but could give evidence to the inquiry conducted by the Court. The High Court held an inquiry into TSB's refusal.

Evidence was on affidavit. Costello J found:

1. At some material time Hoddle was the legal entity that obtained the purchase price.

2. The price was paid into a bank. At Mr Desmond's request, it put the money into the account of Delion. Delion, again at Mr Desmond's request, transferred the money into the Trustee Savings Bank account.

3. That account was owned by Freezone, and it would appear that Freezone became entitled to the proceeds of sale or the profits of the proceeds of sale in some way.

4. It also appears that Mr Desmond had an option to purchase all the shares in Freezone since 1988. The option agreement contained a power to require the Freezone directors to resign.

Costello J thus showed why the Inspector was seeking information about Freezone: it was a necessary part of his statutory function under s. 14. The bank had misunderstood its statutory duty, he held, and so made a direction under s. 10(6) that the bank should comply with the inspector's demand. Costs were awarded against the Trustee Savings Bank.

The proper mechanism for questioning a s. 14 appointed Inspector's demand is by a s. 10(5) and (6) High Court inquiry. Costs went against TSB due to their refusal to comply with the Inspector's demand. In future, the procedure should be to inform the customer that the bank intends to comply with the request and leave it up to the customer to challenge the Inspector. But the customer can not instigate an action under s. 10(5). That is up to the Inspector upon a refusal to comply with his demand. The only mechanism available is an application for judicial review, which O'Hanlon J in his judgment of 25 February 1992 above considered inappropriate. How can this be reconciled with O'Hanlon J's opinion? One way would be to amend s. 10(5), which is now needed because of the unconstitutionality of a part of it, to include a provision for an application to the High Court by other parties. The area needs clarification.

## PRE-INCORPORATION CONTRACT

**Pre-incorporation contracts and liquidators power to ratify** Costello J in *HKN Invest Oy and Another v Incotrade Pvt Ltd and Others* [1993] 3 IR 152, considered pre-incorporation contracts and the power of the liquidator to ratify them.

In August 1991, three Germans, Gunter Knieper, Alfred Eiger and Jurgan Heilser incorporated a bogus loan brokerage called Incotrade Pvt Ltd (Incotrade). In September 1991 they fled the country ahead of the Irish and German police. They left a lot of angry creditors and a number of legal problems regarding the assets they had left behind.

Incotrade went into liquidation. The present dispute concerned the ownership of certain assets including credits standing in bank accounts in the names of Knieper and Eiger. The plaintiffs had obtained judgment against both the company and the individuals, maintaining these assets belonged to the individuals. Execution against them by way of the garnishee proceedings should be permitted. The liquidator claimed these assets were the company's property, available for the company's creditors.

The plaintiffs were Finnish companies who had reached an agreement with the three defendants in July 1991 for the provision of loans to some of the plaintiffs' clients. The plaintiffs agreed to pay commission on the loans in advance of any draw down of the loan. The commission was to be repaid if the loan was not advanced in thirty days. When no loan was forthcoming the Finnish companies sent representatives to Ireland only to find the Incotrade offices deserted and the three Germans gone. The Finnish companies then obtained judgment against Incotrade and the three defendants individually for £251,276.86. They found £84,727.35 standing to the credit of Gunter Knieper and £16,181.31 to the credit of Alfred Eiger at the Allied

Irish Bank branch in Bishopstown. They obtained a conditional Garnishee Order over the bank's indebtedness on 2 March 1992 and then applied to have it made absolute.

Were the accounts in the Bishopstown branch owned beneficially by Knieper and Eiger or by the company?

The accounts comprised money paid as commission (a) prior to incorporation of Incotrade on contracts made before its incorporation; (b) after Incotrade's incorporation on contracts made before its incorporation, and (c) after its incorporation on contracts entered after its incorporation. He then went on to consider the law as regards pre-incorporation contracts.

The common law of pre-incorporation contracts provides that an unformed company has no capacity to contract, and a pre-incorporation contract can not be ratified by the company after incorporation. (It could enter into a new contract which effects the terms of the pre-incorporation contract). S. 37 of the Companies Act 1963 modifies the position: providing that the company can ratify a pre-incorporation contract after incorporation. Here Costello J decided that although ratification could occur informally he could not infer ratification from the mere acceptance by the principal shareholder of sums paid by commission.

Could the liquidator of Incotrade ratify the pre-incorporation contracts under s. 37? He found that although there were no express powers to ratify conferred by the 1963 Act, s. 231(2)(i) empowers liquidators to 'do all such other things as may be necessary for winding up the affairs of the company and for distributing its assets'. Thus s. 231(2)(i) includes a power to ratify pre-incorporation contracts, as by this means assets could be obtained for distribution to the company's creditors which otherwise would not be available.

Could these particular pre-incorporation contracts be properly ratified? The contracts contained provisions that (a) the company would render certain services and (b) that if they did not do so within 30 days the commission would be repayable. Thus the act of ratification would entitle the other party to a return of the money paid to the company as the company had failed to fulfil the obligations it had undertaken in the contract and which the liquidator could not fulfil after ratification. Costello J considered this and found that ratification would mean that as a matter of law the pre-incorporation contracts would have existed from their date of execution. Costello J suggested (and as we later suggest, we think wrongly) it would not affect the rights of either party arising from the manner in which the contract has or has not been performed since then. He thus declared that the liquidator was entitled to ratify the pre-incorporation contracts entered into on behalf of the company prior to its incorporation.

But this left open the question of the beneficial ownership of the monies in the accounts. That could only be determined by application of the principles of equity which applied irrespective of ratification. He determined that the pre- incorporation commission was received as constructive trustees, as such a trust arises where a person who holds property in circumstances in which in equity and good conscience should be held or enjoyed by another. The holder must hold the property in trust for some other (*Hussey v Palmer* [1972] 3 All ER 744). The fact there was fraud involved on the part of these particular promoters did not change the situation in equity as they had acted in breach of trust and not to disestablish the trust. Thus the moneys in the two accounts representing the balance of commission received prior to incorporation on 13 August 1991 were held in trust for the company and could not be the subject of a garnishee order.

Next, he considered the moneys held in the accounts as commission paid after incorporation in respect of pre-incorporation contracts or post-incorporation contracts. These should have been paid over to the company by Knieper and Eiger but were retained for their own use. Here Costello J held that the two gentlemen, whether directors or not, had received the moneys as agents for the company and as such held those moneys on a constructive trust. Costello J refused to make absolute the order of garnishee and discharged the conditional order, and also made a declaratory order that the liquidator was entitled to the monies in these accounts.

There are major potential problems with the ratification of pre-incorporation contracts, and the application of equity as suggested here.

Assume X, intending to contract with C. Ltd, not yet formed, pays over money. X takes a risk. The law, X should be aware, may permit C. Ltd to ratify the contract or not. S. 37 envisages that if X chooses to do so, he may stipulate that he will not pay any money unless a promoter or future director (P) agree to honour the contract if C. Ltd repudiate it after formation. He could even go further if he suspects P's financial probity. He could require P to obtain an indemnity from a bank or insurance company, so that not only will P be bound to honour the contract, but P will have the resources to do so. If X fails to do this, and leaves the matter open, and pays the money, X must appreciate that C. Ltd will probably form binding contracts with trade creditors T, and U. If C. Ltd become insolvent, and go into liquidation, T and U will expect to be paid, as they have binding contracts. Should they be expected to take less, because X paid over money before incorporation? Surely T and U could say, 'X could have asked P to take up this contract but did not do so, and should take the consequences. Why should some of the company's funds be used to diminish what we are paid?

Trade creditors need protection more than those such as X, who choose to pay money to an as yet unformed company, without requiring P or P's bank to agree to honour the contract, if C Ltd either repudiates the contract or can not afford to pay. The presumption behind the statutory provision was that the unmodified common law could lead to unjust enrichment. Have the exceptions to the common law rule now created just such unjust enrichment as they were designed to avoid?

## RECEIVER

**Security for costs, directors duty of good faith and residual powers of directors** Keane J in *Lismore Homes Ltd v Bank of Ireland and Ors* [1992] ILRM 798; [1992] 2 IR 57, had to decide whether or not the plaintiffs should provide security for costs.

The action here arose from a housing development at Weston Park, Newcastle, County Dublin. The land was purchased by the first plaintiff and the construction of 442 houses on the site was to be undertaken by the second plaintiff. The only shareholders in the plaintiff companies were Mr and Mrs James Kennedy. The finance for the acquisition and development of the land was provided by the Bank of Ireland, and the advances were secured by Deeds of Mortgage Debenture over the assets and undertakings of both companies.

In 1989 the bank demanded repayment of all amounts owing to them within 21 days. It relented, made conditions about employing a financial controller, and in particular certain quantity surveyors and architects (defendant parties to the action) and increased its lending. Later, the bank appointed the fifth named defendant as the receiver and manager of all the assets of both the plaintiff companies.

The receiver then sold the principal assets of both companies: land and houses on the land. In April 1990 the plaintiffs brought the present action against the defendants claiming damages for negligence and breach of contract. Each of the defendants then applied for an order requiring the plaintiffs to furnish security for costs and other orders.

S. 390 of the Companies Act 1963 which provides that:

> [w]here a limited company is plaintiff in any action or other legal proceeding, any judge having jurisdiction in the matter, may, if it appears by credible testimony that there is reason to believe that the company will be unable to pay the costs of the defendant if successful in his defence, require sufficient security to be given for those costs and may stay all proceedings until the security is given.

It was argued that these proceedings were not being prosecuted in good faith for the benefit of the companies and were being brought at the instance of Mr and Mrs Kennedy because of their personal liability on foot of guarantees which they had entered into with the defendant bank. The bank claimed that the action was brought to bring pressure to bear on the bank to compromise their possible claims against Mr and Mrs Kennedy and that the other defendants had only been joined to cause them professional embarrassment and so lead to a compromise of the entire matter.

The plaintiffs argued there were special circumstances that the Court should take into account when deciding on the exercise of its discretion here: the defendants' actions had led to the inability of the plaintiffs to pay costs. So security for costs should not be required.

Keane J stated it was for the plaintiffs to discharge the onus of establishing special circumstances. The special circumstance in this case was that the Banks with the other defendants had caused the plaintiffs' financial hardship, and inability to provide security. Keane J held that the plaintiffs had not proved that this was the case. He ordered the plaintiffs to provide security for the costs of the first, second, third and fourth named defendants, and stayed proceedings until this was given.

Though in the event the Kennedys had to provide security for costs, the reasoning is important. Keane J was unimpressed by the claim that Mr and Mrs Kennedy were not bringing the above proceedings 'in good faith for the benefit of the company' but were doing so for their own personal interests. Were such an objection to prevail, a whole new layer of jurisprudence would commence: one speculates how this would have worked in the Telecom litigation. Though a receiver and manager had been appointed, the directors were not *functus officio*. The action brought lay within the residual powers of the directors. This judgment is consistent with Murphy J's dicta in *Wymes v Crowley*, High Court, 27 February 1987: see the 1987 Review, 49-50.

## EXAMINATION

**Confirmation of examiner's proposed scheme of arrangements and duty of good faith in examination proceedings** Costello J in *In re Wogan's (Drogheda) Ltd (No. 2)*, High Court, 7 May 1992, had to decide whether to confirm the examiner's proposed scheme of arrangements. He also considered how to remedy abuse of the process of Court in examination proceedings.

S. 15 of the Companies (Amendment) Act 1990 provides for the first report that an examiner presents to the Court on the company in examinership. Here, the examiner presented a s. 15 report to the Court on the 10 February 1992. At meetings of the members and creditors which took place on the 31 March 1992 he presented a scheme of arrangement. He then presented his report under s. 18 and the court was asked to confirm the scheme of arrangements.

The scheme materially affected the interests of the two main creditors of the company, Hill Samuel (Ireland) Ltd and the Revenue Commissioners. It proposed to write the debt of Hill Samuel worth £462,300, down to £235,000 and treat it as a 7-year term loan. The total due to the Revenue Commissioners was £293,402 on the 13 January 1992. Only a portion of this amount was a preferential debt. The scheme proposed the total payment to the Revenue Commissioners (over a number of years) of £73,465 which was approximately 25% of the amount due.

Both the bank and the Revenue Commissioners voted against the scheme and objected to its confirmation. Most of the creditors of the company were small creditors and were to receive only 10% of the amount due to them under the proposed scheme. A majority in number and value of the unsecured creditors voted to accept the scheme. Costello J refused to confirm the scheme.

First, on the evidence, there had been an abuse of the processes of Court at the time of the original application for protection. An affidavit sworn by the directors after the appointment of the examiner disclosed a financial situation seriously different and materially worse than that in the s. 2 petition. That petition had been verified by one of the directors.

Costello J concluded that the company had failed to pay sums due to the Revenue Commissioners in respect of PAYE and PRSI. This was a deliberate and conscious decision known to at least two directors. At least two of the directors must have known that the petition filed by the company contained information that was incorrect and that the verifying affidavit contained a deliberate untruth relating to the debt due to the Revenue Commissioners. If the Court had been informed of the company's true position and that the directors had for some time been consistently defrauding the Revenue Commissioners, it would not have made the Protection Order on the 13 January 1992 and the company would now be in liquidation.

Costello J discussed the duty of utmost good faith which exists when a s. 2 petition is presented. This duty is owed by all parties involved including the professional advisers. He stated:

> [i]n the light of what has happened in this and in other cases, it seems to me to be desirable that, when making a protection order under s. 2, the order should state that it is subject to any further order the Court may make terminating the appointment of the examiner pursuant to an application to re-enter by the examiner, and that the order should impose a duty on the examiner under s. 15(2) to consider whether any evidence adduced at the hearing was misleading in any material respect and to

re-enter the matter for further consideration should this be so before preparing a report under s. 15.

Secondly, Costello J was unwilling to make orders regarding taxation matters. These required the examiner to obtain a tax clearance certificate from the Revenue Commissioners. The Commissioners were unwilling to do so and so the investor (the scheme involved the investment of a Dublin hardware firm) required the court to Order that the tax liabilities to date be extinguished. In light of the directors' role in defrauding the Revenue Commissioners Costello J held such an order would be unreasonable. He also refused to make other orders about corporation tax and VAT, as they would be detrimental to the Revenue Commissioners, and suppliers.

Thirdly, Costello J adverted to defects in the scheme of arrangements which the examiner negotiated with the new investor of such a nature which precluded its confirmation. These were: (1) aspects of the scheme were not brought to the attention of the principal creditors until the instant proceedings; (2) the obligations in the scheme were ambiguous and imprecise; (3) the scheme ignored two guarantees between the directors and Hill Samuel. Two of the directors entered into separate contracts of guarantee with the bank by which each personally guaranteed up to a limit of £100,000 the repayment of the company's indebtedness to the bank. The directors were of the opinion that the scheme of arrangements would discharge their liabilities under the guarantees and the examiner was of the opinion that the guarantees were not the concern of the scheme. Costello J held that both parties were incorrect in their opinion and that omission of the scheme to deal with the personal guarantees was a serious defect as subrogation rights could arise and thus the whole scheme would be in jeopardy. Also the directors voted on the scheme while under a serious misapprehension, to which the examiner contributed; (4) one of the clauses of the scheme allowed the investor to amend the scheme or to withdraw from it and so the scheme would collapse. Additional costs might be incurred; the creditors would be liable for these. The Court could not conclude that any future amendments were likely to facilitate the survival of the company; (5) the scheme failed to deal satisfactorily with a claim by the mother-in-law of one of the directors to be entitled to £49,200 and accumulated interest. The examiner considered that the money was loaned by two directors and had been repaid. Costello J disagreed, considering that the creditors deserved a full explanation of how the directors and the examiner differed about who loaned the money. The creditors were entitled to have the transaction investigated by a liquidator which would not be possible should the scheme be approved; (6) the scheme provided that the investor could potentially dismiss some or all of the company's employees. If the examiner was required to terminate some or all the contracts of employment the resulting claims for damages for wrongful dismissal would endanger the scheme. One of the main aims of the legislation, he said, was to protect employees of ailing companies. The scheme failed to do this. In essence it was a vehicle to establish what was in reality (if not in name) a new commercial enterprise (new directors, new shareholders and new employees) to the probable detriment of the preferential and secured creditors of the old enterprise.

Costello J thus concluded that the scheme should not be confirmed: it was unlikely to facilitate the survival of the company as a going concern. The Revenue Commissioners submitted then that the company be wound up.

Costello J stressed the duty of the examiner to reconsider any information given at the initial application for a protection order, which may have proved misleading, and to re-apply to the Court. Holding that the making of such an order had proved clearly inappropriate, he found that the examiner had misconceived his function. The Act provides no clear guidelines as to when an examination is appropriate. This has two ramifications. First, there are insufficiently clear legislative grounds for appointing (or refusing) an examinership. While the legislation provides that the Court has discretion to appoint an examiner, it does not specify the grounds on which such discretion should be exercised. Initially, this led to judge-made descriptions of grounds: e.g. re-defining the appropriate circumstances by importing epithets. In *In re Rex Rotary Ltd*, *Sunday Business Post*, 24 May 1992, Finlay CJ stated there must be an 'identifiable' prospect of the statutory object being achieved. In *In re Atlantic Magnetics Ltd* [1993] 2 IR 561, at first instance Lardner J referred to a 'reasonable' prospect of survival. The latter was rejected by the Supreme Court on appeal from Lardner J, settling the test by stating an examiner should only be appointed where the evidence leads to the conclusion that in all the circumstances it appears worthwhile to order an investigation by the examiner of the companies affairs and see can it survive, there being some prospect of survival: see the 1991 Review, 33-5.

Second, s. 2 does not distinguish between when it is appropriate to instigate a liquidation as opposed to an examinership. A company with no chance of survival can obtain the protection of the Court to the detriment of its creditors by simply not acting in good faith when presenting the s. 2 petition. Costello J, identifying this abuse, suggested that in future the Court should make a s. 2 order subject to any further order the court may make terminating the appointment of the examiner. It should also impose a duty on the examiner under s. 15(2) of the Act requiring him to bring any misleading information to the attention of the Court before he goes on to present his report under s. 15. Perhaps this does not go far enough: initially, in s. 2 proceedings, the applicant should be required to prove that the appointment of an examiner rather than a liquidator is appropriate. This would place an added burden on both the Court and the applicant. But because an examinership suspends the contractual rights of the creditors for a period of three months, protections should not be granted lightly.

It is surprising that no creditor has yet been heard to argue that the lack of good faith present in the initial petition, which resulted in that creditor's suspension of contractual rights, is of itself actionable, grounding a claim by the creditor against either the examiner or his advisers (or the directors). Indeed, if an examinership has been initiated 'in bad faith', why has no creditor yet claimed that the examinership was void *ab initio*?

**Examiner's costs, remuneration and expenses, examiner's conduct and vesting of powers in examiner** Costello J, in *In re Clare Textiles Ltd* [1993] 2 IR 213, considered an application by the examiner of Clare Textiles Ltd (in liquidation) for payment of remuneration, costs and expenses.

The examiner applied for an order under s. 29 of the Companies (Amendment) Act 1990 for payment of remuneration, costs and expenses. The Court had previously refused to confirm the proposed scheme of arrangement, and ordered that the company be wound up. The total amount claimed by the examiner was £207,339.72p. Costello J discussed the steps the examiner had taken. At the original petition stage, the company had advanced detailed reasons why it had hope of surviving as a going concern. The parent company's shares were to be sold, new capital injected, and these considerations persuaded the Court. The examiner had requested, and obtained, an order vesting the powers of the board of directors in himself.

The examiner's first duty is to take steps to report to the Court under s. 15. In order to do this he is required by O. 75A, r.14 of the Rules of the Superior Courts 1986 to deliver his report by making an *ex parte* application for leave to deliver it. The examiner is also required to bring to the attention of the Court any particular aspects of the report which may be relevant to the exercise of its functions under the Act. Once having given liberty to deliver a report, the Court may only make an order for a hearing on foot of the report, if the examiner expresses an opinion that (a) the company would not be capable of survival, (b) that the formulation of a scheme of arrangements would not facilitate the company's survival, (c) that an attempt to continue the whole or part of the company's undertaking would not be more advantageous than a winding-up order, or (d) that there is evidence of serious irregularities in relation to the company's affairs.

Here the examiner expressed none of these opinions. The Court had no power to order a hearing on foot of the s. 15 report. The Court could only give the examiner liberty to deliver the s. 15 report: such order being an 'administrative' not a 'judicial' one. Once liberty had been given to deliver the s. 15 report, the examiner had then to carry out the functions detailed in the Act. The examiner in question argued the Court had approved his s. 15 report, the actions detailed therein, and the costs thereof. Costello J disagreed. The Court, he held, neither approves or disapproves of the s. 15 report when giving liberty to deliver. It has no statutory function or power to express any opinion on the report.

This was not the only mistake the Examiner made in which he misconstrued the 1990 Act. The survival proposals put to the Court in the s. 2 petition were dropped. The examiner then set about selling the assets of the company as if he were a liquidator. In the s. 18 report (the scheme of arrangement) the examiner proposed, and detailed the contracts of sale, and provided for the giving of redundancy notices to all the company's employees.

The examiner had no authority to prepare proposals involving the sale of the company's assets, its business and its liquidation. The examiner must use his powers to fulfil his statutory function where the company and the whole or any part of its undertaking is capable of survival. This was not done here. In the examiner's s. 15 report there was no statement (as statutorily required) whether the company was capable of survival in whole or part; only vague unsubstantiated statements about the survival of the business. The Court may make an order (s. 29) for the reasonable expenses properly incurred by an examiner. Costello J held expenses had been properly certified in accordance with the Act, and made the order.

Considering the matter of the examiner's remuneration and costs, Costello J noted s. 29(3) provides that any remuneration and costs which are sanctioned by the Court are to be paid in full before any other claims in the winding-up. The examiner here claimed £103,587. The liquidators indicated that an order for this sum would adversely affect the unsecured creditors and might affect the principal secured creditor.

Costello J considered that the examiner had been carrying out his statutory functions in accordance with the Act up until 25 January (the s. 15 report was presented on 26 January). He was entitled to remuneration up until that date but was not entitled to remuneration for the preparation of the s. 15 report itself as he did not comply with the statutory provisions for a s. 15 report. After that date the examiner was acting outside the provisions of the Act and so was not entitled to any remuneration. Similarly the examiner was not entitled to legal costs after 25 January and whether the examiner was personally liable for the costs after that date was a matter for the liquidator to pursue.

Costello J commented that when the Court appoints an examiner, the order should require him to report either by means of affidavit or in the s. 15 report as to (a) any material errors in the petition or grounding affidavit leading to his appointment and (b) when proposals for the company's survival have been contained in these documents and are not subsequently adopted, the reasons for their non-adoption. The scheme was not confirmed. The Court ordered the company to be wound up.

The examiner's function is misunderstood by some who undertake the position. Currently, there is nothing the Court can do to remedy this. This examiner lost out financially: perhaps this fact will deter others. The vesting of the powers of the directors in the examiner may initially appear innocuous and reasonable, but in the hands of an examiner who misunderstands his function, the result may be unfortunate in the extreme, if, for example, assets are sold and irrecoverably lost. Directors duties to the company and its members continue when the company is under the protection of the Court. An examiner should not be required to undertake any of these duties unless there are special circumstances requiring it.

**Confirmation of scheme of arrangements and lack of good faith in original petition** Costello J in *In re Selukwe Ltd*, High Court, 20 December 1992, had to decide whether to confirm the examiners proposed scheme of arrangements.

The examiner of Selukwe Ltd presented a s.15 report and prepared proposals for a scheme of arrangements. Two of the creditors of the company, the Revenue Commissioners and Allied Irish Banks plc (the Bank), objected to the proposals and asked the Court not to confirm them. The Bank was owed a debt of £50,262.86 plus £7,338.90 interest on an overdraft facility, secured by joint and several guarantees from two of the directors of the company, Mr Stack and Mr Byrne. The proposed scheme envisaged paying only 10% of the bank's debt over a five month period. The directors would be free of personal guarantees. The Revenue Commissioners' objections to the scheme were as follows: (a) The business was carried on unsatisfactorily; proper books and records were not maintained. (b) The directors disregarded the company's obligations to the Revenue. (c) The directors were associated with other companies which had not paid tax due. (d) The directors had not disclosed to the Revenue that a creditors meeting was held in April 1992. (e) The directors failed to pay current taxes due until ordered by the Court to do so.

Costello J found it unfair to deprive the bank of its security of personal guarantees. Thus the Court could not confirm a proposed scheme of arrangement which contained this. He removed this provision. He ordered that the directors' rights of subrogation against the company be limited in order not to defeat the purpose of the scheme.

The Revenue were owed approximately £326,770.26. Under the proposed scheme, they would only receive £99,820, Costello J, though he considered the Revenue's objections well-founded, refused to throw the proposals out. He modified the scheme. Mr Byrne and Mr Stack should cease to act as directors as their conduct in relation to the obligations due to the Revenue was such as to disentitle them from acting. Costello J, confirming the proposed scheme of arrangements subject to these modifications, expressed serious reservations as to the viability of the proposals and considered that there had been a lack of good faith in the presentation of the petition in the first place. The reason he confirmed the scheme was in the hope that 30 jobs might be saved.

Costello J here confirmed a scheme of arrangement which he considered very doubtful and commented on the lack of good faith exhibited by the parties bringing the original petition. The hope that 30 jobs might be saved was his only reason for confirming the scheme. But employees' interests are not the only ones due consideration. While Costello J correctly considered the proposed scheme of arrangement on its merits alone, did the merits outweigh the bad faith exhibited in the initial petition? It is submitted that here they did not, and the proposed scheme should not have been confirmed. The creditors of the company's contractual rights were interfered with, and money was lost by Court confirmation of the scheme. If the company did eventually fail, as was likely, yet more debt would be incurred.

While the interests of the employees of a company in a situation such as this may be more visible, they should not have priority over other considerations such as the viability of the scheme and the interests of the creditors. In any case, the job prospects of the employees would be short-lived if the company failed.

## WINDING-UP

**Costs in an application by the liquidator** In *In re Hibernian Transport Companies Ltd*, Supreme Court, 21 January 1992, Finlay J (Hederman and McCarthy JJ agreeing) considered whether the representative creditor and representative shareholders should be indemnified for costs in appealing to the Supreme Court.

Hibernian Transport Ltd and a subsidiary, Palgrave Murphy Ltd, both went into liquidation in 1970. The two companies were clearly insolvent at this time. By 1983, the insolvent liquidation had produced the unusual result that, when distribution of the assets was finally possible, all the claims of the creditors could be paid in full, and a substantial surplus would be left. The question arose as to whether the creditors of the companies were entitled to interest on the monies outstanding to them for the last 10 years and if so at what rates, before the surplus was distributed to the shareholders.

It was necessary therefore to have the issue decided by the court. For that purpose an order was sought and obtained appointing Shell International

Petroleum Company Ltd as a representative creditor, to argue the creditor's side and appointing John M. Gordon and Peter Markham as representative shareholder's arguing the shareholder's side. Before the hearing in the High Court the liquidator applied to the President of the High Court for an order directing that by reason of their representative capacity both parties to the action should be entitled to costs irrespective of the result of the issue. The President refused to make such an order at that stage but indicated that he would make such an order after the determination of the issue and irrespective of its result.

After the President's determination in this fashion, the main issue was referred to Carroll J, who after a long trial held that the creditors were entitled to interest. But the representative shareholders were unhappy, and appealed the decision of Carroll J. The issue of costs, however, was still outstanding: costs not only of the action before Carroll J, but now of the appeal from Carroll J to the Supreme Court.

This motion was exclusively an attempt by the liquidator (with the consent of the representative shareholders and representative creditors) to persuade the Supreme Court to hold, in advance, that the representative creditor and representative shareholders be indemnified in respect of costs of the appeal from Carroll J's judgment, and that the liquidator himself would be protected by being permitted to include the costs of the appeal from Carroll J's judgment as part of the winding up costs. As part of this, the liquidator asked for a determination (in advance) that if the appeal proved unsuccessful, whether the costs owed to the liquidator and representative creditors should take priority over the money due to the shareholders.

The action discussed here was a motion brought by the liquidator at the request of the representative shareholders and creditors, supported by both.

The questions were: (a) should the representative creditor and shareholder bringing such an action should be indemnified against the costs of such an action, (b) should the liquidator be entitled to include the costs of such action to him, as part of the winding up costs and (c) in the event of an appeal being unsuccessful, whether the costs owed to the liquidator and creditors should take priority over the money due to the shareholders?

It was relevant that the representative shareholders and representative creditors had agreed to the other receiving solicitor and client costs. It was suggested, but not argued fully, that as they had been appointed representatives by the High Court, such an arrangement was within their authority. This Finlay CJ rejected as doubtful in the extreme, although the matter was not fully argued.

Finlay CJ held that it was incorrect for a court to make an order for the provision of costs in advance of the decision, as to do so would be to prejudge the issue. However, given the circumstances, a declaration of intention would be made in this case, as such an action was entirely necessary to ensure the neutrality of the liquidator. No priority with regard to payment should be granted as having regard to the financial situation of the company there were no circumstances which would justify such an order.

Were the problems in this case due to the complexity of the issues or the length of the liquidation? We note with some scepticism that this insolvent liquidation is still in progress after 22 years. Finlay CJ referred to various problems about ownership of money in trust, and taxation issues, and to their complexity, but without minimizing the difficulties, it remains questionable whether current insolvency law is sufficiently well-adapted to protect creditors and shareholders if it permits a liquidation to take so long. Indeed, this judgment refers to the trial of a substantive issue by Carroll J, the appeal therefrom, and an appeal by Motion to the Supreme Court as to what the costs position should be after the substantial motion has been determined by the Supreme Court. Surely the substantive law and the Rules should be altered to make more expeditious and simple procedures obligatory?

What is the difference between (a) interfering with the trial judge's discretion by refusing to make an order for costs before the substantive issue is determined and (b) making a 'declaration' by order? There seems no difference between either course of judicial action: it is a distinction without a difference. The Supreme Court would consider itself as bound by a 'declaration' by 'order' of Finlay CJ as by an 'order'. The same arguments about anticipatory interference with the judicial discretion of any Court hearing the substantive issue apply to both.

If it is appropriate to make an order for costs before the determination of the main issue only in exceptional circumstances (such as a long and complex liquidation) and Finlay CJ was faced with making an order about costs as a side issue in just such circumstances as he declared exceptional (a long and complex liquidation) is it not excessively timid not to make an order for costs? Finlay CJ made it clear that there can be only one reason for making an order for costs at this stage and that is where 'this court should be satisfied that the issues which have been determined in the High Court are of such general legal importance with regard to the liquidation of companies as to make it desirable that they should be finally determined by this court'. The issue of payment of interest to creditors in a liquidation and the unusualness of this situation was the main issue. Finlay CJ said that the main issue involved 'a general principle of considerable importance'. It is surprising he did not follow his own lead.

**Members voluntary winding-up unsupported by report of independent person** In *In re Favon Investment Co. Ltd* [1993] 1 IR 87, it was held that failure to support a members voluntary winding-up with the report of an independent person (required by s. 256 of the Companies Act 1963 as amended by s. 128 of the Companies Act 1990) requires the Court to annul the winding-up.

The shareholders of Favon Investment Company Ltd intended to have a members' voluntary winding-up. The directors failed to make and deliver a statutory declaration of solvency in accordance with the new s. 256 inserted in the Companies Act 1963 by s. 128 of the Companies Act 1990. Under that section a statutory declaration of solvency has no effect: (a) unless a report containing the statements specified in the s. is 'annexed to the declaration'; (b) unless the report is made by an 'independent person' as defined; (c) unless the statutory declaration embodies a statement made by the independent person that he has given and not withdrawn his consent to the issue of the declaration (with his report annexed thereto); and (d) unless a copy of the declaration is attached to the notice of the holding of the general meeting held to wind up the company. Furthermore the statutory declaration (with the report attached to it) must be delivered to the registrar of companies within 15 days of the passing of the winding-up resolution.

Only when the above section had been complied with could it then be a members winding-up. As s. 256 had not been complied with, the winding-up was therefore a creditors' winding-up in accordance with s. 256(11). Although this was the case no creditors meeting had been held and so there was no appointment of a liquidator in a creditors' winding-up under s. 267. This section provides for the appointment of a liquidator by the members, whose nominee may be replaced by that of the creditors. The company had an invalidly appointed liquidator and so could not proceed with the liquidation. The liquidator applied to the court under s. 280 of the 1963 Act seeking an order giving liberty to attach the report of the independent person to the directors statutory declaration of solvency and an order directing the winding-up to proceed as a members voluntary winding up.

Costello J drew attention to the correct mechanism for curing such a defect in a winding-up procedure. S. 131 of the Companies Act 1990 provides for just such eventuality and the liquidator can apply to court under this section to have the situation remedied. The application must be made within seven days of the nomination of the liquidator or within seven days of his becoming aware of the situation. The Court has no power to extend the seven day period. In the instant case no application was brought under s. 131.

Dealing with the s. 280 application, he found that he had no jurisdiction to make the orders requested. The Court had no power to cure the defects in procedures which were adopted by making the order proposed nor could it deem the winding up to be a members winding-up when the statute provided otherwise. The Court had power under s. 280 to annul the resolution to wind up the company. This was the course he adopted. He also ordered the company be bound by any act of the liquidator taken on behalf of the company and that the liquidator be paid his costs of the application and other fees out of the assets of the company. Thus, after this order, the company was free, if it so wished, to proceed to wind-up the company as a members' voluntary winding-up in accordance with the 1963 Act as amended by the 1990 Act.

S. 131 of the Companies Act 1990 was introduced specifically to deal with this situation. Unfortunately no-one on this occasion appears to have known about it. Liquidators appointed in a members voluntary winding up do not have to be professionally qualified, and may not know of the problem, nor how to remedy it within the time provided. However, it seems right that not all liquidators in a members' voluntary winding up should have to be professionally qualified. This should be rectified by legislative intervention, allowing the court to extend the time limit for a s. 131 application in such cases.

Indeed there is a case for radical simplification of solvent voluntary liquidations. This problem has occurred before in *In re Oakthorpe Holdings; Walsh v Registrar of Companies* [1989] ILRM 62; [1987] IR 632: see the 1988 Review, 69.

We note a practical divergence in judicial approach. Carroll J stated in *Oakthorpe Holdings* that the proper applicant under s. 280, where the liquidator's appointment is invalid, should be a contributory. However, the applicant before Costello J in the instant case, was the improperly-appointed liquidator, and the order was granted without reference to whom the proper applicant should have been. This ambiguous position should be addressed.

In *Favan*, Costello J, whilst not specifically dealing with the matter *extenso*, ordered that the invalidly-appointed liquidator should be entitled to his costs and fees (if any) in respect of the aborted liquidation, out of the assets of the company. The Carroll J judgment makes no mention of costs of the application. Again, this divergence requires resolution.

**Validation of payments made by receiver** In *In re McBirney & Co. Ltd*, High Court, 2 July 1992, Murphy J considered the payment of moneys by the receiver to various creditors after a petition for the winding-up of the company had been presented.

Kevin Kelly was provisionally appointed administrator of PMPA, under the Insurance (No. 2) Act 1983. He had power to apply to Court in relation to some 50 companies which were connected to the PMPA for an order under s. 4(2)(a) of the 1983 Act. This enables the administrator to be receiver and manager of all or any part of the property and assets of the connected body concerned and confers on him such powers as the Court think fit. Mr Kelly was then appointed receiver and manager of McBirney and Company Ltd and PMPA Coaches Ltd.

Subsequently, a petition was presented for the winding up of both McBirneys and the coach company. William Horgan was appointed official liquidator of both these companies. After the presentation of the petition, Mr Kelly, as receiver and manager of McBirneys and the coach company, paid creditors of those companies £145,000 and £162,000 respectively. The official liquidator of McBirneys and the coach company contended that the payment of these sums was invalid, relying on s. 218 of the Companies Act 1963, which states:

> [i]n a winding up by the Court, any disposition of the property of the company, including things in action, and any transfer of shares or alteration in the status of the members of the company, made after the commencement of the winding up, shall, unless the court otherwise orders, be void.

Mr Fitzpatrick replaced Mr Kelly as administrator. He contended that s. 218 did not apply to a company over which a receiver and manager is appointed pursuant to the 1983 Act. If the section did apply the court should make an order validating the payments.

Murphy J referred to *In re PMPA Insurance Co. Ltd* [1988] ILRM 109 where it was clearly demonstrated that the position or office of receiver and manager of a connected body is entirely distinct from the position of the administrator of the insurer itself. Acting as a receiver and manager of a connected company is not a facet or aspect of the statutory duty of an administrator appointed under the 1983 Act. The special features of administration and the novelty of that office has no direct bearing on the rights and duties of a receiver and manager appointed over a connected body. Thus the argument of Mr Fitzpatrick based on the novelty of the 1983 Act failed.

Murphy J then considered whether or not the Court should exercise its discretion to validate the payments. In doing so he reviewed the relevant case law referring to *In re Ashmark Ltd (No. 2)* [1990] ILRM 455, *In re Gray's Inn Construction Co. Ltd* [1980] 1 WLR 711 and *In re Leslie Engineers Co. Ltd* [1986] 1 WLR 292. While the parties disputed the validity of the action there was no dispute regarding the liability of either McBirneys or the coach company for the liabilities the receiver did discharge.

The only issue was that in paying particular creditors in full the scheme of the Companies Act for the rateable distribution of the assets of the company amongst its creditors was frustrated. The weight of the authorities above was to the effect that for the Court to exercise its discretion in validating the payments the making of the payment must be shown to be for the benefit of the company or at least desirable in the interests of the unsecured creditors as a body.

Murphy J was of the opinion that while the authorities provided useful guidelines he also had to take into account the special features exhibited by the present case. The total amount of payments made by the Receiver up until 28 March 1984 was £144,978.36. These payments were broken down into eight differing categories by Murphy J lettered (a) to (h) inclusive.

Category (a) represented payments in respect of liabilities which arose prior to the date the Receiver was appointed. These payments represented settlements of claims regarding retention of title clauses and the liquidator did not dispute that they should be validated. Murphy J thus made a validating order.

Category (b) represented payments made after the presentation of the petition in respect of liabilities which arose during the continuance of the receivership. These debts were created to suppliers independent of McBirneys and the coach company or any company associated with them. There were special circumstances involved in this category of payment as the suppliers believed themselves to be dealing with a receiver appointed by the Court and was acting with the Courts authority. Thus these payments were validated by the Court and the liquidator did not dispute this. PMPA coaches had an amount paid to a connected company which was within this category and was not validated for reasons outlined in (g) below.

Category (c) was intended to cover liabilities which arose after the petition date but none did.

Category (d) represented the receivers' fees. The quantum was never determined nor their payment authorised. Thus although there was no dispute as to the entitlement of the receiver to fees it was for the Court to approve those fees at a later date.

Category (e) represented payments in respect of employees which would have been preferential anyway, so a validating order was entirely appropriate.

Category (f) represented fees paid to Auctioneers in respect of reports and services obtained by the receiver regarding the possible sale of McBirneys property. The liquidator pointed out that the receiver had no power to sell property and so had no right to incur such expenses. Murphy J thus refused to validate the payments but also stated that the decision was based on the evidence before him and he had not heard from the auctioneers. Thus it was up to them if they wished to contribute further to the facts known.

Category (g) represented those most strenuously challenged by the liquidator. They related to payments to connected companies. No order was made here validating the payments as there was a distinction made by Murphy J between the outside companies and connected ones. While the outside companies had no knowledge of the particulars of the receivers appointment the connected companies would have known of the details of the receivers appointment. Thus there were no special circumstances to take into account.

Category (h) concerned small amounts which were validated as a matter of commercial prudence.

This case has added to the weight of case law regarding the exercise of judicial discretion contained in s. 218 of the Companies Act 1963. While he considered the case law, Murphy J also considered that the special circumstances of the instant case were of equal if not more weight than the case law. Clearly there were unusual circumstance which prompted Murphy J's departure from established guidelines in order to reach an equitable conclusion. Is there now an extra piece to Oliver J's decision in *In re Leslie Engineers Co. Ltd* where he states:

> I think that in exercising discretion the Court must keep in view the evident purpose of the section which, as Chitty J said in *In re Civil Service and General Store Ltd* (1888) 58 LT 220, 221, is to ensure that the creditors are paid pari passu.

Should there now be added the qualification 'unless there are special circumstances'?

## INSIDER DEALING

**Stock Exchange** The position with regard to 'tippees' who acquire price sensitive information has been changed by the Companies Act 1990 (Insider Dealing) Regulations 1991 (SI No. 151 of 1991) and the Companies Act 1990 (Insider Dealing) Regulations 1992 (SI No. 131 of 1992). The effect of these Regulations is to further restrict the dealings not only of 'tippees' but those who have obtained information from them.

## ACCOUNTS

**Company accounts, groups of companies** The European Communities (Companies: Group Accounts) Regulations 1992 (SI No. 201 of 1992) affect consolidated financial statements relating to periods beginning on or after 1 September 1992. These Regulations, which give effect to the provisions of Council Directive 83/349/EEC of 13 June 1983, deal with definitions of control of companies in the context of group accounting, preparation of and disclosure in consolidated financial statements, and effect certain changes with merger accounting and fair values.

With certain exceptions, accounts in a new or modified format must be prepared where parent and subsidiary undertakings subsist in a group. The definition of 'undertakings' includes bodies corporate, partnerships and unincorporated bodies of persons engaged for gain in the production, supply or distribution of goods, the provision of a service, or the making or holding of investments.

The Regulations alter previous company law by substituting new tests for the parent/subsidiary relationship, adding to the existing tests of legal ownership and control, those of 'the exercise of a dominant relationship' and 'participating interest'.

The Regulations provide certain exemptions, easy to catalogue, impossible to summarise briefly, specified in Regulations 10 to 14. (They involve disparate criteria such as size of the undertaking, whether or not the inclusion of a subsidiary would be 'material', postponement of control by the parent over the subsidiary, and others.)

The Regulations set out the definition and format of group accounts, specifying matters such as the consolidated balance sheet, profit and loss account, and state the overriding requirement that a true and fair view be given of the state of affairs of the group. Regulations 17 to 23 deal with specific problems relating to presentation of accounts in respect of acquisition and merger accounting. Regulations 24 to 26 deal with methods of consolidation. Other matters dealt with are changes in composition of the group (27), valuation (28-31), joint ventures (32), associated undertakings (33-34), participating interest (35). Regulations 36 to 40 modify the existing publications requirements for accounts of groups of companies. A new list of offences and penalties appears in Regulation 41.

The rest of the Regulations, and the schedules to them, deal with specific modifications of the Companies Act 1986 in order to effect the changes made to the Companies Acts 1963 and 1986.

The situations dealt with in this statutory instrument are also dealt with in Financial Reporting Standard 2 (FRS 2) 'Accounting for Subsidiary Undertakings', promulgated by the Accounting Standards Board. FRS 2 replaces Statement of Standard Accounting Practice 14 (SSAP 14). FRS 2 is incorporated into company law in England, but not here. However, it is probable that an Irish court will follow the decision of Woolf J (as he then was) in *Lloyd Cheyham & Co. Ltd v Littlejohn & Co. Ltd* [1987] BCLC 198, who considered the question of professional negligence and departure from the SSAPs (and presumably, therefore, the FRSs). He said:

> [w]hile [SSAPs] are not conclusive, so that a departure from their terms necessarily involves a breach of the duty of care, and they are not as the explanatory foreword makes clear, rigid rules, they are very strong

> evidence as to what is the proper standard which should be adopted and unless there is some justification, a departure from this will be regarded as constituting a breach of duty.

This case does not purport to suggest when derogations from the statutory instrument are justified. The position is that the statutory instrument has the force of law. However, what would be the situation where a difference arises in the interpretation of the two documents? This arises in general considerations of accounting law and professional practice. Specifically it will arise when accountants/lawyers have to consider whether departures (or decisions not to depart) from SSAPs and FRSs may ground a claim for professional negligence or breach of contract. See further on this the judgment of Lardner J in *Kelly and Ors v Haughey Boland & Co.* [1989] ILRM 373.

## 1992 COMPANY LAW PUBLICATIONS

Dr M. Forde's *Company Law* (The Mercier Press, Cork, 1992) contains many useful references to cases and periodical literature not mentioned in other Irish texts. Recent monographs include M. Ashe and Y. Murphy, *Insider Dealing* (The Round Hall Press, Dublin, 1992).

# Conflict of Laws

## CHILD WELFARE

**International child abduction** In the 1991 Review, 81-6 we analysed the Child Abduction and Enforcement of Custody Orders Act 1991, which implemented the Hague and Luxembourg Conventions on the subject. The underlying principle of both conventions is to reduce the incentive for child abduction by requiring the courts of the State into which the child is wrongfully removed to the child's return to the State from which it has been removed. To this general principle there are exceptions. Thus, for example, Article 13(b) of the Hague Convention authorises (though does not require) the non-return of a child where there is a grave risk that to return the child 'would expose [him or her] to physical or psychological harm or otherwise place the child in an intolerable situation'. Article 20 of that Convention also authorises the non-return of a child 'if this would not be permitted by the fundamental principles of the requested state relating to the protection of human rights and fundamental freedoms.' The inclusion of Article 20 in the Convention, as the Law Reform Commission noted, in its *Report on the Hague Convention on the Civil Aspects of International Child Abduction and Some Related Matters* (LRC 12-1985) p. 12, was 'largely the result of an Irish initiative at the Conference' (Mr Justice Walsh was one of the Irish representatives).

In *In re P.K. and C.K., infants; C.K. v C.K.* [1993] ILRM 534, Denham J was faced with a human tragedy. The parties had emigrated from Ireland to Australia in 1989 with their two children. They planned to stay there until 1996, and then to return to Ireland when their elder child would be going to secondary school. The venture worked out very well for the plaintiff wife. She obtained a good job as a sales representative. Matters were far less happy for the defendant husband, who was obliged to drive a taxi for over sixty hours a week for small pay. In February 1992, the plaintiff told the defendant of her friendship with another man. The defendant left the family home by agreement, being let believe that this was a trial separation by the plaintiff who, however, secretly considered it to be a permanent situation. The defendant was still hopeful of a reconciliation. The children remained with the plaintiff, the defendant having access to them. The defendant applied for custody of the children in the New South Wales courts in August 1992, but withdrew the application a few weeks later.

The man with whom the plaintiff had established a relationship visited the family home regularly from June onwards and spent the night there once. He was married with three children of his own. In September 1992 the plaintiff told the defendant that she was going to divorce him and marry this man. The defendant, jealous and upset at the prospect of the children living in the family home with their mother and the man as 'a live-in lover', and feeling that he could not offer the children a home in Australia, abducted them and brought them back to live with his mother and himself in Ireland.

The plaintiff initiated proceedings under the 1991 Act. The defendant did not contest that the removal of the children had been 'wrongful' under Article 3 of the Hague Convention but submitted that the court should not order their return: *first*, because they were not habitually resident in New South Wales at the time of the removal; *second*, because Article 13(b) applied; and, *third*, because Article 20 enabled the court to hold an enquiry into the welfare of the children.

On the question of the children's habitual residence, Denham J was satisfied that it was in New South Wales. She noted that in *Leckinger v Cuttriss*, High Court, 9 July 1992, Blayney J had approved of the equation of the concepts of *habitual* and *ordinary* residence in *V. v B. (a Minor) (Abduction)* [1991] 1 FLR 266. Even if the concepts were not identical, Denham J considered that the children had been both ordinarily and habitually resident in Australia. The children had been there by agreement for three years, with the original plan of staying there until 1996. They were settled in primary school, in a house that the parties had purchased. These factors cumulatively removed any doubt on this point.

Turning to Article 13(b), Denham J was of the view that the test it prescribed had to be read as a whole:

> Thus the question is whether the presence of [the man] in the children's home would put them into an intolerable position by exposing them to physical or psychological harm. There is no evidence that they will be subjected to physical harm, thus the sole question is one of psychological harm.

With respect, this interpretation is not easy to harmonise with the language of Article 13(b), which as we have seen, refers to a grave risk that the child's return 'would expose the child to physical or psychological harm *or otherwise place the child in an intolerable situation*' (emphasis added). It may be that this alternative basis for the option of non-return should be read in accordance with the *ejusdem generis* rule, but that does not reduce it to vanishing point. Clearly Article 13(b) envisages cases *other than* those involving grave risk of exposure to physical or psychological harm.

Of course most intolerable situations are accompanied by a risk of physical or psychological harm to those who are subject to them, but one can conceive of some situations that are intolerable but lack such a risk. Certain situations of danger to the child's moral or religious welfare, for example, do not involve the risk of physical or psychological harm. If they are capable of being characterised as intolerable, then this third category should not be subsumed under the first two categories.

Denham J turned to apply the legal principles to the facts of the case, in relation to which the court had received no evidence from the man with whom the mother had formed the association nor any psychological assessment of the children such as a court would have in a custody hearing. She held there was no evidence that the man would cause the children physical harm; there was, neither, any clear evidence that his presence in the home would cause them psychological harm. In relation to the apprehension that this presence would cause the children moral harm, Denham J said simply:

> Whereas there is the moral question to be considered, I do not consider that such a ground in the circumstances of this case would alone, on the facts before this Court, invoke Article 13(b).

The plaintiff in her affidavit had sworn that she would give an undertaking to the court that she and the man would not live together prior to custody proceedings in New South Wales which would follow their return. Denham J commented:

> Whereas I have some concern about taking an undertaking which cannot be policed by this Court, I consider it in keeping with the policy of this Act that there can be communication between the courts of countries applying this Convention, between the returning court, and the court which will decide the custody issue. Further, that there can and should, be communication between the central authorities.

It is not entirely clear how communication of this type could be effective in protecting the welfare of the children. If an undertaking of this type were subsequently breached, there would seem no way in which the *Irish* court would have any revived jurisdiction in the case, unless the children subsequently were to return to Ireland. Of course an Australian court in custody proceedings would have regard to the fact of the breach of the undertaking but it would not be likely to treat it as a crucial question in determining where the welfare of the children lay. Certainly, it would have no reason to *communicate* with the Irish court, save only to clarify the nature of the undertaking and the court's order — matters which normally should give rise to no confusion.

Denham J, who had spoken in her chambers with the elder child, aged eight, considered it clear that he would be equally happy to live with either parent.

The final issue related to Article 20 of the Convention. Counsel for the defendant had submitted that it allowed the Court to apply Irish fundamental principles; that it was a fundamental principle of Irish law that a child had a right to have his or her welfare vindicated and protected by the Irish court; and that it was also a fundamental principle that the defendant had a constitutional right to litigate the issue of custody before the Irish court.

The essence of this argument was that the 1991 Act should be interpreted as incorporating, through Article 20, the criterion of the paramountcy of the welfare of the child, which underlay the Constitution and the Guardianship of Infants Act 1964.

Denham J rejected this argument. The defendant has not indicated that any constitutional right of children would be breached if they were returned to Australia. He had not indicated that Australian law would not hold an adequate inquiry into the custody of the children.

> There has been no fact before this Court which establishes that such summary procedure would breach a constitutional right of the children. Article 20 specifically enables such a case to be made by the defendant. He has not done that. He has not made the case that the procedures in Australia would not be adequate. He has argued that there must be an inquiry here as to the children's welfare. The only implication one can draw from this argument is that the Australian court would not adequately inquire into the welfare principle. The defendant has not made this case overtly and it is not for this Court to accept such a case for interpretation.

Any excessive delay or inquiry into the process by which the children were returned to their habitual residence would only serve to defeat the objectives of this Act. The Act was designed to protect children from being wrongfully removed from the place of their habitual residence. The corollary was that custody should be determined by the courts of that country. This was done with the welfare of the children in mind.

> This concept of welfare is the foundation of the 1991 Act. There is no evidence that it is in conflict with any rights of the children herein under the Constitution.

Accordingly Denham J made an order for the return forthwith of the children to Australia. The order recited the plaintiff's undertaking that the man with whom she was associating would not live in the home with her and the children pending custody proceedings in New South Wales.

The defendant unsuccessfully sought a stay on Denham J's order. In a brief *ex tempore* judgment, with which the other members of the Supreme Court, O'Flaherty and Egan JJ, concurred, Finlay CJ reasoned as follows. If a stay were granted, of necessity at least five or six weeks would elapse before the appeal could be heard or determined. The appeal raised a new question which would require a full court. The wife would have to return a second time from Australia with no prospect of being funded by her husband. The children, having been removed from Australia would have to remain here and, if the High Court judgment were affirmed, would have to go back after that.

The Chief Justice stated:

> Bearing all these features in mind and bearing in mind particularly that there was a wrongful removal of the children and that what this whole code is about is child abduction in that sense and bearing in mind that there is no doubt that the husband has full access to the courts in Australia who will deal in accordance with the same principles as would these courts with the question of the welfare of these children, the court is satisfied that, in the interests of justice and in the interest of the children as well, . . . it should not grant a stay.

The holding in this case makes it clear just how radical is the change engineered by the 1991 legislation. If the court had applied the 'welfare' test, as that concept is understood in our legislation and under our Constitution, the defendant would have had some prospects of being awarded custody; one suspects that in New South Wales, where the elements of religious and moral welfare are given a somewhat different meaning, the defendant's prospects of being awarded custody would be considerably less. Decisions such as *Smythe v Smythe* (1983) 48 ALR 677 and *Barker v Barker* (1976) 9 ALR 451 would encourage this view. As against this, the Australian courts are somewhat less disposed to presume that a young child's interests are best served by an order for custody in favour of the mother.

It would be a radical proposition to contend that the mere fact that the notion of welfare has a different connotation in Irish constitutional law from that in the law of a foreign country entitles a defendant to invoke Article 20 of the Convention. But it is surely an equally doubtful proposition to argue that, because the same formal principles apply to the determination of the welfare question in Irish law and the foreign law, Article 20 can have no application.

We should here record briefly a casenote of the decision of Blayney J in

*L.(K.) v C.(L.)*, High Court, 9 July 1992, which is published in [1993] 2 Fam LJ 79. The casenote was approved by Blayney J on 13 July 1993. It appears that counsel for the defendant submitted that the court should have regard to the Guardianship of Infants Act 1964 and the paramountcy of welfare principle. In rejecting this submission, Blayney J held that the provisions of the Convention were extremely clear in their terms and, if the terms of the Convention were in effect to deal with the consideration of the merits of the custody of the children, the Convention would lose all its force. The correct view of the matter was that set out in the English High Court decision of *P. v P. (Minors) (Child Abduction)* [1992] 1 FLR 155, to the effect that one of the fundamental principles of the Hague Convention was its acceptance that the court in each of the contracting states was equally capable of deciding on the merits of the case.

The casenote makes no reference to Article 20. It is surprising that Blayney J apparently had nothing specially to say in its regard. When English cases on the Convention are cited in Irish courts, it might be desirable to remember that Article 20 was omitted from the text as given the force of law in Britain. Dicey & Morris, *The Conflict of Laws* (12th ed., 1993) p. 837, explain that, '[i]n the absence of a Bill of Rights or a written Constitution, this Article had no clear meaning in English law. . .'

In the 1993 Review, we shall analyse Keane's J's judgment in *W. (A.C.) & W. (N.C.) v Ireland and Attorney General and W. (M.)*, High Court, 6 July 1993, which also addresses the effect of Article 20 of the Convention.

In *In re W. R. P. (An Infant); W. v W.*, High Court, 19 February 1992, a number of questions arose under the Hague Convention. The first related to Article 3, which provides that the removal or retention of a child is to be considered wrongful where (a) it is *in breach of rights of custody* attributed to a person, an institution or any other body, either jointly or alone under the law of the State where the child was habitually resident immediately before the removal or the retention *and* (b) at the time of the removal or retention *those rights were actually exercised*, either jointly or alone, or would have been, but for the removal or retention. The parties to the litigation, a married couple, had been habitually resident in England for the duration of their marriage but were living apart for three years. The husband had initiated divorce proceedings, which had reached the stage of a conciliation hearing. The mother brought the couple's eleven-year-old son to Ireland, where she went to live with her relations and the father sought the boy's return.

Lardner J acted on affidavit evidence as to the effect of English law of parent — child relationships adduced by the English solicitor instructed by the husband in the divorce proceedings. There the Children Act 1989 replaced the concept of *custody of children* by the concept of *parental responsibility*. Under s. 2(9) a person having parental responsibility may not surrender on transfer any part of it to another person; thus, the solicitor explained, both parents retained joint parental responsibility even if they had to come to an informal agreement as to the exercise by either of them as to their parental rights and duties. Moreover, the power of a parent to give or withhold consent to the removal of a child from the jurisdiction was an incident of parental responsibility.

Lardner J. held that the mother's removal of the child from England was a breach of Article 3. He rejected his wife's contention that the father had not actually been exercising any rights jointly with her in relation in to the boy at the time of the removal. Had this been established, the mother would have established a defence under Article 13 (a) of the Convention.

The mother also resisted return on the basis of Article 13(b). In her affidavit she claimed that her son had serious emotional problems associated with his relationship with his father, that the boy objected to any supervised contact with his father and wanted to remain in Ireland and that he would suffer serious psychological harm if he were returned to England. The father contraverted their allegations in strong terms.

Lardner J interviewed the boy. He found that he was not afraid of his father but that he was particularly fond of his mother and would dislike being separated from her, 'which is quite understandable at his age'. Lardner J found no evidence that returning the boy carried with it any grave risk of physical or psychological harm or that it would necessarily place him in an intolerable situation.

Lardner J accordingly ordered the return of the boy to England under the 1991 Act but he deliberately made no order that he be returned to his father because he wanted to give the mother the opportunity to accompany her son to England and to keep him living in her care at least until the matter of custody or parental responsibility was determined in the English Courts.

The question whether a court must order the return of a child to the applicant is one that caused much discussion when the Convention was being formulated. Lardner J's approach is in accord with the English decisions: see McClean, Note, '"Return" of Internationally Abducted Children', (1990) 106 LQ Rev 375. In other jurisdictions, the practice increasingly appears to be that the courts return the child to the applicant. Such an approach has been criticised: Bruch, 'International Child Abduction Cases: Experience under the 1980 Hague Convention', chapter 25 of J. Eekelaar & P. Sarcevic eds, *Parenthood in Modern Society: Legal and Social Issues for the Twenty-first Century* (1993), at 359.

In *In re Y.A.A., an Infant; M.A. v P.R. (otherwise known as P.A.)*, High Court, 23 July 1992 the defendant brought her daughter from England, the place of the child's habitual residence, to Ireland, in breach of Article 3 of the Hague Convention. She invoked Article 13(b) in her defence against the plaintiff's application for the child's return, arguing that this would expose her to a grave risk of physical or psychological harm from the plaintiff's irascible and violent conduct arising from his drinking and gambling habits.

The parties had married in Dublin in 1987. The plaintiff was a Libyan national and a Muslim; the defendant an Irish national and a Catholic. They had been cohabiting for some years previously. Shortly afterwards they moved to England. The defendant gave evidence, which the court accepted, that the plaintiff had subjected her to a great deal of violence during the marriage and that she was continuously protecting her daughter from potential physical violence from the plaintiff. She said that the child's behaviour had frequently irritated the plaintiff, that she would have to make sudden dives to remove her out of the way of possible blows, that she was often the recipient of blows from him and that she had done everything to prevent the child from getting hurt. Flood J did not make an express finding of fact that the plaintiff had ever actually struck the child but he concluded that there was a grave risk that the child would suffer physical violence 'and quite probably psychological harm'.

Counsel for the plaintiff had submitted that, if the court concluded that there was such a risk, it should, on the authority of *W. v W.*, above, exercise its discretion to return the child to the State of her habitual residence. Flood J rejected this submission. He distinguished *W. v W.* on several grounds. First, it involved the risk of psychological harm: Flood J noted that '[p]sychological damage in unlikely to occur *instanter*; physical damage can.' Secondly, in *W. v W.* Lardner J was satisfied as a matter of probability that the mother could and would return; in the case before him, Flood J was satisfied that the mother would not return and should not be required to do so. Thirdly, there were no proceedings in England to which the defendant or any other person having care for the child could have resort for quick and immediate relief in protection from what Flood J believed to be imminent danger of physical harm. (This is a somewhat surprising proposition, since English law, like Irish law, has the remedies of injunction and specific procedures for domestic violence: cf. B. Hoggett & D. Pearl, *The Family, Law and Society: Cases and Materials* (3rd ed., 1991), chapter 9.) Flood J had 'no faith whatsoever' in the plaintiff's undertaking that he would vacate the matrimonial home to permit the defendant and the child to live there. In his view, to return the child to England on the basis that her future custody, care and welfare should be determined there would not be an exercise of discretion but an abrogation of the court's duty to protect the child from a grave risk of exposure to harm. He accepted that such a discretion could exist:

> It could be exercised in an appropriate case where clearcut evidence existed of a safe and secure residence and scene of care being available

> for the infant and that there existed proceedings before an English court or other social services which could be called into instant action to protect the infant from the . . . apprehended grave risk of physical harm or to which this court could hand over the care and protection of the infant. Were that so, I would give serious consideration to the exercise of such discretion.

In the light of his conclusion Flood J refused the plaintiff's application for the return of the child.

In *G. (R.) v G. (B.)*, High Court, 12 November 1992, [1993] 2 Fam LJ 55, Costello J declined to order the return of three young children, aged between three and ten years on the basis of a grave risk of psychological harm to them under Article 13(b). He accepted the defendant wife's evidence that she was in serious danger of being battered by the plaintiff husband. Costello J considered that the grave risk of psychological harm arose for the children because seeing their mother abused and assaulted was itself psychologically damaging. He did not require any medical evidence to support this conclusion, which he (sensibly) regarded as being dictated by common sense.

Costello J also took into account the wishes of the ten-year-old and eight-year-old children, which favoured staying in Ireland.

In view of his conclusion under Article 13(b), Costello J found it unnecessary to express any view on submissions made by the defendant in relation to Article 20. These might have been of some general interest, since they could well have involved a consideration of the constitutional right to bodily integrity, as well as broader welfare issues.

**Jurisdiction in other custody disputes** In *In re S. and D.R.; L.R. v D.R.*, High Court, 2 April 1992, Costello J was concerned with the question of the jurisdiction of the Irish courts to hear proceedings relating to the custody of children in a case that did not fall within the remit of the Child Abduction and Enforcement of Custody Orders Act 1991. The plaintiff, an Irishwoman, had lived in Ireland until her marriage in 1988 to the defendant, an American citizen. This was the plaintiff's first marriage, the defendant's fifth. After the marriage, the parties lived in the United States but returned regularly to Ireland. They had two children, one of whom obtained an Irish passport and thus was an Irish citizen (as well as an American citizen); the other child, who did not obtain an Irish passport, was an American citizen. In May 1991 the parties again returned to Ireland, intending to stay for about three months. Shortly afterwards, serious problems arose which affected this relationship most adversely. Costello J did not describe these problems in any great detail, though he referred to the plaintiff's allegation that her husband became severely depressed at this time.

The defendant went back to the United States briefly, returned to Ireland and then went back again to the United States. The plaintiff resisted his demand to go back to the United States with the children, claiming that she would not do so on account of the defendant's behaviour.

Before leaving for America the defendant instructed an Irish firm of solicitors, who contacted the plaintiff to warn her that, if she did not go back to the United States with the children, the defendant would initiate proceedings there involving the Hague Convention on Child Abduction. The plaintiff's response was to initiate custody proceedings in Ireland under s. 11 of the Guardianship of Infants Act 1964.

In the autumn of 1991 the defendant initiated proceedings for divorce (on the ground of 'incompatibility') and for custody. The plaintiff unsuccessfully submitted that the custody question should be determined by the Irish courts. In January 1992, the American court granted the divorce decree and held that the husband should have custody of the children, the court finding that the respondent had wrongfully retained them in Ireland. The husband sought to invoke the provisions of the Hague Convention but was informed by the Irish Central Authority that the Convention had not come into force in Ireland until 1 October 1991, six weeks after the alleged 'wrongful retention' had taken place. Under Article 35, the Convention applied only to wrongful retention occurring after the Convention's entry in force in the State in question. In the proceedings before Costello J, counsel for the husband did not seek to argue that the Convention applied, but contended that the court should nonetheless apply the principles enshrined in the Convention.

Costello J first addressed the question of jurisdiction. He thought it 'perfectly clear' that the court had jurisdiction to make custody orders in respect of both children should it consider it appropriate to do so. The court had jurisdiction where the child was an Irish citizen and within the jurisdiction; this was the case with one of the children. The court also had jurisdiction in such matters based on the mere presence of the child within the State; this was the position with the other child. In support of the latter proposition, Costello J cited Binchy's *Irish Conflicts of Law*, 323-6 (1988). Counsel for the defendant accepted that this was the position whilst strenuously arguing that the court should not exercise its undoubted jurisdiction.

Costello J went on to determine where the welfare of the children lay, and held that it would be with their mother. We consider this aspect of the case in the Family Chapter, below, 357-8. He then addressed the problem of the pre-existing custody order in favour of the children's father which the American court had made. He adopted passages from Dicey & Morris's *Conflict of Laws*, Fourth Cumulative Supplement to the 11th ed. (1991), pp 200-202, which he considered to be consistent with the legal principles underlying *Northampton County Council v ABF and MBF* [1982] ILRM 539,

*Kent County Council v C.S.* [1984] ILRM 292 and expressly supported in *W. v W.* [1978] ILRM 121 and *D.A.D. v P.J.D.*, High Court, 7 February 1986. These principles, in summary, permit an Irish court to make a custody order even when a foreign court has already done so, since the welfare of the child is the first and paramount consideration. This entitlement is, of course, subject to the provisions of the 1991 Act which, as we have seen, significantly restrict the Irish court's entitlement to act inconsistently with the foreign court's order.

Costello J, whilst not bound by the decision of the American court, gave it 'great weight'. Nonetheless he was willing to come to a different conclusion as to custody. He stressed the fact that he had had the benefit of hearing both parties, in contrast to the American court. It was true that the wife had been afforded the opportunity to participate in the foreign proceedings, but she had not the financial resources to go. Costello J did not think that her non-attendance should be held against her or affect consideration bearing on the children's welfare.

Counsel for the husband had urged that the family in the case should be treated as an American family, that the husband and wife (and through them their children) were domiciled in America, that the children were American citizens, that the Irish connection with the case was only slight and that, accordingly, the Irish court should relinquish its jurisdiction in favour of the United States court. Costello J did not consider that this was the proper approach to the legal issues that arose in the case:

> The application is one under the 1964 Act and the first and paramount consideration is the children's welfare. I have concluded that the order which should be made, bearing in mind their welfare, is that the mother should have custody of the children, and I cannot abdicate my responsibility to make such an order merely because the connection of the parties with the United States court as a matter of law may be greater than that of the Irish court.

Counsel for the husband indicated that the husband was willing to set aside the American custody order and to have the question re- heard and to pay all the mother's costs and expenses in travelling to attend the new hearing. Costello J did not, however, think that this offer would justify him in refusing to make the order that should be made in the interests of the welfare of the children.

Costello J finally rejected the submission made on behalf of the defendant that the court should apply the principles of the Hague Convention even though they did not apply in Ireland until a few weeks after the alleged 'wrongful detention'. This submission, said Costello J:

> fails to take into account the demands of the 1964 Act. Whatever might have happened last year and whoever is responsible for the breakdown of the marriage, and whether or not the events constituted a 'wrongful detention' within the meaning of the Convention, I am now required by statute to decide the custody dispute by reference to the welfare of the children. As I see it today, for reasons already given, their welfare requires that they remain in the custody of their mother and the events of last year do not detract in any way from this conclusion.

The thrust of recent English decisions is towards extending the principles of the Convention to cases not falling within the geographical scope of the Convention: *D. v D. (Child Abduction: Non-Convention Country)* [1994] 1 FLR 137; *Re S. (Minors) (Abduction)* [1994] 1 FLR 297. It can perhaps be argued that the public policy underlying the Convention is sufficiently strong to justify its extension in this way, not only geographically but also temporally. There is nonetheless a striking difference between the weight that Costello J afforded to the constitutional underpinnings of the welfare test and that identified, so faintly, by Denham J in *C.K. v C.K.* above. Whilst addressing separate issues, these judgments are hard to reconcile from the standpoint of fundamental constitutional values.

## RECOGNITION OF FOREIGN DIVORCES

In the 1988 Review, 73-80 and the 1989 Review, 89-90, we analysed Barr J's decision in *C.M. v T.M.* [1988] ILRM 456 and *C.M. v T.M. (No. 2)* [1991] ILRM 268, to the effect that the domicile of dependency of married women did not survive the promulgation of the 1937 Constitution. In *W. v W.* [1993] ILRM 294, the Supreme Court addressed the implications of such a holding for the traditional rules for recognition of foreign divorces.

The legal background to the case may be sketched briefly. At common law, a foreign divorce would be recognised if *obtained in the common domicile of the spouses*. Coupled with this recognition rule was the general rule that a woman, by marrying, acquired the domicile of her husband, by way of dependency upon him, and that any subsequent changes in his domicile should be attributed to her, regardless of whether this corresponded with her actual situation. In combination, these two rules of private international law had the effect in practice that recognition would be afforded to a foreign divorce, obtained by either spouse, in the country of the *husband's* domicile.

The idea that an Irish wife whose connections remained essentially Irish should be deprived of her status by her husband's establishing a foreign domicile and subsequently divorcing her is difficult to harmonise with the public policy underlying Article 41.3 of the Constitution. Thus, it was not surprising that, in *Gaffney v Gaffney* [1975] IR 133, at 152, Walsh J expressed the view that it was:

> possible that some day [the principle of a wife's domicile of dependency] may be challenged on constitutional grounds in a case where the wife has never physically left her domicile of origin while her deserting husband may have established a domicile in another jurisdiction.

The thrust of this observation was clearly that such a divorce should be *denied* recognition. For further analysis, see Binchy, op. cit., 80-82.

The Domicile and Recognition of Foreign Divorces Act 1986 came into operation on 2 October 1986. S.1 abolished, prospectively, the domicile of dependency of married women and s. 5, again prospectively, introduced the principle (backed by additional grounds for recognition not of present relevance) that a divorce should be recognised if obtained by either spouse in the country where either spouse is domiciled.

In *W. v W.* O'Hanlon J stated a case for the opinion of the Supreme Court in the following circumstances. The plaintiff, born in Ireland in 1939 and of Irish domicile of origin, had emigrated to England in 1957. She returned to Ireland for a few months in 1965 but went back to England and in 1966 married an Englishman, domiciled in England, at a registry office in England. They had a daughter the following year. The couple separated in 1969. The plaintiff went to Australia for two years, after which she returned to Ireland.

The plaintiff met the defendant shortly after her return. When he asked her to marry him, the plaintiff sought the advice of a priest. He suggested that, while she was free to marry in church, the wisest course from the standpoint of civil law would be to obtain a divorce in England from her husband, who continued to be domiciled there. This she did by uncontested petition in 1972. The plaintiff went through a ceremony of marriage with the defendant in a Catholic Church in Ireland in 1973. They had two children. Matrimonial difficulties arose in 1989. The plaintiff obtained a barring order and a maintenance order against the defendant in the District Order. He appealed to the Circuit Court. Following negotiations, a consent maintenance order was made by the Court, the defendant undertaking to stay out of the home during the period originally covered by the barring order.

The plaintiff subsequently sought a decree of judicial separation and ancillary relief. The Circuit Court judge, rejecting the defendant's contention that he was not the plaintiff's husband, gave judgment in favour of the plaintiff. On appeal to the High Court, O'Hanlon J, with the consent of the parties, addressed the question of the marital status of the parties as a preliminary issue. He posed the following four questions of law for the determination of the Supreme Court:

> 1. Did the rule that the domicile of a married woman is the same as that of her husband survive the enactment of the Constitution?
>
> 2. Is the said rule contrary to Article 40.1, Article 40.3 and/or Article 41 of the Constitution?
>
> 3. If the said dependent domicile rule did not survive the enactment of the Constitution, what effect (if any) does the removal of this rule have on the common law in regard to the recognition of foreign divorces which applied prior to 2nd October 1986 and what are the correct rules now to be applied in regard to such divorces and in particular the divorce of the plaintiff from [the man she married in 1966]?
>
> 4. Can the decision of Barr J in *C.M. v T.M.* that the rule of the dependent domicile of married women is unconstitutional be applied retrospectively so as to render void the marriage of the plaintiff to the defendant [in] 1973?

On the first two questions, the Supreme Court was unanimous. Blayney J (Finlay CJ and O'Flaherty J concurring) held that the domicile of dependency of married women was inconsistent with Article 40.1 of the Constitution, which provides that '[a]ll citizens shall, as human persons, be held equal before the law' and so had not been continued in force by Article 50. In the light of Walsh J's statement in *Quinns Supermarket v Attorney General* [1972] IR 1, at 13, as to how Article 40.1 should be interpreted, Blayney J had no doubt that the dependency rule denied equality in two ways. As between a married woman *and her new husband*, the rule placed her in a position of inequality because he retained his independent domicile while she lost hers and became connected by law into a domicile dependent on his. As between a married *and a single woman*, the rule also involved inequality since it 'would continue to attribute an independent domicile to the latter whereas the former, simply by virtue of her marriage, would cease to have an independent domicile'. This latter rationale may perhaps be debated: the mere fact that a person's legal rights or responsibilities change on marrying is not of itself an invidious inequality. If there were good reasons in justice or on the basis of social policy for the domicile of dependency of married women, the fact that married women had a domicile different from that of single women would not, *of itself*, offend against Article 40.1.

Blayney J went on to identify practical disadvantages for a married woman which the dependency rule involved. On her death, the law to be applied in the administration of her movable estate would be that of her husband's domicile, so that if he had left her and established a domicile in a foreign country where she had never been, nonetheless the law of that country would apply. In addition, domicile was 'an important factor in giving a court jurisdiction in matrimonial matters and in this regard also a married woman could be prejudiced by not having an independent domicile'. Perhaps it would have been wise to have identified the *dependency rule* rather than the absence of an independent domicile as the real source of prejudice in this context. Certainly, as we shall argue below, the *particular* rules for recognition of foreign divorces endorsed in the instant case, which are based on independent domicile, are capable of generating a great deal of hardship and injustice for married women. It is quite possible to envisage a gender-neutral substitute for the independent domiciles of *both husband and wife* which would arguably yield less injustice than what the court was willing to concede in its model for future legal development. For example, if there were to be a 'matrimonial domicile', determined by reference to the circumstances of *both* spouses in conjunction with the policies underlying Article 41, and completely devoid of any trace of sex discrimination, this might be a more just approach.

Blayney J went on to conclude that the first question posed by O'Hanlon J should be answered in the negative and that the answer to the second question should be that the rule of the dependent domicile of married women was contrary to Article 40.1. He thought it unnecessary in the circumstances to consider whether it was also contrary to Article 40.3 or 41 (as Barr J had held in *C.M. v T.M.*), and he expressed no view on that part of the question. It is unfortunate that Blayney J favoured this approach. Consideration of the relevance of these constitutional provisions (especially Article 41) to the theoretical basis and practical operation of the doctrine of dependent domicile of married women might well have deepened the Court's analysis of the rule of recognition of foreign divorces.

Egan J delivered a separate judgment, with which Finlay CJ and O'Flaherty J also concurred. His analysis of the domicile question is identical in its structure and conclusions to that of Blayney J. The dependency rule 'quite clearly resulted in married women not being held equal with single women or with men, whether single or married, and this inequality had nothing to do with differences of capacity, physical or moral, or social function'. Egan J considered that there was 'nothing whatever in Article 41 which could or ought disentitle a married woman to the equality which is guaranteed to her by Article 40'. This conclusion is worth comparing with that of Barr J in *C.M. v T.M.* In Barr J's view, the dependency rule was inconsistent with Article 41; in contrast, Egan J considered merely that Article 41 did not save the rule from being defeated by Article 40.1

Egan J went on to observe that there 'was even an element of absurdity' in the dependency rule as its application could mean that a married woman would be held domiciled in a country where she had never set foot and never intended to visit. He noted that Walsh J had cast doubts on the validity of the rule in *Gaffney*, and that in *M.C. v K.E.D. (otherwise K.C.)* [1985] IR 697 at 705. McCarthy J had referred to Walsh J's doubts and observed that he was not to be taken as accepting that the principle had survived the enactment of the Constitution. It is perhaps unfortunate that these Judges' observations were not scrutinised closely in the context in which they were uttered. It seems impossible to derive any support from Walsh J's remarks for the proposition to which the majority in *W. v W.* ultimately subscribed, that the Constitution should be interpreted as warranting a rule of recognition for foreign divorces on the basis of the domicile of only one spouse whose deserted spouse retained an Irish domicile.

Hederman J also held that the dependency rule had ceased to be part of Irish law by virtue of Article 50 of the Constitution on account of its inconsistency with Article 40.1. He observed:

> Although the married state could be regarded in a social function for the purposes of the second paragraph of section 1 of Article 40, it is equally so for both spouses and there can be no sex discrimination between equals. The former rule, Judge-invented, of dependent domicile of a wife discriminated against [the wife] (or distinguished between the spouses) on the grounds of sex only. In paragraph (2) of section 1 of Article 40 a distinction on the grounds of social function is reserved by the Constitution to 'enactments'. A common law rule does not qualify.

This passage might seem to suggest that common law rules, in contrast to statutory provisions, must respect equality *without* due regard to differences of capacity, physical and moral, and of social function. Such an interpretation would appear difficult to support, since it would apparently cast a constitutional shadow over an array of common law rules, such as those exempting physically or mentally disabled persons from civil or criminal disability or treating children more leniently or protectively than adults.

More radically, if being a *spouse* rather than a *husband* or wife is a social function, then it would seem that legislation (or, indeed common law rules) treating husbands differently from wives would offend against Article 40.1. It should be borne in mind that such offence is not necessarily fatal to constitutionality: in the Supreme Court decision of *O'B. v S.* [1984] IR 316, Walsh J (for the Court) observed that:

> [l]egislation which differentiates citizens or which discriminates be-

> tween them does not need to be justified under the proviso [to Article 40.1] if justification for it can be found in other provisions of the Constitution.

The overwhelming tendency of family legislation, from the Married Women's Status Act 1957 onwards, has been for the statutory provisions to be expressed in gender – neutral language. This applies even to aspects of family law, such as custody of children (Guardianship of Infants Act 1964), (see below, 358, 362) matrimonial violence (Family Law (Protection of Spouses and Children) Act 1981) and maintenance (Family Law (Maintenance of Spouses and Children) Act 1976 and the Judicial Separation and Family Law Reform Act 1989). This does not mean that such provisions, neutral on their face, translate in practice into a judicial disregard of the concept of sex roles within marriage. Thus we find a *de facto* preference (at times even articulated in terms of a presumption) in favour of the mother in custody proceedings, at all events where the children are young. Moreover, the judicial determination of maintenance obligations reflects social mores relating to wives who work in the home. Curiously, when it comes to property entitlements, the courts show little desire to interpret gender-neutral principles in a way that will protect the interests of the same women who work in the home.

In the light of the Supreme Court's determination of the domicile issue in *W.W.*, we must consider what are the implications for the constitutional validity of s. 4 of the Domicile and Recognition of Foreign Divorces Act 1986. That section contains a significant distinction between the sexes in the determination of the domicile of a minor. The general rule at common law continues to apply to minors whose parents are living together; their domicile is determined by that of their *father*. The effect of s. 4(1) is that the father's domicile is displaced by the mother's as the determinant of their child's domicile only where the spouses are living apart and either the minor has his or her home with the mother and no home with the father or, such a situation having prevailed, the minor has not since had a home with the father: see Binchy, op. cit., 87-9.

It is hard to see how this preference for the father can withstand constitutional scrutiny. The practical difficulties identified by Blayney J in respect of the domicile of dependency of married women, whilst not identical with those in relation to the domicile of minors, can find some close enough parallels. If, for example, an Irish husband and wife separate, the husband going to live in England, the wife remaining here, and their daughter being sent to live with the wife's parents in Kerry, the daughter's domicile will become English when her father acquires an English domicile. Perhaps it can be argued that, while this type of result is scarcely defensible, it occurs a good deal less frequently in practice than does the simple case of the spouses splitting up with the children remaining in the custody of one or other parents. It is, of course, discriminatory that the father's domicile should control, in cases where the parents are living together or where the children share homes with parents who are living apart. If the Court were disposed to strike down s. 4, an even greater engine of inequality, the traditional common law rules, would revive, unless declared by the Court not to have survived the promulgation of the Constitution. The Court would have the unenviable task of fashioning new, non-discriminatory, rules in relation to children. A possible approach is suggested by Binchy, 'Reform of the Law Relating to the Domicile of Children: A Proposed Statute' (1979) 11 Ottawa L Rev 279.

There is perhaps some force in the argument that no useful parallel can be drawn between the positions of women and children, respectively, in that the immediately attractive alternative to the domicile of dependency of married women, namely, an independent domicile — has no equivalent in relation to the dependent domicile for children (cf. William Duncan's excellent advocacy in 'The Domicile of Infants' (1969) 4 Ir Jur (ns) 36); manifestly this cannot provide a satisfactory solution where the child is so young as to be incapable of forming any relevant intention as to where he or she will permanently reside. Moreover, the nature of the relationship between child and parent, even with relatively mature teenagers, is such that the intention of the child to reside long-term in any country is to a considerable degree compromised by the fact that the child is part of a household where decisions as to the place of residence are made by the parents.

Having disposed of the issue of domicile, the members of the Supreme Court turned to the issue of recognition of foreign divorces. The wife had, after all, obtained a divorce in England at a time when, in O'Hanlon J's judgment, she should be considered to have an Irish domicile, if that question were determined on the premise of her having an independent domicile. The common law rule of recognition was based on the divorce's being obtained in the country of the spouses' *common* domicile. Such was not the case here. The crucial question, therefore, was whether the doctrine of domicile of dependency of married women should be regarded as *interfering with the requirement that the divorce be obtained in the country of the spouses' common domicile* or, on the contrary, as *tacitly involving the principle that a divorce should be recognised if obtained in the country of the domicile of either spouse*, but denying to wives recourse to that principle on account of a discriminatory policy towards them. By a majority, the Court in its result, but, not so clearly in its process of analysis, favoured the latter interpretation and held that the appropriate rule was that recognition should be afforded to a divorce obtained (by either spouse) in the country of the domicile of either spouse.

The manner in which the Judges for the majority reached this conclusion is worth examining. Blayney J's is the most intriguing. He referred in detail to the famous English decisions of *Travers v Holley* [1953] P 246 and *Indyka v Indyka* [1969] 1 AC 33. He acknowledged that they had been decided in a legal and factual context very different from that obtaining in the instant case but nonetheless he found them 'of great assistance because they involved the courts in looking at the nature and origin of the rule as to recognition of foreign divorces and the reason for its adoption'.

Two principles emerged from these decisions. The first was *the policy of avoiding 'limping' marriages* valid in one country and not another. Blayney J noted that this policy could be traced to the seminal decision of *Le Mesurier v Le Mesurier* [1895] AC 517 in a passage which Kingsmill Moore J had cited with approval in *Mayo-Perrott v Mayo-Perrott* [1958] IR 336. The second principle was that the question whether or not a divorce should be recognised 'should be answered by the Court *in the light of its present policy*'. (Emphasis added.) Adopting these guidelines, Blayney J considered that the Court should recognise the divorce obtained by the petitioner. Such a ground could be adopted 'almost without changing the former rule'. While this would leave out of account the domicile of the plaintiff, it would be no innovation: the former rule had done so as well. It had looked to the domicile of the husband only, assuming that that was also the domicile of the wife. And while the courts had usually referred to recognising a foreign divorce granted in the jurisdiction in which both parties were domiciled, 'the underlying practical position was occasionally recognised . . . '

Blayney J saw 'no alternative' to changing the recognition rule to one based on the domicile of either spouse. In his opinion that rule would be consistent with what the present policy of the Supreme Court should be. The Court might not leave out of account the provisions of the 1986 Act, which, having abolished the dependency rule in s. 1, went on in s. 5 (1) to prescribe a rule for recognition of foreign divorces based on the domicile of either spouse. While s. 5 was prospective in its operation, Blayney J thought it wholly consistent with the statute that the Supreme Court, as a matter of public policy, should independently modify the judge-made rule in order to do justice to the plaintiff.

Several features of Blayney J's judgment are worthy of comment. The first relates to his reliance on the policy of preventing 'limping' marriages which he perceived as a major element in the common law recognition rule requiring that the divorce be obtained in the country of the spouses' common domicile. Undoubtedly this policy has some merits and was a factor in the derivation of the common law rule but it would need much closer scrutiny before it should be elevated into the dominant position which Blayney J was willing to concede.

In *Le Mesurier v Le Mesurier*, the policy of preventing limping marriages was invoked in the context of the issue of *jurisdiction*. The House of Lords reasoned that the country with which the spouses had their long-term connections was the most appropriate one to hear and determine proceedings as to their status. Since different communities had different views and laws respecting matrimonial obligations and a different estimate of the grounds which should justify divorce, it was both just and reasonable that the differences of married people should be adjusted in accordance with the laws of the community to which they belonged, and dealt with by the tribunals which alone could administer those laws.

For the *Le Mesurier* approach to prevent or seriously diminish limping marriages it would be necessary that domicile should be the sole jurisdictional test in every country or, failing this, that it should be the sole test for recognising foreign divorces in all countries' systems of private international law. Even at the time when *Le Mesurier* was decided jurisdiction for divorce in many countries was based on connecting factors far more tenuous than domicile. Today, the international picture is more starkly in conflict with the assumptions on which the House of Lords proceeded in *Le Mesurier*. Apart altogether from the divorce mills, such as Nevada and Haiti, the general policy in most countries today is to have fairly wide-ranging jurisdictional grounds, such as residence for a relatively short period within the jurisdiction. Moreover, the grounds for recognition of foreign divorces have been greatly extended in most countries in recent years. The reason why this should have happened is simple. There is today a principle of *favor divortii* internationally, as there used formerly be a principle of *favor matrimonii*. Since, in countries with a divorce regime, 'marriage' today means not a commitment for life but rather the *most recent* commitment, of revocable quality, made by a person in accordance with the laws of a state, it would be quite foolish for such countries to have narrow recognition rules. If a spouse can get a divorce easily at home, why should a state refuse to recognise a divorce obtained abroad in a country with which he or she had little or no connection? Once the intention to divorce, consensually or by repudiation, is manifested, as it inevitably is by the actual resort to the divorce process, there is no public policy objection to recognising the divorce, wherever it is obtained.

The tendency of the contemporary international practice, therefore, to reduce the potential for 'limping' divorces (and thus 'limping' remarriages) by a very broad policy of recognising divorces obtained in states where the parties are not domiciled. Yet in Blayney J's view, the policy of preventing limping marriages should require the Supreme Court to recognise *divorces obtained in the country of domicile of either spouse*. Such recognition rule may or may not be justifiable on other grounds, but it certainly cannot be justified in the basis of preventing limping marriages because it will not do so in many cases.

It must also be asked how, in the light of Article 41, the Irish courts should be engaged in the process of accommodating an international *favor divortii* approach. The only way in which the phenomenon of 'limping' marriages could be effectively dealt with would be for the Irish courts to join the international club and recognise as many divorces as other countries do. But to do that would subvert the policy of protection of marriage which underlies Article 41.

Let us now consider Blayney J's second preferred principle, that the question whether or not a divorce should be recognised 'should be answered by the Court in the light of it present policy'. The process of analysis was that the Court 'm[ight] not leave out of account' the changes brought about by the 1986 legislation, that it would be 'wholly consistent' with that legislation for the Court, as a matter of public policy, independently to modify the judge-made recognition rules 'in order to do justice to the plaintiff' and that, if the legislature considered it right that the statutory abolition of the dependent domicile rule by s. 1 should require the enactment of s. 5(1), it would be eminently reasonable that the Court should do likewise, 'in order to enable the plaintiff's divorce to be recognised'.

Now it is beyond argument that judicially-developed rules for recognition of foreign divorce should not be obsolete, and it is also true that any development of judicial principles involving a clear change from former norms has a potential for injustice or hardship resulting from overturning expectations of those who made important decisions on the basis of the former rules.

It is, however, quite a different proposition that such recognition rules should be altered *with exclusively retrospective effect*, simply because the legislature has replaced common law recognition rules by a quite different set of rules, *which have only prospective effect*. What the court should have been concerned with was the admittedly complicated question of how the retrospective abolition of the domicile of dependency of married women should affect the common law rules for recognising foreign divorces which applied between 1937 and 1986.

Let us take the case of an Irish man and woman, both domiciled in Ireland, who married in Dublin in 1965. The wife deserted her husband and abandoned her children in 1975. Having established residence in England with the intention of staying there permanently, she obtained a divorce there in 1977. If the man had sought advice as to whether the divorce would be recognised here, he would have been told that it would not. Competent legal advice at that time would have been that Irish private international law recognises only divorces obtained in the common domicile of the spouses. That advice would have gone on to note Walsh J's words of warning in

*Gaffney v Gaffney*, casting doubt about the operation of the dependency doctrine in aid of *husbands* who leave wives in Ireland and acquire a foreign domicile. No prudent lawyer would have suggested for a moment to the man that the Constitution required, or that public policy would support, the adoption by the Supreme Court of a rule recognising foreign divorces on the same lines as what is set out in s. 5(1) of the 1986 Act. So far as the shadow of unconstitutionality had been cast over the dependency doctrine, it operated to render divorces obtained in the country of the domicile of one spouse *less* rather than more likely to be afforded recognition. Yet the effect of *W. v W.* is to confer retrospective recognition upon divorces in respect of which, at the time they were granted, no plausible legal argument could have been made in favour of such an outcome. It is curious that retrospective rules of recognition should operate in this way.

A notable aspect of Blayney J's analysis of how the Court should fashion the rules as to recognition of foreign divorces was his concern that the Court's modification of its former rules should be done 'in order to do justice to the plaintiff' and 'in order to enable the plaintiff's divorce to be recognised'. This concentration on the plaintiff's situation as an element, and apparently a not insignificant one, in the formulation of rules of *general* application is puzzling. It is too easy to envisage cases where the new rules of recognition of foreign divorces, applied retrospectively, are going to cause very considerable hardship and injustice. We have already given one instance. Why should spouses in such cases be damaged by the new rules simply to accommodate the plaintiff by a rule that seemed to be just and appropriate in her case?

The Court's approach seems to be a tragic instance of solving a particular problem by the establishment of a general rule which will yield hardship and injustice in other cases. The criticism here is not that the plaintiff's individual circumstances did not call for a rule that was fully fair to her, but rather that the task of the court — a difficult but far from insurmountable one — was to fashion a structure for recognition of foreign divorces that would maximise sensitivity to the particular circumstances of each case.

Why might the Court have considered that the plaintiff's divorce was worthy of recognition? The answer is surely that in 1972 (and for generations before then) a divorce obtained in the country of the husband's domicile was regarded as being eligible for recognition on the basis of the combination of the domicile of dependency rule with the common domicile test. If retrospective abolition of the domicile of dependency of married women were to result in the retrospective non-recognition of divorces obtained in the country of the husband's domicile, this would result in much hardship and injustice. It is understandable that the Court should not wish to bring about such an outcome but this should not have led the court to introduce a rule which created new injustice when there was no need to do so. It should not have been beyond the ability of the court to have devised recognition rules which would have been fair, consistent with the policies underlying Article 41, yet sensitive to particular contexts.

## JURISDICTION

**Contract** The supplemental jurisdictional basis of contract proceedings provided by Article 5 of the Brussels Convention continues to provoke litigation. It will be recalled that, as well as the basis of the defendant's domicile, afforded by Article 2, Article 5 provides that a person domiciled in one contracting state may be sued in another contracting state, 'in matters relating to contract, in the court the place of performance of the obligation in question'. Two issues thus arise: *what* is the 'obligation in question' and *where* is the place of performance of that obligation?

In the 1991 Review, 86-9, we reviewed a number of cases, including the Supreme Court decision in *Unidare plc and Unidare Cable Ltd v James Scott Ltd* [1991] 2 IR 88 and Costello J's decision in *Olympia Productions Ltd v Mackintosh* [1992] ILRM 204. These decisions featured in Lardner J's judgment in *Handbridge Ltd v British Aerospace Communications Ltd*, High Court, 25 February 1992. The plaintiffs sought damages for breach of contract against the defendant. The plaintiffs constructed custom-built computers in the Shannon development area. The defendant was engaged in developing communication systems. The plaintiffs claimed that the defendant had broken its contract to purchase eight thousand computers which the plaintiffs were to manufacture and to deliver to Stevenage in England. There had been extended negotiations between the parties which descended into a quagmire of contested evidence, in which the plaintiffs alleged that a contract had been consummated but not further acted on by the defendant, the defendant denying that matters had gone so far.

Lardner J applied the test laid down by the Court of Justice in *de Bloos v Bouyer* [1976] ECR 1497 that the 'obligation' mentioned in Article 5(1) refers to *the contractual obligation forming the basis of the legal proceedings*. Hence, assuming that there was a completed contract, the breach on which the plaintiffs relied by necessary implication in their affidavits and submissions was the *failure by the defendants to place orders for computers* in accordance with the alleged contract. This view was supported by the form of the terms and conditions of supply or trade, on which the plaintiffs relied. Since the defendant would have discharged this obligation by communicating its orders to the plaintiffs at Shannon, Lardner J held that the Irish courts had jurisdiction to hear the proceedings.

In reaching this conclusion, Lardner J referred to the decision of the House of Lords in *Union Transport Group plc v Continental Lines Ltd* [1992] 1 All ER 161, on which the defendant had relied. The House of Lords there had held that, where there was a dispute concerned with a number of obligations arising under the same contract and forming the basis of the proceedings commenced by the plaintiff, jurisdiction under Article 5(1) should be determined by the *principal* obligation. Lardner J found no material difference between their approach and that favoured in the Irish decisions.

In *Gannon v B & I Steampacket Co. Ltd, Landliner Travel Merseyside Ltd and Edenderry Transport Ltd* [1993] 2 IR 359, the plaintiff was injured when travelling as a passenger in Landliner Travel's coach which collided with Edenderry Transport's lorry. The accident took place in Chester. The plaintiff had booked a ticket with an agent of B & I, who offered to intending passengers a return trip to Liverpool by boat from Dublin to Holyhead and by coach from Holyhead to Liverpool. B & I was an Irish domiciled company. Both Landliner Travel and Edenderry Transport were companies domiciled in Ireland.

The plaintiff's action against the English defendants was in tort; her action against B & I was, however, in contract. She contended that B & I has a responsibility in law for the selection, choice and instruction of the driver and in relation to the coach in which she was travelling in England.

The English defendants challenged the jurisdiction of the Irish courts. It was accepted that the plaintiff could not sue them in Ireland for tort (since it was conceded that the tort was committed in England) unless she could successfully invoke Article 6 (1) of the Brussels Convention which enables co-defendants to be sued in the courts for the place where one defendant is domiciled. B & I was admittedly domiciled in Ireland, but that did not necessarily mean that the proceedings against the English defendants could be maintained here. The Court of Justice, in *Kalfelis v Bankhaus Schröder, Munchmeyer, Hengst & Co.* [1988] ECR 5565, had made it plain that the jurisdiction provided for in Article 6 (1) is an exception to the principle set out in Article 2 that jurisdiction is vested in the courts of the defendant's domicile and that an exception of this kind must be treated in such a manner that there is no possibility of the very existence of that principle being called in question. The Court of Justice had gone on to state that this possibility might arise if a plaintiff were at liberty to make a claim against a number of defendants with the sole object of ousting the jurisdiction of the courts of the State where one of the defendants was domiciled. Such a possibility had to be excluded. For that purpose there must be a connection between the claims made against each of the defendants.

Denham J, in the High Court, held that the plaintiff had a good jurisdictional base for her claim against the English defendants. She was satisfied that the plaintiff could sue B & I in contract, commenting in respect of that claim: 'It may not be successful, but it is reasonable.' She considered that there was no evidence that the plaintiff had improperly removed the English defendants from the jurisdiction of the court that was competent in the case.

The Supreme Court reversed. Finlay CJ (O'Flaherty and Egan JJ concurring) considered that, in cases where Article 6 (1) applied, the Court 'must closely enquire not only as to the making of a claim against a defendant domiciled in this jurisdiction but must also enquire as to the plausibility of such a claim in a *prima facie* fashion.' He accepted that B & I might well be contractually bound, as the plaintiff had alleged, in relation to the selection, choice and instruction of the driver and in relation to the coach but it was also necessary to enquire whether any such obligation could have contributed to the events alleged to have caused the plaintiff's injury. The case involved 'a simple road accident' in which the coach had collided with a lorry when the lorry was doing a u-turn in front of it. There were grounds for suggesting that possibly the coach was being driven too fast or that the driver of the coach or the lorry had failed to keep a proper look-out. There were, however, 'no *prima facie* grounds of any description for suggesting that the driver was a person who, even if individually selected by B & I, was other than an apparently competent driver, having very many years' experience as a coach driver, nor that there was anything wrong with the coach'. When pressed by the court to indicate why the plaintiff was suing B & I at all, apart from the alleged desire to oust the jurisdiction of the English courts on the tort claim against the English defendants, it seemed to the Chief Justice that 'no satisfactory answer was given' by plaintiff's counsel.

Finlay CJ went on to deal with an important procedural point which had a capacity to arise in other cases. B & I had been only a notice party in the original motion by the English defendants, proceedings against whom were now being struck out. On the basis of the Court's holding, it was clear that B & I would have no prospect under Article 6 (2) of adding them as third parties in the Irish proceedings. This would gravely prejudice B & I. The Chief Justice held that that the Court's decision to dismiss the proceedings against the English defendants amounted to a decision that the proceedings against B & I were technically an abuse of the processes of the Court.

**Appearance to contest jurisdiction** In the 1991 Review, 88-9, we examined Morris J's decision in *Campbell International Trading House Ltd v Van Aart* [1992] ILRM 26, and noted that the Supreme Court reversed Morris J: [1992] ILRM 663. The High Court and Supreme Court decisions have since been reported in [1992] 2 IR 305. For insightful analysis of Morris J's decision, see Gerard Hogan, 'Procedure and Practice and the Judgments Convention: Some Further Developments' (1992) IJEL 82, at 82-7.

Briefly, the case concerned proceedings for breach of contract brought in Ireland by the plaintiff against a German-domiciled defendant. The defendant entered an appearance, in which he required delivery of a statement of claim. When this was sent to him, he raised particulars to it; replies were sent six months later. The defendant subsequently applied for the dismissal of the case, arguing that the Irish Court lacked jurisdiction. The whole process from the entry of the appearance to the motion for dismissal took about nine months.

The plaintiff resisted the defendant's application on the basis that the court had jurisdiction under Article 18 of the Brussels Convention, since the defendant had not entered an appearance solely to contest the jurisdiction. Morris J held in favour of the defendant's application, however. There was no machinery under Order 12 of the Rules of the Superior Court 1986 for the entry of an appearance solely to contest the jurisdiction, nor had such been conferred by the Rules of the Superior Courts (No. 1) 1989 (SI No. 14 of 1989), although the 1989 Rules clearly envisaged the existence of this category of appearance. Morris J interpreted the decision of the Court of Justice in *Elefanten Schuh GmbH v Jacqmain* [1981] ECR 1671 as permitting a defendant wishing to raise the issue of jurisdiction to do so at any time prior to delivering his defence within the jurisdiction. In the instant case, the defendant had not delivered a defence. His notice for particulars did not constitute 'a defence addressed to the Court'. Morris J could well envisage circumstances where by reason of the short form of pleadings it might become necessary for a defendant to deliver a notice for particulars and receive replies before he could know whether he wished to raise a jurisdictional point.

Having held that the defendant was not prevented by Article 18 from challenging the court's jurisdiction, Morris J went on to consider that issue and held that Article 5, s. 2 did not constitute a good jurisdictional base as the contractual obligation which the plaintiff claimed to have been breached was one that was to be performed in Germany rather than Ireland.

The plaintiff's appeal was successful. Finlay CJ expressed himself satisfied that, on the facts of the case as established on affidavit, there was 'no evidence of any description' that the defendant, on entering an appearance and requesting delivery of a statement of claim, had done so for the purpose of contesting jurisdiction. That being so, the plaintiff had been entitled to accept or believe that the defendant had submitted by implication to the jurisdiction. The defendant had failed to indicate at any time prior to his motion to have the case dismissed that he was making any challenge to the court's jurisdiction. Accordingly the mere absence of an actual form in the 1989 Rules had no bearing on the case.

It was clear from Article 18 that a defendant seeking to challenge the jurisdiction should so indicate in entering an appearance:

> It may not be necessary to do it any particular form; conceivably it is not necessary to do it exactly contemporaneously with the entry of appearance, but it is certainly necessary to do it by some method, informing the plaintiff of the fact that the purpose of the entry of an appearance is to contest jurisdiction. That could be done, conceivably, by a letter accompanying the appearance, by a letter immediately following the appearance, or by a notice of motion accompanying or following the appearance and contesting the jurisdiction.

In the view of the Chief Justice, this dealt with the argument that in some instances a defendant might wish to have further particulars, beyond those in a plenary summons, before being satisfied as to what was the precise situation in regard to jurisdiction:

> An indication that the appearance is being entered for that purpose in no way prevents such an individual if [he] subsequently abandon or fail in the challenge to jurisdiction, from defending the case on the merits. In my view, that is the real effect — and the only effect — of the decision in *Elefanten Schuh GmbH v Jacqmain* [1981] ECR 1671, which was relied upon by [Morris J] in reaching the view which he did.

This interpretation of *Elefanten Schuh* is closely similar to that proferred by Gerard Hogan in his discussion of Morris J's decision, to which we have referred above.

**Exclusive jurisdiction** In *GPA Group plc v Bank of Ireland* [1992] 2 IR 408, the important question of the proper remit of Article 17 of the Brussels Convention fell for consideration. The matter concerned a dispute about an agreement which contained the following clause:

> *Choice of Law*
> 1. This Agreement is governed by, and shall be construed in accordance with, the laws of England.
>
> 2. *Submission to Jurisdiction*
> (a) For the benefit of the Participants, each of the Borrowers irrevocably agrees that:-

(i) the courts of England are to have jurisdiction to settle any disputes which may arise in connection with the legal relationships established by this Agreement or otherwise arising in connection with this agreement.
(ii) this provision shall not prevent the conduct of proceedings in any other court of competent jurisdiction.

The question arose as to whether this clause excluded the jurisdiction of the Irish courts that would otherwise arise under the Convention. Article 17, entitled Prorogation of Jurisdiction, provides in part as follows:

> If the parties, one or more of whom is domiciled in a Contracting State, have agreed that a court or courts of a Contracting State are to have jurisdiction to settle any disputes which have arisen or which may arise in connection with a particular legal relationship, that court or those courts shall have exclusive jurisdiction. Such an agreement conferring jurisdiction shall be either in writing or evidenced in writing or, in international trade or commerce, in a form which accords with practices in that trade or commerce of which the parties are or ought to have been aware. Where such an agreement is concluded by parties, none of whom is domiciled in a Contracting State, the courts of other Contracting States shall have no jurisdiction over their disputes unless the court or courts chosen have declined jurisdiction. . . . If an agreement conferring jurisdiction was concluded for the benefit of only one of the parties, that party shall retain the right to bring proceedings in any other court which has jurisdiction by virtue of this Convention.

Keane J interpreted the clause as not purporting to confer exclusive jurisdiction on the English courts; thus Article 17 had no application. Keane J did not clearly identify why he so interpreted the clause though his emphasis on paragraph (2) of the second clause suggests that this element greatly influenced him. An entirely separate interpretative process, leading to the same conclusion as that reached by Keane J, can, however, plausibly be proposed. The clause as a whole is drafted in such a way as to suggest that those who drafted it were intending to fit it into the framework of Article 17, so that there would be a choice of exclusive jurisdiction — England — backed by a provision reminiscent of the final sentence of Article 17, which preserves the right of the party for whose benefit the exclusive jurisdiction agreement was concluded to bring proceedings in any other court having jurisdiction by virtue of the Convention. Whereas Keane J interpreted the clause as evincing a non-exclusive intention, and its literal interpretation undoubtedly is consistent with such a holding, nonetheless the echoes of

Article 17 are sufficiently strong to suggest that it was designed to give express, albeit redundant and, in the event overbroad, expression to the supplementary jurisdictional rights protected by the final sentence of clause 17. Otherwise, why the phrase 'For the benefit of the Participants each of the Borrowers irrevocably agrees . . .'?

In *Bank of Ireland Ltd v McGrath*, High Court, 28 May 1992, Barr J rejected the argument of a third party that proceedings against it should be set aside on the basis of an exclusive jurisdiction clause providing that courts of England should have sole jurisdiction. The proceedings had been taken by a man who was acting as its dealer in Ireland. The contract between the third party and the dealer had originally not contained any provisions relating to jurisdiction. The contract did allow for its amendment by the third party on giving due notice of any change to the dealer. The third party subsequently amended the contract by including the exclusive jurisdiction clause but, on the evidence, Barr J held that it had not been preceded by due notice to the dealer. Barr J rejected the third party's argument that Article 17 of the Brussels Convention applied. He declined to order that the proceedings in the High Court be set aside.

**Jurisdiction in proceedings affecting children's welfare** Earlier in this chapter, we discussed several decisions dealing with jurisdictional aspects of proceedings affecting children's welfare. Many of these arose under the Child Abduction and Enforcement of Custody Orders Act 1991.

## INTERNATIONAL SALE OF GOODS

In its *Report on the United Nations (Vienna) Convention on Contracts for the International Sale of Goods 1990* (LRC 42-1992), the Law Reform Commission recommends that Ireland should accede to the Convention and that legislation be enacted to give effect to its provisions. At present international contracts are subject to no distinct codification in Ireland. Matters are determined by reference to the Irish private international law rules relating to contract and personal property. The statutory implementation of the Rome Convention, brought about by the Contractual Obligations (Applicable Law) Act 1991 (analysed in the 1991 Review, 54-80) has introduced a high degree of certainty into the contract side of the equation, as well as ensuring a significant degree of uniformity at Community level. But that legislation does not address personal property issues and provides merely for a process of selection of the law of a particular state to apply to the issue in question; those who engage in international trade would generally prefer to have their contract governed by a uniform set of rules dealing with the details of the contract. This is what the Vienna Convention offers.

The Vienna Convention was the culmination of a movement for harmonisation stretching back for more than a century. The narrow international appeal for the Hague Conventions of 1964 encouraged the United Nations General Assembly to establish a Commission on International Trade Law (UNCITRAL), which in turn led to the adoption of the Vienna Convention in 1980. It entered into force on 1 January 1988. By the time the Law Reform Commission published its Report, thirty-two states had ratified it or acceded to it, including these EC states: France, Germany, Italy, Spain and the Netherlands.

The Convention deals only with the *international* sale of goods. Article 1(1) provides that the Convention:

> applies to contracts of sale of goods between parties whose place of business are in different States:
>
> (a) when the States are Contracting States; or
> (b) when the rules of private international law lead to the application of the law of a Contracting State.

The Convention excludes certain types of sales from its application. The most important exclusion is the sale of goods 'bought for personal, family or household use, unless the seller, at any time before or at the conclusion of the contract, neither knew nor ought to have known that the goods were bought for any such use': Article 2, para.(a). It will be recalled that consumer sales such as these are the subject of distinctive provisions in both Brussels Judgments Convention (see the 1987 Review 70-4 and the 1988 Review, 90-104) and the Rome Contract Convention (see the 1991 Review 54-80).

Article 4 of the Vienna Convention makes it plain that the Convention governs only the formation of the contract of sale and the rights and obligations of the parties arising from the contract. The Convention is not concerned with the questions of the *validity* of the contract or the effect that the contract may have on the *property* in the goods sold. Neither does it apply to the liability of the seller for death or personal injury caused by the goods to any person: Article 5. (It will be recalled that the Liability for Defective Products Act 1991 deals with aspects of such liability in a European context: see the 1991 Review, 420-34.)

Article 6 of the Convention permits the parties to exclude the application of the Convention or to derogate from or vary the effect of its provisions (save for the provision in Article 12 allowing a state to require that a contract be in writing).

The Commission examines the arguments for and against Ireland's acceding to the Convention. In favour of accession is, first, the fact that the strategy of uniform rules is preferable to the traditional choice of law process since it obliterates the need for a court to get to grips with the provisions of a foreign law. All that the judge has to do to decide the case is to examine and apply the provisions set out in the Convention. Second, the Convention has commanded such a significant degree of international support that it has the potential to realise, at some future time, the objective of becoming the law most frequently applied to international sale of goods. The Convention, surely correctly, regarded it as extremely unlikely that other attempts will be made at an international level to create another uniform law. A third consideration in favour of accession is that most of Ireland's major trading partners are already parties to the Convention. The only exception, Britain, was contemplating accession when the Convention published its Report.

A significant argument against accession lies in the inadequacies of some of the provisions of the Convention which, as the Commission notes on p. 84, 'may serve to confuse rather than to clarify and may be the subject of conflicting interpretations.' Article 14 is unclear as to whether or not a price must be fixed before a contract is formed (see the Report, p. 45). Article 19 provides only a doubtful improvement to the conundrum of the 'battle of the forms' (see the Report, pp. 48-9).

The Commission's conclusion that the balance of the argument lies in favour of accession seems entirely reasonable. It is true that the Convention has as yet spawned little litigation but this scarcely indicates a widespread resort to derogation from its terms; it is far more likely that the specificity and general clarity of most of the provisions of the Convention have largely removed the incentive to have recourse to the courts.

The Commission goes on to recommend that Ireland should not make a declaration pursuant to Article 92 that it will not be bound by the provisions of Part II of the Convention on formation of contract or Part III on sale of goods. The Commission can identify no compelling reason to do so; on the contrary, such a reservation would require the courts to have recourse to two systems of law — the Convention and the applicable law under traditional conflicts rules.

The Commission recommends against a reservation under Article 94 that the Convention should not apply to contracts of sale or their formation where the parties have their places of business in Ireland and another specified country with the same or closely related legal rules. Britain would be the obvious candidate here, but the Commission notes that the differences between Irish and British law are in some respects significant.

The Commission also recommends against a reservation under Article 95 relieving the reserving State from being bound by subparagraph (1)(b) of

Article 1, under which the Convention applies to contracts for the sale of goods between parties whose places of business are in different States *when the rules of private international law lead to the application of the law of a Contracting State*. This reservation would not reduce the complexity of a choice-of-law process under private international law; indeed, as the Commission observes, resort to the Convention as the applicable law might minimise rather than exacerbate difficulties of this kind. The Commission rightly rejects the chauvinist attitude that the Convention should be displaced in cases where the applicable law under the traditional approach would be that of Ireland.

Next the Commission recommends that Ireland should not make a declaration under Article 96 that, to the extent that Article 11, Article 29 and Part II of the Convention allow a contract of sale or its modification or termination by agreement or any offer, acceptance or other indication of intention to be made in any form other than in writing, this should not apply where any party has his or her place of business in Ireland. Section 4 of the Sale of Goods Act 1893, in the Commission's view, relates to enforcement rather than formation but, even if Ireland were in a position to avail itself of this reservation, the Commission sees no strong reason for doing so:

> It seems that Article 96 has in mind more important and therefore more stringent formalities. The Irish requirement has little practical significance in the context of the international sale of goods. In any event, even within our domestic law, there appears to be some confusion and uncertainty concerning the specifics of the requirement of a signed memorandum. Similar considerations apply to modification of contractual terms and termination by agreement.

## TORT

In *Donegal Fuel and Supply Co. Ltd v Londonderry Port and Harbour Commissioners*, High Court, 6 May 1992, which we consider in the Constitutional Law Chapter, below, 144-7, an unusual issue of private international law arose. The question was compounded by elements of the historical conflict concerning jurisdiction over the northern part of the island.

Very briefly, the case concerned a pier on the Donegal side of Lough Foyle which was vested in the defendants by legislation in the nineteenth century. In earlier proceedings (on 6 June 1986) Costello J held that the defendants were under a statutory duty to keep the pier open and (on 6 April 1991) he held that the defendants were in breach of that statutory duty, entitling the plaintiffs to damages for loss that they had sustained since 1978.

In the instant proceedings, Costello J came to the conclusion that the statutory provisions imposing that duty had not been carried over into Irish law by Article 73 of the 1922 Constitution. He did not, however, consider that this precluded him from assessing damages in the earlier proceedings:

> The Irish courts have jurisdiction to entertain a claim for damages for breach of a duty imposed by a foreign statute on a foreign corporation when the breach occurs in this State and when the foreign corporation submits to jurisdiction, as happened in the earlier case. The principles on which damages for breach of statutory duty are awarded are the same under Irish law as under the law of the United Kingdom and so my conclusion that the plaintiffs are entitled to damages is unaffected by the fact that their entitlement arises under the law of Northern Ireland rather than the law of the Republic. In assessing damages I will, in the light of this judgment, have to consider whether the measure of damages is affected by the law of Northern Ireland, including the limit, if any, imposed by the Ministerial Order in 1991 which relieved the Harbour Commissioners for liability to maintain the pier.

This sensible approach reflects a departure from the traditional conflict of laws treatment of torts. In being willing to engage in *depecage*, Costello J may be regarded as a modernist. See Binchy, *Irish Conflict of Law* (1988), 578-80.

# Constitutional Law

## ACCESS TO COURTS

**Discovery as action** In *Megaleasing UK Ltd v Barrett (No. 2)* [1993] ILRM 497, the Supreme Court adverted to the question whether discovery could constitute a substantive action: see the Practice and Procedure chapter, 479, below.

**Legal aid: family cases** In *M.F. v Legal Aid Board*, High Court, 4 November 1992; [1993] ILRM 797 (SC), O'Hanlon J in the High Court (affirmed by the Supreme Court in 1993) quashed a refusal by the Legal Aid Board to grant the applicant civil legal aid in connection with judicial separation proceedings instituted by her husband under the Judicial Separation and Family Law Reform Act 1989: see the Practice and Procedure chapter, 487, below.

**Right to present full argument** In *Slattery v An Taoiseach and Ors.* [1993] 1 IR 286, the Supreme Court noted that procedural points about whether the plaintiffs should be given leave to serve proceedings during the vacation had not been used to prevent the plaintiffs presenting their substantive arguments to court: see the discussion of the case below, 218-9.

## AVOIDANCE OF CONSTITUTIONAL ISSUE

The normal rule of avoiding a constitutional issue where possible was applied by Lynch J in *In re Tivoli Cinema Ltd* [1992] ILRM 522; [1992] 1 IR 413: see the Licensing chapter, 427-9, below.

## COMPENSATION FOR BREACH OF RIGHTS

In *A.D. v Ireland and Attorney General*, High Court, 29 July 1992, Carroll J, in a relatively short judgment, rejected the plaintiff's claim that the State had failed to vindicate her right to bodily integrity by not having a comprehensive system to compensate her arising from the violent criminal offences of rape, buggery and assault committed against her.

The perpetrator of the crimes had been charged and convicted and had been sentenced to 18 years imprisonment in respect of the crimes, which had occurred in 1988. That date was significant because it was two years after the government had amended the *ex gratia* Scheme of Compensation for Injuries Criminally Inflicted, which had originally been introduced in 1972. Until 1986, victims of crime were entitled to apply to the Criminal Injuries Compensation Tribunal established by the Scheme for damages arising from the injuries sustained by them, and that the Tribunal could award general damages for pain and suffering in such cases. In 1986, the government decided to restrict the Scheme to awards of special damages. Thus, the plaintiff in the instant proceedings was precluded from claiming general damages for what Carroll J described as the 'considerable' injuries, past and future, suffered by her.

The plaintiff accepted that the State had, under Article 40.3 of the Constitution, defended 'as far as practicable' her right to bodily integrity through providing a police force, a code of criminal law and a justice system. However, the plaintiff argued that the State had failed, under Article 40.3 to vindicate as far as practicable that right.

Carroll J, referring to *Ryan v Attorney General* [1965] IR 294, accepted that the plaintiff's right had been breached through the violent crimes committed against her. She also referred approvingly to both *The State (Healy) v Donoghue* [1976] IR 326 and *Meskell v CIE* [1973] IR 121 as supporting the plaintiff's proposition that:

> if the courts find there is a constitutional right which is being ignored by the State, the courts will also find a remedy in the absence of the State undertaking to observe that right. That breach of a constitutional right gives rise to a claim for damages has been established in the case of *Meskell v CIE* [1973] IR 121.

However, Carroll J added a gloss that the plaintiff could only succeed if she could show there was 'a constitutional right to compensation'. She referred to the argument made by counsel for the State that the State had vindicated the plaintiff's right by the fact that it seeks to prevent crime, that it punishes wrongdoers and that '[i]t provides a civil remedy against a wrongdoer.' Counsel also argued that the plaintiff's claim would be 'to make the State an insurer'.

Ultimately, Carroll J did not accept the argument that the State was obliged to compensate the plaintiff in order to demonstrate its vindication of her right. Her judgment concludes:

> The question of compensation is purely a matter of policy for the

> Government and the Oireachtas. It seem to be a question on which many States have already made a policy decisiuon to have a scheme of compensation. It is an area in which the Government did have a policy which included pain and suffering and have resiled from it since 1986. But no matter how desirable such a policy might seem, it is esentially a matter for the Government and accordingly the plaintiff must fail in her claim.

This approach of Carroll J echoes the similar 'hands off' approach taken by a number of judges in recent years, in which they have deferred to the government or Oireachtas in areas described as policy issues or which would involved the State in some expenditure. For criticism of this general approach, see the discussion of *Cosgrave v Legal Aid Board* [1991] 2 IR 43 in the 1990 Review, 144-7.

However, the specific argument in the instant case that the plaintiff's argument would require the State to be an insurer is worthy of some comment. It echoes arguments in the context of 'private' personal injuries claims that the standard of reasonable care should not be extended to one of absolute liability. It can, of course, be accepted that to impose liability on the State for all personal injuries would involve strict liability but that was not the plaintiff's argument. Her case was confined to injuries criminally inflicted, and the specific context involved crimes of violence. It is surely not beyond the bounds of imagination to develop a limited right to compensation from the State in respect of a limited range of matters, such as those involving violence. This would be consistent, for example, with the limited right to legal aid established in the *The State (Healy) v Donoghue* [1976] IR 326 to which Carroll J referred, where the Supreme Court confined the right to serious criminal cases. This clearly involved a 'policy' choice by the Supreme Court. Indeed, the decision of the Supreme Court in *McKinley v Minister for Defence* [1992] 2 IR 333 (see 613-8, below), delivered only two days before Carroll J's judgment in the instant case, indicates that, where necessary, the courts can be quite inventive and interventionist on occasion. However, it remains that, in most cases, the courts in recent years are reluctant to trample unduly over what are regarded as 'political' or 'non-justiciable' issues. See in this context the decisions in *McKenna v An Taoiseach and Ors.*, High Court, 8 June 1992 and *Slattery v An Taoiseach* [1993] 1 IR 286: 218-9, below.

## DISCOVERY OF DOCUMENTS

In *An Blascaod Mór Teo and Ors v Commissioners of Public Works in Ireland*

*and Ors*, High Court, 27 November 1992 Murphy J placed stringent limits on the extent to which discovery of documents could be obtained concerning advice given to the government about legislation whose constitutional validity was being challenged.

The plaintiffs had instituted proceedings claiming, *inter alia*, that the Blascaod Mór National Historic Park Act 1989 (see the 1989 Review, 4) was unconstitutional. In the course of the proceedings, the plaintiffs sought discovery of correspondence and materials considered at cabinet level and committees thereof, draft bills and heads of legislation concerning the 1989 Act and all communications concerning the Act between any of the defendants. The Master of the High Court declined to order discovery. The plaintiffs sought an extension of the time for appealing the Master's refusal and also sought an order for discovery from the High Court in the same terms as put to the Master. Murphy J allowed the extension of time but refused to order discovery.

On the extension, he held that since the plaintiffs averred that they had intended to appeal the Master's decision within the specified time limit, he would exercise his discretion to permit the extension of time, applying the leading decision in *Éire Continental Trading Co. Ltd v Clonmel Foods Ltd* [1955] IR 170.

On the main issue posed, he took the view that the instant case was not primarily a question of claiming privilege for documents sought, but rather whether the documents were relevant to the proceedings. In this context, he used the decision of the House of Lords in *British Railways Board v Pickin* [1974] AC 765 as the basis for deciding that the documents sought were not relevant. Murphy J acknowledged that the relevance of the *Pickin* case was not readily apparent, since he noted that British constitutional law does not allow of the judiciary making a declaration that legislation was invalid. Despite this, he considered that the analysis in *Pickin* was relevant to the issue he was asked to determine.

Using the analysis in *Pickin*, Murphy J considered that it would appear 'absurd and offensive' to members of the Oireachtas that, whatever purpose or motive the promoters of a Bill might have, such would be regarded as the effective cause of the enactment of any legislation. He accepted the view in *Pickin* that, in legal terms, an analysis of the motivation for legislation would be meaningless in practice and wholly unwarranted by the doctrine of the separation of powers. He concluded that since the validity of legislation must be tested by reference to the document ultimately enacted by the Oireachtas, any documentation dealing with representations to a Minister or member of the Oireachtas concerning proposed legislation was wholly irrelevent for the purposes of discovery.

This conclusion merits some consideration. Undoubtedly, the motives behind legislation might in practice be virtually impossible to ascertain even after full examination of briefing papers and other documentation prepared for a govermnent Minister, and as Murphy J states may in any event be irrelevant to the text of the legislation ultimately approved by the Oireachtas.

However, the total emphasis on textual interpretation seems inappropriate. Recent decisions of the Irish courts have indicated a move away from complete reliance on legislative text to elucidate meaning. The starting point would appear to be the judgment of Henchy J in *Nestor v Murphy* [1979] IR 326, in which he emphasised a teleological approach to statutory interpretation, an approach which is admittedly more in line with the civil law than the common law tradition. More recently, in *McLoughlin v Minister for the Public Service* [1986] ILRM 28; [1985] IR 631, Henchy J referred to an Explanatory Memorandum to a Bill to elucidate the meaning of the Act it became. Since it is well known that the Explanatory Memorandum is prepared by a public servant from the government department sponsoring the legislation, the *McLoughlin* case would appear to be a relevant pointer for the *Blascaod Mór* case.

Finally, an analogy might reasonably be made with the question whether parliamentary debates concerning legislation are relevant to the interpretation of the legislative text. It is notable that, until its decision in *Pepper v Hart* [1992] AC, the House of Lords had refused to examine such parliamentary debates, and that this was judicial orthodoxy at the time of the *Pickin* case approved by Muprhy J in the *Blascaod Mór* case. However, a different approach has been taken in the Irish courts on this question. In *Wavin Pipes Ltd v Hepworth Iron Co. Ltd* [1982] FSR 32, Costello J held that parliamentary debates could in some instances be used at the very least in confirming textual interpretations. This decision seems in line with the *Nestor* and *McLoughlin* cases, and again seems to point to the relevance of motive or intention at least in a limited context. It is on this basis that the sweeping nature of Murphy J's refusal in the *Blascaod Mór* case is open to some criticism.

## ELECTIONS

The Electoral Act 1992 involves a comprehensive consolidation with amendments of the statutory regime concerning Dáil elections, together with some associated necessary amendments to overlapping statutory provisions in connection with presidential, Seanad, European and local elections. However, these other categories of elections remain regulated primarily by the special electoral provisions connected with them, albeit amended by the 1992 Act.

Given the range and complexity of the topics covered by the 1992 Act, it is not possible to discuss in detail in this Review the consequences of the 1992 Act. John O'Dowd's comprehensive Annotation in *Irish Current Law Statutes Annotated* provides an enlightening analysis of the background to the 1992 Act and its connection with the previous regime as well as its relationship with the overlapping statutory regimes for elections other than those to the Dáil. His commentary also analyses numerous constitutional questions raised by the terms of the 1992 Act, though not necessarily discussed during the passage of the Act.

As his annotation indicates, while the 1992 Act is primarily a consolidation of the existing statutory provisions, there are also a number of innovations. We will refer to just some of these in the Review, without in any way providing an exhaustive list of new provisions. These must, of course, be seen against the general constitutional background requiring a secret ballot based on a system of proportional representation by the single transferable vote in multi-seat constituencies.

**Commencement and application to 1992 general election** It may be noted here that the 1992 Act was signed by the President on 5 November 1992, just one day after the Dáil had been dissolved by the President in preparation for the general election held on 25 November 1992. The Act had been debated in the Oireachtas in the knowledge that an election was imminent and concern was expressed that its terms would apply to the forthcoming election. In the event, certain provisions did apply to that election: see the Electoral Act 1992 (Commencement) Order 1992 (SI No. 321) and the Electoral Act 1992 (Commencement) (No. 2) Order 1992 (SI No. 322), the terms of which are discussed by John O'Dowd in his comments on s.1 of the 1992 Act, *ICLSA*. However, the remainder of the 1992 Act was brought into effect generally from 11 December 1992: see the Electoral Act 1992 (Commencement) (No. 3) Order 1992 (SI No. 386).

**Double registration** S. 11(1) of the 1992 Act provides that a person 'shall not be registered as an elector more than once in any registration area nor in more than one such area'. This clearly prohibits double registration of electors, reversing the decision of the Supreme Court in *Quinn v Waterford Corporation* [1991] ILRM 433; [1990] 2 IR 507 which had interpreted s.5(4) of the Electoral Act 1963 as envisaging registration in more than one electoral area: see the 1990 Review, 175-6. As we indicated in the 1990 Review, 175, the 'right' of double registration established in *Quinn* was short-lived, and although McCarthy J's judgment in *Quinn* indicated merely that the Constitution precluded double voting, the Oireachtas has now firmly set its face against double registration.

**Electoral register** S. 13 of the 1992 Act, and the Second Schedule, amended the time scale for the preparation of the electoral register, the qualifying date for which is 1 September, such register to come into effect on 15 February of the following year. S. 15 also provides for a supplemental list of voters who would have been entitled to registration on the qualifying date but who were not actually placed on the electoral list.

**Nomination process** S. 47 of the 1992 Act increased the deposit required from Dáil candidates from £100 to £300, a sum decided after the proposed figure of £500 had been criticised during the Oireachtas debate. The Dáil Elections Free Postage Scheme 1992 (SI No. 338) lay down the procedure by which candidates may claim free postage of their literature. The 1992 Scheme revokes all previous schemes, including the 1990 Scheme.

**Special voters' list** The special voters' list, first introduced by the Electoral (Amendment) (No. 2) Act 1986 for the purposes of facilitating voting by persons who were physically incapabale of attending at a polling station, was subject to substantial criticism on the ground that such a person was required to produce a certificate from a medical practitioner that the voter was of sound mind and capable of comprehending the act of voting. This requirement has not been repeated in ss. 78 to 84 of the 1992 Act, which deals with the special voters' list. However, the 1992 Act continues the requirement that such voters be attended in their home to cast their vote, rather than extending the postal voting provisions to such persons. The Minister for the Environment resisted amendments to provide the postal ballot to such voters. For an unsuccessful constitutional challenge to the regime prior to the 1986 Act, see *Draper v Attorney General* [1984] ILRM 643; [1984] IR 277.

**Format of ballot paper** S. 88 of the 1992 Act provides for some minor changes to the format of a ballot paper to ensure candidates have equal space on it, but other changes suggested by the opposition, such as a random rather than alphabetical listing of candidates or photographs of candidates on the ballot paper, were rejected during the debate on the Act.

**Identification at poll** S. 111 of the 1992 Act authorises the Minister to specify by Regulation the different identification documents which may be produced by a person to satisfy a returing officer of their identity. On the different documents now specified, see the Electoral Regulations 1992 (SI No. 407).

**Counting of votes** Ss. 118, 121 and 122 of the 1992 Act provide for some minor amendments to the procedures for counting votes, and in particular in relation to the procedure by which the returning officer deals with doubtful and rejected ballot papers, as well as the important procedure for distributing surpluses from one candidate to another. In his Annotation for *ICLSA*, John O'Dowd raises some pertinent constitutional issues concerning the vagaries of the rules concerning the distribution of surpluses in the context of close electoral counts, and argues that these may be in conflict with the requirements of Article 16.1.4 and 16.5.2 of the Constitution.

**Election petitions** S. 132 of the 1992 Act provides that election petitions will in future be heard by the High Court, rather than a special election court.

**Canvassing at polling station** S. 147 of the 1992 Act prohibits for the first time canvassing or the display of election literature within 50 metres of any polling station during polling day, thus effecting a dramatic change to the physical environment surrounding Irish polling stations.

## EQUALITY

**Detention powers** In the highly significant decision *The People v Quilligan and O'Reilly (No. 3)* [1993] 2 IR 305, the Supreme Court rejected an argument that s.30 of the Offences against the State Act 1939 infringed Article 40.1 of the Constitution: see the discussion in the Criminal Law chapter, 234-9, below.

**Family** In *McKinley v Minister for Defence* [1992] 2 IR 333, the Supreme Court accepted that the common law action for loss of consortium, confined to a claim by a husband for the loss of the services of his wife, was inconsistent with Article 40.1: see the discussion in the Torts chapter, 613-8, below. And in *W. v W.* [1993] ILRM 294, the Court also found that the dependent domicile rule, by which a wife took the domicile of her husband, infringed Articles 40.1 and 41: see the discussion in the Conflict of Laws chapter, 115-25, above.

## EXTRA-TERRITORIALITY

In *Donegal Fuel and Supply Co. Ltd v Londonderry Port and Harbour Commissioners*, High Court, 6 May 1992, Costello J dealt with an issue concerning extra-territoriality in the context of a dispute whose origins lay in his previous judgment in *Moyne v Londonderry Port and Harbour Commissioners* [1986] IR 299.

In the *Moyne* case, Costello J had held that the Londonderry Port and Harbour Commissioners were in breach of statutory duty in failing to maintain the Carrickarory Pier which was situated on the Donegal side of Lough Foyle, and which came within the jurisdiction of the Commissioners. The plaintiffs in that case were coal importers who had used the Pier and who claimed that the failure to maintain the Pier resulted in loss and damage to them. In the *Moyne* case, Costello J had concluded that the Commissioners were in breach, in particular, of the requirements of the Londonderry Port and Harbour Act 1854 and the Harbours, Docks and Piers Clauses Act 1847. However, he also concluded that the Commissioners could, by means of bye-laws made under s.47 of the Londonderry Port and Harbour Act 1882, restrict the use of any part of the Port, including the Carrickarory Pier.

The *Moyne* proceedings were then adjourned for the assessment of damages, but very little appears to have occurred until a number of developments came together. These arose from moves taken under the terms of the Harbours Act (Northern Ireland) 1970, an Act which purported to alter substantially the make-up and powers of Harbour Commissioners. In relation to the Londonderry Port and Harbour Commissioners, the 1970 Act provided that very substantial changes to their powers and composition could be made by Ministerial Order under the Act. Thus, in 1976, an Order was made which required the then Commissioners, elected under the Londonderry Port and Harbour Act 1920, to be replaced by an appointed body. This change, which clearly predated the Moyne judgment in 1986, was to surface for the first time only in the instant proceedings. But two events occurred which precipitated the instant proceedings. First, in June 1991, the Northern Ireland Department of Commerce made a statutory Order under the Harbours Act (Northern Ireland) 1970, which purported to empower the Commissioners to abandon the maintenance and repair of any port. Under this Order, the Commissioners decided to abandon the Carrickarory Pier in September 1991. However, because the Commissioners were not convinced that the Order made under the Northern Ireland Act of 1970 could operate in Donegal, they also sought in October 1991 to apply to the Department of the Marine for its approval of bye-laws restricting the use of the Carrickarory Pier pursuant to s. 47 of the Londonderry Port and Harbour Act 1882.

It was against that background that the applicants in the instant case sought judicial review on two fronts. First, they sought mandamus directing the Commissioners to repair the Carrickarory Pier. Second, they sought prohibition restraining the Minister for the Marine from approving the bye-laws.

Costello J was thus required to consider to what extent the pre-1922 Acts applicable to the Commissioners had been affected by the Constitution of the Irish Free State and, in particular, to what extent they had been carried over by Article 73 of that Constitution. If they had not, then the applicants would fail in their claims because the Commissioners would be entitled to act under the powers conferred by the Northern Ireland Act of 1970 and the Minister for the Marine would have no function in relation to making bye-laws. Costello J held in favour of the Commissioners and against the applicants on both counts.

He stated that the questions raised in the case could be expressed as follows: 'could the legislature of the Irish Free State in 1923 have passed a law establishing in Northern Ireland a statutory corporation with the powers, duties and functions contained in the pre-1922 statutes and elected in the manner provided for in those statutes?' In this connection, he accepted that although the matter had initially been one of doubt, the Irish Free State Oireachtas, as a member of the Commonwealth, had power to legislate extra-territorially, but that this was subject to well-established principles of international law. See generally *In re the Criminal Law (Jurisdiction) Bill 1975* [1977] IR 129 in this connection. Referring with approval to Brownlie, *Principles of International Law*, 3rd ed., p. 228, Costello J concluded that the state of international law in 1923 was such that the Irish Free State was not empowered to legislate for a matter which was within the exclusive jurisdiction of another State and that the State was precluded from enacting laws which would apply to a corporate body, such as the Commissioners, that was domiciled in another State.

He accepted that the Free State Oireachtas could have legislated in respect of the Carrickarory Pier, as it was situated in Donegal, and that such legislation could have dealt with the operations of a foreign corporation such as the Commissioners. However, he did not consider that such legislation could have imposed a duty to repair on the Commissioners, since such a duty was intimately connected with the levy-raising powers of the Commissioners. In an important passage, Costello J concluded:

> The financial provisions of the pre-1922 statutes could not have been enacted by the Oireachtas as they imposed taxes to be collected in a foreign State and to do so would have constituted and amounted to an unjustifiable interference in the internal affairs of the United Kingdom. The provisions of the pre-1922 statutes imposing duties to repair the pier at Carrickarory and keep it open were so closely linked to those financial provisions as to make it impossible to sever these duties from those provisions and so the sections on which the applicants herein rely could not have been enacted by the Oireachtas and so were not carried over by Article 73.

Of some interest is that Costello J pointed out that this conclusion did not preclude the Irish courts from assessing damages in the connected *Moyne* case. This was because he held that the High Court was empowered to award damages against a foreign corporation where the breach of duty occurred in the State. However, he did state also that, since damages in such a case would be determined by the law of Northern Ireland, the measure of damages in the *Moyne* case might be affected by the 1991 Order made under the Northern Ireland Act of 1970 referred to above.

Costello J's conclusion on the extra-territoriality point led him to conclude that both the mandamus and prohibition proceedings must fail because the Commissioners were under no duty since 1991 to maintain the Carrickarory Pier, and the Minister for the Marine had no continuing power to make bye-laws under the pre-1922 statutes as these had not been carried over.

Finally, he added that, if he was wrong on the extra-territoriality point, the Minister for the Marine also lacked power to make bye-laws because the Commissioners envisaged by the pre-1922 statutes no longer existed. This was because the 1920 Act referred to already required the Commissioners to be elected, whereas since 1976 the Commissioners had been appointed under the terms of the 1976 Order made under the Northern Ireland Act of 1970. For this reason, the present Commissioners were not Commissioners within the meaning of the pre-1922 legislation, even assuming that it had been carried over by the 1922 Constitution.

## EXPRESSION

Article 40.6.1.i of the Constitution was considered by the High Court in *McKenna v An Taoiseach and Ors.*, High Court, 8 June 1992 and in *McCann v An Taoiseach and Ors (No. 2)*, High Court, 5 October 1992: see the discussion below, 217-20.

## FAIR PROCEDURES

The case law on fair procedures in 1992 is discussed in the Administrative Law chapter, 8, above.

## FAMILY

The case law on the family in 1992, many of which involve constitutional issues centering around Articles 41 and 42 of the Constitution, is discussed in the Family Law chapter, 338-76, below.

## INTERNATIONAL RELATIONS

**Conforming to the Council of Europe** In *Desmond and Dedeir v Glackin, Minister for Industry and Commerce and Ors (No. 2)* [1992] ILRM 490; [1993] 3 IR 1, O'Hanlon J followed a line of authority which indicates that, under Article 29.4.3, the courts should as far as possible interpret Irish law in a way that conformed to the requirements of the Council of Europe Convention for the Protection of Human Rights and Fundamental Freedoms: see the discussion in the Criminal Law chapter, 239-42, below.

**Diplomatic immunity** In *Government of Canada v Employment Appeals Tribunal* [1992] ILRM 325; [1992] 2 IR 484, the Supreme Court considered the sovereign immunity of a foreign government against the background of Article 29.3 of the Constitution.

The Court (Finlay CJ, Hederman, McCarthy, O'Flaherty and Egan JJ) concluded that, in light of developments in other jurisdictions since World War II in particular, it was clear that other States had abandoned the notion of an absolute sovereign immunity; and that such an absolute immunity was relevant only to a time when a State was concerned with the conduct of its armed forces, foreign affairs and the operation of its currency. The Court decided it was no longer appropriate to an era when so many States were engaged in the business of trade, whether directly or indirectly; and that the more restrictive form of foreign immunity now recognised by most States was one which attached to the actual public business or policy of a foreign State, so that no immunity attached to private trade conducted by States. In this respect, the Court approved of dicta in *Zarine v Owners of SS Ramava* [1942] IR 148 and of the overall approach indicated by Lord Wilberforce in the House of Lords decision *I Congresso del Partido* [1983] 1 AC 244. The Supreme Court decision is discussed more fully in the 1991 Review, 90-2.

**Maastricht Treaty on European Union** The case law arising from the referendum campaign on the Maastricht Treaty on European Union is discussed below. The effect of the Treaty itself is outlined in the European Community chapter, 326-30, below.

**Signature and ratification** In *Hutchinson v Minister for Justice* [1993] ILRM 602, Blayney J rejected the proposition that the government was in any way bound by its signature of an international Convention. The applicant was a British national serving a life sentence for murder, imposed in 1980, in an Irish prison. He wished to be transferred to an English prison to serve the remainder of his term. His case centered on whether the State had committed itself to be bound by a Council of Europe Convention on the transfer of prisoners.

In 1983, the Council of Europe opened for signature its Convention on the Transfer of Sentenced Prisoners. Article 18.2 of the Convention provided that it would enter into force one month following ratification of the Convention by three States. Article 18.3 provided that subsequently the Convention would enter into force in any other State one month after such State ratified the Convention. France, Spain and Sweden ratified the Convention in 1985, and the Convention entered into force in July 1985. In 1986, the Convention was signed on behalf of the Irish government by the then Minister for Foreign Affairs. The government had not, at any time up to 1992, ratified the Convention, but the applicant sought an order of mandamus to the effect that the government's signature placed it under an obligation to ratify the terms of the Convention.

Blayney J rejected the applicant's argument that such a proposition formed part of the generally accepted principles of international law. He referred to a number of the leading textbooks, including Oppenheim, *International Law*, 4th ed. (1928), *O'Connell on International Law*, 2nd ed. (1970) and Schwarzenberger, *A Manual of International Law*, 6th ed. (1976). The applicant had argued that the concept of 'good faith' in international law required that the State ratify an international agreement to which it was signatory. But the textbooks to which Blayney J referred, in particular *O'Connell*, universally rejected this proposition. On that basis, therefore, he dismissed the applicant's claim that the State's signing of the Convention had any effects in law.

This decision is hardly surprising in view of the dualist theory of international relations which is said to be at the heart of Article 29.5 of the Constitution so far as international relations are concerned: see, for example, Forde, *Constitutional Law of Ireland*, pp. 207-9. Indeed, in the domestic context, the courts have declined to order mandamus to require a Minister to make a Commencement Order in respect of an Act: see *The State (Sheehan) v Government of Ireland* [1988] ILRM 437; [1987] IR 550 (1987 Review, 16-19).

## IRISH LANGUAGE

In *Ní Cheallaigh v Minister for the Environment*, High Court, 4 May 1992, O'Hanlon J, in a judgment delivered in the Irish language *sub nom. Ní Cheallaigh v An tAire Comhshaoil*, dismissed the applicant's claim that the Minister for the Environment had acted in breach of Article 8 of the Constitution in making the Road Vehicles (Registration and Licensing) (Amendment) Regulations 1986. The 1986 Regulations laid out the form that licence plates for motor vehicles were required to take from 1 January 1987.

Under the 1986 Regulations, licence plates must contain a year number, for example, '87' for the year 1987, followed by a letter or letters to indicate the relevant licensing authority with which the motor vehicle was registered, for example 'D' to indicate the vehicle was registered with the Dublin licensing authority.

The applicant had registered her motor vehicle with the Dublin licensing authority, but she attached to her car two licence plates with the letters 'BAC', which represented the Irish language version, Baile Átha Cliath, of the Dublin licensing authority, instead of the letter 'D'as required by the 1986 Regulations. The applicant was prosecuted under the 1986 Regulations, convicted in the District Court and fined £10. The applicant then instituted the instant proceedings claiming that the 1986 Regulations were invalid on the ground that the exclusive use of the English language designation for a licensing authority failed to have regard to the status of the Irish language as the first official language of the State in Article 8 of the Constitution.

As already indicated, O'Hanlon J dismissed the applicant's claim. He first of all referred to the text of Article 8. Article 8.1 provides that the Irish language as the national language is the first official language. Article 8.2 provides that the English language (Sacs-Bhéarla) is recognised as a second official language. Crucially in the instant case, Article 8.3 provides that:

> Provision may, however, be made by law for the exclusive use of either of the said languages for any one or more official purposes, either throughout the State or in any part thereof.

O'Hanlon J applied the views expressed in the Supreme Court in *Attorney General v Coyne and Wallace* (1963) 101 ILTR 17. In particular he cited the dicta of Kingsmill Moore J that the true meaning of Article 8.3 was that either the Irish or English language could be used for official purposes, unless provision was made by law that one of the two official languages only was to be used for some one or more official purposes. In that sense, O'Hanlon J held that the Oireachtas and Minister for the Environment were empowered to determine that the English language be used exclusively to designate the county of registration for motor vehicles under the 1986 Regulations. O'Hanlon J also distinguished the instant case from that arising in *Delap v Minister for Justice*, High Court, 13 June 1990, *sub nom. Delap v An tAire Dlí agus Cirt* (see the 1990 Review, 440-1), in which he held that the applicant was entitled to an Irish language verison of the Rules of the Superior Courts 1986 in order to give effect to his right of access to the courts under Article 40.3. In the *Ní Cheallaigh* case, O'Hanlon J noted that the issue of access to the courts was absent in the instant case. Nor did he consider that there was any attack on the property rights of the applicant by requiring that she place the licence plates required by the 1986 Regulations on her motor vehicle. We may note that Regulations made in 1992 on licence plates would appear to incorporate some use of the Irish language: see the discussion in the Transport chapter, 630, below.

## JUDICIAL LEGISLATING

In *McKinley v Minister for Defence* [1992] 2 IR 333, the Supreme Court took a proactive view of its function where a common law rule is declared inconsistent with the equality guarantee in Article 40.1. In *McKinley*, the Court decided by a 3-2 majority (Hederman, McCarthy and O'Flaherty JJ; Finlay CJ and Egan J dissenting) that the common law action for loss of consortium, which was confined to a claim by the husband for loss of the services of his wife, was inconsistent with Articles 40.1 and 41 of the Constitution.

However, one possible consequence of this finding might have been to stop at this point; indeed, the decision in *Cahill v Sutton* [1980] IR 326 might have indicated that the Court not even reach this issue on the ground that the declaration of invalidity of the comon law rule conferred no benefit on the plaintiff, a woman whose husband had been severely injured in the scrotal region while serving in the Irish Army. In *McKinley*, however, the majority held that, in examining an existing common law heading of claim, the courts were not confined to declaring the existing rule invalid for inconsistency with the Constitution. Having identified the inequality, the majority considered that the courts had jurisdiction to declare that the plaintiff had an equal right to claim for loss of consortium.

This replacement of a narrow and invalid common law rule with an expanded and constitutionally valid head of claim was criticised by the minority, Finlay CJ and Hederman J, as impermissible judicial legislation. Indeed, the majority approach would appear to open up, at least in theory, a large range of possible avenues for significant positive judicial law making. It appears at least possible that *McKinley* may be cited for the proposition that any existing common law rule which falls foul of a constitutional provision because it is too narrow in scope may be 'mended' by its replacement with an expanded, constitutionally valid, rule.

This is, of course, in theory. However much one might argue for this approach to be adopted as a general rule, experience indicates that, while *McKinley* may include some eloquent statements about the 'mending' power of constitutional judicial review, the reality is that the courts have, in the past, baulked at the prospect of wide-ranging social engineering through constitutional judicial review. A similar point to that accepted by the majority in

*McKinley* was firmly rejected by Keane J in *Somjee v Minister for Justice* [1981] ILRM 324, albeit in the context of a statutory rule. Most judges will take the view that, where rights are conferred too narrowly, it is not the function of the judges to extend those rights in the name of equality, rather that this is a matter for the Oireachtas.

This turned out, of course, to be the minority view in *McKinley*. However, it seems more likely that *McKinley* may, in the future, be regarded as either being a case 'decided on its own peculiar facts' or an aberration. One need look no further than the 'hands off' approach of the judges in *Slattery v An Taoiseach* [1993] 1 IR 286 (see pp. 218-20, below) (two of whom made up the majority in *McKinley*) to provide what is probably a more accurate picture of the proactive level of the judiciary. See the more detailed discussion of this in the Torts chapter, 613-8, below.

## LIBERTY

**Inquiry into detention** In *Sheehan v Reilly* [1993] ILRM 427; [1992] 1 IR 368, the Supreme Court emphasised the immediacy of the procedure under Article 40.4.2 for obtaining an inquiry into the legality of a person's detention. The case arose from the following rather involved circumstances.

The applicant had been convicted in November 1990 of certain offences and sentenced to a total of 16 months' imprisonment. Having withdrawn an appeal against these convictions, he began serving the sentence in January 1991. On 2 January 1992, the applicant was convicted by the first respondent, a Judge of the District Court, of an offence under the Larceny Act 1916, and was sentenced to 10 months' imprisonment, to date from the termination of the sentences imposed in November 1990. On 22 January 1992, the applicant applied in person to the High Court for 'a conditional order of habeas corpus . . . and for an inquiry in accordance with the Constitution of Ireland, Article 40.4.2'. The ground for the application was that the first respondent's order of 2 January 1992 was in excess of jurisdiction in that its effect was to impose consecutive sentences totalling 26 months. On 5 February 1992, Carney J ordered that, in lieu of granting an order for habeas corpus, the applicant be permitted to apply for judicial review of the order made on 2 January 1992. The text of the ruling made by Carney J appeared to indicate that he was under the mistaken impression that the applicant's November 1990 conviction had occured in November 1991. On 25 March 1992, Denham J made an order on judicial review quashing the conviction and sentence of 2 January 1992, but remitted the case to the District Court pursuant to O.84, r.26(4) of the Rules of the Superior Courts 1986. By a spoken order on the same date, Denham J also discharged the applicant from custody.

The applicant appealed in person to the Supreme Court, which issued a recommendation that the applicant was entitled to the benefit of the Attorney General's non-statutory scheme under which solicitor and counsel are assigned to argue judicial review applications for those unable to afford legal advice. This scheme first emerged during the legal argument in *Application of Woods* [1970] IR 154 (decided in 1967). Counsel for the applicant then submitted a number of arguments to the Supreme Court, particularly in relation to the course adopted by Carney J in converting the proceedings from an Article 40.4.2 inquiry into a judicial review application.

In the judgment delivered by the Chief Justice for the Court (Finlay CJ, Hederman, O'Flaherty, Egan and Blayney JJ) a major emphasis was placed on the importance of the Article 40.4.2 procedure.

The Chief Justice began by stating that, as the application of 22 January 1992 clearly raised an issue concerning the legality of the applicant's detention, it should have been regarded as one for an inquiry pursuant to Article 40.4.2 of the Constitution, even though it was described by the applicant in somewhat ambiguous terms. He went on to state that an application under Article 40.4.2 must necessarily transcend any procedural form for judicial review or otherwise, and that a High Court judge has a jurisdiction to make speedy and, if necessary, informal inquiries of the jailor or detainer to ascertain the facts, even before reaching a conclusion that a sufficient doubt exists as to the legality of the detention. In the instant case, he noted, because of the absence of any inquiries and the unfortunate error made by Carney J on 5 February 1992 that the November 1990 sentence had been imposed in November 1991, the application was converted into one for judicial review with its consequent procedural delays.

Finlay CJ referred to the Court's decision in *The State (McDonagh) v Frawley* [1978] IR 131 where the then Chief Justice, O'Higgins CJ, had forcefully pointed out that the Article 40.4.2 procedure was not to be used as an alternative procedure for cases which should be dealt with by way of judicial review. While accepting the accuracy of this approach, Finlay CJ pointed out that where, as in the instant case, the application clearly raised the question of the validity of the detention, the conversion into judicial review proceedings was inappropriate.

Finally, on the question of remittal, the Supreme Court accepted that Denham J had jurisdiction to remit the applicant's case to the District Court under O.84, r.26(4) of the 1986 Rules, referring to the decision in *The State (Tynan) v Keane* [1968] IR 348 in this respect (see also the discussion of *Sweeney v Brophy* [1993] ILRM 449; [1993] 2 IR 202, decided by the Court on the same date as the *Sheehan* case, in the Criminal Law chapter, 268-70, below). However, in the particular circumstances of the instant case where the applicant was deprived by the 'converting' order of 5 February 1992 of what appeared to be his immediate right to challenge his detention, the Court considered that it would not be fair or just that he be charged again in respect of the offence in question, and so the Court refused to remit the case to the District Court.

## LIFE OF UNBORN

### Abortion

*The historical background* The Constitution, as originally promulgated, said nothing explicit about abortion. This was not a matter of comment for many years afterwards. It was only when courts in other jurisdictions rapidly developed a constitutional jurisprudence favouring the right to abortion that the question came to be considered whether the Constitution effectively protected the right to life of the unborn.

Some commentators took the view that the Constitution did indeed protect the unborn against abortion; there were some judicial *dicta*, of varying degrees of force and specificity, which lent weight to this view.

Other commentators were less sure that the Constitution afforded adequate protection to the unborn against abortion, since it expressly limited its guarantee of the right to life to 'every citizen' (a term which did not include the unborn) and since a constitutional right of privacy might be invoked as a basis for legalised abortion. International experience showed that no Constitution or Convention, in the absence of explicit protection of the right to life of the unborn, had proved capable of withstanding an argument in favour of legalised abortion: see Michael, 'Abortion and International Law: The Status and Possible Extension of Women's Rights to Privacy' (1981) 20 J of Family Law L 241; Glenn, 'The Constitutional Validity of Abortion Legislation: A Comparative Note' (1975) 21 McGill LJ 673; O'Reilly,'Marital Privacy and Family Law' (1977) 65 Studies 8; Binchy, 'Marital Privacy and Family Law: A Reply to Mr O'Reilly' (1977) 65 Studies 330; Casey, 'The Development of Constitutional Law under Chief Justice Ó Dálaigh' (1978) 4 Dublin ULJ 1, at 10; Binchy, 'The Need for a Constitutional Amendment', in Flannery ed., *Abortion and the Law* (1983), ch. 11; Treacy, 'The Constitution and the Right to Life', id., ch. 7; M. Arnold & P. Kirby, eds., '*The Abortion Referendum*': *The Case Against* (1982); Binchy, 'Ethical Issues in Reproductive Medicine: A Legal Perspective', in M. Reidy, ed., *Ethical Issues in Reproductive Medicine* (1992), ch. 9.

*The Eighth Amendment* In 1983, after extended public debate, the Eighth Amendment to the Constitution added a new subsection to s. 3 of Article 40. The subsection reads as follows:

> The State acknowledges the right to life of the unborn and, with due regard to the equal right to life of the mother, guarantees in its laws to respect and, so far as practicable, by its laws to defend and vindicate that right.

For a comprehensive analysis of the historical background to the amendment campaign and to the public debate surrounding it, see T. Hesketh, *The Second Partitioning of Ireland?* (1990) (Dr Hesketh's book was warmly welcomed by both sides of the debate as an objective, insightful account of events). See also Quinlan, 'The Right to Life of the Unborn — An Assessment of the Eighth Amendment to the Irish Constitution', [1984] Brigham Young LL L Rev 371; Hogan, 'Law and Religion: Church-State Relations from Independence to the Present Day', (1988) 35 Am J of Compar L 47, at 74-83; Charleton, 'Judicial Discretion in Abortion: The Irish Perspective', (1992) 6 Internat J of L & the Family 349, at 350-62; O'Leary & Hesketh, 'The Irish Abortion and Divorce Amendment Campaigns', (1988) 3 Ir Political Studies 43, at 43-55, 58-9; Basil Chubb, *The Politics of the Irish Constitution* (1991), 52-5; Randall, 'The Politics of Abortion in Ireland', ch. 5 of J. Lovenduski & J. Dutshoorn, eds., *The New Politics of Abortion* (1986); Girvin, 'Social Change and Moral Politics: The Irish Constitutional Referendum 1983', (1986) 31 Political Studies 61; Garvin, 'The Politics of Denial and Cultural Defence: The Referenda of 1983 and 1986 in Context', (1988) 3 Irish Review; O'Carroll, 'Bishops, Knights — and Pawns? Traditional Thought and the Irish Abortion Referendum Debate of 1983' (1991), 6 Ir Political Studies 53; Speed, 'The Struggle for Reproductive Rights: A Brief History in its Political Context', in Ailbhe Smyth ed., *The Abortion Papers* (1992), p. 85; Barry, 'Movement, Change and Reaction: The Struggle Over Reproductive Rights in Ireland', *id.*, p. 107.

*Supreme Court prohibits information about foreign abortion clinics* In *Attorney General (Society for the Protection of Unborn Children (Ireland) Ltd) v Open Door Counselling Ltd and Dublin Wellwoman Centre Ltd* [1989] ILRM 19; [1988] IR 593, the defendants engaged in non-directive counselling and referral to abortion clinics in Britain for those women who wanted to consider the abortion option further. The Supreme Court enjoined the defendants from assisting pregnant women within the jurisdiction to travel abroad to obtain abortions by referral to a clinic, by making travel arrangements for them or by informing them of the identity and location of, and the method of communication with, specified clinics. Finlay CJ (Walsh, Henchy, Griffin and Hederman JJ concurring) said that he was:

> satisfied beyond doubt that . . . the defendants were assisting in the

> ultimate destruction of the life of the unborn by abortion in that they were helping the pregnant women who had decided upon that option to get in touch with a clinic in Great Britain which would provide the service of abortion. It seems to me to be an inescapable conclusion that if a woman was anxious to obtain an abortion and if she was able by availing of the counselling services of one or other of the defendants to obtain the precise location, address and telephone number of, and method of communication with, a clinic in Great Britain which provided that service, put in plain language, that was knowingly helping her to obtain that objective.

For consideration of the *Open Door* case, see the 1988 Review, 117, 132.

In *Society for the Protection of Unborn Children (Ireland) Ltd v Grogan* [1989] IR 753, the plaintiff society applied for an interlocutory injunction to prevent officers of certain students unions from publishing similar information about foreign abortion clinics in student guidebooks. Carroll J, invoking the Article 177 procedure, referred to the Court of Justice a number of questions of European Community law (which we consider below) and effectively, though not *expressis verbis*, refused to grant the requested interlocutory injunction.

The Supreme Court, in strong terms, reversed Carroll J. Finlay CJ rejected as 'unsound' the respondents' attempt to distinguish between the one-to-one non-directive counselling situation that arose in *Open Door* and the provision of the same information in a student publication:

> It is clearly the fact that such information is conveyed to pregnant women, and not the method of communication, which creates the unconstitutional illegality, and the judgment of this court in the *Open Door Counselling* case is not open to any other interpretation.

The Chief Justice considered that no question as to the propriety of granting the interlocutory injunction arose in Irish law where an injunction such as was sought in the instant case was 'not only consistent with but [also] in full accord with our constitutional law'.

Walsh J, concurring, observed that:

> [w]hen the present matter came before the High Court it was clear beyond all doubt that the activities complained of were contrary to the Constitution. The decision of the High Court judge to adopt the course which she did, namely, to leave the matter undecided, was in effect to suspend the provisions of the Eighth Amendment for an indefinite period. It is not open to any judge to do anything which in effect suspends the Constitution for any period whatsoever.

Walsh J went on to note that the Eighth Amendment to the Constitution was subsequent in time, by several years, to the amendment of Article 29, when Ireland entered the EEC. He commented that this fact might 'give rise to the consideration of the question of whether or not the Eighth Amendment qualifies the amendment to Article 29'.

This theme was echoed by McCarthy J, concurring, who observed that '[i]t may be that, in enacting the Eighth Amendment to the Constitution as explained by this Court in the *Open Door Counselling* case, the People of Ireland did so in breach of the Treaty to which Ireland had acceded in 1973'. For consideration of the differences in emphasis between Walsh and McCarthy JJ on this issue, see Gráinne de Búrca, 'Fundamental Human Rights and the Reach of EC Law' (1993) 13 Oxford J of Legal Studies 283, at 287-8.

*A European dimension emerges* After the *Open Door* and *Grogan* decisions, the issue of abortion left the Irish courts for a time. Matters did not rest there, however. The defendants in *Open Door* initiated proceedings against Ireland under the European Convention of Human Rights and the Court of Justice addressed the questions posed to it by Carroll J.

On 7 March 1991, the European Commission, by an eight to five majority held in favour of the defendants in the *Open Door* litigation: (1991) 14 EHRR 131. Article 40.3.3 was considered by six of the Commissioners to have been drafted with such generality as to constitute an insufficiently precise proscription of freedom of expression under Article 10(2) of the Convention. (As we shall see, the Court of Human Rights in 1992 upheld the Commission's holding, but on different grounds.)

The Court of Justice, in October 1991, addressed the questions that Carroll J had referred to it under the Article 177 procedure: [1992] ILRM 461; [1991] 3 CMLR 849. These were (i) whether the medical termination of pregnancy was a 'service' for the purposes of Article 60 of the Treaty and (ii) whether a Member State could prohibit the distribution of information about abortion services in another Member State if abortion was lawful under the law of the former.

The Court of Justice answered that abortion was indeed a 'service' if performed in accordance with the law of the State where it was carried out. The court declined, in effect, to answer the second and third questions because there was not a sufficient economic nexus between the students' activities in distributing the information and the actual provision of abortion services in England to bring the prohibition within the scope of Article 59 of the Treaty. The Court stated:

> It is not contrary to Community law for a Member State in which

> medical termination of pregnancy is forbidden to prohibit Students' Associations from distributing information about the identity and location of clinics in another Member State where voluntary termination of pregnancy is lawfully carried out and the means of communicating with these clinics where the clinics in question have no involvement in the distribution of the said information.

For analysis of the Court of Justice's response, see Wilkinson, 'Abortion, The Irish Constitution and the EEC' [1992] Public L 20; Spalin, 'Abortion, Speech and the European Community' [1992] J of Social Welfare & Family L 17; Phelan, 'Right to Life of Unborn v. Promotion of Trade in Services: The European Court of Justice and the Normative Shaping of the European Union' (1992) 55 Modern L Rev 670; de Búrca, op. cit., especially at 316-8. Phelan comments (at 681):

> There was never any question in *SPUC v Grogan*, given Member States' differences, of the ECJ adopting the right to life of the unborn as a fundamental right. But the Court's previous jurisprudence on fundamental rights . . . did not indicate how far it would push the logic of its teleology, or how much of a chasm exists between the Court's and Member States' conceptions of fundamental rights. 'The most basic of all human rights is life itself' [*per* Walsh J, in the Supreme Court decision in *Grogan*]; yet the Court not only denied, as a matter of legal principle, any importance to the manifestation of the most fundamental constitutional right of a Member State (and it is up to the Member State to decide the relative weight of constitutional rights), but it defined the destruction of that right as a service to be promoted to attain the Treaty objectives to which Community fundamental rights aim.

The next crucial development was in relation to the proposed Maastricht Treaty on the European Union, scheduled for implementation in 1992. In December 1991, Ireland obtained the agreement of the other Member States a Protocol to the effect that European Community law should not affect the operation in Ireland of Article 40.3.3. The impact of this Protocol was that there would be no possibility of European Law overriding or modifying the effect in Ireland of Article 40.3.3. Clearly this would forestall any argument that there is a right of access to abortion in Ireland.

Those who opposed legalised abortion naturally welcomed the Protocol, which was in harmony with the values underlyingArticle 40.3.3. We examine the effect of the Protocol in some detail below. First we must consider a development that took place with no forewarning but with enormous impact on the political, social and legal aspects of Irish life.

*The X Case* In *Attorney General v X* [1992] ILRM 401; [1992] 1 IR 1; [1992] 2 CMLR 277, the first defendant, a fourteen-year-old girl, was the victim of sexual abuse by a man in his forties, a friend of her family. She became pregnant as a result. The man had first sexually molested here when she was twelve years old. (Subsequently a man was charged with several counts of unlawful carnal knowledge. He pleaded guilty to two counts and was sentenced to fourteen years' imprisonment. He gave notice of his intention to apply to the Court of Criminal Appeal against the refusal of the trial judge to grant leave to appeal against sentence.)

The girl and her parents (who were also defendants in the case) decided that she should go to England for an abortion. The parents made it known to the gardaí that they were considering this course and raised with them the possibility that someone could be present in England for the purpose of carrying out a scientific (DNA) tests on the aborted foetus by which it was thought that the identity of the father could be ascertained. Legal opinion was sought from the office of the Director of Public Prosecutions. The Director informed the Attorney General, who sought an injunction restraining the first defendant from leaving the jurisdiction and from having an abortion.

*The High Court proceedings* Costello J heard the case. (The first defendant's evidence was given by way of affidavit). No medical witness gave evidence but a clinical psychologist testified that he had understood the first defendant to have indicated a suicidal intent. He considered that the psychological damage to her of carrying a child would be considerable and that the damage to her mental health would be devastating.

Costello J granted the injunction. He considered that the court had a duty to protect the first defendant's life 'not just from the actions of others but from actions she may herself perform'. What the court was therefore required to do was to assess by reference to the evidence the danger to the life of the child and the danger that existed to the life of the mother. He was quite satisfied that there was a real and imminent danger to the life of the unborn and that, if the court did not step in to protect it by means of the injunction sought, its life would be terminated. The evidence also established that if the court granted the injunction there was a risk that the first defendant might take her own life; but that risk was much less and was of a different order of magnitude than the certainty that the life of the unborn would be terminated if the order was not made. Costello J was:

> strengthened in this view by the knowledge that the young girl had the benefit of the care and support of devoted parents who will help her through the difficult months ahead. It seems to me, therefore, that having had regard to the rights of the mother in this case, the court's duty to protect the life of the unborn requires it to make the order sought.

Costello J rejected the defendants' argument that the injunction would infringe the first defendant's right to liberty. The Supreme Court decisions dealing with bail, *People v O'Callaghan* [1966] IR 501 and *Ryan v Director of Public Prosecutions* [1989] IR 399, had not decided that a court might not order a defendant to refrain from doing an unlawful act, if necessary by restraining his or her constitutional right to liberty.

Costello J also rejected the defendants' argument based on an asserted freedom to travel to receive an abortion service in Britain. In his view the Eighth Amendment was clearly an expression of public policy on a moral issue on which there were profound differences and deeply held views throughout the contemporary world. It constituted a permissible derogation under Community law which was proportionate in giving effect to its aim to protect the right to life of the unborn. 'Indeed', he observed, 'in the absence of such a power the protection afforded to the right to life which the Constitution acknowledges would in many cases be worthless.' In reaching this conclusion, Costello J regarded the jurisprudence of the European Court of Human Rights as relevant, though he did not identify its precise significance. (As we shall see below, the European Court took a somewhat different view on the proportionality issue in this general context.)

*The Supreme Court judgment* The proceedings, which had been held *in camera*, had generated very considerable public attention. In a situation of high emotion, the government encouraged the defendants to appeal against Costello J's judgment and offered to pay their legal costs. The defendants did appeal to the Supreme Court which discharged the order on 26 February 1992. The Court gave its reasons eight days later.

By a majority of four (Finlay CJ, McCarthy, O'Flaherty and Egan JJ) to one (Hederman J), it was held that Article 40.3.3 permits abortion where there is a real and substantial risk to the life, as distinct from the health, of the mother which can be avoided only by an abortion. The majority held, further, that this ground was established in the instant case. On the question whether it was permissible, in other cases, to grant injunctions against travelling abroad to have an abortion, the Court divided somewhat differently. Finlay CJ, Hederman and Egan JJ considered that it was; McCarthy and O'Flaherty J took the opposite view.

*The substantive issue* The substantive issue in the case concerned the lawfulness or unlawfulness of abortion under Article 40.3.3. The role of the Attorney General in this matter was crucial. Counsel for the Attorney General conceded without argument that Article 40.3.3 envisaged cases in which abortion would be lawful. He argued that the subsection could not be interpreted in isolation from the other provisions of the Constitution, and that this global approach applied to the interpretation of the phrases 'due regard' and 'as far as practicable', which would have to be harmonised with the other rights and obligations guaranteed or identified by it. Counsel relied (*inter alia*) on the following passage from Walsh J's judgment in *McGee v Attorney General* [1974] IR 284, at 318-9:

> In this country, it falls finally upon the judges to interpret the Constitution and in doing so to determine, where necessary, the rights which are superior or antecedent to positive law or which are imprescriptible or inalienable. In the performance of this difficult duty there are certain guidelines laid down in the Constitution for the judge. The very structure and content of the Articles dealing with fundamental rights clearly indicate that justice is not subordinate to the law. In particular, the terms of s. 3 of Article 40 expressly subordinate the law to justice. Both Aristotle and the Christian philosophers have regarded justice as the highest human virtue. The virtue of prudence was also esteemed by Aristotle, as by the philosophers of the Christian world. But the great additional virtue introduced by Christianity was that of charity — not the charity which consists of giving to the deserving, for that is justice, but the charity which is also called mercy. According to the Preamble, the people gave themselves the Constitution to promote the common good, with due observance of prudence, justice and charity so that the dignity and freedom of the individual might be assured. The judges must, therefore, as best they can from their training and their experience interpret these rights in accordance with their ideas of prudence, justice and charity. It is but natural that from time to time the prevailing ideas of these virtues may be conditioned by the passage of time; no interpretation of the Constitution is intended to be final for all time. It is given in the light of prevailing ideas and concepts.

This passage received the endorsement of O'Higgins CJ in *The State (Healy) v Donoghue* [1976] IR 325, at 347.

In the light of these principles, laid down by the Supreme Court, counsel for the Attorney General submitted that the phrases 'due regard' and 'as far as practicable' made it necessary, when interpreting Article 40.3.3, to take into account the mother's other constitutional rights and duties, 'as a mother, or a sister, as a daughter, as a parent perhaps', as well as the rights of the mother's parents where the mother was of the age of the first defendant. Counsel for the Attorney General submitted that these principles translated into a right to an abortion where the continuation of the life of the unborn constituted a risk of immediate or inevitable death to the mother. He argued that, in the circumstances of the instant case, the evidence had not established a risk of that magnitude.

Finlay CJ accepted all of these submissions, save that relating to the scope of permissible abortion. He regarded the principles set out in *McGee* and *Healy* as 'particularly and peculiarly appropriate and illuminating in the interpretation of a subsection of the Constitution which deals with the intimate human problem of the right of the unborn to life and its relationship to the right of the mother of an unborn child to her life.'

The Chief Justice recorded his specific endorsement of the submission that the doctrine of harmonious interpretation of the Constitution involved a consideration of the interrelation of the constitutional rights and obligations of the mother with those of other people 'and, of course, with the right to life of the unborn child as well'. Such a harmonious interpretation, carried out in accordance with the concepts of prudence, justice and charity, as they had been explained in *McGee*, led Finlay CJ to the conclusion that, in vindicating and defending as far as practicable the right of the unborn to life but at the same time giving due regard to the right of the mother to life:

> the court must, amongst the matters to be so regarded, concern itself with the position of the mother within a family group, with persons on whom she is dependent, with, in other instances, persons who are dependent upon her and her interaction with other citizens and members of society in the areas in which her activities occur.

The Chief Justice stated that, '[h]aving regard to that conclusion' he was satisfied that the test proposed on behalf of the Attorney General insufficiently vindicated the mother's right to life and that the proper test was that, if it was established as a matter of probability that there was a real and substantial risk to the life, as distinct from the health, of the mother, which could be avoided only by the termination of her pregnancy, such termination was permissible.

Egan J's judgment most closely resembles that of Finlay CJ's. Having referred, without comment, to the criminal prohibition on abortion contained in s. 58 of the Offences Against the Person Act 1861 and to the interpretation of that section in *R. v Bourne* [1939] 1 KB 687, Egan J stated as follows:

> The wording of the Eighth Amendment which guarantees to defend and vindicate the right to life of the unborn recognised by the inclusion of the words 'with due regard for [*sic*] the equal right of [*sic*] life of the mother' and the words 'as far as practicable' that an abortion will not in every possible circumstances be unlawful.

Egan J went on to say, that he 'would regard it as a denial of a mother's right to life if there was a requirement of certainty of death in her case before a termination of a pregnancy would be permissible'. The true test, in his opinion, was that a pregnancy might be terminated if its continuance as a matter of probability involved a real and substantial risk to the life of the mother. He concluded his analysis of this issue by stating:

> The risk must be to her life but it is irrelevant, in my view, that it should be a risk of self-destruction rather than a risk to life for any other reason.

McCarthy J provided an analysis as to the approach to be adopted to Article 40.3.3, which found no direct support in the other judgments of the majority. He stated:

> The right of the girl here is a right to a life in being, the right of the unborn is to a life contingent; contingent on survival in the womb until successful delivery. It is not a question of setting one above the other but rather of vindicating, as far as practicable, the right to the life of the girl/mother (Article 40. s. 2, subs. 2), whilst with due regard to the equal right to life of the girl/mother, vindicating, as far as practicable, the right to life of the unborn (Article 40, s. 3, subs. 3). If the right to life of the mother is threatened by the pregnancy, and it is practicable to vindicate that right, then because of the due regard that must be paid to the equal right to life of the mother, it may not be practicable to vindicate the right to life of the unborn.

In McCarthy J's view, it was:

> not a question of balancing the life of the unborn against the life of the mother. If it were, the life of the unborn would virtually always have to be preserved, since the termination of pregnancy means the death of the unborn; there is no certainty, however high the probability, that the mother will die if there is not a termination of pregnancy. In my view, the true construction of the Amendment, bearing the mind the other provisions of Article 40 and the fundamental rights of the family guaranteed by Article 41, is that, paying due regard to the equal right to life of the mother, where there is a real and substantial risk attached to her survival not merely at the time of application but in contemplation at least throughout the pregnancy, then it may not be practicable to vindicate the right to life of the unborn. It is not a question of a risk of a different order of magnitude; it can never be otherwise than a risk of a different order of magnitude.

McCarthy J considered that the purpose of the Eighth Amendment could:

> be readily identified — it was to enshrine in the Constitution the protection of the right to life of the unborn thus precluding the legislature from an unqualified repeal of s. 58 of the Act of 1861 or otherwise, in general, legalising abortion. The guarantee to the unborn was qualified by the requirement of the regard to the right to life of the mother and made less than absolute by recognising that the right could only be vindicated as far as practicable.

O'Flaherty J also provided an analysis that found no express support from the other judges of the majority. He examined the view that Article 40.3.3 had not brought about any fundamental change in the law. He noted that s. 58 of the 1861 Act already made it an offence unlawfully to bring about the miscarriage of a woman. He also referred to s. 58 of the Civil Liability Act 1961, which, for the avoidance of doubt, declares that the law relating to wrongs, applies to an unborn child for its protection in like manner as if the child were born, provided the child is subsequently born alive. (For consideration of this provision, see McMahon & Binchy, *Irish Law of Torts* (2nd ed., 1990, 604-7).

Echoing the words of the Chief Justice, but elaborating on their scope, O'Flaherty J said that Article 40.3.3 could:

> not, of course, be taken in isolation from its historical background which I have already briefly sketched: it must also be considered as but one provision in the whole Constitution. The Constitution has at its core a commitment to freedom and justice. It treats the family with such respect and in language of such clarity and simplicity, that any attempt to summarise or paraphrase it must be inadequate.
>
> Can it be that a Constitution which requires the State to look to the *economic* needs of *mothers* is unconcerned for the health and welfare and happiness of mothers? I am certain that reading the Constitution as a whole, as I believe one must do, then the answer is clearly not. A broad dimension must be given to the Constitution and a narrow or pedantic approach to its provisions has to be put aside.

O'Flaherty J explained his belief that Article 40.3.3 was clear in the following three aspects:

> (i) Abortion, as such, certainly abortion on demand, is not something that can be legalised in this jurisdiction.
> (ii) Promotional propaganda in respect of abortions abroad is prohibited. *Attorney General (SPUC) v Open Door Counselling* [1988] IR 593.
> (iii) The legislators when they come to enact legislation must have due regard to the woman's right to life — a right protected by the Constitu-

> tion in any event. Until legislation is enacted to provide otherwise, I believe that the law in this State is that surgical intervention which has the effect of terminating pregnancy *bona fide* undertaken to save the life of the mother where she is in danger of death is permissible under the Constitution and the law. The danger has to represent a substantial risk to her life though this does not necessarily have to be an imminent danger of instant death. The law does not require the doctors to wait until the mother is in peril of immediate death.

The majority's analysis and holding on the substantive issue provoked an outpouring of public controversy and of legal and political assessment. This was because, until the *X.* decision, the Eighth Amendment had been universally interpreted as having been promulgated with the purpose of rendering the direct taking of unborn life unlawful in all circumstances. That was the basis on which its proponents had sought support for it, and it was the basis on which much of the opposition to it was founded. There is no record of any proponent of the Amendment ever having argued in its favour on the basis that it would permit abortion in any circumstances. The opposition to the Amendment had concentrated on two main arguments. First, it was claimed that the Amendment would render unlawful a range of necessary medical treatments for pregnant women which would, or could, result in the death of their unborn children indirectly, as an unsought side effect. Second, some argued that the Amendment should be opposed on the basis that it would render unlawful abortions carried out to preserve the life or health of the mother, or in cases of rape, youthful pregnancy, incest or foetal abnormality. McCarthy J was thus quite mistaken in his belief that the purpose of the Amendment could be 'readily identified' as being merely to preclude the legislature from 'an unqualified repeal' of s. 58 of the 1861 Act; the true object was 'to make abortion an impossibility in this State . . .': Editorial, *Irish Times*, 6 March 1992. After 1983, the medical profession clearly understood that abortion was not lawful in the State: see the Medical Council's *Guide to Ethical Conduct and Behaviour and to Fitness to Practice* (1984), p. 21.

Of course the intent of any law-maker, whether at the statutory or constitutional level, may not always prevail over the interpretation given to the particular law by the judiciary. The question, therefore, arises as to the adequacy of the Supreme Court's interpretation of the Eighth Amendment in *X.*

The proponents of the Amendment (of which the second author of this Review was one) argued that the terms of the Amendment clearly excluded the direct taking of an innocent life. The Amendment, they said, makes it plain that there is no hierarchy of entitlement to be protected from a direct attack on one's life. It is no more legally justifiable under the Amendment to kill directly an unborn living human being than it is to kill directly a born living human being. Article 40.3.3 puts this argument beyond doubt by the words 'equal right to life of the mother'. It is clear that the law does not distinguish between the lives of born people, so as to authorise the direct taking of the life of a born person, even where considerable advantages to others would flow from such a termination. There is no calculus whereby a court is required to weigh the totality of the constitutional rights and obligations of other persons against the constitutional protection of a born person's life from direct extinction.

There is, however, a clear distinction of principle between directly taking a person's life and acting in a way that is directed to some other purpose which has the indirect result of leading to the death of that person, or of another, as an unintended side-effect. The most obvious example is in the area of the treatment of sick or terminally-ill patients. If the purpose of a particular treatment is curative or palliative and death results indirectly as an unintended side-effect, the treatment will be consistent with the protection afforded the patient by Article 40.3.

In the context of the medical treatment of pregnant women, this distinction is of very considerable relevance since certain treatments, notably chemotherapy where the pregnant woman has cancer, can impact indirectly on the foetus, at times fatally.

The purpose, and effect, of the Amendment is to preserve this vital distinction, the proponents of the Amendment maintain. That is why the Amendment contains the requirement of *due regard* for the equal right to life of the mother and a guarantee to defend and vindicate the right to life of the unborn *as far as practicable*. This distinction between a direct attack on the life of the unborn and treatment for the mother that results indirectly in the death of the unborn has governed medical practice in the State both before and since the Amendment.

As to the empirical question of whether abortion is ever medically necessary to preserve the life of the mother, the Medical Council in 1993 reasserted its long-held position that such a necessity remained to be proved.

Incredibly, in the light of the extended public discussion of the legal issues prior to the promulgation of the Eighth Amendment, the Attorney General made no attempt to distinguish between the direct taking of unborn life and the death of an unborn as an indirect result of necessary medical treatment for the mother. Indeed, such limited discussion of the issue of medical treatment by counsel for the Attorney General as is reported in the summary of the legal argument in the Supreme Court proceedings appears to involve a conflation of indirect and direct, without regard to any difference in principle between the two. Witness the following reported interchange:

> McCarthy J: Are you saying that there is only one answer: the child must be aborted if the mother is in immediate danger of death? If this is so, where does 'as far as practicable' enter the equation? Do you accept that the Eighth Amendment envisages a 'lawful abortion' in Ireland?
>
> [Counsel for the Attorney General]: Yes, I accept that. For example, a mother suffering from a cancerous condition which requires chemotherapy has the right to have her pregnancy terminated. The pregnancy may be terminated if, but only if, there is an inevitable danger to the right to life of the mother.

The expression 'termination of pregnancy' is ambiguous, since it could mean either an abortion, where the child is abstracted from the mother's womb, or, alternatively, medical treatment of the mother, such as chemotherapy, which risks injuring the foetus and which in some instances can result indirectly in the death of the foetus.

It is not clear from the argument of counsel for the Attorney General which of these processes is envisaged. From the medical standpoint, there is no need in such cases to carry out an abortion, with inevitably fatal consequences for the unborn.

The failure by counsel for the Attorney General to draw any distinction between direct termination of the life of the unborn and death resulting indirectly from treatment of the mother may well have contributed to the inadequate analysis by the majority of the issues at the heart of the Eighth Amendment.

Some commentators deny that there is any sound moral or legal basis for this distinction. As a matter of law they argue that if a person does an act where there is a very substantial likelihood, or certainty, that this will result in harm to another, even as an indirect and unsought side-effect, legal responsibility should inevitably arise in respect of that harm unless some particular defence excuses or justifies the act. Undoubtedly it is true that liability does, and should, attach to one who acts with an unjustifiable purpose, where the act also inevitably (or very foreseeably) causes harm to an unintended target. Thus, an assassin who throws a bomb into a crowd intending to kill a particular victim but knowing that others must also die will not be excused on account of his lack of any desire that they should lose their lives. The law attributes a criminal intent to him in such circumstances, designating it an 'oblique' intent.

Peter Charleton has noted that:

> in all the cases where the courts have found a breach of the criminal law the primary purpose . . . was itself unlawful.

> Cases of oblique intention necessarily involve a wrongful act as the accused's primary purpose. . . It is not inconsistent to argue that where the primary purpose of the accused is, in itself, lawful, an undesired but foreseen consequence does not come within the scope of an unlawful intention: 'Judicial Discretion in Abortion: The Irish Perspective,' (1992) 6 Internat J of L & the Family 349 at 360.

Mr Charleton's analysis is, of course, pertinent to s. 58 of the Offences Against the Person Act 1861, but more importantly it assists in one's understanding of the Eighth Amendment, which does not refer to the matter of intention but rather is drafted in such a way as to render the direct termination of unborn life unlawful whilst ensuring that medical treatment designed to assist mothers is lawful even where it results indirectly in the death of the foetus. See further Kingston & Whelan, op. cit., at 282.

In *X*, counsel for the Attorney General is reported as having encouraged the Court, in pursuit of a harmonious interpretation of the Constitution, to look to other constitutional rights, values and obligations when interpreting the Eighth Amendment. He argued that the Court should take account specifically of the defendant's 'rights and duties as a mother, as a sister, as a daughter, as a parent perhaps'. To this Finlay CJ responded by enquiring whether the rights of the defendant's parents should be 'weighed when favouring the [first defendant]'s life over the life of the unborn'. Counsel for the Attorney General replied:

> Yes I do not say that is so. *The mother's right may be superior to the right to life of the unborn because of the other constitutional rights and duties.* But we must look at the circumstances in which it calls for determination. (Emphasis added.)

It is hard to interpret these words as meaning other than that, in the light of a mother's other constitutional rights and duties, her right to life, in some circumstances, may be *superior* to the right to life of the unborn child. This is, no doubt, a stance that has received support in the law of some other countries (cf. *R. v Bourne* [1939] 1 KB 687; [1938] 3 All ER 615), but it clearly is not possible under the Eighth Amendment, which expressly provides that the mother and her unborn have an *equal* right to life.

The judgments of the majority were to the effect that the words 'due regard' and 'as far as practicable', in conjunction with an assessment of the totality of constitutional rights and duties of the mother and of others, led to the conclusion that it was permissible to extinguish directly the life of the unborn. That conclusion is consistent only with an *inequality* between the mother's right to life and that of the unborn.

Could it be argued that the mother and the unborn are not similarly situated in that the mother has a wider repertoire of constitutional rights and obligations, apart from the right to life, than does the unborn? The majority accepted this argument but if it is tested in another context it may be shown to be false. It is clear, or at all events prior to his decision seemed clear, that a one-year-old baby girl's right to life, equal to that of her mother, may not be sacrificed even if the mother's constitutional rights and obligations, which are likely to range vastly more widely than those of her infant daughter, would be greatly facilitated by directly terminating the daughter's life. The equality of the right to life here gives the daughter effective protection; it is not capable of being defeated by other constitutional rights and obligations. If a one-year-old infant's rights to life cannot thus be swept away, it is hard to see how an unborn's right to life can be destroyed by reference to such considerations unless the mother's right to life is superior. The Eighth Amendment expressly denies any such superiority. Just as considerations relating to 'practicability' do not justify the direct taking of a one-year-old infant's life, they do not permit it in respect of the life of an unborn.

The next major error in the Court's reasoning was to accept the submission of counsel for the Attorney General that Walsh J's remarks in *McGee v Attorney General* [1974] IR 284, at 319 were relevant to the interpretation to be afforded to the terms 'due regard' and 'as far as practicable'. Walsh J was speaking at the highest level of generality on the question of the jurisprudential basis of the natural law rights recognised as anterior to positive law. Walsh J, in a passage not quoted in Finlay CJ's judgment, had identified the natural law thus recognised as a theological concept: 'the law of God promulgated by reason and . . . the ultimate governor of all the laws of men'. The Constitution, he considered, intended the natural human rights to which it referred to be in the theological category 'rather than simply an acknowledgment of the ethical content of law in its ideal of justice'. Walsh J went on to refer to the fact that while the Constitution speaks of certain rights being imprescriptible or inalienable, or being antecedent and superior to positive law, *it does not specify them.* This is so in the case of Article 40.3.

There are clear grounds for interpreting the passage from Walsh J's judgment which the Chief Justice quoted as referring to the court's task of *articulating the nature and scope of the unspecified personal rights* to which Article 40.3 refers. Walsh J's reference to the virtues of justice, prudence and charity is anchored upon the Preamble to the Constitution. The idea that these remarks give the judiciary a *carte blanche* to modify a calibration of constitutional rights which the Constitution itself expressly prescribes seems untenable.

Finlay CJ appears to have proceeded on the basis that the concepts of 'due regard' and 'practicability' should be interpreted by reference to changing social attitudes. The implications of such an approach, not only for abortion law in this State, but also for the law relating to the direct termination of the lives of innocent people who have been born, are significant and controversial.

There was no empirical evidence that social attitudes to the issue of abortion had changed between 1983 and 1992 and the political voices in favour of legalised abortion within the State were, if anything, even fainter in 1992 than in 1983. But let us assume, for the purposes of our analysis that the opposite was the case and that a clear majority of the Irish people was in favour of legalised abortion in March 1992 on the basis that the unborn's right to life was inferior to that of the mother. What implications, if any, should such a change of values have on the interpretation of the Eighth Amendment?

As a matter of constitutional interpretation it is clear that any such change of values could not have the effect of altering the explicit calibration of equality prescribed by Article 40.3.3, any more than a clear majority sentiment against the prohibition of divorce legislation could override the express terms of Article 41.3.2. A Court may not seize upon the expressions 'due regard' and 'as far as practicable' and use them as a channel for replacing the equality of the right to life by a norm of inequality. Such a process violates the requirement of fidelity to the norms unambiguously acknowledged in the Constitution. There is a need here for intellectual honesty at the highest judicial level. The central problem with the majority holding in *X* is that it sought to justify an impermissible alteration of fundamental values by reference to a text that did not warrant such a process.

A wider jurisprudential issue is raised by the Court's reliance on Walsh J's judgment in *McGee*. The idea that fundamental principles of natural law relating to human rights are to be determined by a sense of what the majority of the community at any particular time may favour is one that could very easily slip into a caricature of human rights by opinion poll. If that is what Walsh J envisaged, clearly it would have to be rejected; but that is not, and could not reasonably be interpreted to be, what he was suggesting. What Walsh J would seem to have been rejecting was a sterile ultra-formalistic theory of original intent as a basis of constitutional interpretation. There is no reason to interpret his remarks as warranting the surrender of the judicial obligation to give effect to the authentic natural law principles that underlie the fundamental rights provisions of the Constitution.

It would be wrong to suggest that Walsh J's approach is non-problematic or that it in any sense finally resolves the question of how the courts should discharge this obligation. There is room for much debate on this question, especially in the contexts of the notion of 'prevailing ideas' and the reference to the judges' 'training and . . . experience'. All that the majority of the Supreme Court could contribute to this debate, on the fundamental question of the right to life, was to quote what Walsh J had said, declare that it was relevant to the issues arising in the case, and let the reader *infer* that the Court must have accepted a radical and unprecedentedly broad interpretation of the role of public opinion in defeating an express provision of the Constitution.

The Court's decision has proved controversial in other respects also. One implication of the judgment is that an abortion would be lawful at any stage of pregnancy. The point here, of course, is not that the life of every viable unborn infant may be terminated on demand or that, where it is alleged that the mother's life is at risk, the viable unborn must in every case be aborted rather than delivered safely. The problem with the Supreme Court decision is that it presents no *principled* argument against the destruction of the life of an unborn at any stage of the forty weeks' gestation. No doubt, the practicability criterion would point to safe delivery rather than abortion in most instances, but not in all. In a case where a mother asserts a suicidal intent if the child's life is not terminated, nothing in *X* would suggest that a court is obliged to decline to authorise the termination of the unborn life. The fact that the unborn is capable of being born alive is not crucial; the reason the child's life may be taken is that the mother's assertion of suicidal intent takes priority in terms of prescribing solutions. If the problem is characterised as the *continuation of the unborn child's life*, rather than simply its continuation within its mother's womb, and if the unborn child's right to life is regarded as being in principle capable of direct termination, then the fact that the child is capable of living outside the womb will not, of itself, be a compelling guarantee against a judicial order in favour of terminating its life.

It is worth reflecting on why the Court said nothing about the rights of the unborn at different stages of pregnancy. It could be, of course, that the majority simply forgot to address the question. Another explanation is, however, possible. In other jurisdictions, important legal distinctions are made on the basis of the gestational age of the unborn. Perhaps the most obvious example is the decision of the United States Supreme Court in *Roe v Wade* (1973) 410 US 113, which differentiated radically between the rights of the unborn on the basis of the particular trimester in which the abortion takes place. It would have been hard for the Supreme Court in *X* to have engaged in a sliding scale of protection from abortion on the basis of the gestational age of a particular unborn without addressing the question of the value and significance of that life. The Eighth Amendment makes it clear that the lives of all unborn are equally valuable; it does not permit a court to engage in a process of attributing or denying value to a life at any particular stage.

Finlay CJ's judgment may be contrasted with that of McCarthy J in a number of important respects. First, McCarthy J places no emphasis on Walsh J's observations in *McGee* on the interpretation of the natural law and of rights guaranteed by Article 40.3. McCarthy J's understanding of the proper remit of practicability does not profess to depend on a changing social calibration of the virtues of prudence, justice and charity. Secondly, McCarthy J's analytic cornerstone is that *due regard* to the mother's life permits the direct taking of the life of the unborn and that any anxiety about this outcome is neutralised by the practicability proviso.

There is a difficulty with McCarthy J's analysis in this context: no explanation is proffered as to why *due* regard to an *equal* right to life permits or requires the court to *favour* that life to the extent of authorising the direct taking of the other life. McCarthy J's analysis seems consistent only with the proposition that the mother's right to life is not equal to the right to life of the unborn. That proposition is not in harmony with the Eighth Amendment.

A third feature of McCarthy J's analysis is his rejection of Costello J's conclusion that an injunction should be granted because of the relative magnitudes of the risk to the life of the unborn (which was certain in the case of an abortion) and the mother (which was less than certain). McCarthy J was clearly impressed, and apparently puzzled, by the fact that such an approach would lead to the result that the life of the unborn 'would virtually always have to be preserved.' It seems that McCarthy J regarded this result as so self-evidently indefensible that some other analysis, permitting the direct destruction of the life of the unborn, had to be preferred.

McCarthy J was right to sense that the conclusion that an abortion was not lawfully authorised could not depend *merely* on a calculating of competing risks. The reason why it is not lawful under the Amendment directly to take the life of an unborn is not reducible simply to that process of calculation; prior values are involved. McCarthy J's error lay in his handling of these values, whereby he gave priority to the mother's right to life, contrary to the specific requirements of the Amendment.

A fourth notable element in McCarthy J's judgment is the uncertainty as to the *scope* of abortions that he envisages as lawful under the Amendment. A key passage is his statement that 'the true construction of the Amendment, bearing in mind the other provisions of Article 40 and the fundamental rights of the family guaranteed by Article 41, is that, paying due regard to the equal right to life of the mother, when there is a real and substantial risk attached to her survival not merely at the time of application but in contemplation at least throughout the pregnancy, then it may not be practicable to vindicate the right to life of the unborn'. This statement does not expressly distinguish between the mother's life and health, as the Chief Justice does, but the word 'survival' has a starkness that does not easily encompass considerations of health *per se*.

There is, however, an aspect of McCarthy J's test which seems narrower than that of Finlay CJ. This is the requirement that the real and substantial risk should not merely attach to the mother's survival at the time of application but should also be 'in contemplation at least throughout the pregnancy'. The reason for this limitation is hard to fathom. It would not seem supported by the wording of the Amendment on any plausible interpretation.

If McCarthy J was on this point narrower than the Chief Justice, in another respect he appeared to favour the possibility of a radically broader scope of abortion under the Amendment. Having criticised the Oireachtas for not having legislated on the subject, he went on to pose a series of questions:

> What are pregnant women to do? What are the parents of a pregnant girl under age to do? What are the medical profession to do? They have no guidelines save what may be gleaned from the judgments in this case. What additional considerations are there? Is the victim of rape, statutory or otherwise, or the victim of incest, finding herself pregnant, to be assessed in a manner different from others . . .? Does the right to bodily integrity . . . involve the right to control one's own body?

He went on to observe that legislation might be both negative and positive: negative, 'in prohibiting absolutely or at a given time, or without meeting stringent tests'; positive by requiring positive action. He observed finally that it was not for the courts to programme society, adding that that was partly, at least, the role of the legislature. The courts were not equipped to regulate these procedures.

What is one to make of all this? Why is McCarthy J raising the possibility of abortion in cases of underage pregnancy, rape, unlawful carnal knowledge and incest and on the basis of the right to control one's own body? How can the absence of legislation be relevant to any of these situations if the Amendment is to be interpreted (as McCarthy J indicated earlier in his judgment) as authorising abortion only in the case of a real and substantial risk attaching to the mother's survival? If one returns to this earlier passage and peruses it carefully, one discovers that McCarthy J did not in fact state expressly that the Amendment authorised abortion only in this case. What he said was that the true construction of the Amendment was that in such a case it might not be practicable to vindicate the right to life of the unborn.

The use of the words 'true construction' certainly suggests that the construction should be limited to the stated ground, but it may be argued that it does not require this conclusion. McCarthy J was addressing a case in which the right to abortion on the ground of an asserted risk to the mother's life was being claimed. His conclusion that the true construction of the Amendment was that in such a case it might not be practicable to vindicate the right to life of the unborn did not commit him to holding that it *would* be practicable in all other cases.

In truth McCarthy J appears to have been attempting in his later remarks to open up the possibility that the Oireachtas might have power to extend eligibility for abortion to some or all of the cases he mentioned. His profession of the inappropriateness of the courts' function in 'programm[ing] society' and the propriety of the legislature's role was no doubt designed to cede to the legislature the primary function of balancing constitutional rights. (One is reminded here of Henchy J's approach to the reconciliation of the right of free speech and the right to a good name in *Hynes-O'Sullivan v O'Driscoll* [1989] ILRM 349; [19881 IR 436: see our comments in the 1988 Review, 442-3.)

O'Flaherty J's judgment also gives rise to reflection. Several features are striking. First, it is noteworthy for its failure to make any reference to the fact that Article 40.3.3 recognises that the unborn child's right to life is equal to that of the mother's. It is fair to observe that a person who read O'Flaherty J's judgment without access to the text of Article 40.3.3 would have no inkling that it recognised such an equal right.

The second noteworthy feature of O'Flaherty J's judgment is that he also envisages legislation providing for abortion in circumstances other than where the mother's life is threatened. As we have seen, O'Flaherty J stated that he believed Article 40.3.3 to be clear in this respect:

> Abortion, as such, certainly abortion on demand, is not something that can be legalised in this jurisdiction. . . .

We may note here that O'Flaherty J only clearly excluded abortion *on demand* from the legislative programme. Thus, for example, legislation prescribing abortion on grounds such as the mother's health, her young age, rape, incest, or (perhaps) bodily integrity or privacy could possibly be lawful. O'Flaherty J makes no attempt to distinguish between abortion on demand *de jure* and *de facto*. Relatively few countries expressly authorise abortion on demand and fewer still use language so stark as the term abortion 'on demand'. What happens in most countries where abortion is legal is that the legislature uses terminology that suggests restrictiveness but in practice results in abortion on demand. This is the experience in Britain, where abortion on demand is available under the rubric of the mother's health, and in the United States, where the mother's right to privacy is the basis for wide-ranging abortion.

O'Flaherty J went on to state (as we have noted) that:

> [t]he legislators when they come to enact legislation must have due

> regard to the mother's right to life — a right protected throughout the Constitution in any event. Until legislation is enacted to provide otherwise, I believe that the law in this State is that surgical intervention which has the effect of terminating pregnancy *bona fide* undertaken to save the life of the mother where she is in danger of death is permissible under the Constitution and the law. The danger has to represent a substantial risk to her life though this does not necessarily have to be an imminent danger of instant death. The law does not require the doctors to wait until the mother is in peril of immediate death.

This passage requires close scrutiny. O'Flaherty J's failure to mention that the mother's right to life is equal to that of her unborn child is here particularly striking. The words '[u]ntil legislation is enacted to provide otherwise' seem crucial. They appear at least consistent with the view that the Oireachtas has power to extend the grounds of abortion beyond life-threatening cases virtually all the way to the terminus of abortion on demand, provided only that it stops just short of that terminus. This notion of legislative power to do what the judiciary cannot is strikingly reminiscent of what McCarthy J suggested less explicitly. O'Flahertys J's words would also seem capable of encompassing a legislative entitlement to restrict, or even exclude completely, the entitlement to abortion stated judicially in *X*. The general tenor of his judgment is not easy to harmonise with this interpretation, however.

Egan J's more sober consideration of the subject is closer to that of the Chief Justice. His reference to the probability of a real and substantial risk to the mother's life does not, however, in express terms distinguish the mother's life from her health. This might not have been thought to be of any great significance had it not been that Egan J's brief summary of the *Bourne* decision evinces no apparent unease about the breadth of the ground for abortion favoured in that case. In *Bourne*, mental health was equiparated with life. Egan J's reference to *Bourne* suggests that he may have regarded the decision as representing good law in the State. That is a view that has received little or no endorsement by commentators over the years.

Undoubtedly the most eminent analyst of the majority's interpretation of the Eighth Amendment in *X* is Mr Justice Brian Walsh, of the European Court of Human Rights and a Judge of the Supreme Court from 1962 to 1991. In a lecture on *Justice and the Constitution* delivered at University College Galway on 11 November 1992. Mr Justice Walsh observes that the Eighth Amendment

> confers no immunity for taking life and its stated objective is the preservation of and respect for life. It is perfectly consonant with the

> idea of the safeguarding of the mother's life without intentional and direct intervention to terminate the life of the foetus. The claim that it admits of direct termination has never been fully argued. In the *X* case it was conceded. There was no *legitimus contradictor* to argue against such a construction and therefore the court's decision can only bind the particular case as it was based on a conceded and unargued construction. It is well established that neither a constitutional provision nor even a statutory provision can be construed on the basis of a concession if it were to be binding *in rem*.

**Application of the law to the facts** The majority, which held that abortion was lawful where there was a real and substantial risk to the mother's life, also held that the first defendant was entitled to have an abortion on the facts of the case. This was based primarily on evidence that the first defendant had made threats to commit suicide and on the evidence of 'a very experienced clinical psychologist' whose opinion was that there was a real likelihood that she would commit suicide.

Finlay CJ said that it was:

> commonsense that a threat of self-destruction such as is outlined in the evidence in this case, which the psychologist clearly believes to be a very real threat, cannot be monitored in th[e same] sense [as monitoring the progress of a physical condition] and that it is almost impossible to prevent self-destruction in a young girl in the situation in which this defendant is if she were to decide to carry out her threat of suicide.

The majority proceeded on the basis that (*per* Finlay CJ) '[u]pon the facts proved in the High Court, the first defendant was . . . raped, and as a result of such rape became pregnant. . . .' Hederman J counselled judicial caution on this issue:

> The fact that this girl is pregnant clearly proves that somebody is guilty of unlawful carnal knowledge of a girl under the age of fifteen years. The proof of such an offence does not depend on the absence of consent of the girl. So far as the allegation of rape is concerned it must for the purpose of this case remain an allegation as neither the High Court nor this Court can decide whether or not there was a rape by the person alleged by the first defendant or any person.

Hederman J went on to identify certain aspects of the case which affected the cogency of the evidence. Neither the High Court nor the Supreme Court had either heard or seen the mother of the unborn child. There had been 'no evidence whatever of an obstetrical or indeed of any other medical nature'.

On the issue of the threat to the mother's life, there had been a 'remarkable paucity' of evidence:

> What has been allowed is the evidence of a psychologist based on his own encounter with the first defendant and on what he heard about her attitude from other persons, namely the Garda Síochána and her parents. This led him to the opinion that there is a serious threat to the first defendant by an act of self-destruction by reason of the fact of being pregnant. This is a very extreme reaction to pregnancy, even to an unwarranted pregnancy. . . If there is a suicidal tendency then this is something which has to be guarded against. If this young person without being pregnant had suicidal tendencies due to some other cause then nobody would doubt that the proper course would be to put her in such care and under such supervision as would counteract such tendency and do everything possible to prevent suicide. I do not think the terms of the Eighth Amendment or indeed the terms of the Constitution before amendment would absolve the State from its obligation to vindicate and protect the life of a person who had expressed the intention of self-destruction. This young girl clearly requires loving and sympathetic care and professional counselling and all the protection which the State agencies can provide or furnish. There could be no question whatsoever of permitting another life to be taken to deal with the situation even if the intent to self-destruct could be traced directly to the activities or the existence of another person.

It has to be said that Hederman J's analysis is far more convincing than that of the majority. The Chief Justice's discussion of the issue was widely criticised by several professional commentators, including Professor Patricia Casey, Professor of Psychiatry at University College Dublin: see *Irish Medical News*, vol. 9, No. 10, 16 March 1992; *Irish Independent*, 20 March 1992. Particularly worthy of note is the statement of Eastern Health Board psychiatrist, Brian McCaffrey, that the adequacy of the *X* case ruling must be open to question on account of the Court's failure to hear medical evidence from a duly qualified registered medical practitioner. The difficulties in the Court's approach to threatened suicide were identified by Dr Paul O'Mahony, author of a major study on the prevention of prison suicides, former research psychologist with the Department of Justice, now lecturer in psychology at Trinity College Dublin: 'Legal recognition of suicide intent invites manipulation', *Irish Times*, 13 March 1992.

On the broader question of whether it is ever necessary to terminate unborn life, the Medical Council published a *Statement on Guidelines re Abortion* on 3 March 1993, at which it stated that the necessity for abortion to preserve the life or health of the mother remained to be proved. This position was strongly endorsed by Dr Eamon McGuinness, Chairman of the Institute of Obstetricians and Gynaecologists. The fact that the Medical Council came to this conclusion is particularly noteworthy in view of the strong legal and political pressures created by the *X* decision. The criterion which the majority applied in *X* (without the evidence of any medically or psychiatrically qualified witness) was based on a premise that the Medical Council did not accept as having any established empirical validity. Subsequent to the Medical Council's *Statement*, the Irish Medical Organisation at its annual conference in April 1993 passed motions re-affirming doctors' respect for all human life and in favour of a policy against abortion. The UNICEF Report, *Progress of Nations 1993*, showed that Ireland is the safest country in the world for a mother to have a child: fewer mothers die bearing children here than anywhere else in the world, including such countries as the United States and Britain, with well-developed economies and liberal abortion regimes.

**Injunctive power against travel abroad for abortion** Since the majority of the Court in *X* held in favour of the defendant on the substantive issue, the question whether the Constitution authorised or required the granting of an injunction against travel abroad for an abortion in cases where abortion would not be lawful within the State as strictly *obiter*. Nonetheless all the members of the Court stated their views upon it.

Finlay CJ's position is not entirely clear. He rejected the contention that a pregnant woman had an absolute right to travel, which could not be restricted in defence of the right to life of the unborn. But he considered that the requirement of practicability in Article 40.3.3 encompassed the limitation, already applicable to the injunctive power in general, that the court should avoid making a futile or unenforceable order. (See, however, *Kutchera v Buckingham International Holdings Ltd* [1988] ILRM 501; [1988] IR 6, analysed in the 1988 Review, 84-9). The Chief Justice accepted that, in a great number of instances, an injunction would be impossible to supervise or enforce, save by *ex post facto* punishment or sanctions; the imposition of such penalties, 'except to the extent that they might provide a deterrent would not be an effective defence of the right of the unborn to life'.

Nonetheless, in the instant case, since the defendants had demonstrated an anxiety to abide by the lawful order of the Court, the orders made by the High Court, until discharged on appeal, had been 'wholly effective to achieve the purpose for which they were made'. While this approach might not be shared by many others, the Chief Justice did not consider that a mere expectation that a significant number of people might be unwilling to obey the orders of a court could deprive that court from 'attempting, at least, in appropriate cases to discharge its constitutional duty by the making of an injunction restricting, to some extent, the right to travel of an individual'.

It is hard to discern the precise holding on this question. Perhaps the Chief Justice envisaged that in some cases the *likelihood* of obedience to an order would justify the court in making an order. In other words, there should be no general rule that injunctions of this kind could not constitutionally be granted but instead the court should engage in a process of investigation and assessment of the facts of any particular case in order to estimate the likelihood of compliance in the particular circumstances. If a defendant made it clear that she intended not to comply with the order, or if this likelihood was otherwise established, then the court could not lawfully make the order. There is something faintly ridiculous about this distinction, which would give to the defendant the power to render unconstitutional a proposed injunction by uttering words of defiance to it.

Hederman J was of the view that, unless Costello J's injunction was upheld to its full extent, the Court could not effectively discharge its constitutional obligation of protecting unborn life:

> If the defendants were to travel out of the jurisdiction and the first defendant had an abortion, the court could only deal with the question of contempt of court if the defendants returned to the jurisdiction, but could not restore the unborn life.

Egan J was also of the opinion that injunctions might be granted against travelling abroad for an abortion. He did not rely on any immutable principle of a hierarchy of constitutional rights, whereby the superior right should prevail in the case of conflict:

> The right to life of the person (as in *The People v Shaw* [1982] IR 1) was held to be superior to the right to liberty of another, but, quite clearly, the right to life might not be the paramount right in every circumstances. If, for instance, it were necessary for a father to kill a man engaged in the rape of his daughter in order to prevent its continuance, I have no doubt but that the right of the girl to bodily integrity would rank higher than the right to life of the rapist.

Egan J considered that the right to travel abroad to have an abortion 'must surely rank lower than the right to life of the unborn'. It might well be that proof of an intention to commit an unlawful act could not amount to an offence but in the instant case there was a *stated intention* of depriving the unborn of its right to life. It might well be that instances of a declared intention and proof of such would be very rare indeed and there was also the position that the supervision of a court order would be difficult but these considerations, in his view, had to yield precedence to the defence and vindication of the right to life.

The three judges of the majority on this issue can thus be seen to have lacked any unanimity on the range of circumstances in which an injunction may be ordered. Hederman J referred to no limitation on the injunctive power; the Chief Justice narrowed the scope to cases where the injunction is likely to be effective; and Egan J considered that the crucial test was whether the defendant had actually declared an intent to have an abortion abroad. It should be noted that, whereas Egan J's test is narrower than that of Finlay CJ in requiring an express declaration of intent, it is potentially wider in not requiring proof of likelihood of non-compliance. One wonders what principle underlines distinguishing between a declaration of intent and other credible manifestations of intent. Is it based on the unambiguity of proof of intent (a matter of evidential cogency) or does it encompass the notion that express defiance of the values encapsulated by Article 40.3.3 has to be met by a judicial response, even where this may not be fully effective?

It is interesting to contrast Egan J's approach in this regard with that of Finlay CJ, for whom manifestation (including intimation) of defiance of the values underlying the administration of justice should render an injunction unconstitutional.

The two dissenting judges also differed among themselves. McCarthy J presented the more extensive analysis. He noted that the right to travel had been identified in *The State (M.) v Attorney General* [1979] IR 73 as an unenumerated constitutional right guaranteed under Article 40. He continued:

> If the purpose of exercising the right to travel is to avail of a service, lawful in its own location, but unlawful in Ireland, is the right curtailed or abolished because of that local illegality and/or because of the guarantee in the Amendment? If it were a matter of a balancing exercise the scales could only tilt in one direction, the right to life of the unborn, assuming no threat to the life of the mother. In my view, it is not a question of balancing the right to travel against the right to life; it is a question as to whether or not an individual has a right to travel — which she has. It cannot, in my view, be curtailed because of a particular intent. If one travels from the jurisdiction of this state to another, one, temporarily, becomes subject to the laws of the other state. An agreement, commonly called a conspiracy, to go to another state to do something lawfully done there cannot, in my opinion, permit of a restraining order. Treason is thought to be the greatest of crimes. If I proclaim my intent to go to another country, there to plot against the government here, I may, by some extension of the law against sedition, be prosecuted and,

> consequently, subject to detention here, but I cannot be lawfully prevented from travelling to that other country there to plot the overthrow, since that would not be a crime in the other country. I go further. Even if it were a crime in the other country, if I proclaim my intent to explode a bomb or shoot an individual in another country, I cannot lawfully be prevented from leaving my own country for that purpose.
>
> The reality is that each nation governs itself and enforces its own criminal law. A court in one state cannot enjoin an individual leaving it from wrongdoing outside it in another state or states. It follows that, insofar as it interferes with the right to travel, there is no jurisdiction to make such an order.

This analysis confuses several quite separate issues. These are: (1) the propriety of involving the criminal law to punish a manifestation of an intent to commit a crime; (2) the propriety of prohibiting by injunction an act that is not unlawful in the foreign state where it is intended to occur; (3) the extra-territorial remit of a state's criminal law; (4) the extra-territorial dimensions of constitutional protection for particular fundamental human rights, notably the right to life; and (5) the possible limits on the constitutional right to travel, in the light of a harmonious interpretation of the totality of rights protected by the Constitution.

Let us assume for the purposes of argument that the criminal law may not be invoked to punish the manifestation of an intent to commit a crime, unless that manifestation has translated itself into a significant element of preparation for its commission. We need not here address the question whether the constitutional guarantee of liberty is inconsistent with a statutory amendment of the law of attempt so that criminal liability attaches to conduct *earlier* than that falling within the present scope of attempt to or with the statutory creation of a new offence of preparation to engage in specified criminal activity. It is one thing to punish an intent to commit a crime; it is quite another to penalise actual conduct, albeit in the early stages of translating thought into action.

In the instant decision, the proceedings were of a civil, not a criminal, nature, so no question of punishing an offence arose. There may be jurisprudential arguments in favour of extending the *Ryan* philosophy into the area of the civil law of injunctions generally or in specific contexts, and there may well also be sound legal objections to developing any such analogy. McCarthy J makes no attempt to adduce these arguments and instead wrongly concludes that the criminal law principles apply in the civil context. This is particularly hard to explain, since Costello J had expressly refuted such an error.

At the heart of McCarthy J's analysis is the erroneous premise that the constitutional protection of fundamental rights necessarily stops at our shorelines in all cases. The question of the international remit of constitutional protection is one of great juridical complexity to which there are not easy obvious answers. McCarthy J's analysis gives no indication of an understanding of these complexities.

Some of the issues of policy and principle are identified by Binchy, 'Constitutional Remedies and the Law of Torts', in J. O'Reilly, ed., *Human Rights and Constitutional Law* (1992) 201. Suffice it here to note that, far from being self-evident that the constitutional protection is limited to the intra-state activity and its intra-state effects of extra-state activity, it is on the contrary obvious that constitutional rights are protected, at least in certain respects, when they are violated outside the jurisdiction. For example, if an Irish woman, domiciled and resident in Ireland, is encouraged to go on a short sea journey from Galway forty miles into the Atlantic, with the promise of returning to port in a couple of hours and she is raped or tortured while on board the boat, in violation of her constitutional right to bodily integrity, the Constitution may be invoked *after* the event: cf. *Meskell v Corás Iompair Éireann* [1973] IR 121.

No argument against the granting of an injunction directed at preventing such a violation of bodily integrity can therefore rest on the mere fact that it is about to take place outside the jurisdiction.

This is not to suggest, of course, that all actual or threatened conduct, regardless of where its takes place in the world, is capable of falling under the protective cloak of the Irish Constitution. That is not in issue; what is in question is the proper approach for determining how and where the line should be drawn.

This type of question is not at all new: it arises (albeit in somewhat less complex circumstances) in the context of choice of law in tort: see W. Binchy, *Irish Conflicts of Law* (1988), chapter 32. The twentieth century has witnessed a growing philosophical sophistication in the judicial analysis of how to choose between competing legal systems where a tort involves more than one state. The old approach, which found much favour internationally, was to apply the *lex loci delicti* — the law of the place where the tort was committed. This rule had the virtue of simplicity in most cases, but the simplicity was bought at a huge price in some instances, since the place where the tort was committed might be entirely contingent or unconnnected with the reality of the parties' relationship or the social policies and norms underlying the particular tort. If, for example, an Irish family goes on holiday to a foreign country and an acccident occurs where the father carelessly leaves a gun within easy access of his child, justice might not obviously be done if the Irish court, in negligence proceedings brought by the injured child, were to apply the law of the country where the accident took place, which (let us assume) prohibited any such claims between family members.

If the plaintiff in the Irish proceedings were to invoke Article 40.3.2, and to quote Barron J's opinion, in *Sweeney v Duggan* [1991] 2 IR 274 (191 Review, 459) that this subsection gave 'a guarantee of a just law of negligence', it would scarcely be a *sophisticated* answer for the court to reply that, although such a law as existed in the foreign state would indeed be unconstitutional if it were enacted in Ireland, no constitutional argument arose because the accident occurred outside Ireland. One would hope that the court would verse itself in the elaborate jurisprudence, led by such scholars as Currie and Cavers (cf. Binchy, *op. cit.*, 16-21), and address the highly complex but hugely important task of fashioning appropriate criteria for determining the international remit of constitutional protection with regard to particular rights in particular contexts.

It is ironic that only six years previously the Supreme Court had addressed this precise question in *Grehan v Medical Incorporated and Pine Valley Associates* [1986] ILRM 627; [1986] IR 528. Walsh J (for the court) spelt out an entirely new choice of law philosophy for tort. In his view:

> the Irish courts should be sufficiently flexible to be capable of responding to the individual issues prescribed in each case and to the social and economic dimensions of applying any particular choice of law rule in the proceedings in question.

No one imagines that this approach is easy; *a fortiori* where constitutional rights are concerned. But McCarthy J's notion of a stark and unmitigated territorialism in respect of constitutional protection is a disappointing achievement for a judge who displayed such creative abilities in several other constitutional cases.

The final area of weakness in McCarthy J's analysis of the injunction issue is the remarkably undeveloped quality of the concept of the constitutional right to travel which he propounded. One might have expected some considerations of the values underlying the concept; instead the phrase is incanted ritually and without any normative context or vitality.

The right to travel encompasses several important human values: autonomy in decision-making, empowerment of private choice over public plans, and the liberty to go here, there or nowhere in particular. In totalitarian societies the right to travel is compromised or destroyed because the state has no interest in accommodating individual life plans. A person's decision to go or stay must give way to the grander vision of the state. The right to travel is also associated with important economic values, especially in relation to employment, and these have had a significant effect on the historical development of the law of domicile (cf. *In re Bushbey*, 112 NYS 262, at 263; *per* Crosby, Surrogate, 1908).

*Pace* McCarthy J, the right to travel is manifestly subject to some clear limitations. I have no right to travel onto someone else's property without his or her permission. There is no general constitutional right to trespass. (It is arguable that the Constitution permits trespass in the exercise of certain other rights — free speech, for instance — in particular circumstances: cf. McMahon & Binchy, op. cit., 433. It also is the view of two members of the Law Reform Commission, Mr Justice Hederman and Mr John Buckley, that the constitutional right to bodily integrity of a trespassing child would be violated if the occupier owed the child a duty less extensive than the duty of care in negligence: cf. the Law Reform Commission's *Report on Occupiers' Liability* (LRC 46–1992), paras. 4.22-4.24). These considerations in no sense support the far wider proposition that there is a constitutional right to travel anywhere at any time.)

It seems clear that a particular act which involves travel as integral to its occurrence may have legal significance that extends beyond the travel component. The *very process of travelling* may do damage to another's constitutional rights in certain circumstances. For example, a highly infectious person who travels on a train with people who are particularly vulnerable to infection may by doing so violate their right to life or bodily integrity. Again, speaking in the wider human context, travel may be *integrally related to the accomplishment of a particular goal* which involves damage to the constitutional rights of others. In the case of abortion, which is available lawfully abroad, the purpose of the travel is to accomplish such a goal. A judge who invokes the right to travel as a supreme constitutional norm has to explain why the right is capable of embracing the specific category of travel which is directed necessarily at accomplishing the goal of damaging another's constitutional rights.

This raises the question of the scope of Costello J's order. If it had been confined to travel for the purposes of obtaining an abortion, how would this have compromised the constitutionally protected right to travel? McCarthy J's analysis offers no guidance.

Pregnancy involves unique issues in relation to the right to travel, since the mother and the unborn child are conjoined in a relationship of unilateral dependency. A pregnant woman who wishes to travel necessarily brings her child with her. An important distinction must be drawn between a case where a pregnant woman wishes to travel in circumstances where the journey or its after-effects may indirectly damage the foetus, without any intention on the part of the mother to bring about this result, and the entirely separate case where a pregnant woman travels to have an abortion. In the first case, the mother is asserting a constitutional right to travel which, considered in its own terms, including its purpose, raises no constitutional difficulty. This genuine constitutional right would be balanced against the right to life of the unborn. In the second case, the position is quite different from a constitutional standpoint. The mother's purpose in travelling is to have an abortion. The journey cannot be fully understood as a human act without regard to that purpose. McCarthy J's judgment betrays no sensitivity to this crucial distinction.

O'Flaherty J's disposition of the travel issue was somewhat more rhetorical and less analytic than McCarthy J's. He stated that the State's role in relation to women who found themselves unwillingly pregnant:

> should be a positive rather than a negative one. In particular I do not believe that the Court should grant an injunction to intervene to this extraordinary degree with the individual's freedom of movement. In this case the injunction granted also involves, in my judgment, an unwarranted interference with the authority of the family.
>
> It should be decided that once an injunction is granted by a court it is an order that must be obeyed. If there is a failure to obey the order, then that disobedience may be punished by the imposition of various penalties, including the possibility of imprisonment or fines. To say that it is unlikely that such penalties would ever be invoked in this case is no answer; the fact is that such severe remedies are available.
>
> Such a regime is impossible to reconcile with a Constitution, one of the primary objects of which, as stated in its Preamble, is to assure the dignity and freedom of the individual.

O'Flaherty J offers no explanation as to why there should be no restraint on freedom of movement where the only purpose of that movement is to violate another's constitutional right. His reference to the authority of the family is intriguing. If it implies that Article 41 gives a distinct legal entitlement to parents to facilitate the termination of the life of their unborn child which does not inhere in other facilitators, this is an argument that would need some further development; in adumbrated form it is less than convincing. It would, incidentally, impact on other relevant areas of constitutional controversy, notably the question of the provision of abortion information and assistance.

**The aftermath of the *X* decision** The Supreme Court judgment in *X* provoked great controversy. Clearly it was unacceptable to those who had sought the Eighth Amendment since it held that abortion was legal in certain circumstances. The proponents of the Amendment argued that respect for democratic values made it essential that the people be given a new opportunity in a referendum to state their opposition to legalised abortion or, as the case might be, their support for the *X* decision. From a different standpoint, pressure came on the Government to seek to alter the Protocol to the Maastricht Treaty, since the *X* decision made it plain that a residual injunctive power existed in relation to abortion abroad. This pressure went so far as to seek the effective reversal of the earlier Supreme Court decision, in *Open Door* and *Grogan*.

The Government unsuccessfully sought a modification of the Protocol and contented itself with a Solemn Declaration in its regard, which was formally adopted by the EC foreign ministers on 1 May 1992. We examine the scope of the Protocol and Solemn Declaration below, in the context of subsequent constitutional developments.

**Morris J's judgment** After the Court of Justice in *Grogan* imately returned to the High Court, where Morris J gave judgment on 7 August 1992. For analysis, see Kingston & Whelan, 'The Protection of the Unborn in Three Legal Orders' (1992) 10 ILT 279-80.

Morris J first rejected the argument by the defendants that a pregnant woman had the right to receive information relating to clinics in Britain which provided abortion services. This argument was based on Community law. Morris J considered that a provision in Irish law prohibiting the giving of such information was not in conflict with the Treaty of Rome. He relied on the Supreme Court's holdings and statements of law in *Open Door* and in *Grogan* to the effect that this was unconstitutional. Of course a particular action may be unconstitutional without being contrary to the Treaty of Rome and *vice versa*; Morris J's conclusion might have been more attractive if he had held, on the basis of these two Supreme Court decisions, that the giving of information was unconstitutional and that this was so notwithstanding the Community law dimensions to our Constitution.

Morris J went on to reject the argument that the State's failure to provide post-abortion medical treatment facilities to women who had abortions in Britain violated their right to bodily integrity. Nothing in the evidence tendered on behalf of the defendants supported the suggestion that such care was not available; on the contrary the evidence established to Morris J's satisfaction that this treatment was readily available. Even if it had not been so, Morris J could not see how this would be relevant to the defendants' conduct; it could not logically be suggested that the medical profession in Ireland would more readily provide medical attention to women who had attended clinics recommended by the defendants in their publications rather than if they had attended other clinics. Morris J's conclusion on this issue may be contrasted with that of the European Court of Human Rights, which relied on an opinion of an expert in public health, adduced on behalf of the clinics, which the Irish Government had chosen not to contradict. (The persistent failure of the Irish Government in cases before the European court to adduce expert evidence on matters of empirical or normative controversy is a regrettable feature of its litigation strategy. Henchy J's words of warning in *Norris v Attorney General* [1984] IR 36 have clearly not been heeded.)

Morris J next rejected an argument based on Article 40.1 of the Constitution to the effect that there was an unconstitutional inequality of treatment between those who had an economic association with British abortion clinics (to whom Community law applied, with the effect, the defendants claimed, of rendering lawful their provision of information about the abortion clinics) and those without such association (whose conduct was not rendered lawful by Community law). Morris J pointed out that the Supreme Court decision in *Open Door* had made it clear that information of this nature was unconstitutional and prohibited by Irish law irrespective of the existence or absence of such an association. (It should be noted that Protocol No. 17, not yet in force at the time of Morris J's judgment, appears to exclude the application of Community law in the determination of the question of the constitutional validity under Article 40.3.3 of the provision of such information. Whether it affects Article 40.3.3 as amended by the Thirteenth and Fourteenth Amendments is a question we examine below.)

The defendants sought unsuccessfully to rely on the *X* decision as establishing a class of person and a circumstance in which abortion could be regarded as permissible. They argued that a person in a situation falling within the parameters of *X* would be entitled to receive information as to British abortion clinics and that therefore their conduct was in consequence lawful. Morris J identified 'a profound distinction' between distribution of this information to the community at large and to university students in particular, on the one hand, and the communication of such information to 'a clearly defined and extremely restricted type of person identified in the [*X*] test.' It had not been suggested that the defendants had wished to confine their activities to the distribution of information to that class. The European Court of Human Rights, in contrast, in *Open Door* used this class as an element in its proportionality weighting against the injunction.

Morris J also dismissed the defendants' contention that the plaintiffs' failure to have earlier sought to have them committed for contempt should disentitle them to an injunction. The plaintiffs had been entitled to wait for clarification by the Court of Justice on the Article 177 reference. (For criticism, see Kingston & Whelan, op. cit., at 280).

Morris J rejected the defendants' argument based on the Solemn Declaration of 1 May 1992 (of which more anon), since the Maastricht Treaty, in relation to which it applied, had not yet come into force.

Morris J granted a permanent injunction in the same terms as the interlocutory injunction granted by the Supreme Court. He directed the papers to be sent to the Director of Public Prosecutions to enable him to determine whether the case was an appropriate one for prosecution for contempt of court. (No prosecution in fact resulted).

**Open Door's application under the European Convention** We mentioned earlier that the clinics against whom an injunction was ordered by the Supreme Court took proceedings against Ireland under the European Convention. These were successful before the Commission (*Open Door Counselling v Ireland* (1991) EHRR 131) and also before the Court: *Open Door Counselling and Dublin Well Woman v Ireland* (1992) 15 EHRR 244. For incisive analysis, see Hogan, 'The Right to Life and the Abortion Question under the European Convention on Human Rights', in Liz Heffernan ed., *Human Rights: A European Perspective* (1994) at 104, and Kingston & Whelan, op. cit., at 96, 280.

The particular argument that succeeded before the Commission failed before the Court. This was to the effect that Article 40.3.3 was so unclear in its scope that, in the absence of clarifying legislation, it was not possible to know whether the activities contemplated by the clinics were or were not unlawful and that accordingly the restriction was not 'proscribed by law' under Article 10(2) of the Convention. The Court rejected this argument. Taking into account 'the high threshold of protection of the unborn provided under Irish law generally' and the manner in which the Irish courts had interpreted their role as the guarantors of constitutional rights, the possibility that legal action might be taken against the clinics must have been reasonably foreseeable, with appropriate legal advice. This conclusion was reinforced by the legal advice that one of the clinics had actually received before injunction was sought, which was to the effect that such a prospect existed. See further Hogan, op. cit., at 109-10.

The Court then addressed the question of which Articles were relevant to its deliberations. Clearly Article 10 was of importance. It provides as follows:

> 1. Everyone has the right to freedom of expression. This right shall include freedom to hold opinions and to receive and impart information and ideas without interference by public authority and regardless of frontiers. . .
> 2. The exercise of these freedoms, since it carries with it duties and responsibilities, may be subject to such formalities, conditions, restrictions or penalties as are prescribed by law and are necessary in a democratic society, in the interests of national security, territorial integ-

> rity or public safety, for the prevention of disorder or crime, for the protection of health or morals, for the protection of the reputation or rights of others, for preventing the disclosure of information received in confidence, or for maintaining the authority and impartiality of the judiciary.

The Government submitted to the Court that Article 10 should be interpreted against the background of Articles 2, 17 and 60 of the Convention. Article 2(1) provides that:

> [e]veryone's right to life shall be protected by law. No one shall be deprived of his life intentionally save in execution of a sentence of a court following his conviction of a crime for which this penalty is provided by law. . . .

Article 17 provides that nothing in the Convention may be interpreted as implying for any State, group or person any right to engage in any activity or perform any act aimed at the destruction of any of the rights and freedoms set forth in the Convention or at their limitation to a greater extent than is provided for in the Convention. Finally, Article 60 provides that nothing in the Convention is to be construed as 'limiting or derogating from any of the human rights and fundamental freedoms which may be ensured under the laws of any High Contracting Party or under any other argument to which it is a Party'.

In a crucial passage, the Court characterised the case as one involving the protection of morals rather than of *life*. It stated (in para. 63):

> The Court cannot accept that the restrictions at issue pursued the aim of the prevention of crime since . . . neither the provision of the information in question nor the obtaining of an abortion outside the jurisdiction involved any criminal offence. However, it is evident that the protection afforded under Irish law to the right to life of the unborn is based on profound moral values concerning the nature of life which were rcflected in the stance of the majority of the Irish people against abortion as experienced in the 1983 referendum. The restriction thus pursued the legitimate aim of the protection in Ireland of the right to life of the unborn in one aspect. It is not necessary in the light of this conclusion to decide whether the term 'others' under Article 10(2) extends to the unborn.

This disposition of the right to life of the unborn under the Convention carries no credibility. The mere fact that a particular constitutional provision protects morals does not mean that it does not also protect life. In the case of Article 40.3.3, the provision is all about the protection of life. Indeed the Court's own characterisation of the Amendment as involving the protection of morals makes it plain that the protection was 'based on profound moral values *concerning the nature of life* . . .' (emphasis added). Of course philosophical debate attaches to the existential significance of life. That debate is as old as humanity. To characterise it as a morals issue is to trivialise what is surely one of the most profound questions that the human mind can address.

Very significant consequences follow from the refusal of the Court to address the question of the protection afforded to the lives of the unborn by the Convention. Most obviously, the scope of permissible restrictions on freedom of expression based on the protection of morals may well be narrower than that of permissible restrictions based on the protection of life. The Court's conclusion (which we describe below) that the protection of morals did not justify the injunction granted by the Supreme Court leaves entirely unresolved the question whether the protection of the right to life of the unborn is a sufficient (or, indeed, necessary) justification under Article 10(2). This issue was central to the case; by leaving it unresolved, the Court, in effect, determined it against the unborn, *sub silentio*.

There are further radical implications, extending well beyond the issue of abortion, which flow from the Court's characterisation of 'profound moral values concerning the nature of life' as falling within the zone of protection of morals rather than of life. In the past twenty years or so, there has been a growing tendency in many countries among some groups, to regard certain individuals as less than fully human or as lacking sufficient status to have their lives protected when their continued existence presents difficulties for others. There is also the view that certain lives would be better terminated than allowed to continue. Among those who have come under critical scrutiny are infants with significant disabilities ('defective newborns'), persons who are in a coma with little or no chance of regaining full consciousness, patients with Alzheimer's disease and the seriously mentally disabled. There is already a significant diversity of value positions within Europe in relation to all of these people. The Court's judgment in *Open Door* gives clear warning that their right to life will not necessarily be protected under Article 10(2) or Article 2 and that their protection in any national law will be subjected to a proportionality test on the basis that the issue is one of morals and not of the protection of life. The Court's reference to 'profound moral values concerning the nature of life' does not appear to envisage merely a scientific disagreement as to the physical ingredients of human life but rather to encompass ethical norms regarding particular aspects of human existence, against a broad tapestry of ontological debate. If the very fact of the social phenomenon of a diversity of approaches to these questions is, of itself, sufficient to neutralise Article 10(2) and, it would seem, Article 2, the future prospects for the Convention as a source of protection for human rights are not propitious.

In *Open Door* the Irish Government argued that the injunction was necessary in a democratic society for the protection of the right to life of the unborn and that Article 2 of the Convention, which, it said, protected unborn life, should be taken into account when interpreting Article 10. The Court responded by observing that:

> at the outset . . . in the present case it is not called upon to examine whether a right to abortion is guaranteed under the Convention or whether the foetus is encompassed by the right to life as contained in Article 2. The applicants have not claimed that the Convention contains a right to abortion, as such, their complaint being limited to that part of the injunction which restricts their freedom to impart and receive information concerning abortions abroad.
>
> Thus the only issue to be addressed is whether the restrictions on the freedom to impart and receive information contained in the relevant part of the injunction are necessary in a democratic society for the legitimate aim of the protection of morals as explained above. It follows from this approach that the Government's argument based on Article 2 of the Convention does not fall to be examined in the present case. On the other hand, the arguments based on Articles 17 and 60 fall to be considered. . . .'

The Court's analysis is again seriously flawed. The fact that the clinics had not asserted that the Convention contained a right to abortion in no sense foreclosed the necessity to address the relevance of Article 2. The *Government* had invoked Article 2 in defence of the Supreme Court's order. The Court's refusal to address the issue that undoubtedly arose under Article 2 has been criticised: see, e.g., Wilson Finnie, 'Jurisprudence of the European Court of Human Rights 1992', [1993] Juridical Rev 192, at 193.

There is an alarming possible explanation for the Court's strategy. If the majority of the Court were of the (albeit tentative) opinion that there probably is a right to abortion under the Convention (based perhaps on considerations of the mother's life, health, privacy, employment rights, freedom of association or sex equality), then clearly Article 2 would not offer a justification to the Irish Government with regard to the Supreme Court order in *Open Door*. The Court might therefore conclude that it was politically prudent not to address Article 2 in this case since it was going to hold in favour of the clinics on another ground. If there was any strong sense among the majority that the unborn were protected under Article 2, it would make no sense to decline to address the Government's argument based on Article 2.

The issue of abortion had not previously confronted the Court. The Commission's handling of the subject, in *Bruggeman and Schenten v Federal Republic of Germany* (1977) 3 EHRR 244 and *Paton v United Kingdom* (1980) 3 EHRR 408, evinced a considerable reluctance to confront the crucial questions squarely; what it had to say would give little encouragement to supporters of Article 40.3.3. Whelan and Kingston (op. cit., at 95) note that:

> the Commission still has a role to play in ensuring that all the rights guaranteed by the Convention are safeguarded; it could be argued that overly restrictive anti-abortion measures may constitute an invasion of privacy. It may also be argued that obliging a woman to go through a pregnancy which has the effect of turning her into a physical or mental wreck constitutes cruel or inhuman treatment, contrary to Article 3 of the Convention.

The Court's strategy in *Open Door* keeps these arguments secure for another day.

Having thus cleared the way to consider the case exclusively in terms of restrictions aimed at the protection of morals, the Court considered itself free to invoke the proportionality test. In the light of precedent (notably *The Observer and the Guardian v United Kingdom* (1991) 14 EHRR 153, para. 59), the Court sought to determine whether there existed a pressing social need for the measures in question and, in particular, whether the restriction complained of was proportionate to the legitimate aim pursued.

The Court held that the Government had not passed this test. While the restriction was limited to the provision of information, it was not a criminal offence under Irish law for a pregnant woman to travel abroad to have an abortion. Furthermore, the Court noted, the injunction limited the freedom to impart and receive information with respect to services that were lawful in other Convention countries and might be 'crucial to a woman's health and well-being'. The Court was struck by the absolute nature of the injunction, which restrained the provision of information to pregnant women concerning abortion facilities abroad, 'regardless of age or state of health or their reasons for seeking counselling on the termination of pregnancy.' The 'sweeping nature' of this restriction had been highlighted in the *X* decision; it had been conceded by counsel for the Government that the injunction no longer applied to women who, in the circumstances as defined in *X*, were free to have an abortion in Ireland or abroad. The Court observed that '[o]n that ground alone', the restriction appeared over-broad and disproportionate.

The Court's references to the 'age or state of health' of the mother and her reasons for seeking counselling on the termination of pregnancy are significant in suggesting that the majority of the Court was of opinion, or at least strongly sympathetic to the argument, that the Convention should be interpreted in a way that was consistent with a perception of access to abortion as a right requiring protection under the Convention, in circumstances going well beyond the issue of protection of the mother's life.

The Court went on to identify several other factors which confirmed its assessment that the restriction was over-broad and disproportionate. The clinics had engaged in non-directive counselling; there could be little doubt that following it there were women who decided against abortion. Accordingly, the link between the provision of information and the destruction of unborn life was 'not as definite as contended.' Such counselling had been tolerated by the State authorities until after the Supreme Court's judgment. Furthermore, the information that was provided was not made available to the public at large.

The information that the injunction sought to restrict was already available, in magazines and telephone directories or for persons with contacts in Britain. It could be obtained 'in a manner which was not supervised by qualified personnel and thus less protective of women's health.' Moreover, the injunction appeared to have been largely ineffective in protecting the right to life of the unborn, since it had not prevented large numbers of Irish women from continuing to obtain abortions in Britain.

In addition, the available evidence, which had not been disputed by the Government, suggested that the injunction had created a risk to the health of women seeking abortions at a later stage of their pregnancy due to lack of proper counselling, and who were not availing themselves of customary medical supervision after the abortion had taken place. (This conclusion may be contrasted with that of Morris J, above). Moreover, the injunction might have had more adverse effects on women who were not sufficiently resourceful or who had not the necessary level of education to have access to alternative sources of information. These were 'certainly legitimate factors' to take into consideration in assessing the proportionality of the restrictions.

The Court's analysis of the proportionality issue is a good example of Morton's fork. The ban on information about British abortion clinics was condemned because (among other reasons) Irish law did not make it an offence to have an abortion abroad; yet it seems clear that, even with such an extension of the criminal law, the ban would still be struck down by the Court: see Hogan, op. cit., at 113 and Búrca, op. cit., at 315. The ban was condemned as being at the same time unduly efficacious (in its detrimental health implications) and inefficacious (in its capacity to control conduct).

The Court went on to dispose summarily of the Irish Government's argument that Article 10 should not be interpreted in such a manner as to limit, destroy or derogate from the right to life of the unborn which enjoyed special protection under Irish law, which fell within the scope of Articles 17 and 60 of the Constitution:

> Without calling into question under the Convention the regime of protection of unborn life that exists under Irish law, the Court recalls that the injunction did not prevent Irish women from having abortions abroad and that the information it sought to restrain was available from other sources. Accordingly, it is not the interpretation of Article 10 but the position of Ireland as regards the implementation of the law that makes possible the continuance of the current level of abortions obtained by Irish women abroad.

This is a most curious argument. It is one thing to contend (as the Court did earlier in its judgment) that the relative inefficacy of an injunction is a factor to be taken into account in determining whether the restriction it creates is proportionate to the legitimate aim pursued; it is quite another thing to invoke this inefficacy as a way of destroying the basis of the protection of human rights that are ensured under the laws of High Contracting Party, which, Article 60 promises, will not be 'limited or derogated' from by the Convention.

The Court's disposition of the issue amounts to a refusal to consider the difficult questions that necessarily arise under Article 60 in the context of Article 40.3.3 of the Constitution. If the right to life of the unborn is indeed a human right or fundamental freedom, then Article 60 ensures that nothing in the Convention is to be construed as limiting or derogating from it. Article 60 does not state that the right will be protected only to a proportionate extent; thus the Court's proportionality-based analysis, in which the question of the efficacy of the restriction arose for consideration, would not be relevant to Article 60. The willingness of the Court to decline to address the important issues arising under Article 60 and instead to characterise the question as one of causation rather than of human rights and fundamental freedoms echoes the Court's avoidance of the issue of whether the unborn were 'others' for the purposes of Article 10(2) by characterising the question as one of morality.

What is singularly lacking in the Court's judgment as a whole is an acknowledgement of the facts of international life and the practical difficulties they present for a state which adheres to a particular value relating to an aspect of human rights where surrounding states adhere to an opposing norm. A policy of wide-ranging day-to-day controls on the first state's borders would undoubtedly be stigmatised as oppressive and would certainly not meet with the approval of the Court of Human Rights. On the other hand, the absence of stringent legal controls can be seized upon, as it was in *Open*

*Door*, as demonstrating the absence of a strong public policy on the issue. Whatever the state does, therefore, will be regarded as grounds for stigmatising its solution as offending against the proportionality doctrine. The state's offence, in truth, is to adhere to a value that is actively opposed by most other states. In *Open Door*, the crucial debate was not between protection of unborn life and free speech but rather as to the Convention's impact on the issue of abortion.

**The November referenda** In November 1992 the Government put three issues to the people in three separate referenda. These dealt with what had come to be referred to as the 'substantive issue' of abortion, the question of travel abroad for the purpose of having an abortion and the matter of the provision of information relating to foreign abortion facilities. Public discussion of these issues was reduced by the sudden calling of a general election, which was held on the same day as the referenda were determined.

*1. The 'substantive issue'* The referendum on the substantive issue of abortion proposed the addition to Article 40.3.3 of the following:

> It shall be unlawful to terminate the life of an unborn unless such termination is necessary to save the life, as distinct from the health, of the mother where there is an illness or disorder of the mother giving rise to a real and substantial risk to her life, not being a risk of self-destruction.

The Government adopted a curious strategy in relation to explaining the intended import of this proposed amendment. Initially the Minister for Health, Dr O'Connell, maintained that it distinguished between the direct taking of unborn life by means of abortion, which would in all cases be unlawful, and necessary medical treatment for the mother that resulted indirectly in the death of the unborn, which would not be unlawful: see Geraldine Kennedy, 'Conflicting views on when abortion is legal under wording', *Irish Times*, 10 October 1992. The Government in press briefings endorsed this interpretation: see Denis Coughlan, 'Direct abortions ruled out by Government as Fine Gael backs referendum moves', *Irish Times*, 10 October 1992. A few days later, the Minister for Justice, Mr Flynn, changed this stance. His opaque language, when closely analysed, revealed that the proposed amendment did indeed contemplate conferring express constitutional legitimacy on a range of abortions.

Undoubtedly the wording of the proposed amendment had such an effect. The expression 'terminate' clearly embraced the intentional destruction of the life of the unborn. Ironically, it was not quite so clear that the wording would have legitimated medical treatment of the mother resulting *indirectly* in the death of the unborn. Of course, in one sense, there is a clear causal nexus between the treatment and the indirect consequence, but the expression 'terminate' suggests a degree of direct connection between the actor and the result which is not easily reflected in situations where an unintended and indirect consequence of a person's actions results in the death of the unborn. Little hinges on this point, however since Article 40.3.3 as promulgated in 1983 ensures that no liability attaches to treatment with such indirect effect.

The proposed amendment clearly sought to subtract from the range of circumstances recognised in the *X* decision as warranting an abortion those cases where there was a risk of 'self-destruction'. It is difficult to identify a principled basis for this distinction. Pragmatic considerations as to how several different grounds for abortion might work out in practice appear to have influenced the Government in this context: see Hogan, 'Law, Liberty and the Abortion Controversy', in A. Whelan ed., *Law and Liberty in Ireland*, at p. 116.

The distinction drawn in the proposed amendment between the mother's life and health reflected the judgment of Finlay CJ in *X*. As we have noted, the other judges for the majority on the substantive issue did not expressly make such a differentiation; McCarthy and O'Flaherty JJ seemed to envisage legislative grounds for abortion ranging beyond life and health, whereas Egan J's discussion of the *Bourne* decision indicated no discomfort on his part with the equiparation between 'life' and 'mental health'.

The Amendment was opposed by the Pro-Life Campaign on the basis that it would have involved the people in giving their authorisation for abortion. The Campaign argued that, since the Supreme Court's decision in *X* had been directly contrary to the intent of the electorate when voting for the Eighth Amendment, there was now a democratic obligation to give the people an opportunity to re-iterate their opposition to legalised abortion or to accept the *X* holding. Mr Justice Walsh, in his lecture *Justice and the Constitution*, to which we have already referred, stated:

> Any proposal to alter the Constitution should only result from a careful and extensive examination of the need for such a change. In the present case there are all the appearances of an overhasty and superficial reaction without regard for the right of the electorate to be offered a choice. Legitimacy of government requires that if the People's views on fundamental principles are to be ascertained they must be asked the question directly. If they do not so wish, then they must be offered a choice of a test that will better guarantee and defend th[e unborn's] natural rights both now and in the future. The only choice now on offer is a little abortion or extensive abortion, and even within that 'Hobson's

> choice' there are dangerous ambiguities. Is 'necessary' to be construed objectively or subjectively? Is the permitted termination of the unborn life to be justified by a risk to life any time in the future however distant?

Opposition to the proposed Amendment was also heard from those who favoured legalised abortion. Much of this opposition extended beyond a preference for the ground stated in *X* and criticised the proposed Amendment for its distinction between the mother's life and health. In other words, the basis of this critique was that the Constitution should authorise abortion on health grounds.

At all events the proposed Amendment was roundly defeated, by 1,079,297 votes (62.7%) to 572,117 (33%) on a 68% turnout of the electorate. The number of spoiled votes, 81,835, was strikingly high.

*2. The 'travel' amendment: introduction* The Twelfth Amendment to the Constitution, passed by 1,659,367 votes (62.39%) to 624,059 (37.61%) (with 74,454 spoiled votes), adds an extra provision to Article 40.3.3, to the effect that '[t]he subsection shall not limit freedom to travel between the State and another state'. The purpose of the amendment, as advocated by the Government, was to remove the possibility of criminal or civil sanctions (notably injunctions) attaching to women going abroad to have an abortion. For analysis of the amendment, see Gerard Hogan's *Annotation* [1992] ICLSA.

Public discussion of this amendment and of the 'information' amendment, which we consider below, was not at a detailed level, in which the exact implications of the proposed change could be examined and debated. Three factors led to this curtailment of discussion. First, as we have mentioned, the three referenda were held on the same day as a general election. This meant that the time available on the media for debate of the issues raised by the referenda necessarily was shortened. Secondly, the initially uncertain meaning of the proposed amendment on the substantive issue took several days of public debate to resolve; the substantive issue was understandably given greater time and attention than the travel and information amendments. Thirdly, there was a reluctance on the part of the Government to spell out in detail what was its understanding of the effect of these amendments in specific cases.

It is necessary therefore to examine the wording of the Thirteenth Amendment with fresh eyes, in order to try to see what exactly it has achieved. The amendment, as we have seen, prevents Article 40.3.3 from limiting *freedom to travel* between the State and another State. In 1992, the expression 'travel' became, in effect, a code-word for having a foreign abortion, but from the legal standpoint it does not have this connotation. We have examined this question in detail in our analysis of the *X* decision. The essence of our critique of the judgments of McCarthy and O'Flaherty JJ (especially the former's) was that there is a distinction between a legal control on travel in general and a legal control on a particular instance of travel where the process of travel is designed to, and integral in achieving the purpose of, violating another's constitutional rights.

What is striking about the manner in which the Twelfth Amendment is drafted is that it does not confer any constitutional entitlement on the *receipt* of 'abortion services' abroad. If the intention had been to confer constitutional legitimacy on the extinction of life of an unborn abroad, in those countries where abortion is lawfully available, one might have expected that this radical change would be clearly indicated.

It must be borne in mind that Article 40.3.3 recognises that the unborn have a right to life that is equal to the right to life of their mothers, and that the Supreme Court, in *Open Door, Grogan* and *X*, has interpreted Article 40.3.3 as conferring protection on the unborn against having their lives terminated abroad. It is hard to argue that a freedom to travel implicitly embraces the right to terminate the life of an unborn on the basis of a foreign law permitting abortion on demand simply because one has a freedom to travel to a country with such an abortion regime. Denham J, dissenting, in *Attorney General at the Relation of the Society for the Protection of Unborn Children (Ireland) Ltd v Open Door Counselling Ltd* [1994] 1 ILRM 256, appeared to favour an interpretation of this breadth, and to derive from it further implications in relation to the entitlement to receive information about the identity and location of abortion clinics abroad. We shall be examining in detail the Supreme Court's judgment in these proceedings in the 1993 Review. Suffice it here to note that the Twelfth Amendment does not confer a constitutional right to abortion on demand, on condition that one has one's abortion abroad.

It is to be noted that the language of the amendment is to the effect that Article 40.3.3 'shall not limit' freedom to travel 'between the State and another state'. It thus ensures that the freedom to travel between the State and a foreign state is preserved, without in any way reducing the geographical remit of the protection afforded by Article 40.3.3 of the Constitution to the right to life of the unborn. The Amendment does not purport to restrict *the scope of the application* of Article 40.3.3 to the territory of the State. (The contrast in language with Protocol No. 17 is here instructive.) It seems that, as a result of the passage of the Twelfth Amendment, a court may not use its injunctive power to *enjoin the process of travelling abroad* even where the intent to have an abortion when abroad is plain. The amendment does not, however, give any right to have an abortion when abroad. Article 40.3.3 continues to apply to that matter, unmodified by the amendment.

It may be useful to consider briefly the relationship between the Twelfth

Amendment, Protocol No. 17 and the Solemn Declaration. As we have indicated in our discussion of Protocol No. 17, the precise effect of the protocol on the injunctive power has yet to be judicially determined. The Twelfth Amendment does not indicate whether 'freedom to travel' between the State and another state (i) refers exclusively to an Irish constitutional law right; (ii) connotes a right that is derived from an assessment of the interrelationship between the Irish Constitution and European law or (iii) refers exclusively to a Community right. Let us therefore examine the terms of the Protocol and the Solemn Declaration and then return to a consideration of the precise remit of the Twelfth Amendment.

*The Protocol* Protocol 17, which the Government negotiated in December 1991, is to the following effect:

> [n]othing in the Treaty on European Union or in the Treaties establishing the European Communities, or in the Treaties or Acts modifying or supplementing those Treaties, shall affect the application in Ireland of Article 40.3.3 of the Constitution of Ireland.

It seems beyond argument that the effect of the Protocol is to ensure that the constitutional protection of unborn life prescribed by Article 40.3.3 cannot be modified by Community law so as, for example, to strike down or alter legislation prohibiting abortion in Ireland. (We do not here address the question, considered above, as to the defects in the Court's analysis and holding in *X*. For present purposes the only point at issue is whether Community law can override or modify anti-abortion legislation regarding abortions within the State; the answer is that it cannot.)

The more controversial question relates to abortions taking place *outside* Ireland. The question here is whether the Protocol attaches to Irish legal controls, consistent with or even required by the Constitution, in respect of (i) *the giving of information* in Ireland as to foreign abortion services which assists in the destruction of an unborn life; (ii) *going abroad to have an abortion*, and (iii) *having an abortion abroad.*

The answer to this complex question must depend on the words 'in Ireland'. They could refer to the Irish legal system as a whole, in contrast to other legal systems in the Community. The difficulty with this interpretation is that, if that had been the intent, it would have been easy to say so clearly. Moreover, the words appear to have a specifically *geographical* connotation, limited to Ireland, as opposed to any other place within the confines of the Community.

If the words are to be interpreted geographically, how does that temporal delimitation operate? The Protocol throws no light on the issue. One approach that has been suggested (by Gerard Hogan, 'Protocol 17', chapter 14 of Patrick Keatinge, *Maastricht and Ireland: What the Treaty Means* (1992), at pp 115-6) concentrates on *presence of a party within the jurisdiction*. Thus, an injunction made against a woman in Ireland against her travelling abroad for an injunction would fall within the scope of the Protocol but an injunction made against an Irish woman, with similar intent but by the time of the injunction already outside the jurisdiction (though not necessarily in the country where she intended to have the abortion) would fall outside the scope of the Protocol.

The arbitrary outcomes flowing from this distinction, which depends on accidents of location and timing, lead one to conclude that this must not have been the intent of those formulating the Protocol. It is true that Irish private international law, reflecting earlier English precedent, has based jurisdiction on the mere presence of a party within the State: see W. Binchy, *Irish Conflicts of Law* (1988), 124-6, 326-7; *Rainford v Newell-Roberts* [1962] (IR) 95, *In re Magees, Infants* (1892) 31 LR (Ir) 513. Apart from the fact that this is stigmatised as an exorbitant ground of jurisdiction by Article 3(2) of the EEC Convention on Jurisdiction in Civil and Commercial Matters, there is no compelling reason why it should be the test for determining the remit of Protocol No. 17. The idea that the territorial restriction it prescribes is intended to distinguish between those within and outside the jurisdiction is entirely reasonable if it is understood in broader terms than those of strictly defined, contingent personal location at a particular time. What these terms are we consider in a moment but first we must consider another approach, which concentrates, not on the location of a party at any particular time but rather on the *occurrence of conduct within the State*. If the Protocol's geographic remit has to be determined by some tangible criterion, why should it not be that of human conduct, since the normative core of the law is to guide and direct human action?

On this approach, it might be argued that the provision of information in Ireland about the identity and location of abortion clinics in Britain is undeniably an action taking place entirely in Ireland and is one that has been identified by the Supreme Court in *Open Door* and *Grogan* as being an unconstitutional assistance in the destruction of the unborn life. It would seem very hard to argue that this conduct falls outside the scope of the Protocol.

The process of travelling abroad to have an abortion is somewhat more difficult to assess, adopting the same approach. It is undeniably conduct occurring (in its early stages at least) in Ireland. Moreover, it is conduct relevant to Article 40.3.3. This is plain from the judgments of Finlay CJ, Hederman and Egan JJ in *X*. But it is also conduct that is less integrally connected with Ireland than is the provision of information in Ireland as to the identity and location of abortion clinics in Britain. Once an informer informs, his or her conduct is complete. The full lethal effects have yet to occur, abroad, but the informer's role will by then be history. There are loose parallels here with the traditional application of the *lex loci delicti*; some courts have taken the view that the *locus* should be identified as the place where the defendant acted rather than where the consequent harm was suffered.

It could perhaps be argued that in the case of a woman travelling to Britain to have an abortion the continuum of her conduct cannot be artificially severed so as to regard Article 40.3.3 as applying to her conduct in Ireland in seeking to initiate that travel. The injunctive power envisaged by Finlay CJ, Hederman and Egan JJ was not based on the occurrence in Ireland of any particular conduct. This issue was not crucial because the questions in *X* concerned the extra-territorial remit of Article 40.3.3 and the propriety of enjoining the act of travelling to have an abortion abroad. Nothing said by these judges, however, gives support for the view that the protection afforded the unborn by Article 40.3.3 was referable only to the presence in Ireland of the defendant or the occurrence (past or apprehended) of any conduct in Ireland.

On the conduct-focused interpretation of the Protocol, if a court were faced with an application for an injunction with regard to travel from Ireland for the purpose of an abortion it would have regard to the fact that it could not respond to the whole picture relating to the proposed conduct without regard to the foreign element, namely the intended abortion abroad, and that accordingly it would have to take account of Community law in deciding whether or not to grant the injunction.

If that is so, could it not also be contended that court should equally have regard to Community law in injunction proceedings against the provision of information in Ireland of the identity and location of foreign abortion clinics? After all, the ultimate likelihood of an abortion abroad may (in some cases at least) be equally strong. The best reply is that, from the standpoint of an analysis of *conduct*, which we are here considering, the conduct consisting of giving such information is located far more centrally in Ireland than is the conduct consisting of getting onto a boat or plane in Ireland with the intention of having an abortion. In truth, the argument in favour of an injunction under Article 40.3.3 against travelling abroad for an abortion does not depend crucially on any conduct here, but, rather is directed towards the apprehended future conduct abroad. It would seem clear that, under the majority holding in *X* on the injunction issue, an Irish court would still have competence to grant an injunction against having an abortion abroad in a case where the woman had already travelled abroad.

Many people will understandably be dissatisfied with a technical analysis based either on the location of the defendant or of the conduct in which the defendant has engaged or may engage. Clearly geography is crucially relevant to Protocol No. 17, but is it to be determined by such a technical process as either of the alternatives we have examined? Of the two, the conduct-centred analysis seems more convincing. It may be, however, that the Court of Justice, when interpreting the Protocol, will dispense with a technical analysis in favour of a more robust, polic-driven, assessment of the purpose of the Protocol which was clearly to ensure two goals: that Irish public policy on abortion in Ireland would not unduly trench upon those from other countries with different values relating to abortion. In the light of the established constitutional jurisprudence at the time the Protocol was negotiated, a reasonable dividing-line would have ensured that injunctions such as had been granted in *Open Door* and *Grogan* would have been secure from modification by Community law. The Supreme Court's analysis of the travel issue (on which the Court divided three to two) had yet to be given, in *X*, three months after the Protocol had been negotiated.

*The Solemn Declaration* It is at this point that the Solemn Declaration becomes particularly relevant. It is drafted as follows:

> The High Contracting Parties to the Treaty on European Union signed in Maastricht on the 7th day of February 1992;
> Having considered the terms of Protocol No. 17 to the said Treaty on European Union which is annexed to the Treaty and to the Treaties establishing the European Communities;
> Hereby give the following legal interpretation: that it was and is their intention that the Protocol shall not limit freedom either to travel between Member States or, in accordance with conditions which may be laid down, in conformity with Community law, by Irish legislation, information relating to services lawfully available in Member States.
> At the same time, the High Contracting Parties solemnly declare that, in the event of a future constitutional amendment in Ireland which concerns the subject matter of Article 40.3.3 of the Constitution of Ireland and which does not conflict with the intention of the High Contracting Parties herein before expressed, they will, following the entry into force of the Treaty or European Union, be favourably disposed to amending the said Protocol so as to extend its application to such constitutional amendments if Ireland so requests.

The first, and most important, point to note about the Solemn Declaration is that it does not appear to be legally binding. This is the view of most commentators: see, e.g., Hogan, 'Protocol 17', chapter 14 of P. Keatinge ed.,

*Maastricht and Ireland: What the Treaty Means* (1992), at pp 118-9, Kingston & Whelan, 'The Protection of the Unborn in Three Legal Orders — Part III' (1992) 10 ILT 166, at 169 and (more tentatively) Robinson, 'European Dimensions of the Abortion Debate', in *Abortion, Law and Conscience* (1992) 273, at 279-80.

Secondly, the Solemn Declaration betrays the pragmatic political considerations that inspired its creation. The purported legal interpretation as to what the intention of the High Contracting Parties had been when the Solemn Declaration was signed is clearly inconsistent with what their actual intention had been. As Kingston and Whelan (op. cit., at 169) note,

> [m]ost observers . . . would agree that the protocol was negotiated in response, very largely, to the decision of the Court of Justice in *SPUC v Grogan*, which raised the possibility of the distribution of abortion information in Ireland on behalf of clinics established in other EC Member States. Thus, provision of information by way of assistance seems certainly to have been intended to be governed by the Protocol.

These authors and several other commentators point out that, if, as the Solemn Declaration claims, the Protocol was not *intended* to affect travel, the action of the Attorney General in seeking an injunction against travel in *X* would have been inconsistent with that intent. Moreover, as Gerry Whyte observes, the Government's attempt, after the *X* decision, to persuade the other Member States to accept a modification of the Protocol 'was arguably premised on the belief that the Protocol, as it stood, did affect rights to travel and, receive information': *Abortion Law and Conscience*, p. 266.

Eoghan Fitzsimons (*Irish Times*, 6 May 1992) has invoked Article 31(3) of the Vienna Convention on the Law of Treaties 1969 (to which Ireland is not a party) in support for the view that the Court of Justice would take account of the Solemn Declaration on the basis that it represents a post-Treaty agreement between its parties as to its interpretation. Kingston & Whelan (op. cit., at 169-70) respond that:

> [t]he Declaration is not binding on the Court, however, and it is a matter for speculation whether Fitzsimons' argument is undermined by the characterisation [by Hogan, op. cit., at 119] of the Solemn Declaration as a 'retrospective claim', at odds with the evident intention of the parties. Arguably, the argument must turn on whether the Court of Justice would favour (should a case arise) the *imputed* or the *actual* intention of the parties to the Treaty. We can only guess at the choice the Court would make'.

Let us now turn to examine the precise content of the Solemn Declaration.

There is a striking similarity between its terms and the language subsequently used in the Twelfth Amendment.

It could perhaps be argued that the latter paragraph of the Solemn Declaration indicates an intent, at the time of drafting the Protocol, that the Protocol should refer only to the exact words that were in Article 40.3.3 and that accordingly Community law would not be prevented by the Protocol from attaching to any amended Article 40.3.3. As against this, it can be replied that little weight should be attached to any aspect of the Solemn Declaration in view of its unconvincing retrospective ascriptions of intent. It may be, however, that the Court would take the view that the question of the meaning of the reference to Article 40.3.3 in the Protocol can be severed from the other questions of the interpretation and that, even if it is the case that the Solemn Declaration involved a false retrospective ascription of intent, this does not prevent the Court from deriving some assistance from the Solemn Declaration on the other questions of interpretation.

The following passage from Gerard Hogan's analysis of the precise interrelationship of Community and Irish law (op. cit., pp 119-20) is of considerable assistance:

> On the one hand, legal certainty would seem to require that our community partners should only be bound by the version of Article 40.3.3 as existed at the time of the ratification of the Treaty. On the other hand, it may plausibly be argued that the intention of the Protocol was to commit these matters entirely to the provenance of Irish constitutional law. If this argument is correct, it would mean that the Protocol includes any future changes to Article 40.3.3, at least where those changes were in harmony with the original version of that provision.

Mr Hogan considers that here is 'much force' in both of these arguments. If we take the second of them, there would no doubt be some debate about when the 'spirit' of Article 40.3.3 has been violated by a change to it, bearing in mind that every amendment would necessarily have some impact on its scope. Nonetheless, it is easy to envisage certain amendments that would clearly not be within its spirit; some analogies maybe drawn here with the variation of a contract as distinct from its substitution by an entirely new one: see *British & Beningtons Ltd v N.W. Cachar Tea Co. Ltd* [1923] AC 48.

Let us try to assemble the various strands of analysis at this point. The position appears to be as follows. Article 40.3.3, as originally formulated, enables the court, in an appropriate case, to enjoin travel abroad for the purpose of an abortion. Whether or not there is a right or freedom under Community law to travel abroad for an abortion in a state where it is lawful is not clear. In *Grogan*, Advocate General van Gerven appeared to consider that a general restriction or a right to travel for an abortion would be contrary to Community law; whether a more focused restriction would be consistent with Community law, on his analysis, is not clear: see Kingston & Whelan, op. cit., at 167.

Nor is it clear whether the Protocol excludes Community law from applying to controls on travel for this purpose. We have canvassed the competing approaches to resolving this question.

Finally, the effect of the Twelfth Amendment is also a matter of debate. On one view, it removes the power whilst conferring no constitutional entitlement whatsoever to have an abortion abroad. Accordingly, on this view, Article 40.3.3 continues to afford protection against abortions abroad. The point is of some considerable significance in a wider context since, if there were a constitutional entitlement to have an abortion abroad, this would impact on the scope and intensity of constitutional protection of the right to life of the unborn in Ireland. The use of the term 'freedom' rather than 'right' might suggest on reference to Community law, but those who argue that the Twelfth Amendment has by this term introduced a constitutional entitlement to have an abortion in other states of the European Union have a heavy onus in seeking to compromise so profoundly the protection afforded the right to life of the unborn. Neither a literal nor purposive interpretation would warrant such a radical conclusion.

When one turns to examine the relationship between the Twelfth Amendment and the Protocol, the first question, of interpretation, concerns the reference to Article 40.3.3. If it is to Article 40.3.3 as originally formulated, then the revised Article 40.3.3 is not protected by the Protocol from the application of Community law. It is a separate question whether the Twelfth Amendment (in conjunction with the Thirteenth Amendment) permits the partial or full application of Community law, *as a matter of Irish constitutional law*. The observations of Walsh and McCarthy JJ in *Grogan* make it plain that Irish constitutional law need not necessarily be consistent with Community law. Thus, even if as a matter of Community law, there is a right (or freedom) to travel abroad for an abortion, the Irish court, in assessing the revised Article 40.3.3, in conjunction with the reception of Community law into our Constitution, is free to hold that the protection of the unborn would be improperly compromised by such a degree of absorption of Community law. The political pressures on Irish courts to avoid such an international conflict are, of course, intense and must be taken into account in assessing probable future legal developments.

3. *The 'information' amendment* The Thirteenth Amendment, adopted by a majority of 992,833 (59.88%) to 665,106 (40.12%) (with 74,494 votes spoiled), comprises an addition to Article 40.3.3, in the following terms:

> This subsection shall not limit freedom to obtain or make available, in the State, subject to such conditions as may be laid down by law, information relating to services lawfully available in another state.

For analysis of the amendment, see Gerard Hogan's *Annotation* [1992] ICLSA.

The meaning of this amendment was raised in *Attorney General at the Relation of the Society for the Protection of Unborn Children (Ireland) Ltd v Open Door Counselling Ltd* [1994] 1 ILRM 256, where, however, the majority (Finlay CJ, Hederman, Egan and Blayney JJ; Denham J dissenting) declined to address this issue, since it considered that the matter had not been fully argued and decided in the High Court. We have already indicated that we shall discuss this case in detail in the 1993 Review.

It is clear that the Thirteenth Amendment does not render lawful the activity of abortion referral. The Supreme Court, in *Open Door*, held that abortion referral constituted assistance in bringing about the termination of unborn life. The Government's information booklet, delivered to every home before the referendum, made it clear that the amendment would not permit abortion referral. Nothing in the language of the amendment supports the argument that abortion referral has been rendered lawful.

The crucial question of interpretation in relation to the Thirteenth Amendment concerns the scope of information that is encompassed by the expression 'information relating to services lawfully available in another state'. The proponents of the amendment argue that the effect of the passage of the amendment is to permit the transmission of information as to the identity and location of abortion clinics abroad, which the Supreme Court held to be contrary to Article 40.3.3 in *Open Door* and *Grogan* on the basis that it constituted assistance in the ultimate termination of the life of the unborn. They point to the fact that in *Grogan* the Court of Justice held that abortion clinics were providing 'services' for the purposes of Community law.

The opponents of the amendment contend that it should not be so interpreted. They point out that Article 40.3.3 confers generous protection to the right to life of the unborn, recognising that the unborn's right to life is equal to that of the mother. The idea that the unborn's right to life could be reduced to a right of such fragility that it could lawfully be extinguished by geographic relocation to a place fifty miles away is so fundamentally inconsistent with the values underlying Article 40.3.3 that the expression 'information relating to services lawfully available in another state' should be interpreted harmoniously with the protection of unborn life to the maximum extent. On this approach, it would be permissible to give and receive full factual information about the nature of abortion and its physical and psychological effects, for example, but it remains contrary to the law to give information as to the identity and location of abortion clinics, since this constitutes assistance in bringing about the destruction of unborn life, as the Supreme Court held in *Open Door* and *Grogan*.

It may be argued that an amendment achieving only this limited result was scarcely worth the trouble. To this it can be responded that it removed the widespread misunderstanding that *all* information about the subject of abortion was censored. Under Article 46.1, as Barrington J noted in *Finn v Minister for the Environment* [1983] IR 154, at 164, the people have 'power to clarify or make more explicit anything already in the Constitution'. Whether this interpretation harmonises with the political realities, including the Government's explanation of what the amendment was seeking to achieve, may be debated.

Other issues relating to the amendment concern the questions whether it is self-executing and the permissible scope of conditions that the Oireachtas may impose. In the Supreme Court hearing in 1993 ([1994] 1 ILRM 256), Denham J, was of the view that the amendment was indeed self-executing. The majority taking no position on the question.

It is necessary to say a few words in conclusion about the relationship between the Thirteenth Amendment and Community law. First, there is the question whether the words of the amendment itself seek to embrace Community law within the ambit of Article 40.3.3. The expression 'freedom' rather than 'right', as in the Twelfth Amendment, might suggest that it does, but again the case against this interpretation is strong, in the light of how the Supreme Court characterised the giving of information about the identity and location of foreign abortion clinics in *Open Door* and *Grogan*. The point here is not, of course, that these decisions cannot, in effect, be overruled by a constitutional amendment but rather that the interpretation of any constitutional amendment must take account of how subversive of the right to life the provision of this type of information was regarded in these decisions.

The next question is whether the Protocol protects Article 40.3.3 in the light of the revision effected by the Thirteenth Amendment. If the Protocol protects revisions of Article 40.3.3 which capture the spirit of the original, then the Thirteenth Amendment would appear to constitute such a revision. (There is, however, a problem of severance: if, for example, the Thirteenth but not the Twelfth Amendment was in the same spirit as the original, is it possible to hold that Community law applies in one respect but not the other?)

It is now necessary to examine the position on the hypothesis that the Thirteenth Amendment is not protected by the Protocol *and* that Community law applies. (It should be noted that the latter does not flow inevitably from the former: it is possible that the Thirteenth Amendment, in conjunction with the Eighth Amendment, prescribes constitutional norms that are not in harmony with Community law. Walsh and McCarthy JJ raised this possibility with regard to the Eighth Amendment and, as we have seen, the Thirteenth Amendment has not necessarily altered the position on this issue.) If, therefore, Community law applies, does this mean that a restriction on information as to the identity and location of foreign abortion clinics is necessarily inconsistent with Community law? Advocate General van Gerven in *Open Door* thought not (see Kingston & Whelan, op. cit., at 168). This is an opinion that has provoked much controversy: see, e.g., Phelan, op. cit., at 685, de Búrca, op. cit., at 306ff.

## LOCUS STANDI

**Attorney General** In *Attorney General v Mr Justice Hamilton* [1993] ILRM 81; [1993] 2 IR 250, the Supreme Court dealt with the standing of the Attorney General in a judicial review from a ruling of the tribunal of inquiry into the beef processing industry: see 212-17, below.

**General rule** In *Desmond and Dedeir v Glackin, Minister for Industry and Commerce and Ors (No. 2)* [1993] 3 IR 67, the standing of the plaintiffs to challenge the validity of s. 10 of the Companies Act 1990 was raised: see the discussion in the Company Law chapter, 74-81, above.

## OIREACHTAS

**Allowances and pensions** The Oireachtas (Allowances to Members) and Ministerial and Parliamentary Offices (Amendment) Act 1992 enables further effect be given to a number of recommendations of the Review Body on Higher Remuneration in the Public Sector, which had been chaired by Dermot Gleeson SC. The Act also deals with the issue of Ministerial pensions. The Act came into force generally on its signature by the President on 18 March 1992, but certain sections required Commencement Orders and others had retrospective effect to take account of amendments being made to existing statutory provisions. It can also be noted that the somewhat unwieldy title of the Act provides for some even more unwieldy titles of the Statutory Instruments made under it, as can be seen below.

In relation to what might be described as ordinary expenses, Gleeson had recommended that the regime concerning expenses of Oireachtas members be brought more into line with that for other taxpayers. This was implemented in ss. 3 and 4 of the 1992 Act. The Oireachtas (Allowances to Members) and Ministerial and Parliamentary Offices (Amendment) Act 1992 (Allowances) Regulations 1992 (SI No. 62) gave effect to the new regime from 6 April

1992. Further amendments were introduced by the Oireachtas (Allowances to Members) and Ministerial and Parliamentary Offices (Amendment) Act 1992 (Allowances) (No. 2) Regulations 1992 (SI No. 397). S. 11 of the 1992 Act, substituting a new s. 2 of the Oireachtas (Allowances to Members) Act 1962, confirms the existing regime of free telephone and postal facilities from Leinster House and introduces a new contribution scheme for calls other than from Leinster House. The new contribution scheme came into effect on 1 April 1992: see Oireachtas (Allowances to Members) Act 1962 (Commencement) Order 1992 (SI No. 141). The details of the contribution scheme are contained in the Oireachtas (Allowances to Members) (Amendment) Regulations 1992 (SI No. 142).

The other major issue dealt with by the 1992 Act is the pensions paid to former Ministers who continue to be members of the Oireachtas after they lose Ministerial office. This issue had become a matter of public controversy in the late 1980s when Desmond O'Malley and Robert Molloy of the Progressive Democrats Party had declined to accept the Ministerial pensions to which they were entitled and had proposed changing the existing regime. The matter is now dealt with in s. 7 of the 1992 Act, which inserted new sections 13A and 13B into the Ministerial and Parliamentary Offices Act 1936. The main effect of s. 7 of the 1992 Act is that such pensions will not normally be paid in the future to a former Minister until the age of 55. It should be noted, however, that s. 7 of the 1992 Act operated prospectively, from the election of the Taoiseach following the general election which first occurred after the Act was passed (see s. 6 of the 1992 Act). In other words, it became operative on the election of the Taoiseach in January 1993 in the wake of the November 1992 general election. The 1992 Act thus did not affect existing pensions payable under the Ministerial and Parliamentary Offices Act 1936. The relevant amendments to the existing pension scheme were effected by the Houses of the Oireachtas (Members) Pensions (Amendment) Scheme 1992 (SI No. 300) and the Houses of the Oireachtas (Members) Pensions (Amendment) (No. 2) Scheme 1992 (SI No. 354). S. 10 of the 1992 Act also introduced a severance payment in respect of former holders of ministerial and parliamentary offices.

Finally, one other item dealt with in the 1992 Act was the introduction of a 'termination allowance' for ordinary members who lose their seat. This is dealt with in s. 5 of the Act, which came into effect on 1 November 1992: Oireachtas (Allowances to Members) and Ministerial and Parliamentary Offices (Amendment) Act 1992 (Section 5) (Commencement) Order 1992 (SI No. 355). The details of the allowance are prescribed in the Oireachtas (Termination Allowance) Regulations 1992 (SI No. 356).

**Legislation: expression of principles** In *Ambiorix Ltd and Ors v Minister* *for the Environment and Ors (No. 2)* [1992] 2 IR 37, Lynch J rejected a claim that the Urban Renewal Act 1986 was in breach of Article 15 of the Constitution for granting an unconstitutional delegation of the power to legislate to Ministers: see the Local Government chapter, 461-3, below.

## PRESIDENT

In April 1992, the government advised the President to exercise her right of pardon under Article 13.6 of the Constitution in respect of Nicky Kelly, who had been convicted in 1976 of an armed robbery usually known as the Sallins Mail Train robbery: see *Irish Times*, 29 April 1992. The granting of the Presidential pardon in this case brought to an end a long campaign by Mr Kelly to clear his name in what had become as famous a miscarriage of justice as the Birmingham Six and Guildford Four cases had been in Britain. For some background on the Sallins case, see the 1989 Review, 358-61. On the legal effect of a pardon and some criticisms, see Michael McDowell's article (1991) 1 ICLJ 9. We may also note that, arising from the Sallins case, a mechanism for reopening criminal cases though a referral by the Minister for Justice to the Court of Criminal Appeal was introduced by the Criminal Procedure Act 1993, to which we will return in the 1993 Review.

## PRIVACY

In *Desmond and Dedeir v Glackin, Minister for Industry and Commerce and Ors (No. 2)* [1993] 3 IR 67, the right to privacy was raised: see the discussion in the Company Law chapter, 74-81, above.

## PROPERTY

**Retrospection** In *Chestvale Properties Ltd and Hoddle Investments Ltd v Glackin* [1992] ILRM 221; [1993] 3 IR 35, Murphy J rejected a claim that the Companies Act 1990, in allowing inspections concerning transactions effected before the Act came into force, was in breach of Articles 40.3 and 43 of the Constitution: see the Company Law chapter, 69-74, above.

**Unjust attack** In *Hempenstall and Ors v Minister for the Environment* [1993] ILRM 318, the plaintiffs claimed that certain Regulations made by the Minister for the Environment under the Road Traffic Act 1961 had had the effect of reducing the value of their taxi licences and that this constitued an unjust attack on their property rights. In the course of a review of the operation of taxi and hackney cab licences, the Minister made Regulations in 1991 which placed a moratorium on the issuing of hackney cab licences. A press statement issued with the Regulations indicated that this would be a temporary moratorium and, after further review of the situation, the Minister lifted the moratorium in the Road Traffic (Public Service Vehicles) (Amendment) Regulations 1992 (SI No. 172). It was the 1992 Regulations which the plaintiffs claimed constituted an unjust attack on their property rights. This was because there was at all times a thriving trade in the sale of taxi licence plates, and each plaintiff had paid over £35,000 each for their licence plate. They claimed that, as result of the lifting of the moratorium on the issuing of new hackney cab licences, the value of their taxi licences would be severely diminished.

Costello J rejected the plaintiff's arguments, primarily on a finding of facts. He accepted the evidence adduced that, in fact, the sale of taxi licence plates did not appear to have been affected by the lifting of the moratorium on hackney cab licences under the 1992 Regulations. On this basis, therefore, he found that there was no attack on the plaintiff's property rights.

Moreover, while he accepted (as the Minister had) that the taxi licence constituted a valuable property right, Costello J did not necessarily consider that, even if the value of the taxi licence had been adversely affected by the 1992 Regulations, this would have constitued an unjust attack on the plaintiffs' rights. He held that since the taxi licence was a property right created by law, its value could be affected by a subsequent law, and there was an implied condition attaching to such property rights that they may be affected by subsequent laws. This approach mirrors the issues which arose in *Hand v Dublin Corporation* [1991] ILRM 556; [1991] 1 IR 409 (1991 Review, 104-5) and *Cox v Ireland* [1992] 2 IR 503 (1991 Review, 105-7), though neither cases are referred to in Costello J's judgment.

## REFERENDA

**Information on polling cards** S. 1 of the Referendum (Amendment) Act 1992 laid down the format of the information to be placed on polling cards in relation to the referendum held on 18 June 1992 on the Eleventh Amendment of the Constitution, which dealt with the Maastricht Treaty on European Union and the Agreement on European Community Patents. The information given consisted primarily of the text of the proposed constitutional amendments, which were approved in the June 1992 referendum: see the European Community chapter, 326-7, below and the Commercial Law chapter, above,

33-4. The Referendum (Special Difficulty) Order 1992 (SI No. 128) dealt with the problems associated with posting the polling cards to voters during a postal strike which occurred at the time preceding the referendum.

S. 2 of the 1992 Act is of a more significant general impact. It provides that, in future referenda, a statement of information may be prescribed by resolution of both Houses of the Oireachtas, subject to the procedural matters referred to in s.1 of the 1992 Act.

It may be noted that the procedure laid out in s. 2 of the Referendum (Amendment) Act 1992 was not used for the three referenda held on 25 November 1992 concerning Article 40.3.3, as to which see the discussion, below, 214, 217. Instead, s. 1 of the Referendum (Amendment) (No. 2) Act 1992 laid down the format of the information to be placed on polling cards for the three referenda, primarily because of the fact that three separate information cards were required, and the Act laid down the colouring scheme for the cards. S. 2 of the Referendum (Amendment) (No. 2) Act 1992 specifically provided that the procedure in s. 2 of the Referendum (Amendment) Act 1992 would not apply to the three referenda in question.

Finally, it may be noted that the three referenda were held on the same date as the 1992 general election, 25 November 1992, rather than the original date specified, 3 December 1992. Since the Dáil had been dissolved (on 4 November 1992) after the Referendum (Amendment) (No. 2) Act 1992 had been passed (on 30 October 1992), the Minister for the Environment was authorised by s. 9 of the Referendum Act 1942 to bring forward the referenda to the date of the general election. This was effected by the Dáil Election and Referenda Regulations 1992 (SI No. 340).

**Non-interference by judiciary** A number of unsuccessful challenges to aspects of the referendum campaign concerning the Maastricht Treaty on European Union are discussed below, 217-20.

## RETROSPECTIVE CRIMINAL LAWS

The operation of Article 15.5 of the Constitution was considered in *Chestvale Properties Ltd and Hoddle Investments Ltd v Glackin* [1992] ILRM 221 (see the Company Law chapter, 68-73, above) and in *McGrath v Garda Commissioner (No. 2)* [1993] ILRM 38 (see the Garda Síochána chapter, 383, below).

## SEPARATION OF POWERS

**Cabinet confidentiality** In *Attorney General v Mr Justice Hamilton* [1993] ILRM 81; [1993] 2 IR 250, the Supreme Court, by a 3-2 majority, held that, under Article 28.4 of the Constitution, there was an absolute ban on disclosure of the contents of discussions at cabinet, at least in the context of a tribunal of inquiry having the powers contained in the Tribunals of Inquiry (Evidence) Acts 1921 and 1979.

The background to the case was the establishment of a tribunal of inquiry into the beef processing industry, pursuant to resolutions passed by both Houses of the Oireachtas on 24 May 1991. The background to the resolutions and their effect is discussed in *Goodman International v Mr Justice Hamilton* [1992] ILRM 145; [1992] 2 IR 542 (see the 1991 Review, 109-11).

The respondent, President of the High Court, had been appointed the chairman and sole member of the tribunal of inquiry. In the course of the tribunal's hearings, a former Minister for Justice was examined by counsel for the tribunal concerning the details of discussions which took place at meetings of the cabinet, that is the executive branch of government, on 8 June 1988. Counsel for the Attorney General objected to these questions on the ground that discussions at government were absolutely confidential pursuant to Article 28.4 of the Constitution. The respondent indicated that he intended to pursue the questioning of the former Minister, and the Attorney General was then given an opportunity to apply for judicial review of this ruling.

In the High Court, O'Hanlon J upheld the respondent's ruling and found that cabinet discussion were open to scrutiny. This decision was reversed by the Supreme Court.

O'Hanlon J had relied on a line of Supreme Court decisions concerning claims for executive or public interest privilege in applications for discovery of documents, in particular *Murphy v Dublin Corporation* [1972] IR 215 and *Ambiorix Ltd v Minister for the Environment* [1992] ILRM 209; [1992] 1 IR 277 (see the 1991 Review, 338-9). O'Hanlon J concluded that these decisions militated against an absolute claim for confidentiality in government deliberations, and that they were relevant to the instant case since it also concerned the balance to be struck between an individual's legal rights and the claims of the executive. He felt that the claim to an absolute blanket of confidentiality put forward by the Attorney General in the instant case would not have due regard to the rights of the individual guaranteed by the Constitution, and if such a ban had been intended it would have been spelt out in clear terms in the Constitution, as it had been in relation to the freedom from arrest for Oireachtas members in Article 15.13. He concluded his judgment with a comment which received considerable publicity at the time:

> It has not been unknown in the history of government in other countries for totally corrupt governments to come to power and for the members to enrich themselves dishonestly at the cost of the public purse. Were

> such a situation to arise at some unforeseen future time in our own country and were the information to leak out of discussions at cabinet level at which such a nefarious plot was being considered, the legal submissions now advanced on behalf of the [Attorney General] would — if accepted as correct — prevent any future tribunal of inquiry appointed by the Houses of the Oireachtas from obtaining the information it needed to establish guilt where guilt existed.
>
> I do not consider that our Constitution has failed to protect the public interest in the manner suggested. It would hardly be a model of its kind if it were so deficient in such an important respect.

This strong statement in support of the conclusions reached by O'Hanlon J echo the similar sentiments he had expressed in connection with freedom of speech in his judgment in *The State (Lynch) v Cooney* [1983] ILRM 89; [1982] IR 337, in which he found s. 31 of the Broadcasting (Authority) Act 1960 to be unconstitutional. It will be recalled that, in Lynch, the Supreme Court reversed his finding in that case in a judgment which placed considerably less emphasis on the importance of individual rights and leaned towards emphasising the importance of the common good and institutional stability. With the benefit of hindsight vision, it might be said that the omens in the instant case were not good. At least, that is how it turned out. The Supreme Court, by a 3-2 majority, reversed O'Hanlon J.

The Court first dealt with a preliminary point, on which it was unanimous. It had been argued that the Attorney General lacked *locus standi* to maintain these judicial review proceedings. The Court rejected this suggestion on the ground that the proceedings related to an issue which the Attorney had claimed was fundamental to the whole operation of government and, if his contention was correct, he had the clearest duty to intervene. The Court also dismissed as irrelevant the point that the issue concerned an implication from an express constituional provision as opposed to a fully expressed constitutional provision, thus rejecting the suggested distinction between the instant case and the two recent Article 40.3.3 cases, *Attorney General (SPUC Ltd) v Open Door Counselling Ltd* [1987] ILRM 477; [1988] IR 593 (see the 1987 Review, 97-8) and *Attorney General v X.* [1992] ILRM 401; [1992] 1 IR 1 (discussed 158, above).

The Court then moved on the to substantive issue on which, as already indicated, it was divided 3-2 (Finlay CJ, Hederman and O'Flaherty JJ; McCarthy and Egan JJ dissenting).

On the question of the leading case law on discovery of documents, *Murphy v Dublin Corporation* [1972] IR 215 and *Ambiorix Ltd v Minister for the Environment* [1992] ILRM 209; [1992] 1 IR 277, on which O'Hanlon J had relied in the High Court, the majority view was that none of these cases had directly raised the issue of government or cabinet discussions. In any event, the majority argued, since they concerned the exercise of the judicial power, the principles invoked in them could not automatically be applied to the question of evidence adduced before a tribunal of inquiry appointed on foot of resolutions passed by the Houses of the Oireachtas.

However, the major part of the judgments delivered in the Supreme Court involved a much more expansive discussion than a review of the discovery cases. All five judges delivered reasoned judgments in which they examined the issue raised in the context of the Constitution as a whole. Given that this left the judges at large, it is not perhaps surprising that they arrived at different conclusions as to what the Constitution, read as a whole, might indicate.

The majority view emphasised the need for orderly government. For example, the Chief Justice's analysis of the obligation on government Ministers in Article 28.4, to meet and act as a collective authority and to be collectively responsible for any decision made, led him to conclude that this:

> involves, as a necessity, the non-disclosure of different or dissenting views held by members of the government prior to the making of decisions.

Finlay CJ buttressed this view by an extended discussion of the implications of the doctrine of the separation of powers deriving from Article 6 of the Constitution, as well as the need to interpret the Constitution 'in its entirety in the manner most likely to make it an effective instrument for the ordering of society and the governing of the Nation'.

He also addressed an 'historical' point made by counsel for the Tribunal, and supported by the minority judges, McCarthy and Egan JJ. This was that, since Articles 26.2.2 and 34.4.5 had expressly inserted provisions prohibiting the expression of dissenting opinions in Supreme Court decisions concerning post-1937 legislation, this indicated that express bans on disclosure of information were required, and that implying such bans was inconsistent with the overall tenor of the constitutional text. However, Finlay CJ considered that Articles 26.2.2 and 34.4.5 laid down no such general proposition and were properly to be interpreted by reference to the historical context in which they had been inserted after the Supreme Court decision in *In re the Offences against the State (Amendment) Bill 1940* [1940] IR 470.

In a related 'historical' issue, the majority held that, having regard to the indications that it was the invariable practice of the Houses of the Oireachtas not to seek information from government Ministers on cabinet discussions, this supported the claim to confidentiality in the instant case. In his last judgment before his untimely death, McCarthy J, in reply, adverted to the fact that many past government ministers, notably Noel Browne (*Against the*

*Tide*), Gemma Hussey (*At the Cutting Edge*) and a former Taoiseach, Garret FitzGerald (*All in a Life*) had published memoirs which included references to discussions at Cabinet level. While not citing these as definitive evidence of the non-existence of the absolute confidentiality claimed by the majority, McCarthy J indicated that he was 'not prepared to accept that former members of government would consciously breach the constitutional norm'. Drawing on his own forensic experience, McCarthy J also cited the evidence given in the Central Criminal Court in the second 1970 'Arms Trial', citing it as *The People v Luykx*, though without adding '*and Ors*' in the title; McCarthy J had been senior counsel for one of the defendants in this trial.

Ultimately, of course, the majority view upholding the claim to absolute confidentiality prevailed. Having accepted the Attorney General's arguments, the Chief Justice summed up the effect of the Court's decision towards the end of his judgment as follows:

> I would, therefore, conclude that the claim for confidentiality of the contents and details of discussions at meetings of the government, made by the Attorney General in relation to the inquiry of this tribunal, is a valid claim. It extends to discussions and to their contents, but it does not, of course, extend to the decisions made and the documentary evidence of them, whether they are classified as formal or informal decisions. It is a constitutional right [*sic*] which, in my view, goes to the fundamental machinery of government, and is, therefore, not capable of being waived by any individual member of government, nor in my view are the details and contents of discussions at meetings of the government capable of being made public, for the purpose of this inquiry, by a decision of any succeeding government.

This paragraph is clearly stated in absolutist terms and, like the passage quoted above from the judgment of O'Hanlon J in the High Court, it received a large amount of publicity in the aftermath of the Supreme Court decision in the case. It was criticised for its absolutism in that it appeared to support the proposition that all cabinet discussions were absolutely confidential for all time. Thus, some commentators queried whether the decision placed a constitutional question mark over the provisions of the National Archives Act 1986. It was also pointed out that cabinet 'leaks' amounted almost to a national pastime. See, for example, Vincent Browne, *Sunday Tribune*, 23 August 1992.

Undoubtedly, the majority decision is difficult to reconcile with existing case law, particularly the general thrust of the discovery cases. However, two points need to made in particular in relation to the passage quoted from the Chief Justice's judgment. First, it must, like all judgments, be read *secondum subjectam materiam*, in other words, against the background of the precise issue raised in the case. The passage quoted twice refers to the context of a claim for confidentiality in relation to the proceedings of a tribunal of inquiry. This places the first limit on the potential breadth of the decision. That point was also reflected in the majority's analysis of the previous discovery cases, which had all related to proceedings wholly in the judicial sphere. The second point to note is that the Chief Justice makes no reference to the release of cabinet papers, but simply to evidence of cabinet discussions in the context of a tribunal of inquiry. Again, the context indicates that this will involve 'live' controversies, and thus the decision of the majority is somewhat narrower in that light.

In summing up, however, it must be said that the majority decision is open to misreading, perhaps in part because of the trenchant nature of the language used by the judges themselves. However, a parallel might be drawn with the case law on Article 40.3.3, *Attorney General (SPUC Ltd) v Open Door Counselling Ltd* [1987] ILRM 477; [1988] IR 593 (see the 1987 Review, 97-8) and *Attorney General v X.* [1992] ILRM 401; [1992] 1 IR 1, discussed in the *locus standi* context in the instant case. Any commentator who had suggested that the judges in the first case would have supported the arguments made by the defendant in the second case might have been regarded as somewhat fanciful. However, that is precisely what happened: the precise circumstances were, apparently, highly influential to the outcome. In that light, the decision in *Attorney General v Mr Justice Hamilton* [1993] ILRM 81; [1993] 2 IR 250 may not prove as wide-ranging as it might at first blush.

**Division or separation** In a phrase which will undoubtedly gain currency in the future, O'Hanlon J stated in *Desmond and Dedeir v Glackin, Minister for Industry and Commerce and Ors (No. 2)* [1993] 3 IR 67 (see further the Company Law chapter, 74-81, above) that the protection of a free society would not be better served by the operation of affairs of State in water-tight compartments.

**Justiciable controversy** The issue of justiciable and non-justiciable controversies arose in three decisions challenging the government's campaign during the referendum on the Treaty on European Union, the Maastricht Treaty (the Treaty is discussed in the European Communities chapter, 326-30, below). In each case, the High Court and Supreme Court declined to become involved in what the judges saw as political controversies.

In the first of the three cases, *McKenna v An Taoiseach and Ors*, High Court, 8 June 1992, the plaintiff, a citizen of Ireland and member of a political party, sought injunctive relief concerning the manner in which the government was conducting its referendum campaign on the Maastricht Treaty. The plaintiff argued that the government was acting in breach of the Constitution by conducting a partisan campaign in favour of the Treaty; that it was obliged in such circumstances to provide funding for a 'no' campaign; that it was misleading the public on the contents and effects of the Treaty; and that the government had infringed the plaintiff's constitutional rights, *inter alia*, to express freely her convictions and opinions. Since the referendum was due to be held on 18 June 1992, the plaintiff's application for interlocutory relief was treated as if it was the trial of the action to enable the High Court adjudicate on the merits of the claim. In an *ex tempore* judgment, Costello J dismissed the claim for relief.

Costello J displayed some sympathy for the plaintiff's grievance that, as a person involved in a small political party opposed to the government's campaign, her campaign would be deprived of the benefits which the government had conferred on itself from public funds. However, he considered that this grievance was in the political and non-justiciable sphere and that the judiciary was not empowered by the Constitution to remedy such a grievance since to do so would, he considered, weaken the judicial role. Thus, since the plaintiff's complaint was one of political misconduct (and Costello J made it clear that he would express no view on that complaint) she had failed to establish any constitutional impropriety.

He also held that it would be inappropriate for him to express any view on the plaintiff's specific complaint that the government's booklet 'A Short Guide to the Maastricht Treaty' was misleading, since this complaint was the staple of political debate and not a matter on which the courts should adjudicate.

On the question of communication rights, Costello J stated that, even if the plaintiff could establish that the government's campaign had rendered less effective the communications she wished to make to fellow citizens, this did not involve any infringement of her constitutionally protected right to communicate. Nor did he consider that it deprived her of her right to have equality of voting in the referendum vote.

In the second case involving the Maastricht referendum campaign, *Slattery and Ors v An Taoiseach and Ors* [1993] 1 IR 286, the plaintiffs argued that the government had failed to provide the citizens of the State with sufficient information on the Maastricht Treaty which would enable them to cast their votes in the referendum in an informed manner.

The Bill containing the text of the proposed amendments to Article 29.4.3, the Eleventh Amendment of the Constitution Bill 1992, had been published in April 1992. The plaintiffs instituted proceedings on 5 June 1992, three days after a referendum on the Treaty in Denmark had been defeated (of course, a subsequent referendum held in Denmark in 1993 approved the

Maastricht Treaty). As we noted in the context of the *McKenna* case, above, the date fixed for the referendum in Ireland was 18 June 1992.

A preliminary hurdle for the plaintiffs was that they sought leave to serve notice of application for interlocutory relief during the Trinity vacation, which commenced on 5 June 1992 and which was to end on 17 June. In the High Court, Costello J held that the plaintiffs had not made out a case for obtaining leave to serve notice of application during the vacation, there being no valid reason why they had not instituted proceedings prior to 5 June. In any event, however, Costello J would have refused leave on the ground that the plaintiffs were unlikely to succeed in obtaining any relief at the interlocutory stage, having regard to the judgment he had delivered only minutes before in the *McKenna* case, above.

The plaintiffs unsuccessfully appealed to the Supreme Court. Reflecting the views expressed by Costello J in the *McKenna* case, the Court (Hederman, McCarthy and Egan JJ) held that to grant the plaintiffs interlocutory relief on the ground that the government had failed to provide information on the effects of the Maastricht Treaty would be a wholly unwarranted intrusion by the courts into the legislative domain provided for under the Constitution. Citing the decisions in *Wireless Dealers Association v Minister for Industry and Commerce*, Supreme Court, 14 March 1956 and *Finn v Attorney General* [1983] IR 154, the Court pointed out that under the Constitution the Oireachtas had the sole power to set in train the procedure for amending the Constitution; and that the plaintiffs had not made out any case that the government had acted in breach of the Constitution in carrying through the decision of the Oireachtas to propose an amendment to Article 29.4.3 of the Constitution in order to accede to the Maastricht Treaty.

In a concurring judgment, McCarthy J noted that the plaintiffs had been able fully to avail of their right of access to the courts since the High Court and the Supreme Court had not confined themselves to the question of whether leave to serve notice of application during the Vacation should be granted.

The third case concerning the Maastricht referendum campaign was *McCann v An Taoiseach and Ors (No. 2)*, High Court, 5 October 1992. Here the plaintiff, a citizen and practising barrister, unsuccessfully sought injunctive relief concerning a broadcast due to be made by An Taoiseach on Radio Telefís Éireann concerning government policy in the referendum campaign on the Maastricht Treaty. RTE had been requested by the government to make arrangements for the broadcast under s. 31(2) of the Broadcasting Authority Act 1960 on the ground that it constituted a Ministerial announcement. The plaintiff argued that the broadcast would not constitute an announcement as it would be a highly partisan one in favour of the Treaty; and that, alternatively, RTE was obliged to provide time for a reply to An

Taoiseach's broadcast. Carney J dismissed the claims in June 1992, his reasoned judgment being delivered in October 1992.

Carney J considered that the word 'announcement' in s. 31(2) of the 1960 Act should be construed broadly, and stated strongly that it was An Taoiseach's right and duty to support the government's policy and to encourage his audience to vote for that position with every argument he can muster. He added that An Taoiseach was entitled to do this in the context of a broadcast under s. 31(2).

As to the claimed right of reply, Carney J noted that the 1960 Act did not make provision for a right of reply to a Ministerial broadcast, and he contrasted this with the requirement of impartiality concerning general affairs broadcasts imposed on RTE by s.18 of the 1960 Act, as amended by s.3 of the Broadcasting Authority (Amendment) Act 1976. Carney J also rejected, in a terse and laconic passage, the plaintiff's argument that there was any right of reply implicit or explicit in the Constitution. Although he did not cite any authority in support of this conclusion, he could have referred in this context to the judgment of Costello J in *McKenna v An Taoiseach*, High Court, 8 June 1992, discussed above. It will be recalled that in *McKenna*, Costello J had invoked the separation of powers to preclude judicial intervention in what he considered were political controversies. Resonances of this approach can be seen in the judgment of Carney J in the *McCann* case, where he cited with approval the dicta of Walsh J in *Crotty v An Taoiseach* [1987] ILRM 400; [1987] IR 713 (on which see generally the 1987 Review, 91-3) to the effect that statements of government policy as such are not restrainable by the courts.

These three decisions reflect the unbroken line of recent authority, some of which was expressly cited in Slattery, in which the courts lean against any interference with the mechanics of the legislative process. It seems unlikely, therefore, that the courts are prepared to suggest that either Article 40.1 or Article 40.6.1.i requires the State to provide funding for views which are different from those expressed by the government of the day. While any legislation providing such funding would probably survive a constitutional challenge, the courts seem unwilling to enter that particular arena by establishing a positive right to State funding. Even in the judicial domain, the courts have in recent years appeared reluctant to impose financial constraints on the State, as *Cosgrove v Legal Aid Board* [1991] 2 IR 43 (1990 Review, 144-7) illustrates.

**Replacement of invalid rule: consortium** In *McKinley v Minister for Defence* [1992] 2 IR 333, the Supreme Court replaced the common law action for consortium, which was confined to a claim by the husband for loss of the services of his wife, with a 'constitutional' action for consortium open to both husband and wife. On the implications of this approach, see the discussion earlier in this chapter, 144, above.

## SEVERABILITY

In *Desmond and Dedeir v Glackin, Minister for Industry and Commerce and Ors (No. 2)* [1993] 3 IR 67, the severability test in *Maher v Attorney General* [1973] IR 140 was applied: see the discussion of the case in the Company Law chapter, 74-81, above.

## SUPREME COURT JURISDICTION

In *Hay v O'Grady* [1992] ILRM 689; [1992] 1 IR 210, the Supreme Court noted that, although O.58 of the Rules of the Superior Courts 1986 provides that appeals to the Supreme Court shall be by way of re-hearing, this was to be interpreted as involving a re-hearing of the legal issues arising in the court of trial and did not extend to a re-hearing of the oral evidence given at the trial court. The Court concluded that it had itself, in effect, limited its jurisdiction under Article 34.4.3 of the Constitution in the case law on this topic. The decision is dicussed in detail in the Practice and Procedure chapter, 470, below.

## TRIAL OF OFFENCES

**Burden of proof** *Hardy v Ireland*, High Court, 10 September 1992; Supreme Court, 18 March 1993 was an unsuccessful challenge to the validity of s. 4 of the Explosive Substances Act 1883. The plaintiff's argument that s. 4 of the 1883 Act invalidly transferred the burden of proof from the prosecution to the defence in respect of the offence of possession of explosives was rejected successively by Flood J in the High Court and by the Supreme Court. In this respect, the decision of Costello J in *O'Leary v Attorney General* [1991] ILRM 454; [1993] 1 IR 102 (see the 1990 Review, 178-82) was particularly influential. The decision in *Hardy* will be discussed in detail in the 1993 Review. For an earlier decision in this case, see *Hardy v Special Criminal Court* [1992] 1 IR 204 (discussed in the 1991 Review, 154-5).

**Function of judge and jury** In *The People v Davis* [1993] ILRM 407; [1993] 2 IR 1, the Supreme Court held that, under Article 38.5 of the

Constitution, a trial judge was precluded from directing a jury to arrive at a guilty verdict, though the judge was entitled to direct an acquittal: see the discussion of the case in the Criminal Law chapter, 271-3, below.

**Majority jury verdicts** In *O'Callaghan v Attorney General* [1993] ILRM 267 (HC); [1993] ILRM 764 (SC); [1992] 1 IR 538 (HC); [1993] 2 IR 17 (SC), the Supreme Court rejected a challenge to the constitutionality of the majority jury verdict procedure introduced by s. 25 of the Criminal Justice Act 1984. When s. 25 was being debated in the Oireachtas in 1984, doubts had been expressed about its constitutional validity. These had led the late Professor John Kelly, the author of the leading text on Irish constitutional law and also a T.D., to query whether the radical departure in s. 25 from the traditional unanimity rule could withstand constitutional scrutiny: see Kelly, *The Irish Constitution*, 2nd ed., p. 420. The *O'Callaghan* decision has dispelled any doubts on this front.

The case arose in the following way. The plaintiff had been tried in the Circuit Criminal Court on charges of larceny and robbery and was convicted by a 10-2 majority of the jury. His appeal to the Court of Criminal Appeal was unsuccessful: see *The People v O'Callaghan*, Court of Criminal Appeal, 30 July 1990 (discussed in the 1990 Review, 210). He then instituted the present proceedings claiming that s. 25 of the 1984 Act, which permits majority jury verdicts provided that at least 10 members of the jury are agreed on the verdict, was repugnant to Article 38.5 of the Constitution. In the High Court, Blayney J dismissed the claim, and this decision and Blayney J's reasoning was approved by the Supreme Court.

Blayney J began his judgment by placing the presumption of constitutionality before the plaintiff. Quoting with approval from the judgments in *Pigs Marketing Board v Donnelly Ltd* [1939] IR 413 and *In re the Offences against the State (Amendment) Bill 1940* [1940] IR 470 he stated that, as s. 25 of the 1984 Act had been enacted since the adoption of the Constitution, the plaintiff undertook a heavy burden of establishing that it was clearly repugnant to the Constitution.

As to the substance of the plaintiff's claim, Blayney J relied substantially on existing analyses of the nature of jury trial guarnateed by Article 38.5 of the Constitution. He referred in particular to dicta in the seminal decisions of the Irish and United States Supreme Courts, respectively, *de Burca v Attorney General* [1976] IR 38 and *Apodaca v Oregon*, 506 US 404 (1972). From these, he stated that the essence of trial by jury was that a decision as to the guilt or innocence of the accused is made by a group of fellow citizens and not by a judge or judges.

However, he pointed out that in the *de Burca* case, Walsh J had opined that unanimity was not an essential feature of trial by jury. The case then turned on whether any kind of majority was acceptable. Again, Blayney J turned to existing precedent on this point, in this instance the decision in the *Apodaca* case: the crucial point was that a majority verdict was no less one of the jury provided it was arrived at by a substantial majority of the jurors. On this test, the majority verdict provision s. 25 of the 1984 Act, which required a decision by at least 10 jurors, maintained the substantial majority required by the Constitution. Blayney J did indicate that there was a bottom line somewhere below this: if the majority required was substantially lowered, then a jury decision it might lose the character of being a decision of the jury. This would appear to suggest that 7-5, and probably 8-4, would not meet constitutional standards, but that 9-3 or 9-2 might be acceptable.

The other point raised in the case concerned the minimum deliberation period required under s. 25. The 1984 Act provides that the jury must have deliberated for two hours before reaching a majority verdict. Blayney J held that this did not could not be interpreted as an interference with jury deliberations, as the basis for its decision continued to be the evidence given at the trial.

As indicated already, on appeal by the plaintiff, the Supreme Court (Finlay CJ, Hederman, O'Flaherty, Egan and Costello JJ) in its decision in February 1993 upheld the reasoning and conclusions of Blayney J.

The judgment of the Court, delivered by the Chief Justice, adopted with approval the comments of Walsh J on the nature of jury trial in *de Burca v Attorney General* [1976] IR 38. It will be recalled that Blayney J had relied on these dicta in the High Court. The Supreme Court's judgment also cited with approval dicta of Henchy J in his dissenting judgment in *The People v O'Shea* [1983] ILRM 549; [1982] IR 384, the decision on appeals against acquittals in the Central Criminal Court. From these, the Supreme Court stated that the essential feature of a jury trial was to interpose between the accused and the prosecution a reasonable cross-section of people acting under the guidance of a judge, who would bring their experience and common sense to bear on resolving the issue of the guilt or innocence of the accused. The Court considered that a requirement of unanimity was not essential to this purpose.

The Court's judgment added a novel point to those mentioned by the High Court in favour of majority verdicts, namely, that they held an advantage for both the accused and the prosecution of reducing the chances of disagreement. Since the two hour requirement in s. 25 of the 1984 Act constituted sufficient time for a minority to win others over to their point of view, the Court considered that this constituted a protection and could not be regarded as an interference with the decision-making process of the jury. The Court agreed that Blayney J had been correct in stating that a decision might lose its character of being a decision of the jury if the majority required was substantially reduced, and also agreed with his conclusion that s. 25 of the 1984 Act did not fall below the, unspecified, threshold indicated by the phrase 'substantially reduced'.

Finally, the Court dealt with another matter not addressed in the High Court, namely that the majority jury requirement appeared to impinge on the traditional rule that jury deliberations be regarded as completely confidential. The Court upheld the importance of this rule, referring with approval to the dicta of the Court of Criminal Appeal to this effect in *The People v Longe* [1967] IR 369. Indeed, the Supreme Court added that jury deliberations should not be published after a criminal trial. However, the Court concluded that s. 25 did not breach the confidentiality rule since it was concerned only with the verdict and not with the deliberations of the jury. The Court alluded to its own decision in *Attorney General v Mr Justice Hamilton* [1993] ILRM 81; [1993] 2 IR 250 (212-17, above), with which there were some obvious parallels, though it did not make any specific comments on the analogy.

It is clear that the *O'Callaghan* decision seems to have proofed s. 25 of the 1984 Act against any further constitutional challenge. It must also be said that the decision is in line with Irish dicta and United States authority on the matter. Nonetheless, it remains that the decision represents a simple policy choice by the Supreme Court on the benefits of majority decisions. Two criticisms may be made of the Court's approach in *O'Callaghan*.

First, the Court appeared to present its decision as being of benefit to defendants in criminal cases, on the grounds that it reduced the chances of disagreement. It might be hard to convince the plaintiff in the instant case of the benefits for him in this particular line of argument: perhaps if asked he would have been happy to have obtained a re-trial after a jury disagreement. No doubt, of course, the Supreme Court's argument on this point was intended to be more normative than the analysis suggested here, but if that is so then one might have expected that the Court would have supported its normative suggestion with empirical research as to whether the introduction of majority verdicts has, in fact, led to less disagreement. Unfortunately, the Court's effective ban on the publication of any information on the deliberations of juries might make such research difficult to come by in an Irish context. It seems more appropriate that the government of the day bring forward justifications of this kind after, perhaps, the publication of its own research on the topic. Sadly, the Oireachtas debate on s. 25 of the 1984 Act was marked by assertion rather than facts on the reasons for introducing s. 25. It was stated by the then Minister for Justice that jury disagreements had been increasing in the years immediately preceding the Oireachtas debate, though the evidence for this seemed to be more anecdotal than factual. The inclusion of s. 25 in the 1984 Act might have owed more to the fact that it contained many provisions which had been included in the ill-fated Criminal

Justice Bill 1967, which in turn had been modelled on the British Criminal Justice Act 1967, the Act that had introduced majority verdicts in Britain. It might be said that the reasoning of the Supreme Court in *O'Callaghan* equally lacks a basis in fact for the assertions made by the Court on the benefits of majority verdicts. In the absence of such grounding evidence, the existence of s. 25 could be said to reflect the overall lack of research on which many decisions in the criminal justice area are arrived at.

The second criticism which might be levelled at the Court in *O'Callaghan* was its over-reliance on existing Irish dicta indicating that unanimity was not required in criminal jury trials. It is, of course, trite law that the mere existence of a long-established rule does not preclude its change on constitutional grounds. It is also true to say that the courts have found it difficult to take a consistent approach on the 'historical' approach to constitutional interpretation. In the context of jury trials, the Supreme Court found in *de Burca v Attorney General* [1976] IR 38 that the long-established restrictions on jury selection were unconstitutional, while in *The People v O'Shea* [1983] ILRM 549; [1982] IR 384, the Court, by a 3-2 majority, overturned the well-established principle that there could be no appeals against acquittals in criminal trials. The dissenting judges in that case, Finlay P and Henchy J, had stated that the principle was so well-established that the judges should not permit the prosecution to appeal against not guilty verdicts. Ironically, Henchy J's general comments on the jury in *O'Shea* were quoted by his fellow-dissentient in that case Finlay CJ in the *O'Callaghan* case (albeit in a collegiate judgment of the Court) to support the case for a statutory provision which removed a well-established principle of Irish criminal law. The selective use of dicta is an accepted practice in common law courts, but it is unfortunate that they were used in the instant case to justify the constitutional approval of the demise of the unanimity rule. It is also notable that the judgment in *O'Callaghan* is strong on citation of dicta in support of the specific conclusion arrived at but that virtually nothing was said on the historical existence of the unanimity requirement and its overall significance as a principle supporting fairness of procedures. This may be contrasted with the decision of the Supreme Court only two months earlier in another case concerning jury trial, *The People v Davis* [1993] ILRM 407; [1993] 2 IR 1 (see the Criminal Law chapter, 271-3, below). In *Davis*, the Chief Justice delivered a judgment with which all other members of the Court (four of whom made up the Court in *O'Callaghan*) agreed and in which he cited with approval the ringing declaration from Carroll CJ in *Youman v The Commonwealth*, 189 Ky 152 (which in turn had been cited with approval by Kingsmill Moore J in *The People v O'Brien* [1965] IR 142 and in the judgment of the Court of Criminal Appeal delivered by O'Higgins CJ in *The People v Madden* [1977] IR 336): 'It is much better that a guilty individual should escape punishment than that a court of justice should put aside a fundamental principle of the law in order to secure his conviction.' Both in *O'Callaghan* and *Davis*, the Chief Justice cited with approval similar extracts on the nature of jury trial from the *de Burca* and *O'Shea* cases, but only in *Davis* did he cite the views of Carroll CJ in the *Youman* case. It might be argued that the quotation amounts to nothing more than rhetoric, but such rhetoric, or its absence, can often be an indicator of the strength of feeling of the judges pronouncing them or omitting them, as the case may be. It might be concluded that, in *Davis*, the Court feld strongly on the matter in issue, whereas in *O'Callaghan* the Court was not prepared to think as highly of the unanimity requirement.

**Minor offences** In *Desmond and Dedeir v Glackin, Minister for Industry and Commerce and Ors (No. 2)* [1993] 3 IR 67, the High Court and Supreme Court held that s. 10(5) of the Companies Act 1990, which authorised the High Court to try a person for refusal to answer questions put by an inspector as if the person was in contempt of court, was repugnant to Article 38.1 of the Constitution. This was because it permitted the High Court to try summarily an offence which was not minor in character. The case is discussed in detail in the Company Law chapter, 74-81, above.

# Contract Law

## MISTAKE

In *Bank of Ireland v O'Shea*, High Court, 31 July 1992, Denham J applied broad equitable principles to the law of mistake, which led to an unconventional result which has the aura of justice in relation to the particular facts of the case. The defendant signed a guarantee for £50,000 in respect of a family company which owned a ship. When the ship was being put up for sale the Gulf War broke out, resulting in the collapse of the shipping market. After some prompting by the defendant and other members of his family, the plaintiff disposed of the vessel by way of a judical sale in the Netherlands and proceeded against the defendant on the basis of the guarantee.

The defendant contended that the plaintiff was in breach of its duty of care in negligently disposing of the vessel at an undervalue. The family, having encouraged the plaintiff to adopt a stance that indicated it would proceed to a judicial sale, in order to frighten off other creditors, had later tried go encourage the plaintiff to stay its hand, Denham J held that the plaintiff had not acted tortiously:

> The reality is that this was a commercial venture that got caught in the fall-out from the Gulf crisis. . . . Perhaps the sale of the ship could have been conducted more satisfactorily, or deferred. Perhaps the matter could have been conducted so as to achieve a better commercial result. But the time was one of crisis and war. The bank did not precipate the judicial sale. . . . The bank became involved in the judical sale as a result of a request from the O'Shea family.

Denham J made no reference to the decisions of *Holohan v Friends Provident and Century Life Office* [1966] IR 1, *Lambert v Donnelly*, High Court, 5 November 1982 or *McGowan v Gannon* [1983] ILRM 516 (as to which see Keane's *Company Law in the Republic of Ireland*, 2nd ed., 1990, para 24.08) presumably because she considered that the plaintiff had acted reasonably in selling at the time and in the mode it adopted. Denham J went on to hold, however, that the defendant should be liable only for £16,667 under the guarantee. This was because the defendant had signed the document under a mistaken, reasonable, belief that he was agreeing to guarantee only a third of the £50,000. The defendant had given evidence that he had believed the guarantee was a joint and several one, in which his father, his brother and himself each was liable only for a third of the full amount advanced to the company. Before attending the bank to sign the relevant papers, the defendant had asked the plaintiff to supply the relevant papers to him for his solicitor to examine. This was done of all papers except the guarantee. The defendant was told that it was the usual guarantee. Denham J considered that a lay person reading the contract of guarantee would probably be confused because, although signed by one person, it referred throughout to 'Guarantors':

> It was thus misleading, in the circumstances. It is not the agreement which he thought he was signing.

The defendant had 'agreed to guarantee a third of the [sum]', the document he signed 'did not embody the agreement made between the parties'.

From a doctrinal viewpoint it is hard to see how contractual liability (for a third of the full sum) could derive from a situation where there was no *consensus ad idem* and where the defendant was acting under a mistaken belief. Nowhere in her judgment does Denham J ascribe any mala fides or impropriety to the plaintiff. The case seems best understood as involving an equitable tempering of the full rigour of the law of guarantees in order to weaken the blow of the sale at such an unfortunate time.

Immediately below, we discuss *Hunnisett v Owens*, High Court, 15 May 1992, another decision of Denham J. We argue that the decision can best be understood as one relating to the absence of an offer rather than the existence of a mistake, common or unilateral.

## OFFER AND ACCEPTANCE

In *Hunnisett v Owens*, High Court, 15 May 1992 the parties were involved in settlement negotiations of a negligence action for personal injuries resulting from a traffic accident. The defendant's solicitor understood a discussion with the plaintiff's solicitor as a concluded agreement to settle the case for £10,000 plus special damages. But Denham J found that the plaintiff's communication had gone no further than to enquire whether an offer to settle on these terms, which had earlier been made, was still on the table as a basis for negotiation. In coming to this conclusion Denham J relied in part on memoranda prepared by the solicitors at the time.

Denham J considered that both solicitors were honourable and truthful, but that they had been at cross purposes:

> There was no meeting of minds. The two memos alone showed that they came to a different conclusion as to what they had done. [The plaintiff's solicitor] recollects the discussion, and I accept his evidence. There was no offer, and consequently no contract.

The last line of this quotation more accurately captures the essence of the holding than does the reference to the absence of a meeting of minds. In the absence of an offer, express or implied, there simply could be no contract. This was not a case where each of the parties made a communication which each of them regarded as a constituent contractual component, whether offer or acceptance.

## RECTIFICATION

**Agreement to settle litigation** In *R. McD. v V. McD.* [1993] ILRM 717, Barron J was faced with a confused set of facts in an action by the plaintiff wife for rectification of the heads of an agreement concluded in settlement of the wife's proceedings against the defendant, her husband, for maintenance, custody and the distribution of property. The parties' legal advisors had been in negotiation on the eve of the proceedings for a long period, culminating in agreement at 2 a.m. The heads of the agreement dealt with the several matters at issue in the litigation but contained no provision as to costs. The plaintiff's action for rectification was dismissed by Barron J.

The evidence presented difficulty, not because of any particular direct conflict between witnesses, but on account of the clouded memories and impressions of some of them. Counsel for the plaintiff had no specific memory of any discussion about costs. He was of the view that the negotiations must have been upon the basis that the defendant was paying the costs because otherwise he would have discussed the question of the costs with his client and this he had not done. Neither had he discussed the matter with the plaintiff's solicitor. He was of the opinion that the heads of agreement included 'the hard core' of an agreement between the parties. Counsel for the defendant, however, said that the heads of the agreement included the entirety of what the parties had agreed. Applying the principles of the *Irish Life* decision, which we discuss immediately below, Barron J held that there had been no common intention on the matter of costs. In the absence of any such consensus, rectification should not be ordered.

**Contract for sale of ground rents** In the section on Specific Performance, below, pp. 230-31, we discuss the decision in *Ferguson v Merchant Banking Ltd* [1993] ILRM 136, where Murphy J declined to order rectification of a contract for the sale of ground rents.

## SPECIFIC PERFORMANCE

The sale of ground rents has generated litigation more than once in this country. In the 1989 Review, 133-5, we analysed the Supreme Court decision of *Irish Life Assurance Co. Ltd v Dublin Land Securities Ltd* [1989] IR 253, where rectification was refused in respect of a contract for the sale of ground rents which included a valuable holding which the plaintiff had intended to exclude but had erroneously left in. A somewhat similar dispute arose in *Ferguson v Merchant Banking Ltd* [1993] ILRM 136. The defendant company was being wound up. The liquidator was anxious to realise and dispose of ground rents. He agreed to sell to the plaintiff, not only the particular sites out of which the ground rents issued but also various 'bits and pieces'. The contract drawn up by the defendant included an acre of land which turned out to be of some considerable value. The liquidator had not intended to include this in the contract but the plaintiff's principal was aware of the particular portion of land, believed (reasonably) that it was unlikely to be of considerable value and understood at all times that it was intended to be incorporated in the sale. He thus did not appreciate that an error had occurred of which he might take advantage.

Murphy J granted the plaintiff specific performance. He regarded the defendant's position in the instant case as far weaker than that of the vendor in *Irish Life*. The liquidator could not say, as the vendor in *Irish Life* could, that he had been conscious of the vendor's ownership of the contested piece of land and had made a positive decision to exclude it, so that the documentation that was ultimately prepared failed to implement his true intent. The position was that the liquidator had simply not known of the existence of the valuable tract. In one important respect, however, the cases were the same: in neither had there been a pre-existing concluded agreement establishing the common intent of the parties with a sufficient degree of particularity. Here, the so-called pre-existing contract, as the vendor understood it, amounted to no more than an agreement to sell the lands comprised in the various estates which were subject to the leases by which the ground rents were created together with so much of the surrounding of ancillary lands as the vendors believed to be of no value. In refusing rectification, Murphy J expressed the view that '[c]learly such a bargain would be too imprecise to constitute a contract.'

Murphy J went on to refuse rescission of the contract. Relying on the clear observations of Russell LJ in *Riverlate Properties Ltd v Paul* [1975] Ch 33, at 140, which had received Keane J's benediction at trial in *Irish Life* ([1986] IR 332, at 351-3), Murphy J stressed that the purchaser had believed that the disputed tract was included in the contract, that he had not appreciated that it was of significant value and that he was not aware that an error had occurred on the part of the vendor. It may be argued that, even if the purchaser had been aware of the land's true value, nothing in Russell LJ's observations would have warranted rescission. It is one thing for a purchaser to be aware that the reason why certain lands are included in a sale is because the vendor regards these as being of little or no value. It is quite another thing for the purchaser to be aware that a sale is *contingent on the lands' not being of value*. If rescission could be granted in the first type of situation, there could be no such thing as a good bargain and the law would be placing its weight behind bad commercial judgment at the expense of those with sound economic judgment.

Murphy J went on to address the question of the relationship between recission by reason of mutual mistake and the avoidance of liability where it is established that there never was *consensus ad idem*. He noted that a distinction between them could be made in theory but in practice it was difficult to imagine a case where there was no *consensus ad idem* to an apparent contract save in the context of some element of unilateral or mutual mistake.

In the circumstances of the present case, in contrast to those arising in *Mespil Ltd v Capaldi* [1986] ILRM 373 and *Magee v Pennine Insurance Co. Ltd* [1969] 2 QB 507, there had been no fundamental error or absence of agreement on any fundamental term. The liquidator had agreed to sell the property which was already defined in the legal documents executed by him. No material provision had been overlooked or neglected in that documentation. There had been no want of consensus and no mistake as to what in substance was being sold:

> An error or misunderstanding may have arisen as to the extent of the undeveloped property and certainly an error on the part of the vendor as to the potential value thereof. These are not considerations which would give rise to a right of rescission in law or in equity in the absence of some abuse or sharp practice on the part of the vendor.

Since the vendor's claims for rectification or rescission failed it 'follow[ed]', in Murphy J's view, that the plaintiff was entitled to specific performance. Of course an award of specific performance is a discretionary remedy, but nothing would seem to have been served in the instant case by leaving the purchaser only to a damages remedy.

## UNDUE INFLUENCE

In the Family Law chapter, below, 371-2, we analyse Sheridan J's decision in *Allied Irish Banks plc v English* (1992) 11 ILT 208, dealing with the protection of the interests of elderly people who are induced to pledge their assets, or give their consent to a transaction affecting their interests in the family home.

## SEPARATION AGREEMENT

In the Rectification heading, above, p. 199, we discuss the decision of *R. McD. v V. McD.* [1993] ILRM 717, where Barron J dismissed an action for rectification of the heads of an agreement concluded in settlement of family litigation.

## EXISTENCE OF CONTRACT

In *Scafform Ltd v Dawson and Professional Event Management Ltd*, High Court, 1 May 1992, the plaintiff agreed to source out seats for the defendant, to be used in a televised broadcast in Dublin, on a gigantic screen, of the World Cup matches in June 1990. In April he received a quotation from a British supplier. The plaintiff's managing director neither accepted the quotation immediately nor communicated it to the defendant until about six weeks had elapsed. This amounted, Flood J held, to a breach of contract. As a result of the delay, the defendant was obliged to accept a quotation from another company at a higher price.

Flood J held that the plaintiff could not recover the difference in price. The defendant's acceptance of the second quotation had been 'a Hobson's choice'. In the circumstances there had been 'no real mutual assent and no real mutual offer and acceptance to create a contractual acceptance of the [second quotation] such as would constitute a waiver of the plaintiff's . . . breach of contract.'

# Criminal Law

## APPEALS

**Accuracy of transcript** In *The People v McKeever*, Court of Criminal Appeal, 16 July 1992 (discussed in a different context below, 271), the Court was faced with an unusual point concerning the transcript of the defendant's trial.

The defendant claimed that an entire question and answer recorded in the transcript had not, in fact, been put in the trial. The question was central to the defendant's arguments as to whether he had been accurately described by a witness to the robbery in respect of which he had ben charged. The Court quoted with approval dicta in *Attorney General v Joyce and Walsh* [1929] IR 526 to the effect that a transcript certified for the purposes of an appeal under s. 97 of the Courts of Justice Act 1924 should as far as possible be accurate, but that inevitably there might be some inaccuracies where, for example, evidence is misheard by the stenographer. In the instant case, the Court concluded, after an examination of the full transcript, that there was nothing in the instant case to support the defendant's claim that the question and answer recorded in the transcript had not been put in the trial.

**Additional evidence** In *The People v Barr (No. 2)*, Court of Criminal Appeal, 2 March 1992 (the full appeal in which is discussed below, 257-9), the Court (O'Flaherty, Keane and Flood JJ) refused to admit fresh evidence under O.86 of the Rules of the Superior Courts 1986 for the purposes of the defendant's appeal. Applying the decision in *Attorney General v M'Gann* [1927] IR 503 and a passage from *Cross on Evidence*, 7th ed., p. 309, the Court held that where the fresh evidence seeks to contradict evidence given by a trial witness on a collateral issue only, the Court will not admit it for the purposes of the appeal.

**Appellate court function** In *The People v Quilligan and O'Reilly (No. 3)* [1993] 2 IR 305 (see 234-9, below), the Supreme Court held that the trial judge's determination that the appellants' statements were voluntary could not be challenged since it was based on the trial judge's assessment of the veracity of the Gardaí who had questioned the appellants. This decision is in line with the general approach taken by appellate courts in civil cases.

In *The People v G.*, Court of Criminal Appeal, 13 November 1992 (discussed below, 224-5) the Court applied its own decision, affirmed by the Supreme Court, in *The People v Egan (L.)* [1990] ILRM 780 (see the 1990 Review, 193-4) in the context of review of jury findings. The same approach was applied by the Court in *The People v McCarthy and Ors*, Court of Criminal Appeal, 31 July 1992 (see 264-5, below).

**Case stated** In *Director of Public Prosecutions (Murphy) v Regan* [1993] ILRM 335, O'Hanlon J reluctantly declined to hear a case stated where the applicant prosecutor had failed to serve a notice in writing on the defendant as required by s. 2 of the Summary Jurisdiction Act 1857: see the discussion in the Practice and Procedure chapter, 474-6, below.

**Points not raised in trial** In *The People v Moloney*, Court of Criminal Appeal, 2 February 1992, the Court (O'Flaherty, Keane and Flood JJ), in an *ex tempore* judgment, noted that it was reluctant to hear points not canvassed at trial even where there had been a change in legal representation, though it was prepared to do so where the justice of the case so required (see also p. 264). The Court took a similar view in *The People v Hardy*, Court of Criminal Appeal, 22 June 1992 (the substantive issues in which are discussed below, 265-6).

**Re-trial** In *The People v Brophy* [1992] ILRM 709 and *The People v Synnott*, Court of Criminal Appeal, 29 May 1992 (see below, 253-4), the Court of Criminal Appeal declined to order re-trials after quashing convictions.

**'Trawling' of transcript** In *The People v Ryan*, Court of Criminal Appeal, 30 November 1992 (see 259-60, below) the Court expressly disapproved of the practice of basing grounds of appeal on a 'trawl' through a trial transcript for errors not thought worthy of mention during the trial itself. See also its earlier decision in *The People v Moloney*, above.

## ARREST

**Detention under Offences against the State Act** *The People v Quilligan and O'Reilly (No. 3)* [1993] 2 IR 305 is a seminal decision which raised two fundamental issues: whether s. 30 of the Offences against the State Act 1939 was unconstitutional and whether a mandatory jury warning was required on the danger of convicting on an uncorroborated confession. The Supreme Court answered both questions in the negative. We will discuss later in this

Chapter the confessions point (see 255-7, below). For the moment, we will deal with the unsuccessful challenge to s. 30 of the 1939 Act. The circumstances of this long-running case were as follows.

The appellants had been arrested and detained in Garda custody under s. 30 of the Offences against the State Act 1939 on suspicion of involvement in a burglary. In the course of the burglary in question, the occupier of the property had been killed. The appellants were questioned by the Gardaí in relation to the burglary and killing, as a result of which the appellants made incriminating statements. The appellants were charged with burglary and murder. At their trial in the Central Criminal Court in 1985, the Director of Public Prosecutions applied to have the burglary charges postponed and the appellants were tried on the murder charge only. The trial judge (Barr J) held that, since the offences in question were non-subversive, the detentions under s.30 of the 1939 Act were invalid. He held that the appellants' statements were thus inadmissible and he directed an acquittal. On appeal by the Director, the Supreme Court held in a 1986 decision that this finding was not correct: see *The People v Quilligan and O'Reilly* [1987] ILRM 606; [1986] IR 495. However, in a further 1988 decision the Supreme Court declined to order a retrial on the murder charge: see *The People v Quilligan and O'Reilly (No. 2)* [1989] ILRM 245; [1989] IR 46 (1988 Review, 168-72).

The appellants were then tried on the burglary charge in the Central Criminal Court in 1989. The trial judge (Costello J) held that the trials should be allowed to proceed. On the voir dire he held, having heard the evidence of the appellants and the Gardaí involved in their questioning, that the incriminating statements had been voluntary. The defendants gave evidence in the substantive trial denying participation in the burglary and stated that the incriminating statements were the result of intimidation and threats. In his charge to the jury, the trial judge dealt with the appellants' allegations and told the jury of their function in relation to the veracity of the incriminating statements. However, he declined to give a warning that it would be dangerous to convict on the statements without corroborative evidence.

On appeal to the Supreme Court, the appellants argued that s. 30 of the 1939 Act was unconstitutional and also appealed on the other grounds which had been rejected by the trial judge. As already indicated, the Supreme Court (Finlay CJ, Hederman, McCarthy, O'Flaherty and Egan JJ) dismissed the constitutional claim.

Counsel for the appellants argued that s. 30 infringed both Article 40.1 and Article 40.3 of the Constitution. The argument concerning Article 40.1 was that s. 30 resulted in a discrimination as between one citizen and another by delaying the time when an arrested person is brought before a court. The Court rejected this on the basis that this discrimination was not invidious in nature, bearing in mind that a person detained under s. 30 enjoyed a range of protections also enjoyed by a person detained at common law. The Court listed these protection in the context of rejecting the argument based on Article 40.3. Here, the Court held that s. 30 of the 1939 Act did not constitute a failure by the State to protect the personal rights of the citizen under Article 40.3, because, again, a person detained under s. 30 enjoyed a range of protections which had been built up over the years. In an important passage (and drawing on dicta of Walsh J in the first judgment in this case, *The People v Quilligan and O'Reilly* [1987] ILRM 606; [1986] IR 495) the Court listed the protections which, it held, precluded a finding of unconstitutionality. Since the passage constitutes an up-to-date summary of the protections available in relation to a detention under s. 30, it deserves to be quoted in extenso:

> Where a person has been arrested pursuant to s. 30 of the Act of 1939 he has got, in the view of this Court, the following protections.
>
> 1. If the arresting Garda does not have a bona fide suspicion based on reason [*sic*] of one or other of the matters provided for in the section, the arrest is unlawful and he may be released by an order pursuant to Article 40 of the Constitution: *The State (Trimbole) v Governor of Mountjoy Prison* [1985] ILRM 465; [1985] IR 550.
> 2. At the time of the arrest, the suspect must be informed, if he does not already know, of the offence pursuant to the Act of 1939 (or scheduled for its purpose) of which he is suspected, otherwise his arrest will be unlawful: *The People v Walsh* [1980] IR 294.
> 3. The person detained has, during his detention, a right to legal assistance, and the refusal to grant it to him when reasonably requested can make his detention unlawful: *In re the Emergency Powers Bill 1976* [1977] IR 159 and *The People v Healy (P.)* [1990] ILRM 313; [1990] 2 IR 73,
> 4. The right to medical assistance: *In re the Emergency Powers Bill 1976.*
> 5. The right of access to the courts: *In re the Emergency Powers Bill 1976.*
> 6. The right to remain silent and the associated right to be told of that right: *The People v Quilligan and O'Reilly* [1987] ILRM 606; [1986] IR 495
> 7. The Judges' Rules, with their provision in regard to the giving of cautions and the abstention from cross-examination of a prisoner, apply to a person in detention under s. 30: *The People v Quilligan and O'Reilly* [1987] ILRM 606; [1986] IR 495.

8. A person detained under s. 30 must not, in the words of Walsh J in *The People v Quilligan and O'Reilly* [1987] ILRM 606; [1986] IR 495, 'be subject to any form of questioning which the courts would regard as unfair or oppressive, either by reason of its nature, the manner in which it is conducted, its duration or the time of day or of its persistence into the point of harassment, where it is not shown that the arrested person has clearly indicated that he is willing to continue to be further questioned.'
9. If the detention of a person arrested under s. 30 is extended by a Chief Superintendent for a further period after the first period of 24 hours, he must entertain also the necessary bona fide suspicion of the suspect that justified his original arrest and must be satisfied that his further detention is necessary for the purposes provided for in the section: *The People v Eccles, McShane and Phillips* (1986) 3 Frewen 36.

The Court also rejected the claim that s. 30 infringed the right to silence, which counsel for the appellants argued was an unspecified right under Article 40.3. In rejecting this claim, the Court again relied on the quoted list of protections enjoyed by a person detained under s. 30 of the 1939 Act. The Court did so on the assumption that the right to silence was one protected under Article 40.3, though without making a determination on this point.

The Court also rejected another argument concerning s. 30. Counsel for the appellants had drawn attention to the fact that the Emergency Powers Act 1976, which allows for up to seven days detention when brought into operation, had been enacted under the emergency provisions of Article 28.3.3 of the Constitution. It had been apparently conceded in argument by the then Attorney General in the Article 26 challenge to the 1976 Act, *In re the Emergency Powers Bill 1976* [1977] IR 159, that without the cover of Article 28.3.3 such a law would have been virtually impossible to defend on constitutional grounds. The 1939 Act does not, of course, have the benefit of the cover of Article 28.3.3: it is not 'emergency legislation', and stands or falls on ordinary constitutional criteria. However, the Supreme Court in the instant case was not prepared to draw any inference as to the possible invalidity of s. 30 of the 1939 Act from this aside on the 1976 Act. The Court considered that the gap between two days and seven days was sufficiently large to justify distinguishing the two situations, and that, whatever the status of the concession concerning the Emergency Powers Act 1976, s. 30 of the 1939 Act stood up against any constitutional challenge.

While the *Quilligan and O'Reilly (No. 3)* decision provides a useful list of the protections available to a person detained under s. 30 of the 1939 Act, the rejection of the constitutional challenge to the detention powers it contains is somewhat disappointing. It must be remembered that these protections have been grafted onto s. 30 in the last few years by judicial development rather than by protections developed by the legislature. What evidence there is of legislative intention is that the detention power in s. 30 was to operate without any recourse to protections for those detained under its provisions.

The decision of the Supreme Court on s. 30 must also be assessed in light of the Court's decision on the other fundamental point raised in the case: the question of confessions. It would be naive to look at s. 30 as merely involving a postponement of the production of a detained person before a court of law. Virtually all judicial dicta on s. 30, included the analysis by the Court in *Quilligan and O'Reilly (No. 3)*, have tended to analyse s. 30 as merely a 'delaying' or 'holding' power and have perpetuated the view that it would flout constitutional fundamentals if s. 30 were used with the avowed purpose of questioning or interrogating. Of course, no Garda in evidence will state that s. 30 was used with the intention of interrogating a person, but the reality is that s. 30 is, as a matter of practice, used to interrogate.

There are only so many instances in which the detention powers are used to take a person 'off the streets' so that they do not interfere with collection of evidence by the Gardaí. As far back as 1981, the then Garda Commisisoner stated that: 'It is generally accepted that something in the order of 80% of all crime solved is achieved by questioning suspects': McLaughlin, (1981) 16 *Ir Jur* 217. Since then, s. 4 of the Criminal Justice Act 1984 has introduced extensive new powers of detention, and we have already seen that an earlier decision in the instant proceedings confirmed that s. 30 of the 1939 Act could be used in the 'non-subversive' context: see *The People v Quilligan and O'Reilly* [1987] ILRM 606; [1986] IR 495. The instant case also illustrates that detention powers are used in order to obtain statements, or confessions, from the detained person. The analysis by the Court in the instant case is flawed, therefore, because of the failure to recognise the reality of s. 30. This is compounded by the decision of the majority in the Supreme Court on the confessions point, discussed below, 255. The Court managed to isolate the issue of detention from the questioning phase when the two are, in practice, bound inextricably together.

Perhaps only a fundamental review of recent miscarriages of justice will result in a more coherent analysis of the problems posed by powers such as s. 30. The Court in *Quilligan and O'Reilly (No. 3)* may, silently, have wrestled with the problem that to admit that detention powers are used for interrogation purposes would undermine judicial rhetoric to the effect that we operate in an accusatorial system in which the prosecution is required to establish guilt by means of independently obtained evidence rather than evidence from the mouth of the accused. The 80% statistic referred to by the

Garda Commissioner is difficult to square with the claims for an accusatorial system, unless we assume that in all such cases the accused people freely waived their right to refuse to answer questions put by the Gardaí. A trenchant criticism of the existing regime is contained in a Report by the Irish Council for Civil Liberties, *Police Interrogation Endangers the Innocent* (1993).

It is also of interest to note that the Criminal Procedure Act 1993 provides for a trial judge to advise a jury to have due regard to the absence of corroboration in cases where a person's confession is not corroborated. In light of this, some of the reasoning in *Quilligan and O'Reilly (No. 3)* has become redundant. We will return to the 1993 Act in the 1993 Review.

**Reasons for arrest** In *D.P.P.(Cloughley) v Mooney* [1993] ILRM 214, Blayney J discussed to what extent an arresting Garda is required to explain the basis for the arrest to the arrestee: see 297-8, below.

**Stop and search power** Although the power to stop and search is clearly different in nature to the arrest power, O'Hanlon J made a comparison between the two in *Director of Public Prosecutions v Rooney* [1993] ILRM 61, discussed below, 304-5. However, in *The People v Glass (No. 2)*, Court of Criminal Appeal, 23 November 1992, the Court drew a distinction between arrest powers and those on which a warrant to search is based: see the discussion below, 294, 302-3.

## CONTEMPT OF COURT

Two significant cases in 1992 dealt with the scope and extent of contempt law in Ireland, *Desmond and Dedeir v Glackin, Minister for Industry and Commerce and Ors* [1992] ILRM 490; [1993] 3 IR 1 and *Wong v Minister for Justice*, High Court, 30 July 1992. We will also refer to two other short judgments which deal with this area.

*Desmond and Dedeir v Glackin, Minister for Industry and Commerce and Ors* [1992] ILRM 490 was a contempt motion in judicial proceedings arising from the appointment of the first respondent as an inspector pursuant to the Companies Act 1990. For the substantive issues raised in the judicial review proceedings, see *Desmond and Dedeir v Glackin, Minister for Industry and Commerce and Ors (No. 2)* [1993] 3 IR 67 (discussed in the Company Law chapter, 74, above).

The applicants had, as indicated, instituted judicial review proceedings challenging the validity of the appointment of the first respondent as an inspector pursuant to the Companies Act 1990. The appointment had been made by the second respondent, the Minister, to investigate the purchase and subsequent sale of a site in Ballsbridge, Dublin, formerly operated as a bakery by Johnson, Mooney & O'Brien Ltd. The site had been purchased for over £4m and one year later had been sold to Bord Telecom Éireann, a State sponsored body, for over £9m. This transaction had become the subject of a large amount of public comment prior to the appointment of the inspector, and the first applicant, Mr Desmond, had a beneficial interest in some of the companies involved in the sale.

On an *ex parte* application to the High Court (Flood J), the applicants obtained leave to seek judicial review of the inspector's appointment and also mandatory interim relief prohibiting the inspector from seeking to question the first applicant further on his involvement in the transactions leading to the sale of the site to Telecom Éireann. The affidavit grounding the application alleged that the respondents had obtained certain information from the Central Bank in breach of the Central Bank Acts and the interim relief included an injunction prohibiting the use of any such information.

The first respondent, in response to a request for comment from the media, had expressed surprise that the applicants had sought such relief. The second respondent, the Minister for Industry and Commerce, gave an extensive live radio interview to Radio Telefís Éireann in which he stated, *inter alia*, that he was amazed by the application for interim relief, agreed in response to a question posed by the interviewer that the effect of the injunction was that the High Court had facilitated the blocking of the inspector's investigation under the 1990 Act, and also stated that he hoped that the Supreme Court would provide the same facility to him (the Minister) if an appeal were brought. He also criticised the High Court for accepting the averment in the applicants' grounding affidavit that he (the Minister) had acted in breach of the Central Bank Acts. The applicants sought to have the respondents attached for contempt of court. The gravaman of the application concerned the Minister's radio interview. In an extensive judgment, O'Hanlon J declined to attach the respondents for contempt.

He dealt first with whether the evidence before the Court established that the offence of scandalising the courts had been committed, on the nature of which he cited with approval dicta from the leading decision of the Supreme Court in *The State (DPP) v Walsh* [1981] IR 412. O'Hanlon J concluded that this offence had not been established on the evidence since, although the impugned comments were made about pending proceedings, they had been made about an actual decision and were made at an early stage of the judicial review proceedings in question. He commented that while the Minister's choice of language in the radio interview had been 'unfortunate', he should be allowed a degree of latitude and had not exceeded the bounds of fair and permissible criticism. This approach is in line with that adopted by Carroll J in *Weeland v Radio Telefís Éireann* [1987] IR 662 (see the 1987 Review, 90-1).

O'Hanlon J then moved on to discuss whether the *sub judice* rule had been breached. Approving the decision of the Court of Appeal of New South Wales in *Attorney General for New South Wales v J. Fairfax & Sons Ltd* [1980] 1 NSWLR 362, he noted that it was unlikely that the comments in the instant case were intended to make it more difficult for the judge hearing the judicial review to made a fair decision. Thus a risk to the administration of justice had not been established, but he also pointed out that this did not dispose of the matter, as a statement could constitute contempt either in the sense of prejudging an issue in pending proceedings or by pillorying one of the parties to those proceedings.

On this aspect, O'Hanlon J recalled that the applicants' affidavit grounding the application for judicial review clearly made trenchant criticism of the Minister and that he had been entitled to reply in careful and moderate terms to these. O'Hanlon J considered that the Minister had been ill-advised to give a response on a live radio broadcast, but on the other hand he accepted that the matter was of ongoing public interest. In what he described as these 'exceptional circumstances' and having regard to the provisions protecting freedom of expression in Article 40.3 of the Constitution, he concluded that contempt had not been made out under this heading.

It is noteworthy that, on this aspect of the case, O'Hanlon J was referred to the seminal contempt litigation arising from the Thalidomide case. It will be recalled that, in *Attorney General v Times Newspapers Ltd* [1974] AC 273, the House of Lords had held that the *Sunday Times* were in contempt of court by publishing a series of articles which were highly critical of the manufacturers of Thalidomide at a time when there were numerous claims for damages pending in the British courts arising from the use of the drug. Subsequently, in its landmark decision in *Times Newspapers Ltd v United Kingdom* (1979) 2 EHRR 245, the European Court of Human Rights held that this aspect of British contempt law was in breach of Article 10 of the Council of Europe Convention on Human Rights and Fundamental Freedoms, which guarantees freedom of expression. In the *Desmond* case, O'Hanlon J reviewed in detail the speeches of the Law Lords and the judgment of the Court of Human Rights in the *Sunday Times* case.

O'Hanlon J stated that an Irish court should assume that Irish law on contempt was consistent with Article 10 of the European Convention on Human Rights and Fundamental Freedoms, approving the dicta of Henchy J to that effect in *The State (DPP) v Walsh* [1981] IR 412. While this comment obviously reflects a consistent line of authority in this area, O'Hanlon J's comment might properly be described as obiter in the context of his ultimate conclusion in *Desmond*. As we have already noted, he concluded that the instant case involved 'exceptional circumstances', and he noted that a similar phrase had appeared in the speeches of Lord Reid and Lord Simon of

Glaisdale in *Attorney General v Times Newspapers Ltd* [1974] AC 273. To that extent, therefore, while O'Hanlon J appeared to lean in favour of the Court of Human Rights decision in the *Sunday Times* case, he ultimately concluded that the instant case could be decided on the basis of common law contempt of court principles, with some added flavourings from the Irish Constitution. In that context, the influence of the European Convention on Human Rights remains in the background.

The influence of the common law principles were also in evidence in the judgment of Denham J in *Wong v Minister for Justice*, High Court, 30 July 1992, another case in which the *Sunday Times* found itself at the wrong end of the law on contempt of court. The general principles laid down by O'Hanlon J in the *Desmond* case as well as a number of passages from the speeches in *Attorney General v Times Newspapers Ltd* [1974] AC 273 were accepted and applied by Denham J in her judgment. The *Wong* case is of particular interest because of the distinction drawn by Denham J between contempt involving the risk of prejudice and contempt affecting the general administration of justice.

The applicant in *Wong* had instituted judicial review proceedings to quash a decision made by the Minister for Justice under the Aliens Acts 1935 to 1970 refusing him permission to remain in Ireland. These proceedings were adjourned from 3 June 1992 to 30 July 1992 to provide an interpreter for the applicant and also to facilitate discovery of documents. On 28 June 1992, the *Sunday Times* published an article under the heading 'Triads "behind illegal aliens"'. The article referred to the applicant's judicial review proceedings and asserted that evidence would be given in the case on behalf of the Department of Justice that a Hong Kong Triad gang 'may be behind an alleged attempt to bend the Republic's strict immigration laws'. The article also stated that a Garda working in the Aliens' Registration Office in the Department of Justice had been suspended after it was revealed that stamps had been incorrectly applied to the passports of Hong Kong residents. It also stated that, at a previous court hearing, evidence had been given that the applicant's British passport was stamped in an irregular manner.

The applicant sought to attach for contempt the *Sunday Times* and the journalist who had written the article. The applicant stated that the assertion in the article that his judicial review case would involve evidence as to Hong Kong Triads was entirely wrong, that this would prejudice the hearing of his case in the High Court and that, since he had been held up to public obloquy by the article, his right of access to the courts had been affected and the general administration of justice had thus suffered.

The *Sunday Times* editor, Andrew Neil, stated on affidavit that it was not his newspaper's policy to publish material which was in contempt of court. Both he and the journalist who had written the article offered a full apology in the event the court found the article in contempt. The journalist who had written the article as well as the newspaper's solicitor accepted on affidavit that the article was inaccurate in asserting that the judicial review case would involve evidence about Hong Kong Triads and they accepted that the case would not in any way involve that point. However, they also stated that they believed that, since the judicial review case was to be heard by a High Court judge, as opposed to a jury, the inaccuracies in the article would not prejudice the judge's decision in the case and thus it did not amount to contempt.

Denham J accepted the *Sunday Times*' defence that the article did not create any real possibility, let alone a real risk, that the judge hearing the judicial review application would have been influenced in his or her deliberations. However, she found that there was a contempt arising from the other point raised by the applicant. Although the article would not influence the outcome of the judicial review, it had held the applicant up to public obloquy and that affected his right of access to the courts and thus the general administration of justice suffered. It was thus in contempt of court. In an important passage, Denham J stated:

> The basis of this ground is wider than solely the concern that the Court will be biased as a result of the report. The basis is that the administration of justice suffers as a result of a litigant mid-trial being held up to such public obloquy. If such false reporting were to be the norm then the administration of justice would suffer.

This reflects the views expressed in *Attorney General v Times Newspapers Ltd* [1974] AC 273 that litigants, or potential litigants, should not be inhibited from bringing cases to court for fear that by doing so they could be held up to public obloquy.

Denham J also noted that, unlike the *Desmond* case, discussed above, the issue of triad gangs 'had no part or parcel to play in the judicial review proceedings before the Court, nor were they the subject of ongoing public debate at the time this article was published'. This distinction between the cases led her to conclude that there had been a contempt in the instant case, but, as the fallacy of the facts had been accepted the apologies tendered had adequately purged the contempt. It may also be noted that counsel for the applicant had, in effect, accepted that the motion for contempt was intended primarily to draw attention to the false reporting contained in the article rather than to seek any more drastic redress.

While the outcome in the *Wong* case was a relatively mild one for the newspaper concerned, the case points out that, even where an article does not present any risk that a court will be prejudiced by the inaccuracies contained in the article, a contempt of court may arise if the article might tend simply to subject a litigant to public obloquy.

Two further cases concerning contempt should be mentioned for completeness, though they did not raise substantial issues of law.

In *Byrne v Crowley and Ors*, High Court, 25 March 1992, the contempt motion arose in the context of a claim by the plaintiff, the well-known broadcaster Gay Byrne, against the defendants, in which the plaintiff had made various claims against the personal representatives of his deceased accountant, Charles Russell Murphy, and against alleged partners in the accounting practice of his deceased accountant. The defendants who were alleged to be partners of Mr Murphy initially brought a contempt motion against Mr Byrne in October 1989 alleging that, through persistent public references to his connection with the late Mr Murphy and to the then pending proceedings, Mr Byrne had prejudiced those proceedings. That motion for contempt precipitated settlement of the claim by Mr Byrne as well as settlement of the motion with all the moving parties apart from one of the defendants, Mr Campbell. The settlement included a statement read to Court in which the plaintiff acknowledged that the defendants who compromised were not partners of the late Mr Murphy, were not guilty of improper behaviour and were not guilty of any misappropriation of funds. While Mr Campbell refused to compromise the action, notice of discontinuance of the action was served on him on the same date as the settlement of the claim against the other defendants. Mr Campbell then proceeded with the contempt motion.

Ultimately, Carroll J dismissed the motion for contempt, on the ground that, in the light of the compromise and discontinuance of the action, the application was primarily an academic exercise. She could not, in that context, understand why Mr Campbell had persisted in his application to have the contempt motion heard, nor did she 'did not know what he hoped to achieve.' Equally, however, Carroll J also criticised the plaintiff, Mr Byrne, for having given an interview in which he had discussed the merits of the then pending litigation, though she considered that if the case was still live the most that would have been done on foot of this would have been to warn Mr Byrne not to discuss the merits of the case in the future. She also commented that Mr Byrne 'really cannot have it both ways' by claiming, in his replying affidavit to the motion for contempt, that his case 'is and was at all times' that Mr Campbell was a partner of the late Mr Murphy when the compromise of the action had been based on a statement that none of the relevant defendants were ever Mr Murphy's partners. Carroll J commented that: 'It seems to me that these two litigants are stubborn people unwilling either of them to give an inch when the reality of the situation is that the case is over.' She therefore considered that the appropriate order was to dismiss the application.

Finally, in *McCann v An Taoiseach and Ors*, High Court, 22 June 1992, Carney J dealt with a contempt motion initiated by the judge himself arising from the coverage on Radio Telefís Éireann of the instant proceedings in which the plaintiff sought, unsuccessfully, to prevent An Taoiseach making a Ministerial broadcast concerning the Maastricht Treaty referendum: see *McCann v An Taoiseach and Ors (No. 2)*, High Court, 5 October 1992 (discussed in the Communications chapter, 189-90, above). The RTE coverage of the proceedings had suggested that Carney J might have been influenced in his judgment of the case by the actions of independent radio stations granting broadcasting time to those opposed to the Maastricht Treaty. In fact, no reference had been made in the proceedings to independent radio stations. In addition, the RTE coverage had suggested that Carney J had stated during the hearing of the case that, although he was unlikely to prevent the Ministerial broadcast, RTE should consider 'in the interests of fairness' whether it should allow the 'No' lobby broadcasting time. Carney J interpreted this aspect of the coverage as indicating that he had 'entered into the arena': see *Irish Times*, 17 June 1992.

In his judgment on the contempt motion, Carney J indicated that he considered that this coverage amounted to a serious contempt and damaging to the administration of justice. He noted, however, that RTE had been entirely co-operative and that it had not tried to minimise the gravity of the situation in any way. While he reiterated that the coverage amounted to a serious contempt, he accepted that it had not been intentional or malicious, that the damage had been immediately repaired by RTE's coverage of the initiation of the contempt motion. In that light, as the damage had been fully repaired, Carney J concluded that no further action was required. He concluded:

> The Constitution, in Article 34, requires that justice shall be administered in public. Most citizens delegate the monitoring of the work of the courts and of the Oireachtas to the press. Kieron Wood, during his tenure of office as Legal Affairs Correspondent of RTE, has reported informatively and attractively on all major cases coming before the courts. Because his reporting of one case has gone wrong, and very wrong, he should not on that account in the future become defensive, bland or dull.

## CRIMINAL DAMAGE

The Criminal Damage Act 1991 (Section 14(4)) (Commencement) Order 1992 (SI No. 226) brought s. 14(4) of the 1991 Act into effect on 10 August 1992. The result of this Order was that the common law offence of arson was abolished from that date, and replaced with the offences contained in s. 2 of the 1991 Act. The rest of the 1991 Act had come into force on 27 January 1992 in accordance with s. 16(2) of the Act. The provisions on arson were delayed pending the passing of legislation in Britain in order to match the changes effected by the 1991 Act to the Criminal Law (Jurisdiction) Act 1976. On the 1991 Act generally, see the 1991 Review, 134-6.

## DELAY

Three more cases on delay were considered in 1992.

The first case on this point was *The People v Quilligan and O'Reilly (No. 3)* [1993] 2 IR 305, the circumstances of which are outlined above, 234. The Supreme Court dealt with two arguments concerning delay, applying the criteria laid down in *The State (O'Connell) v Fawsitt* [1986] ILRM 639; [1986] IR 362 (see the 1987 Review, 120-3, the 1988 Review, 147-51 and the 1991 Review, 143-5).

The first argument was a general one, concerning the delay between 1985 and 1989 in having a burglary charge dealt with. This had arisen because the appellants had, in the first instance, been charged with murder and burglary. The prosecution applied in 1985 to have the murder charge dealt with first. The appellants were acquitted on this charge. The prosecution appealed this acquittal to the Supreme Court, which did not finally determine the matter until July 1988 when it ordered that no retrial on the murder charge could take place: see *The People v Quilligan and O'Reilly (No. 2)* [1989] ILRM 245; [1989] IR 46 (1988 Review, 168-72). The burglary charge then proceeded in 1989. The Supreme Court rejected the delay argument on the ground that no prejudice to the appellants had been established arising from the delay.

The second argument on delay concerned the second appellant only. A witness who had testified in the 1985 trial that the second appellant had been at another location which would have made it impossible for him to have been at the scene of the burglary had died before the 1989 trial. Having regard to this, the Supreme Court held that the second appellant's trial in 1989 should not have proceeded having regard to the prejudice which arose from the absence of this witness. Accordingly, his appeal appeal on the burglary conviction was allowed on this ground.

The second case on delay was *Claffey v Director of Public Prosecutions*, High Court, 27 November 1992. Here, the plaintiff claimed a declaration that a second criminal trial against him for burglary and malicious damages should not proceed. The charges related to a burglary occurring in Co. Wexford in August 1988. A person giving the plaintiff's name had been arrested at the time and given an address in Dublin. It was not until October 1989 that the plaintiff was arrested in Dublin in respect of these charges. Due to an error, he failed to appear at his first remand hearing in Wexford in January 1990, and he first appeared at a remand hearing in February 1990. He was sent forward for trial to Wexford Circuit Court and successfully applied for a transfer to the Central Criminal Court. His first trial commenced in October 1990, but the prosecution attempted to adduce evidence of identification which had not been included in the book of evidence and on the plaintiff's application the trial judge discharged the jury. A re-trial was fixed for December 1990, but the plaintiff began the instant plenary proceedings seeking a declaration that a re-trial in such circumstances would be in breach of his right to a speedy and fair trial. Murphy J dismissed the plaintiff's claim.

On the question of delay, the plaintiff referred to the decision of Lardner J in *O'Connor v Director of Public Prosecutions* [1987] ILRM 723 and to the *ex tempore* decision of the Supreme Court in *Dawson v Hamill* [1991] 1 IR 213. The latter case is discussed below. On this issue, Murphy J noted that nothing had occurred between August 1988 and the plaintiff's arrest in October 1989 which prejudiced his ability to conduct his defence, and rejected this point.

However, the plaintiff raised a connected issue in his case, to the effect that since the prosecution in the first trial had been given notice that the plaintiff would be challenging the identification evidence sought to be adduced in the trial, this would also unfairly prejudice the plaintiff's defence in the second trial. Murphy J dismissed this argument also, rejecting the parallel with the decision of Finlay P (as he then was) in *The State (O'Callaghan) v Ó hUadhaigh* [1977] IR 42, where the the present Chief Justice had prohibited the prosecution of renewed charges where the Director had entered a *nolle prosequi* with a view to frustrating a court ruling. In the instant case, Murphy J concluded that what had occurred in the first trial might be 'of some slight benefit to the prosecution' but he considered that the plaintiff's case fell 'short by a substantial margin of establishing that his right to fair procedures would be infringed by proceeding with the pending indictment.' On this basis, he therefore dismissed the plaintiff's claim.

The third case concerning delay was *D.P.P. (Finn) v Bouchier Hayes*, High Court, 19 December 1992. Here, the defendant had been charged summarily with offences under the Road Traffic Acts, alleged to have been committed in April 1991. The summons was applied for in May 1991 and issued in December 1991. The case came on for trial in the District Court in March 1992, when the defendant raised the issue of the delay in proceeding with the prosecution. The prosecution stated that the delay between May and December 1991 had been due to an industrial dispute in the District Court, and offered to adduce evidence to that effect if allowed an adjournment to do so. The District Judge declined to allow an adjournment for this purpose and dismissed the case for failure to produce sworn evidence to explain the delay. On a case stated Carroll J held the District Judge had erred in his approach and she remitted the case to the District Court.

Distinguishing the instant case from that in *The State (Cuddy) v Mangan* [1988] ILRM 720 (see the 1988 Review, 151), Carroll J considered that the 11-month delay in the instant case from the date of the offence to the date of trial fell into the realm of being unconscionable or unreasonable per se, but she did accept that the delay fell into the category which required an explanation.

As to what was a reasonable explanation or time delay, Carroll J expressly declined to follow the approach taken by Barr J in the *ex tempore* decision *Director of Public Prosecutions v Burnby*, High Court, 24 July 1989, in which a period of six months was suggested as a guide time. Carroll J considered that in light of the fact that the statutory period for applying for a summons is six months from the date of the alleged offence, it should not be a requirement that service of the summons take place within or close to that time.

She considered that a reasonable time for both issue and service would have to be allowed. In a very helpful elucidation of this, she stated that if the application for a summons is made at an early stage of the statutory period, then a longer period for issue and service might be allowed than where a summons was not applied for until the end of the statutory period. Thus, Carroll J concluded that that if the overall lapsed time between offence and trial is reasonable, there can be no objection to differing periods between the offence, the application for the summons, the issue of the summons, the service and the trial.

In the instant case, Carroll J concluded that the District Judge had erred in finding that any unexplained delay was unreasonable or unconscionable, and that he also erred in refusing to allow an adjournment to the prosecution to adduce evidence on the delay. She remitted the case to the District Court to hear evidence as to why the delay had occurred and as to any question of prejudice.

It may be noted that the issue of delay also re-emerged in the judgment of Lynch J in *Director of Public Prosecutions v Corbett (No. 2)* [1992] ILRM 674: see below.

## DISTRICT COURT

**Amendment of summons** The extensive nature of the power of a District

Court judge to amend a summons under r.88 of the District Court Rules 1948 was underlined by the judgment of Lynch J in *Director of Public Prosecutions v Corbett (No. 2)* [1992] ILRM 674. This was a second case stated arising from the prosecution of the defendant under, *inter alia*, s. 49 of the Road Traffic Act 1961. The first case stated arising from this prosecution was decided by Barr J in 1991: *Director of Public Prosecutions v Corbett* [1991] 2 IR 1: see the 1991 Review, 143-4.

To reiterate the circumstances briefly, as indicated, the defendant was charged, *inter alia*, with an offence under s. 49 of the Road Traffic Act 1961, the summons originally alleging the offence took place on 19 September 1989. The summons was applied for on 9 February 1990, and the hearing was set for 3 May 1990 in the District Court. At the hearing, the defence sought to have the case struck out for prejudice to the defendant arising from the delay involved. No evidence being led on this point, the District Court dismissed the application. The prosecution then applied, under r.88 of the District Court Rules 1948, to change the date of the alleged offence on the summons from 19 September 1989 to 18 September 1989, and to change the number of the defendant's dwelling on the summons from '27' to '25'. The District Court refused to amend the summonses and dismissed the charges. On a case stated, Barr J remitted the case to the District Court, rejecting arguments that there had been prejudicial delay and holding that the District Court judge had a quite wide discretion under the 1948 Rules to amend the summons in this case: see the 1991 Review, 143-4.

On the remittal of the case to the District Court, the case was again dismissed at a hearing on 24 June 1991. At that hearing, it appears that many of the issues raised in the first hearing and the first case stated were reiterated to the District Court judge, including the question of delay and the amendment to the summonses against the defendant. On the second case stated to Lynch J, he followed the essential reasoning in the judgment delivered by Barr J on the first case stated and found against the defendant in this respect.

However, one additional matter was also raised in the second case stated. This was the argument that a court was precluded by the Courts (No. 3) Act 1986 from amending a summons once the six-month-time period from the date of the offence had elapsed, since an amendment to the summons in such a case would result in a discrepancy between the basis on which a complaint is made under the 1986 Act and the basis on which the substantive trial is conducted. Lynch J also rejected this argument. He stated:

> However it seems to me that once it is clear, as it appears to be in this case (although the District Court may prefer to hear the evidence first), that the offences alleged in the amended summonses will still be the substantive offences alleged in the application for the summonses, the

> amendment should be made. That substantive offence in relation to the summons still subsisting and now the subject of the case stated before me is that on one occasion, mistakenly stated to be 19 September 1989 but in fact on 18 September 1989, the [defendant] drove a mechanically-propelled vehicle at Main Road, Phoenix Park with excess alcohol in his blood.

This passage should also be seen in the context of a comment made by Lynch J earlier in his judgment that '[t]he day is long past when justice could be defeated by mere technicalities which did not materially prejudice the other party.' In this light it is not surprising that he concluded that the amendments sought by the prosecution were well within the jurisdiction of the District Court judge under r.88 of the District Court Rules 1948.

## ENTRY POWERS

In *Minister for Social Welfare v Bracken*, High Court, 29 July 1992, Lavan J applied the principles laid down by the Supreme Court in *Director of Public Prosecutions v McCreesh* [1992] 2 IR 239 (see the 1991 Review, 131-2) in interpreting the limits on the powers of entry conferred on social welfare inspectors under the Social Welfare (Consolidation) Act 1981: see the discussion of the case in the Social Welfare chapter, 543-5, below.

## EVIDENCE

In addition to the case law on evidential matters referred to below, the provisions of the highly significant Criminal Evidence Act 1992 are also discussed under the relevant headings to which they relate, namely, children (corroboration); competence and compellability of spouses; documentary evidence (hearsay); oaths; and video links.

**Accomplice: corroboration** In *The People v Diemling*, Court of Criminal Appeal, 4 May 1992, the Court addressed the question of what constitutes an accomplice such that the accomplice warning is required: see the discussion below, 287-8.

**Alternative evidence available** In *Minister for Agriculture and Food v Cahill*, High Court, 12 November 1992 (discussed in the Safety and Health chapter, 528, below) O'Hanlon J held that, where certain evidence was ruled inadmissible for non-compliance with statutory procedures, a trial judge is required to consider whether on the remaining evidence it was open to convict on the charges brought.

**Children** S. 28 of the Criminal Evidence Act 1992 provides for the abolition of the rule in s. 30 of the Children Act 1908 requiring corroboration of a child's unsworn evidence. Instead, a discretionary rule is introduced by which the trial judge may warn a jury of the dangers of convicting on a child's evidence alone. For discussion of the similar rule in s. 7 of the Criminal Law (Rape) (Amendment) Act 1990, see the *The People v Reid* [1993] 2 IR 186, discussed in the 1991 Review, 151-2. See also the discussion below, 261, of s. 27 of the 1992 Act which abolishes the need for an oath or affirmation for children and other persons with a mental disability. S. 28 came into effect on 7 October 1992, three months after its signature by the President: s. 1(2) of the Act.

**Comment on accused not giving evidence** In *The People v Maples*, Court of Criminal Appeal, 30 March 1992, the Court (Egan, Barron and Denham JJ), in an *ex tempore* judgment, ordered a re-trial in a case in which prosecution counsel had referred on a number of different occasions to the failure of the defendant to give evidence in the case. The Court held that this was in breach of the requirement in s. 1(b) of the Criminal Justice (Evidence) Act 1924 that no comment be made by the prosecution on the failure of the accused to testify. The Court considered that, in the particular circumstances, the trial judge's direction to the jury to disregard the comments by counsel were not sufficient to cure this defect.

**Competence and compellability of spouses** Part IV of the Criminal Justice Act 1992 (ss. 20 to 26) involves a substantial amendment to the existing law on the competence and compellability of spouses. In relation to competence of spouses, Part IV follows in broad terms the recommendations contained in the Law Reform Commission's 1985 Report on Competence and Compellability of Spouses as Witnesses (LRC 31-1985) and thus replaces the very narrow terms of the Criminal Justice (Evidence) Act 1924. However, on the question of compellability of spouses, particularly at the instance of prosecution, Part IV rejected the relatively conservative views contained in the 1985 Report and takes account of the highly significant decision of the Court of Criminal Appeal (delivered by Walsh J) in *The People v T.* (1988) 3 Frewen 141, discussed in the 1988 Review, 151-3. Part IV came into effect on 7 October 1992, three months after its signature by the President: s. 1(2) of the Act.

S. 21 of the Act provides that, in general, a spouse of an accused is competent to give evidence either for the prosecution or defence. Ss. 24 and 25 of the Act makes this subject to the usual rule that co-accused, now including spouses who are co-accused, are not always competent or compellable witnesses against each other where they are charged in the same proceedings, that is, where separate trials have not been ordered.

S. 22 of the Act deals with compellability. Here, a distinction is drawn between 'a spouse' and 'a former spouse'. The latter is defined in s. 20 of the Act so that it 'includes' a person who, in respect of their marriage to the accused, has either entered into a separation agreement or has been granted a decree of judicial separation, whether granted inside or outside the State. The word 'includes' in this definition appears to contemplate other categories of 'former spouse', possibly such as those who have obtained divorces (that is decrees of dissolution of marriage) in other States. Obviously, in the absence of divorce legislation in Ireland, the main category of 'former spouses' are those specifically referred to in s. 20.

S. 22 of the Act provides that a 'spouse' is compellable at the instance of the prosecution only in relation to cases involving violence by the accused against the spouse, against a child of the spouse or the accused or against a person under 17 years of age, or involving a sexual offence committed against a child of the spouse or the accused or against a person under 17 years of age. Attempts to commit such offencss are also included within the scope of s. 22. This provision constitues a legislative implementation of the principles contained in *The People v T.* (1988) 3 Frewen 141, above. A 'former spouse' is, on the other hand, compellable under s. 22 in connection with all offences in which the other 'former spouse' is the accused, subject to the fact that the offence in question occurred after separation and also subject to the 'co-accused rule' in s. 25 of the Act.

Finally, s. 26 of the Act provides that nothing in Part IV shall affect any aspect of 'marital privacy'. This phrase is not defined, but it echoes both the prohibition against disclosure of communications between spouses contained in the (now repealed) Criminal Justice (Evidence) Act 1924 as well as the recognition of marital privacy as a constitutional right in *McGee v Attorney General* [1974] IR 284. In light of the decision in *The People v T.* (1988) 3 Frewen 141, above, it seems unlikely that an accused could, per se, argue against the admission of evidence on the ground that certain information that had passed between spouses came within the marital privacy context; it seems more likely that the rights of a complainant would, from the principles in *The People v T.*, take priority over marital privacy. Beyond that general approach, however, the precise extent of s. 26 remains to be sketched out.

**Complaint of sexual assault** The circumstances in which a complaint of sexual assault is admissible were considered in three Court of Criminal Appeal decisions in 1992, *The People v Brophy* [1992] ILRM 709, *The People v Synnott*, Court of Criminal Appeal, 29 May 1992 and *The People v G.*, Court of Criminal Appeal, 13 November 1992. In each case, infirmities in the evidence resulted in the verdicts being quashed, and for different reasons, no re-trials were ordered in any of the them.

In the first of these cases, *The People v Brophy* [1992] ILRM 709, the defendant had been convicted in the Circuit Criminal Court of indecent assault of a 14-year-old girl and sentenced to five years imprisonment. The verdict was a majority verdict, a matter also discussed in the defendant's appeal.

During the trial, it emerged that the complainant had not made a complaint of sexual assault at the first opportunity available to her, which appeared to be to her mother. She had mentioned the matter to some friends and to her father. The prosecution took the view that, although this precluded the complainant from giving evidence as to the terms of the complaints, she was free to give evidence of the fact of making these complaints. There appeared to be some confusion in the court of trial on this point, which resulted in the complainant giving some evidence on the making of the complaint. Counsel for the defence then sought to have the jury discharged on this ground, but the trial judge declined to do so. The Court of Criminal Appeal (O'Flaherty, Keane and Barron JJ) acknowledged that the discharge of a jury was an 'extreme remedy' but it concluded that this was justified in the instant case where the prosecution rested, ultimately, on the evidence of the complainant and where there were certain discrepancies between her evidence and those of the defence, including the evidence of the defendant.

The Court laid down a clear rule on evidence as to complaints in its judgment, namely that such evidence was either admissible or inadmissible, that there was no half-way house in this respect and that if it was admissible then evidence both as to the making the complaint and its terms were admissible. The Court expressly approved the decision of the Court for Crown Cases Reserved in *R. v Lillyman* [1896] 2 QB 167 in this respect. In the instant case, the Court held that, since the complainant had not made a complaint at the first available opportunity, evidence concerning her ultimate making of a complaint was not admissible. The Court also noted that such complaint was to be clearly distinguished from the making of a formal criminal complaint to the police, and that the police were not to be inhibited in any way by the rule concerning complaints from making inquiries on foot of a complaint to them.

We may note that the Court decided not to order a re-trial in this case on the basis that, even if the defendant was convicted, he would be unlikely to be given a sentence which would require him to serve more than the one year he had been in prison on foot of the original conviction.

In the second case concerning evidence by a complainant of a sexual assault, *The People v Synnott*, Court of Criminal Appeal, 29 May 1992, the Court (Finlay CJ, Keane and O'Hanlon J), in an *ex tempore* judgment, quashed a conviction in which evidence as to complaint was led where, as in *Brophy*, the complainant had not made a complaint at the first available opportunity. Expressly following the approach in the *Brophy* case, above, the Court strongly disapproved of any arrangement between counsel in which an attempt would be made to mention the complaint in any form during the complainant's evidence. It is thus clear from these two cases that such evidence will either take the full form of referring to the complaint and the terms of the complaint or else no reference whatever can be made to it. We may also note that, in the *Synnott* case, the Court concluded that no re-trial should be ordered having regard to the trauma which had been suffered by the complainant, who was aged about 12 years, in giving her evidence in the first trial and also to the fact that the defendant, as in *Brophy* had served one year in prison of a sentence of four years imposed.

In the third case concerning evidence by a complainant of a sexual assault, *The People v G.*, Court of Criminal Appeal, 13 November 1992, the defendant had been charged on four counts of the indecent assault of his daughter. The assaults were alleged to have taken place between 1986 and 1988. During the daughter's cross-examination in the trial court, she accepted that the defendant had sent her to a child psychologist during the time it was alleged she was being sexually assaulted but that, at that meeting, she had not made any complaint of sexual assault to the psychologist. In her re-examination by the prosecution, the daughter stated that since that initial meeting with the psychologist, she had re-attended and that the psychologist had recommended that she go to the Gardaí.

Counsel for the defendant applied to have the jury discharged on the ground that the daughter's evidence on re-examination amounted to evidence of a complaint of sexual assault, that it was inadmissible since it was not sufficiently close in time to the events complained of, and that the jury would be highly prejudiced by its admission since they might consider that the psychologist had accepted the complaint and had advised the daughter to go to the Gardaí. The trial judge declined to discharge the jury but warned them that the evidence had been inadmissible and to discount it. The defendant went into evidence and denied the allegations made by his daughter. The defendant was convicted on all counts. On his application for leave to appeal, the Court of Criminal Appeal (Finlay CJ, Keane and Carney JJ) granted the application and allowed the appeal.

Addressing first its general approach on appeals, the Court stated that it would not interfere with a jury verdict in a case such as the present merely on the ground that the defendant had vehemently denied the accusation, since there was credible evidence to support the verdict and it could not otherwise be said to be perverse. The Court expressly followed its own decision, affirmed by the Supreme Court, in *The People v Egan (L.)* [1990] ILRM 780 (see the 1990 Review, 193-4).

However, in this instance the Court was prepared to overturn the verdict on the basis of a specific point concerning the evidence of complaint by the defendant's daughter. The Court considered that, having regard to what it described as that fact that the case was 'extraordinarily finely balanced' between the strength of the evidence for the prosecution and defence, the inclusion of what was undoubtedly the inadmissible evidence of complaint to the psychologist had created a risk of prejudice in the jury's mind. The Court considered that this risk was too great to make it safe to leave the jury's verdict undisturbed, and the Court stated that it had also been influenced in this regard by the fact that the daughter's evidence on this point had been specifically referred to in the prosecution's closing speech to the jury.

Finally, the Court indicated at the end of its judgment that, as prosecution counsel indicated that it was unlikely that the defendant would be charged again, the Court did not make an order for his re-trial but admitted him to bail pending the entering of a *nolle prosequi* in the Circuit Criminal Court. The Court appeared to express some disapproval of the fact that no definitive decision had been made on whether to charge the defendant again.

**Confession: no corroboration required** In its highly significant decision, *The People v Quilligan and O'Reilly (No. 3)* [1993] 2 IR 305, the Supreme Court held, by a 3-2 majority, that no mandatory jury warning was required on the danger of convicting on an uncorroborated confession. The facts of the case have already been set out in the context of the discussion on s. 30 of the Offences against the State Act 1939, 204-9, above.

Counsel for the appellants had submitted to the Supreme Court that, in light in particular of recent experience with miscarriages of justice concerning uncorroborated confession evidence, the Court should move to a mandatory warning requirement in the same way that the Court in *The People v Casey (No. 2)* [1963] IR 33 had developed a mandatory warning requirement for visual identification cases. The majority in the Court (Finlay CJ, Hederman and O'Flaherty JJ) rejected this general proposition, though they appeared to accept that a warning might be required in individual cases. McCarthy and Egan JJ in dissent argued that a general Casey-like warning was required.

The majority suggested that the introduction of a general warning on the dangers of convicting on the evidence of an uncorroborated statement to Gardaí was really a matter for the Oireachtas (as we will see below the Oireachtas has since acted on this area). But the reasoning of the majority in *Quilligan (No. 3)* can be seen from this passage in the judgment of Hederman J:

> While it may be said that members of the Garda, by reason of their profession, have a special interest in bringing law-breakers to book, it would not on that account be reasonable, in effect, to equate them with accomplices in a crime.

This seems a somewhat difficult argument to follow. Can Hederman J be suggesting that the presence of the mandatory warning in visual identification cases means that the courts treat the witnesses in those cases in the same way as accomplices? Surely not. The reason for the warning in the *Casey* case, as the judgments in that case indicate, was the experience with what would now be described as miscarriages of justice in a number of cases immediately preceding *Casey*. The absence of a warning was accepted by the judges as having led to miscarriages of justice and as risking further miscarriages of justice. The warning was introduced to attempt to bring home to juries the need to measure carefully the reliability of visual identification evidence. The reason for introducing the warning was not necessarily to place a slur on those who had given visual identification evidence in any of these miscarriage of justice cases, nor could it be interpreted as placing a general slur on all those witnesses who, in future cases, gave evidence in respect of which a warning was given to the jury.

Clearly, therefore, the passage quoted from Hederman J's judgment in the *Quilligan and O'Reilly (No. 3)* case must have had something different in mind when he talked about a mandatory warning having the effect of treating Gardaí as accomplices. The difference between visual identification cases and confession cases is, of course, that confession evidence emanates almost invariably from quite protracted questioning or interrogation by members of the Garda Síochána. In these cases, therefore, there is a common source of the evidence, whereas in visual identification cases the source is much more happenstance in origin. What the passage from Hederman J's judgment might be expressing, therefore, is a fear that a mandatory warning in confession cases would involve a general slur against all evidence emanating from police questioning. This may very well be an accurate assessment of the possible effect of such a warning, but does this justify declining to issue such a warning if experience indicates a need for one?

Of couse, this question itself begs the question. McCarthy and Egan JJ considered that recent experience justified a change in the common law rules so that juries should be warned of the dangers of convicting on an uncorroborated confession. The majority considered that such a radical change was not necessary. Finlay CJ, Hederman and O'Flaherty JJ did, however, suggest that in the individual circumstances of a particular case, such as where a verbal statement only was in evidence, the trial judge might consider warning the jury on the dangers of convicting without corroborative evidence. This, however, did not arise in the instant case, as the statements which had ultimately admitted in evidence at their trial were written.

One might wonder why the majority felt that this change in the existing regime was required whereas the admittedly more radical change was rejected. The majority do not appear to give any justification for their suggested discretionary warning rule, and indeed it might be argued that such a discretion is more likely to give rise to confusion and appeals than to clarity and fairness. If the discretionary warning was thought desirable, there must be some basis on which it was suggested, but none is to be found in the majority judgments. The minority judgments pass at least a minimal 'transparency' test in that they are firmly basis on an assessment, ultimately subjective, of the effect of recent miscarriages of justice.

However, in any event, the majority view has now been superceded by s. 10 of the Criminal Procedure Act 1993. This provides for a trial judge to advise a jury to have due regard to the absence of corroboration in cases where a person's confession is not corroborated. We will return to s. 10 of the 1993 Act in the 1993 Review.

**Documentary evidence: hearsay** Part II of the Criminal Evidence Act 1992 (ss. 4 to 11) reverses some of the rigours of the hearsay rule by providing that information contained in a document compiled in the ordinary course of business can be admissible in criminal proceedings as evidence of facts contained in the document. Part II of the 1992 Act gives effect to the recommendations of the Law Reform Commission in its 1987 Report on Receiving Stolen Property (LRC 23 — 1987) (see the 1987 Review, 147-54). Part II came into effect on 7 October 1992, three months after its signature by the President: s. 1(2) of the Act.

S. 5 of the 1992 Act follows the recommendatons of the Commission both in terms of its general admissibility of documentary evidence and also in terms of the exceptions which it provides for. As Claire Jackson points out in her Annotation, *Irish Current Law Statutes Annotated*, a novel feature of s. 5 is that it permits persons ordinarily resident outside the State to swear evidence before a Judge of the District Court and that such evidence will be admissible where contained in a document later presented before the trial judge. This would be particularly important in the context of crimes against tourists. Ss. 7 and 10 of the 1992 Act provide for adjustments to the advance notice requirements of the Criminal Procedure Act 1967 where documentary evidence is proved under the terms of the 1992 Act. Part II of the 1992 Act came into force on 7 October 1992 in respect of offences occurring after that date: see s. 1(2) and (4) of the Act.

**Effect on jury of inadmissible evidence** In *The People v Barr (No. 3)*,

Court of Criminal Appeal, 21 July 1992, the effect on a jury of inadmissible DNA evidence was considered. The case also raised the impact of inaccurate media coverage of a criminal trial.

The defendant had been convicted of indecent assault and buggery. In the course of the trial, the prosecution introduced DNA profiling, or genetic fingerprinting, which had been conducted on swabs taken from the complainant. After two witnesses had been examined concerning the techniques involved, it emerged that the person who had performed the actual DNA profile was not available to give evidence. Defence counsel then applied to have the jury discharged on the ground of possible prejudice. Prosecution counsel stated he would no longer be relying on the DNA evidence, and that it had been introduced primarily as a test case for DNA profiling. The trial judge declined to discharge the jury, but he ruled that the evidence was not admissible and warned the jury to ignore the DNA evidence. This was to be the basis for one ground of appeal.

A second ground of appeal concerned headlines in the daily newspapers' reporting of the case, the coverage being particularly intense due to the DNA evidence, a novelty in Irish criminal trials. One of the headlines stated, *inter alia*, 'Genetic printing barred in rape trial'. When this was brought to the trial judge's attention, defence counsel applied again to have the jury discharged for possible prejudice. The trial judge declined the application but warned the jury to ignore the newspaper coverage and reminded them that the trial was not one for rape. It later emerged that the trial judge had, on an approach from a newspaper reporter, approved the contents of the newspaper reports, but not the headlines.

The Court of Criminal Appeal (McCarthy, Keane and Denham JJ) dismissed the grounds of appeal concerning both points mentioned, though not without some critical comments on the procedure adopted on both issues.

As to the incompleted DNA evidence, the Court held that, as the trial judge had warned the jury to disregard it once the prosecution indicated that it did not seek to rely on it, it (the Court) would not presume that the jury would reject that direction and convict an accused person on the speculation that some forensic evidence would have proved some unspecified fact. It is of interest to contrast this approach with that adopted by the Court in the somewhat different circumstances which arose in *The People v G.*, Court of Criminal Appeal, 13 November 1992 (discussed 254-5, above).

The Court stated that it had been improper for the trial judge to discuss in any way the trial with representatives of the media. In particular, the Court felt that the trial judge should not have vetted in any way the newspaper reports of the trial, albeit this had been influenced by the desire to ensure there should be no report which would influence the outcome of the trial. However, the Court again concluded that, in light of the judge's warning to the jury concerning the DNA evidence, the Court would not presume that the headlines had affected the jury's verdict.

As to the way in which the DNA evidence had been introduced by the prosecution, the Court was particularly strong in its disapproval. It unreservedly condemned any suggestion that a court of trial could be used as a testing area for the admissibility of evidence, forensic or otherwise, and it emphasised the desirability of careful assessment in advance of trial of the need to call particular evidence. In spite of these strong criticisms, however, it is of interest to note that the Court did not overturn the convictions in this case.

**Fingerprints** Two important points concerning fingerprint evidence arose in *The People v Ryan*, Court of Criminal Appeal, 30 November 1992.

The defendant had been charged with attempting to cause grevious bodily harm to a neighbour of his. It was alleged during the trial by the neighbour and other prosecution witnesses that the defendant attacked the neighbour with a sword. The defendant's son, aged 15 years, appearing as a defence witness, gave evidence that he had never seen the sword in question in the family home. On cross-examination by the prosecution, he denied ever touching the sword, and stated that he could not explain how his fingerprints had been found on it. The prosecution introduced a fingerprint expert who testified that he found eight points of comparison between the son's fingerprints and the prints found on the sword. Defence counsel objected to the admission of this evidence on the ground that the practice was that there be 12 points of comparison. The trial judge admitted the fingerprint evidence. The defendant was subsequently found guilty. On appeal, in addition to challenging the admissibility of the fingerprint evidence concerning his son, the defendant argued that the cross-examination of the son had been unfair. It was also argued that the evidence concerning the defendant's own fingerprints had been inadmissible as it was obtained in breach of the Regulations as to the Measuring and Photography of Prisoners 1955, in that there was no evidence adduced that the prison officer who had taken the prints had been authorised to do so by a Garda Superintendent. The Court of Criminal Appeal (Blayney, Lynch and Lavan JJ) dismissed the appeal.

As to points of comparison between fingerprints, the Court considered that, while the practice of requiring 12 points of comparison was a good one where it concerned an accused, in this instance it was a witness and not the accused who was involved, and the fact that there were only eight points of comparison was a matter going to the weight of the cross-examination rather than the admissibility of the evidence. The usual practice of requiring 12 points of comparison thus received approval, perhaps obiter, from the Court.

In relation to the defendant's fingerprints, the Court held that the trial judge had a discretion as to whether to introduce the evidence even assuming, without deciding the point, that there was a breach of the 1955 Regulations, applying its decision in *The People v McGrath* (1965) 99 ILTR 59. This was so, the Court held, particularly having regard to the fact that no objection was taken at the trial to the admission of this evidence, a point which the Court picked up later in its judgment, as we will note. While the Court applied well-established principles in holding that illegally-obtained evidence is admissable on the discretion of the trial judge, it is unfortunate that it was, apparently, not addressed on the vires of the 1955 Regulations themselves, purportedly made under the Penal Servitude Act 1891. It is of interest to note that during the debate on s. 6 of the Criminal Justice Act 1984, which introduced a new fingerprinting-taking power for persons held in Garda custody under s. 4 of the 1984 Act, the vires of the 1955 Regulations was expressly doubted by the then Minister for Justice: see the Annotation to s. 6 of the 1984 Act, *Irish Current Law Statutes Annotated.* Given the admitted uncertainty over the 1955 Regulations it is doubly unfortunate that they have not been revoked since 1984 by any subsequent Minister for Justice; it also seems striking that the procedure under the 1955 Regulations was used in the instant case rather than the procedure under the 1984 Act.

On the third point argued concerning the son's cross-examination, the Court concluded that the fact that the prosecution put a line of cross-examination to the defendant's son without forewarning the defence of this line of questioning did not create unfairness to the defendant. The Court and noted that while each case must be judged on its own facts, the instant case was quite different from the situation in *The People v Cull* (1980) 2 Frewen 36, where the prosecution cross-examined the accused in a manner not indicated in the book of evidence.

Finally, it may be noted that the Court reiterated a well-known practice point. Referring to its decision in *The People v Coughlan* (1968) 1 Frewen 325, it noted that some of the grounds argued had resulted from a 'trawl' through the trial transcript for errors not thought worthy of mention during the trial itself. The Court expressly disapproved of this practice.

**Forensic evidence** The Criminal Justice (Forensic Evidence) Act 1990 (Commencement) Order 1992 (SI No. 129) brought the 1990 Act into effect on 5 June 1992. The 1990 Act provides extensive powers to the Gardaí for the taking of fingerprints, swabs and other material from detained persons for forensic purposes. The Act was given particular urgency with the emergence of DNA profiling. The Act will facilitate the conducting of DNA profiling in the State, whereas previously such tests had been conducted in Britain: for an example of the unsuccessful use of DNA profiling, see *The People v Barr (No. 3)*, Court of Criminal Appeal, 21 July 1992, above, 257-9.

On the 1990 Act generally, see the 1990 Review, 206-7. The Criminal Justice (Forensic Evidence) Act 1990 Regulations 1992 (SI No. 130) lay down the detailed procedures to be followed where samples are taken under the 1990 Act.

**Hearsay** The effect of Part II of the Criminal Evidence Act 1992 on the hearsay rule is discussed above, 257.

**Hostile witness** In *O'Flynn v Smithwick* [1993] ILRM 627, Costello J discussed the common law rules on hostile witnesses in the context of the taking of depositions in a preliminary examination: see the discussion below, 294.

**Oaths** S. 27 of the Criminal Evidence Act 1992 substantially altered the test in s. 30 of the Children Act 1908 as to admitting into evidence the testimony of a child under 14 years of age or of a person with a mental disability of any age, giving effect to the recommendations on this point in the Law Reform Commission's 1990 Reports on Child Sexual Abuse (LRC 32 — 1990) and on Sexual Offences against the Mentally Handicapped (LRC 33 — 1990), both discussed in the 1990 Review, 246-58. S. 27 came into effect on 7 October 1992, three months after its signature by the President: s. 1(2) of the Act.

The test under the 1908 Act had been whether the child had sufficient intelligence and whether the child understood the duty of telling the truth. S. 27 replaces this with a test under which the court must be satisfied that the child or person with mental disability 'is capable of giving an intelligible account of events which are relevant' to the criminal proceedings. This provision will be of particular relevance to cases of sexual assaults, but it should be noted that its terms apply to all criminal proceedings. See also the discussion above, 251, concerning s. 28 of the 1992 Act, which deals with corroboration of a child's testimony.

**Sexual assault: corroboration** In *The People v Barr (No. 3)*, Court of Criminal Appeal, 21 July 1992 (discussed above, 257-9), the defendant had been charged with indecent assault contrary to s. 10 of the Criminal Law (Rape) Act 1981.

In his final charge to the jury, the trial judge had given a warning to the jury that it was unsafe to convict the defendant if they could not find corroboration in the evidence adduced. The defendant was convicted on both counts. On appeal, the Court of Criminal Appeal (McCarthy, Keane and Denham JJ) upheld the trial judge's accomplice warning.

The Court noted that the trial in the instant case had taken place after s.

7 of the Criminal Law (Rape) (Amendment) Act 1990 had come into effect, and thus a trial judge was not required to warn the jury of the danger of convicting on uncorroborated evidence (see the 1990 Review, 260-1). A warning was therefore a matter for the trial judge's discretion (see also *The People v Reid* [1993] 2 IR 186, discussed in the 1991 Review, 151-2). The defendant had objected to the form of the particular warning given by the trial judge. The Court of Criminal Appeal concluded, however, that having regard to the particular warning in the instant case, the trial judge had dealt correctly and adequately with the question of what evidence might constitute corroboration.

A similar decision to give a warning in the post-1990 Act situation was upheld by the Court (Egan, Keane and Budd JJ) in its *ex tempore* judgment in *The People v Riordan*, Court of Criminal Appeal, 22 July 1992.

**Similar fact** The circumstances in which similar fact evidence might be admissible were adverted to by the Supreme Court in *Smyth and Anor v Tunney and Ors (No. 3)*, Supreme Court, 26 June 1992 (discussed in the Practice and Procedure chapter, below, 469-70).

**'Test case' evidence** In *The People v Barr (No. 3)*, Court of Criminal Appeal, 21 July 1992 (discussed above, 257-9), the Court unreservedly condemned the suggestion that a court of trial could be used as a testing area for the admissibility of evidence, forensic or otherwise.

**Video links** Part III of the Criminal Evidence Act 1992 (ss.12 to 19) provides that, in a sexual offence or an offence involving violence or a threat of violence, evidence may be given by any person, other than the accused, by means of video links with the court of trial.

The provisions of Part III should be seen, in part, against the background of the procedural recommendations of the Law Reform Commission in their two reports on Child Sexual Abuse (LRC 32 — 1990) (see the 1990 Review, 246-53) and Sexual Offences Against the Mentally Handicapped (LRC 33 — 1990) (see the 1990 Review, 253-8). The Commission was particularly concerned that the formality of courtroom procedure would not defeat justice in cases where young children or those with a mental disability were required to give evidence. This is particularly the case in sexual offences.

Ss. 13(1) and 19 of the Act provides that, in the case of a person under 17 years of age or a person with a mental disability over 17 years of age, a live video link may be used 'unless the court sees good reason to the contrary', whereas, in any other case 'the leave of the court' is required. S. 14 also provides that questions put to a witness giving such video link evidence may be passed through an intermediary who can then use appropriate language where needed to convey the meaning of the question to the witness.

Ss. 15 and 16 deal with the further refinement of video link evidence. Ss. 15 and 16 provide that a video link taken during a preliminary examination in the District Court may subsequently be used at the court of trial. Where this procedure is adopted, the Criminal Justice (Legal Aid) Act 1962 has been amended to provide that legal aid to employ counsel will be possible at such a preliminary examination. Where the facilities are not available in the District Court to conduct a video link during the preliminary examination, s. 17 provides that the matter may be transferred to an appropriate Circuit Court.

More specifically, however, s. 16(1)(b) of the Act also renders admissible video recordings of any statement by a victim of an offence to which Part III applies (where that victim is under 14 years or else has a mental disability) where the statement is made to a member of the Garda Síochána or to 'any other person who is competent' for that purpose. In relation to the second situation, this provision would appear to envisage admissibility of video recordings made between such a victim and, for example, a child psychologist ('person who is competent') in a child sexual abuse assessment unit. It should be noted that, in either case, s. 16(2) of the Act provides that the evidence will not be admitted in evidence if the trial judge considers that it should be excluded, particularly if it is considered that its admission would 'result in unfairness to the accused'.

S. 18 of the 1992 Act relieves a witness giving evidence under Part III of the requirement to identify the accused but only where there is evidence that the witness was known to the accused prior to the date of the alleged offence. S. 19 of the Act adapts the references to persons under 17 years of age to include references to persons with a mental disability of over that age.

It may be noted that since s. 13 of the 1992 Act applies to offences of violence as well as sexual offences, its impact will be greater than simply curing the defects referred to in the Law Reform Commission's reports referred to. It may also be of great importance in the context of evidence in cases of violence where the victim is in fear of the accused discovering the whereabouts of the victim. The availability of a video link may be highly significant in that context.

Unlike the rest of the 1992 Act, Part III requires Ministerial Orders to come into effect, which is explained by the technology associated with its operation. Ss. 12 and 18 of the 1992 Act were fully brought into force on 15 February 1993: Criminal Evidence Act 1992 (Sections 12, 13, 18 and 19) (Commencement) Order 1993 (SI No. 38 of 1993). The same Order brought s. 13 of the Act on television links for children, and the connected provision in s. 19 for persons with a mental disability, into effect on the same date in respect of proceedings in the Central Criminal Court and the Dublin Circuit

Criminal Court. This was extended to the Dublin Metropolitan District of the District Court as from 30 September 1993 by the Criminal Evidence Act 1992 (Sections 13, 15(4), 16, 17 and 19) (Commencement) Order 1993 (SI No. 288 of 1993). This later Commencement Order also brought into effect on 30 September 1993: s. 15(4) of the Act in relation to the Dublin Metropolitan District of the District Court (legal aid in preliminary examinations to which Part III applies): s. 16 of the Act in relation to the Dublin Metropolitan District of the District Court (video recording of the evidence of a person under 17 years of age as provided for in s. 16(1)(a), but the taking of video evidence from a person under 14, envisaged by s. 16(1)(b), was not brought into force); s. 17 in its entirety (transfer of proceedings); and s. 19 of the Act insofar as it is connected to s. 16(1)(a).

**Visual identification: unreliability** In *The People v Quirke (No. 3)*, Court of Criminal Appeal, 22 July 1992, the Court (Egan, Keane and Budd JJ), in an *ex tempore* judgment, quashed the defendant's conviction for indecent assault. The principal evidence in the case was of the complainant, and the Court emphasised that the divergence between her initial description of her assailant to the Gardaí and her later description in the defendant's trial were such that the defendant's conviction was unsafe. The Court also took account of the divergence between her evidence in the two trials of the defendant. For earlier proceedings, see the 1991 Review, 150.

**Visual identification: warning adequate** In *The People v Moloney*, Court of Criminal Appeal, 2 March 1992, the Court (O'Flaherty, Keane and Flood JJ), in an *ex tempore* judgment, held that the visual identification warning in the instant case had been adequate. The Court noted that the trial judge, consistently with the approach taken in *The People v Casey (No. 2)* [1963] IR 33, had not 'slavishly' followed any formula in his warning. See further the 1991 Review, 154 on this area.

**Visual identification: warning not required** In *The People v McCarthy and Ors*, Court of Criminal Appeal, 31 July 1992, the Court considered an unusual situation in which it was decided that a warning concerning visual identification was not required.

The defendants were charged with rape and actual bodily harm arising out of one incident. The complainant gave evidence in which she identified the defendants as having raped her in sequence. The first defendant admitted that he had been at the scene involved, but denied that he had had sexual intercourse with the complainant. In statements to the Gardaí and at the trial, the second and third defendants, brothers, admitted that they had had sexual intercourse with the complainant but alleged that it had been with her consent.

The complainant was extensively cross-examined on her account. In his closing address, counsel for the defendant noted that the second and third defendants had given a similar explanation of their involvement in the event and had had no opportunity to concoct a story before giving their statements to the Gardaí. The trial judge, in his summing up, pointed out that a number of hours elapsed before the second and third defendants had given their statements to the Gardaí. The defendants were convicted on the counts of rape and actual bodily harm. On appeal by the defendants, the Court of Criminal Appeal (McCarthy, Keane and Budd JJ) dismissed their appeals.

On the question of visual identification, the Court pointed out that, in relation to the first defendant, this was not a case in which visual identification was challenged for accuracy in the ordinary sense, since the first defendant admitted he had been at the scene in question. Accordingly a specific warning to the jury on the dangers of convicting on visual identification, on the lines laid down in *The People v Casey (No. 2)* [1963] IR 33, was not required.

The Court went on to state that the case against the first defendant turned on the issue whether the complainant's evidence that he had raped her was believed by the jury. Having regard to the fact that, overall, the trial judge had fairly put the defendants' case in his direction to the jury (subject to some minor complaints), the Court concluded that it would not interfere with what essentially was a matter for the jury, who had an opportunity to see the complainant's evidence at first hand.

Finally, the Court pointed out that, while counsel for the second and third defendants was entitled to put every legitimate case to the jury in closing submissions, it was equally the duty of the trial judge to draw the jury's attention to whether any such defence case was based on a statement of fact that was not true or not wholly true. Thus, the trial judge's direction as to the time lapse before the second and third defendants made their statements to the Gardaí came within the scope of this duty, and he had acted correctly in so doing.

## EXPLOSIVE SUBSTANCES

In *The People v Hardy*, Court of Criminal Appeal, 22 June 1992, the Court (Finlay CJ, Lynch and Lavan JJ), in an *ex tempore* judgment, upheld the defendant's conviction for possession of explosive substances in suspicious circumstances, contrary to s. 4 of the Explosive Substances Act 1883.

The defendant was found to be in possession of sodium chlorate and of mercury tilt switches. Evidence was given at the defendant's trial that these could be used as component parts in what are commonly called car bombs.

During closing submissions, reference was made by the prosecution to two legal definitions of explosive substance in connection with the defendant's possession of sodium chlorate. First, it was pointed out that s. 9 of the 1883 Act defined explosive substance by reference to any material which could be used in aiding or causing an explosion. Second, it was pointed out that sodium chlorate was designated as being an explosive substance for the purpose of the Explosives Act 1875 by the Explosives (Ammonium Nitrate and Sodium Chlorate) Order 1972. In the Special Criminal Court's ruling finding the defendant guilty, reference was made to the 1972 Order only.

The Court of Criminal Appeal considered whether there was any risk of injustuce in upholding the defendant's conviction under s. 4 of the 1883 Act in these circumstances. The Court concluded that there was no risk of injustice having regard to the surrounding circumstances in which the defendant had been found to be in possession of the sodium chlorate (which he stated was for weedkilling) together with the mercury tilt switches; had been found at a port with a passport not in his own name and had attempted to run away from customs officials when he was stopped.

For other unsuccessful proceedings initiated by the defendant arising out of his trial, see *Hardy v Special Criminal Court* [1992] 1 IR 204 (discussed in the 1991 Review, 154), *Hardy v Ireland*, High Court, 10 September 1992; Supreme Court, 18 March 1993 (referred to in the Constitutional Law chapter, 191, above) and *Hardy v Ireland (No. 2)*, High Court, 25 June 1993 (which we will discuss in the 1993 Review).

## EXTRADITION

**Attorney General** The role of the Attorney General in the unsuccessful extradition application in the *Fr Ryan* case (see the 1988 Review, 155-6) is considered in Gerard Hogan's excellent article in (1992) 2 ICLJ 128.

**Procedural irregularity** In *O'Sullivan v Director of Public Prosecutions*, High Court, 10 July 1992, the applicant successfully sought an order of prohibition in relation to his trial in the Special Criminal Court on foot of an extradition warrant. The applicant had been indicted in 1976 on charges of unlawful possession of firearms and ammunition, but during his trial in the Special Criminal Court he absconded. He was not located again until 1991 when he was arrested by police in Wales. A warrant for his arrest from the Special Criminal Court had been issued in 1976 in respect of the firearms charges, and it was sought to execute this by means of the reciprocal backing of warrants extradition procedure contained in the UK Backing of Warrants (Republic of Ireland) Act 1965. In the course of seeking the applicant's extradition, a second warrant for the applicant's arrest came to light which had been issued by the Special Criminal Court in connection with 29 other charges, and this warrant was placed with the warrant concerning the firearms charge before the British Magistrate dealing the applicant's extradition. It later transpired that, in connection with these 29 charges, the defendant had either been found not guilty or the charges had been dropped at some time between 1976 and 1991, but this was not known to the authorities when the applicant's extradition was being sought.

Having been extradited to this jurisdiction, the applicant sought to prohibit his trial on the firearms charge on the ground that the extradition order was tainted with the warrant connected with the 29 charges. O'Hanlon J agreed that the courts were required to ensure strict observance of the legal and constitutional rights of those affected by the extradition procedure, citing *The State (Quinn) v Ryan* [1965] IR 70, *R. v Bow Street Magistrates, ex p Mackeson* (1981) 75 Cr App R 24 and *The State (Trimbole) v Governor of Mountjoy Prison* [1985] ILRM 465; [1985] IR 550 in this regard. He considered that it was a matter for the State to establish that all proper procedures had been applied in the applicant's extradition hearing in Wales. In the absence of a full transcript of that hearing, O'Hanlon J accepted that it was difficult to determine whether in fact the warrant connected with the 29 spent charges had influenced the Magistrate's decision to extradite the applicant. However, there was sufficient evidence to indicate that that warrant could have had a bearing on the decision, even if the firearms charge was the major consideration in the extradition decision. In those circumstances, O'Hanlon J granted the applicant a prohibition order. However, it is notable that O'Hanlon J stated at the end of his judgment that he did not rule out the possibility that the applicant might be charged on the firearms offence at some time in the future; he did not make a determination on that issue.

## FIREARMS AND OFFENSIVE WEAPONS

In *The People v McBride*, Court of Criminal Appeal, 7 April 1992 the Court (McCarthy, Lavan and Carney JJ) dealt with two issues arising under the Firearms and Offensive Weapons Act 1990. The defendant had been charged under s. 9(5) of the 1990 Act with possession in a public place of one pick-axe handle, one baseball bat and one short iron bar with a grip, with the intention by him unlawfully to cause injury to, incapacitate or intimidate one Aidan Conway. The defendant had been driving a car which was with another car in which Conway was being carried. When the cars approached a Garda checkpoint, all the occupants of the other car ran away, the defendant attempted to avoid the checkpoint but was arrested. The defendant was convicted after a trial in the Special Criminal Court and this conviction was upheld by the Court of Criminal Appeal.

The items mentioned were found in the back of the defendant's car. The Court of Criminal Appeal rejected the argument that, since the car was an item of personal property, the defendant could not be charged with possession of the items in a public place. The Court took the view that once the car was in a public highway, this was sufficient to satisfy the requirements of the 1990 Act.

The second point raised in the case was whether there was sufficient evidence to indicate that the items referred to were intended by the defendant to intimidate Conway. The defendant pointed out that Conway was in another car at the time the defendant was stopped at the Garda checkpoint. While the Court of Criminal Appeal accepted that this was a matter in some cases of inference from the surrounding circumstances, it noted that s. 9(5) of the 1990 Act provides that an offence is committed where the article or articles in question are intended to cause injury or intimidate 'in a particular eventuality or otherwise. . . .' In the instant case, the Court was prepared to accept the inference drawn by the court of trial that the two cars were acting in concert and that this was sufficient to indicate the requirement concerning intimidation.

## JUDICIAL REVIEW

**Retrial after *certiorari*** In *Sweeney v Brophy and DPP* [1992] ILRM 479 (HC); [1993] ILRM 449 (SC); [1993] 2 IR 202 (HC & SC), the Supreme Court confirmed a long line of authority on the circumstances in which a retrial may be ordered after a conviction has been quashed on judicial review. However, an important rider was also added to the existing law in this area, namely that on discretionary grounds a court would decline to remit a case to the District Court under O.84, r.26(4) of the Rules of the Superior Courts 1986, thus bringing the matter to an end. The decision was delivered on the same date as that in *Sheehan v Reilly* [1993] ILRM 427; [1993] 2 IR 81, discussed in the Constitutional Law chapter, 152-4, above, in which the same issue arose.

In *Sweeney*, the applicant had been convicted of assault before the respondent Judge of the District Court. The applicant sought *certiorari* to quash the verdict on the ground that a number of improprieties had occurred during the hearing of the case. The respondents did not oppose the application for *certiorari* but sought to have the matter remitted to the District Court under O.84, r.26(4) of the Rules of the Superior Courts 1986. In the High Court (see the 1991 Review, 169), Barron J had declined to remit the case.

He held that the improprieties which had occurred did not make the trial void *ab initio*, but rather that the resulting conviction was voidable so that *certiorari* lay to quash it. Since the applicant had been put in peril in a trial which had initially been valid, Barron J concluded that he was entitled to plead *autrefois acquit* and it was thus not appropriate to remit the case.

On appeal by the Director of Public Prosecutions, the Supreme Court (Finlay CJ, Hederman, O'Flaherty, Egan and Blayney JJ) unanimously upheld this decision.

The only reasoned judgment was delivered by Hederman J, with whom the other members of the Court concurred. He first referred to a passage from the judgment of Walsh J in the leading decision *The State (Tynan) v Keane* [1968] IR 348 in which Walsh J had outline the different situations in which *certiorari* would result in remittal and those in which it would not, that is where certiorari would not result in an acquittal and those in which *certiorari* would have the effect of an acquittal. Hederman J then also referred to a passage in the judgment of Henchy J in *The State (Holland) v Kennedy* [1977] IR 193, in which the general basis on which *certiorari* is granted was discussed. It had been suggested that the judgment of Henchy J in *Holland* was inconsistent to some extent with that of Walsh J in *Tynan*. Hederman J rejected this argument. In a helpful summary of the law applicable to the circumstances of the instant case, Hederman J concluded:

> . . . *certiorari* is an appropriate remedy to quash not only a conviction bad on its face or where a court or tribunal acts without or in excess of jurisdiction but also where it acts apparently within jurisdiction but where the proceedings are so fundamentally flawed as to deprive an accused of a trial in due course of law. . . [*C*]*ertiorari* is not appropriate to a routine mishap which may befell any trial; the correct remedy in that circumstance is by way of appeal. However, if there is a breach of the fundamental tenets of constitutional justice in the hearing or failure to hear the evidence in the case, the trial can properly be categorised as one that has not been held in due course of law and any conviction arising therefrom should be quashed so as to entitle the defendant to plead *autrefois acquit*.

The decision in *Sweeney* confirms the view that, in some instances, *certiorari* amounts, in effect, to an acquittal where the jurisdictional error is voidable, that is, where the court had jurisdiction entering into the case but has fallen into jurisidictional error through fundamental procedural flaws. Where the jurisdictional error is *ab initio*, it appears that *certiorari* will still leave open the possibility of a remittal under the 1986 Rules.

However, in *Sweeney* Hederman J added an important rider to the existing jurisprudence. Even where the error is an *ab initio* one, he suggested that, in the exercise of the Court's discretion to remit under the 1986 Rules, it would be appropriate to take into account whether the person involved had 'endured enough' and whether the prosecution could not be 'acquitted of all blame for some, at least, of what went wrong at the trial.' While in the context of the *Sweeney* case, these comments were obiter, such an approach had already been taken by the Court in its *ex tempore* decision in *Dawson v Hamill* [1991] 1 IR 213. Perhaps because the *Dawson* case was *ex tempore*, it was not expressly cited by the Court in *Sweeney*.

In *Dawson v Hamill*, Lynch J had remitted a prosecution under the Road Traffic Acts to the District Court after he had quashed an acquittal which for involved a voidable error in jurisdiction: [1990] ILRM 257; [1989] IR 275 (see the 1989 Review, 175-7). However, on appeal to the Supreme Court by the applicant the Supreme Court held that, in the particular circumstances where there was extensive time lag between the *certiorari* application and the original events involved in the prosecution, the Court would exercise its discretion not to remit a case to the District Court under O.84, r.26(4) of the 1986 Rules. Thus, the *Dawson* case is an instance of the Supreme Court applying the approach suggested, obiter, by Hederman J in *Sweeney*.

We may also note here that the approach in both *Dawson* and *Sweeney* is consistent with recent decisions of the Supreme Court in comparable areas: see for example the decision in *McGrath v Garda Commissioner* [1990] ILRM 817 (1990 Review, 330-1). It thus appears that *Sweeney* has the potential for creating a new situation in which, on a discretionary basis, *certiorari* can amount to an acquittal in respect of *ab initio* void decisions. For a highly informative analysis of this area, see Kevin Costello's article, (1993) 3 ICLJ 145.

**Suitability of judicial review** We might note here one other aspect of the *Sweeney* case worth mentioning. The passage form the judgment of Hederman J quoted above indicates that judicial review is not the appropriate remedy where the error under challenge is a minor one; in such circumstances an appeal would be the appropriate remedy to seek. This issue arose in the judgment of O'Hanlon J earlier in 1992 in *Lennon v Clifford* [1993] ILRM 77. Here the applicant had been convicted in the District Court with two offences of failing to make a tax return and he sought on judicial review to challenge the adequacy of the evidence on which he was convicted. Citing the decision of the House of Lords in *Chief Constable of the North Wales Police v Evans* [1982] 3 All ER 141, O'Hanlon J held that judicial review did not lie in such circumstances, as any error (if such existed) did not go to jurisdiction. See further the discussion of the case in the Revenue Law chapter.

## JURY

**Admissibility of confessions** In *The People v Quilligan and O'Reilly (No. 3)* [1993] 2 IR 305 (the circumstances of which are discussed, 233, 255, above), the Supreme Court, by a 3-2 majority, (Finlay CJ, Hederman and O'Flaherty JJ; McCarthy and Egan JJ dissenting) applied its decision in *The People v Conroy* [1988] ILRM 4; [1986] IR 460 to the question of determining the admissibility and reliability of confessions. The Court affirmed that it was not the jury's function to assess the voluntariness of statements (this being for the trial judge on the *voir dire*), but rather to assess whether the evidence given was truthful. In the instant case, the Court held that the jury had been adequately addressed on the issue by the trial judge and that he had also adequately addressed the jury on all the allegations of ill-treatment raised by the appellants in their evidence.

**Discussion of case** In *The People v McKeever*, Court of Criminal Appeal, 16 July 1992 (discussed in relation to majority verdicts above, 274), the Court emphasised the need for all juries to be warned not to discuss the case with any person other than another member of the jury. In the instant case, no such warning had been given, but the Court held that, since there was nothing to indicate that any irregularity had occurred arising from this failure, the verdict reached in the case should be allowed to stand. In this respect, the Court expressly approved the 'harm' test established by the English Court of Appeal (Criminal Division) in *R. v Prime* (1973) 57 Cr App Rep 632.

**Effect of inadmissible evidence** In *The People v Barr (No. 3)*, Court of Criminal Appeal, 21 July 1992, the Court considered the impact of inadmissible evidence on a jury: see 227-9, above.

**Judge directing guilty verdict** The decision of the Supreme Court in *The People v Davis* [1993] ILRM 407; [1993] 2 IR 1 is a timely reminder that a judge in a criminal trial must not direct a jury to arrive at a verdict of guilty.

The accused was tried on a charge of murder in the Central Criminal Court. He pleaded not guilty to murder but guilty to manslaughter. This plea was not acceptable to the prosecution, and a plea of not guilty was entered. The evidence indicated that the accused had consumed a large quantity of alcohol on the night in question. He and a friend, Brady, had become involved in a late night fight with others and were being taken away from the fight, against their will, by some companions. The defendant got free and procured a knife intending to attack the person he believed had started the fight. He in fact stabbed his friend Brady a number of times and Brady died as a result.

The trial judge directed the jury that, as a matter of law, they could only bring in a verdict of murder in the instant case since the consumption of alcohol would not in any way be regarded as a defence to the murder charge such as would overturn the presumption of an intention to kill or cause serious injury as required by s. 4 of the Criminal Justice Act 1964. The trial judge expressly directed the jury to arrive at a verdict of guilty of murder, which the jury did. On appeal by the accused, the Supreme Court (Finlay CJ, Hederman, O'Flaherty, Egan and Blayney JJ) directed a retrial.

Delivering the only reasoned judgment, with which all the other judges concurred, the Chief Justice began by quoting with approval the dicta of Walsh and Henchy JJ respectively in *de Burca v Attorney General* [1976] IR 38 and *The People v O'Shea* [1983] ILRM 549; [1982] IR 384 (comments which, we have seen, were also to be quoted just over two months later in the judgment of the Court in *O'Callaghan v Attorney General* [1993] ILRM 764; [1993] 2 IR 17: see the Constitutional Law chapter, 222-6, above).

Drawing on these dicta, Finlay CJ stated that the right to a jury trial in Article 38.5 of the Constitution 'has as a fundamental and absolutely essential characteristic the right of the jury to deliver a verdict'. He went on that, in the interets of justice, however, the trial judge has a right and duty to withdraw a case from the jury and direct them to enter a not guilty verdict where the judge is satisfied that a verdict of guilty could not be supported. But, he said, there is no corresponding right or duty to direct a jury to enter a verdict of guilty, even in limited or exceptional circumstances to prevent what might appear to be a preverse verdict.

Finlay CJ acknowledged that this situation might appear anomolous, but he concluded that the mischief which would flow from any invasion of the right of a jury to consider and arrive at its verdict, and even to arrive at what might seem to be a perverse verdict, would be much greater than any conceivable harm that could arise from the inability of the judge to direct a guilty verdict.

The decision in *Davis* is, of course, an important one in that expresses a minimum requirement to which trial judges must comply. There are, of course, situations in which a trial judge does not overtly direct a jury in the manner prohibited by the *Davis* decision, but rather will present evidence in such a away as to indicate how a jury should decide a case. The *Davis* decision would appear to support a trial judge who attempts to veer a jury towards a not guilty verdict, but what of the situation of the trial judge who presents the prosecution evidence in such a way that the jury is moved towards a guilty verdict. Existing precedent in this area, such as *The People v Doran* (1987) 3 Frewen 125 (see the 1987 Review, 142), indicates that such an approach by a trial judge is acceptable. In light of the *Davis* decision, this now seems open to doubt. Of particular interest in this context is that, towards the end of his judgment in *Davis*, the Chief Justice quoted with approval the following comment of Carroll CJ in *Youman v The Commonwealth*, 189 Ky 152, which in turn had been cited with approval by Kingsmill Moore J in *The People v O'Brien* [1965] IR 142 and in the judgment of the Court of Criminal Appeal delivered by O'Higgins CJ in *The People v Madden* [1977] IR 336: 'It is much better that a guilty individual should escape punishment than that a court of justuce should put aside a fundamental principle of the law in order to secure his conviction.'

**Judge drawing attention to weakness in defence case** In *The People v McCarthy and Ors*, Court of Criminal Appeal, 31 July 1992, the Court stated that a trial judge was obliged to point out any obvious defects in defence counsel's submissions: see the precise circumstances discussed above, 234, 264-5.

**Judge substituting new charge** The limits on the power to substitute new charges was adverted to by Carroll J in *Director of Public Prosecutions v Ó Súilleabháin* [1993] ILRM 14: see 296-7, below.

**Majority verdicts and Constitution** In *O'Callaghan v Attorney General* [1993] ILRM 267 (HC); [1992] 1 IR 538 (HC); [1993] ILRM 764; [1993] 2 IR 17, the Supreme Court rejected a challenge to the constitutionality of the majority jury verdict procedure introduced by s. 25 of the Criminal Justice Act 1984: see the discussion in the Constitutional Law chapter, 222-6, above.

**Majority verdicts procedure** Two cases in 1992 discussed the procedural aspects of the majority verdict mechanism under s. 25 of the Criminal Justice Act 1984.

The first case on majority verdicts was *The People v Brophy* [1992] ILRM 709. Here, the trial judge had indicated to the jury prior to the ending of the two-hour-period provided for deliberations in s. 25 of the Criminal Justice Act 1984 that they could arrive at a majority verdict if they continued their deliberations for the two-hour-period. The jury brought in a 10-2 majority verdict. On appeal, the Court of Criminal Appeal (O'Flaherty, Keane and Barron JJ) rejected the argument that the trial judge was precluded by s. 25 of the 1984 Act from making such a comment to the jury. In doing so, the Court expressly approved the approach taken by the Court in its decision in *The People v O'Callaghan*, Court of Criminal Appeal, 30 July 1990 (see the 1990 Review, 209-11). The Court also noted in *Brophy* that, in its *ex tempore* decision in *The People v Glass*, Court of Criminal Appeal, 19 March 1991 (see the 1991 Review, 170), it had also rejected the argument that the judge should inform the jury of its entitlement to reach a majority verdict at the beginning of its deliberations.

The second case on majority verdicts was *The People v McKeever*, Court of Criminal Appeal, 16 July 1992. The defendant had been charged in the Circuit Criminal Court on three counts arising from the same incident: robbery of £35; possession of a firearm with intent to commit an indictable offence, namely robbery; and possession of a firearm with intent to endanger life. At his trial, the defendant was acquitted on the charge of possession of a firearm with intent to endanger life, but was convicted by a majority of 10-2 on the other two charges.

On appeal, the Court of Criminal Appeal (O'Flaherty, Lynch and Denham JJ) considered, *inter alia*, the manner in which the trial judge had accepted the majority verdict. At the end of the two-hour-period referred to in s. 25 of the 1984 Act the trial judge informed the jury that, sufficient time having elapsed, he could accept a majority verdict. He was immediately informed by the jury foreman that they had reached a 10-2 majority verdict, and he had there and then accepted that verdict. The Court of Criminal Appeal held that the trial judge had not infringed s. 25 in so doing, so that the verdict could not be challenged on this ground. However, the Court did add that it might be better, where the trial judge applies s. 25 of the 1984 Act and where the judge is thereupon informed that a majority verdict has been reached, for the jury to be asked to retire for a further short time to consider the matter in private. It is of interest that this rider by the Court corresponds to the steps suggested in the 1967 English Practice Direction on majority verdicts. Indeed previous indications from the Irish case law discussed in previous Reviews (see the 1988 Review, 174, 1990 Review, 210 and the 1991 Review, 170) also seem to reflect the English Practice Direction. It thus seems that, in the absence of an Irish Practice Direction, the procedures set out in the English Practice Direction are likely to be followed in Irish courts.

## LEGAL AID

In *Cahill v Reilly*, High Court, 24 March 1992, the applicant was serving a custodial sentence when he was served with a summons that he drove a mechanically propelled vehicle without insurance. He was brought from custody before the respondent judge of the District Court. The applicant was not legally respresented. After the prosecuting Garda had opened the case against the applicant, the applicant admitted that he had no insurance. The respondent then found the applicant guilty on the charges brought. On being informed that the applicant had a number of previous convictions in this type of offence, the respondent imposed a sentence of imprisonment. The applicant applied for judicial review of the respondent's order on the ground that he had failed to inform the applicant of his right to legal aid under the

Criminal Justice (Legal Aid) Act 1962. Denham J granted the relief sought.

She first noted that, once the applicant had indicated that he had no insurance on the date in question, the requirements of r.64(1) of the District Court Rules 1948 had been met and the respondent was accordingly entitled to find the applicant guilty. Crucially, she considered that it was only at this stage in the trial that the issue of a custodial sentence became a probability, since only then did the respondent hear of the applicant's previous convictions. Denham J referred to a number of passages from the judgments delivered in *The State (Healy) v Donoghue* [1976] IR 326, and in particular the judgment of Griffin J in which he stated that the issue of being informed of a right to legal aid really arises where 'a sentence of imprisonment is likely'. In the instant case, Denham J did not therefore consider that the right to be informed of the right to legal aid arose until after the applicant had been convicted. Prior to that, a sentence of imprisonment was not 'likely'. Indeed, Denham J expressly stated:

> I am not deciding that in all cases where there is a statutory sentence of imprisonment possible that the accused has the right to be told of his right to be legally represented or to apply for legal aid.

In the instant case, Denham J quashed the conviction but remitted the case to the District Court under O.84, r.26(4) of the Rules of the Superior Courts 1986.

## OFFENCES

**Arson abolished** The replacement of the common law offence of arson arising from the full implementation of the Criminal Damage Act 1991 is referred to above, 245-6.

**Criminal damage** The replacement of the common law offence of arson arising from the full implementation of the Criminal Damage Act 1991 is referred to above, 245-6.

**Offences against property** The Law Reform Commission *Report on the Law Relating to Dishonesty* (LRC 43–1992) presents a comprehensive analysis of the substantive and procedural aspects of the subject. The common law and statutory background is inauspicious; the Commission rightly observes (para 36.22) that the law of theft:

> ended up in a straitjacket whose seams were loosened here and there to

> afford sufficient movement to capture glaring cases not captured within the basic shape of the jacket. Consolidating legislation merely reproduced the same basic 'cut' of straitjacket, complete with unsightly bulges.

Generations of law students have unhappy memories of trying to come to terms with judicial metaphysics which stretched the concepts of 'possession' and 'taking' far enough to ensure the conviction of dishonest persons whose conduct scarcely fell within the parameters of the offence of larceny. Those engaging in false pretences were, on the other hand, treated somewhat leniently, while servants and those in fiduciary positions were generally subjected to a somewhat robust jurisprudence. The meaning of a 'document', for the purposes of the law of forgery, is deeply obscure, raising questions that tantalise philosophers and confound judges. For a stimulating analysis of the subject of larceny and related offences, see P. McCutcheon, *The Larceny Act 1916* (1988).

*Theft* The Commission recommends that the offence of theft should be committed by one who:

> a. without the consent of the other, unless the consent is obtained by deception or intimidation;
> b. dishonestly appropriates property'.

This definition seeks to incorporate the better elements of the statutory reform effected in England by the Theft Act 1968, while mitigating some of its less desirable aspects. Clearly the limitation of the *actus reus* of theft in the Larceny Act 1916 to cases of *taking and carrying away* means that other dishonest appropriations can fall outside the scope of the criminal law. The concept of *appropriation* embraces these other forms of dishonest conduct by extending the *actus reus* to a more abstract generic level, but there is a price to pay, as the Commission recognises. It is difficult to know when an interference with another's property goes beyond mere trespass or criminal damage into the realm of appropriation. If appropriation is to be equiparated with conversion this will involve the court, as the Commission acknowledges, in making 'fine distinctions'. Secondly, as again the Commission admits, the notion of appropriation blurs the distinction between attempt and commission. This weakness in the English legislation was long ago identified and criticised: see Elliott, 'Theft and Related Problems—England, Australia and the USA Compared', (1977), 26 ICLQ 110, at 113-4.

The Commission has valiantly sought to come to terms with the troublesome issue of the relationship between appropriation and the owner's consent. The lack of clarity in the 1968 Act generated much confusion: cf. *DPP v Lawrence* [1972] AC 626; *R. v Morris* [1984] AC 320; *R. v Gomez* [1991] 4 All ER 394. The Commission's definition requires the absence of the consent of the owner, save where consent is obtained by deception or intimidation. Thus, a false pretence which enables the dishonest party to acquire ownership through appropriation of the property would constitute theft. Under existing law, the dishonest party could not be charged with larceny for this type of fraudulent conduct.

The Commission wisely does not follow the English lead in relation to the ingredient of dishonesty. The Criminal Law Revision Committee thought that the word 'dishonestly' was preferable to 'fraudulently and without a claim of right made in good faith', on the basis that dishonesty was a familiar concept which was easy to understand. At first the judges sought to define the concept. In *R. v Feely* [1973] QB 530, at 537, the Court required that jurors should apply 'the current standards of ordinary decent folk' when deciding whether the accused had acted dishonestly. In time, the courts added an extra requirement, whereby the jury had to apply this test both objectively and subjectively, so that, even if they were satisfied that what the accused had done was dishonest according to the ordinary standards of reasonable and honest people, they could not convict unless they were also satisfied that the accused realised that what he or she was doing was dishonest by those standards: *R. v Ghosh* [1982] QB 1053.

The Commission proposes instead that 'dishonesty' should be defined in terms of the absence of a claim of legal right, thus perpetuating the approach adopted by s. 1 of the Larceny Act 1916, as interpreted judicially: see Lowe, 'The Fraudulent Intent in Larceny' [1956] Crim L Rev 78, Smith, 'The Fraudulent Intent in Larceny: Another View' [1956] Crim L Rev 238. It might perhaps be preferable to accomplish this goal more directly by dispensing with any reference to dishonesty in the definition of the offence, since it could constitute a source of confusion to juries, who would have to be instructed by the trial judge that they must give the concept an artificially restricted construction. It would be far simpler for the statutory provision to require an absence of a claim of legal right, with no reference to dishonesty.

The Commission recommends the removal of the requirement to prove an intent to deprive the owner permanently of property in offences of dishonesty. This recommendation will need further consideration before it can be integrated with the Commission's recommendation that theft should be defined in terms of *appropriation* of another's property, since it is far from clear whether temporary borrowings constitute appropriations of property in particular cases. If I take another's bicycle and use it to convey me for two miles, have I stolen it under the Commission's recommendations? The answer would seem to be yes. If this is so, then appropriation embraces not merely conversion of another's property but also a wide range of trespassory takings that are not conversions: cf. McMahon & Binchy, op. cit., 534-7. One may wonder whether a concept so lacking in certainty and clarity of definition would be sure to withstand a constitutional challenge.

With regard to the *subject-matter* of theft, the Commission is satisfied to follow the lead of the 1968 legislation in relation to land, flora, wild creatures and choses in action. The theft of confidential *information* is not an offence in England (*Oxford v Moss* (1978) 68 Cr App R 183). The Commission recommends that it should be. The principal inspiration for this recommendation appears to be the Commission's dissatisfaction with the artificiality of the present law whereby prosecutions are based on the incidental violations of tangible property rights:

> In our view it is wrong to resort to a charge of stealing an exam paper when the actual mischief to be addressed is acquisition of knowledge of the questions, to charge larceny of electricity when the mischief is unauthorised use of a computer or, in any of these cases, to seek out an agreement and charge conspiracy to defraud, the last refuge of a prosecutor. (Para. 20.46)

There are, however, formidable objections, identified by the Commission, to criminalising the theft of information. The Commission quotes from Hammond's leading analysis ('Theft of Information' (1984) 100 L Q Rev 252, at 263-4), to the effect that the public's overriding 'right to know' qualifies the legal protection of confidential information in certain situations. Whether it does so in any particular case can involve a complex public policy assessment as to the likely social and economic costs entailed in granting or withholding protection:

> The criminal law is too blunt an instrument for this task. It does not offer a 'quick fix' for the kinds of issues at stake.

Apart from the possible context of computer 'hacking', the Commission acknowledges that it may be argued that no clear social need has been shown for extending the criminal law of theft into the area of information misappropriation and that enlargement of the traditional civil remedies relating to the interference with intellectual property rights might be the more satisfactory solution. It must be said that the case against criminalising the theft of information seems a good deal stronger than that in favour of the change.

The Commission recommends that it should be an offence to retain property obtained by mistake where there is an obligation, in civil law, to restore it. This proposal mirrors the approach in England (s. 5(4) of the 1968

Act) and the United States (*Model Penal Code*, Article 223.4). It means that an employee who discovers that he or she has been overpaid will be a criminal if he or she succumbs to the temptation to spend (or even simply retain) the excess amount. The Commission sees no moral significance between this type of case and one where the accused has set out to steal:

> Life includes a wide range of temptations, some of which can be very pressing. It is true that where property is, as it were, thrust on a person by mistake, that person may find it hard to resist the temptation to hold onto it; but the temptation to steal in other specific contexts can be equally pressing. (Para. 21.14)

Under the Married Women's Status Act 1957, s. 9(3), one spouse may be guilty of theft from the other spouse only where they are no longer living together or where the property is taken when leaving or deserting the other spouse. The Commission recommends the removal of these restrictions, with the requirement that the consent of the Director of Public Prosecutions be obtained before a prosecution may be taken. This solution was recommended by the Commission in relation to prosecutions for interspousal rape and implemented by the Criminal Law (Rape) (Amendment) Act 1990, s. 5(2): see the 1990 Review, 259-60.

*False pretences, deception and other dishonest conduct* Under the Larceny Act 1916, s. 32, a person may be convicted on the offence of obtaining 'any chattel, money or valuable security' by false pretences. See *McCutcheon*, op. cit., paras 143-51. The false pretence must be one of past or present fact; thus neither misrepresentation of law or of opinion nor promises as to the future fall within the scope of the offence. The Commission recommends that the criminal law should capture misrepresentations of these kinds, as well as extending liability to nondisclosure that involves the creation or reinforcement of a false impression in the victim. The Commission, following the lead of England and the United States, recommends that the expression 'false pretence' should be replaced by 'deception'.

The Commission does not favour the retention of a separate offence of deception. Instead, as we have seen, appropriation through deception is part of the Commission's proposed offence of *theft*. But the Commission goes on to recommend a *general* offence of dishonesty, whereby one who dishonestly causes another to suffer financial prejudice or a risk of prejudice or who dishonestly makes a gain for himself or herself will be criminally responsible. Dishonesty here would encompass only the absence of 'a claim of right'. (One assumes that the Commission intends to limit this to a claim of *legal*, rather than moral, right, since that is the criterion proposed in relation to theft.

Otherwise the law would contain a distinction between the offences of theft and dishonesty that would be hard to justify on any principle and for which no argument is adduced in the Report.)

The Commission argues in favour of its proposed general offence of dishonesty as follows:

> We see little point in confining [it] to deception. . . . Deception, like furtive taking, is simply a means of obtaining property without true consent. If the offence of assault can co-exist with several specific offences of violence against the person, why should not a general offence of dishonesty also co-exist with such specific offences as theft, deception and forgery?
>
> The common denominators are the absence of a claim of right and the causing of financial prejudice. Once these can arise together, without deception, there is no point in confining dishonesty to offences of deception. (Para. 36.31)

The difficulty with the breadth of the proposed offence is, however, that not only does it extend to cases where there is no deception, but it also embraces cases where there is no dishonesty, in the normal sense of that term. A person will be liable for causing, *or even risking*, financial prejudice to another without claim of right. A drunken driver, for example could be prosecuted for this offence, a consequence so curious that one is forced to examine again the rationale for the offence.

In truth, the proposed offence has been inflated into one encompassing a huge range of intentional conduct that causes or risks financial loss. The Commission produces no clear argument in support of such a fundamental extension to the criminal law. It identifies no conduct that is at present outside the scope of the criminal law and which needs an offence of this kind in order to render it unlawful. There is something to be said for a generic offence of *dishonesty* which seeks to target all manifestations of dishonesty, though there are formidable difficulties in providing a workable definition of dishonesty, as the English experience has shown. The Commission's solution of identifying dishonesty as the absence of a claim of right is perfectly managable in relation to the proposed offence of theft, since theft requires appropriation of another's property. Once criminal liability attaches to the absence of a claim of right, in conjunction with any conduct that knowingly causes or risks causing another person financial loss, we have moved from dishonesty to a vast expanse of conduct that never previously was considered so anti-social as to warrant a criminal sanction.

As well as this umbrella offence, the Commission recommends the creation of the offences of obtaining services by deception, of making off without payment, and of using a cheque or credit card after the supplier has communicated or sought to communicate to the user notification of the revocation of permission to use it. The latter recommendation represents a narrowing of the scope of the offence proposed by the Commission in its earlier Discussion Paper on the subject, which would have made it an offence to use a cheque or credit card without authority in obtaining anything capable of being dishonestly appropriated, even where the terms of revocability had been agreed with the card user on receipt of the card and the supplier had not necessarily sought to communicate to the user notification of the revocation of permission to use it. The undesirability of the generic offence of dishonesty here becomes particularly apparent. If it was right to have *narrowed* the scope of the specific offence, how is it justifiable that conduct falling outside the scope of the specific offence recommended in the Report can still be prosecuted under the generic offence?

*Computer crime* Much has been written in the past decade about the need to reform the law to respond to computer crime. See, e.g., Webber, 'Computer Crime and Jay-Walking on the Electronic Highway', 26 Crim LQ 217 (184), the Scottish Law Commissioner's *Report on Computer Crime* (Scot. Law Com. No. 106, 1987), the Law Reform Commission of Tasmania's Report No. 47, *Computer Misuse* (188) and the English Law Commission's Working Paper No. 110, *Computer Misuse* (1988). The Criminal Damage Act 1991 already deals with several modes of interference (see the 1991 Review, 135) and the Data Protection Act 1988 with others (see Robert Clark, *Data Protection Law in Ireland* (1990), 125-31 and the 1988 Review, 390-9).

The Commission sees little force in the arguments in favour of further legislative change. Nevertheless it recommends the inclusion of a provision, partly modelled on s. 115 of the Australian Territory Ordinance, to the effect that a person who, by any means, dishonestly uses, or causes to be used, a computer or other machine with intent to obtain by that use a gain for himself, herself or another person or to cause loss to another person, is guilty of an offence.

It should be noted that the appropriation of information, whether in respect of a computer or otherwise, is to constitute theft under the Commission's recommendations. The need for the distinctive offence in relation to dishonest computer use is not entirely clear. Conduct of this kind, to the extent that it does not constitute theft, would appear to fall squarely within the terms of the generic offence of dishonesty proposed by the Commission. A caveat should, however, be recorded. The Commission does not clarify whether the concept of dishonesty in its proposed computer offence is to have the same meaning as in its proposed generic offence. There is no reason to assume that it should necessarily do so; it is unlikely that the concept is so understood in the Australian Capital Territory, whose provision is recommended for inclusion in our law.

*Forgery and counterfeiting* The Commission makes detailed proposals for reform of these offences, largely modelled on England's Forgery and Counterfeiting Act 1981.

*Blackmail* The present law of blackmail is contained in ss. 29 to 31 of the Larceny Act 1916. These prescribe several offences, of great specificity, involving demands with menaces. They have a somewhat antique air and it is not too hard to find anomalies in cases that fall between the cracks of the legislative platform: see McCutcheon, *op. cit.*, 92-104, Campbell, 'The Anomalies of Blackmail' (1939) 55 LQ Rev 382.

In England, s. 21(1) of the Theft Act 1968 redefined the offence in terms that would excite the attentions of linguistic philosophers but was scarcely likely to appeal to the more pragmatic judicial minds in the Court of Appeal. A person is guilty of blackmail if he or she makes any unwarranted demand with menaces (subject to certain conditions). A demand is unwarranted when the person making it does so in the *belief* that he or she has *reasonable grounds for making the demand* and that the *use of the menaces is a proper means of reinforcing the demand.*

Judicial attention has concentrated on the accused's belief as to 'proper means'. In *R. v Harvey* (1980) 72 Cr App Rep 139, the English Court of Appeal interpreted this as connoting a belief that the means are *lawful*. This interpretation has been dismissed by the commentators, who generally advocate a more subtle psychological *renvoi*, involving an enquiry into whether the defendant believed that people generally would regard the means as 'proper'—in the moral order.

The Commission steers clear of recourse to moral norms by recommending that the approach of s. 21 be adopted with one alteration: instead of making an 'unwarranted' demand the offence would consist of demanding or attempting to demand, with menaces 'and without a claim of (legal) right'.

The difficulty with this definition is that, in contrast to s. 29(1)(i) of the 1916 Act, it renders unlawful all demands with menaces where the person making the demand has not a claim of legal right. (The brackets around 'legal' do not appear to be based on a willingness of the Commission to countenance claims of non-legal right.) It is clear from the case law on s. 29(1)(i) that it is very hard to draw a clear legal line in economic disputes, especially in trade-protection and trade-union contexts, based on the criterion of a 'reasonable and probable cause'. It is a bold step, however, for the Commission to propose that the criminal law should attach to demands where the person making the demand lacks a claim of legal right. Many trade unions will make demands which they know are not protected by the law. They do so, not because they wish to become criminals but rather because the traditional law relating to strikes and other industrial action has tilted towards the protection of employers' interests. The civil law in this area is notoriously complex and uncertain. The Industrial Relations Act 1990 has gone some way towards a reasonable, pragmatic compromise (see the 1990 Review, 347-56), but significant residual areas of controversy remain. At present, a trade union engaging in robust industrial action has some hope of avoiding liability for blackmail. Under the Commission's recommendation the scope for exemption would be significantly reduced.

*Dishonesty in the management of companies* The Companies Act 1990 extended the scope of criminal liability in relation to the management of companies: see the 1990 Review, 56-117. The Commission recommends the addition of a further summary offence. This would consist of controlling a company at a time when an offence of dishonesty is committed by a director, officer, servant or agent of the company in circumstances where the person in control had reasonable cause to believe that such an offence would be or was being committed, having regard to the nature and extent of the control thus exercised. It would be a defence to this offence that the defendant had acted reasonably in seeking to prevent the commission of the offence. The Commission presents little supporting argument in relation to this proposal. This makes it difficult to assess what justification for it the Commission perceived. Certainly, its scope is enormous. An offence would be committed even where the servant's dishonesty was unrelated to the economic goals of the company. The proposed offence is one of negligence. There is a widely held view that the criminal law should not embrace negligence save (perhaps) in exceptional cases. The proposed offence would turn those in charge of companies into criminals in certain situations that have always been regarded as quintessentially falling within the exclusive remit of the civil law. If an employer fails to take adequate steps to protect his or her employees from the dishonesty of a co-employee, that may result in an action for negligence but should it really also expose the employer to criminal prosecution?

*Investigation of dishonesty* The Commission does not favour the establishment of a Serious Fraud Office similar to the English model, which proved so controversial. It goes so far as to question the need for its establishment in England as an independent entity. The Commission does not believe that the volume of cases would warrant such a step here. In its view, resources would be better directed into the Garda Fraud Squad.

The Commission goes on to recommend the introduction of investigatory provisions such as those in s. 2 of the English Criminal Justice Act 1987, 'appropriately adapted'. That section requires persons interviewed by he Director of the Serious Fraud Office to answer questions. The (limited) protection against self-incrimination afforded by subs. (8) satisfied the Commission as to its constitutional validity in the Irish context. The Commission also recommends that that Gardaí be given a power of arrest without warrant for all offences of dishonesty.

*Prosecution of dishonesty* The Commission makes several recommendations in aid of the prosecution. First it proposes that, where there has been a series of appropriations by an accused from one victim, the law should permit a charge or count to be laid in respect of the general deficiency arising either in isolation or together with changes in respect of particular appropriations, notwithstanding any duplicity involved. It goes on to deal with the problem for prosecutors presented by a solicitor or other trustee of a fund, consisting of intermingled clients' money, who dips into the fund improperly; it is impossible in such a case to say that any *particular* client's money has been taken. The Commission recommends that a person should be presumed to have caused financial prejudice or the risk of such prejudice when, having been entrusted with moneys for applying in a particular manner, he or she fails to do so or to account for them when an account is sought. Such a person would be eligible to be charged in respect of a deficiency in the relevant account, not exceeding the total amount entrusted, on a date unknown during the period of the entrustment, notwithstanding the fact that no particular appropriation of the money entrusted can be proved.

The Commission does not explain what offence the accused would commit in such circumstances. It seems that it envisages that it would be theft, but such conduct would in any event fall within the proposed generic offence of dishonesty. In order to be constitutional, the statutory presumption proposed by the Commission would have to pass the test laid down by Costello J in *O'Leary v Attorney General* [1991] ILRM 454; [1993] 1 IR 102: see the 1990 Review, 178-82. Questions that arise include the following. Is it fair to establish a presumption that the accused caused financial prejudice where the person suffering such prejudice is not identified? So far as the presumption relates to carrying a *risk* of financial prejudice, how does that assist the prosecution's case that the accused in fact appropriated any property? Does failure to account for moneys connote a *refusal or omission* to account or does it also embrace an *inadequate or unconvincing* account? If the latter, how precisely is the trial judge to instruct the jury? Is the presumption a legal or evidential one? How may it be rebutted?

The Commission goes on to recommend that the Director of Public Prosecutions should have power to elect whether offences of dishonesty are to be prosecuted summarily or on indictment. The Commission's recommendation to the same effect in its Discussion Paper had provoked the criticism by Michael McDowell SC that to deny the accused a right to elect for trial by jury would be unconstitutional. The Commission seeks to meet this objection by the argument that:

> [t]he Oireachtas is entitled to rely on the integrity of the Director of Public Prosecutions in the exercise of a statutory power of election, so that this power will be exercised consistently with constitutional requirements. If it were not so exercised on any occasion, the District Judge would be charged with the task of protecting the accused's constitutional rights and refusing to try an accused summarily for a minor offence not fit to be so tried. If he or she failed to do so, an eventuality which we have no reason to contemplate would occur with any frequency, the accused's constitutional rights would fall to be protected by the superior courts.

One may doubt whether it is wise to propose such a further complication to the judicial task in relation to minor offences. The courts have so far been less than impressive in seeking to articulate the ingredients of a minor and a non-minor offence: see our comments in the 1987 Review, 108-9.

The Commission, echoing the approach it favoured in its Report on Child Sexual Abuse, recommends that in relation to offences of dishonesty, the preliminary examination should be dispensed with. Depositions would still be taken in the District Court and the accused would be able to derive any support they might provide in any application by him or her to the court of trial for an order directing his or her discharge.

The Commission, constrained by Article 38.5 of the Constitution, does not follow the example of the majority of the Roskill Committee in England which recommended abolition of jury trial in fraud prosecutions. All that the Commission proposes is that a conviction for any offence of dishonesty, regardless of the penalty imposed, should constitute a ground for disqualification from jury service. In order to improve expertise in fraud trials, the Commission recommends the establishment of a Judicial Studies Board, the arranging of seminars on such subjects as information technology and accountancy, at which judges would attend, making accountancy a compulsory subject in training for the Bar and making post-qualification training in accountancy and information technology available for practising lawyers.

The final recommendations of substance are that ten years' imprisonment should be the maximum penalty for offences of dishonesty other than robbery and blackmail and that, in respect of a prosecution for an offence of dishonesty, it should be possible for the jury to convict on any other offence of dishonesty.

*Indecent assault* In *Doolan v Director of Public Prosecutions* [1993] ILRM 387, O'Hanlon J held that indecent assault was an aggravated form of assault at common law and was thus an offence known to the law. This apparently simple conclusion arose against a complex background of legislative provisions. We will also note later that, to some extent, the *Doolan* case is already more of historical than contemporary interest.

The applicant had been tried on indictment in the Circuit Criminal Court, the indictment containing two counts. The first count was indecent assault on a named female, the particulars being 'contrary to common law as provided for in section 10 Criminal Law (Rape) Act 1981. Contrary form of the statute in such case made and provided'. The second count was assault, the particulars being 'contrary to common law and contrary to form of the statute in such case made and provided'. The applicant's counsel argued that there was no offence known to the law as indecent assault. This argument was rejected by the Circuit Court judge (Judge Moriarty). The applicant entered a plea of guilty to the second count. The applicant then applied on judicial review for an order of prohibition, on the grounds that the offence of indecent assault was unknown to the law and, in the alternative, that having accepted the guilty plea to the second count on the indictment, the trial court was precluded from proceeding with Count No. 1, the indecent assault charge, since it amounted to a charge of simple assault, albeit of a higher category to that in Count No. 2. O'Hanlon J dismissed the application for judicial review on both grounds argued.

On the first ground, the applicant argued that legislation such as s. 52 of the Offences against the Person Act 1861 or s. 6 of the Criminal Law Amendment Act 1935, both of which had been replaced by s. 10 of the Criminal Law (Rape) Act 1981, were fundamentally flawed since they provided for a penalty for indecent assault without creating new offences by express terms, and that this invalidated the indictments in the instant case.

O'Hanlon J did not accept this argument. He reviewed the history of assault, noting that it was a misdemeanour at common law, and indictable at common law according to the aggravating features associated with the particular form it might take. Having regard to the wide meaning given to assault (which could incorporate what was strictly speaking a battery) he pointed out that, historically, it was thought right to regulate by statute the penalties that could be imposed for different circumstances of assault, and that this had involved a statutory regulation of the penalty to be imposed for the old common law misdemeanour of assault. Accordingly, he concluded that the statutes in question were not in any respect defective, since they merely set penalties for different forms of common law assaults. Thus, he concluded that the indictments in the instant case disclosed an offence known to the law. He cited in support the judgment of Finlay P (as he then was) in *The State (Foley) v Carroll* [1980] IR 150.

O'Hanlon J also rejected the applicant's second argument which had suggested, in effect, that the indictment was bad for duplicity. Citing *R. v Bostock* (1893) 17 Cox CC 700, he accepted that it had been unnecessary in the instant case to include assault in Count No. 2 on the indictment, because if a person was found not guilty of indecent assault then a conviction for assault could be made. However, he concluded that it was permissible to include alternative charges in the indictment, provided that convictions were not entered on both counts. He noted that s. 14 of the Interpretation Act 1937 was aimed at prohibiting dual convictions arising out of the same episode rather than dual charges arising out of the same episode. Alternatively, he noted that the prosecution could also seek to have Count No. 2 removed from the indictment, notwithstanding the guilty plea entered by the applicant, since in any event the applicant would have been entitled to change his plea up to sentencing stage. This conclusion reflected the views he had expressed less than a week earlier in his judgment in *O'Brien v Patwell* [1993] ILRM 614 (discussed below, 292-3).

We noted at the beginning of the discussion of the *Doolan* case that it may be regarded as having more historical than contemporary interest. This, perhaps surprising, suggestion arises form the terms of the Criminal Law (Rape) (Amendment) Act 1990, which came into effect after the events in the *Doolan* case. On the 1990 Act in general, see the 1990 Review, 258-62. S. 2 of the 1990 Act replaces 'indecent assault' with 'sexual assault'. It also expressly provides that sexual assault is a felony. This apparently new approach in drafting technique precludes the type of argument that was, of course, rejected in the *Doolan* case.

## PARTIES

**Accomplice** In *The People v Diemling*, Court of Criminal Appeal, 4 May 1992 the Court held that being an accessory after the fact was sufficient participation to constitute being an accomplice, thus necessitating that the accomplice warning be given to the jury. The judgment of the Court (Hederman, Carroll and Flood JJ) delivered by Hederman J was lengthy but the salient facts may be described, briefly, as follows.

The defendant had been charged with the false imprisonment and murder of one Evans. One of the principal prosecution witnesses was the defendant's daughter. She stated that she had come to Ireland from England on holiday in 1988, that she had met the defendant, her father, and that he had brought her to the place where he was then holding Evans. She stated that she treated Evans for the effects of beatings inflicted on him. After a number of days, she became aware that Evans was dead and stated that his body had been burned beside the place where he had been held. She did not report the matter to the Gardaí at first, but later came forward. The defendant denied that these events had taken place or that Evans was dead.

In the further course of evidence, the suggestion was made that the defendant had been a member of the SAS or similar military unit, but this was withdrawn by the prosecution and the trial judge directed the jury to disregard this suggestion.

The defendant was found guilty on both counts. He was sentenced to life imprisonment for the murder and to seven years imprisonment for the false imprisonment. On appeal to the Court of Criminal Appeal, the defendant argued that the trial judge should have given the jury an accomplice warning in connection with his daughter's evidence. He also argued that the suggested involvement in the SAS or similar military unit rendered the trial unsafe. The Court of Criminal Appeal allowed the appeal on the murder verdict and directed a re-trial, but upheld the false imprisonment conviction.

Delivering the Court's judgment, Hederman J noted that, by her own account, the defendant's daughter was fixed with knowledge of Evans' death, and was aware that he had been beaten. As a result, the Court held, she was therefore aware that the death amounted to homicide; and her subsequent activities in assisting concealment of evidence constituted her an accessory after the fact. Applying the reasoning in *The People v Carney* [1955] IR 324, the Court concluded that, since an accessory can have a sufficient degree of complicity to be an accomplice, this was a matter which the trial judge should have left to the jury to determine, and he should have also warned them on the dangers of convicting on the evidence of an accomplice. The trial judge had thus erred in withdrawing this matter from the jury, and a re- trial on the murder charge was ordered on this ground. However, the Court upheld the false imprisonment conviction on the ground that there was no evidence to support the submission that the defendant's daughter was an accomplice in the unlawful detention of Evans.

On the second ground put forward, the Court held that, since the suggestion that the defendant had been in the SAS had been immediately withdrawn by the prosecution, the trial judge had not erred in refusing to discharge the jury; and his warning to them was regarded as sufficient to prevent any lack of fair procedures.

Finally, for completeness, a note attached by the Court Registrar to the informal headnote circulated with the unreported judgment pointed out that an appeal against severity of sentence on the false imprisonment conviction was withdrawn.

## PROCEDURE

**Additional counts** The power to add charges to an indictment conferred on a Judge of the District Court by s. 8 of the Criminal Procedure Act 1967 was considered by O'Hanlon J in *O'Brien v Patwell* [1993] ILRM 614 (see below, 292-3).

**Amending summons** In *Director of Public Prosecutions v Winston*, High Court, 25 May 1992, the defendant had been charged with an offence under s. 49 of the Road Traffic Act 1961, as amended by the Road Traffic (Amendment) Act 1978. At his trial in the District Court, it was submitted that the summons against the defendant misstated the townland in which the offence was alleged to have taken place, and the District Court judge acceded to an application by the defence to have the case dismissed on that ground. On a case stated to the High Court, O'Hanlon J held that the trial judge had erred in dismissing the case and he remitted the matter to the District Court.

O'Hanlon J took the view that the power of a District Court judge to amend a summons pursuant to r.88 of the District Court Rules 1948 was not dependent on a formal application by the prosecution to have the summons amended. He considered that r.88 was designed to discourage the taking of purely technical objectioins and that the District Court judge would refrain from doing so only where 'the variance, defect or omission is one which has misled or prejudiced the defendant or which might affect the merits of the case. But O'Hanlon J also added that, even where the judge considers that a defect falls into the category in which an amendment should not be made under r.88, he did not consider that a complete dismissal on the merits should always follow. In a significant comment, O'Hanlon J suggested that:

> the position of the accused person could be protected either by making the amendment subject to adjourning the proceedings to a later date, or by dismissing without prejudice to the complaint being again made, and it appears to me that a dismiss on the merits based on a purely technical objection to the form of the complaint should be very much the exception rather than the rule.

This approach reflects recent case law which discourages giving an accused person in a summary trial the full benefit of relatively minor defects in a summons: see for example *DPP (Nagle) v Flynn* [1987] IR 534, discussed in the 1987 Review, 138.

*Autrefois acquit* In *The People v Quilligan and O'Reilly (No. 3)* [1993] 2 IR 305 (the circumstances of which are discussed, 234-9, above), the

Supreme Court considered the legal effect of a verdict of not guilty of murder in the Central Criminal Court which had been set aside on appeal by the Supreme Court: see *The People v Quilligan and O'Reilly* [1987] ILRM 606; [1986] IR 495. The Supreme Court had declined to order a retrial on the murder charge: see *The People v Quilligan and O'Reilly (No. 2)* [1989] ILRM 245; [1989] IR 46 (1988 Review, 168-72), but the appellants faced burglary charges arising out of the same events as had been dealt with in the murder trial. The Supreme Court held that the appellants could not plead autrefois acquit or *res judicata* in relation to the murder trial or the findings of law made by the trial judge in the murder trial, since the not guilty verdict in that case had been set aside by the first Supreme Court decision referred to. Thus, the findings of law in the original trial could not in any way affect the trial judge who presided over the burglary trial.

*Defence request for forensic examination* *Rogers v Director of Public Prosections* [1992] ILRM 695 concerned an application by the defence for a forensic examination of a motor vehicle. The case arose as follows.

During a pursuit of a stolen car in August 1991, Gardaí in the chasing patrol car stated that they recognised the driver of the car as the applicant. After the patrol car had been rammed and the stolen car abandoned, the applicant was arrested in the subsequent chase and was charged on the same date with the unlawful taking of a motor vehicle. The book of evidence was served on the applicant in October 1991, the District Court having declined jurisdiction in September 1991. In late October 1991, the solicitor for the applicant enquired if the car involved in the chase was available for forensic examination. The Gardaí replied that the car had been returned to its owner shortly after the August incident. The applicant applied on judicial review for an order of prohibition in respect of his trial on the ground that, as he was deprived of the opportunity to have the car forensically examined, his trial would not be in due course of law and that fair procedures would not be observed. It emerged in the judicial review proceedings that the car had been forensically examined by the Gardaí prior to its return to the owner and that no fingerprints had been found in the car. O'Hanlon J dismissed the application for an order of prohibition.

The applicant had relied on the decision of Lynch J in *Murphy v Director of Public Prosections* [1989] ILRM 71 (1988 Review, 172-3), but O'Hanlon J distinguished it. In *Murphy*, the applicant had sought a forensic examination at an early stage and prohibition had been granted where the Gardaí had replied that no examination was, in effect, required. O'Hanlon J held that where, as in the instant case, a forensic examination is carried out promptly by the Gardaí and no mention is made of a forensic examination by the defence until over two months after charges had been brought, there was no breach of fair procedures such as would justify the court in halting the prosecution pending against the applicant.

While rejecting the application in the instant case, O'Hanlon J also made some comments of general interest on the subject. He stated that the interests of the innocent owner of stolen property should be taken into consideration where stolen property becomes the subject matter of criminal proceedings, any forensic examination (whether by the prosecution or defence) should take place within a reasonable time, having regard to all the circumstances, so that the property can then be returned as expeditiously as possible to its true owner. This emphasis on the interests of the victim of a crime against property appears to mirror the current legislative emphasis on victim's interests in crimes involving violence, such as is contained in the Criminal Justice Act 1993 (which will be discussed in the 1993 Review).

**Fitness to plead** In *O'Connor v Judges of the Dublin Metropolitan District Court* [1992] 1 IR 387, the timing of an initial examination as to whether an accused was fit to plead arose. In this case, the applicant had been charged with various offences and his case had reached the preliminary examination stage. During the hearing of the preliminary examination in the District Court, the District Court judge dealing with the matter was informed that the applicant's mental condition was such that his legal representatives were unable to take any proper instructions from him. The judge proposed postponing any further steps in the preliminary examination until an inquiry was conducted into the applicant's fitness to plead. The applicant's legal advisers objected to this move, and sought judicial review of the District Court judge's decision on the ground that fitness to plead should be left exclusively as an issue for the court of trial. This line was based on the procedures introduced in Britain by the Criminal Procedure (Insanity) Act 1964, as interpreted in *R. v Webb* [1969] 2 QB 178 and *R. v Burles* [1970] 2 QB 191.

On judicial review, O'Hanlon J held that the judge had taken the appropriate course of action in the case. O'Hanlon J relied to a great extent on dicta of the Supreme Court judges in *The State (C.) v Minister for Justice* [1967] IR 106, which indicated that what was proposed was the appropriate course under the Criminal Procedure Act 1967. He thus held that a preliminary examination could not properly continue in circumstances where the judge dealing with the matter was not satisfied that the accused person was fit to plead. In such a case, O'Hanlon J concluded that the matter should either be investigated by the District Court judge or else the Director of Public Prosecutions should discontinue the prosecution for the time being conditional on the applicant's mental state. In the light of the *C.* case, O'Hanlon J felt precluded from examining the alternative procedure suggested by the applicant's counsel derived from the practice in Britain.

*Murray v Director of Public Prosecutions*, High Court, 13 May 1992, involved the aftermath of a finding of unfitness to plead where a person has been returned for trial under the Criminal Procedure Act 1967. The applicant's next friend sought to have the applicant's pending trial prohibited on the ground that he was not fit to plead by reason of mental infirmity. While Denham J in her judgment accepted that the applicant's mental condition at the time of the application rendered him unfit to plead, the medical evidence adduced indicated that this might not always be the case. On this ground, she was not prepared to make an order which would have the effect of permanently prohibiting the Director from proceeding with the trial. She concluded that the question as to whether the applicant was, ultimately, fit to plead would be a matter for the trial court. This indicates that, once the preliminary examination has been passed, the issue of unfitness to plead passes to the trial court for determination.

*Indictment: duplicity* In *O'Brien v Patwell* [1993] ILRM 614, O'Hanlon J rejected an argument that an indictment was bad for duplicity.

The applicant had been sent forward for trial in the Central Criminal Court on four counts: indecent assault contrary to common law and s. 10 of the Criminal Law (Rape) Act 1981; unlawful carnal knowledge of a girl under 15 years of age, contrary to s. 1 of the Criminal Law Amendment Act 1935; unlawful carnal knowledge of a named female forcibly and against her will contrary to common law; and buggery contrary to s. 61 of the Offences against the Person Act 1861. The fourth count had been added by the respondent District Court Judge under s. 8 of the Criminal Procedure Act 1967 at the conclusion of the preliminary examination. The applicant sought judicial review of the order sending him forward for trial on the grounds that: (i) it was not permissible to send him forward on the second and third counts since they constituted the same offences and thus breached s. 14 of the Interpretation Act 1937 — which prohibits double punishment in respect of the 'same offence' — and that the prosecution should be put to its election; and (ii) the respondent Judge had no jurisdiction under s. 8 of the 1967 Act to add a charge unless this was in substitution for an existing charge. O'Hanlon J dismissed the application.

Referring to the Court of Criminal Appeal decisions in *The People v Dermody* [1956] IR 307 and *The People v Coughlan* (1968) 1 Frewen 325, O'Hanlon J held that the second and third counts on the indictment did not constitute 'the same offence' within s. 14 of the Interpretation Act 1937, since consent was not a defence to the charge under s. 1 of the Criminal Law Amendment Act 1935, whereas it was a defence to the third count. Thus the indictment was not bad for including both counts. In any event, he noted, the prohibition in s. 14 of the 1937 Act was directed at punishment twice-over for a single incident, not against two charges arising from a single episode. He was to reaffirm this same point less than a week later in his judgment in *Doolan v Director of Public Prosecutions* [1993] ILRM 387 (discussed above, 286-7).

As to the power conferred by s. 8 of the Criminal Procedure Act 1967, he held that it was not confined by its terms to the substitution of one count for another, and the respondent Judge had thus been entitled to add a new count to the indictment if satisfied that evidential material put before him justified him in doing so. He noted that a similar power vested in the Director of Public Prosecutions by the 1967 Act had been held not to be repugnant to the Constitution by the Supreme Court in *O'Shea v Director of Public Prosecutions* [1989] ILRM 309; [1988] IR 655 (see the 1988 Review, 166-8).

**Indictment: particulars of sexual assault** In *The People (D.P.P.) v Barr (No. 3)*, Court of Criminal Appeal, 21 July 1992 (discussed in a different context above, 257-9), the defendant had been charged with indecent assault and buggery. The indictment stated that the indecent assault was contrary to common law as provided for in s. 10 of the Criminal Law (Rape) Act 1981, the particulars alleging that on a specified date the defendant indecently assaulted a named female.

It was accepted that the form of the indictment conformed as nearly as possible to the requirements of the Criminal Justice (Administration) Act 1924, but the defence argued that the prosecution was required to specify the particular acts alleged to constitute the indecent assault. In the course of her evidence in the defendant's trial, the complainant stated that the defendant had, *inter alia*, touched her breasts and inserted a stick into her anus and vagina. The defendant was convicted on both counts. On appeal, the Court of Criminal Appeal (McCarthy, Keane and Denham JJ) dismissed the appeal.

The Court approved the decision in *Jemmison v Priddle* [1972] 1 QB 489, in which an identical argument had been rejected. The Court held that since the form of the indictment in the instant case conformed as nearly as may be to the forms in the appendix to the 1924 Act, and since the actions alleged against the defendant could be described as components of a single activity or a chain of similar events, it was not necessary for the indictment to specify separately each act of alleged assault. The Court did add, however, that, as a matter of fairness, it might be that the prosecution would be bound, if requested to do so, to specify the relevant acts alleged to constitute the indecent assaults. This point will doubtless prove influential in future practice in this area.

**Judge and jury** Cases concerning the role of the judge and jury in a criminal trial are discussed above, 271-3.

**Original witness statements** In *The People v Glass (No. 2)*, Court of Criminal Appeal, 23 November 1992, the Court (O'Flaherty, Lynch and Carney JJ), in an *ex tempore* judgment, rejected the argument that the defence is entitled to a 'general delivery up of original statements' under the Criminal Procedure Act 1967. The Court held that only in circumstances where a witness's evidence appears to be in conflict with their original statement of evidence would the issue of putting this contradiction to the witness arise. On another issue raised in the case, see the discussion below, 302-3.

**Preliminary examination** In *O'Flynn v Smithwick* [1993] ILRM 627, Costello J considered some procedural aspects with the relatively little-used depositions element of the preliminary examination.

The applicant had been charged on indictment with, *inter alia*, shooting with intent to cause grevious bodily harm. In the course of the preliminary examination of the case before the respondent, the President of the District Court, the prosecution served notice on the applicant under s. 7 of the Criminal Procedure Act 1967 of its intention to examine by deposition certain witnesses. The applicant requested from the prosecution the statements on which the depositions were to be based. The prosecution replied that, in relation to three witnesses, no statements were available; 'memos' to this effect, based on notes taken by the investigating Gardaí, were furnished to the applicant. During the taking of depositions, the prosecution applied to have the three witnesses in question treated as hostile, the respondent acceded to this application and the witnesses were then cross-examined. The applicant sought judicial review of the procedures leading up to and including the taking of depositions from these three witnesses. Costello J refused the relief sought.

He held that s. 7(2) of the Criminal Procedure Act 1967 did not require that the party requiring the attendance of a witness for the purpose of depositions should forward a statement to the other side of the evidence to be given, so that it did not prohibit either the prosecution or the defence from requiring the attendance of a witness who had refused to be interviewed by either the Gardaí or the accused. Despite this, however, he went on that fair procedures required that where an accused has no pre-knowledge of a witness's statements, the prosecution should furnish the accused with any relevant notes, as was done in the instant case, and that the District Judge may be required to adjourn the taking of depositions to enable the accused instruct legal advisers so that an informed cross-examination may take place.

The applicant had also argued that the Supreme Court decision in *The State (Williams) v Kelleher* [1983] IR 112 indicated that s. 7 of the 1967 Act precluded the prosecution from adducing matters at deposition which have not been included in the information supplied to the accused. Costello J rejected that any dicta in the *Williams* case supported this argument, but he did accept again that an adjournment may be required in such circumstances in order to comply with fair procedures.

As to the procedure for dealing with hostile witnesses, Costello J held that the common law rules by which a party's own witness could be regarded as hostile and thus be cross-examined by that party were based on a wide range of criteria, and he referred approvingly in this context to the decision in *Price v Manning* (1889) 42 Ch D 372, as well as referring to the decision in *The People v Taylor* [1974] IR 97. He considered that these common law rules were not in any way affected by s. 3 of the Criminal Procedure Act 1865, which concerns the power to discredit a hostile witness. Thus, the grounds on which a witness could be treated as hostile were not limited to circumstances in which the witness gave evidence inconsistent with a previous statement; and the first respondent had thus not erred in treating the three witnesses in the instant case as hostile.

**Separation of charges** In *The People v Quilligan and O'Reilly (No. 3)* [1993] 2 IR 305 (the circumstances of which are discussed, 204-9, above), the Supreme Court held that there had been good grounds in the instant case for having burglary and murder charges separated. The appellants had, in 1985, been tried and acquitted on the murder charge laid against them. The Supreme Court upheld the fairness of later trying them on the burglary charge which had been put back pending determination of the murder charge.

**Service of case stated** In *Director of Public Prosecutions (Murphy) v Regan* [1993] ILRM 335, O'Hanlon J reluctantly declined to hear a case stated where the applicant prosecutor had failed to serve a notice in writing on the defendant as required by s. 2 of the Summary Jurisdiction Act 1857: see the discussion in the Practice and Procedure chapter, 474-6, below.

**Test case for DNA evidence** In *The People v Barr (No. 3)*, Court of Criminal Appeal, 21 July 1992 (discussed above, 257-9), the Court unreservedly condemned the suggestion that a court of trial could be used as a testing area for the admissibility of evidence, forensic or otherwise.

## ROAD TRAFFIC

**Breathalyser test** In *Director of Public Prosecutions v Gaughran* [1993] ILRM 472, the defendant had been charged with driving with an excess of alcohol under s. 49 of the Road Traffic Act 1961, as amended. Prior to his arrest under s. 49, the defendant had been breathalysed by the arresting Garda. At his trial in the District Court, the charge was dismissed on the ground that no evidence was given that the arresting Garda had informed the defendant of his obligation to give a breath test under s. 12 of the Road Traffic (Amendment) Act 1978 and of the consequences of a refusal to take such a breath test. On a case stated, O'Hanlon J held that the District Court judge erred in this decision and he remitted the case to the District Court.

O'Hanlon J held that a crucial factor in the instant case was that this was not a case where the defendant had refused to take a breathalyser test and had then been charged with refusal to take a test under s. 12 of the 1978 Act. In those circumstances, he considered that there was no obligation on the arresting Garda to inform the defendant of the statutory basis on which he was requiring him to take a breathalyser test. In this respect, he followed the decision of Keane J in *Director of Public Prosecutions v Brett*, High Court, 19 March 1991. In that case, Keane J had also distinguished this type of case from that discussed by the Supreme Court in its *ex tempore* decision in *Director of Public Prosecutions v McGarrigle*, Supreme Court, 22 June 1987. In that case, where a defendant had been prosecuted under s. 13 of the 1978 Act for failure to provide a blood or urine sample, the Supreme Court had held that the charge was correctly dismissed where the defendant was not informed that the sample is being required under s. 13 and of the consequences of a failure to provide the sample. However, the *Gaughran* case did not involve that situation, and thus O'Hanlon J remitted the charge to the District Court.

**Opinion grounding arrest** In *Director of Public Prosecutions v Ó Súilleabháin* [1993] ILRM 14, the defendant had been charged with the following offences: driving with an excess of alcohol under s. 49 of the Road Traffic Act 1961, as amended by s. 10 of the Road Traffic (Amendment) Act 1978 and s. 3 of the Road Traffic (Amendment) Act 1984; failing to provide a blood sample to a registered medical practitioner, contrary to s. 33 of the Road Traffic (Amendment) Act 1978, as amended by s. 5 of the Road Traffic (Amendment) Act 1984; and dangerous driving, contrary to s. 53 of the 1961 Act, as amended by s. 51 of the Road Traffic Act 1968 and s. 3 of the Road Traffic (Amendment) Act 1984.

At the trial in the District Court, the arresting Garda had given evidence that he was on duty in Kildare St, Dublin, at about 2.35 a.m. on the morning in question when he heard a loud crash from a particular direction and went towards this. He saw a car half on the footpath and half on the road, that the car was badly damaged and that it had struck a wall. The defendant, who was standing beside the car, acknowledged that he had been driving the car and the arresting Garda also gave evidence that he got a strong smell of intoxicating liquor from the defendant's breath. The Garda then stated that he informed the defendant that he was committing an offence under s. 49 of the

1961 Act and thereupon arrested him under that section. He was brought to a Garda station where he was unable to give a urine sample and refused to give a blood sample.

The District Court judge dismissed the charges under s. 49 of the 1961 Act and s. 33 of the 1978 Act on the ground that the arresting Garda had not given sufficient evidence to indicate that he had formed the opinion that the defendant was incapable of driving the car in question as required by s. 49 of the 1961 Act. She also substituted the offence of driving without due consideration, contrary to s. 51A of the 1961 Act, in place of the dangerous driving charge, and convicted the defendant on the s. 51A charge alone. On case stated to the High Court, Carroll J found that the District Court judge had erred on both points.

As to the opinion required of the arresting Garda, Carroll J interpreted the language used by the Garda as indicating that he had informed the defendant that the defendant had committed an offence when he was driving the car rather than that he was committing an offence as he stood beside the car after the crash. Having determined that issue of interpretation in favour of the Garda, Carroll J concluded that his indication to the defendant that he had 'committed an offence under s. 49 of the Act' was sufficient evidence to indicate that he had formed an opinion that the defendant was incapable of driving the vehicle. In this respect, Carroll J placed emphasis on the surrounding circumstances to which the Garda had testified, and thus drew a direct comparison with the circumstances in, and rationale of the decision in, *Director of Public Prosecutions v O'Connor* [1985] ILRM 333. For a case distinguishing *O'Connor*, see *Director of Public Prosecutions v Lynch*, High Court, 7 November 1990 (1990 Review, 243).

As to the substitution of driving without due consideration, Carroll J held that the District Court judge had no jurisdiction to make such an order. She noted that s. 53 of the 1961 Act permitted the substitution by the trial court of careless driving, the offence created by s. 52 of the 1961 Act, for dangerous driving. But s. 53 did not permit the trial court to substitute the driving without due consideration offence created by s. 51A of the 1961 Act. Carroll J pointed out that a trial judge was not, other than provided for by law, authorised to charge a person with an offence, citing dicta to that effect from *Attorney General (McDonnell) v Higgins* [1964] IR 374.

**Reasons for arrest: 'drunk driving'** In *Director of Public Prosecutions v Mooney* [1993] ILRM 214; [1992] 1 IR 548, Blayney J discussed whether an arresting Garda had sufficiently informed the arrested person of the basis for an arrest under s. 49 of the Road Traffic Act 1961. The circumstances were as follows.

The defendant had been stopped by a Garda while driving his car. The

Garda later stated that he got a smell of intoxicating liquor from the defendant and that his speech was slurred. A breathalyser test proved positive. The Garda formed the opinion that the defendant was committing an offence under s. 49(2) or (3) of the 1961 Act. He arrested the defendant under s. 49(6) of the 1961 Act and informed the defendant that he was being arrested pursuant to s. 49(6) of the 1961 Act for the offence of 'drunk driving'. The defendant was charged under s. 49(3) with the offence of attempting to drive when he was in excess of the permitted level of alcohol. At his trial in the District Court, it was argued that the defendant had not been validly arrested since the offence of 'drunk driving' was, if anything, an offence under s. 49(1) of the 1961 Act and not the offence under s. 49(3) with which the defendant had been charged, and that, accordingly, the defendant had not been propely informed of the basis on which he was being arrested. This point was accepted by the District Court judge. On case stated to the High Court Blayney J held that the District Court judge had erred in this conclusion.

Blayney J considered that the description 'drunk driving' applied equally to offences under s. 49(1), (2) and (3). He held that the clear reason why driving under the three different circumstances described in these subsections was prohibited was that, if the concentration of alcohol in a person's system was over the permitted level, it would be likely to impair the person's ability to have proper control of a motor vehicle. He concluded therefore that, in substance, there was very little difference between the three subsections.

Looking at the purpose of the rule that the arresting Garda inform the person of the reason for an arrest, Blayney J referred to a passage from the speech of Viscount Simon in the House of Lords decision in *Christie v Leachinsky* [1947] AC 573, as approved by O'Higgins CJ delivering the majority judgment in *The People v Walsh* [1980] IR 294. Blayney J noted that the rule is based on ensuring that the arrested person knows in substance why they are being arrested, rather than that they are given a technical explanation. Thus, he held that the use of the phrase 'drunk driving' in the instant case was a sufficient communication of the reason for the arrest.

Blayney J also added, possibly *obiter*, that in light of the positive result from the breathalyser test, the defendant must have been well aware of the basis for his arrest, and so it must be doubtful whether the Garda was required to explain the basis on which he was being arrested.

See to the same effect in a different context the decision of O'Hanlon J in *Director of Public Prosecutions v Rooney* [1993] ILRM 61, discussed below, 304-5.

## SENTENCING

**Acquittal on lesser charge** In *The People v McKeever*, Court of Criminal Appeal, 16 July 1992 (discussed earlier, 233, 271) the defendant had been charged in the Circuit Criminal Court on three counts arising from the same incident: robbery of £35; possession of a firearm with intent to commit an indictable offence, namely robbery; and possession of a firearm with intent to endanger life. At his trial, the defendant was acquitted on the charge of possession of a firearm with intent to endanger life, but was convicted on the other two charges. He was sentenced to two concurrent terms of six years imprisonment. The Court (O'Flaherty, Lynch and Denham JJ) allowed the defendant's appeal against severity of sentence. It considered that the sentence of six years may not have reflected the acquittal of the defendant on the most serious charge, and in these circumstances it was reduced to four years, to run from the date of the offences and the defendant's arrest.

**Attempted rape** In *The People v Riordan (No. 2)*, Court of Criminal Appeal, 29 July 1992, the Court (Egan, Keane and Budd JJ), in an *ex tempore* judgment, reduced a sentence for attempted rape from five years penal servitude to three years. The Court noted that the defendant had been acquitted of rape in his trial. While it accepted the view of Lord Goddard in *R. v Morris* [1951] 1 KB 394 that, in the absence of a statutory provision leading to a different conclusion, a common law misdemeanour remained punishable at the discretion of the Court, the Court also referred with approval to the decision of the Northern Ireland Court of Appeal in *R. v Taylor* [1958-9] NI 135, also a case of attempted rape. In the *Taylor* case, the Court of Appeal had tempered the view of Lord Goddard with the comment that, since Parliament had provided in s. 38 of the Offences against the Person Act 1861 that the maximum sentence for assault with intent to commit a felony was two years imprisonment, it was difficult to think that Parliament intended to leave a general discretion without limit to sentencing courts. In the *Riordan* case, the Court of Criminal Appeal pointed out that, in this jurisdiction, the reasoning in the *Taylor* case could be supported by reference to s. 10(1) of the Criminal Law (Rape) Act 1981, which provided that the maximum sentence for indecent assault was ten years imprisonment. The Court regarded indecent assault as being extremely close to the offence of attempted rape. It was on this basis that the Court reduced the sentence from five to three years. We should note here that the offence of indecent assault was replaced by new offences in the Criminal Law (Rape) (Amendment) Act 1990: see the 1990 Review, 258-62.

**Collection of fines** In *The People v Connors*, Court of Criminal Appeal,

11 March 1992, the Court (Hederman, Barr and Lavan JJ), in an *ex tempore* judgment, criticised the failure by the State to collect fines imposed on the defendant for previous offences. The practice had apparently developed by which such fines were not collected where a custodial sentence was executed and that this was also deemed to execute all elements of a particular warrant, including the fines imposed. The Court did not consider that such practice was acceptable, and that all elements of a sentence including the fine imposed 'must be obeyed by the appropriate State authority' and there could be no question of a general policy directive that fines are not to be collected.

**Consecutive sentence** In *The People v Bollard*, Court of Criminal Appeal, 25 May 1992, the Court (McCarthy, Carney and Flood JJ), in an *ex tempore* judgment, reduced a sentence of penal servitude from five years to three years. The defendant had been convicted in the Circuit Criminal Court with a co-accused of wounding and assault occasioning actual bodily harm, and the trial judge imposed a sentence of seven years on the co-accused and one of five years on the defendant. In fact, the maximum sentence permissible was five years, and in the circumstances, the Court of Criminal Appeal reduced the sentence on the defendant to three years, on the basis that the trial judge had intended there be a disparity between the defendant and his co-accused. However, the Court noted that the defendant had committed other offences while he was on bail awaiting trial on the instant charges and had been sentenced in the District Court in respect of those other matters before the instant sentencing. The Court acknowledged that the mandatory consecutive sentencing provisions contained in s. 11 of the Criminal Justice Act 1984 did not apply to the instant offences, as s. 11 is confined to offences in respect of which a person is given a sentence of imprisonment as opposed to one of penal servitude. Nonetheless, the Court declined to interfere with the trial judge's order in the instant case that the defendant's sentence run consecutively to the sentences imposed on him in the District Court, commenting that the sanction in relation to offences committed while on bail should be more severe than would otherwise be the case.

**Drugs supply** In *The People v Melia*, Court of Criminal Appeal, 11 May 1992, the Court (Hederman, Barron and Denham JJ), in an *ex tempore* judgment, upheld a sentence of seven years for possession of heroin (diamorphine) which had been imposed on the defendant to run consecutively to a sentence of ten years for possession of firearms. Although the defendant was acknowledged to have been a heroin user and had also pleaded guilty to the drugs charges, the Court also took account of the fact that the amount found in his possession had a sale value of between £25,000 and £50,000, and had been packed in amounts which indicated that it would be sold in very small quantities to young people. In those particular circumstances, the Court concluded that it would not interfere with the sentence imposed. However, the Court noted that, in view of the defendant's own use of drugs, every effort should be made to assist him to overcome this problem while in prison.

**Indecent assault** In *The People v C.K.*, Court of Criminal Appeal, 16 November 1992, the Court (Blayney, Lynch and Lavan JJ), in an *ex tempore* judgment on an appeal in an indecent assault case, confirmed a sentence of five years imposed on the applicant. The sentence had been imposed in November 1990 and had in fact been suspended in full. However, the defendant later committed the same offences and in December 1991 the sentence was reimposed. The defendant appealed his original sentence, but was out of time. The Court indicated that it would not have hard the appeal but for the consent of the Director of Public Prosecutions. The Court was told that the sentence was on foot of a first offence, that the defendant had a son suffering from cerebral palsy and that the defendant's imprisonment would impose a large burden on his family. However, the Court considered that the sentence had been an appropriate sentence and declined to alter it in the instant case.

**Indecent assault: lack of treatment** In *The People v Nealon*, Court of Criminal Appeal, 16 November 1992, the Court (Blayney, Lynch and Lavan JJ), in an *ex tempore* judgment on an appeal in an indecent assault case, rejected an argument that the Court should take account on appeal that there was no psychosexual treatment available for the defendant. The Court stated that the appropriate course for the defendant was to initiate an inquiry under Article 40.4.2 into the legality of his detention. However, the Court did reduce the applicant's sentence of ten years, the maximum for the offence, to one of nine years on the ground that the trial judge had not taken into account the defendant's guilty plea.

**Leniency or clemency** In *The People v Gilmore*, Court of Criminal Appeal, 9 November 1992, the Court (Finlay CJ, Keane and Carney JJ), in an *ex tempore* judgment, applied the principles laid down in *The People v Walsh* (1989) 3 Frewen 248 (see the 1991 Review, 180) and in *The People v Connington*, Court of Criminal Appeal, 17 December 1990 (see the 1991 Review, 174 and 179) in holding that the behaviour of a defendant after the imposition of sentence was not a matter to be considered by it on appeal but was a matter for the executive to take into account in granting clemency. However, the Registrar's note circulated with the judgment in *Gilmore* indicated that the applicants' appeal against sentence was successful on 7 December 1992. They had both pleaded guilty to robbery in the Special

Criminal Court and been sentenced to seven years imprisonment. The Court of Criminal Appeal reduced the sentence to five years.

## STOP AND SEARCH POWERS

**Constitutional validity** In *O'Callaghan v Ireland*, High Court, 1 April 1992; Supreme Court, 24 May 1993, the High Court and, on appeal, the Supreme Court, upheld the constitutional validity of the stop and search powers conferred on Gardaí by s. 23 of the Misuse of Drugs Act 1977, as amended by s. 12 of the Misuse of Drugs Act 1984. We will discuss in detail the Supreme Court decision in this case in the 1993 Review.

We will discuss here two judgments of O'Hanlon J concerning different aspects of other stop and/or search powers conferred on the Gardaí.

**Search warrant** In *The People v Glass (No. 2)*, Court of Criminal Appeal, 23 November 1992, the Court (O'Flaherty, Lynch and Carney JJ), in an *ex tempore* judgment, dealt with issues arising from the issuing of a search warrant under under s. 29 of the Offences against the State Act 1939, as inserted by s. 5 of the Criminal Law Act 1976. S. 29 of the 1939 Act provides that a Garda Superintendent may issue a search warrant authorising the search of a premises where he has reasonable grounds for believing that an offence under the 1939 Act, or a scheduled offence, or an offence under the 1976 Act has been or is about to be committed.

Premises belonging to the defendant had been searched on foot of a warrant issued under s. 29 of the 1939 Act. As a result of the search, a number of cars were found and the defendant was charged with receiving the cars and of malicious damage to one of the cars. The defendant was convicted in the Circuit Criminal Court and sentenced to five years imprisonment. On appeal, the defendant argued that the warrant issued under s. 29 of the 1939 Act must state the offences in respect of which the Superintendent has reasonable grounds to believe that the issuing of the warrant is justified. The defendant argued by analogy with the requirement on the Gardaí to inform an arrested person of the grounds on wich a person is arrested, and he relied on the judgment of Walsh J in *The People v Quilligan and O'Reilly* [1987] ILRM 606; [1986] IR 495 in this respect. The Court in the instant case rejected this analogy, on the basis that the rule requiring a reason be given to an arrested person is that the arrested person is entitled to decide the best course of action to take in relation to preparing a defence to any possible charge. In the case of a search warrant, however, the Court considered that the Superintendent would not be aware at the time of the issuing of the warrant whether there would in fact be any items of evidence to be found in the premises to be searched. In that sense, one could comment that the Court did not consider that the matter had come into sufficient focus to identify a person in respect of whom any criminal charges might be brought. This distinction has been employed by the courts in the context of whether a person in a police station is under arrest, on which see the judgment of Walsh J in the *Quilligan* case also.

On another aspect of the case, see above, 294.

**Stop power at common law** In *Director of Public Prosecutions v Cowman* [1993] 1 IR 335, O'Hanlon J discussed the common law power of a Garda to stop a member of the public. A Garda had approached the defendant in public. The Garda later gave evidence that he saw the defendant stagger, that he got the smell of intoxicating liquor from him and that when he asked the defendant for his name and address, the defendant became very agitated. The Garda stated he then formed the opinion that the defendant had taken drugs due to his demeanour and unreasonable behaviour and that he then informed the defendant he was arresting and detaining him under the Misuse of Drugs Acts 1977 and 1984 for the purpose of searching him. The Garda stated that the defendant resisted arrest with some violence. When the defendant was brought to a Garda station, he was found to be in possession of a dagger-type knife, an eight-inch blade and a wooden handle.

The defendant was charged with a number of offences: of being guilty of a breach of the peace; of being drunk and disorderly; of assault of the Garda; and possession of a knife contrary to s. 9 of the Firearms and Offensive Weapons Act 1990.

At the defendant's trial in the District Court, the arresting Garda was asked by the District Court judge why he had approached the defendant in the first place. The Garda replied: 'I don't know, I just had a feeling about him.' The judge dismissed the charges against the defendant on the ground that this was an insufficient basis on which to approach the defendant and that the subsequent arrest was thus unlawful. On case stated to the High Court, O'Hanlon J held that the judge had erred in law in this conclusion. He considered that such a view would severely restrict the Gardaí in their investigation of crime, and that a Garda could not approach a member of the public without already having formed an opinion that some grounds existed for suspecting that person had already committed or was about to commit a crime. He continued:

> I do not consider that any such restriction is imposed by law on the right of a member of the Garda Síochána to approach members of the public from time to time as he thinks fit for the purpose of speaking to them and having communication with them on an informal basis.

On this basis, O'Hanlon J remitted the case to the District Court to enter continuances in the case.

It is important to bear in mind that this case was decided in the context of a decision by the Garda in question to approach the individual in question not with a view to arrest but rather for the 'informal' discussion referred to by O'Hanlon J. It is not, therefore, authority for a wider proposition conferring stop and search powers on the Gardaí. It might be best described as a case on 'stop powers'. The more extensive 'stop and search' powers can only be conferred by specific legislation, as the second judgment by O'Hanlon J in this area makes clear.

**Dublin Police Act 1842** In *Director of Public Prosecutions v Rooney* [1993] ILRM 61; [1992] 2 IR 7 (delivered a week before his judgment in Cowman, above), O'Hanlon J discussed the nature of the power to stop and search under the Dublin Police Act 1842.

The defendant, while walking on a street in Dublin, had been approached by a member of the Garda Síochána and was asked what money he had in his hand. On showing a £10 and £5 note, he was asked if he had any other money and he said 'No'. The Garda then put his hand in the defendant's pocket, the defendant lifting his hands out of the way to allow the Garda reach towards the pocket. The Garda found a £20 note which he believed was a forgery. The defendant was charged with possession of forged bank notes, contrary to s. 8 of the Forgery Act 1913.

At his trial in the District Court, objection was taken to the admission of the Garda's evidence on the ground that the Garda had failed to inform the defendant of the legal basis on which he was searching the defendant. The prosecution relied on s. 29 of the Dublin Police Act 1842, which (as adapted) provided that a member of the Garda Síochána 'may . . . stop, search and detain . . . any person who may be reasonably suspected of having or conveying in any manner any thing stolen or unlawfully obtained. . . .' On a consultative case stated to the High Court, O'Hanlon J remitted the case to the District Court, holding that the defence submission had been correct.

O'Hanlon J used by way of analogy the rule in *Christie v Leachinsky* [1947] AC 573 (as followed in *The People v White* [1947] IR 247) which requires a Garda to inform a person of the basis for an arrest. O'Hanlon J accepted that, although the power to stop and search contained in s. 29 of the 1842 Act was less drastic in its effect than a power of arrest, it nonetheless amounted to a substantial and significant interference with the liberty of the subject. He concluded that, if the constitutional guarantees of liberty of the person were to be adequately defended and vindicated, it required that before the power of search in s. 29 could be lawfully exercised, the person stopped was entitled to be informed of the nature and description of the statutory power being invoked, namely that he was suspected of having or conveying something stolen or unlawfully obtained, and that the person also be informed of the search power contained in s. 29 of the 1842 Act.

O'Hanlon J also noted, however, that it was not required to arrest the person prior to exercising the power to search, unless this was necesary for some other reason, thus underlining the distinction between the stop power and the arrest power.

Of course, it has been shown in cases such as *The People v Coffey* [1987] ILRM 727 and *The People v McGinley (D.)* (1987) 3 Frewen 233 (1991 Review, 130) that in some instances arrest and detention are synonymous. Nonetheless, it seems clear that an express power to stop and search will be sufficient to distinguish it from an arrest, so that the legal principles associated with the arrest power will not come into play. However, in light of O'Hanlon J's decision in *Rooney*, the stop and search power is now clearly subject to its own particular procedural protections. We will discuss this in the context of the Supreme Court decision in *O'Callaghan v Ireland*, High Court, 1 April 1992; Supreme Court, 24 May 1993 (referred to above, 303) in the 1993 Review.

## VICTIMS

The position of the victim of crime in the overall context of Irish criminal procedure was alluded to in *Rogers v Director of Public Prosecutions* [1992] ILRM 695 (see 290-1, above).

## YOUNG PERSONS

**Summary trial on indictable offence** *Hutch v Governor of Wheatfield Prison and Ors*, High Court, 28 February 1992; Supreme Court, 17 November 1992 is an important decision on the statutory sentencing limits in respect of a young person who is tried summarily for an indictable offence.

The applicant had been charged with a number of indictable offences, involving stealing and malicious damage to property. With his consent, he was tried summarily in the District Court. He was convicted and sentenced to three terms of one year's imprisonment in respect of three of the charges, two of the terms to run consecutively. The trial judge imposed these sentences in purported exercise of powers in s. 2 of the Criminal Justice Act 1951, which empowers the District Court to try summarily certain indictable offences, including the offences with which the applicant was charged. However, the applicant sought judicial review on the ground that s. 5 of the

Summary Jurisdiction Over Children (Ireland) Act 1884 limited the District Court to imposing a sentence of three months on a young person tried summarily for an indictable offence. 'Young person' is defined by s. 9 of the 1884 Act, as amended by s. 28 of the Children Act 1941, as a person between the age of 15 and 17. The applicant fell into this age category.

In the High Court O'Hanlon J granted the judicial review sought and quashed the sentences, holding that they were *ultra vires* s. 5 of the 1884 Act. On appeal by the respondents, this decision was upheld by the Supreme Court (Finlay CJ, O'Flaherty and Egan JJ).

Delivering the only reasoned judgment, Finlay CJ noted that s. 5 of the 1884 Act constituted a specific enactment establishing a very definite and important right for young persons. Since s. 2 of the 1951 Act conferred a general jurisdiction on the District Court without reference to the 1884 Act, he concluded that the maxim *generalia specialibus non derogant* applied, applying dicta in the House of Lords decision in *Seward v 'Vera Cruz'* (1884) 10 App Cas 59 on this point (for a recent Irish decision on the maxim, see *The People v T.* (1989) 3 Frewen 141, discussed in the 1989 Review, 151-3). It followed, he said, that the special provision in s. 5 of the 1884 Act — whose continued validity had been recognised by the amendment to the definition of a 'young person' effected by s. 28 of the 1941 Act — had not been impliedly repealed by the general provision in s. 2 of the 1951 Act. Consequently, s. 2 of the 1951 Act could not be regarded even as an optional jurisdiction which could be exercised by a court of summary jurisdiction over young persons who came within the terms of the 1884 Act. Therefore, the Chief Justice concldued that the sentences imposed in the instant case had been *ultra vires*.

# Defence Forces

## MILITARY DISCIPLINE

An excellent overview of the background to the Courts-Martial Appeal Act 1983 and the effects of that Act is provided in Raymond Murphy's article (1992) 2 Irish Criminal Law Journal 94.

**Court-Martial** In *In re Murphy*, Courts-Martial Appeal Court, 17 November 1992, certain aspects of court-martial procedure were considered. The accused, a Private in the Irish Army, had been charged with desertion. Prior to his court-martial, he had requested that he be defended by one Captain Milner, but it emerged that this officer was unavailable. The accused was informed by the Convening Authority (that is, the person making the arrangements for the court-martial) that another officer, Captain White, was available. The accused asked the Convening Authority to ask Captain White if he was willing to act for him. Captain White agreed to act for the accused. The Convening Authority subsequently served on the accused a copy of the charge sheet, and under Article 20(3) of the Rules of Procedure (Defence Forces) 1954, asked the accused if he wished to be represented by a particular officer or if he wished the Convening Authority to assign an officer. In reply, the accused gave Captain White's name. Article 20(3) requires the Convening Authority to assign a suitable officer if requested to do so by an accused. At his court-martial, the accused pleaded guilty to being absent without leave, and this plea was accepted. He was ordered to be discharged from the Defence Forces. As already indicated, his appeal concerned procedural aspects of the court-martial, in particular the manner in which Captain White had come to represent him.

The Courts-Martial Appeal Court (Blayney, Lynch and Lavan JJ), dismissing the appeal, held that the Convening Authority had not acted in breach of Art. 20(4) of the 1954 Rules since although the accused's original choice of officer was unavailable, the Convening Authority had not been requested to assign an officer to the accused, but rather the accused had requested that Captain White act for him. The Court also distinguished the instant case from *The State (Freeman) v Connellan* [1987] ILRM 470, in which the accused had been deprived of legal representation.

The Court also noted that it had, pursuant to s. 17 of the Courts-Martial Appeals Act 1983, taken into account additional evidence by the accused that he had been subjected to violence by his wife, and that he had feared that she might become violent to their children and that this had led him to stay in England with his children. However, the Court concluded that, even if the Court-Martial had had this evidence available to it, it was unlikely that it would have affected its decision. See also Raymond Murphy's note on the case in (1993) 3 ICLJ 190.

# Education

## DUBLIN INSTITUTE OF TECHNOLOGY

The Dublin Institute of Technology Act 1992 provided for the creation of the Dublin Institute of Technology (DIT). The DIT Act came into effect on 1 January 1993: Dublin Institute of Technology Act 1992 (Commencement) Order 1992 (SI No. 336).

In effect, the DIT Act created a unitary and independent structure for a number of third level Dublin colleges, most of which had been under the control of the Dublin Vocational Education Committee. The colleges concerned are specified in the First Schedule to the DIT Act, namely the College of Catering, Cathal Brugha St.; the College of Commerce, Rathmines; the College of Marketing and Design, Mountjoy Square; the College of Technology, Bolton St.; the College of Technology, Kevin St.; and the College of Music, Adelaide Rd. S. 3 of the DIT Act also provides that other institutions may, by Order of the Minister for Education, be incorporated into the DIT at any stage in the future.

The DIT Act sets out the structures of the DIT itself, including a chief executive (Director), a governing body and an academic council. The relevant provisions are modelled on those contained in recent legislation in this area, notably the University of Limerick Acts 1980 and 1989 and the Dublin City University Acts 1980 and 1989 (see the Annual Review, 190-1). These Acts, together with the DIT Act and the Regional Technical Colleges Act 1992, discussed below, are part of the overall updating of the general legislative framework for education in Ireland, ranging from the primary, through the second and on to the third level.

## HIGHER EDUCATION GRANTS

S. 3 of the Local Authorities (Higher Education Grants) Act 1992 amends s. 2 of the Local Authorities (Higher Education Grants) Act 1968 by providing for improved access for mature students to higher education grants. The details of eligibility for mature students will be set out in Regulations to be made by the Minister for Education under s. 2 of the 1968 Act, as amended by s. 3 of the 1992 Act. S. 4 of the 1992 Act also amends s. 2 of the 1968 Act by providing for recognition of second level terminal results obtained outside the State, that is, other than the Leaving Certificate, for the purpose of qualifying for higher education grants. S. 5 of the 1992 Act provides that it applies to places obtained in third level colleges in 1992 and subsequent years. S. 6 provides that Regulations made under the 1968 Act, as amended, are subject to the negative annulment procedure in the Oireachtas.

## INTERMEDIATE EDUCATION

The Registration Council (Constitution and Procedure) (Amendment) Rules 1992 (SI No. 33), made under the Intermediate Education (Ireland) Act 1914, provide for Dublin City University and the University of Limerick to have nominees on the Registration Council.

## LEGAL EDUCATION

The statutory provisions concerning the Incorporated Law Society's examinations are referred to in the Solicitors chapter, 549, below.

## NCEA DESIGNATION OF COLLEGES

**Garda College** The National Council for Educational Awards Act 1979 (Designation of Institutions) (No. 2) Order 1992 (SI No. 304) designated the Garda Síochána College, Templemore as being an institution to which the 1979 Act applied, and it thus came within the remit of the NCEA.

**Griffith College** The National Council for Educational Awards Act 1979 (Designation of Institutions) Order 1992 (SI No. 240) designated Griffith College, Dublin as being an institution to which the 1979 Act applied, and it thus came within the remit of the NCEA.

**Newman College** The National Council for Educational Awards Act 1979 (Designation of Institutions) (No. 3) Order 1992 (SI No. 398) designated Newman College, Dublin as being an institution to which the 1979 Act applied, and it thus came within the remit of the NCEA.

## NATIONAL UNIVERSITY OF IRELAND

**Pension scheme** In *Linehan v University College Cork,* High Court, 31 January 1992, the applicant unsuccessfully sought judicial review of a decision of the Pensions Committee of University College Cork to refuse him a particular form of pension under the statutes of the National University of Ireland (NUI). The case arose against the following background.

The applicant had been a college lecturer in the law faculty of University College Cork. Owing to his health giving way, he was unable to carry out fully his lecturing duties in the year 1981-2. During the academic year 1985-6, he gave no lectures during the latter part of the year but continued to give tutorials. In Spring 1985, the applicant applied for sabbatical leave in order to study in Harvard University, but this was refused. The UCC authorities became concerned about the applicant's health and at a meeting in July 1985 with the college President and Secretary, they suggested that he retire and that in such event a lump sum would be payable to him or that he could resign on health grounds and that he could be dismissed on that basis. Some negotiations took place concerning this, but nothing came of them.

In February 1986, the applicant was suspended by the college, and he then instituted High Court plenary proceedings challenging this. These proceedings were compromised by agreement in July 1986, under which the college agreed to a decree for £40,000 together with a contribution of £5,000 towards the applicant's legal costs. The settlement also provided that the applicant would resign from his position as college lecturer with effect from 30 June 1987, that he would be paid his usual salary until then, that he would deliver an irrevocable letter of resignation to the college and that he would not attend at the college from 1 July 1986 save to remove his personal effects or on invitation. A letter of resignation was duly forwarded by the applicant in July 1986.

The applicant subsequently attended Harvard University during the year 1986-7 and was awarded an LL.M. degree. However, he became ill in May 1987 and returned to Ireland. In July 1987 he wrote to the college inquiring about his pension entitlements. It emerged that there were two types of pensions that might be of relevance to the applicant. NUI statute 79 of 1968 provided that an employee who is incapable of discharging his duties by reason of infirmity of mind or body or whose incapacity is, in the opinion of the Pensions Committee, likely to be permanent must retire and on so retiring would be entitled to a pension. Under NUI statute 108 of 1976, a pension was also payable in respect of a person who had left the service of the college other than by reason of dismissal for misconduct or for dereliction of duty. This pension was payable only on the employee reaching 60 years of age. After lengthy correspondence between the applicant and the college and the taking of medical examinations by the applicant, the Pensions Committee concluded that the applicant was entitled to a pension under NUI statute 108 of 1976 when he reached the age of 60.

The applicant then instituted the instant judicial review proceedings claiming, in effect, that he was entitled to a pension under NUI statute 79 of 1968. Barron J dismissed the claim.

Barron J first expressed some doubt as to whether judicial review was the appropriate remedy to seek in a case in which the basis for the claim appeared to be in contract. On this point, see the 1990 Review, 12-14 and the 1991 Review, 14. However, since the respondent college indicated that it wished the issues raised by the applicant to be determined by the court, Barron J proceeded with the case.

As to whether the applicant was entitled to a pension under NUI statute 79 of 1968 by reason of incapacity arising during employment which is likely to be permanent, Barron J stated that there was 'undoubtedly evidence from which the appropriate authority might have so decided' in relation to the applicant. However, he also noted that the applicant had at the relevant time 'refused to acknowledge any such incapacity'. He noted that the applicant's 1986 High Court proceedings were based on his full capacity. On this basis, Barron J concluded that the applicant 'cannot now turn around and claim that he was in fact incapacitated'. Barron J also pointed out that the applicant had retired by agreement under the terms of the settlement of those 1986 proceedings.

Nor did he accept the applicant's alternative argument that, since he became ill in May 1987 before his term of employment actually came to an end, the terms of NUI statute 79 of 1968 applied to him. Barron J held that, once the applicant had resigned through the letter of July 1986, any subsequent incapacity was incapable of bringing his employment to an end since it 'was already prospectively at an end'. He considered that NUI statute 79 of 1968 only applied to a person in employment and who, if the application for a pension fails, will continue in employment. Barron J concluded that the applciant did not fall into this position as, whatever happened, his employment would have ended in June 1987. On this basis, he dismissed the applicant's claim.

## RECOGNITION OF QUALIFICATIONS

**Veterinary Medicine** The European Communities (Recognition of Qualifications in Veterinary Medicine) (Amendment) Regulations 1992 (SI No. 253) amended the 1980 to 1987 Regulations of the same title to give effect to Directives 89/594/EEC and 90/658/EEC.

## REGIONAL TECHNICAL COLLEGES

The Regional Technical Colleges Act 1992, which is complementary to the Dublin Institute of Technology Act 1992, discussed above, provides that the

11 Regional Technical Colleges (RTCs) as well as two other colleges referred to in the First Schedule to the RTC Act, shall operate on an independent, self-governing, basis. The Act came into force on 1 January 1993: Regional Technical Colleges Act 1992 (Commencement) Order 1992 (SI No. 337). Previouly, the RTCs had been under the control of the Vocational Education Committees in their respective county areas. The RTC Act provides that each RTC shall have their own structures, including chief executives (Directors), governing bodies and academic councils. As with the DIT Act, these provisions are largely modelled on the provisions in University of Limerick Acts 1980 and 1989 and the Dublin City University Acts 1980 and 1989 (see the Annual Review, 190-1). Similarly, s. 3 of the RTC Act also provides that other institutions may, by Order of the Minister for Education, be added to the current list of institutions covered by the RTC Act.

## VOCATIONAL EDUCATION

The Vocational Education (Grants for Annual Schemes of Committees) Regulations 1992 (SI No. 443), made under the Vocational Education Act 1930, provided for the grants to Vocational Education Committees for 1992.

# Electricity and Energy

## PETROLEUM

**Whitegate offtake** The Petroleum Oils (Regulation or Control of Acquisition, Supply, Distribution or Marketing) (Continuance) Order 1991 (SI No. 336) continued through 1993 the regime outlined in the 1988 Order of the same title: see the 1988 Review, 198.

# Equitable Remedies

## INJUNCTIONS

**Interlocutory injunctions** In 1992, the courts had to grapple with the legal principles relating to interlocutory injunctions on several occasions. For a thorough analysis of the decisions (in particular, the Supreme Court judgment in *Curust*), see Hilary Delany (1993) 15 DULJ 228.

In *Phonographic Performance (Ireland) Ltd v Chariot Inns Ltd*, High Court, 7 October 1992, which we analyse in the Chapter on Commercial Law above 39, Keane J granted an interlocutory injunction to the plaintiffs, acting on behalf of the record companies, against the defendants, from playing sound recordings in their nightclub. The litigation raised the question of which procedure under the Copyright Act 1963 was appropriate to resolve the dispute between the parties: the plaintiffs had sought to operate the machinery of s. 32; the defendants preferred s. 31.

Keane J had no doubt that the plaintiffs had raised a serious question to be tried in accordance with the test laid down by the Supreme Court in *Campus Oil Ltd v Minister for Industry and Energy (No. 2)* [1983] IR 88. As regards the balance of convenience, Keane J was of the opinion that, if the plaintiffs were ultimately vindicated, it was unlikely that they would recover the full damages from discotheque operators *other than the defendants*, who would be likely to adopt the same course as the defendants if an interlocutory injunction were not granted. He was of the view that, if an injunction were granted and the defendants ultimately were successful, the defendants would be able to enforce against the plaintiffs their undertaking as to damages.

Keane J commented:

> The defendants will, I am satisfied, be almost wholly inhibited in the operation of the discotheque, but I think that it is somewhat unreal to suggest that a large and well equipped licensed premises in [Ranelagh] will have to go out of business because of the suspension for a time of their discotheque operation.

Keane J expressed himself to be 'accordingly' satisfied that more damage would be caused by a refusal than by a granting of the injunction and that, in particular, the award of damages to the plaintiffs, if they should ultimately succeed at the trial of the action, would not adequately compensate them for the losses which they would have sustained. He added:

> It follows that I need not reach any conclusion as to where the balance of convenience lies, although were I to determine that issue I would conclude that it lay in favour of granting the injunction.

The passage is of interest in that it appears to suggest that the consideration as to inadequacy of damages *necessarily* outweighs the consideration of the balance of convenience. The earlier precedents fall short of such a stark proposition, wisely, it is respectfully suggested. Of course the prospect of a plaintiff's being left in a position where he or she will not be able to recover adequate compensation is a factor that will weigh heavily in the perusal of the scales of balance of convenience but the established case law suggests that the inadequacy of damages should in no sense be regarded as a trump card.

Keane J's reliance on the possibility that the plaintiffs might not be able to recover damages from *other* defendants has been criticised by Paul Coughlan [1993] 1 (European Intellectual Property Review, D-10) and Hilary Delany, op. cit. at 238. Mr Coughlan observes that:

> [a]s the defendant would be liable in damages for only those acts of copyright infringement which it performed, and could hardly be held accountable for the activities of independent third parties who might have followed its lead, taking into account the possible actions of such persons in determining the case for and against an interlocutory injunction as between the parties to the action would seem to place an excessive weight on extraneous considerations.

Ms Delany perceives in this approach some similarly with the importance that O'Hanlon J appeared to attach, in *Howard v Commissioners of Public Works*, High Court, 3 December 1992 (considered below, 461) to wider considerations than those which arose between the parties, such as EC grants earmarked for the Burren project that was challenged by the applicants and the potential damage to local employment projects.

*GPA Group plc v Bank of Ireland* [1992] 2 IR 408 reveals the inefficacy of interlocutory proceedings to prevent payment pursuant to a letter of credit. Keane J gave effect to policy, enunciated by Kerr J in *Harbottle Ltd v National Westminster Bank Ltd* [1978] QB 146, at 155-6, that it should be in exceptional cases that the courts would interfere with the machinery of irrevocable obligations assumed by banks.

> They are the life-blood of international commerce. . . . They must be allowed to be honoured, free from interference by the courts. Otherwise, trust in international commerce could be irreparably damaged.

In *GPA*, the plaintiff sought an interlocutory injunction restraining the defendant bank from making a payment on foot of a letter of credit to the European Organisation for the Safety of Air Navigation (Eurocontrol). The plaintiff argued that the demand certificate did not comply with the terms of the letter of credit in two important respects: the letter of credit did not envisage payment on the basis of a consent judgment and it was drafted so as to operate solely in the event of Eurocontrol's succeeding in an action for the amount of route changes against GPA and not any other party.

Keane J rejected both arguments. The court could not resolve issues between GPA and Eurocontrol, since Eurocontrol was not a party to the proceedings. Other litigation might well be necessary to resolve them. It was now 'perfectly clear' that the bank was not entitled to withhold payment of the letter of credit because of a dispute between the parties as to whether or not it was intended to operate, when the documents furnished were on their face in conformity with the terms of the letter itself. Whilst in an application for an interlocutory injunction, the court, if satisfied that the plaintiff had raised a serious question as to the violation of its rights, would go on to consider where the balance of convenience lay. In a case of this nature, however, where the question as to whether the bank was obliged to make payment depended solely on the construction of the letter of credit and the documents furnished by the party seeking payment, it would defeat the policy considerations identified in *Harbottle Ltd v National Westminster Bank Ltd* if the court were to enjoin the bank from payment until the trial's ultimate disposal of the action. Accordingly, he refused to grant an interlocutory injunction.

In *Boyle v An Post* [1992] 2 IR 437, Lardner J granted the relatively infrequent remedy of a mandatory interlocutory injunction requiring the defendant to make arrangements to pay the seven plaintiffs, its employees, their salaries even though the defendant's payroll system computer had to be shut down on account of an industrial dispute which did not involve the plaintiffs. Lardner J quoted with approval the following passage from *Halsbury's Laws of England* (4th ed.), note 24, para. 948:

> A mandatory injunction can be granted on an interlocutory application as well as at the hearing, but, in the absence of special circumstances, it will not normally be granted. However, if the case is clear and one which the court thinks ought to be decided at once, or if the act done is a simple and summary one which can be easily remedied, or if the defendant attempts to steal a march on the plaintiff, such as where, on receipt of notice that an injunction is about to be applied for, the defendant hurries on the work in respect of which complaint is made so that when he receives notice of an interim injunction it is completed, a mandatory injunction will be granted on an interlocutory injunction.

He also quoted an extended passage from O'Higgins CJ's judgment in *Campus Oil Ltd v Minister for Industry and Energy (No. 2)* [1983] IR 88, at 105, wherein the Chief Justice had observed that '[i]t frequently happens that neither the applicant's right nor the fact of its violation is disputed by the person whose acts are sought to be restrained. In such a case an injunction may be given almost as of course. . . .'

The instant case clearly fell within the principle stated in *Halsbury*. It was an exceptional case where one could say with assurance that at the hearing of the substantive action the plaintiffs were bound to succeed.

Lardner J rejected the defendant's argument that the case could properly be dealt with by an award of damages. The personal financial circumstances of the plaintiffs were such that the ultimate recovery of damages, even with interest, would not compensate them for the hardship, distress and anxiety that they would suffer in the meantime. He accepted that arranging and paying wages and salaries would cause the defendant difficulties but these difficulties were not in his view insurmountable. The balance of convenience fell in favour of granting a mandatory injunction in favour of the plaintiffs.

In *Curust Financial Services Ltd v Loewe* [1993] ILRM 723, analysed by Hilary Delany (1993) 15 DULJ 228, the Supreme Court, reversing Barron J, refused to grant an interlocutory injunction to the plaintiff company restraining the defendant from supplying paint to another company, in breach of the defendant's contract to supply the plaintiff with paint of this kind. The parties for a number of years had had a good business relationship. When it broke down, the defendant proceeded to supply another company with the paint. The plaintiff, in professed compliance with its contract with the defendant, indicated its desire to assign the right of manufacture of the paint to an unidentified fourth party, and sought the defendant's assurance that it would not intimidate that party into refusing to go through with the assignment. That assurance was not forthcoming, the defendant already having taken the position that its contractual relationship with the plaintiff had ceased. Under the contract, assignment required the prior consent of the defendant, which consent could not be unreasonably refused: cf. [1993] ILRM, at 731. Barron J, in granting the interlocutory injunction, held that a triable issue arose and that damages would not be an adequate remedy. The Supreme Court agreed with Barron J on the first only of these points. The defendant had argued that the contract was void, having regard to Article 85(1) of the Treaty of Rome. Such a defence placed on the plaintiff the onus of establishing as a triable issue the existence of an exemption or avoidance of this prohibition. One of the plaintiff's senior executives averred in an affidavit his belief that the agreement had no material effect on intra-Community trade since the plaintiff had only a tiny share of the sales of paint of the relevant kind in the relevant part of the territory of the Community, which was Ireland and Britain. The Supreme Court agreed with Barron J's characterisation of this as being only slight evidence but nonetheless sufficient to raise a triable issue.

The Supreme Court also agreed with Barron J that an injunction should not be refused merely because the assignment was not in compliance with the terms of the contract. In this context Finlay CJ considered that the court should, at the interlocutory stage, proceed on the basis that the plaintiff might succeed in the plenary hearing in establishing its case that the contract was still viable and that accordingly the defendant's failure to give an assurance of non-interference in the plaintiffs attempt to secure a viable assignment was wrongful.

The Supreme Court differed from Barron J on the question whether damages would be an adequate remedy. The Chief Justice, admitting that this was 'the most difficult issue' arising on the appeal, identified several reasons for holding that damages would be adequate. There had been no suggestion that the defendant would not be in a position to pay an award of damages, if it were ultimately granted. The loss to be sustained by the plaintiff if an injunction were not ordered was 'purely and simply a commercial loss arising from a diminution in trade' and, therefore ostensibly capable of quantification. Difficulties in quantification were not a ground for holding that damages were not an adequate remedy. The principle that an injunction should be awarded in preference to damages save where the damages were very small was appropriate to a permanent rather than interlocutory injunction. In the instant case the Chief Justice did not consider that there was a real risk that the plaintiff company would collapse if an interlocutory injunction were not granted.

Egan J concurred with Finlay CJ's judgment. O'Flaherty J concurred with the Chief Justice's holdings on the existence of a triable issue and on the adequacy of damages as a remedy. As to the first point, he observed that, although it had not been argued that the instant case was such, there were instances where a breach of contract was so clear or the party attempting to resist the injunction so devoid of merits that the court should immediately grant the injunction. He cited in support *Doherty v Allman* (1878) 3 App Cas 709, *Dublin Port & Docks Board v Brittania Dredging Co. Ltd* [1968] IR 136 and *Irish Shell Ltd v Elm Motors Ltd* [1984] ILRM 595; [1984] IR 200, at 225.

On the question whether damages would be an adequate remedy, O'Flaherty J considered that the deciding element was the fact that the plaintiff was not going to be deprived of access to the market in paint of the particular kind but rather would be obliged to share it in competition with the third party to whom the defendant was supplying paint.

## TRUST

**Constructive trust** In *HKN Invest Oy v Incotrade Pvt Ltd* [1993] 3 IR 152, which is considered in greater detail in the Company Law Chapter, above, 84-7, Costello J held that monies received by promoters by way of commission before incorporation on pre-incorporation contracts which the company was empowered to ratify, had been received on a constructive trust. Citing *Hanbury's Modern Equity*, 218 and *Hussey v Palmer* [1972] 3 All ER 744, at 747, Costello J said:

> A constructive trust will arise when the circumstances render it inequitable for the legal owner of property to deny the title of another to it. It is a trust which comes into existence irrespective of the will of the parties and arises by operation of law. The principle is that where a person who holds property in circumstances in which in equity and good conscience should be held or enjoyed by another he will be compelled to hold the property in trust for another.

Costello J considered that this principle was in no way dependent on the existence of a dimension of fraud. If a promoter who received such commission were adjudicated a bankrupt and the contract were subsequently ratified, the court should uphold the company's claim against that of the bankrupt's creditors:

> The commission was never beneficially owned by the promoter — he held it in trust for the company which he was forming and which was to perform the services he had agreed would be performed. If this was not the case (a) considerable injustice could be suffered by the company, its shareholders or creditors who were deprived of the commission whilst (b) the creditors in the bankruptcy would obtain a greater interest in the property than the Bankrupt himself enjoyed.

Costello J considered that this principle applied even if the company did not formally ratify the contract. Nor could the fraud of the promoters affect the position.

**Trustees of pension scheme** In *In re Lynch*, High Court, 17 July 1992, Denham J was called on to determine whether ten annuities bought by trustees on the lives of certain pensioners were 'buy-out' contracts or instead had been purchased for the benefit of a pension scheme. In the case of the former, the trustees of a pension scheme may discharge the scheme's obligation to a particular pensioner by buying for him or her a suitable contract from a life assurance company, known as a buy-out contract. After having done so, the trustees have no further obligation to the pensioner in respect of the benefits secured. Under the latter approach, trustees may purchase for the benefit of a scheme an annuity contract to match the scheme's liability to a particular pensioner. Here the annuity contract is one of the investments of the pension scheme.

Denham J's perusal of the deed governing the scheme convinced her that the latter situation arose. No clause in the deed explicitly permitted the trustees to purchase buy-out contracts save one dealing with dissolution of the scheme. It was reasonable to envisage the purchase of buy-out contracts in such circumstances since, if the scheme was wound up, the trustees would not be in place to administer a pension.

The references in the deed to annuities should in the context of the deed as a whole be interpreted as not referring to buy-out annuities. Denham J was satisfied, moreover, that the trustees had never bought buy-out contracts. The facts established clearly that the annuities had been bought *as part of the pension scheme* and matched against named persons. This was good management of monies rather than indicative of the purchase of buy-out contracts.

## ESTOPPEL

In *In re J.R., a Ward of Court* [1993] ILRM 657, analysed by Paul Coughlan (1993) 15 DULJ 188, Costello J had to deal with an application by the committee of an elderly ward of court to approve the sale of his dwelling house. The ward was now seventy-three years old. He had been admitted to a psychiatric hospital two years previously. There was no real prospect of his recovery. In 1978 he had met the respondent, a married woman whose husband had left her seven years previously. She was aged thirty-four when she met the ward. Both were at the time undergoing psychiatric treatment. The respondent had suffered two brain tumours which so weakened her that she could not work. She went to live with the ward shortly after she met him. The couple lived together in unmarried cohabitation until the ward went again to a psychiatric hospital in 1990. During these twelve years, the ward maintained the respondent out of his resources and gave her an allowance to augment her disability pension.

After the ward went to hospital the house fell into a progressive and serious state of disrepair. The respondent resisted the committee's application for permission to sell it, claiming that she had a legal interest in the property. She gave evidence, which the court accepted, that, when she went to live with the respondent, he represented to her that he would look after her and that she would be sure of a home for the rest of her life. He continued to make these representations to her and she acted on them.

In 1988, on the respondent's birthday, the ward made a will in which he bequeathed all his property to the respondent. He handed her a folder containing the will and said to her: 'It's not my house now, its our house and eventually it will be your house.'

Costello J gave a detailed review of the law relating to promissory and proprietary estoppel. He held that the respondent had acted on the ward's representation, to her detriment. The Privy Council case of *Maharj v Chand* [1986] AC 898 showed that detriment may exist when a representee leaves a permanent home on the faith of a representation that another will be offered in its place. In the present case there was no evidence of where the respondent had been living in 1978 but Costello J stated that he was entitled to assume that she had a house or flat which she gave up to go to live with the respondent and that 'accordingly' she had made out a case of promissory estoppel as she had acted on the representation made to her. It would be 'plainly inequitable' for the ward now to deny that she had a right to live in his house. It seemed to Costello J that the respondent had an equity which entitled her to stay in the house for as long as she wished and that the court was obliged to give effect to it.

The events on the respondent's birthday in 1988 conferred no additional rights on her, however. Costello J considered that the ward's words to the respondent showed an intention to give a gift of an interest in the house to her, but the gift was an imperfect, and thus an unenforceable, one. Nor did a constructive trust arise, giving the respondent an immediate beneficial interest, since the ward intended merely that the respondent should have a right to reside in the house during his life, followed by ownership of it after his death. If the ward had intended the respondent to have an immediate beneficial interest, he would have arranged to transfer the property either to her alone or jointly with her. The doctrine of estoppel had no application to the events of that day since the respondent could not show that she had acted in any way to her detriment arising from the representation made to her then.

Costello J's resolution of the case was an excellent example of the application of the spirit of equity. He approved the sale of the house but ordered that another smaller house be purchased suitable for the respondent's needs. It would be bought in the ward's name but subject to the court's declaration that the respondent had a right to reside in it for as long as she wished.

A couple of aspects of Costello J's judgment are worthy of comment. When holding that there had been an imperfect gift, Costello J expressed the view that the ward had intended by his words to give a gift of an interest in the house to the respondent; yet, when rejecting the argument based on a constructive trust, Costello J held that the ward did not confer an immediate beneficial interest since he intended that she have a right of residence during his life, followed by ownership on his death. It might be asked what interest the ward intended to confer if not a beneficial interest. The answer would seem to be that Costello J was seeking to distinguish between a full proprietary beneficial interest and a right of residence.

Broader jurisprudential issues also arise. The decision raises the question whether promissory and proprietary estoppel are here merged into a broader general principle, as has occurred in Australia and (perhaps) in Ireland in the Supreme Court decision of *Webb v Ireland* [1988] IR 353: see O'Dell, 'Estoppel and Ultra Vires Contracts' (1992) 14 DULJ 123, at 133-8; cf. Coughlan, op. cit., at 190-1. Alternatively, it can be argued that the case would have more convincingly lent itself to a proprietary estoppel characterisation, since it is hard to see how the respondent suffered any detriment in going to live with the ward: see Paul Coughlan's comprehensive analysis of the issues, op. cit., at 192ff. In this decision, Costello J has gone some distance to creating the equivalent of the Family Home Protection Act 1976 in relation to cohabitees; no doubt the particular facts of the case, which were short on detriment but otherwise of striking poignancy, led Costello J to a holding which would not be applied unthinkingly in other instances that may come before the Court.

In the 1990 Review 330-1, we discussed the decision of *McGrath v Garda Commissioner* [1991]ILRM 817; [1990] 1 IR 69, which held that it would amount to an unfair procedure for the Commissioner to proceed with a disciplinary hearing alleging corrupt or improper practice after essentially the same issues which would arise at the hearing had been fully heard and determined by a court of competent jurisdiction, wherein he had been acquitted of the charges brought against him. In the 1988 Review, 337-8, we analysed the Courts (No. 2) Act 1988, which was designed to confer retrospective validation on acts done by a District Justice who had stayed on the Bench beyond his actual retirement age.

The case of *McCarthy v Commissioner of the Garda Síochána* [1993] 1 IR 489 involved an intermingling of these two strands of law. The applicant for judicial review, a member of the Garda Síochána, had been tried and acquitted of certain offences impugning his honesty. An enquiry was subsequently held under the Garda Síochána (Discipline) Regulations 1971 resulting in the applicant's dismissal. In this enquiry allegations of breaches of discipline were investigated which included the issues that had been disposed of by the jury in the applicant's favour. On the authority of *McGrath*, the applicant would be expected to succeed in his application for judicial review but, as matters transpired, the District Justice who had been involved in the early stages of his trial was the person whose overstay on the

Bench had precipitated the 1988 Act. It was argued on behalf of the Commissioner that the applicant's return for trial had been a nullity, that he had never been in jeopardy of conviction and accordingly that he could not make use of his acquittal to block the disciplinary procedure.

Flood J rejected this argument. He referred to the counter-argument on behalf of the applicant that the acquittal generated a legitimate expectation on the applicant's part that the verdict constituted an end to that chapter in his life, insofar as any fraud or dishonest intent could or would be alleged against him. Counsel for the applicant had called in aid of this proposition the judgments of Finlay CJ in *Webb v Ireland* [1988] ILRM 565; [1988] IR 353, (which we analyse in the 1987 Review, 162-4) and of Murphy J in *Garda Representative Association v Ireland* [1989] ILRM 1; [1989] IR 193 (which we analyse in the 1988 Review, 24-6). Flood J stated:

> Fundamental to our criminal procedure, and indeed to the liberty of the individual, is the presumption of innocence. The finding by a jury of a verdict of not guilty in respect of criminal charges is more than a verdict of not guilty. It is a certificate of the person's uninterrupted innocence.
>
> To all persons concerned in the . . . indictment trial it was an accepted assumption that, on the return of the verdict of not guilty, there was vested in the applicant a certificate of that uninterrupted innocence.... The verdict of that jury was unappealable in fact. No court and no power in the land could challenge it. It was the applicant's shield against any allegation of dishonesty on his part in relation to the matters which had been the subject matter of consideration and adjudication by his twelve peers, the jurymen of that trial. The trial, on its face, was perfectly fair, all-embracing, valid and concessive. It seems to me that to rip the certificate of innocence from the hands of the applicant and metaphorically to shred it and declare it a total nullity and to claim that it never in fact existed all by reason of a clerical error made in 1977 as to the age of a District Justice would be wholly inequitable. To permit the State or any arm of the State to purport in any other proceedings to retry the applicant on the same facts in relation to the same events would in my opinion be an oppressive and unfair procedure.

Accordingly, Flood J granted an order of *certiorari*, a declaration that the applicant had been unlawfully dismissed and an order of his re-instatement.

The Commission appealed to the Supreme Court in an *ex tempore* judgment on 25 June 1992 the Supreme Court unanimously dismissed the appeal, on the ground that the disciplinarly proceedings after the applicant's acquittal had been oppressive and unfair.

## IMPROVIDENT TRANSACTION

In *McQuirk v Branigan*, High Court, 9 November 1992, a Circuit Appeal, an elderly widow living in 'a relatively modest thatched house', agreed to make available to her grandson a strip of her garden which, in conjunction with a part of her daughter's neighbouring land, would make up an appropriate site for his new house. The architectural technician retained to prepare the necessary maps for the transfer called to the plaintiff to inspect the site; when he did so, the plaintiffs daughter and grandson also attended. Discussions took place in which the architectural technician pointed out that the proposed site would not be sufficiently wide for a bungalow and that more land would be required. He indicated how much land should be taken. He also pointed out that an arrangement which the plaintiff was disposed to adopt in regard to her back garden would have the effect of her losing the land immediately outside her back doorway. He suggested that the plaintiff should retain a one metre strip around her house and shed.

Morris J was satisfied that the architectural technician had acted in an entirely proper manner and had done everything required of him. He was also satisfied that the plaintiff had agreed to give some additional ground to her grandson; but he did not accept that the plaintiff 'was ever at any stage a willing party' to the arrangement, which had been thrust upon her, having been decided upon by the three other parties to the meeting without the opportunity of her having any input into the arrangements.

A deed of transfer was in due course prepared by the family's solicitors and signed by the plaintiff. The deed incorporated the extension of the area transferred in relation to the bungalow site. As regards the back garden, the accompanying map appeared to divest the plaintiff of her interest in the entire area, without retaining the *cordon sanitaire* proposed by the architectural technician.

Morris J was satisfied that the arrangement made at the meeting as to the site for the bungalow should not stand. He declined, however, to direct that the register be altered so as to reflect a transfer of the original strip since this would mean in effect that the plaintiff, by divesting herself of land to the boundary of her shed behind her house, would be deprived of the opportunity of repairing that part of her home. He had 'no doubt whatever' that an arrangement such as this was an improvident transaction viewed from her point of view. It had been made without the benefit of independent legal advice 'or indeed any advice' and in circumstances in which a Court should intervene. Had the plaintiff been in receipt of advice, it would have reflected the views expressed by the architectural technician on site.

Morris J therefore affirmed the Circuit Court Judge's order.

# European Community

The year 1992 saw the welcome reappearance of the Journal of the Irish Society of European Law, under its new title the *Irish Journal of European Law*. The 1992 volume of the Journal contains a number of highly informative articles covering the application of Community Law in Ireland during the period 1983 to 1989 as well as law reports of cases in the Irish courts raising issues of European law.

## TREATY ON EUROPEAN UNION

The Eleventh Amendment to the Constitution Act 1992, which became law on foot of the referendum held on 18 June 1992 which had approved its amendments to Article 29.4 of the Constitution, provided primarily for the ratification by the State of the 1992 Treaty on European Union (hereafter TEU), commonly known as the Maastricht Treaty. It also provided for the ratification of the 1989 EC Agreement relating to Community Patents, an aspect discussed in the Commercial Law chapter, 42, above.

It is not possible in this Review to discuss in detail the many important substantive changes effected by the TEU. Some of its provisions are referred to, albeit briefly, below, 328-31. Before dealing with these, however, we will outline the amendments to Irish law effected by the Eleventh Amendment Act and also discuss the effect of the TEU in establishing both the European Union (EU) and, perhaps surprisingly, the European Community (EC).

**Amendments to Constitution** The Eleventh Amendment Act inserted Article 29.4.3, 5 and 6 into the Constitution, and also repealed the third sentence of Article 29.4.3, the provision under which Ireland had initially acceded to the Treaties of the European Communities and subsequently acceded to the Single European Act Treaty in 1987. Because the Eleventh Amendment Act effected such substantial changes to Article 29.4, it may be helpful to reproduce here the amended text, including the now repealed third sentence of Article 29.4.3:

> 3 The State may become a member of the European Coal and Steel Community (established by Treaty signed at Paris on the 18th day of April, 1951), the European Economic Community (established by

Treaty signed at Rome on the 25th day of March, 1957) and the European Atomic Energy Community (established by Treaty signed at Rome on the 25th day of March, 1957). The State may ratify the Single European Act (signed on behalf of the Member States of the Communities at Luxembourg on the 17th day of February, 1986, and at the Hague on the 28th day of February, 1986). [*No provision of this Constitution invalidates laws enacted, acts done or measures adopted by the State necessitated by the obligations of membership of the Communities or prevents laws enacted, acts done or measures adopted by the Communities, or institutions thereof, from having the force of law in the State. Note: this third sentence was repealed by the Eleventh Amendment Act, and replaced by subs. 5, below.*]

4 The State may ratify the Treaty on European Union signed at Maastricht on the 7th day of February, 1992, and may become a member of that Union.

5 No provision of this Constitution invalidates laws enacted, acts done or measures adopted by the State which are necessitated by the obligations of membership of the European Union or of the Communities, or prevents laws enacted, acts done or measures adopted by the European Union or by the Communities or by institutions thereof, or by bodies competent under the Treaties establishing the Communities, from having the force of law in the State.

6 The State may ratify the Agreement Relating to Community Patents drawn between the Member States of the Communities and done at Luxembourg on the 15th day of December, 1989.

As to Article 29.4.5, apart from minor grammatical changes, this provision retains the crucial phrase 'necessitated by the obligations of membership' which had appeared in the original Article 29.4.3. On the question of what is 'necessitated', see the discussion in *Lawlor v Minister for Agriculture* [1988] ILRM 400 (1987 Review, 92-4), *Greene v Minister for Agriculture* [1990] ILRM 364; [1990] 2 IR 17 (1989 Review, 99-101) and *Condon v Minister for Agriculture*, High Court, 12 October 1990 (1990 Review, 283-4). See also *Whelan*, (1992) 2 ISLR 60, referred to in the 1991 Review, 205. However, these decisions must now be seen in the light of the enormously important decision of the Supreme Court in November 1993 in *Meagher v Minister for Agriculture* [1994] 1 ILRM 1, which will be discussed in the 1993 Review.

**European Communities (Amendment) Act 1992** The 1992 Act provides for the incorporation into Irish law of the relevant provisions of the TEU consequent on the June 1992 referendum. The 1992 Act was brought into force on 1 November 1993: European Communities (Amendment) Act 1992 (Commencement) Order 1993 (SI No. 304 of 1993). This commencement was made possible when the German government deposited its instrument of ratification in October 1993 after the German Constitutional Court had found that the TEU was consistent with German law. The TEU itself also thus took effect in accordance with its terms on 1 November 1993.

**Overview of TEU** The text of the Treaty on European Union (TEU), as published in the Official Journal of the European Communities, runs to 112 pages: OJ, No C191, 29.7.1992, p.1. The substantive Articles of the Treaty are divided into seven titles, widely differing in size, running to 67 pages of text in the Official Journal. The remaining 45 pages comprise 17 Protocols and 34 Declarations which are appended to the Treaty. Some of these Protocols are of some size and deal with significant issues such as Social Policy (discussed below, 330-1), while others concern matters of significance only to one Member State or another, such as the Protocol on Article 40.3.3 of the Irish Constitution: see the Constitutional Law chapter, 202, above.

The Articles of the TEU are lettered rather than numbered, and run only from Article A to S. This might seem surprising in a Treaty of 67 pages of printed text, but the reason for this becomes clear when one realises that the bulk of the TEU in fact consists of amendments to the existing Treaties rather than entirely novel provisions.

Title I of the TEU, which consists of Articles A to F, the Common Provisions, runs to a little over one page in the Official Journal. Article A establishes 'the European Union' and provides that '[t]he Union shall be founded on the European Communities, supplemented by the policies and forms of cooperation established by this Treaty.' The supplementing policies contained in the TEU include the provisions on a Common Foreign and Security Policy, contained in Title V, and those on Cooperation in the Fields of Justice and Home Affairs, in Title VI. Between them, Titles V and VI run to less than 5 pages in the Official Journal. We will discuss below, the nature of the European Union thus established.

The remainder of the TEU's 67 pages consist of amendments to the existing Treaties establishing the Communities. Title II consists of amendments to the Treaty Establishing the European Economic Community, Title III consists of amendments to the Treaty Establishing the European Coal and Steel Community while Title IV consists of amendments to the Treaty Establishing the European Atomic Energy Community. Of the other Titles, by far the most significant, both in substantive provisions and in length, is Title II.

**Nature of European Union (EU)** As we have seen, on the coming into force of the TEU on 1 November 1993, the European Union (EU) was established. What is the nature of this European Union?

It is clear from Article A of the TEU that the European Union is, in large part, a creature of the existing European Communities, and the principles already established by Community law, or *acquis communautaire*. This is supported by the fact that much of the TEU consists, in fact, of amendments to the existing Treaties.

Given the well-documented nervousness of some of the Member States to move towards a federalist model of 'ever closer union between the peoples', the EU is clearly not a federal State. The final text of the TEU is somewhat more conditional than some of the drafts which had been prepared during 1991 in particular. While the intention at one time may have been to move from 'Communities of States' straight to full 'European Union', this was clearly not acceptable to all Member States. The result is that the European Union is an entity with certain, limited, powers in its own right, for example in the context of the adoption, under Title V of the TEU, of a common foreign and security policy (e.g. in a UN context) and, under Title VI, of common positions on home affairs policy (e.g. on combatting crime). Previously, foreign policy had been a matter of political co-operation under the Single European Act, while home affairs had been dealt with within the extra-Treaty Trevi meetings.

These two areas have been excluded by the TEU from the jurisdiction of the Court of Justice, thus indicating the quite tentative nature of the activities of the European Union. Indeed, the relevant provisions of the TEU on these two areas are not included in the TEU provisions which have been incorporated into Irish law by the European Communities (Amendment) Act 1992, above. However, we may note that the coming into force of the TEU resulted in a change of name for the Council of Ministers. From 5 November 1993, the Council is to be known as the 'Council of the European Union'. However, at the time of writing, no name change has taken place for what remains the Commission of the European Communities.

In his Annotations to the Eleventh Amendment Act and to the European Communities (Amendment) Act 1992 for *Irish Current Law Statutes Annotated*, Anthony Whelan considers in further detail the juridical nature of the European Union.

**EEC Treaty becomes EC Treaty** Title II of the TEU runs to 38 pages in the Official Journal. It consists of a single Article, Article G, but this disguises the fact that it provides for substantial changes to the Treaty Establishing the European Economic Community, whose title is, moreover, amended to become the Treaty Establishing the European Community (hereafter the EC

Treaty). The numerous amendments effected to what is now the EC Treaty attempt to preserve the Article numbering system in the former EEC Treaty. The full text of the EC Treaty, as amended by the TEU, was also published in the Official Journal: OJ, No. C191, 29.7.1992, p.1.

Title II of the TEU includes amendments to Article 2 of the EC Treaty, which sets out the aims and objectives of the EC. The provisions on Citizenship of the European Union are now included in a renumbered Article 8 of the EC Treaty.

Title II of TEU also inserts the central provisions on Economic and Monetary Union, creating Articles 102a to 109m of the EC Treaty, which run to ten pages in the Official Journal. The full EMU process begins with the establishment of the European Monetary Institute and culminating, perhaps by 1997 or 1999, in a single currency controlled by a European Central Bank. This controversial and enormous task is, of course, hedged around with various convergence criteria established in the TEU itself. However, whatever the fate of these provisions, other amendments effected by the TEU are likely to have a more immediate and long term impact.

Provisions are included in Title II of the TEU on topics which indicate a development of the existing Community competences, such as those on Culture (Article 128), Public Health (Article 129), Consumer Protection (Article 129a), Trans-European Networks (Article 129b), Competitiveness of Industry (Article 130), Economic and Social Cohesion (Article 130a) (linked with the creation of a Committee of the Regions by Article 198a), the Environment (Article 130r) and Development Cooperation with Developing Economies (Article 130u). Of these, the provisions on Economic and Social Cohesion and the Committee of the Regions were regarded as having a particular significance for Ireland as one of the peripheral economies in the EC/EU.

Finally, we may note that Title II of the TEU also increased the powers of the European Parliament in two ways. First, it expands the areas to which the existing 'Co-operation Procedure' contained in Article 189c of the EC Treaty (first introduced by the Single European Act) applies. Secondly, it introduces a 'Co-Decision Procedure' by which, under Article 189b of the EC Treaty, the Parliament can, in limited circumstances, veto a Directive against the wishes of the Council of Ministers, but only after attempts to avoid conflict cannot be resolved by a newly-created Conciliation Committee.

**Protocol on Social Policy** We mentioned above that the Protocols to the TEU include a Protocol on Social Policy, which precedes the text of the Agreement on Social Policy between 11 of the 12 Member States, excluding the United Kingdom.

The Agreement on Social Policy had originally been included in the body of the Treaty itself, but the refusal of the United Kingdom government to support certain aspects of the social policy agenda resulted in it being relegated to an 'Agreement Between Eleven'. Since the text of the Agreement envisages the Eleven agreeing Directives which will only apply to those 11 States, this clearly raises spectres of a 'two tier' Social Europe. In his Annotation on the Eleventh Amendment Act for Irish Current Law Statutes Annotated, Anthony Whelan carefully considers this difficult aspect of the TEU. Whether the Eleven will wish to proceed with the United Kingdom in certain aspects of social policy remains to be seen. It may be noted, however, that in the aftermath of the 1989 Social Charter agreed between the same Eleven, a number of Directives were subsequently agreed between the Twelve under the Single European Act, even though these strictly speaking involved implementation of Social Charter action items: see the Commission's Second Report on Implementation of the Social Charter, Social Europe.

## ABUSE OF DOMINANT POSITION

In *Masterfoods Ltd (t/a Mars Ireland) v HB Ice Cream Ltd* [1993] ILRM 145, Keane J, in an extremely detailed judgment, rejected claims that certain agreements amounted to an abuse of a dominant position in breach of EC or Irish competition law: see the Commercial Law chapter, 27-30, above.

## CONCERTED PRACTICE

In *Curust Financial Services Ltd and Anor v Loewe-Lack-Werk Otto Loewe GmbH & Co. KG and Anor*, High Court, 3 July 1992; [1993] ILRM 723 (SC) (discussed in the Equitable Remedies chapter, 318-9, above), the question arose as to whether an exclusive manufacturing and distribution agreement constituted a concerted practice or agreement under Article 85 of the Treaty of Rome. The *Masterfoods* case, above, also involved such an argument.

## IMPLEMENTATION OF EC REQUIREMENTS IN IRISH LAW

The following regulations and orders made in 1992 pursuant to the provisions of s. 3 of the European Communities Act 1972 (or other statutory powers) involve the implementation of Community obligations.

Air Pollution Act 1987 (Combustion Plant) Regulations 1992 (SI No. 273): see the Safety and Health chapter, 534, below.

Control of Exciseable Products Regulations 1992 (SI No. 430): see the Revenue chapter, 515, below.

European Communities (Antioxidant in Food) (Purity Criteria) (Amendment) Regulations 1992 (SI No. 63): see the Safety and Health chapter, 537-8, below.

European Communities (Appliances Burning Gaseous Fuels) Regulations 1992 (SI No. 101): see the Safety and Health chapter, 538, below.

European Communities (Application of the Rules on Competition to Air Transport) Regulations 1992 (SI No. 379): see the Transport chapter, 620, below.

European Communities (Award of Public Supply Contracts) Regulations 1992 (SI No. 37): see the Commercial Law chapter, 46, above.

European Communities (Award of Public Works Contracts) Regulations 1992 (SI No. 36): see the Commercial Law chapter, 46, above.

European Communities (Cereal Seed) (Amendment) Regulations 1992 (SI No. 29): see the Agriculture chapter, 15, above.

European Communities (Cereal Seed) (Amendment) (No. 2) Regulations 1992 (SI No. 382): see the Agriculture chapter, 15, above.

European Communities (Classification, Packaging and Labelling of Dangerous Preparations) Regulations 1992 (SI No. 393): see the Safety and Health chapter, 526-7, below.

European Communities (Classification, Packaging and Labelling of Pesticides) (Amendment) Regulations 1992 (SI No. 416): see the Safety and Health chapter, 528, below.

European Communities (Community Transit) Regulations 1992 (SI No. 433): see the Transport chapter, 627, below.

European Communities (Companies: Group Accounts) Regulations 1992 (SI No. 201): see the Company Law chapter, 101-2, above.

European Communities (Consolidated Supervision of Credit Institutions) Regulations 1992 (SI No. 396): see the Commercial Law chapter, 33, above.

European Communities (Construction Products) Regulations 1992 (SI No. 198): see the Safety and Health chapter, 538, below.

European Communities (Control of Oestrogenic, Androgenic, Gestagenic and Thyrostatic Substances) (Amendment) Regulations 1992 (SI No. 427): see the Agriculture chapter, 14, above.

European Communities (Cosmetic Products) (Amendment) Regulations 1992 (SI No. 400): see the Safety and Health chapter, 527, below.

European Communities (Credit Institutions: Accounts) Regulations 1992 (SI No. 294): see the Commercial Law chapter, 33, above.

European Communities (Customs) Regulations 1992 (SI No. 207): see the Revenue chapter, 515, below.

European Communities (Customs) (No. 2) Regulations 1992 (SI No. 431): see the Revenue chapter, 515, below.

European Communities (Customs) (No. 3) Regulations 1992 (SI No. 432): see the Revenue chapter, 515, below.

European Communities (Customs and Excise) Regulations 1992 (SI No. 394): see the Revenue chapter, 515, below.

European Communities (Dangerous Substances) (Classification, Packaging, Labelling and Notification) (Amendment) Regulations 1992 (SI No. 426): see the Safety and Health chapter, 526-7, below.

European Communities (Egg Products) Regulations 1992 (SI No. 419): see the Agriculture chapter, 16, above.

European Communities (Fees for Health Inspections and Controls of Fresh Meat) Regulations 1992 (SI No. 177): see the Agriculture chapter, 13, above.

European Communities (Flavourings for Use in Foodstuffs for Human Consumption) Regulations 1992 (SI No. 22): see the Safety and Health chapter, 536, below.

European Communities (General Authorisations for Exports of Agricultural Products) Regulations 1992 (SI No. 266): see the Agriculture chapter, 14, above.

European Communities (Identification of Foodstuff Lot) Regulations 1992 (SI No. 110): see the Safety and Health chapter, 537, below.

European Communities (International Carriage of Passengers) Regulations 1992 (SI No. 341): see the Transport chapter, 628, below.

European Communities (Introduction of Organisms Harmful to Plants or Plant Products) (Prohibition) (Amendment) Regulations 1992 (SI No. 214): see the Agriculture chapter, 15, above.

European Communities (Labelling of Additives for Use in Foodstuffs) Regulations 1992 (SI No. 23): see the Safety and Health chapter, 536, below.

European Communities (Licensing and Supervision of Credit Institutions) Regulations 1992 (SI No. 395): see the Commercial Law chapter, 33, above.

European Communities (Live Poultry and Hatching Eggs) Regulations 1992 (SI No. 362): see the Agriculture chapter, 16, above.

European Communities (Low Voltage Electrical Equipment) Regulations 1992 (SI No. 428): see the Safety and Health chapter, 538, below.

European Communities (Machinery) Regulations 1992 (SI No. 246): see the Safety and Health chapter, 538-9, below.

European Communities (Major Accident Hazards of Certain Industrial Activities) (Amendment) Regulations 1992 (SI No. 21): see the Safety and Health chapter, 527, below.

European Communities (Marketing of Feedingstuffs) (Amendment) Regulations 1992 (SI No. 143): see the Agriculture chapter, 15, above.

European Communities (Marketing Standards for Eggs) Regulations 1992 (SI No. 254): see the Agriculture chapter, 16, above.

European Communities (Mechanically Propelled Vehicle Emission Control) Regulations 1992 (SI No. 363): see the Transport chapter, 627, below.

European Communities (Merchandise Road Transport) (Amendment) Regulations 1992 (SI No. 217): see the Transport chapter, 631, below.

European Communities (Motor Vehicles Type Approval) Regulations 1992 (SI No. 178): see the Transport chapter, 627, below.

European Communities (Motor Vehicles Type Approval) (No. 2) Regulations 1992 (SI No. 345): see the Transport chapter, 627, below.

European Communities (Non-Automatic Weighing Instruments) Regulations 1992 (SI No. 424): see the Commercial Law chapter, 46, above.

European Communities (Non-Life Insurance) (Amendment) Regulations 1992 (SI No. 244): see the Commercial Law chapter, 37, above.

European Communities (Operation of Air Cargo Services) Regulations 1992 (SI No. 11): see the Transport chapter, 620, below.

European Communities (Pesticide Residues) (Feedingstuffs) Regulations 1992 (SI No. 40): see the Agriculture chapter, 15, above.

European Communities (Preservatives in Food) (Purity Criteria) (Amendment) Regulations 1992 (SI No. 64): see the Safety and Health chapter, 538, below.

European Communities (Prevention of Supply of Certain Goods and Services to Libya) Regulations 1992 (SI No. 146): see the Commercial Law chapter, 41, above.

European Communities (Prohibition of Trade with the Republics of Serbia and Montenegro) Regulations 1992 (SI No. 157): see the Commercial Law chapter, 41, above.

European Communities (Prohibition of Trade with the Republics of Serbia and Montenegro) (No. 2) Regulations 1992 (SI No. 203): see the Commercial Law chapter, 41, above.

European Communities (Quality of Bathing Water) (Revocation) Regulations 1992 (SI No. 154): see the Safety and Health chapter, 534, below.

European Communities (Quick-frozen Foodstuffs) Regulations 1992 (SI No. 290): see the Safety and Health chapter, 538, below.

European Communities (Recognition of Qualifications in Veterinary Medicine) (Amendment) Regulations 1992 (SI No. 253): see the Education chapter, 312, above.

European Communities (Retirement of Farmers) Regulations 1992 (SI No. 148): see the Agriculture chapter, 17, above.

European Communities (Review Procedures for the Award of Public Supply and Public Works Contracts) Regulations 1992 (SI No. 38): see the Commercial Law chapter, 46, above.

European Communities (Right of Establishment and Freedom to Provide Services in Hairdressing) Regulations 1992 (SI No. 315): see the Commercial Law chapter, 35, above.

European Communities (Road Passenger Transport) (Amendment) Regulations 1992 (SI No. 216): see the Transport chapter, 631, below.

European Communities (Road Traffic) (Compulsory Insurance) (Amendment) Regulations 1992 (SI No. 347): see the Transport chapter, 628, below.

European Communities (Seed of Fodder Plants) (Amendment) Regulations 1992 (SI No. 199): see the Agriculture chapter, 15, above.

European Communities (Seed of Fodder Plants) (Amendment) (No. 2) Regulations 1992 (SI No. 234): see the Agriculture chapter, 15, above.

European Communities (Seed of Fodder Plants) (Amendment) (No. 3) Regulations 1992 (SI No. 370): see the Agriculture chapter, 15, above.

European Communities (Seed of Oil Plants and Fibre Plants) (Amendment) Regulations 1992 (SI No. 301): see the Agriculture chapter, 15, above.

European Communities (Social Welfare) Regulations 1992 (SI No. 152): see the Social Welfare chapter, 543, below.

European Communities (Surveillance of Certain Textile Products Imports) Regulations 1992 (SI No. 34): see the Commercial Law chapter, 41, above.

European Communities (Surveillance of Imports of Certain Iron and Steel Products) Regulations 1992 (SI No. 105): see the Commercial Law chapter, 41, above.

European Communities (Telecommunications Services) Regulations 1992 (SI No. 45): see the Telecommunications chapter, 51, below.

European Communities (Therapeutic Substances Act 1932) (Cesser of Application) Regulations 1992 (SI No. 406): see the Health Services chapter, 393, below.

European Communities (Transferable Securities and Stock Exchange) Regulations 1992 (SI No. 202): see the Commercial Law chapter, above.

European Communities (Units of Measurement) Regulations 1992 (SI No. 255): see the Commercial Law chapter, 46-7, above.

European Communities (Value-Added Tax) Regulations 1992 (SI No. 413): see the Revenue chapter, 514-5, below.

European Communities (Vehicle Testing) (Amendment) Regulations 1992 (SI No. 324): see the Transport chapter, 630-1, below.

European Communities (Vocational Training for Drivers of Vehicles Carrying Dangerous Goods) Regulations 1992 (SI No. 204): see the Safety and Health chapter, 529, 540, below.

European Communities (Waste Oils) Regulations 1992 (SI No. 399): see the Safety and Health chapter, 536, below.

European Communities (Wildbirds) (Greenland Whitefronted Goose, Shoveler and Curlew) Regulations 1992 (SI No. 228): see the Agriculture chapter, 17-8, above.

Food Standards (Fruit Juices and Fruit Nectars) (European Communities) (Amendment) Regulations 1992 (SI No. 27): see the Safety and Health chapter, 537, below.

Health (Emulsifiers, Stabilisers, Thickening and Gelling Agents in Food) Regulations 1992 (SI No. 24): see the Safety and Health chapter, 536, below.

Local Government (Water Pollution) Regulations 1992 (SI No. 271): see the Safety and Health chapter, 534-5, below.

Mechanically Propelled Vehicles (International Circulation) Order 1992 (SI No. 384): see the Transport chapter, 628, below.

Quality of Bathing Water Regulations 1992 (SI No. 155): see the Safety and Health chapter, 534, below.

Road Traffic (Compulsory Insurance) (Amendment) Regulations 1992 (SI No. 346): see the Transport chapter, 628, below.

Road Traffic (Construction, Equipment and Use of Vehicles) (Amendment) Regulations 1992 (SI No. 325): see the Transport chapter, 627, below.

Value-Added Tax (Payment of Tax on Intra-Community Acquisitions of Means of Transport) Regulations 1992 (SI No. 412): see the Revenue chapter, 514, below.

Winter Time Order 1992 (SI No. 371): see the Commercial Law chapter, 47, above.

In addition to the above Regulations, some EC Directives and EC-related law were implemented by primary legislation.

The Environmental Protection Agency Act 1992 provides for the implementation by Ministerial Regulation of certain EC Directives: see the Safety and Health chapter, 529-33, below.

The Finance Act 1992 and the Finance (No. 2) Act 1992 gave effect to a number of measures required as part of the coming into being of the Internal Market on 1 January 1993: see the Revenue Law chapter, 500, below.

## JURISDICTION OF COURTS

In *Gannon v B & I Steampacket Co. Ltd, Landliner Travel Ltd and Edenderry Transport Ltd* [1993] 2 IR 359 (discussed in the Conflict of Laws chapter, 127-8, above) the Supreme Court considered the application of the Jurisdiction of Courts and Enforcement of Judgments (European Communities) Act 1988.

## SERVICES

The 1991 decision of the Court of Justice in *Society for the Protection of Unborn Children (Ireland) Ltd v Grogan (No. 2)* [1992] ILRM 461 is considered along with the 1992 decisions of the High Court and Supreme Court in *Attorney General v X* [1992] ILRM 401; [1992] 2 IR 1 in the Constitutional Law chapter, 154-208, above.

# Family Law

## NULLITY OF MARRIAGE

**Incapacity to form a normal marriage relationship** The past twelve years have witnessed the development of the ground of inability to form a 'caring or considerate', or 'normal', marriage relationship as a ground for annulment. Initially, the jurisprudence was at the level of the High Court (beginning with *R.S.J. v J.S.J.* [1982] ILRM 263 (Barrington J) and *D. v C.* [1984] ILRM 173 (Costello J), but it received the benediction of the Supreme Court in *F. (otherwise H.C.) v C.* [1991] ILRM 65: see the 1990 Review, 291-7.

It would be quite wrong to believe that the mere invocation of this ground is a passport to a decree of annulment. In *M.G. O'D. v C.D. O'D.*, High Court, 8 May 1992, O'Hanlon J refused a decree to a petitioner alleging that he suffered from inability to enter into or sustain a normal marriage relationship on account of his psychological incapacity and emotional immaturity. The petitioner also alleged duress and 'absolute unprepared[ness] and . . . unwillingness to enter the married state.'

The petitioner had been studying for the priesthood from 1956 until 1966, when he left shortly before the time for ordination. He had given his father a promise before his death that he would help in looking after the large family which his father was leaving behind. On leaving the order, however, he elected not to go back to his family home but instead embarked on further university study, acquiring teaching qualifications.

His courtship of the respondent, who was nine years his junior, was a matter of disputed evidence. The petitioner alleged that he had emerged from the religious life as a gauche, immature person, accustomed to submitting his will in all things to the will of others. The respondent was the daughter of the vice-principal of the school where the petitioner had obtained part-time work; the respondent claimed that the father had encouraged their relationship, that the respondent had 'set her cap' at him, and that he had been dragooned against his will into an engagement he did not want to enter. He claimed that on one occasion he had broken off the engagement but the respondent's mother had told him that the respondent might have a nervous breakdown and her father, who had a bad heart, might die. The petitioner's brother confirmed that, on his way to the church, the petitioner had made a remark indicating a great desire not to go through with the ceremony.

The petitioner's sister gave evidence to the effect that the petitioner was tense and seemed to be under pressure when she was at home from abroad on holidays during the engagement. She said that she tried to raise the matter of the engagement with the respondent's mother but the mother had told her not to interfere, saying that her daughter was a very nervous person who could suffer a nervous breakdown.

Some formidable evidence pointed the other way. The respondent's neighbour gave evidence that the wedding service had in her opinion been a happy affair and that the parties had seemed happy and affectionate when at her own wedding five years later. More weighty was a series of letters sent by the petitioner to the respondent during their engagement, including the days immediately before the ceremony. The petitioner's attempt to characterise them as 'the vapid bleatings of an adolescent' met with no approval from O'Hanlon J, who observed that at this time the petitioner was well past the period of adolescence, having been out in the world for two years after leaving his life of religion. During that period he had associated with other girls and had gone to dances and parties with them. He was making his way in the university quite successfully and 'was no longer an innocent abroad'. The romantic passages in his letters were interspersed with very business-like and factual accounts of his ordinary activities and of the travel and accommodation arrangements for his family when the wedding was taking place. O'Hanlon J accepted that the petitioner appeared to have suffered sensations of panic when the die was cast and he was actually face to face with marriage with all its implications of intimate association with the girl of his choice; but O'Hanlon J was not prepared to accept that the petitioner had entered into the marriage by reason of pressure put on him by the respondent or her parents. He believed that the parties had each entered into the marriage bond 'in the belief that they were deeply in love with the other party and for no other reason.'

After the ceremony the parties had lived together in harmony for about five years. Their first child, a daughter, was born in 1970. Four years later, after the respondent's sister had died in tragic circumstances and her father had also died, the respondent moved back to live with her mother for the time being, bringing her infant daughter with her. The petitioner spent some time with her and some time in the family home. Reports came back to the respondent of other women visiting the petitioner and leaving in the early morning. When taken to task, the petitioner angrily denied any involvement and threatened to move for annulment. He initiated proceedings for a church annulment but did not then take them any further.

The parties resumed cohabitation and a second child, a son, was born in 1975. Shortly afterwards they separated. The husband revived his proceedings for a church annulment which was granted two years later on the ground of his lack of due discretion. In High Court proceedings around the same time, the respondent was awarded custody of the children and maintenance. In 1980 the parties were briefly reconciled. From 1979, at the latest, and 'in all probability' far earlier, the petitioner had a series of sexual relationships with other women. He went through a ceremony of marriage in 1989 with a divorcée.

The respondent strongly opposed the petition for nullity. Evidence given by a consultant psychiatrist who had interviewed both parties, in O'Hanlon J's view 'gave little support to the petitioner's claim based on alleged incapacity'. In rejecting, without hesitation, the ground of duress, O'Hanlon J expressed the belief that the petitioner had freely chosen to marry, 'although in all probability he was the victim of last-minute fears, and misgivings such as might affect many persons when brought face-to-face with what is intended to be a life-long commitment.'

As to the 'more difficult' ground of the petitioner's alleged incapacity to form a normal marriage relationship, O'Hanlon J had no 'doubt whatever' that the petitioner's personality and psychological make-up had been 'profoundly affected by the early years of his life', when he had been living a cloistered life, but the deterioration and eventual collapse of the marriage, O'Hanlon J thought, should be attributed to his faults and weaknesses of character rather than to any inherent incapacity on his part to enter into and sustain a normal marriage relationship:

> He may be regarded as having left his original family somewhat in the lurch when he emerged from the seminary, having promised his father he would help to look after them, and from that time forward I believe he consulted his own interests and desires at every stage and was unwilling to make the sacrifices necessary to make his marriage work. . . . He had sufficient capacity to have affairs with other women and ultimately to embark on a new matrimonial relationship with one of them which he claims has been completely successful for some years past.

Even if he had come to a different conclusion on this aspect of the case, O'Hanlon J would have held that, the marriage 'being voidable on this ground and not void *ab initio*', a decree should be refused on the basis of approbation and delay. Approbation, because the petitioner had approbated the marriage when fully aware of the problems that had arisen between the parties and the legal remedies available if either physical or psychological incapacity could be established. Delay, because the petitioner 'had been taking legal advice from the early 1970s and reading up all the legal texts he could lay hands on dealing with matrimonial law and nullity in particular.' He had prepared nullity proceedings in 1983 and sworn a long affidavit in support of his claim at that time, but had then let the matter lie dormant for seven years. He had, moreover, cohabited with the respondent as late as 1981-2. Further, his delay had meant that the court was deprived of the important evidence of the respondent's father and the priest who officiated at the ceremony, both of whom were now long dead.

The final ground for nullity was that, because of the singular nature of the petitioner's religious formation, he was absolutely unprepared and wholly unwilling to enter the married state. O'Hanlon J summarily rejected this on the basis that the evidence gave it no support. It would seem mistaken to enshrine this disposition of what is a novel ground for nullity as conferring any judicial endorsement of it. True, O'Hanlon J did not expressly reject it but the reason seems abundantly plain: that, even if it had any validity — a matter on which O'Hanlon J saw no reason to comment—it found no support from the evidence.

O'Hanlon J's judgment is refreshing in its willingness to address the question of personal responsibility for relational disharmony. If a spouse wishing to rid himself of a marriage had only to repudiate the other spouse and then invoke that repudiation as evidence of his incapacity to form a caring and considerate relationship, the law of nullity would lose its fundamental rationale, which is to distinguish between freely chosen conduct and cases of genuine incapacity. A determinist philosophy of interpersonal relationships is incompatible with the law of nullity.

In *W.K. v M.C. (otherwise K.)*, High Court, 31 July 1992, Lavan J granted a decree of nullity on the ground of the respondent's incapacity to form a normal marriage relationship. The case was a clearcut one since there was strong evidence that the respondent suffered from a schizophrenic illness. Somewhat more troubling was the question whether the petition should be dismissed on the basis of approbation or delay; we consider that aspect of the case below, 349-50.

In *P.K. v M.B. (otherwise M.K.)*, High Court, 27 November 1992, Costello J gave a decree of nullity of marriage where the respondent was suffering from a paranoid psychosis at the time of the ceremony which made it impossible for her to sustain a normal marriage relationship. The parties had gone through a ceremony of marriage eleven years previously. The respondent had displayed a capacity for violence shortly afterwards. She consulted one psychiatrist in 1985 and a second the following year. The second psychiatrist treated her for a condition of paranoid psychosis for some months. The following year, after much disharmony, culminating in a scene in which the petitioner threw a chair at the respondent, the parties finally separated.

Costello J had no hesitation in accepting the second psychiatrist's diagnosis. While the first psychiatrist had not made the same diagnosis, he had considered that he was counselling the respondent rather than treating her as a patient. He had seen her on only two occasions and had not witnessed her, as the second psychiatrist had, in a hysterical outburst. A third psychiatrist had examined the respondent pursuant to the Master's order in 1991. He had not diagnosed paranoid psychosis but he accepted that when she was attending the second psychiatrist she must have been psychiatrically ill at the time. Costello J reached the conclusion, which the third psychiatrist also accepted, that the second psychiatrist had been in the best position of the three to make a correct diagnosis of her condition. Costello J went so far as to state that he 'could have no reasonable doubt' that the respondent suffered from this condition.

In determining whether or not the grounds for annulment was made out, Costello J used the expression 'normal marriage relationship', derived from his own judgment in *D. v C.*, above. He went on to express the view that the respondent 'lacked the capacity due to a psychiatric illness to form and sustain a lasting marriage relationship'. Should any significance be attached to the reference to a *lasting* marriage relationship? Nothing in Costello J's judgment suggests that he was seeking to explore new ground in using this expression. The notion of a normal marriage relationship imports permanence of commitment since that is the very basis of the marriage relationship. Moreover, in *D. v C.*, Costello J spoke of an inability *to enter and sustain* a normal marriage relationship. It seems, therefore, that the use of the word 'lasting' was not intend to have any particular juridical novelty.

Costello J noted that counsel for the respondent had sought to draw an analogy with impotence by arguing that, if the respondent had acquired the capacity to maintain a normal marriage relationship at some time subsequent to the date of the wedding, a decree should be refused, just as it would be where a condition of impotence existing at the time of the marriage was later cured. (Indeed, with impotence, the fact that the condition is *capable* of being cured, though not yet actually cured, should on principle prevent the court from granting a decree (*Dickinson v Dickinson* [1913] P198) though courts do not press this requirement very strongly: Duncan & Scully, *Marriage Breakdown in Ireland: Law and Practice* (1990), para. 2.033.) Costello J rejected the argument on the evidence, which was to the effect that the respondent had *not* acquired the requisite capacity subsequent to the wedding. The tenor of his remarks suggests that he was not unreceptive to the argument as a matter of law, though it would be wrong to read too much into his treatment of a point that was destined to fail on the facts.

In *K.W.T. v D.A.T.*, High Court, 18 March 1992, Murphy J dismissed a petition for nullity of marriage based on the alleged incapacity of both parties to enter into and sustain a normal marital relationship with each other. The parties had gone through a ceremony of marriage in 1972. They had three children; they separated in 1989. The essence of the petition was that, beneath the attractive surface of a marriage blessed by intellectual attainments, vocational successes and a glamorous lifestyle, there was a fundamental flaw which negated the very basis of the matrimonial relationship. This, the parties said, was their inability to discuss problems together. The respondent summarised the problem as she saw it:

> We both learnt to skirt issues. We did not open them out. We did not face them. We were careful and we were polite. There were no rows. There was no meeting of minds. . . . There was no emotional closeness in the relationship.

This was substantially the conclusion reached by two distinguished psychiatrists who examined both of the parties at considerable length. The psychiatrists were emphatic that the marriage was doomed from the outset. The respondent was so immature and insecure that she had a special need for emotional support if a marriage relationship was to be sustained. The petitioner did not have the exceptional emotional maturity and generosity that would have been needed for the relationship to succeed.

Murphy J considered that O'Hanlon J's decision in *P.C. v V.C.* [1990] 2 IR was of particular importance as its facts had much in common with the instant case. One of the psychiatrists in the instant case had also given evidence in *P.C. v V.C.*, where he had concluded that the marriage was doomed from the outset by reason of elements of immaturity in the character and temperament of both parties and an inability on both sides to form an maintain a functional, viable marriage relationship. Murphy J considered that the case-law had established that a decree of nullity might be granted 'where by reason of elements of immaturity alone and notwithstanding the absence of any psychiatric disorder the parties to the purported marriage d[id] not have in combination with each other an adequate emotional capacity to sustain a viable marriage relationship.' O'Hanlon J's decision in *P.C. v V.C.* was a very helpful and instructive application of that principle but in the final analysis it was the duty of the judge to determine whether, *as a matter of degree*, the inadequacy of the emotional relationship was such as to render the purported marriage a nullity.

Murphy J identified two points of difference between the cases. In *P.C. v V.C.* the parties had shared a home for less than eighteen months, in contrast to the period of eighteen years in the instant case. Their relationship had been interrupted by constant and dramatic disagreements, in contrast to the courtesy and lack of any obvious unpleasantness which had characterised the relationship of the parties in the instant case.

Murphy J noted that it had only been in recent times that the nature of the matrimonial relationship had been more fully explored to establish and identify factors which had been at all times essential ingredients in that very special relationship. Much of this analysis had been carried out by psychiatrists, psychologists and social workers. It followed that their evidence in such cases was of paramount importance. Nevertheless, at the end of the day, Murphy J considered that he could not abdicate his function to the experts, however distinguished, even though they had argued that the parties lacked an emotional capacity to sustain the marital relationship.

The fact that the marriage, at least in its outward form, had survived so long without apparent discord or obvious mental distress suggested that an adequate if less than satisfactory relationship had been achieved. Moreover, one of the psychiatrists had apparently concluded that the respondent had eventually achieved emotional maturity, though at a time when it was too late to save the marriage. This made it clear that the respondent's emotional inadequacy had not been irreversible 'and to that extent presumably it was possible that their combined problems could have been resolved or ameliorated if during their lives together some event occurred which resulted in one or both of the parties obtaining requisite advice and assistance at an earlier date'. With some hesitation Murphy J concluded that the inadequacy of the emotional response of the parties one to the other was not such a degree as would justify the court in granting a decree of nullity.

Murphy J's judgment is of interest in a number of respects. First, it provides a necessary brake on a potentially overbroad interpretation of the ground of relational incapacity which a cursory reading of *P.C. v V.C.* might have encouraged: see our observations in the 1989 Review, 220-3. It must be acknowledged that not all of the points of difference between *P.C. v V.C.* and the instant case can be pressed too far. The external appearance of a successful marriage extending over several years could scarcely constitute a barrier to granting an annulment if, as a matter of fact, albeit not publicly known, one or both of the parties lacked capacity.

Secondly, it is worth noting that Murphy J's articulation of the test by which capacity is to be assessed referred to capacity 'to sustain a viable marriage relationship'. Perhaps viability here may be equiparated with the notions of a 'caring or considerate' or 'normal' marriage relationship. Certainly the judgment gives no indication that Murphy J intended to establish a new ground to extend the *R.S.J.* principle in any radical way. Clearly an incapacity to form a caring, considerate or normal marriage relationship would be quite inconsistent with the viability of the relationship. It is nonetheless interesting that in *P.K. v M.B. (otherwise M.K.)*, above, as we have seen, Costello J spoke of incapacity to form a 'lasting' marriage relationship, apparent as an aspect of the general incapacity to form a normal marriage relationship, which he had recognised in *D. v C.* nine years previously.

In *S. v K.*, High Court, 2 July 1992, Denham J granted a decree of nullity based on the incapacity of the parties to enter into and sustain a normal mental relationship with each other. The account of the parties' lives involved a poignant tale. The petitioner had been treated with great harshness when growing up. He had been wrongly blamed for his father's illness, required to sleep in a maid's room and locked in a room during the day to study. When he failed his medical examinations, his parents evicted him from the family home. The respondent's early life also had its hardships. Her adoptive mother had died two months before the respondent sat her Leaving Certificate examination. Her adoptive father then disappeared. It was assumed he committed suicide.

The parties began to go out together in 1967. The respondent became pregnant and they went through a ceremony of marriage. They did not tell their friends of the pregnancy, on the petitioner's urging. This isolated the respondent and caused her distress.

Home life thereafter was chaotic. The petitioner worked hard at completing his medical studies, which he did successfully in 1970. The respondent, who inherited a substantial sum from her father's estate seven years after his disappearance and presumed death, showed signs of mental difficulties from the earliest days of her time living with the petitioner. She was admitted to hospital for nearly five months' psychiatric care in 1971. The position afterwards was no better:

> Year by year the situation between the petitioner and the respondent and her behaviour at home was more chaotic, more violent. She had no friends or family with whom she had a relationship. She was intolerant of many things, she was unable to mother or care for her children or the petitioner.

At this time she was drinking heavily. When the petitioner commenced practice as a general practitioner from home, to facilitate the home situation, the respondent was unable to cope with the practice and abused the patients. The respondent remained under psychiatric care thereafter. She gave up drink in 1979. She left the family home a year later to live with a man with whom she had become friendly when attending Alcoholics Anonymous. The petitioner established a relationship with another woman in 1988.

The psychiatric evidence was to the effect that the respondent suffered from an inherent, possibly inherited, psychiatric disorder which was activated by stress initially at the time of her first pregnancy and relationship with the petitioner. She was a person who would have difficulty maintaining a stable relationship; her prospects of doing so would depend on her partner, who would have to be enormously stable and understanding.

The psychiatrist who was appointed by the Master to examine the petitioner described him as a perfectionist, highly organised and of authoritarian disposition. In the psychiatrist's opinion, the petitioner had been immature at the time of courtship and marriage ceremony and would not have recognised the respondent's needs, but at the time of examination had become mature, stable and capable of forming a good relationship with a mature, stable, warm and affectionate person.

Denham J granted a decree of nullity on the basis that both parties had not had the capacity to enter into and sustain a normal marital relationship with each other. There were, she found, inherent personality factors, neither voluntary nor self-induced, which made them incapable of entering into or sustaining such a relationship. Although the petitioner had been as supportive in running the house and rearing the children as his medical studies would allow, he had acted in an impersonal, domineering and judgmental way towards the respondent and was immature. The respondent had an inherent and constitutional predisposition to psychiatric illness, a schizo-affective disorder, triggered by her pre-marital pregnancy and the circumstances surrounding it and her purported marriage to the petitioner.

In holding that both parties lacked the capacity to enter into or sustain a normal marriage relationship, Denham J made it clear that each of them suffered from this incapacity in its own right, regardless of the particular personality of the other. But she went on to hold, on the analogy with impotence, that the incapacity could be in relation to a particular person. She noted that the fact that the parties had subsequently entered into relationships with other persons did not detract from the factual and legal situation pertaining to their relationship with each other.

In the 1989 Review, 222, in our discussion of *P.C. v V.C.* [1990] 2 IR 91, we argued that the ground of incapacity to form a 'caring and considerate', or 'normal', marriage relationship should not be transformed into a completely different ground of incompatibility, resting on entirely different philosophical premises. Denham J makes it clear that she is faithful to the true philosophical basis underlying *R.S.J. v J.S.J.* and *D. v C.* since she makes an express finding in respect of each of the parties of an incapacity to enter into or sustain a normal marital relationship: compare conclusions no. 5 and no. 7 of her judgment. Nevertheless, her reference to the analogy with impotence (*quoad hunc vel hanc*) should not be pressed too far, as we indicated in the 1989 Review, 222.

Denham J's observations on the onus of proof in nullity proceedings are of interest. She acknowledged that the petitioner carried 'a heavy burden to discharge' to show that the marriage was invalid. She went on to quote Hanna

J's statement in *McM. v McM.* and *McK. v McK.* [1936] IR 177, at 187 that a petition based on impotence must be established 'clearly, unequivocally and beyond reasonable doubt. . . .' She commented that this might well be the high water mark of the law on the burden of proof in this type of case; in practice, the courts had been requiring a high but less demanding burden than in criminal cases. She noted that there had been *obiter dicta*, including McCarthy J's statement in *N. (otherwise K.) v K.* [1986] ILRM 75, at 94, to the effect that the burden of proof is that of the balance of probabilities. Her own test did not go so far:

> In view of the Constitutional protection of the institution of marriage it is quite clear that there is a heavy burden of proof on the petitioner. There is a severe and heavy burden on the petitioner, of a quasi-criminal trial nature.

This would appear to be very close to Hanna J's high water mark and considerably heavier than the balance of probabilities. It is worth noting that in *P.K. v M.B.(otherwise M.K.)*, above, Costello J raised, but did not resolve, the question whether the appropriate standard of proof was that requiring proof beyond reasonable doubt; on the facts of the case the petitioner had established the ground for annulment in accordance with this standard.

In *A.B. v E.B.*, High Court, 14 October 1993, Budd J referred to Henchy J's view, in *Banco Ambrosiano v Ansbacher & Co.* [1987] ILRM 669, at 701, that allegations of fraud in civil litigation should be determined on the balance of probabilities. Budd J could see no reason why the same measure should not be applied in cases of nullity of marriage. We will discuss this decision in the 1993 Review.

**Impermanent commitment** In the 1990 Review, 301-6, we analysed Carroll J's judgment in *H.H. (otherwise H.C.) v J.F.F.D.S.*, High Court 19 December 1990, refusing the application for a decree of nullity. The Supreme Court (*sub nom. H.S. v J.S.*) affirmed on 3 April 1992.

It will be recalled that the essence of the petitioner's case was that she had gone through a ceremony of marriage with her Portuguese boyfriend to enable him to obtain a visa for the United States, on the basis that if the marriage did not work out they would divorce. She also asserted that she had been too immature to give a valid matrimonial consent. Carroll J held against the petitioner on both these grounds.

On appeal, Finlay CJ (Hederman, McCarthy, O'Flaherty and Egan JJ concuring) endorsed Carroll J's approach. The Chief Justice was satisfied that an intention by a party, when entering into a marriage, to terminate it by divorce, should both parties not want it to continue, did not render the marriage invalid:

> There are a great number of persons whose religious convictions or moral code would raise no bar to obtaining a divorce in an appropriate jurisdiction in the event of a marriage not proving to be successful, and it cannot, in my view, be said that such persons by reason of that particular belief, and even by reason of an expressed intention that in the event of the marriage not working out a divorce would be availed of, have not entered into a valid marriage.

The respondent had not participated in the proceedings. It was 'extremely improbable' that a court could safely reach any decision on the question of the nullity of the marriage, *based on the petitioner's account of what she thought or believed the respondent's understanding or attitude to have been.* This made the case peculiarly one in which the trial Judge would have an opportunity of judging the petitioner before her and thus one in which the Supreme Court should be particularly slow to disturb or vary the inferences that she had drawn from the evidence.

Taking this approach, the Chief Justice considered that Carroll J's factual conclusions were well supported on the evidence and that her legal conclusions were correct:

> . . . [N]either immaturity in a general sense nor irresponsibility can of itself and to a general degree only, constitute a ground for nullity, though in particular cases personality disorders, including immaturity or irresponsibility arising from psychiatric or personality disorders may affect true consent, or may affect the capacity of a person to maintain a lasting marriage relationship. The capacity to maintain a lasting marriage relationship must, however, be distinguished from an intention that, if it was not convenient or successful to try and do so, . . . the attempt could be abandoned.

It seems clear from the decision that a private *agreement* between the parties to divorce if the relationship does not work out satisfactorily does not invalidate a marriage. The Chief Justice's observations suggest that if one of the parties has such an intention, which is not communicated to the other, this similarly will not render the marriage void or voidable. Where does this leave Kenny J's holding in his dissenting judgment in *S. v S.*, Supreme Court, 1 July 1976? Kenny J there held that the secret intention by one party never to consummate the marriage invalidated the marriage on the basis that the intention to have sexual intercourse was 'a fundamental feature of the marriage contract'. If we imagine a case where a man goes through a ceremony of marriage in order to obtain the entitlement to live in a particular country, with the secret intention of abandoning his wife within weeks or days of the marriage, does the validity or invalidity of the marriage depend on whether the parties consummated the marriage?

The best answer would appear to be that a secret intention to use marriage simply as a momentary means to an independent end should fall within Kenny J's formula. The difficulty with any such general test, of course, is that it involves the court in judgment calls in a grey area. The price of this is lack of certainty and the danger of differing approaches among trial judges. Nevertheless, there is also a significant price to be paid for certainty and an *a priori* refusal to go into grey areas. That price is paid by those parties whose personal circumstances fall within the broad scope of Kenny J's test. For further consideration of this general theme, see Wrenn, 'Redefining the Essence of Marriage' (1986) 46 Jurist 532, at 533-4, Davis, 'Fraud and Annulment of Marriage' (1988) 2 Austr. J of Family L 138, Jessup, 'Fraud and Nullity of Marriage in Australia' (1989) 3 Austr. J of Family L 93.

**Approbation and delay** In *W.K. v M.C. (otherwise K.)*, High Court, 31 July 1992, where Lavan J granted a decree of nullity on the basis of the respondent's incapacity to form a normal marriage relationship on account of a schizophrenic illness, he held that the petitioner had not been guilty of delay or approbation in failing to initiate nullity proceedings for several years after the ceremony of marriage in 1976. The petitioner had been unaware of the respondent's condition in 1976. He first learned of her illness in 1979. He had acted honourably at all times towards her and had tried to look after her at home, against medical advice that she should be hospitalised. The respondent had eventually left the home and returned to her mother in 1985. The parties' son had been born in 1977.

Lavan J was concerned that the petitioner had stated on oath that he would not have petitioned for nullity of marriage if the respondent's mother had not sought maintanance and other property orders against him in favour of her daughter. Nonetheless Lavan J did not consider that this should defeat the petitioner's entitlement to a decree. This was 'an exceptional case' which did 'not establish any principle of law in relation to either delay or approbation'.

Lavan J stated that he accepted as applicable to the case the principles set out by Hederman J in the Supreme Court decision of *D.B. (otherwise O'R.) v N. O'R.* [1991] ILRM 160; [1991] 1 IR 536. Our comments on the approach there favoured may be found in the 1989 Review, 300-1. Once again, the question arises as to how to characterise the *R.S.J.* ground for annulment: does it render the marriage voidable (in which case approbation is a bar) or void (in which case ratification may be available as a bar)? Of course, if ratification is co-extensive with the bar of approbation in its range of operation, this question of characterisation will be of no importance, but there is reason to believe that the two bars are not co-extensive. In *D.B. (O'R.)*

*v N. O'R.*, Hederman J accepted that the bar of *delay*, but not *approbation*, was available in a case involving lack of consent (resulting from duress rather than mental capacity). He observed that 'approbation can never be relevant where there is no true consent . . .' This would appear to leave to the bar of delay the exclusive task of defeating the petition in appropriate cases, with ratification playing no role.

Earlier in this chapter, above, 338-41, we discussed the decision of *M.G. O'D. v C.D. O'D.*, High Court, 8 May 1992, where O'Hanlon refused a decree of nullity on the basis of the petitioner's incapacity to form a normal marriage relationship. We noted that O'Hanlon J would in any event have dismissed the application on the basis of the petitioner's approbation and delay.

## GUARDIANSHIP OF CHILDREN

**The welfare test in custody disputes** The Supreme Court decision of *S. v S.*, 21 February 1992 is an important signpost to the direction of judicial thinking on the values underlying the concept of children's welfare in custody disputes. The case represents the first instance for well over a decade in which the Court has been called on to address this question at any deep level.

The statutory context may be shortly described. S. 3 of the Guardianship of Infants Act 1964 provides in part that, in any custody proceedings, the court is to regard the welfare of the infant as the first and paramount consideration. S. 2 defines 'welfare' as comprising 'the religious and moral, intellectual, physical and social welfare of the infant'. It may be noted that s. 2 makes no reference to the psychological welfare of the infant. That aspect is not of course ignored by the courts, but falls within the scope of some of the other elements, notably physical and intellectual welfare: see A. Shatter, *Family Law in the Republic of Ireland* (3rd ed., 1986), p. 355.

The reference to the religious and moral welfare of children inevitably raises the question of how the courts should regard parental conduct that is inconsistent with permanence in matrimonial commitment, such as where a parent leaves the home without justification and goes to live with another person. The courts have constantly stressed that the children are not to be treated as symbols of victory in a matrimonial contest and that an award of custody 'is not a prize for good matrimonial behaviour', as Kenny J put it in *J.J.W. v B.M.W.*, 110 ILTR 45, at 47 (High Court, 1971, reversed by Supreme Court, 1971). But it is equally clear that parental conduct may impact on a child's welfare. In what way, therefore, should the courts approach the welfare implications of one parent's abandonment of the other in favour of a new relationship? Three possible solutions have been suggested in the decisions. *First*, that such conduct should be assessed in accordance with the prevalent norms of society; *second*, that the religious and moral values of the parents should be the appropriate test by which to assess the child's welfare and *third*, that the parent's conduct should be considered in terms of the example it offers the child.

The decisions do not distinguish clearly between these three rationales. Thus we find Finlay P, in the High Court decision of *McD. v McD.*, 19 February 1979, stating:

> The capacity of children to become good members of the society in which they live, their moral welfare as I have defined it and their religious welfare as I have defined it all depend in any given case upon the nature and standards of the society in which they live, its commonly accepted moral norms and the moral and ethical code of the religion in which they are being brought up.
>
> These children were . . . intended to live and grow up for the present at least in this country and to be brought up as practising members of the Catholic Church.
>
> . . . [S]ociety in Ireland accepts as a fundamental and integral unit the family and the Constitution therefore protects and safeguards the integrity of the unit. In addition I would consider the moral code of that society as well as the moral and ethical code of the Catholic Church [which] considers as fundamental the sanctity of marriage and condemns and disapproves of adultery.

Similarly, in the Supreme Court decision of *E.K. v M.K.*, 31 July 1974 (extracted in Binchy's *Casebook on Irish Family Law* (1984), p. 441), Walsh J said that:

> . . . the life which is being led by the mother in this case is a manifest repudiation of the social and religious values with which the children should be inculcated which she believes she can teach them while at the same time clearly repudiating them herself in the sight of her own children.

In *J.J.W. v B.M.W.*, above, where the wife had gone to live with another man, Kenny J articulated the third of the rationales identified above:

> The main argument against the wife is the fact that she is living with a man to whom she is not married and so she is committing a serious sin judged by Christian standards. As he will take the place of the father,

> the children will have a deplorable example before them all the time. They will quickly learn that their mother is living in a way condemned by the Church to which she belongs and in which they are being brought up. Court orders for divorce will not alter this. It is difficult to imagine the children giving a great deal of attention to what they are taught about Christian marriage when they have this model before them, and example by parents is worth more than years of sermons, instruction and public piety.

Most of the cases in which the issue has been discussed involve situations where the *mother* has gone to live with another man. The reason for this is not that the courts look on such conduct by wives in a worse light than when husbands are involved. The explanation is that, in cases where a husband has gone to live with another woman, the prospects of his being awarded custody are usually slight enough since the courts have a tendency to presume that the mother is the appropriate custodian in the absence of strong countervailing considerations: see Binchy, 'The Sex of a Parent as a Factor in Custody Disputes', (1983) 77 Incorp. L. Soc. of Ireland Gazette 269. A father of young children who has left his wife and established a new relationship may have difficulty in convincing the court that the *moral, religious* and *physical* welfare of his children will best be served by awarding him custody. Normally he cannot credibly make a case on the basis of economic advantage since the court will (quite reasonably) be concerned as to why he should have left his wife in worse financial circumstances than himself.

In *S. v S.*, the parties had married in 1973, when the wife was twenty-five years old and the husband thirty-four. Both were Catholics. They had three girls, ranging from thirteen to seven years at the time of the proceedings. In 1988 the wife left the family home, taking her children with her. She had by this time formed a sexual relationship with another man, who was married with children. She intended to live with him when her children were older. The wife obtained an order for judicial separation from Morris J in December 1991. In related custody proceedings Morris J ordered that the husband should have sole custody of the children with provision for access by the wife, not including overnight access.

Morris J provided graphic portraits of the spouses. Of the husband, he said:

> I believe that he is a thrifty, hardworking, responsible, retiring man. He is a non-drinker and a non-smoker. His interests are his farm and his work and to a far lesser extent GAA administration activities and, in the past, political activities. He is not one interested in socialising. He believes strongly in traditional values and in his religion. I believe that

> in this, in as much as he may be criticised in being strict, this strictness relates to instilling into the children the virtues of honesty and decency. On the negative side I believe that it could be said of him, in so far as the children are concerned, that he may find it difficult to relate to them in children, childy [*sic*] matters.

Morris J's opinion of the wife was as follows.

> I believe that she is concerned with enjoying her life to the full in so far as it relates to social activities, golf clubs, public houses, the choral society and to socialising generally. She is bitterly disappointed about the life that her marriage gives her and desperately wants to get away from that life and the life that it offers her, and she is anxious to get into a life which offers her more activity and excitement. I believe that she grew to dislike her husband over the past three or four years before she left him, because she regarded him as an impediment in the enjoyment of her life. . . .
>
> I believe that the wife has no proper appreciation of the commitment which marriage involves and I believe that she put her own enjoyment above all other considerations.

Morris J went on to hold that the wife had been having an affair in the presence of the children and that the man involved would be seen by them as a substitute figure for their father, which would be of no value to them. He also held that the wife, for the purpose of pursuing her enjoyment, had left the children alone for prolonged periods of time at night, without a baby-sitter, while she was in a public house. She had, moreover, deliberately turned the children against their father in an effort to bolster an utterly false allegation of sexual abuse which she had made against her husband.

Morris J identified a number of factors in support of awarding custody to the father. While living with him, the children would be brought up by a person who had a high appreciation of traditional moral values which would be passed to them. They would have a stable, loving home, even though they would have to be looked after by a housekeeper between 7 a.m. and the time they went to school. They would, moreover, have the companionship of their cousins who lived about half a mile away. They would have the company of their father every weekend and every evening during the week.

In support of the wife, Morris J acknowledged that she was fond of the children and that 'she would undoubtedly give them an enjoyable life, introducing them to the enjoyment of living, and they would at least in the short-term be happy'. Against her, Morris J considered it almost inevitable that the children would be brought into close association with the man with whom the wife was having a relationship and who in Morris J's opinion had 'nothing to offer them' in the role of foster father. Furthermore, the wife's lifestyle and values would be detrimental to the children and show them 'a very bad example'. Morris J went so far as to express the belief that the children 'would adopt the habits of drinking and might well get into the habit of loose living at an early age'.

The varying approaches of the Supreme Court judges are worthy of attention. Four judgments were delivered: by Finlay CJ, McCarthy O'Flaherty and Egan JJ. All were agreed that the award of custody in favour of the husband should be upheld but the points of emphasis differed from judge to judge.

Finlay CJ contented himself in stressing the fact that the inferences from the primary facts which Morris J had drawn were 'peculiarly and to a very large extent, if not exclusively,' based on his opportunity to observe the demeanour of the parties and other witnesses. He observed that, whilst general principles concerning question of custody could be gleaned from the decisions of the courts in individual cases, 'those principles are very particularly to be applied to the special facts of each case which vary greatly'. The findings made by the Supreme Court in *MacD. v MacD.* (1979) 114 ILTR 59 concerning the qualities, character and approach of the mother to the upbringing of her children, as well as the ages of the children, made *MacD.* wholly different in detail from the instant case.

Egan J, concurring, observed that:

> [t]here is no perfect solution to the problem and the more decided cases I read the more convinced I become that, although legal principles are clear, their application depends very much upon the facts of each particular case.

He noted that it had been conceded that the wife was very fond of her children but added that there could be no doubt that her lifestyle and conduct were a bad example to them. As against his, Egan J considered that it had to be said that life with their father on the farm would be lonelier for the children even though they had cousins nearby.

Egan J went on to observe that:

> [t]he evidence seems to indicate a reluctance on the part of the children to reside with their father and this is an unhappy feature of the case as one would be anxious that they should be happy. There is also the fact that they are girls, which means that there could be advantages for them in being looked after by their mother rather than by their father.

In spite of these considerations, Egan J concluded that the best interests of the children would be served by awarding custody to the father:

> He is a good man and hopefully the children will grow to be happy with him in time. In any event, happiness is not always synonymous with welfare. No matter how much the mother loves her children she is a bad example to them and, in her capacity as a mother, she must be strongly criticised for leaving her children alone for periods at night, even though only occasionally. Neither is it in the children's welfare that she seems to have turned them against their father without good cause.

McCarthy J delivered a short concurring judgment. Having referred briefly to three earlier decisions of the Supreme Court, he said:

> No doubt there are many other cases where comments have been made upon the role of mother or father in the care and custody of young children and, particularly, young girls. In my view, save for a clear expression of general principle, little assistance is to be gained in resolving any one case of child custody by reference to the facts of another.

O'Flaherty J evinced a certain degree of discomfiture with the approach favoured by his colleagues. While not dissenting from it, he noted that initially he would have wished to have an order made providing for the custody of the children to be given jointly to the parents but he had come to accept that this might not be a practical solution.

O'Flaherty went on to observe that:

> [t]here must be a better solution to cases like this than to have protracted High Court proceedings with an appeal to this Court. Here are parents who have fallen out; the children, of course, inevitably must suffer as little as possible. I would remit the matter to the Local District Court or Circuit Court to monitor the progress of this case. A final order cannot be made. Hopefully the parties will be able to agree but, if they do not, the matter of access will have to be decided, if not from month to month, perhaps from half year to half year. The local district judge or circuit judge is best qualified to preside over any incidental matters of dispute that may arise between the parties. He is available at a local venue, easily accessible. I think it shocking that the parties have engaged in such lengthy, debilitating proceedings in the High Court to establish what, with some goodwill and give and take on each side, should have been worked out by agreement.

O'Flaherty J went on to agree with Egan J's view that, while the principles were clear, their application had to depend on the facts of each particular case. He concluded as follows:

> I do not wish to apportion blame because that is a redundant exercise. I would urge the parents to recognise their duties and obligations to the children and the fact that the law lays down that their welfare is the first and paramount consideration. They should leave aside past bitterness and seek anew an accommodation of their differences that will give the children the hope and confidence that they need in those most crucial years of their lives.

The decision of the Supreme Court in *S. v S.* raises a number of issues of general significance, ranging beyond the facts of the case. Perhaps the most central is the question of the extent to which parental values and conduct remain a significant factor in the determination of where the welfare of the children lies. Morris J had no doubt about the answer to this question. The mother's value preferences and conduct made it contrary to her children's welfare that she should have custody of them. This view clearly prevailed in the Supreme Court, since all five of the judges endorsed Morris J's order. Nevertheless differences of emphasis may be discerned in the judgments.

Finlay CJ was satisfied that Morris J had properly applied the relevant principles in regard to the welfare of the children. He provided no express analysis of his own as to how parental values and conduct can impact on children's welfare. Egan J also expressed support for Morris J's holding in relation to specific aspects of the case. On the question of conduct, he twice ventured the view that the mother was 'a bad example' to her children but, like the Chief Justice, he did not elaborate on this in any detail. McCarthy J had nothing to say on this matter.

It is hard to read the several judgments in the Supreme Court without forming the view that the judges were reluctant to articulate any explicit legal norms relating to the religious and moral welfare of the children. To resort to the position that every case depends on its particular facts is not simply unenlightening; it is positively misleading as it suggests that the welfare of children is not a matter on which general principles may properly be articulated. If parental extra-marital cohabitation is contrary to children's moral and religious welfare in one case, it is hard to see how it should not also be contrary to children's welfare in other cases, of otherwise similar facts. O'Flaherty J's judgment is of particular interest as it reflects the fashion for joint custody orders for separated parents which swept America over a decade ago, as well as evincing a distaste for the judicial role in custody proceedings which also has found support in some quarters. The joint custody solution proved unsatisfactory since it represented a cosmetic disguise for reality, which was that children will normally spend most of their time with one of their parents. Some non-custodial parents liked to be called 'joint' custodians of their children but the general view in America today is that the legal system is more convincing when its orders reflect rather than disguise reality. For analysis, see Scott & Derdeyn, 'Rethinking Joint Custody' (1984) 45 Ohio State LJ 455, Schulmann & Pitt, 'Second Thoughts on Joint Custody: Analysis of Legislation and Its Implications for Women and Children' (1982) 12 Golden Gate U L Rev 538 (1982), Reece, 'Joint Custody: A Cautious View' (1983) U Cal Davis L Rev 775.

The distaste for the judicial role in custody proceedings raises far deeper questions as to the role of the courts in family law. The role of the courts in most family law contexts is to protect the rights of individual family members, and of families, from injustice. When a court hears a custody dispute, its role is to identify where the welfare of the child lies and to fashion its orders in such a way as best to advance the welfare of the child. If the court withdraws from this role, there is no guarantee that negotiations between the parents will yield a result that is best for the child. The stronger party may well be able to lay down terms in which considerations of the child's religious and moral welfare are far from central. The experience of mediation as a substitute for judicial resolution of family law issues indicates that power imbalance and the absence of judicial supervision can lead to significant injustice to children. For consideration of some of these themes, see Morris, 26 Santa Clara L Rev 745 (1986), Folberg, 19 Columbia J of L & Social Problems 413 (1985), Misteravich, 70 U Detroit Mercy L Rev 37 (1992), Grillo, 100 Yale L J 1545 (1991), Bruch, 2 Internat J of L & the Family 106 (1988).

In *In re S.* and *D.R.; L.R. v D.R.*, High Court, 2 April 1992 — a decision that we analyse in greater detail in the Conflicts of Law Chapter above, 112-5—Costello J addressed the question of the custody of two children, aged three and one. He considered that, under Irish domestic law (uncomplicated by the international dimensions of the case), the question of custody was 'simple and straightforward'. The plaintiff was a loving and caring mother who had looked after the children since their birth. She was now living in her parents' home. Conditions were crowded but there was a reasonable prospect that she would obtain accommodation from the local authority in the near future should an award of custody be made. She was in receipt of welfare payments for herself and the children, augmented by financial assistance from her parents and her sister. If the children were returned to the custody of their father in the United States of America they would undoubtedly live in a larger house and the income available for their maintenance would be higher. But these considerations were 'of little significance' when weighed against the other factors in the case. The father, though he loved the children and would do his best to care for them, would be out at work every day from Monday to Friday. A woman had offered to help to look after the children, should he obtain custody.

Costello J considered it

> obvious. . . that these arrangements would be a very poor substitute for the love and care which children of such a young age should obtain from their mother and which they would obtain from the plaintiff. . . . It seems perfectly clear to me that their moral, intellectual, physical and social welfare requires that their mother should retain their custody.

Costello J observed that as both parents were practising Catholics, 'the children's religious welfare is a neutral factor in the case'.

The decision involves a strong reiteration of what is in effect a presumption that young children's welfare lies with their mother. Although attempts have been made internationally over the past two decades, at both the judicial and legislative levels, to introduce a principle of gender neutrality in custody decision-making, these have been strikingly unsuccessful.

One wonders how the Supreme Court would respond to the argument that Article 40.1 renders unconstitutional a decision as to custody based on a perception that mothers, as a category, are more suitable custodians of very young children than are fathers. Costello J's language suggests that his decision was indeed based on just such a generic perception. The allegedly unconstitutional discrimination, it should be noted, is the creature of judicial rather than legislative enterprise, since the Guardianship of Infants Act 1964 is, on its face, entirely devoid of gender discrimination with respect to marital children. (The position relating to non-marital children, starkly discriminatory as between the sexes under the 1964 legislation, still retains an important degree of gender discrimination under the Status of Children Act 1987: see *K. v W. (No. 1)*, [1990] ILRM and *K. v W. (No. 2)*, 1990 ILRM 791, and our comments in the 1989 Review, 248-57 and the 1990 Review, 316-22).

In view of the body of judgments, at both High Court and Supreme Court level, over the last twenty-five years in which there is a clear judicial perception of mothers *as a category* as more suitable custodians of young children, it is hard to see the Supreme Court radically over-turning this approach. It is far more likely that the Court would seek to dispose of a constitutional challenge by denying that there is any rule of law, or even legal presumption, operating in favour of mothers as a category. Formally this may be so, but it would be disingenuous to explain away what is a clear preference in such an incomplete manner. It is, of course, possible that the Court would face this issue squarely and hold, *as a matter of empirical fact*, that the welfare of young children is better served as a general rule by placing them in the custody of their mother. Such a conclusion would require formidable scientific evidence. For a stimulating analysis, see Berns, 'Living Under the Shadow of Rousseau: The Role of Gender Ideologies in Custody and Access Disputes' (1991) U Tasmania L Rev 233.

Whatever approach the Court adopts, one hopes that it will not reduce this important issue to one 'dependent on the facts of the particular case' — a tendency apparent in *S. v S.*, above. Of course every custody dispute has to be decided by having regard to its unique facts, but the court nevertheless has to confront the question whether it is ever permissible to proceed on the basis that most women or most men have capacities distinctive to their sex which tilt the welfare issue in their direction.

In *In re R.M. Infant; E.M. v A.M.*, High Court, 16 June 1992, the question of the custody of a child arose in an international context. Flood J took the rare step of awarding custody to a parent whose home was outside the jurisdiction, where there was no question that the parent resident in Ireland had wrongfully removed the child from abroad to Ireland.

The parties had married in Ireland in 1983, having previously cohabited for a period of about a year and a half followed by a short separation. The mother, who was 23 years old at the time of this wedding, was from a small lumber town in Oregon, 'in what can only be described as an idyllic woodland setting'. She had previously married at the age of seventeen, borne a child and been divorced by the age of nineteen. In 1986, the mother gave birth to a second child, a boy. After a period of domestic disharmony, the father left the matrimonial home in 1987. The parties co-operated well for the next three years. The boy stayed with his mother during the week, while the father had him to stay for weekends. The father contributed £3,000 per annum maintenance for his son but made no other payment to his wife. Relations were so good at the time that the father spent a period of at least one summer with his wife in her parental home in Oregon.

In 1990 a dispute arose as to the boy's schooling. The father obtained an order for sole custody. In proceedings later that year the parties agreed that they should have joint custody and that the child should reside at each of their homes at times to be agreed. This arrangement worked out in practice much as it had previously, with the child spending the weekdays with his mother and the weekends with his father. An attempted reconciliation by the mother was rejected by the father. This led to deepened embitterment. The wife, through her solicitor, 'laid a very grave charge, relating to [the boy] against her husband'. She subsequently withdrew this unreservedly (and it had no influence on Flood J's assessment of the case) but it further soured the relationship between the parties.

At this time the wife's studies at third level, on which she had embarked some years previously, were not going well. Her income consisted of child support from her husband and her former husband, as well as donations from her own family. Flood J found that she was living in 'conditions of extreme penury'. Aware that her husband was going to object to the boy's spending the forthcoming summer in Oregon, she took him to Oregon without his permission. Her husband for some weeks was not fully aware of his son's whereabouts. He successfully took proceedings in the High Court in May 1991 for sole custody. These required further proceedings in Oregon before he could be reunited with his son.

Flood J recorded that:

> [s]ubsequently in a matter of weeks the mother returned to this country, sought and was given extremely limited rights of access under supervision which were later extended but were in all of a very limited and frustrating character. She faced contempt proceedings . . . in which, however, she purged her contempt.

The father invoked these events in support of his objection to his son's being taken out of the jurisdiction. Flood J conceded that this was not an unreasonable contention but he did 'not think it followed that it would be repeated in the future'. Flood J was of the view that the mother:

> was a girl who in the past had acted more with her heart than with her head. During the period of three years from [the] father's departure from the matrimonial home she was in fact living on very restricted funds, with no contribution for her maintenance from her lawful husband, and in the nine months next preceding her flight in May 1991 in a situation of increasing frustration produced by her financial circumstances, lack of appreciation of what she conceived as her generosity in staying in Dublin with [the child] so that he could be near his father. Added to these facts was the misconception [generating the allegation against the father which she subsequently withdrew]. In this, her plight, she chose to go to America and her family, the only haven from her frustration and source of relief from her penury. I am satisfied the very fact that the process of law succeeded in taking her child from her and bringing it back from America to Ireland — albeit at great expense — has clearly and irrevocably impressed on her mind that she has to obey the orders of this court. I am reinforced in that view in the evidence given by her mother that she would take every step in her power to ensure that the orders of this court were obeyed by her daughter. Accordingly I would not give high precedence to this aspect of the matter in my consideration and deliberation as to what is in [the child]'s best interest in terms of future custody.

Turning to the general question of where the child's welfare lay, Flood J found that the mother could give 'a greater stability of lifestyle' to her son, having regard to his age, than could his father. A child psychiatrist had gone to Oregon to see the mother's 'maternal ambience'. He had stayed there for three days. He found the family to be a very close and mutually caring one with a sense of stability and great concern for the child. He 'felt that [the child] would feel more safe and secure in the USA'. The child psychiatrist had only been in a position to talk to the child's father and not the child's paternal grandmother or aunt. He found that the father's home was well kept, tidy and pleasant and that the father had a deep sense of care for his son.

The child psychiatrist found the mother to be a sympathetic person who was soft and sensitive in her relation to her child. He felt that the boy's fundamental attachments were with his mother, who was unequivocally caring and supportive. He found the father to be a very strong personality, deeply attached to his son by a very intense relationship. The child psychiatrist described it as a very energetic and energised relationship to which the child reciprocated; father and son had a great affection for each other. Nevertheless the child psychiatrist's conclusion was that the child needed continuing parenting by his mother in a situation which permitted of his attachment to his father to be available to him and to be renewed at regular intervals.

Flood J, who had heard evidence from the child's maternal grandmother, was clearly greatly impressed by her deep concern for the welfare of the child. The child's paternal aunt, who also gave evidence, manifested a detestation of the boy's mother which did not impress the Judge, who came to the conclusion that, on balance the child would get greater comfort from his extended maternal family.

Flood J concluded, having regard to the age of the child, that he needed parenting by his mother. The extended family ambience of her Oregon home, coupled with adequate educational facilities and the companionship of children of his own age, supported this conclusion. Accordingly he awarded custody to the mother, giving the father generous access. He directed the child's maternal grandmother to undertake to the court to supervise and secure her daughter's compliance with the terms of the award of custody and to advise the Chief Registrar of the High Court if her daughter and grandson left the United States in breach of the custody order.

A number of features of this decision may be noted. First, it again involves a clear preference for mothers of young children, a matter we have discussed, above, 358-9. Secondly, the central role of the child psychiatrist is worthy of comment. Of course the court should have regard to all expert evidence when determining where the welfare of a child lies, but psychiatric and psychological experts have no necessary expertise outside their own disciplines. The statutory definition of 'welfare' in s. 2 of the Guardianship of Infants Act 1964 clearly embraces factors on which psychiatric and psychological evidence would be of only marginal relevance. In the instant case, it would seem that these other factors were not of any particular significance.

Accepting that psychiatric evidence can be of considerable assistance, what factual data should form the basis of that evidence? Of course, the psychiatrist can examine the relevant parties — the child and the two parents, for example. But beyond this point, matters become controversial. If one of the parents alleges that the other parent engaged in violent or abusive conduct, is the psychiatrist permitted to proceed on the basis that this assertion is true? If he or she is so permitted, then his or her conclusion may be based on factual assumptions which are not necessarily the same as those on which the court has proceeded and, in the case of hearsay or other inadmissible evidence, the psychiatrist's conclusion may be one at which the court could not legitimately arrive in the absence of such evidence.

Alternatively, if the psychiatrist engages in what is, in effect, an inquisitorial process, akin to that of a judge in a civil law jurisdiction, does this not compromise, if not actually usurp, the function of the court? Flood J did not himself savour the ambience of Oregon but relied on the experience of another fact-finder who was willing to express conclusions on the ultimate issue of where the child's welfare lay. Courts have had a traditional reluctance to surrender to expert witnesses the function of determining the ultimate issue. While this general reluctance has undoubtedly weakened internationally in recent years (cf. *Cross on Evidence* (7th ed., by Colin Tapper, 1990), pp.499-500), there is good reason to be cautious about too ready a judicial willingness to let expert witnesses determine, rather than assist in the determination of, what is in the last analysis a justiciable issue. We have seen above, 344, that in *K.W.T. v D.A.T.*, High Court, 18 March 1992, Murphy J was rightly concerned about the need to preserve the judicial function when receiving evidence from psychiatrists, psychologists and social workers.

**Challenge to paternity** In *M.D. v G.D.*, High Court, 30 July 1992, Carroll J, on a consultative case stated from the District Court, had to deal with a situation where a wife, having entered into a separation agreement, by deed, with her husband, reserving her rights under the maintenance legislation, and having participated in proceedings under the Guardianship of Infants Act 1964 in which her husband had been granted access to their daughter, sought a discharge of the access order two days after it had been granted, alleging that the husband was not the father of the child. When she sought to introduce evidence in these later proceedings on the paternity question, the District Judge took the view that the proceedings constituted an abuse of the procedures of the court; that, even if he had jurisdiction to determine the matter, the wife had to show a change of circumstances in the two days; that he had no jurisdiction to make an access order in favour of the husband if it was established that he was not the father of the child; that the issue of paternity, if within the knowledge of the wife, should have been raised by her in the access proceedings; and that the issue was now *res judicata*, the wife being estopped from denying that the husband was the father. The District Judge also considered that the wife might be estopped by the deed of separation from denying the husband's paternity and that he had a discretion to exercise in this regard. He was of the view, finally, that, whilst the welfare of the child was the paramount consideration, it was not the sole consideration and he was entitled to make a determination on the admissibility of evidence as to paternity and thereafter to determine the matter having regard to the paramountcy of the welfare of the child.

Carroll J held that it *could* be regarded as an abuse of procedures to seek a discharge of an access order two days after it had been made. Although s. 12 of the 1964 Act contained no restriction on how quickly such an application might be made, the court should not ignore the system of appeals which applied to such cases. If a decision had been made on the merits and there had been no change in circumstances, then an appeal was normally the appropriate method to deal with the matter; but there might be cases where, even in the absence of such a change of circumstances, an application to vary or discharge might be made. In matters relating to children it was never advisable to lay down stringent practice rules; the matter should remain flexible and subject to the exercise of the District Judge's discretion as to whether an abuse of procedures was involved.

Carroll J considered that, in determining whether he had jurisdiction and, if so, whether the wife must show a change of circumstances subsequent to the granting of access, the District Justice had to take into account 'first of all' the welfare of the child, the circumstances then existing, the lapse of time, the question whether appeal was too late and other relevant matters.

As regards the range of orders permitted by s. 11(1) of the 1964 Act, Carroll J was of opinion that a District Judge was entitled to make an access order to allow a child access *to persons other than the child's natural parents*:

> It is the welfare of the child which is paramount. For example, if there were a child in the custody of its mother who lived with her parents, and the father had limited access, then the mother dies; if the father claims and gets custody, it seems to me that access by the maternal grandparents, if contested, could be granted under s. 11(1) on the basis that it would be for the benefit of the child to maintain links with its grandparents. In this case, it may not be to the benefit of the child to be

> cut off from contact with the only father she has ever known. In those circumstances a court would be justified in making an order for access under s. 11(1). This subsection gives very wide powers and is not cut down by subsection (2). An order to be made under s. 11(2)(a). This section refers to the right of a parent to access to a child. This is a different matter to the right of a child to have access to an adult who is not its parent if this would be for its benefit. Under subsection (1) it is the right of the child with which the Court is concerned, not the right of the adult.

Accordingly, Carroll J considered that it was not correct to say that there was no jurisdiction to make an order in favour of the husband, though she thought that it would be more correct to describe the orders as being in favour of the *child*, granting her access to her mother's husband.

Carroll J's interpretation of s. 11(1) is novel and difficult to harmonise with the actual language of the sub-section, on the basis of a literal interpretation. There are, however, good policy arguments in favour of the approach adopted by Carroll J, so far as they would facilitate the award of access to persons who are not guardians of the child. Moreover, Carroll J's child-centred view of access has wider implications in relation to the constitutional validity of the limitations on unmarried father's rights of guardianship prescribed by the Status of Children Act 1987. An attack on the legislation could include the argument that guardianship is a compendium of the rights of a *child* rather than an adult.

Carroll J did not take the view that the paternity of the husband was an element going to the jurisdiction of the court under s. 11(1). If this rule arose, the other side should be given notice; an adjournment might in some instances be appropriate but the rule should not be foreclosed merely because it had not been raised at the outset.

Carroll J held that the paternity issue was not *res judicata*, whether by reason of the wife's failure to raise it in the first application or by reason of her evidence in that hearing. Neither was the wife estopped from raising the question by virtue of the separation deed or because she had issued maintenance proceedings. The District Judge had not been correct in holding the evidence relating to the blood test inadmissible. Citing the Supreme Court, decision in *J.P.D. v M.G.* [1991] ILRM 217 (analysed in the 1990 Review, 314-6), Carroll J observed that:

> [t]he Court should be concerned in ensuring that truth should prevail. If the husband is not the father of his wife's child, that is a truth which should be established.

O'Hanlon J's decision in *S. v S.* [1983] IR 68, sub nom. *A.S. v R.B., W.S. and Another* [1984] ILRM 66, not cited here, is of central relevance. See O'Connor, (1983) 1 ILT 76 and Binchy, (1983) 17 Ir. Med Times No. 6, p. 26, for analysis of *S. v S.*

Finally Carroll J agreed with the District Judge that, while the welfare of the child was the first and paramount consideration, it was not the only consideration and that the District Judge was entitled to determine the matter accordingly.

**Child sexual abuse investigations** In *D.K. v A.K.* [1993] ILRM 710, which we examine in the Practice and Procedure Chapter, below, 469, Costello J declined to strike out a statement of claim under O.19 of the Rules of the Superior Courts 1986 as being scandalous, frivolous or vexatious or in the exercise of the court's inherent jurisdiction to strike out a claim. The plaintiff, who had custody of his son, was the subject of an allegation of sexual abuse brought against him by his wife. The child was admitted to one hospital and referred to another hospital, where he was attended by a doctor. The plaintiff subsequently took proceedings against (*inter alia*) the governors of the two hospitals and the doctor, claiming damages for libel, negligence and breach of constitutionally protected rights, including his right to a good name.

As to the claim in libel, it was clear that absolute privilege attached to statements made by a witness to a solicitor taking his proof of evidence for the purpose of a trial: *Watson v McEwan* [1905] AC 480. In the instant case, the doctor's report was made the day before the date on the letter of request from the plaintiff's wife's solicitors. Moreover, these solicitors had indicated that the report would be made available to the *plaintiff's* solicitors; Costello J considered that it could be argued that the requirements of the proper administration of justice would not demand privilege to extend so far.

On the negligence issue, counsel for the doctor argued that she had not owed the plaintiff a duty of care. Costello J considered that it could not be said that the trial judge would certainly hold in the defendant's favour on this point; accordingly it would be wrong to strike out the plaintiff's claim before this controversial issue had been determined with the benefit of oral evidence and full legal argument.

We do not wish to anticipate how a court would ultimately dispose of this question. Some recent decisions in England display a pronounced hostility towards the idea that the law of defamation should be supplemented by any other lines of attack, such as conspiracy (*Lonrho plc v Fayed (No. 5)* [1994] 1 All ER 188). Moreover there is a clear reluctance in that jurisdiction to inhibit police enquiries by the imposition of a duty of care in negligence: *Hill v Chief Constable of West Yorkshire* [1989] AC 53, *Alexandrou v Oxford* [1993] 4 All ER 328, *Osman v Ferguson* [1993] 4 All ER 355. Judicial thinking on the defamation point in New Zealand is similar: *Bell-Booth Group Ltd v A.G.* [1989] 3 NZLR 148. A case running in the opposite direction is the House of Lords decision in *Spring v Guardian Assurance plc* (1994) 144 New L J 971. The Law Reform Commission, in its *Report on Child Sexual Abuse* (LRC 32-1990), recommended that legislation impose a duty on (*inter alios*) doctors to report cases of child sexual abuse to the relevant health board. Due care would be essential whether the decision was to report or not to report: lack of due care in making a report would generate civil liability, failure to report through lack of due care would generate criminal liability. See 1990 Review, 246-7.

In relation to the claim based on infringement of the plaintiff's right to a good name, Costello J noted that this plea might give rise to an issue to be decided at the trial relating to the priority to be given between the court's duty to vindicate constitutionally protected rights, on the one hand, and, on the other hand, its duty to ensure the proper administration of justice by the enforcement of rules relating to the confidentiality of communications with lawyers in the preparation of proceedings.

Costello J was disposed to go somewhat more deeply into the jurisprudential dimension of the question. The plaintiff's claim raised an issue as to whether a defamatory utterance that involved both the common law tort of libel and the 'constitutional tort' of infringement of a constitutionally protected right gave rise to *two separate causes of action*. This issue had not yet been authoritatively decided and the claim certainly could not be dismissed as being an abuse of the court's process. Furthermore the court would have to address the question whether the law of privilege in libel actions was modified in any way if the libel involved an infringement of a plaintiff's constitutionally protected right to a good name, as well as the issue whether the law relating to the limitation of damages recoverable in a negligence action was modified in any way when the negligent act amounted to an infringement of the right to a good name. For consideration of some of these issues, see Binchy, 'Constitutional Remedies and the Law of Torts', in J. O'Reilly, ed., *Human Rights and Constitutional Law* (1992), 201. It is an unfortunate fact that, in the wake of the important decision of the Supreme Court in *Conway v Irish National Teachers Organisation* [1991] ILRM 497; [1991] 2 IR 305, no clear answer is forthcoming to the latter question. See the 1991 Review, 448-53.

Finally, Costello J declined to strike out the plaintiff's claim against the doctor based on a contractual nexus. The plaintiff had argued that the plaintiff's wife had entered the contract with the doctor for the care, treatment and diagnosis of her son on behalf of both herself and her husband. Without expressing any concluded view upon it, he did not consider this argument so devoid of merit as to warrant dismissal *in limine*.

Declining to discuss the proceedings against the second hospital, because it was arguably vicariously liable for any wrongful act the doctor might have committed, or against the first hospital, because it could be vicariously liable for any negligent acts of its staff, Costello J observed:

> If it is not claimed that [the doctor] was the servant or agent of [the first hospital] then no claim for damages for libel and no claim for damages for infringement of constitutionally protected rights would be against [it].

**The unmarried father's guardianship rights** Later in the chapter, below, 369-71, we discuss O'Hanlon J's decision in *In re J.W. ; G.W. v D.G., P.L. and B.L. and An Bord Uchtála and the Catholic Protection and Rescue Society*, High Court, 1 May 1992, dealing with the important question of the entitlement of unmarried fathers to be appointed guardians of their children where their mothers propose to have them adopted.

## ADOPTION

**Compulsory adoption in the international context** In *In re A.N.M. (an Infant); Eastern Health Board and T.M. and A.M. v An Bord Uchtála* [1992] ILRM 568, Carroll J addressed the question whether the Adoption Acts 1952 to 1988 applied to a child of alien parents. A married couple, resident and domiciled in Ireland, had applied to the Delhi Council for Child Welfare in 1979 to adopt a child. They were appointed joint guardians of a baby girl in 1980 by the Delhi court. They brought the child to Ireland, with the consent of the Department of Justice. The Minister for Justice issued a certificate of naturalisation to the child in 1985 on the application of the husband as parent rather than guardian of the child. She received an Irish passport.

The couple applied to adopt the child. An Bord Uchtála, satisfied as to their appropriateness as proposed adoptive parents, made a declaration under s. 2 of the Adoption Act 1988 that, if the Court made an order under s. 3 of that Act, it would (subject to s. 2(2)) make the adoption order sought by the couple. The Delhi Council for Child Welfare did not wish to participate in the proceedings.

Carroll J reviewed the history of adoption legislation in the State, and in particular the Adoption Act 1988, upheld as constitutional in *In the Matter of the Adoption (No. 2) Bill 1987* [1989] ILRM 266; [1989] IR 656: see the 1988 Review, 246-52. She concluded that the 1988 Act did not apply to the case of a foundling born abroad, regardless of whether Irish citizenship had been conferred on the child.

Carroll J's reasoning is worthy of close analysis. She quoted a passage from Finlay CJ's judgment (for the Court) in the Article 26 Reference, in which the Bill was interpreted as reflecting the terms of Article 42.5 of the Constitution, relating to the failure of parental duty towards children. She stated:

> It is clear from the judgment that the Supreme Court's consideration was directed towards the adoption of a child whose parent(s), apart from any natural rights, had rights and duties under the Constitution. It is obvious that the Supreme Court did not consider the constitutionality of the Act in the context of the failure of parents outside the jurisdiction to carry out their duties. Parental duties may vary from civilisation to civilisation and what are perceived as parental duties in one society may be very different from what are considered parental duties in another. Alien parents not within the jurisdiction could not have constitutional duties under the Irish Constitution. There is no common good involved in the State supplying the place of alien parents.
>
> Therefore even though alien children were not expressly excluded from the Act, it is obvious that the Oireachtas did not intend to legislate to take away the rights of alien parents.
>
> The requirement in s. 4(4) that all appropriate measures should be taken to ascertain the identity or whereabouts of the parents concerned makes no sense when a child had been born out of the jurisdiction.
>
> The fact that the child is now an Irish citizen is irrelevant in considering the application of the Act. Regardless of her present status, her parents were alien parents and the State did not intend to abrogate the rights of those parents.

Carroll J considered that the description of the husband in the certificate of naturalisation as parent of the child was 'clearly incorrect, thus rendering the certificate liable to be revoked'.

The whole subject of inter-country adoption raises important issues relating to human rights and dignity, to cultural norms at a global level, and to justice as between rich and poor people and between rich and poor societies. The recent Hague Convention on the matter, in the formulation of which Professor William Duncan played a leading role, addresses these themes sensitively.

Carroll J's judgment gives an indication of an appreciation of the complexity of the issue. It may be contrasted with the Supreme Court's analysis in its decision on 8 March 1993, reversing Carroll J. We will examine the Supreme Court's decision in the 1993 Review. Suffice it here to say that its formalistic disposition of the matter as involving no more than a question of statutory interpretation failed to do justice to the significant constitutional issues that arose. Carroll J was clearly correct in discerning that the Adoption Act 1988 had not envisaged an extra-territorial application. It is quite another matter, however, to assert that Article 41 affords constitutional protection only to those who are nationals, domiciliaries or residents of Ireland. The troublesome task for the courts is to address the international dimension of the constitutional protection of fundamental rights with a seriousness of purpose that befits the jurisprudential complexity of the subject rather than to pretend that the matter can be dealt with by parsing the language of sub-sections of the legislation. For consideration of how the courts might approach the task, see Binchy, 'Constitutional Remedies and the Law of Torts', in J O'Reilly ed., *Human Rights and Constitutional Law* (1992), 201.

**The position of unmarried fathers** In the 1989 Review, 248-57 and the 1990 Review, 316-22, we analysed the important decisions of *K. v W. (No. 1)* [1990] 1 LRM 121 and *K. v W. (No. 2)* [1990] ILRM 791 on the subject of the application by an unmarried father to be appointed guardian of his child under s. 6A of the Guardianship of Infants Act 1964 (inserted by s. 12 of the Statutes of Children Act 1987) where the child would be adopted with the mother's consent if the father was not appointed guardian. The Supreme Court judgment in *K. v W. (No. 1)* appears to involve a subtle shift away from the approach favoured in *The State (Nicolaou) v An Bord Uchtála* [1966] IR 567: see our observation in the 1989 Review, 252-5.

In *In re J.W.; G.W. v D.G., P.L. and B.L. and An Bord Uchtála and the Catholic Protection and Rescue Society*, High Court, 1 May 1992, O'Hanlon J was called on to apply the revised principles in a case which, on its facts, bore many resemblances to the *K. v W.* litigation, save that the father's claim to be guardian appears to have been somewhat less strong than in *K. v W.*

The plaintiff was aged twenty-one, living with his parents, a younger sister and a brother in a three-bedroomed house (one of the bedrooms being described in evidence as a 'box-room'). He had left school at sixteen with the group certificate and had worked in several different jobs; at the time of the hearing of his application he was employed by a window installation firm earning £160 per week. As to his personal profile, O'Hanlon J observed that '[h]e smokes, takes a drink at the week-end, plays football and badminton and generally leads the type of social life enjoyed by young men of his age group'. He had one conviction, for stealing a van, for which he had been given the benefit of probation.

The mother, aged around nineteen, had been to secondary school, performed very creditably in her Leaving Certificate examination and completed a business studies course. She was working as a receptionist with a commercial firm.

The parties had met in 1989. They formed a relationship and had sexual intercourse from time to time, but apparently infrequently. The mother went to work in Italy in the summer of 1990; while there she learned that she was pregnant. On her return to Ireland, the parties discussed the possibility of an abortion but the mother was advised on medical grounds that it was far too late to contemplate this course.

The mother wanted to have her child adopted but this was opposed by the father. The parties became engaged in December 1990 but the mother broke it off within three days. It appeared from the evidence that the father was willing and perhaps eager at all times to resume his relationship with the mother probably with a view to marriage, but that this held no attraction for the mother. The father accepted, in evidence, that it was no longer likely that the relationship would be restored.

The baby, a girl, was born in February 1991. She was placed for adoption three months later with adoptive parents who already had an adopted child.

There was no real contest between the father and the adoptive parents as to where the welfare of the child would best be served. The father, who said that he went to Mass 'now and again', expressed the hope that any future wife of his would accept his daughter. In the meantime, if he were granted custody of the child, his sister would share one of the bedrooms with the baby and he and his brother would move into the box-room. His mother would be very happy to look after the child (as she confirmed in evidence), since he would normally be out at work all day.

A child psychiatrist gave evidence that the father displayed a sound and normal personality with 'appropriate' feelings and thinking on the subject of parenting. This witness acknowledged that separating the child from her adoptive parents would cause her trauma. This anxiety about trauma was confirmed by a psychologist, called on behalf of the mother and the adoptive parents.

The adoptive parents lived in a four-bedroomed house. The adoptive mother was on leave of absence from her work, which would continue for about two years. They had a very warm relationship with the infant. They were, moreover, practising Catholics.

O'Hanlon J had no doubt that the welfare of the child demanded that she be left in the care and custody of her adoptive parents. Apart from the ties of blood between the girl and her father, it appeared to O'Hanlon J that on every other score the scales were weighted very heavily in favour of the adoptive parents. The home circumstances of the father would be far from ideal. The accommodation was not adequate and virtually all the responsibility for rearing the baby would fall on her grandparents. The psychologist's evidence indicated that this was 'a burden that should not normally be placed on them and quite often proves too much for them'. The adoptive parents provided a loving and caring and stable environment, where all the baby's maternal needs were provided for, with her physical, emotional and psychological welfare entrusted to a couple who had 'received the highest testimonials from those who ha[d] seen the new family and the new home'. To break that bond would be seriously damaging and there were no circumstances which would justify taking such a course.

## THE FAMILY HOME

**Judicial transfer of the family home to wife** In *M.C. v A.C.*, High Court, 31 July 1992, in an application by a wife under s. 5 of the Family Home Protection Act 1976 and under s. 15 of the Judicial Separation and Family Law Reform Act 1989, Lavan J made a transfer order of the family home to the wife. He applied the principles articulated by Costello J in *E.D. v F.D.*, High Court, 23 October 1980, extracted in Binchy's *Casebook on Irish Family Law* (1984), pp. 201, 345, and by Barron J in *O'N. v O'N.*, High Court, 6 October 1989, which we analyse in the 1989 Review 244-7.

In the instant case the husband had not paid the mortgage and had increased his bank loans, using the family home as security. Lavan J considered that he could only reasonably conclude that, in so conducting himself, the husband had engaged in 'a conscious and deliberate act intended to deprive his wife and children of their home'. The husband was, in Lavan J's opinion, acting imprudently and incurring substantial debts to avoid his responsiblilities to his wife and children and with the express intention of forcing a sale of the family home to his benefit.

The parties had been separated by judicial decree eighteen months previously on the ground of the husband's adultery. The wife had been granted custody of their three children. The judgment is not explicit as to whether the wife's claim was under s. 5(1) or (2); the circumstances mentioned in the judgment make it plain that subs. (1) must have been in question.

Lavan J invoked the protections accorded the wife under *both* the 1976 and the 1989 Acts but made the transfer order in respect of the family home exclusively pursuant to s. 5 of the 1976 Act. It is interesting to note that he must have regarded the policy underlying s. 15 of the 1989 Act as pointing in the same direction as s. 5 of the 1976 Act.

**Undue influence** In *Allied Irish Banks plc v English*, Circuit Court (South Eastern Circuit, 1992) 11 ILT 208, Judge Sheridan addressed the question of the appropriate course of conduct in securing a non-owner-spouse's consent to an equitable mortgage by deposit of title deeds. The case concerned a guarantee for his son's overdraft of £3,000 made by the defendant who provided as security the land certificate of his property. The defendant's wife had signed a consent to the deposit by her husband of the title deeds. In evidence the defendant's wife stated that she had participated in the process because otherwise she would have had a row with her husband; that she knew nothing about her son's loan; and that she had no recollection of being informed of the nature and extent of the document she had signed.

Judge Sheridan dismissed that the bank's action, on foot of the guarantee, for a declaration that the equitable mortgage stood well charged on the lands. Invoking an earlier decision of his own, *AIB Ltd v Ryan*, Circuit Court, 4 February 1986, he came to the conclusion that the letter of guarantee must necessarily be suspect. He was:

> not satisfied that . . . the guarantee and deposit of title deeds were given under circumstances whereby the bank required this elderly man and indeed his wife to seek independent advice. In any event as far as the equitable mortgage is concerned, there was no consent by Mrs Buckley prior to the mortgage of the family home. I feel that in all the circumstances where in particular elderly people are induced to pledge their only assets without getting anything in return, it should be clearly brought to their attention by a suitable letter or memorandum as to precisely what the transaction involves and they should be told to seek legal advice subject to the fact that the matter can proceed if they refuse to take such legal advice.

Judge Sheridan's approach, sensitive to human realities, anticipates that favoured by Geoghegan J in *Bank of Ireland v Smyth* [1993] 2 IR 102, which we shall be analysing in the 1993 Review. Judge Sheridan's requirements for informed consent concentrate on the vulnerability of the parties resulting from their age. This focus is not apparent in Geoghegan J's judgment.

More recent English developments worthy of note in this context are the House of Lords decision in *Barclays Bank v O'Brien* [1994] 1 FLR 1; [1993] 4 All ER 417 and the Court of Appeal decision in *CIBC Mortgages plc v Pitt* [1994] 1 FLR 17; [1993] 4 All ER 433. See Doyle, 'Borrowing Under the Influence', 15 Business L Rev 6 (1994).

## SPOUSAL MAINTENANCE

In *K. v K.*, Supreme Court, 13 February 1992, the Court gave some important guidance as to the circumstances in which a spouse who is in desertion may be awarded maintenance. In earlier proceedings the Supreme Court had affirmed MacKenzie J's grant of a judicial separation to the husband on the basis of cruelty by the wife which had justified his leaving the family home.

The wife was found to be suffering from a condition of morbid jealousy, a mental disease which gave her illusions of misconduct on the part of her husband. The wife had been awarded £225 per week maintenance in respect of the parties' three children, who continued to live with her; no maintenance had been awarded to her on her own behalf. In subsequent proceedings brought before Costello J in 1991, the wife sought in order for maintenance on her own behalf, as well as an upward variation of the maintenance awarded in respect of the children. Costello J in an *ex tempore* judgment rejected these claims. The Supreme Court upheld Costello J's rejection of the first claim but made an order increasing the amount of maintenance for the children.

Counsel for the wife argued that she was entitled to be awarded a maintenance order, first, because constructive desertion did not apply to the provisions of s. 5 of the Family Law (Maintenance of Spouses and Children) Act 1976, as amended by s. 20(5) of the Judicial Separation and Family Law Reform Act 1989. The Supreme Court had absolutely no hesitation in rejecting this contention. Finlay C J (Hederman and McCarthy JJ concurring) considered that the virtually identical definitions of 'desertion' contained in s. 3(1) of the 1976 Act and s. 2 of the 1989 Act were 'plain' and 'unambiguous' and clearly envisaged a situation such as had arisen in the instant case. These definitions provide that 'desertion' includes 'conduct on the part of one spouse that results in the other spouse with just for cause leaving' and living apart from the spouse who remains. S. 3(1) includes the words 'separately and' between 'living' and 'apart'. This difference appears to have no special significance: Duncan & Scully, op. cit., para. 7.047. There is little doubt that the Chief Justice's rejection of the wife's argument or this issue was entirely justified.

The more significant argument on behalf of the wife related to s. 38(2) of the 1989 Act, which amended s. 5 of the 1976 Act in an important respect. S. 5(2) had originally provided that a spouse guilty of desertion (actual or constructive) should not be entitled to be awarded maintenance for his or her own benefit. S. 38(2) transformed this absolute prohibition into one that applies in all cases save where, 'having regard to all the circumstances, including the conduct of the other spouse, the court is of opinion that it would be repugnant to justice not to make a maintenance order'.

What kind of case would warrant an award of maintenance to a deserting spouse? Finlay CJ considered that s. 38(2) placed 'a heavy onus' of an applicant spouse seeking to avoid what was otherwise an absolute ban on maintenance. He rejected the wife's argument that, on account of the finding that she suffered from the mental disease of a morbid jealousy, she should be equated with a person of unsound mind unable to administer or look after her own affairs and therefore deserving of special protection from the courts. The Chief Justice considered it:

> clear . . . that the [wife]'s capacity to look after her own affairs and to deal with any business matters she had to deal with, is quite unimpaired by the particular condition of morbid jealously from which she suffers, and that, whilst that may have been the cause of her cruelty to her husband, which forced him out of the matrimonial home, it is clear from the history of this matter that it has not impaired her capacity to assert and, where possible, to achieve her rights, nor the vigour with which she has prosecuted them.

Finlay CJ considered that Costello J had had a sound basis on which to hold against the wife's application for maintenance. The evidence on which her case substantially depended was that on which MacKenzie J had adjudicated in 1989. There was no obligation for Costello J in his *ex tempore* judgment to have set out the precise findings of primary fact on which he reached his conclusion.

On the question of an increase in the maintenance order on behalf of the children, Finlay CJ made it clear that the High Court, in an application for variation of a maintenance order, 'cannot and must not' commence *de novo* to reach a new view on the general question of maintenance, but should merely try to ascertain whether the situation has changed since the making of the maintenance order so as to warrant an increase or decrease in the amount of maintenance.

When MacKenzie J was determining the maintenance order on behalf of the children, he took into account the fact that the husband was paying nearly £2,000 per annum for the eldest child who was at a boarding school. The wife, when seeking a variation order, pointed to the fact that this child was no longer a boarder and was now attending a non-fee-paying school. Finlay CJ rejected this argument. He was:

> satisfied that the mere fact that . . . the husband had by a change of the schooling arrangements been saved an obligation to pay school fees in regard to the eldest child who had been at a boarding school, cannot of itself constitute a ground for increasing the maintenance payable for the children. The mere fact that for a different form of maintenance a higher figure was previously being paid by the husband does not in any way automatically entitle the wife to be paid a greater sum in respect of maintenance based on a different form of education as far as the children are concerned.

This conclusion gives pause for thought. The fact that the husband had an extra £2,000 as part of his assets was surely a factor to which regard should properly be given when assessing his maintenance responsibilities to his children. The sum of £225 per week had been fixed on the basis that the husband was committed to the payment of £2,000. To seek to compartmentalise the several aspects of parental maintenance of children and to hold that the appropriate amount payable in relation to one aspect (food or clothing, for example) should be determined without regard to what is being paid in relation to another (education) would ignore the integrated unity of a parent's obligation to support his or her children. This is not to suggest that the children would have an *inevitable* entitlement to share in the £2,000; the court could well come to the conclusion that £225 per week represented the proper level of maintenance taking all the circumstances into account.

The Chief Justice went on to vary the order upward to £265 per week on the basis of taking judicial notice of the fact that there had been 'an inflationary move in the reduction of the value of money, though not a very large one, since 1989', and on the basis that the Court should raise an inference from the evidence accepted by Costello J that there was 'as a matter of probability, from common experience, some additional expense as the children have grown older'. He also made some small allowance for costs in respect of transporting the children to school and for costs in purchasing books for them.

This resort to judicial notice is of interest. The phenomenon of virtually unending inflation has been a feature of the past couple of decades and there would seem nothing wrong with courts' dispensing with the requirement of proof of that general picture. It is another thing, however, for a court, without evidence on the matter, to come to a judgment as to the extent of that inflation when assessing a parent's changing maintenance obligations over a period of a year. The changing value of money in the recent past is surely a matter on which evidence would be appropriate. This is an everyday feature of tort litigation, and family litigation is also familiar with evidence of this type: see Duncan & Scully, op. cit., paras. 9.087ff.

An important issue arises in relation to the Court's disposition of the matter of constructive desertion. It may be questioned whether it is desirable to restrict, as narrowly as the Court did, the operation of the proviso to the otherwise absolute rule that a deserting spouse is not entitled to maintenance. The problem centres on how mental disease or other incapacity operates in the context of matrimonial relief. A spouse who seeks matrimonial relief has been considered entitled to obtain that relief in cases where the respondent spouse has behaved in an objectively cruel way, such as would justify the applicant spouse in leaving the home. The fact that the respondent spouse is free of subjective responsibility on account of his or her lack of mental capacity is considered not to be a reason for denying the applicant spouse relief. Thus, a wife who is the victim of violence at the hands of a mentally ill husband is entitled to leave him (or to have him barred from the home) and to obtain a decree of judicial separation and an order for maintenance. It is another thing, however, that a spouse against whom a decree for judicial separation has been made should be deprived of his or her entitlement to maintenance. The entitlement to live apart from one's spouse is a separate question from the obligation to maintain one's spouse.

Finlay CJ proceeds on the basis that, in determining what constitutes constructive desertion, the court should disregard mental disability on the part of the spouse alleged to be guilty of constructive desertion, unless that disability constitutes a disease of the mind or, if it does not, unless it has the effect of rendering that spouse incapable of looking after his or her affairs and of dealing with business matters. This seems to be an ungenerous test. There are many people in our community whose lives are affected by mental disability but who are nonetheless capable of conducting their business affairs. The idea that simply because they retain that capacity they should automatically be denied maintenance seems a harsh, and demonstrably unacceptable, test. Take the case of a couple married for forty years. The wife develops a mental condition of morbid jealousy relative to her husband which drives him from the home. Is she to be deprived of any entitlement to maintenance simply because she is able to manage her business affairs? Many wives are not in a good position to maintain themselves adequately. They may have sacrificed career advancement in the interests of the husband or children. The fact that they retain the mental capacity to conduct their business affairs will be of no consolation to them in such circumstances.

# Fisheries

## ANGLING LICENCES

The Fisheries (Amendment) Act 1991 (Fisheries Co-Operative Societies) Order 1992 (SI No.126) provided for the establishment of the fishery co-operative societies envisaged in the 1991 Act, as to which see the 1991 Review, 253. The Fisheries (Amendment) Act 1991 (Fisheries Co-Operative Societies) Rules 1992 (SI No.127) lay down the detailed rules for the co-operative societies.

## AQUACULTURE LICENCES

S. 54 of the Fisheries Act 1980 authorises the Minister for the Marine to designate by Order an area for which licences to engage in aquaculture can be granted. S. 54 of the 1980 Act is hedged around with a number of procedural requirements before such an Order can be made. For discussion of this area, see *Courtney v Minister for the Marine* [1989] ILRM 605 (1988 Review, 256).

But s. 54 of the 1980 Act is merely one of many statutory provisions concerning licensing of fishery activities, and the connection between these various provisions arose for discussion in the judgment of Johnson J in *Madden and Ors v Minister for the Marine* [1993] ILRM 436; [1993] 1 IR 567.

In this case, the applicants had read a notice in their local newspaper indicating that a company, Vestobrook Ltd (the notice party in the instant case), intended to apply to the Minister for the Marine under s. 19 of the Foreshore Act 1933 for permission under s. 3 of the 1933 Act to moor cages on an area of the foreshore at Ballyvaughan Bay, Clare, for the cultivation of trout. As required by s. 19 of the 1933 Act, the notice also stated that objections to the grant of permission should be made to the Department of the Marine. The applicants lodged objections with the Department, and these were acknowledged by letter of 1 February 1989. The first applicant then requested, by letter of 7 May 1989, a copy of the environmental impact assessment carried out in respect of the area concerned. This was furnished by the Department by letter dated 18 May 1989. In response to a further request from the applicants' solicitor, the Department by letter of 20 June

1989 sent him a copy of a licence issued on 1 June 1989 by the Minister to Vestobrook Ltd pursuant to s. 3 of the 1933 Act and s. 15 of the Fisheries (Consolidation) Act 1959 (the latter relating to fish culture licences) which in turn had replaced a licence issued to the company under s. 3 the 1933 Act by the Minister on 28 April 1989.

The applicants argued that the Minister had acted *ultra vires* in attempting to use the 1933 and 1959 Acts to grant what amounted to aquaculture licences and thus circumvent the more stringent terms of the 1980 Act concerning objections. Johnson J agreed with the applicants.

Johnson J was critical of the attitude of the Department of the Marine to the applicants between February and June 1989. He noted that, in the letter of 18 May 1989 enclosing the environmental impact assessment, there was no reference to the fact that a licence had already been granted to Vestobrook Ltd in April 1989. Johnson J commented that 'it appears that the respondent [Minister] deliberately concealed this fact from the applicant'. Having noted that no notice of an application under s. 15 of the 1959 Act is required by an applicant but that stringent procedural requirements are laid out in s. 54 of the 1980 Act, Johnson J commented that '[t]here is no doubt that from the outset in this matter the respondent [Minister] acted in such a way as to avoid the jurisdiction of the courts and to avoid all public inquiries'. While this comment could not be taken literally, since judicial review was always available to the applicants, Johnson J was clearly indicating here that he considered that the Minister appeared to be attempting to avoid the right of appeal by way of rehearing to the High Court which is available under s. 54 of the 1980 Act. It is notable that the use of that right of appeal had led to the overturning of an Aquaculture Designation Order in 1988 in the *Courtney* case, referred to above.

Johnson J accepted the argument by the Minister that the reference in s. 15 of the 1959 Act to a fish culture licence was wide enough to encompass fish farming as envisaged by Vestobrook Ltd in the instant case. However, he also considered that s. 54 of the 1980 Act, by providing in express terms for the designation of areas for aquaculture purposes and by including various procedural protections, had been passed with the express purpose of taking account of the development of fish farming on a scale not envisaged at the time the 1959 Act had been passed. He thus rejected the argument made by the Minister that the 1980 Act gave him, in effect, a free choice as to whether to use the 1980 Act or the 1959 Act as a mechanism for granting licences of the kind given in the instant case. In this context, he referred with approval to the oft-quoted dicta of Walsh J delivering the judgment of the Supreme Court in *East Donegal Co-Op Ltd v Attorney General* [1970] IR 317 that the Minister was required to consider each case on its merits. In the instant case, Johnson J held that the Minister was required not merely to consider the interests of Vestobrook Ltd but also the interests of objectors such as the applicants. In this light, he concluded that the Minister had acted *ultra vires*, especially as he had decided not to hold any public inquiry, as he was empowered to do, under the 1933 Act.

He commented that the 1959 Act could be used where private fishery rights only were involved, but that where public rights were involved, as in the instant case, the 1959 Act was inappropriate. He thus quashed the Minister's decision on the ground that he had incorrectly exercised his discretion to proceed under the 1959 Act and also on the ground that he had failed to provide the applicants with the reasoning on which he had based his decision, at a time in May 1989 when he had already granted a licence but had, in effect, represented to the applicants that no licence had been granted.

## FISHERY HARBOUR CENTRE

The Fishery Harbour Centres (Amendment) Act 1992 amended the Fishery Harbour Centres Act 1968 in order to include Berehaven Sound within Castletownbere Harbour, Cork. This was done to facilitate the collection, by the Harbourmaster of Castletownbere Fishery Centre, of harbour dues from foreign ships anchored in Berehaven Sound, which previously had been included in Bantry Bay. The Fishery Harbour Centre (Castletownbere) (Amendment) Order 1992 (SI No. 243) amended the 1970 Order of the same title by including Berehaven Sound within the definition of Castletownbere Fishery Centre.

## REGIONAL FISHERIES BOARDS

The Election to Regional Fisheries Boards (Amendment) Regulations 1992 (SI No. 352) amend the 1981 Regulations concerning the elections to be held to the boards. The Fisheries Regions (Amendment) Order 1992 (SI No. 353) amends the 1980 Order of the same title and the boundaries of the regions in question.

# Gaming and Lotteries

## BOOKMAKERS

In *Director of Public Prosecutions v Boyle* [1993] ILRM 128, Murphy J held that failure by a bookmaker to pay excise duty on a bet as required by s. 24 of the Finance Act 1926 (as amended by s. 69 of the Finance Act 1982) was a criminal offence, not a civil matter: see the discussion in the Revenue chapter, 521-2, below.

## GAMING MACHINE

In *Director of Public Prosecutions v Cafolla*, Supreme Court, 9 March 1992, the Supreme Court (Finlay CJ, McCarthy and Egan JJ), in an *ex tempore* judgment, held that a machine in an amusement arcade which is in perpetual motion and not as such activated by the insertion of a coin is a slot machine under s. 4(1)(a) of the Gaming and Lotteries Act 1956, as amended by s. 1(a) of the Gaming and Lotteries Act 1979. The Court therefore held that the operation of such a machine constituted unlawful gaming within s. 4 of the 1956 Act. The Irish Times Law Report of the Court's decision is helpfully reproduced in (1992) 2 Irish Criminal Law Journal 203.

## LOTTERY

In *Flynn v Denieffe, Independent Newspapers plc and Eason & Son Ltd* [1993] ILRM 417; [1993] 2 IR 28, the Supreme Court provided some definitive guidance on what constitutes a lottery under the Gaming and Lotteries Act 1956. The case arose against the following background.

The second defendant, Independent Newspapers plc, was the proprietor of a number of newspapers distributed in the State. In 1989, game cards bearing the name 'Scoop' were distributed to all households in the State, accompanied with publicity material announcing that this was 'the world's first newspaper board game', that 'Scoop' amounted to a series of games and that the chances of winning prizes in the game were increased if persons played the game in all three newspaper titles under the control of Independent Newspapers. In order to win a prize, participants were required to move a number of places on the game board indicated by the board itself, then answer a general knowledge question and return the card to Independent Newspapers together with a claim form contained in one of the relevant newspapers. The three defendants were prosecuted for variously promoting, distributing and selling material relating to a lottery, contrary to s. 21 of the 1956 Act.

On a case stated to the High Court, Murphy J held ([1989] IR 722) that 'Scoop' did not constitute a game of skill and was a lottery within the meaning of s. 2 of the 1956 Act. On appeal to the Supreme Court, the defendants did not assert that the game was one of skill, but asserted that it was not a lottery since it was not a requirement that participants purchase a newspaper in order to compete in the game. The Supreme Court (O'Flaherty, Egan and Blayney JJ) were in agreement on the principles applicable to the case, but differed on their application to 'Scoop'.

As to the relevant principles, the judges referred with approval to the leading English cases, the Court of Appeal decision in *Reader's Digest Association v Williams* [1976] 3 All ER 737 and that of the House of Lords in *Imperial Tobacco Co. Ltd v Attorney General* [1981] AC 718. From these, the Court held that the essential attributes of a lottery were: (a) the distribution of prizes; (b) that this was to be done by means of chance; and (c) that there must be some actual contribution made by the participants, or at least by a substantial number of the participants.

As to how these applied in the instant case, Egan and Blayney JJ (O'Flaherty J dissenting) concluded that it was not sufficient for the defendants to argue that, for some participants, the game did not constitute a lottery. The majority held that although not every participant was required to purchase a newspaper in order to take part in the game, it was sufficient that a substantial number did actually purchase a newspaper in order for the game to be classed as a lottery for the purposes of s. 2 of the 1956 Act. This approach by the majority is comparable with the 'form and substance' view in revenue cases; their approach may very well reflect the marketing reality of what the second defendant had intended to achieve with the publicity surrounding 'Scoop'. The result, of course, is that such games are unlikely to feature in Irish newspapers without a change in the relevant provisions of the Gaming and Lotteries Act 1956.

# Garda Síochána

## ADMISSIONS AND APPOINTMENTS

In *Beirne v Commissioner of An Garda Síochána* [1992] ILRM 699 (HC); [1993] ILRM 1 (SC), the Supreme Court addressed for the first time the precise nature of the termination of a trainee garda's training assignment.

The applicant sought judicial review of the termination by the respondent Commissioner of his traineeship in the Garda College. The termination arose out of a series of incidents on a football outing from the Garda College. An investigation of the incidents was made, and other students alleged in statements that the applicant had assaulted one student, threatened to assault another and had to be restrained. None of these statements were made available to the applicant, but he accepted during the investigation that he had consumed about seven pints of Guinness and that arising from this there had been some incidents with other students and a misunderstanding, but that a full investigation would indicate that these had been exaggerated out of all proportion. The applicant was informed that a report would be made to the Commissioner but was not told that a recommendation was made that his traineeship be terminated. In the High Court, Flood J granted the relief sought ([1992] ILRM 699) and this decision was upheld on appeal by a majority in the Supreme Court (Finlay CJ and Egan J; O'Flaherty J dissenting).

The crucial issue was whether the power to terminate the traineeship was essentially contractual or statutory in nature. The majority held that the Commissioner's power derived from the Garda Síochána (Admissions and Appointments) Regulations 1988, which were made under s. 14 of the Police Forces Amalgamation Act 1925. While the majority accepted that the 1988 Regulations empowered the Commissioner to lay down conditions of contract for trainees, including the power to terminate for misconduct, they concluded that this power could not be separated from the statutory basis on which it rested.

The statutory power to terminate being discretionary, the majority held that judicial review lay to quash it on the usual grounds. In the circumstances, the termination of the applicant's traineeship had not been in accordance with fair procedures, as he was not given an opportunity to deal with the statements from the other students nor was he aware that he was liable to have his traineeship terminated arising from the investigation of the incidents.

In his dissenting judgment, O'Flaherty J was of the view that judicial review did not lie because the termination arose from a breach of the contract terms between the respondent and the applicant, and that no question of discretion arose.

## DISCIPLINE

**Effect of acquittal** Two cases decided in 1992, *McCarthy v Commissioner of An Garda Síochána* [1993] 1 IR 489 and *McGrath v Commissioner of An Garda Síochána (No. 2)* [1993] ILRM 38, indicated somewhat different approaches by High Court judges to the effect of an acquittal in criminal proceedings on the subsequent holding of a disciplinary inquiry by the Garda authorities.

In *McCarthy v Commissioner of An Garda Síochána* [1993] 1 IR 489, the applicant successfully applied to have his dismissal from the force quashed. The background was as follows. The applicant garda had been charged with a number of offences under the Larceny Act 1916 alleging embezzlement and fraudulent conversion of public monies. Having pleaded not guilty to these charges, the applicant was acquitted after a jury trial. Subsequently, however, the Garda authorities conducted an inquiry pursuant to the Garda Síochána (Discipline) Regulations 1971 alleging various breaches of discipline by the applicant. It was accepted that many of these matters overlapped with those in respect of which the applicant had been acquitted in his jury trial. In the inquiry under the 1971 Regulations, the applicant was found to be in breach of discipline on a number of counts and, on foot of these findings, the Garda Commissioner subsequently purported to dismiss him from the Force under the 1971 Regulations.

Flood J quashed the applicant's dismissal. This was not altogether surprising given the similarity between the circumstances in the instant case and those in *McGrath v Commissioner of An Garda Síochána* [1990] ILRM 5 (HC); [1989] IR 241 (HC); [1990] ILRM 817 (SC); [1991] 1 IR 69 (SC) (see the 1989 Review, 275-6 and the 1990 Review, 330-1), on which Flood J expressly relied. In effect, the *McGrath* case is authority for the proposition that the holding of a disciplinary inquiry under the 1971 Regulations into matters in respect of which a person had been acquitted could be regarded as improper. In the *McCarthy* case, Flood J appeared to elevate this conclusion to an almost absolute principle of law, by focusing on the not guilty verdict of the jury in the applicant's criminal trial. Flood J stated:

> Fundamental to our criminal procedure, and indeed to the liberty of the individual, is the presumption of innocence. The finding by a jury of a verdict of not guilty in respect of criminal charges is more than a verdict of not guilty. It is a certificate of the person's uninterrupted innocence.

And in connection with the particular verdict in the appicant's trial, he continued:

> The verdict of that jury was unappealable on fact. No court and no power in the land could challenge it. It was the applicant's shield against any allegation of dishonesty on his part in relation to the matters which had been the subject matter of consideration and adjudication by his twelve peers. . . .

This passage would appear to preclude any disciplinary proceedings following an acquittal in a criminal trial, although the *McGrath* case left open such a possibility, albeit in limited circumstances: see the 1990 Review, 331 and the subsequent proceedings arising in the case, discussed below. To that extent, this passage from Flood J's judgment might not have the wide-ranging effect which a first reading would indicate. This is further supported by reference to the one significant respect in which the *McCarthy* case differed from the *McGrath* case.

In *McCarthy*, the preliminary examination for the applicant's criminal trial had been conducted by District Justice Seamus Mahon. It will be recalled that, in *Shelly v Mahon* [1990] 1 IR 36 (see the 1989 Review, 94-5) and *Glavin v Governor of Training Unit Mountjoy Prison* [1991] ILRM 478; [1991] 2 IR 421 (see the 1990 Review, 155-7), the Supreme Court held that certain decisions of District Justice Mahon were null and void by reason of an error in calculating his correct age, thus leading the District Court judge to continue in office beyond his retirement age. In both the *Shelly* and *Glavin* cases, the decisions in question related to preliminary examinations conducted by District Justice Mahon which had been followed by criminal trials in which the applicants had been convicted of criminal offences. In the *McCarthy* case, counsel for the Garda Commissioner had argued that, since District Justice Mahon had conducted the preliminary examination in the instant case, the applicant's trial had, in effect, been a nullity and thus the *McGrath* case was not a relevant authority since the applicant had never been put in jeopardy. Counsel for the applicant noted, however, that s. 1(2)(a) of the Courts (No. 2) Act was intended to validate all defective Orders of District Justice Mahon which did not involve conflicts with the constitutional rights of a citizen, and that the validation of an acquittal would not conflict with the applicant's rights. This argument appealed to Flood J, and it was in this context that he referred, in the passages quoted above, to the status of a not guilty verdict as a certificate of uninterrupted innocence. He then went on to reject the argument for the Commissioner in particularly strong language:

> It seems to me that to rip the certificate of innocence from the hands of

> the applicant and metaphorically to shred it and declare it a total nullity and to claim that it never in fact existed, all by reason of a clerical error made in 1977 as to the age of a District Justice, would be wholly inequitable. To permit the State or any arm of the State to purport in any other proceedings to retry the applicant on the same facts in relation to the same events would in my opinion be an oppressive and unfair procedure.

As indicated, it may be that the particular context in which this case was argued may make the approach of Flood J, and in particular his description of the effect of a not guilty verdict, almost *sui generis*. If taken literally, the concept of a certificate of 'uninterrupted innocence' would be inconsistent with the jurisprudence of the Irish courts indicating that not guilty verdicts were capable of being appealed: see *The People v O'Shea* [1983] ILRM 549; [1982] IR 384. Of course, the *O'Shea* decision was itself the product of a 3-2 decision in the Supreme Court, and has since proved controversial: see *The People v Quilligan (No. 2)* [1989] ILRM 245 (1988 Review, 168-72) and *The People v Quilligan (No. 3)* [1993] 2 IR 305 (discussed above). Nonetheless, Flood J's dicta in *McCarthy* are problematic given that the *O'Shea* line of authority was not discussed.

The question remains whether the combined effect of *McGrath* and *McCarthy* is, in effect, that disciplinary proceedings after acquittals are entirely precluded. It should be noted that, in an *ex tempore* judgment, the Supreme Court in *McCarthy* upheld Flood J's decision on the ground that the disciplinary proceedings in the instant case were oppressive and unfair: see the reporter's note in [1993] 1 IR at 499. This certainly seems consistent with *McGrath,* but does not resolve the precise effect of a not guilty verdict. It might be better to conclude, however, that the dicta of Flood J should be treated with some reserve, particularly in the light of the subsequent proceedings in the *McGrath* case, to which we now turn.

In his judgment in *McGrath v Commissioner of An Garda Síochána (No. 2)* [1993] ILRM 38, Murphy J was faced with the reality that, in *McGrath v Commissioner of An Garda Síochána* [1990] ILRM 5 (HC); [1989] IR 241 (HC); [1990] ILRM 817 (SC); [1991] 1 IR 69 (SC) (see the 1989 Review, 275-6 and the 1990 Review, 330-1), the Supreme Court had expressly appeared to allow for the holding of a disciplinary inquiry even after an acquittal, provided that the inquiry did not overlap with the essential focus of the criminal trial. It is sufficient to note for present purposes that the applicant in this case had been acquitted on charges of embezzlement. In the first set of proceedings, which culminated in the Supreme Court, he succeeded in having certain charges prohibited, but not those which alleged 'improper practices' under the Garda Síochána (Discipline) Regulations 1971.

The Garda authorities then proceeded to hold another inquiry under the 1971 Regulations. However, further difficulties arose as this inquiry also seemed to be infected with material arising from the applicant's criminal trial, resulting in a further successful application to the High Court for an order of prohibition granted by Lardner J in an *ex tempore* judgment delivered in February 1991. In the course of that judgment, Lardner J indicated that the safest course for the authorities to adopt was to proceed anew with a fresh inquiry strictly limited to the 'improper practices' issue. The authorities therefore informed the applicant that the inquiry under the 1971 Regulations was being discontinued. By this time, the Garda Síochána (Discipline) Regulations 1971 had been revoked and replaced by the Garda Síochána (Discipline) Regulations 1989. The inquiry proceeded under the 1989 Regulations, and the applicant then sought a further order of prohibition. It was these proceedings that came before Murphy J, and he declined to prohibit the holding of the inquiry under the 1989 Regulations.

The applicant had argued that the discontinuance of the inquiry under the 1971 Regulations was equivalent to the entering of a *nolle prosequi*, and he cited the decision of Finlay P (as he then was) in *The State (O'Callaghan) v Ó hUadhaigh* [1977] IR 42 as indicating that it should not be used in an unfair manner. Murphy J did not accept the analogy with the *nolle prosequi* situation and considered, on the contrary, that the actions of the authorities in the instant case had been to ensure that the applicant's procedural rights were upheld.

The applicant also argued that the 1989 Regulations could not be used because what was alleged against him under the Regulations concerned matters which pre-dated the coming into effect of the 1989 Regulations. However, on this point Murphy J noted that the substance of the discipline charges against the applicant were virtually identical to those under the 1971 Regulations and so no injustice was done to him. In any event, Murphy J concluded that although there was a retrospective element in the 1989 Regulations this did not fall foul of Article 15.5 of the Constitution since the disciplinary offences could not be equated with criminal offences. He also referred to his own judgment in *Chestvale Properties Ltd v Glackin* [1992] ILRM 221 (see the Company Law chapter, 68-73, above) as authority for the view that retrospective legislation is not *per se* unjust or inconstitutional.

The approach taken by Murphy J in *McGrath (No.2)* would seem to be quite different to that of Flood J in the *McCarthy* case, above. In that respect, the decision of Murphy J would appear to be more consistent with existing case law, and it may be that the particular circumstances of the *McCarthy* case, referred to already, make it a decision almost on its own facts rather than one of more wide-ranging effect.

## PAY

The Garda Síochána Pay Order 1992 (SI No. 153) is an extremely lengthy document which comprises 40 Schedules, setting out the rates of pay for different grades within the Garda Síochána from 1975 to 1991. The salary of the Garda Commissioner is specified in the Order as £54,831.

# Health Services

## CONTRACEPTION

**Introduction** The Health (Family Planning) (Amendment) Act 1992 and the Health (Family Planning) (Amendment) Act 1993 involved substantial amendments to the statutory regime concerning the sale and use of contraceptives in the State. Because the 1992 and 1993 Acts were enacted in such close proximity, we will discuss both in this Review. In brief, the 1992 and 1993 Acts involve two main elements. First, a shift from strict controls over all forms of contraceptives to an approach which moves medical preparations, such as the oral pill, into a different statutory regime. Second, the Acts also extend the availability of non-medical contraceptive devices, in particular contraceptive sheaths, that is, condoms. The focus on condoms must be seen against the background of a change in official policy on combatting the AIDS virus. The 1992 and 1993 Acts came into effect on their signature by the President on 23 July 1992 and 1 July 1993, respectively.

***McGee* case** The availability of contraception was first regulated in statute by the Health (Family Planning) Act 1979, which had been introduced as a belated response to the decision of the Supreme Court in *McGee v Attorney General* [1974] IR 284. It will be recalled that, in *McGee*, the Supreme Court held that the ban on the importation of contraceptive devices in s. 17 of the Criminal Law Amendment Act 1935 was inconsistent with the right of privacy or of marital privacy contained in Articles 40.3 and 41 of the Constitution. A number of failed attempts to respond legislatively to the *McGee* decision had preceded the 1979 Act. See also the decision in *Irish Family Planning Association v Ryan* [1979] IR 295, which concerned a booklet on family planning methods which included reference to contraceptive methods other than natural family planning.

**The 1979 Act** The Health (Family Planning) Act 1979 was famously described in the Oireachtas debate by its proposer, the then Minister for Health and later Taoiseach, Charles Haughey, as 'an Irish solution to an Irish problem'. The Act sought to restrict the use of contraceptives, defined in s.1 of the Act as including both medical preparations or devices (such as the oral pill or spermicides) or non-medical devices (such as condoms) to married persons of 18 years of age and over. S. 2 of the 1979 Act imposed a duty on the Minister for Health to arrange for a family planning service, with particular emphasis on natural family planning methods. S. 3 of the Act dealt with the content of family planning services, but excluded any information or instruction involving the use of contraceptive devices. S. 4 of the 1979 Act required that contraceptives, as defined in s. 1, could only be obtained on prescription from a registered medical practitioner and that they would be dispensed by a pharmacist. S. 4 also required the medical practitioner to be satisfied that the contraceptive would be used for 'bona fide family planning purposes.' Ss. 5 and 6 of the 1979 Act dealt with importation of contraceptives into the State; s. 9 empowered the Minister to fund research into family planning methods, but again excluded methods relating to the use of contraceptives.

Although the 1979 Act formally remains in place, most of its substantive provisions have now been repealed, s.1 being substantially amended by the 1992 and 1993 Acts, ss. 2, 3 and 4 being repealed by the 1992 Act, ss. 5 and 6 being repealed by the 1993 Act and s. 9 being amended by the 1992 Act. The shortcomings in the Irish practice of legislative amendment by substitution are, perhaps, most clearly in evidence in connection with the topic under discussion.

**1985 Act** Before discussing the 1992 and 1993 Acts, we should note that the brief but, at the time, controversial, Health (Family Planning) (Amendment) Act 1985 amended s. 4 of the 1979 Act by removing the need to obtain a prescription in respect of condoms and contraceptive spermicides. However, it remained the position that registered pharmacists, medical practitioners and health board outlets were alone permitted to sell condoms. As we will see, the 1985 Act was repealed and replaced by s. 4 of the 1992 Act.

**Background to 1992 and 1993 Acts** As Paul Ward's Annotation to the 1992 Act in *Irish Current Law Statutes Annotated* indicates, the 1992 Act arose partly out of a successful prosecution of the Irish Family Planning Association, operating an outlet for the sale of condoms in the Virgin Megastore in Dublin, but which was not licensed under the 1979 and 1985 Acts. It was clear that the IFPA was in breach of the legislation and were correctly convicted in the District Court and, on appeal, in the Circuit Court: see *Director of Public Prosecutions v Irish Family Planning Association*, Irish Times, 15 and 27 February 1991. However, it appeared that the adverse media and public reaction to the conviction caused the then government to prepare amending legislation, which eventually led to the 1992 Act. Despite this acknowledged connection with the changes effected in the 1992 Act, the extensive changes apparent in the 1992 and 1993 Acts should also be seen against the background of changing government policies concerning the AIDS virus, in particular an increased emphasis on the use of condoms as an officially-supported means to prevent the spread of sexually transmitted diseases.

**Contraceptive defined** The AIDS connection can be seen in the successive changes in the definition of the word 'contraceptive' in both the 1992 and 1993 Acts. S.2 of the 1992 Act amended the definition of 'contraceptive' in s. 1 of the 1979 Act to mean any appliance or instrument, including contraceptive sheath, prepared or intended to prevent pregnancy resulting from sexual intercourse between human beings. This definition excluded the oral pill and other medical preparations such as spermicides which had been included in the original s. 1. These excluded items are now dealt with as 'medical preparations' under s. 65 of the Health Act 1947, which was amended by s. 7 of the 1992 Act to include them. S. 65 of the 1947 Act authorises the Minister for Health to regulate the sale of 'medical preparations', much of which is now governed by EC Directives on this topic: see the Pharmacy heading below. The effect of s. 2 of the 1992 Act is that the Health (Family Planning) Acts 1979 and 1992 now apply primarily to condoms, diaphragms and IUDs. But ss. 1 and 2 of the 1993 Act went further in restricting the definition of 'contraceptive' by excluding contraceptive sheaths entirely from that definition, and for the first time defining contraceptive sheath to include one intended for use by a male person or a female person, thus including the 'femidom'. This change in definition is relevant in the context of s. 3 of the 1993 Act, discussed below.

**Availability and outlets** S. 4 of the 1992 Act repealed all of the 1985 Act as well as s.4 of the 1979 Act. In the process, it removed the requirement in s.4 that a medical practitioner be satisfied that the contraceptives were to be used for bona fide family planning purposes. S. 4 of the 1992 Act provided that contraceptives could now be sold to any person over 17 years of age or who was married. It also extended the range of premises authorised to sell the limited range of contraceptive devices now covered by the Acts, principally, medical practitioners, pharmacists, health board outlets and others licensed by the Minister for Health. S. 5 of the 1992 Act specifically prohibited the sale of condoms in certain outlets, such as sports centres and restricted their sale to persons over 17 years of age or to those who were married, but this section was repealed by the 1993 Act. S. 3 of the 1993 Act now authorises the Minister for Health to prohibit by Regulations the sale by vending machines of contraceptive sheaths (as defined in the 1993 Act, that is, including 'femidoms'). In effect, this section for the first time envisaged the sale of condoms by vending machines and also removed any statutory age limit for condoms.

The Health (Family Planning) Regulations 1992 (SI No. 132), made under the 1992 Act, required health boards to provide comprehensive family planning services. They laid down the detailed conditions under which contraceptives, including condoms, could be advertised or displayed. This latter aspect of the Regulations was superceded by the terms of the 1993 Act.

**Standards for sheaths** S. 4(3) of the 1992 Act authorised the Minister for Health to specify by Regulations the standards to which condoms must comply. This has been superceded by s. 4 of the 1993 Act which again authorises the Minister to lay down standards by Regulations, and this also applies to the expanded definition of contraceptive sheath in the 1993 Act. On standards generally, see the Safety and Health chapter, 538-9, below.

**Importation restrictions removed** S. 6 of the 1992 Act dealt with the importation of contraceptives, as defined in the 1979 and 1992 Acts. After the 1992 Act, the requirement to obtain a licence to import contraceptives applied only to diaphragms and IUDs, and no longer applied to condoms. Since s. 8 of the 1993 Act repealed ss. 5 and 6 of the 1979 Act and also s. 6 of the 1992 Act, the remaining licensing requirements on the importation of diaphragms and IUDs were removed.

**Family planning services** S. 8 of the 1992 Act repealed ss. 2 and 3 of the 1979 Act and imposed a general duty on the Minister for Health to secure the orderly organisation of comprehensive family planning services. The detailed provisions are laid down in the Health (Family Planning) Regulations 1992 (SI No. 132). S. 8 of the 1992 Act can also be seen in conjunction with s. 3 of the 1992 Act, which amended s. 9 of the 1979 Act so that funding by the Minister of research into methods of contraception does not exclude methods which involve the use of contraceptives. S. 9 as originally worded was confined in its terms to methods of contraception that did not relate to the use of contraceptives.

## MAINTENANCE ALLOWANCES

**Disability** The Disabled Persons (Maintenance Allowance) Regulations 1992 (SI No. 212), made under the Health Act 1970, provided for an increased maintenance allowance for persons with a disability.

**Infectious diseases** The Infectious Diseases (Maintenance) Regulations 1992 (SI No. 213), made under the Health Act 1947, made improved provision for those with an infectious disease who were being cared for.

## MEDICAL COUNCIL

**Fitness to Practice Committee** In *Georgopoulus v Fitness to Practise Committee of the Medical Council*, High Court, 3 March 1992, the role of the Fitness to Practice Committee in formulating the basis for an inquiry into allegations of professional misconduct arose for discussion. The case arose in the following way.

By letter dated 15 February 1990, the applicant, a registrar in neurosurgery in Beaumont Hospital, Dublin, had made complaints amounting to professional misconduct against a consultant neurosurgeon in Beaumont Hospital, Mr John P. Phillips. The letter referred to a number of unnamed cases in which Mr Phillips had been involved. Arising from these complaints, the Board of Beaumont Hospital entered into protracted correspondence with both the applicant and Mr Phillips concerning the allegations of misconduct. In the course of correspondence, the applicant indicated that, under advice from his Medical Defence Union, he would only communicate information concerning particular patients to a medically qualified person and not to non-medical personnel such as the Chairman of the hospital board. Ultimately, by letter dated 12 April 1990, details of particular cases involving Mr Phillips were forwarded by the applicant to the Assistant Medical Administrator of the hospital.

In the meantime, the Chairman of the Board of Beaumont Hospital had applied under s. 45 of the Medical Practitioners Act 1978 to the Fitness to Practise Committee of the Medical Council to hold an inquiry into the allegations concerning Mr Phillips and had also indicated that, if the allegations against Mr Phillips were not established, then the use by the applicant of the medical information referred to in his letter of 15 February 1990 could also require the holding of an inquiry under s. 45 of the 1978 Act.

After a lengthy inquiry into the allegations against Mr Phillips, the Fitness to Practise Committee concluded that Mr Phillips had no case to answer. The Committee then instituted an inquiry into the applicant under s. 45 of the 1978 Act, the grounds for the inquiry referring to both the applicant's letter of 15 February 1990 and also to his letter of 12 April 1990. The applicant contended that, since Beaumont Hospital had referred only to his letter of 15 February 1990 in its application to the Committee, the Committee had acted *ultra vires* s. 45 of the 1978 Act in including any reference to the second letter. Carroll J did not accept this argument. She stressed the link between the applicant's initial complaint and the outcome of the inquiry into Mr Phillips, which she described as 'at all times interlinked'. She described the letter of 12 April 1990 as 'an elaboration' of the letter of 15 February and 'very similar to a reply for notice for particulars'. Although she noted that the Committee had not used the precise wording used in the first letter, she did not therefore consider that the Fitness to Practise Committee had added any grounds of complaint to those contained in that letter of 15 February. Rather it had merely clarified the complaints by incorporating the later letter, and thus had not acted *ultra vires* the 1978 Act. For subsequent proceedings arising from the circumstances discussed in this case, see *Georgopoulus v Beaumont Hospital Board* [1994] ILRM 58. This case will be discussed in the 1993 Review.

## MEDICAL PREPARATIONS

The European Communities (Therapeutic Substances Act 1932) (Cesser of Application) Regulations 1992 (SI No. 406) provide that the Therapeutic Substances Act 1932 shall not apply to therapeutic substances intended for human use. Such use is dealt with by means of the Medical Preparations (Licensing, Advertising and Sale) Regulations 1984, as amended, which implement the relevant EC Directives in this area, such as 89/342/EEC and 89/381/EEC.

## PHARMACY

A most helpful discussion of Irish pharmacy law is contained in Weedle and Cahill, *Medicines and Pharmacy Law in Ireland* (Kenlis Publications, 1991). The authors provide a thorough discussion of the impact of EC Directives on the Irish legislative code for medicinal products in particular up to 1991.

# Labour Law

## UNFAIR DISMISSAL

**Characterisation of 'dismissal'** In *Clarke v Brady*, 3 ELR 133 (1992), the Employment Appeals Tribunal held that the claimant, a bar employee, had been dismissed (unfairly) where the manager had put him on what he described as 'protective notice' and told him that he should look for another job. The omission to use the magic word 'dismissal' in no way prevented this conclusion.

**Dismissal for membership of a trade union or activities on its behalf** S. 6(2) of the Unfair Dismissals Acts 1977 and 1991 deems a dismissal to be unfair if it results wholly or mainly from one or more of a number of specified causes, including, in paragraph (a), the employee's membership or proposed membership or his engaging in activities on behalf of a trade union. In *O'Callaghan v Energy Sealants Ltd*, 3 ELR 230 (1992), the claimant had been dismissed from his position as sales manager. The respondent company argued that this was on account of his failure to reach agreed sales targets. (The claimant's selection of the time for his holidays had also antagonised his employers as it was during a busy sales period). The claimant contended that his dismissal was directly related to the referral of a salary dispute between him and the respondent company to the Rights Commissioner Service after he had sought assistance from his trade union when he could not personally resolve the dispute. He invoked s. 6(2).

In a very brief determination, the Employment Appeals Tribunal rejected the claim, stating that it was satisfied that 'the dismissal of the claimant did not result *wholly or mainly* from the employee's membership of a trade union or his engaging in activities on behalf of a trade union, as defined in s. 6(2)(a). . . .' The emphasis on the words 'wholly or mainly' indicated that the Tribunal must have considered that the claimant's trade union membership or activities played some role in his dismissal, contrary to the respondent company's argument.

In *White v Betson*, 3 ELR 120 (1992), a case ultimately reducing itself to a contested issue of fact, the Tribunal held that the claimant had been unfairly dismissed for trade union membership. The respondent contended that the dismissal related to the claimant's poor work performance and denied that correspondence had been received from the claimant's trade union regarding his conditions of employment before the decision was made to discharge him. The Tribunal held that this communication antedated the dismissal.

**Cesser of fixed-term contract** S. 2(2)(b) of the Unfair Dismissals Act 1977 provides that:

> dismissal where the employment was under a contract of employment for a fixed term or for a specified purpose (being a purpose of such a kind that the duration of the contract was limited but was, at the time of its making, incapable of precise ascertainment, and the dismissal consisted of the expiry of the term without its being renewed under the said contract or the cesser of the purpose, and the contract is in writing, was signed by or on behalf of the employer and by the employee and provides that this Act shall not apply to a dismissal consisting only of the expiry or cesser aforesaid.

In *Sheehan v Dublin Tribune Ltd*, 3 ELR 239 (1992), a fixed term contract contained a clause, entitled 'Contractual period', to the following effect:

> The arrangement is for a two year period and is, again, on a contractual basis. It is fully understood again that on the termination of this contractual arrangement no residual obligations shall exist towards you nor shall you have any claim on the company, arising from the termination of such contract, including any claim for compensation for loss of office.

The Tribunal held that s. 2(2)(b) did not apply because the contract of employment had not specifically provided that the Unfair Dismissals Acts 1977 and 1991 should not apply to a dismissal consisting of the expiry of the term. Strict compliance with s. 2(2)(b) is thus required. The contractual provision would undoubtedly have prevented most employees from having any expectation of succeeding in unfair dismissal proceedings, but nonetheless was not drafted in a way that brought the contract within the scope of s. 2(2)(b).

**Temporary or permanent employment** In *Madden v Cavan Mineral Water Co. Ltd*, 3 ELR 139 (1992), the Tribunal held that the claimant, a lorry driver, had been unfairly dismissed where he had 'had good grounds for feeling that he was a permanent employee of the respondent, notwithstanding the fact that it may have been in [the director]'s mind that the job was of a temporary nature'. There was a significant conflict of evidence so it is difficult to know precisely what the Tribunal perceived to be these 'good grounds'. The moral for employers is nonetheless clear. Any ambiguity as to temporary or permanent status, if capable of being construed reasonably by an employee as involving permanent status, may generate liability for unfair dismissal where an employer purports to dispense with the employee's services on the basis that the employer had only temporary status.

## Misconduct

*Dangerous acts and horseplay* In *O'Mahony v Whelan t/a Pallet Providers*, 3 ELR 117 (1992), the Employment Appeals Tribunal held that the claimant's conduct had justified summary dismissal. The claimant, an operative, had thrown another worker on a pile of blocks close to a rotary saw which had been switched off but was still moving. The other worker had provoked the claimant by kicking over a pile of blocks near him. When the foreman intervened to tell the claimant to cool down, the claimant responded physically. The Tribunal held that the respondent was 'justified in making a rule which protected his workforce' and that a breach of this rule was 'a serious offence'.

*Dunphy v Largo Food Exports Ltd*, 3 ELR 179 (1992) is an important warning to employers that if they do not nip horseplay in the bud, they may find it difficult to defend an unfair dismissal claim when they eventually seek to bring it under control. The claimant, a factory worker, had been dismissed for throwing a large roll of clingfilm at another employee, resulting in his being brought to hospital. The staff had been informed six months previously that horseplay would lead to dismissal. The claimant gave evidence that she had reported earlier incidents of horseplay to the management but that she had not noticed any improvement in the situation. She contended that her conduct on the fateful day had followed an incident in which the other worker, a man, had pulled her hat off from her head and thrown it in the bin and had pulled her hair.

The Tribunal held that the claimant's dismissal had been unfair because horseplay had been an ongoing problem in the factory and had not been brought under control. The decision makes it difficult for employers to know precisely what is the best course in dealing with horseplay. Clearly a warning of dismissal is not enough if this is not followed by an improvement in the position. The solution suggested by the decision would appear to be that the employer is free, if not indeed obliged, to deliver on the threat of dismissal sooner rather than later — a curious result of a successful unfair dismissal claim. The decision is perhaps an example of how what might appear a just and sensible holding in the case before the court can have unintended, though foreseeable, deleterious downstream effects: cf. Wrigglesworth, 'Legislation and Injury Control' (1978) 18 Med Sci & L 191 (1978).

*Breach of trust* In *Parsons v Liffey Marine Ltd*, 3 ELR 136 (1992) the claimant, an apprentice working with sixteen other apprentices, falsified a medical certificate by changing the duration of the period concerned, and then initially maintained that he had not done so. His employer dismissed him. A director of the company told the Tribunal that a lot of trust was put on the individual apprentices to put in the correct hours on their time sheets; he did not now trust the claimant; had he admitted his wrongdoing immediately he would only have been suspended.

The Tribunal held that the claimant had been unfairly dismissed, since the penalty imposed was disproportionate to the offence:

> It was unfortunate that the claimant did not see fit to tell the truth to the respondent when first confronted but the important thing is that he ultimately did admit the truth of the matter.

One wonders whether such delayed disclosure really was 'the important thing'. The director of the company surely had a point in stressing the need for trustworthiness at an earlier stage. It has to be noted that alteration of the medical certificate did not gain the claimant any extra financial or other benefit since the doctor who originally examined him actually offered a certificate for two weeks, which was declined by the claimant, who wanted to take advantage of available overtime work in the second week. When his medical condition worsened at the start of the second week, he altered the certificate to bring it into line with what the doctor had earlier offered.

In *Lee v Transirish Lines Ltd*, 3 ELR 150 (1992) the claimant, an operatives manager, had received a VAT payment on behalf of his employer, amounting to £109, which he had kept for some time before paying over that amount to his employer. In the meantime when questioned about the matter, he had told a number of lies. He was subsequently interviewed and told that, if he admitted to the misconduct and undertook not to let it happen again, the matter would be considered closed. When, however, he made the admission, he was given the option of resignation or dismissal. He chose the former but later took proceedings alleging constructive dismissal.

Counsel for the employer accepted that the claimant had never intended to deprive the employer of the money. Nonetheless, he argued, what had transpired was not a silly little mistake or a relatively minor event. The claimant had abused trust and exposed an innocent third party to very serious risk. A reasonable employer would have to have complete confidence in all employees at this level.

The Tribunal held that there had been a constructive dismissal which 'in *all* the circumstances' had been unfair. This laconic phrase offers the only enlightenment on the Tribunal's reasoning process. The emphasis on *all* the circumstances suggests that the Tribunal may have given some weight to the claimant's contention that his employer had used the opportunity to dismiss him in order to recruit a person to do his job at a considerably lower salary. The Tribunal held that the claimant's contribution to his dismissal by his conduct amounted to 25%.

In *Martin v Audio Video Services Centre Ltd*, 3 ELR 216 (1992), the Tribunal held that the appropriate questions to ask in a case of dismissal for dishonest misappropriation were (1) whether the employer had 'an honest belief that the claimant was dishonest, based on reasonable grounds arising from a fair and adequate investigation' and (2) whether the employer had complied with the rules of natural justice. In the instant case the employer had failed both tests. Although it had used sophisticated detection equipment, in the form of a video camera recorder, the video film had not shown the claimant handling money. There were thus no reasonable grounds for a belief in the claimant's dishonesty. The claimant had not been confronted with the demand for an explanation, when he passed two senior employees with a plastic bag containing a video machine. This failure violated the principles of natural justice, in the view of the Tribunal.

*Absenteeism* In *Hanly v Horan*, 3 ELR 104 (1992), the Tribunal held that frequent absenteeism by an experienced farm manager justified his dismissal (but not summary dismissal) where his absence led to the death of sick pigs that he had a responsibility to feed and tend. This tangible causal connection between the absenteeism and the damage makes the holding eminently defensible.

In *Hynes v GEC Distributors (Ireland) Ltd*, 3 ELR 95 (1992), the Tribunal held that the dismissal of the claimant, a driver, had not been unfair where he had been absent from work for 113 days of his seventeen months' employment. This was compounded by his failure to submit certain medical certificates and Social Welfare cheques, and further exacerbated by the discovery by his employer that he had been playing hurling while on sick leave.

*Failure to carry out instructions* In *Lawlor and Zambra v Togas Fashions Ltd (in liquidation)*, 3 ELR 88 (1992), the claimants, who were machinists, were dismissed without notice for failing to carry out instructions. They contested this, claiming that they had merely sought to clarify how much they would be earning for the particular work assignment. They also challenged the employer's contention that they had received previous warnings.

The Tribunal accepted the employer's evidence on the issue of warnings. Nonetheless it held that the dismissal had been unfair 'on procedural grounds'. What these grounds are is by no means clear and the Tribunal's determination throws no light upon it. One wonders about the merits of such laconic dispositions of important issues. If a determination by the Tribunal has no clear basis, how are employers and employees to work out good procedures?

**Limitation period** In *Reilly v An Post*, 3 ELR 129 (1992), the appellant had been dismissed from his position as a cleaner and the dismissal had been confirmed by the internal appeals board within An Post. Ten months later the Labour Court found in his favour. An Post replied that it was not bound by this determination (which was its entitlement) and that it was not accepting it.

Well after the limitation period (of six months from the time of dismissal) within which an appeal might be lodged with the Employment Appeals Tribunal, the claimant proceeded down that route. He alleged that An Post had been guilty of innocent misrepresentation in agreeing to go to the Labour Court.

The Tribunal, and the Circuit Court on appeal, rejected this contention. Judge O'Connor was satisfied that there had been no misrepresentation. The claimant, in resorting to the Labour Court, was responding to 'a desperate situation'. Having let time run out, this was his only redress.

**Legitimate expectation** In *Bredin v Donegal County Council*, 3 ELR 222 (1992), the claimant had been employed as a fire officer. Until 1985, the retirement age had been sixty. At that time the Local Government Staff Regulations Board and the Irish Congress of Trade Unions agreed to the introduction, at national level, of annual medical checks for fire officers and compulsory retirement at fifty five. The Department of the Environment issued a circular letter relating the early retirement scheme and Donegal County Council decided to implement it, with allowance for a transitional period.

The claimant, who was not even given a medical examination, was required to retire before the age of sixty. He argued that others similarly situated had been permitted to continue in employment; that he had had the expectation of working to the age of sixty and that his employer had never concluded an agreement with him to the contrary.

The Employment Appeals Tribunal held that the claimant had been unfairly dismissed. He had had a legitimate expectation that he would be employed beyond the age of fifty five and should have been given an opportunity to prove his fitness to work on.

The Tribunal stated that it fully appreciated the reasons for the move towards a retirement age of fifty five and the introduction of medical checks. These sprung from Barron J's decision in *Heeney v Dublin Corporation*, High Court, 16 May 1991, which we analyse in the 1991 Review, 398-9. The tension between the goals of tort law and of labour law are very evident here. Barron J had little sympathy for the idea that negotiations to implement safer work practices should take a long period to reach consummation. The Tribunal, on the other hand, concentrated its attention on the expectation of the employee. One can envisage a case with facts somewhat different from *Bredin* where the conflict between tort and labour law could not be resolved so easily. Where there is a risk of personal injury to employees which the employees are happy to undergo, the conflict reduces itself to one of paternalism against employment continuity.

**Jurisdiction and Procedure** In *Sutcliffe v McCarthy* [1993] 2 IR 48, the plaintiff had taken proceedings to have his dismissal investigated by a Rights Commissioner, invoking s. 13 of the Industrial Relations Act 1969. The Rights Commissioner had found in his favour and made an award of compensation. The plaintiff had appealed to the Labour Court on quantum. He then discovered that his claim could have gone straight to the Employment Appeals Tribunal, as provided by s. 8 of the Unfair Dismissals Act 1977. He thereupon issued fresh proceedings, this time involving the Minimum Notice and Terms of Employment Act 1973 and the Unfair Dismissals Act 1977. The Tribunal held that it had no jurisdiction to hear the claim as the plaintiff had been put to his election by s. 8(10) of the 1977 Act, which provides that a dispute in relation to an unfair dismissal is not to be referred to a Rights Commissioner under s. 13(2) of the 1969 Act. The plaintiff, in the view of the Tribunal, could (i) have maintained a claim before a Rights Commissioner in respect of a matter falling within s. 13(2) (which thus excluded a claim based on a allegation of wrongful dismissal); (ii) have brought a claim for unfair dismissal before a Rights Commissioner or before the Tribunal as provided by the 1977 Act; or (iii) have simply brought proceedings for damages for breach of contract at common law. Having exercised his election in favour of the first of these options, he was precluded from recasting his claim under another when dissatisfied with the outcome of the first proceedings.

In proceedings for *certiorari* by way of judicial review, O'Hanlon J quashed the order of the Tribunal and remitted the matter back to it. In his opinion, the original proceedings before the Rights Commissioner should be regarded as a *nullity*, since the Rights Commissioner was specifically precluded by s. 8(10) of the 1977 Act from dealing with precisely the kind of dispute that was brought before him in the instant case. The Rights Commissioner could have dealt with such a claim under s. 8(1) using the procedure prescribed by s. 8(2), but this had not been done.

## WRONGFUL DISMISSAL

In *Robinson v Corneil*, High Court, 10 April 1992, Keane J addressed the question of the common law principles relating to termination of employment. The parties had been cohabiting for some time. The defendant employed the plaintiff as manager of her company and drew up a document, addressed 'to whom it may concern', stating that the employment was full-time, commencing on a specified date, and of a duration of not less than five years. The document was signed by the defendant, professedly in her capacity as managing director of the company.

The defendant purported to dismiss the plaintiff summarily on grounds that Keane J held to be unsustainable. In assessing damages, Keane J proceeded on the basis that the document did not reflect the true nature of the contract, which was highly informal but which still involved the plaintiff in full-time duties. His employment constituted a responsible position 'which would therefore entitle him to reasonable notice. . . .' Keane J held that six months' notice was the appropriate duration.

## CONTINUITY OF EMPLOYMENT

Paragraph 5(1) of the European Communities (Safeguarding of Employees' Rights on Transfer of Undertakings) Regulations 1980 (SI No. 306 of 1980) provides that:

> [t]he transfer of an undertaking, business or part of a business shall not in itself constitute a ground for dismissal by the transferor or transferee and a dismissal, the grounds for which are such a transfer, by a transferor or a transferee is hereby prohibited. However, nothing in this Regulation shall be construed as prohibiting dismissals for economic, technical or organisational reasons entailing changes in the workforce.

These Regulations give effect to the EC Transfer of Undertakings Directive.

It is clear from the decisions of the Court of Justice that a transfer must involve the retention of the business transferred of its identity (*Spijkers v Gebroeders Benedik Abattoir CV and Alfred Benedik En Zonen V* [1986] ECR 119) and that a transfer takes place where there is '*a change in the legal or natural person* who is responsible for carrying on the business and who by virtue of that fact incurs the obligations of an employer *vis-à-vis* employees of the undertaking, regardless of which or not ownership of the undertaking is transferred' (*Lands-organisationen i Danmark Tjenerfor-bundet i Danmark v My Molle Kro* [1987] ECR 5465). In *Bannon v Employment*

*Appeals Tribunal*, 3 ECR 203 (1992) Blayney J, granting an order of *certiorari* quashing the determination of the Employment Appeals Tribunal, ruled that both these elements existed where the company for which the claimant worked as a security guard hived off the security duties it performed at a shopping centre to an outside security firm on a contract basis, which was followed by the dismissal of the claimant for redundancy. Blayney J considered that the business retained its identity: the new firm was supplying the same security services as had been provided by the old, and the recipients of those services, the tenants, were identical. The transfer involved a change in the natural or legal person who was responsible for the carrying on of the business; the fact that the contracting out was a temporary arrangement rather than an absolute transfer did not alter the position. Blayney J noted that *Landsorganisationen* involved the lease of a restaurant, which was similarly a temporary arrangement.

In *Landsorganisationen* the transfer had followed a breach of the terms of the lease by the lessee. In *Guidon v Harrington*, 3 ELR 146 (1992), the Employment Appeals Tribunal applied the decision in holding that a transfer occurred where, it appears, there had not been a breach of a clause in the lease by the lessee.

In *Reddin v Harrison*, 3 ELR 245 (1992), the Tribunal held that there had been continuity of service where the four claimants worked for the same family and transferred between the various boutiques owned by the family, as required. One of the family gave evidence that each of the boutiques was owned by a separate company; everything about these companies was separate, including separate book accounts and VAT numbers; while there was some group buying for the shops, the more usual practice was for individual shops to purchase for themselves. It appeared that, if one shop took stock from another shop, an invoice would be issued in respect of the goods. The claimants, when they had been transferred between the boutiques, had not received redundancy.

The Tribunal held that the claimants had been 'effectively employed' by the defendant family as indicated by the evidence of their transferability between boutiques as the need arose. It found that they had been unfairly dismissed from the last boutique where they worked; there had not been a genuine redundancy situation as there were other people employed in the other boutiques subsequently.

Another decision raising the issue of continuity of service is *Daly v Dublin Futures Exchange Ltd*, 3 ELR 236 (1992), where the Tribunal held that the claimant, a salesman, had been in continuous employment when he had changed from working for one company to working for that company and another company, dividing his working days equally between them, but doing sales work for the first and hiring work for the second.

## MINIMUM NOTICE AND TERMS OF EMPLOYMENT ACT 1973

In *Dodd v Local Stores (Trading) Ltd*, 3 ELR 61 (1992), the Employment Appeals Tribunal held that the claimants' continuity of service had been preserved where a liquidator had been appointed by the High Court. A stumbling block to such a holding might appear to have been prevented by the High Court decision in *Irish Shipping Ltd v Byrne* [1987] IR 486; but the claimants (whose lawyers' industry was expressly commended by the Tribunal) argued that the Tribunal should have regard to two earlier High Court cases, *Donnelly v Gleeson*, 11 July 1978 and *In re Evanhenry Ltd*, 15 May 1986. These had recognised that an employee may be retained on the same terms as his or her original contract by being specifically requested to stay on and that the effect of a winding-up order as a notice of discharge may be waived.

In the instant case, the liquidator had had no contact and the union and its members heard of his appointment only 'through the grapevine'. The Tribunal considered that the presumption as to termination following the appointment of the liquidator could be rebutted in the circumstances and that the effect of the winding-up order as a notice of discharge had been waived, thereby preserving the claimants' continuity of service.

In *Bates v Model Bakery Ltd* [1993] ILRM 22, the Supreme Court endorsed the approach it had adopted in *Becton Dickinson Ltd v Lee* [1973] IR 1, to the effect that into every contract of employment must be read an implied term that the service of a strike notice of a length no shorter than that required for notice to terminate the contract does not in itself amount to notice to terminate the contract or constitute a breach of the contract and that to take action on foot of the strike notice likewise does not amount to a breach. In *Becton Dickinson* the Court conceded that this implied term could be overridden by an express provision to the contrary or by circumstances where by necessary implication a provision to the contrary had to be read into the contract.

The issue in *Bates* concerned the legal character of a communication by the defendant employers to the plaintiffs following a strike. The strike was designed to encourage the employer to adhere fully to a recommendation of the Labour Court for a wage increase for employees in the bakery trade. The employers had ultimately granted this increase but had been dragging their heels for a period of five months subsequent to this recommendation. In the meantime there had been an unofficial strike relating to an entirely different matter which had been resolved by an agreement in which the representative of the employees had undertaken that they would adhere to a particular grievance procedure for the processing of any dispute that might arise, which involved certain steps not taken in the subsequent strike. The employers wrote to the employees, including the plaintiffs, advising them that the strike had 'effectively frustrated' their contract of employment. The letter continued:

> You will have been aware and we advised you specifically several times that any unauthorised withdrawal of your labour would very quickly result in the destruction of our bakery trade. Accordingly, we have no option but to regard your employment contract as having been frustrated. . . .'

The question at issue in the case was whether this communication constituted a dismissal by reason of redundancy under section 7(2) of the Redundancy Payments Act 1967. The Supreme Court held that it did. It interpreted the agreement after the earlier strike as relating to *future* disputes. In contrast, the issue as to the payment of the wage increase was an on-running dispute to which the bakery had never really faced up. The strike notice came within the scope of the *Becton Dickinson* decision. There thus had been no repudiation of the contract or resignation by the employees. Accordingly the bakery's communication had constituted a dismissal to which section 7(2) of the 1967 Act applied.

The Courts did not analyse the issue of frustration because the defendants did not ultimately seek to rely upon the doctrine. *Becton Dickinson* had not been concerned with that issue but rather the question whether strike notice of a duration at least as long as that required for termination of a contract constituted a *breach* of contract. In *Bates* the employers' argument contained in their communication to the employees was in essence that the bakery trade was unusual in that a strike of even a short duration would cripple the efficacy of the employer's business, so that jobs would have to be discharged. The thrust of this contention was that the trade was one that could not survive a strike *regardless of its merits*. This thus argued for a 'no fault' justification for dismissing the employees, and did not depend on the application of *Becton Dickinson* principle.

O'Flaherty J did go so far as to describe the circumstances in which frustration of contract occurs, though he ultimately attached no importance to it since he considered that the term had not been used in its strict legal meaning by the defendant, and it was clear that the defendant was not seeking to argue that the strike came within the doctrine of frustration. He said:

> Frustration occurs whenever the law recognises that, without default of either party, a contractual obligation has become incapable of being performed because of some supervening illegality or because the cir-

> cumstances in which performance is called for would render it something radically different from that which is undertaken by the contract.

Of course it would be hard for employees who chose to strike to invoke the doctrine of frustration since they would be likely to be parried by the defence that the frustration was *self-induced*. But is it open to an employer to invoke the doctrine? On the face of it, there is a certain attraction to the argument that an employer in an industry or trade of special vulnerability should be permitted to invoke that vulnerability when employees strike. It is a fact of life that some businesses will not collapse even when the employees go on an extended strike; but it is equally true that other businesses are not capable of withstanding even a relatively short strike. In such circumstances, if the vulnerable business discharges employees because it cannot continue to employ them viably, why should it not be permitted to invoke the doctrine of frustration?

The most attractive answer would seem to be located in the domain of social policy rather than abstract principle. If an employer were able to fire employees where a strike was biting, this would run counter to the policy of treating strikes as lawful where they are preceded by the due notice requirements.

## JUDICIAL REVIEW

In *Beirne v Commissioner of An Garda Síochána* [1993] ILRM 1 the majority (Finlay CJ and Egan J) upholding Flood J, held that the termination of the training assignment of a trainee member of the Garda Síochána, by reason of his alleged misconduct, was susceptible to judicial review. Whereas O'Flaherty J, dissenting, considered that the contractual relationship predominated with respect to trainees, the majority did not consider that it had the effect of excluding the public law dimension.

The Chief Justice noted that the function of the Commissioner in admitting a person to enrolment in the Garda Síochána was purely statutory in its definition. The standards applied in training, the qualification and characteristics required of persons subjected to that training and the regulation of the training itself were 'matters of particular and immediate public concern and . . . directly relevant to the public question of the ordering of society and the regulation of discipline within society'.

# Land Law

## CONVEYANCING

In its *Report on Land Law and Conveyancing Law (5) General Proposals* (LRC 44 – 1992), the Law Reform Commission makes several recommendations for reform under three broad headings: (1) Simplifying conveyancing generally; (2) rectifying anomalies arising from modern legislation; and (3) amendments to landlord and tenant law.

**Simplifying conveyancing generally** The Commission here addresses four matters. The *first* relates to the need for recourse to company seals. The Commission recommends that the execution of documents relating to land by bodies corporate incorporated outside the State should be accepted as being validly executed by the registering authorities where they have been validly executed in accordance with the legal requirements of the jurisdiction in which the body is incorporated. This proposal is based on difficulties experienced in relation to some European countries, notably the Netherlands, whose law has no requirement of company seals. There is a certain redundancy in requiring foreign companies to have resort to a procedure which has no meaning or utility in their domestic legal system.

The *second* recommendation relates to the appointment of new trustees and the vesting of property of incorporated associations. Most sporting, cultural and community organisations in Ireland are not incorporated. Their property, which often consists of just one premises, must be held by trustees. Frequently the process of appointing new trustees is overlooked; this requires rectification when the property is being sold. Ss. 10 and 12 of the Trustee Act 1893 provide the machinery for dealing with the situation but compliance is far from regular. Accordingly, the Commission recommends that, so far as unincorporated associations are concerned, s. 10 be amended to provide that, save as otherwise provided by its constitution or rules, the right to appoint new trustees of the association's property should be vested in the members assembled in general meeting and that new trustees may be appointed at that meeting, after due notice. This resolution would require the support of the majority of the members present and voting. The Commission recommends that s. 12 of the 1893 Act be amended so as to provide that a copy of the resolution, certified by the chairman of the meeting, should operate as a vesting deed for the purposes of s. 12.

*Third*, the Commission recommends that the requirement to use words of limitation in an assurance of unregistered land be abolished. This change was made in England by s. 60(i) of the Law of Property Act 1925 and in Ireland in respect of *registered* land by s. 123 of the Registration of Title Act 1964. The Commission argues that retention of the traditional rule in regard to unregistered land 'merely continues a trap into which conveyancers of interests in land fall, from time to time, with subsequent expense to their clients (or themselves) in remedying the defect'.

The *fourth* matter addressed by the Commission is one raising important issues of social policy in relation to the family. It appears that Mr Mervyn Taylor TD wrote to Mr Justice Keane, when he was President of the Commission, in May 1990, suggesting that a joint tenant should be able to sever unilaterally a joint tenancy by giving notice that the property would henceforth be held under a tenancy in common. His concern arose in cases where spouses who held the family home as joint tenants had separated and the husband had left the home, his wife and children remaining there. If the wife died first, her interest in the home would pass to her husband automatically by way of survivorship and the position of the children might be undermined. In such cases it might be impossible to secure the husband's consent, during his wife's lifetime, to any severance of the tenancy and conversion into a tenancy in common, so as to give the children a vested interest in the property. Mr. Taylor suggested that in such a case the interests of the children would be protected if their mother could unilaterally execute a simple deed of severance, which would not require the consent of the husband.

The Commission concludes that this proposed solution might create more problems than it solved. It points out that, if a family home is held under a tenancy in common, the husband is free to dispose of his interest in the property either by a transfer made during his life or by his will to a third party, which would not benefit his wife and children. The Commission expresses the view that the wife, where she has grounds for a separation in the situation exemplified by Mr Taylor, should take advantage of the provisions of the Judicial Separation and Family Law Reform Act 1989 and apply to the court for an order in respect of the property which, if successful, would avoid the risk that the property would pass to the husband on his wife's death. The Commission adds the observation — of particular interest in the light of constitutional events in early 1994 — that '[t]his type of situation will hopefully be ameliorated by the implementation of the Government's proposed legislation providing for ownership of the Family Home'.

**Rectification of anomalies arising from modern legislation** The Commission makes three recommendations under this heading. The *first* is that the Planning Acts be amended to give a Planning Authority jurisdiction to grant planning permissions for the development of land within a three-mile zone below high water mark from its land boundary. The functional area of a Planning Authority extends to the maritime boundary: *Browne v Donegal County Council* [1980] IR 132; problems thus arise at present in cases where a Planning Authority gives purported permission for a development, for example a jetty, part of which is within the Planning Authority's jurisdictional area and part of which, being below the high water mark, is not. Section 28 of the Local Government (Reorganisation) Act 1985 offers a solution by way of Ministerial order but the Commission regards this as 'somewhat piecemeal'. It prefers the general amendment that it proposes.

*Secondly*, the Commission recommends that the Companies Acts be amended to provide for the establishment of a register of charges for companies incorporated outside the State which have not established a place of business in the State but which own land in the State. The Commission considers it important that people dealing with these companies showed have notice of charges against land they own here.

*Thirdly* the Commission recommends that s. 90 of the Registration of Title Act 1964 be amended to entitle a person who has the right to be registered as owner of registered land to grant a lease of the land and that the right to transfer, charge or lease the land should extend to part or parts of the land. This recommendation derives from a lacuna in s. 90, identified in Brendan Fitzgerald's *Land Registry Practice*, p. 235 (1989). One of the malign effects of the present statutory framework is that a registered owner may not enter into a sale and leaseback arrangement with a financial institution.

**Amendments to landlord and tenant law** The Commission proposes six amendments under this heading. The *first* flows from the Supreme Court decision in *Fitzgerald (Trustees of Castleknock Tennis Club) Ltd v Corcoran* [1991] ILRM 545, analysed in the 1991 Review, 288-9. The effect of that decision is that a tennis club (or other spoirting or recreational club) may acquire the fee simple in the clubhouse and ancillary areas. While acknowledging that there is 'no doubt' that the Supreme Court reached the correct conclusion in interpreting the law, the Commission is apprehensive about what could happen if a club, having acquired the fee simple, sold off the clubhouse and ancillary areas for development:

> A well-motivated and substantial membership would presumably require the proceeds for the sale to be invested in a new clubhouse and improved facilities. A club is, however, under no obligation to expend the proceeds in this way and a club with a less well-motivated or small

> membership could simply wind itself up and divide the proceeds among the members — hardly what the legislators would have wished.

The Commission recommends that the legislation be amended to provide that the lessee of a sporting or recreational club should not have the right to buy out the fee simple. If this recommendation is considered to run counter to the general policy of the ground rents legislation, the Commission proposes a fall-back solution: that the legislation be amended to provide that, on any acquisition of the fee simple, any covenant requiring the lands to be used for or in connection with outdoor sport or recreation should continue to affect the lands as a covenant under s. 28 (2) of the Landlord and Tenant (Ground Rents) (No. 2) Act 1978.

The *second* recommendation under this heading also relates to section 28. In its earlier *Report on Land Law and Conveyancing Law (1) General Proposals* (LRC 30 – 1989), the Commission drew attention to an anomaly under sub. s. (2) of s. 28, whereby, on acquisition of a fee simple by a person having an interest in land, all covenants, including collateral covenants, cease to have effect: see the 1989 Review, 303. Other anomalies were subsequently identified in John Wylie's *Landlord and Tenant Law*, pp. 1031-3. To meet all of these anomalies and to bring the section into harmony with what was probably the true intention of the Oireachtas, the Commission recommends that the beginning of s. 28(1) be amended to provide: 'Where a person who has enlarged his interest in land into a fee simple by acquiring the fee simple in the land and every intermediate interest in the land, all covenants. . . .'

The *third* recommendation is that s. 5(3) of the Landlord and Tenant (Amendment) Act 1980 be amended to provide:

> i. that, where an individual lessee has transferred the lessee's interest in a tenancy to a limited company, without the lessor's consent, the right to a new tenancy under the Act should remain vested in the individual, and
>
> ii. that the protection of the section be extended to the situation where the lessee's interest is vested in a company but the trading in the premises is carried on by an individual who is the principal of the company.

S. 5(3) was primarily designed to cover the situation where an individual holding a lessee's interest incorporated a company to carry on trading and failed to transfer the lessee's interest in the property to the trading company. The Commission is concerned about the position of the landlord who is required to accept as a lessee a company of which the landlord may know nothing without having any opportunity to check on the company's financial strength. Under the Commission's proposal, if the lessee requires to have the new lease to be taken by the company, the landlord will be entitled to treat that application as an application for consent to assignment which can be dealt with in the usual way.

*Fourthly*, the Commission recommends that s. 13(1)(a) of the Landlord and Tenant (Amendment) Act 1980 be amended to require the relevant property to have been a 'tenement' within the meaning of the Act during the whole of the period of the three years ending at the relevant time. The Commission identifies two instances where the property might not have been a 'tenement' for the whole of the three year period. A landlord may have made a letting for temporary convenience stating the nature of the temporary convenience and the temporary convenience may have ceased to exist; or a tenancy dependent on the continuance in any office, employment or appointment of the lessee might no longer be so if the office ceased to exist or other arrangements were made which resulted in the waiver of this condition.

*Fifthly*, the Commission recommends that s. 17 (2) of the Landlord and Tenant (Amendment) Act 1980 be amended to entitle a landlord to refuse to grant a new tenancy, subject to compensation for the tenant where the landlord requires the premises for occupation as a residence for himself or any person *bona fide* residing or to reside with him or for occupation as a residence for a person in the wholetime employment of the landlord. This would bring the provisions into line with those in the Housing (Private Rented Dwellings) Act 1982.

*Finally*, the Commission recommends that s. 15 of the Landlord and Tenant Act 1984 be amended to ensure that rent reviews should operate on a five yearly pattern, commencing on the date of the commencement of the lease. This proposed change is designed to remove the incentive to lessors and lessees to resort to delaying tactics designed to exploit a rising market or to obtain a deferment of the time for the first review.

## JUDGMENT MORTGAGES

In the 1989 Review, 310-12, we analysed Costello J's decision in *Irish Bank of Commerce Limited v O'Hara*, High Court, 10 May 1989. It will be recalled that the case concerned a substantial judgment mortgage registered against the defendant's house in Killiney, County Dublin. The affidavit had described the property by its name and the road on which it was situate, adding 'Killiney, Borough of Dun Laoghaire, Barony of Rathdown and County Dublin'. It thus gave information (as to name and road) more extensive than was required by s. 6 of the Judgment Mortgage (Ireland) Act 1850, but failed to mention the parish in which the property was situate, as that section required.

Costello J held that this non-compliance was not fatal since the particulars given achieved the purpose for which the statute was designed, which was to identify with precision the location of the lands affected by the judgment mortgage and to enable persons subsequently dealing with the judgment debtor and his or her lands to be warned of its existence. The Supreme Court affirmed on 7 April 1992. It interpreted s. 6 as requiring the inclusion of the name of the parish only in cases where the property is situate in a 'town or county of a city' or a 'town'. This was based on what Finlay CJ called 'the true grammatical interpretation' of the provision as well as precedent: *Credit Finance Co. Ltd v Grace*, Supreme Court, 9 June 1972; *Dardis & Dunns Seeds Ltd v Hickey*, High Court, 11 July 1974, extracted in J. Wylie's *Casebook on Irish Land Law*, p. 479.

The question thus was whether the premises were in a town. In *Dardis & Dunns Seeds* Kenny J, noting the absence of a definition of the word 'town' in the 1850 Act, had commented that therefore its meaning had to be ascertained 'by reference to the law as it was and the English language as used in 1850'. He quoted from Coke's definition of 'town' as a collection of houses which 'hath or in time past hath had, a church and celebration of divine service, sacraments and burials': Litt. 115b. He went on to endorse Palles CB's statement in *Archer v The Earl of Caledon* [1894] 2 IR 473, at 476, at that '[t]own', . . . like every other word in the English language, will bear a different signification according to the object with which it finds a place in any particular piece of legislation.'

In *O'Hara's* case, the Supreme Court gave no clear interpretation of how 'town' should be understood for the purposes of s. 6 of the 1850 Act. Instead it proceeded on the questionable basis that, to establish non-compliance with the section, the applicant would have to establish that 'by reason of the reference to the Borough of Dun Laoghaire contained in the description of the premises set out in the judgment mortgage affidavit the court must conclude that it was a town for the purposes of the Act of 1850'. This approach seems mistaken. It is hard enough that the onus should be on a defendant to establish non-compliance with the requirements of the section. To require him further to establish by reference only to what was in the plaintiff's affidavit that the court must conclude that 'the Borough of Dun Laoghaire' was a town for the purposes of the 1850 Act would not appear to be right. If in fact the Borough of Dun Laoghaire (however described) was a town for the purposes of the Act, then the defendant would have established non-compliance with s. 6. It is a entirely separate question whether the plaintiff's affidavit was defective in its description of the town (if such, indeed, it was).

The Chief Justice, whilst offering no definition of 'town' for the purposes of the 1850 Act, endorsed Kenny J's view, in *Dardis & Dunns Seeds Ltd v*

*Hickey*, that its meaning must be ascertained by reference to the law as it was and the English language as it was used in 1850. Whilst so doing, he did not exclude the possibility that by subsequent statutory enactment the meaning of the word 'town', as contained in the 1850 Act, could be made applicable to a unit or category of area or locality not envisaged or dealt with in the law existing at the time of the enactment of the 1850 legislation. He found no such extension in the provisions of the Local Government (Dublin) Act 1930, which established the Borough of Dun Laoghaire and concluded that 'therefore' there had been no evidence before the High Court that the premises were situate in a town of a city or in a town.

With respect, this analysis is not entirely convincing. The crucial question — of the meaning of a town in 1850 — is left unresolved, unless one has regard to Coke's definition, which Kenny J quoted with apparent approval in *Dardis & Dunns Seeds Ltd v Hickey*. The idea that the Borough of Dun Laoghaire is not (or does not incorporate) a town is palpably unconvincing. Courts have taken judicial notice of facts a good deal less obvious than this.

Judges are well aware that Dun Laoghaire was for a period designated 'Kingstown', following the embarcation of King George IV on 3 September 1821. This title might put even the most sceptical court on notice of the character of Dun Laoghaire close to two centuries ago. With respect to Mr Christopher Doyle, whose excellent analysis (11 Ir L Times (ns) 52 (1993)) should be noted, the question is not whether there was evidence that Dun Laoghaire 'was such a place [viz. a town] in 1850' (cf. id., at 54), but rather, whether in accordance with the meaning of 'town' envisaged by the 1850 legislation, Dun Laoghaire was a town when the affidavit was sworn.

Having held against the defendant on the narrow question of whether the premises were situate in a town, Finlay CJ went on to address the far broader ground on which Costello J had decided the case in favour of the plaintiff. He was satisfied that Costello J's approach was correct. This was 'certainly a case in which it would be quite unreal and, therefore, unjust' to declare the entry of the judgment mortgage invalid by reason of the absence of the name of the parish, having regard to all the other identifications that were so clearly set out in the judgment mortgage affidavit. The Chief Justice acknowledged that 'greater care may have to be taken in any individual case to ensure that no possibility of mistake can occur by reason of any non-compliance with the strict terms of the section in identifying the lands than might be relevant in questions as to the identification of the judgment debtor. . . .'

In *S. O'Connor & Son Ltd v Whelan* [1993] 1 IR 560, the question arose as to whether an affidavit in support of proceedings to have a judgment mortgage declared well charged should be rendered invalid for failure to comply with the general requirement, in O.40, r.4 of the Rules of the Superior Court 1986, that affidavits 'shall be confined to such facts as the witness is able of his own knowledge to prove, and shall state his means of knowledge thereof. . .' In this case, the secretary of the plaintiff company, in an affidavit which complied in every respect with the requirements of s. 3 of the Judgment Mortgage (Ireland) Act 1858, deposed that the defendant was beneficially entitled to the lands and premises against which the judgment mortgage was being registered, but did not set our her means of knowledge. The defendant filed no replying affidavit and did not dispute the facts.

Denham J held that the failure to comply with O.40, r.4 did not invalidate the process. She noted that the affidavit had complied with long practice and, indeed, the printed forms. The fact of long practice was not in itself a reason to uphold the affidavit but was a factor to consider. The affidavit to register the judgment mortgage was a 'special type of affidavit for a special purpose'. The 1858 Act specifically required certain persons to sign the affidavit. It was 'inferred that the company secretary will know the company business of his own knowledge.'

Denham J stated:

> This is a special technical affidavit which does not require the assessment as to means of the knowledge because the statute sets out who is entitled to swear such an affidavit in that situation, and it also sets out what should appear in the affidavit. The Act of 1858 did not require a means of knowledge clause. In the circumstances where the statute has set out who may swear the affidavit a means of knowledge clause is tautologous. In fact, if one looks at the appendices to the Rules of the Superior Courts and sees there the draft affidavits for specific purposes, it is clear that in certain other technical affidavits the means of knowledge assessment is omitted.

The Supreme Court in an *ex tempore* judgment on 20 December 1991, dismissed the defendant's appeal.

## LANDLORD AND TENANT

**Requirement to insure premises** In *Sepes Establishment v KSK Enterprises Ltd* [1993] ILRM 46, O'Hanlon J was called on to determine the extent to which an express term in a lease providing that the lessor was to insure the premises against loss or damage by fire 'in some insurance office or with underwriters of repute' had to be read as being subject to an implied term that the lessor owed a duty to the lessee not to insure on a basis that imposed an unnecessarily heavy burden on the lessee. English decisions were not easy to reconcile. In *Bandar Property Holdings Ltd v J.S. Darwen (Successors) Ltd* [1968] 2 All ER 305, Roskill J had rejected the argument that the business efficacy of the contract required the ascription of such an implied term. Forbes J had taken an approach similar to Roskill J's, in *Gleniffer Finance Corporation Ltd. v Barmar Wood and Products Ltd*, 37 P & C R 208 (1979), differing from the general philosophy articulated by Cairns LJ in *Finchbourne Ltd v Rodrigues* [1976] 3 All ER 581, to the effect that the parties could not have intended that the landlord should have an unfettered discretion to adopt the highest conceivable standard and to charge the tenant for it.

O'Hanlon J tilted towards Roskill J's approach. He considered that:

> if a lessee can establish that a lessor has clearly gone wrong in an important respect when effecting the insurance cover for which the lessee is ultimately to be liable, some scope must be allowed for the lessee to dispute the amount with which he is being charged.
>
> However, if the lessor is clearly acting in a *bona fide* manner (as was the plaintiff in the present case, in my opinion), and is guided by persons who are presumed to be experts in the field whether as insurance brokers, valuers, engineers, architects, quantity surveyors and the like, . . . a lessee challenging the figures put forward undertakes a very heavy onus of proof in seeking to establish that the figures charged are not fair or reasonable. I would respectfully agree with the decision of Roskill J in the *Bandar Property* case that it is not sufficient to show that a quotation for a somewhat smaller figure can be obtained from another source.

How much leeway does this give a lessor? Let us take a case where a lessor, aware of the fact that a particular reputable insurance company is very much on the expensive side, consciously decides to insure the premises with this company. Is that decision permissible under O'Hanlon J's criterion? It seems so. It would be hard to stigmatise such a choice as 'clearly go[ing] wrong in an important respect'. *Bona fides* is scarcely incompatible with the desire to savour the upper end of the reputable insurance market.

O'Hanlon J went on to hold that a lessor should not be put to the exceptionally high cost of having a bill of quantities prepared for the purpose of estimating the cost of reinstatement for insurance purposes. He was, moreover, satisfied that the Measuring Practice Guidance Notes adopted by the Auctioneers' Associations and the Society of Chartered Surveyors provided 'a useful and reasonable guide' for estimation of building costs and for the other purposes mentioned in the handbook.

**The meaning of 'buildings' in the 1980 Act** In *Dursley v Watters* [1993] 1 IR 224, Morris J laid down a number of important guidelines in the interpretation of key concepts in the Landlord and Tenant (Amendment) Act

1980. S. 16 of that Act provides that:

> . . . where this Part applies to a tenement, the tenant shall be entitled to a new tenancy in the tenement beginning on the termination of his previous tenancy. . . .'

S. 5(1) provides (in part) that, in the Act, 'tenement' means:

> (a) premises complying with the following conditions:
>
> (i) they consist either of land covered wholly or partly by buildings or by a defined portion of a building;
> (ii) if they consist of land covered in part only by buildings, the portion of land not so covered is subsidiary and ancillary to the buildings. . . .

In *Dursley v Watters*, the applicant sought a declaration that he was entitled to a new tenancy under the Act, in respect of a car wash premises. These comprised part of the forecourt and surrounding area of the respondent's garage premises. The cars were washed manually with a pressure jet, rather than the more usual automatic rotating machinery. The applicant had been carrying on the business for four years at a weekly rent of £60.

Morris J first addressed the question whether the small shed, holding tank (to catch water draining away from the cars), cage (to protect the washing equipment when not in use) and small lock-up hut (measuring seven feet by five feet) which was used as an office constituted 'buildings'. Following O'Hanlon J's lead in *Terry v Stokes* [1993] 1 IR 204, he pointed to the fact that the 1980 legislation (in contrast to earlier Acts) had used the term 'buildings' rather than 'permanent buildings'. Accordingly it was of no relevance that the hut was capable of being removed and placed elsewhere, and had been delivered on site in a semi-prefabricated state. Nor was its size significant; in *O'Reilly v Kevans* (1935) 69 ILTR 1, a one storey building roofed in corrugated iron in a dilapidated condition had been held to constitute a building and Morris J could see no distinction which could be validly drawn between the two types of structure. He therefore held that the hut was a 'building'.

Following Maguire CJ's analysis in *Mason v Leavy* [1952] IR 40, at 45, where oil storage tanks sunk in the ground were held to be buildings in spite of the fact that they were subterranean and lacked a roof, Morris J held that the holding tank was also a 'building'. He was likewise satisfied that the small shed and cage constituted buildings.

The next question was whether the remaining land was subsidiary and ancillary to the buildings. Morris J considered that the lock-up hut, used as an office, was 'at most a convenience to the carrying on of the business'. None of the actual work associated with the cleaning of the cars was carried out in it. The office contributed little or nothing to the overall business carried on at the premises. The business was of a kind that could have been carried on without the presence of the hut. Morris J thought it significant that, when the applicant advertised, he used the telephone number of the respondent's premises, and did not suggest that customers should contact him at the office on site. No advertising placard had been attached to the hut and none of the work was done in it. The applicant's records were left at his home.

Morris J distinguished *Terry v Stokes* on the basis that, in that case, radiators were actually repaired in sheds before being returned to their vehicles. Moreover, the equipment used for repairing them was kept in the sheds.

Morris J came to the same conclusion in relation to the holding tank. While undoubtedly it was more convenient to carry on the work with the holding tank, the work was in no way dependent upon it. The evidence showed that the applicant had continued to work as usual after the respondent had removed the tank to a point on the forecourt where it could no longer be used in connection with the washing process. The only inconvenience the applicant had suffered was that the water had drained away out onto a shore or gutter adjacent to the road. Morris J was also of the view that the small shed and cage were merely a convenience for the storage of the equipment when not in use and that it could not be said that the balance of the land was subsidiary or ancillary to them. Accordingly the applicant was not entitled to a new tenancy.

**Forfeiture procedure** In *Bank of Ireland v Lady Lisa Ireland Ltd* [1993] ILRM 235, O'Hanlon J held that, where a landlord proposes to forfeit a lease in reliance on a proviso in the lease giving a right of re-entry for non-payment of rent or breach of any other covenant in the lease, the 're-entry' involved may be effected in only one of two ways — either by physical re-entry or by the issue and service of proceedings for recovery of possession of the premises. Thus a notice of re-entry and forfeiture for non-payment of rent served by the plaintiff on the defendant was not of itself sufficient to constitute re-entry; it would have been necessary for the plaintiff to have set in motion a valid claim for an order of possession. This the plaintiff had not in fact accomplished since it had brought the proceedings by way of summary summons under O.2, r.1 of the Rules of the Superior Courts 1986. This Rule had scarcely changed in form, and not at all in substance, since the 1905 Rules. *Keating v Mulcahy* [1926] IR 214 and *Meares v Connolly* [1930] IR 333 were clear authorities to the effect that proceeding by summary summons was not permissible in claims for possession based on a notice to quit. In the latter decision, O'Byrne J had specifically held that the court had no power to allow the plaintiff to amend. Accordingly O'Hanlon J dismissed the plaintiff's claim.

**Law reform proposals** We discuss above, 408-10, the Law Reform Commission's six recommendations for amendments to the landlord and tenant code.

## SUCCESSION

**Adopted children** One of the more interesting aspects of the law of succession is the battlefield between the freedom of testators to have their say and the public policy of society to thwart that ambition, in the interests of the testators' families. That contest is inevitably complicated by the passage of time: the norms of yesteryear, reflected in the decisions of testators of that generation, give way to new attitudes. To what extent should courts today seek to disturb the intentions of those whose world was a different place? Or, from another standpoint, to what extent should the discredited values of the past be permitted to triumph over contemporary norms of justice in inheritance?

These battles are often fought in the arena of interpretation of the testator's intention. Rules of construction are of course based in part on the desire to give effect to the actual intentions of testators, but not always so. Notions of public policy may at times underlie these professedly 'testator-centred' presumptions.

In *In re Stamp, Deceased; Stamp v Redmond* [1993] ILRM 383, the testator, aged eighty-four years, made a will in 1954 in which he left his property on trust for his son Patrick, 'provided always that if he shall die without leaving issue then upon trust for my grandson . . .' who was the son of Patrick's brother. The testator died a few months later. Patrick married in 1956. He and his wife had no children of their own but they adopted two daughters, in 1965 and 1967.

Lardner J was called on to interpret whether the words 'die without issue' comprehended the two adopted daughters. The only relevant statutory provision is the Adoption Act 1952, s. 26(2), which is in the following terms:

> In any disposition of real or personal property made, whether by instrument *inter vivos* or by will (including codicil), after the date of an adoption order —
>
> a. any reference (whether express or implied) to the child or children

> of the adopter shall, unless the contrary intention appears, be construed as, or as including, a reference to the adopted person;
> b. any reference (whether express or implied) to the child or children of the adopted person's natural parents or either of them shall, unless the contrary intention appears, be construed as not being, or as not including, a reference to the adopted person.

S. 26(2) is less than helpful to the adopted daughters since it clearly relates to the property rights of adopted persons where a will is made *after* the adoption order has been made. The limited scope of s. 26(2) suggests that the Oireachtas did not intend to change the common law rules of construction so far as wills made before an adoption was concerned.

Lardner J did not approach the case on the basis that the section resolved the issue one way or the other. Instead he considered that, '[i]f the language used in the will can be read in its ordinary natural sense so as to make sense with respect to the surrounding circumstances, no rule of construction is applicable to ascertain the testator's intention'. The words in the will dispensed with the need for resorting to rules of construction. The word 'issue' was 'not so esoteric or so much a word used in some specialist field as to have no ordinary meaning in common usage.' On the contrary, its ordinary meaning was issue of a marriage or descendants; it would be so understood by persons of ordinary education. Moreover, in 1954, when the will was made, it had been well settled for many years that a bequest to 'issue' *prima facie* connoted descendants of every degree, when not restrained by context. *Berry v Fishes* [1903] IR 484 so held, as did the later decision of the Supreme Court in *O'B. v. S.* [1984] IR 316.

Lardner J went on to note that it appeared from the attestation clause that the will had been made in a solicitor's office. This rendered it likely, in his view, that 'issue' had been used in its well settled sense. From a consideration of all its terms and of the context, Lardner J concluded that this was the sense in which the testator had used the words and that his intention was to be found expressed in these words. S. 26 of the 1952 Act did not require him to reach a different conclusion. Moreover, counsel was agreed that the Status of Children Act 1987 did not affect the case. Lardner J thought it 'perfectly clear, even now, that adopted children are not regarded as children of a marriage. . . .'

Lardner J's reference to the fact that the will had been made in a solicitor's office gives pause for thought. A court should be cautious about attributing to a testator an intent in relation to a legal term of art on the basis that the testator received professional legal advice, unless there is reason to believe that the lawyer explained the nuances of the term to the testator and acted on the instructions of the testator in the light of that explanation. In the present case there was no evidence of any such interchange. The decision of McWilliam J in *Revenue Commissioners v Shaw* [1982] ILRM 433 is helpful in this context. See further W. Binchy, *Irish Conflicts of Law* (1988) 70-1.

**Grant of administration** The problem of wrongdoers benefiting by inheritance from their victims has an ancient pedigree. S. 120 of the Succession Act 1965 deals with this issue by excluding certain wrongdoers, such as those guilty of murder or manslaughter of their victims. See James Brady, *Succession Law in Ireland* (1989), s. 7.10.

A somewhat less stark issue of policy concerns the grant of administration. In *In the goods of Glynn: Ireland and the Attorney General v Kelly* [1992] ILRM 582, the defendant had been convicted of the murder of the sister of a testator. She had been the life tenant of an estate, and the defendant had to undertake to maintain her if he was to derive a benefit under the will. Her death at his hands had accelerated his succession in remainder.

The defendant had been named as executor in the testator's will. An application was brought by the State under s. 27(4) of the Succession Act 1965 for the appointment of the Chief State Solicitor as executor in substitution for the defendant. S. 27(4) provides as follows:

> Where by reason of any special circumstances it appears to the High Court . . . to be necessary or expedient to do so, the court may order that administration be granted to such person as it thinks fit.

Gannon J declined to make the order but the Supreme Court reversed. S. 27(4) gave a broad judicial discretion that was in marked contrast with its predecessor, s. 78 of the Probates and Letters of Administration Act (Ireland) 1857, which was limited to a specific handful of instances, such as the residence of the executor outside the jurisdiction or the testator's failure to appoint an executor willing and competent to take probate, there being also a necessity for other special circumstances. McCarthy J (Finlay CJ and Egan J concurring) considered that it would appear 'utterly wrong' to permit the defendant, even in the most formal manner, to administer the estate. He invoked a precedent of some notoriety, *In the Estate of Crippen* [1911] P 108, in aid.

## WILLS

**Void condition** In *In re Fitzgibbon deceased: Mackessy v Fitzgibbon* [1993] 1 IR 520, the testator devised and bequeathed his farm, dwelling house, out-office and stock and goods and chattels therein and thereon to his grand nephew 'provided he lives and works on the land but if he does not then I leave my land together with my dwelling house and out-office, goods and chattels, cattle and stock to my niece . . .absolutely'. The testator then made a number of pecuniary legacies. There was no residuary clause. The executrix brought a constriction summons.

Carroll J proceeded on the basis of two principles: first, the presumption in favour of early vesting, which treats a condition as *prima facie* subsequent rather than precedent, and second, the principle that, where a vested estate is to be defeated by a condition on a contingency that is to happen subsequently, the condition must be such that the court can see from the beginning precisely and distinctly upon the happening of what event it is that the preceding estate is to determine.

Carroll J was satisfied that the condition was subsequent rather than precedent: it provided for two requirements which, if not fulfilled, would lead to a forfeiture.

As to the question whether the composite condition 'living and working' was void for uncertainty, Carroll J found the earlier decisions in the area to be of assistance. In *In re Hennessy deceased* (1963) 98 ILTR 39, Budd J held that a devise of land to a son 'if he wishes to farm it and carry on same as he thinks best' was void since it did not define with any precision the degree of personal commitment required of the son to the farming enterprise. In *Sifton v Sifton* [1938] AC 656, the House of Lords also held void for uncertainty a provision in a will that payments be made to a woman 'only so long as she shall continue to reside in Canada'. The requisite intensity and continuity of residence were entirely unclear. In *Moffatt v McClear* [1923] 1 IR 16, a bequest to the testator's brother 'provided he or any of his sons come to live at Magherahan within one year of my death' on the same ground. A similar clause was held void in *Motherway v Coghlan* (1956) 98 ILTR 134.

Carroll J concluded that, in the instant case, the condition was void for uncertainty on the same line of reasoning in these cases.

In *Fitzsimons v. Fitzsimons* [1993] ILRM 478; [1992] 2 IR 295, Keane J had to interpret a seemingly straightforward provision in a will, where the plaintiff, who had been given sixty-seven acres of Kildare farmland by his father during the father's lifetime, was devised a further 109 acres (subject to his mother's life estate), conditional on his 'being the beneficial owner for a life estate of the lands [earlier] transferred,' the will going on to provide that, 'in the event of [his] having . . . sold the said lands', certain trusts should take effect. The plaintiff wished to sell just an acre and a half of the lands he had received during his lifetime. The question raised in the case was whether, if he did so, he would lose his interest in remainder in the 109 acres.

Counsel for the plaintiff argued that the condition was void on two grounds: first, that it was a purported restraint on the alienation of the lands transferred earlier and, secondly, that it was void for uncertainty in failing to indicate whether the devise under the will would be forfeited by a sale of *part only of the lands* or by *a disposition of less than the entire beneficial interest*, such as a mortgage of all or part of the lands.

Keane J rejected both of these contentions and held that the plaintiff could succeed to the farm on his mother's death only if he held all of the sixty seven acres. There was no restraint on alienation since manifestly the condition did not prevent the plaintiff from selling all or any part of the lands; the condition thus could not be regarded as equivalent to a similar condition imposed on a gift or devise of fee simple lands. Nor was the condition void for uncertainty; on the contrary, it was precise and unambiguous in its scope. If one were to construe the clause as permitting the sale of part only of the lands, the question would immediately arise as to the extent to which any sale would be permissible under the terms of the will:

> On any view, the sale of a substantial part of the lands would be a breach of the condition. How then is one to determine the extent of a sale necessary to bring the condition into operation? The result would be to create rather than avoid uncertainty.

Whilst the testator would almost certainly have been perfectly happy with the proposal before the court, it had clearly been the testator's desire to avoid a situation where the farm went to the plaintiff when he had already disposed of the lands given to him earlier. In order to ensure that sales of the type before the court could be made by the plaintiff, it would have been necessary for the testator to create a series of elaborate and precisely defined exceptions to the straightforward condition he chose to impose. It was, in Keane J's opinion, perfectly understandable that neither the testator nor his solicitors had considered this necessary or even desirable.

**Construction** In *In re Howell, deceased; Howell v Howell* [1992] 1 IR 292, the testator's will provided as follows:

> I give, devise and bequeath my farm land in the townlands of Drumpeak and Corinshigo together with the furniture and machinery thereon to my brother Joseph. I give, devise and bequeath all my stock and any other assets I may have to my brother Richard.

Joseph predeceased the testator. The question arose as to whether the gift to Richard was a full, comprehensive residuary gift or whether the phrase 'any other assets' should be construed as meaning *any assets other than the farm, furniture, machinery and stock.*

Carroll J held that the latter construction was correct. The scheme of the will indicated that the testator had intended to divide his estate between his two brothers, with Joseph getting the farm, furniture and machinery and Richard getting the stock and any other assets. There was no indication that the testator's mind had ever been directed to the residue or what would happen if one or other brother predeceased him. The presumption of intestacy was here in conflict with the presumption in favour of equality. The latter presumption was more in accord with the intention of the testator so far as it could be gleaned from the will.

In reaching her conclusion, Carroll J found little assistance from precedents such as *In re Aitkinson; Matheson v Pollock* [1942] IR 268 and *In re Mulcair; McCarthy v Mulcair* [1960] IR 321. She echoed the *dictum* of Werner J in *Matter of King* (1910) 200 NY 189, at 192 that 'no will has a twin brother'. As Lowry LCJ pointed out in *Heron v Ulster Bank Ltd* [1974] NI 44, the opinions of other courts on similar words are rarely binding precedents but more often examples, sometimes of the highest authority, of how judicial minds nurtured in the same discipline have interpreted words in similar contexts.

Earlier in this chapter, above, 417-9, we discuss *In re Stamp, Deceased; Stamp v Redmond* [1993] ILRM 383, which raised an important issue of construction in relation to adopted children.

**Alteration** The folly of home-made wills is well demonstrated by the facts and outcome of *In re the Estate of Myles Deceased* [1993] ILRM 34. The testatrix of a hand-written will had engaged in a series of unwise changes to its original draft. She had crossed out a number of its paragraphs and added writings in the margins. There was some evidence that the will had been properly witnessed but no clear evidence that the several changes were witnessed. An application for liberty to apply for a grant of probate of the will came before Lardner J.

Lardner J held that the deletions, if made after the execution of the will, had not effected a revocation of any part of it as they had not been executed in the manner required by s 86 of the Succession Act 1965. He was quite uncertain as to when these deletions and the writing in the margins had occurred. There was a rebuttable presumption that an obliteration or interlineation was made after execution (*In the Goods of Adamson* (1875) LR 3 PD 253). This presumption might be rebutted by reasonable evidence, including evidence afforded by the will itself (*In re Hindmarch* (1866) LR 1 PD 307). Lardner J referred to *In the Goods of Benn* [1938] IR 313, where Hanna J had decided that the court might rely on its own judgment on the internal evidence as presented by the fabric of the will and also upon the evidence of a handwriting expert as to the appearance of the writing in the document and whether the interlineation had been inserted before or after execution.

In the instant case there was a dearth of such testimonial support for the court. Moreover, no evidence had been adduced relating to external events which might have assisted the court in determining the time or times at which the changes were made. One of the attesting witnesses had given evidence that the deceased had crossed out part or parts of the will before signing it but she could not recall which part or parts had been so crossed out.

In a crucial passage, Lardner J said:

> It seems to me that I cannot disregard this evidence. If it is accepted it tends to rebut the presumption. But one is left in an altogether uncertain mind as to what part or parts were crossed out before execution and what was the extent of the will at the time of execution. The applicant by applying for probate takes on the burden of proving on the balance of probabilities what constituted the will at the time of execution. I do not find that burden has been discharged by the evidence which has been adduced.

In the circumstances Lardner J declined to give liberty to apply for a grant of probate.

An interesting evidential issue arises here of competing burdens. No doubt the applicant had the burden of proving what constituted the will at the time of execution, but the rebuttable presumption that an alteration was made after execution must be given effect by a court in assessing the question of what constituted the will. There was admittedly much uncertainty in the present case as to the time or times at which changes were made to the will. In such circumstances the court might have simply decided the case on the basis of the rebuttable presumption which would appear not to have been rebutted by the evidence.

One could imagine a case where an applicant culpably failed to adduce evidence which would have had the effect of rebutting a presumption. In such circumstances the court would rightly dismiss the application and would in no sense be a prisoner to the presumption. But that was not the case here. Lardner J was understandably exercised by the poor quality of the evidence but there is no suggestion that he had any doubts as to the *bona fides* of the application.

Cases such as this reveal how presumptions of this type can operate ineffectively when they collide. The presumption that alterations were made after execution no doubt is designed in part to reflect the likelihood that a change of mind occurred some time during the period between the execution of a will and the testator's death, which can be several years in duration in many cases, rather than in the short period during which the will was being drawn up. But there is also a policy underlying the presumption, which is to discourage fraud. If the presumption were the other way, there would be a huge incentive to commit fraud. Even if there were no presumption one way or the other, it might be thought that this would still facilitate some degree of fraud.

The effects of a rebuttable presumption is to *require* the court to make a particular finding unless the evidence the other way is preponderant. In a case such as Lardner J had to decide, this finding would seem a somewhat artificial one, serving the needs of the underlying general anti-fraud policy rather than in any sense responding to the particular factual circumstances.

# Law Reform

This chapter appears below, 633.

# Licensing

## INTOXICATING LIQUOR

**Amalgamation** In *Application of Oshawa Ltd* [1992] 2 IR 425, the Supreme Court held that it was possible to amalgamate two adjoining premises, both licensed for the sale of intoxicating liquor, and retain one of the licences for the amalgamated premises while extinguishing the other.

As already indicated, the applicant had purchased two adjoining premises, both of which held licences for the sale of intoxicating liquor. The two premises were amalgamated into one premises, and the applicant sought a licence for the amalgamated premises under s. 6 of the Licensing (Ireland) Act 1902, as amended by s. 24 of the Intoxicating Liquor Act 1960. In the Circuit Court on 1 December 1987, the application was granted (over objections from local vintners) and the Circuit Court judge made an order providing for the extinguishment of one of the two licences attaching to the formerly separated premises, such extinguishment taking effect if the Revenue Commissioners granted the licence on application by the applicant. At the same time the Circuit Court judge also made an order granting another applicant (Tennis Village Cork Ltd) a licence; that order being possible on the basis that the licence attaching to the second premises owned by the applicant which had been amalgamated into the new premises would also be extinguished if Tennis Village Cork Ltd sought a licence from the Revenue Commissioners. Tennis Village Cork Ltd sought such a licence and this was granted by the Revenue Commissioners in December 1987. The Revenue Commissioners granted the applicant its licence for the amalgamated premises on 16 February 1988.

On a case stated from the Circuit Court, the objectors argued that a licence could only be granted under s. 6 of the 1902 Act, as amended by s. 24 of the 1960 Act, in respect of amalgamated premises where one of the premises had been unlicenced, but not in the case of two adjoining licenced premises. However, the Supreme Court (McCarthy, O'Flaherty and Egan JJ) did not actually reach this argument because of the way it analysed the status and timing of the Revenue Commissioner's grant of a licence.

The Court noted that the application in the Circuit Court under s. 6 of the 1902 Act, as amended, did not have the effect of creating or of extinguishing any licence, since this was a matter for the Revenue Commissioners. In the instant case, since the Revenue Commissioners had granted a licence to

Tennis Village Cork Ltd in December 1987, the Court held that the licence in the former adjoining premises had been extinguished by the time the applicant sought the licence from the Revenue Commissioners for the amalagamated premises, and therefore the former adjoining premises was unlicensed within s. 6 of the 1902 Act at that stage. Thus, it was not therefore necessary for the Court to determine the case on the argument put forward by the objectors, and the order of the Circuit Court was affirmed for the reasons given.

**Retrospectove renewal prohibited** In *Connolly v Collector of Customs and Excise*, High Court, 5 October 1992, the applicant unsuccessfully sought an order of mandamus directing the respondent to grant him a retrospective renewal of his intoxicating liquor licence. The applicant had purchased a licensed premises in 1981, and had obtained renewals of his licence during the years 1982 to 1985. He had also paid the respondent the duty payable on the licence for those years.

The applicant did not seek a renewal of his licence from the District Court for the years 1986-87 or 1987-88, nor did he reply to requests for payment to the respondent of the applicable duty for those years. When the Courts (No. 2) Act 1986 came into effect (see the 1988 Review, 291), the applicant was sent renewal and pay notices by the respondent for the years 1988-89, 1989-90 and 1990-91, but he did not reply to these notices either. During these years, the applicant continued to carry on the business of a publican.

In September 1991, the applicant applied to the Circuit Court for a new licence for his premises under s. 2 of the Licensing (Ireland) Act 1902, as amended by s. 23 of the Intoxicating Liquor Act 1960. The applicant could only obtain such a licence if he could show that the premises had been licensed at some time within the immediately preceding five years. Accordingly, he sent to the respondent the duty payable in respect of the premises' licence for the year ending 30 September 1986, and he received a receipt for this sum stating it was 'in respect of arrears, publican's licence duty 1985/86'. However, the respondent subsequently refused to issue a licence for the premises for the year ending September 1986, on the ground that such a publican's licence could not be issued retrospectively. It was in those circumstances that the applicant applied for mandamus requiring the respondent to issue the licence in question, so that he could proceed with his application to the Circuit Court.

As already indicated, this was unsuccessful, Blayney J accepting the respondent's submissions. The applicant had argued that it was irrelevent when the duty was paid, and pointed to an order made by Barrington J in an *ex tempore* judgment in *The State (Brookfield Securities Ltd) v Collector of Customs and Excise*, High Court, 22 June 1981. However, it was noted that the order in that case concerned a premises in respect of which duty had been paid during the currency of the licensing year. Blayney J examined the powers of the respondent to renew licences under s. 1 of the Licensing (Ireland) Act 1833 and s. 11 of the Spirits (Ireland) Act 1854, both of which provided that such renewal may be granted 'to the same persons . . . as shall have been licensed in the year last immediately preceding'. Blayney J construed this as referring to the date of the application to the respondent for the renewal of the licence, rather than, as the applicant had argued, the year in respect of which the application for the licence was being made. He felt that the clear intention of the legislation was that the licence renewal be given to the person who was the licensee during the previous year, that is during the year prior to the date of the application for renewal. On that basis, he concluded that the applicant was not entitled to a licence for 1985-86.

It is notable also that Blayney J pointed out that, as mandamus was a discretionary remedy, there were grounds for refusing the applicant the remedy 'because of the very extraordinary conduct of the applicant in totally ignoring the licensing laws for almost six years before bringing this application.' However, because of the other reasons for refusing the order, Blayney J did not give a final view on this matter.

**Theatre licence** In *In re Tivoli Cinema Ltd* [1992] ILRM 522; [1992] 1 IR 413 involved a number of issues concerning the suitablilty of a theatre premises for the granting of a full intoxicating liquor licence.

The applicant company had refurbished a cinema premises for use as a theatre, known as the the Tivoli Theatre, in Francis St, Dublin. The planning permission for use as a theatre authorised the use of the mezzanine floor for the sale of wine only. The mezzanine floor comprised less than one tenth of the total floor space of the theatre premises. A wine licence was obtained for this purpose, but the owner of the Tivoli wished to obtain a licence to sell all forms of intoxicating liquor. One William Lowe was the owner of licensed premises with a full seven day licence for the sale of intoxicating liquor, and this premises was situated 472 yards as the crow flies and 510 yards by road from the Tivoli. Lowe's premises was compulsorily acquired by Dublin Corporation in December 1989. The liquor licence had been renewed in September 1989, although Lowe had ceased trading in June 1989. Lowe entered into a lease of the premises with Dublin Corporation in January 1990, and this expired in June 1990. During this period, he did not trade in the premises. The seven day licence expired in June 1990 on the expiry of the lease. In October 1990, the company agreed with Lowe to purchase any interest Lowe had in the seven day licence. The company then applied to the Circuit Court to acquire a seven day licence for the ground floor, the mezzanine floor and the first floor theatre of the Tivoli premises under s. 3

of the Licensing (Ireland) Act 1902, as amended by s. 23 of the Intoxicating Liquor Act 1943. This provides that a licence may be granted 'for suitable premises in the immediate vicinity' of a premises in respect of which, by reason of the expiration of a lease, an intoxicating liquor licence has been extinguished. A licence was granted under s. 3 of the 1902 Act, as amended, in November 1990.

Various local objectors appealed this decision to the High Court, relying on a large number of grounds. Lynch J allowed their appeal on two of these grounds, thus resulting in the refusal of the licence to the company.

Lynch J considered that the premises were not suitable within s. 3 of the 1902 Act for a full seven day licence. He accepted that it was suitable for a theatre licence limited to the mezzanine floor area under the 1927 Act, but noted that this was not what had been applied for. He also took into account that the mezzanine comprised less than one tenth of the total floor space available in the premises, and concluded that the premises in its entirety was not suitable for a full licence. He accepted that the current owner of the Tivoli was not interested in using the premises as a public house, but Lynch J took account of its possible use in the future in the hands of another owner. A second ground on which Lynch J allowed the appeal from the Circuit Court was that he considered the number of existing premises in the surrounding area, 14 within a radius of 250 yards, to be sufficient for the ordinary licensed trade in the area.

It may be of interest to note here the other grounds put forward but which were rejected by Lynch J.

He rejected the argument that, merely because the grant of a seven day licence would apparently conflict with the planning permission limiting the sale of wine to the mezzanine area, this warranted the refusal of the licence. He noted that the planning and liquor licensing codes were separate codes in this respect, although he did conclude that, if a licence was granted in conflict with a planning permission this could be restrained by injunctive relief under the planning code (as to which see the Local Government chapter, below). He considered that this might then become a factor in determining whether to renew a licence if the holder was to continue such wrongful use. The unsatisfactory overlap between the planning and licensing codes which such considerations throw up was expressly adverted to by Johnson J in *Application of Chariot Inns Ltd*, High Court, 12 April 1991 (see the 1991 Review, 297).

Lynch J also rejected the argument that the Tivoli was not in the 'immediate vicinity' of the Lowe premises within the meaning of s. 3 of the 1902 Act, given the physical proximity of the two and also that they were situated in the same civil and Roman Catholic parishes as well as the same historic liberty of St Sepulchre. He did not consider that the intermediate presence of a substantial traffic artery affected this matter. Lynch J had also the benefit of reference to numerous decisions on this oft-litigated issue, though he did not specifically cite them in his judgment. Examples were the judgments of O'Hanlon J in *In re McGrath*, High Court, 4 August 1987 and *In re Charton Investments Ltd*, High Court, 4 August 1987 (see the 1987 Review, 240).

Lynch J also rejected the objectors' argument that the Lowe licence had not been extinguished or surrendered by reason of its due expiration within the meaning of s. of the 1902 Act. Lynch J held that, although Lowe had not traded in the premises since June 1989 and that the licence expired in June 1990, this did not bring him outside the terms of s. 3 of the 1902 Act. He stated that in this respect, Lowe was in a stronger position than the licensee in *In re Irish Cinemas Ltd* (1967) 106 ILTR 17, in which s. 3 was held to apply also.

Finally, it may be noted that Lynch J had raised an issue as to whether the case was governed by the terms of an Act entitled An Act for Regulating the Stage in the City and County of Dublin 1786. As adapted under the Adaptation of Enactments Act 1931 and the Constitution (Consequential Provisions) Act 1937, this Act appeared to limit the operation of theatres to grantees of letters of patents from the Governor General of the Irish Free State, or the Government of Ireland. Lynch J had also raised the point as to whether the 1786 Act had survived the enactment of the Constitution. Having heard arguments from counsel for the Attorney General, which included a suggestion that on appeal from the Circuit Court the High Court did not have full jurisdiction in constitutional matters, Lynch J declined to deal in any way with this aspect of the case. This was essentially on the ground that, as he had dealt with the case under the licensing code, it would constitute a moot to discuss this other issue. He relied on the decision of the Supreme Court in *McDaid v Sheehy* [1991] ILRM 250; [1991] 1 IR 1 (see the 1990 Review, 464-5) in this regard. No doubt, this seems a sensible approach given the complexities of the licensing issues raised in the case, but it remains an intriguing possibility that, at least in Dublin, the 1786 Act may in some future litigation raise its head in connection with the regulation of theatres.

# Limitation of Actions

## PERSONAL INJURY

**Constitutional aspects** In *Tuohy v Courtney*, High Court, 3 September 1992 Lynch J addressed the important question of whether the statutory code of limitation of actions is unconstitutional in prescribing an unmodifiable six-year cut-off period in actions in tort, other than personal injuries and in contract. In 1991, legislative reform in the wake of Law Reform Commission recommendations introduced a 'discoverability' test for personal injuries litigation, whereby time does not start to run against a plaintiff until he or she could reasonably have known of the injury, the fact that it constituted a tort and the identity of the defendant: see the 1991 Review 299-302. In *Morgan v Park Developments Ltd* [1983] ILRM 156, Carroll J had taken the view that the Constitution required that a plaintiff in an action for property damage should not be deprived of a right of action before he or she could reasonably have been aware of his or her entitlement to sue. The Supreme Court in *Hegarty v O'Loughran* [1990]1 IR 148, though not called on to address the constitutional issue in relation to personal injuries litigation, was clearly unsympathetic to Carroll J's approach: see the 1990 Review, 389-94.

The plaintiff in *Tuohy v Courtney* purchased a leasehold interest in a house in 1978. He learned in 1983 that the lease contained certain obligations, to insure, repair and paint, which had not previously been brought to his attention by his solicitor. He was thus, in Lynch J's view, in a position analogous to that of a plaintiff who had suffered personal injury but was not aware that the injury was significant. The clock does not begin to run against such a plaintiff until he learns that the injury in question was significant: s. 2(1)(b) of the 1991 Act. In 1985, the plaintiff discovered that the leasehold interest, which he had reasonably believed to be the virtual equivalent of a freehold estate, was in fact of very much less value. By this time, more than six years had elapsed since the 1978 purchase.

Lynch J rejected the plaintiff's constitutional challenge to the unmodified six-year limitations period. He stressed the democratic and parliamentary values underlying Articles 6 and 15.2 of the Constitution, which led him to conclude that the 1957 legislation 'therefore enjoys a *strong* presumption of constitutionality and the onus is on the plaintiff to prove *in a compelling manner* that the impugned provisions of the Act are unconstitutional. . . .' (emphasis added). This articulation of the onus of proof is unusual: earlier decisions have not expressed the presumption of constitutionality so strongly even in cases dealing with areas where a broad parliamentary discretion is more clearly permissible under Articles 6 and 15.2. We have argued that limitation of actions is an area where legislative calibration of the balance of justice should not be too easily disturbed by the courts. The Supreme Court's willingness to invoke the *O'Domhnaill v Merrick* principle has compromised legislative choice unduly in our view: see the 1991 Review, 302.

Lynch J went on to observe that it had never been suggested that the time-limiting of causes of actions was *in itself* contrary to the Constitution:

> It is in the interests of society that there should be some limitation on the bringing of actions. The old Latin maxim, *interest rei publicae ut sit finis litium* remains as true today as when first formulated.

There was no doubt that s. 11 of the 1957 Act could operate in a harsh manner in circumstances such as arose in the instant case; but that in itself could not be conclusive. Lynch J echoed Murnaghan J's endorsement, in *Moynihan v Greensmyth* [1977] IR 55, at 64, of the old adage that hard cases make bad law.

Lynch J quoted a passage from Finlay CJ's judgment in *Hegarty v O'Loughran* [1990] 1 IR, at 156, part of which is the following:

> In legislation creating a time limit for the commencement of actions, the time provided for any particular type of action; the absolute or qualified nature of the limits; whether the court is vested with a discretion in certain cases in the interests of justice; and the special circumstances, if any, in which exceptions from the general time limit are provided are with others all matters in the formulation of which the legislature must seek to balance between on the one hand, the desirability of enabling persons with causes of action to litigate them and on the other hand, the desirability of finality and certainty in the potential liability which citizens may incur into the future.

It is hard to read these words as indicating any great support for a time limit which does not permit extension, by way of judicial discretion or by way of absolute entitlement, in cases where the plaintiff could not reasonably have known of his or her right of action. The Chief Justice's observations have, however, a certain delphic quality which makes it difficult to take a confident view on the matter.

Lynch J interpreted s. 3(2) of the 1991 Act as an express re-enactment by the Oireachtas of a six year time limit in actions founded on tort other than actions in respect of personal injuries or fatal injuries and 'an express reiteration by the Oireachtas of their will that actions such as the present action insofar as it is founded on tort should be subject to a limitation period of six years with provision for the extension of that period in the case of disability, acknowledgement, part payment, fraud and mistake and not otherwise'. Lynch J also thought that it followed from this express enactment in relation to tort and the failure to make any variation in the similar provisions relating to contract, that the Oireachtas wished the time limits in relation to actions founded on contract to remain as the 1957 Act provided.

Lynch J's conclusion seems entirely correct. The issues of justice are so finely balanced, with some hardship resulting from every conceivable legislative model for limitation of actions, that a court should long hesitate before stigmatising as unconstitutional a particular legislative solution which is rationally defensible and well thought out. If this issue is squarely addressed by the Supreme Court, one may expect the Court to give the same answer as Lynch J provided in *Tuohy*.

**Definition of 'injury'** In *Maitland v Swan and Sligo County Council*, High Court, 6 April 1992, which we examine in the Torts Chapter below, 557, the defendant surgeon operated on the plaintiff in 1969, removing her right ovary. The plaintiff learned of this removal by 1971, at the latest. It was not until 1983 that she found out that she did not have a normal left ovary. She sued the surgeon for negligence. Her plenary summons was issued in 1985.

On behalf of the surgeon, it was contended that the limitation period had expired. Under the Statute of Limitations (Amendment) Act 1991, the clock begins to run from the time the plaintiff ought reasonably to have known that he or she has been injured, that the injury in question was significant and that the injury was attributable in whole or part to the act or omission alleged to constitute negligence, nuisance or breach of duty.

Counsel for the defendant argued that the alleged injury was the removal of the plaintiff's right ovary, of which fact the plaintiff became aware no later than 1971. Even if she believed that she had a viable left ovary, she must have known that the removal of her right ovary was a significant injury in that it deprived her of the benefit of an alternative gonad should any harm happen subsequently to her left ovary.

Barr J rejected this argument. He noted that s. 2 of the Act did not define 'injured'; in the context of the Act, he considered it to be synonymous with the word 'harmed'. In his view, a person undergoing necessary surgery, skillfully and successfully performed, did not suffer an injury in the context of the Act. Such an operation was a curative, beneficial process and had no element of harmfulness in it, even if the procedure involved the removal of an important organ with in consequence a degree of permanent disablement for the patient. The removal of the plaintiff's right ovary was not, in itself, evidence of negligence and would not suggest negligence to a lay person. It was only in 1983 that the plaintiff could reasonably have known that the 1969 operation, apparently curative and beneficial, was in fact harmful to her.

Barr J's analysis is surely correct. It would seem clearly mistaken to characterise a medical operation as an injury; undoubtedly its therapeutic purpose would have to be taken into account. A whole range of physical contacts should not be treated as injurious when the context in which they occur is taken into consideration. A person who submits to having his or her ears pierced has not been injured though undoubtedly it would be injurious to pierce someone's ears without his or her consent. The answer to the question whether a particular contact constitutes an injury will not always be found by reference to the question of consent, however. There are some kinds of contact which are injurious in spite of their being rendered lawful by reason of consent. A rugby player whose leg is broken by a tackle within the rules has unquestionably been injured. He has no right of action, not because he has not been injured, but because the injury was not caused unlawfully.

It need hardly be pointed out that, from a policy standpoint, it would be unfair to plaintiffs injured during medical treatment to hold that the clock started when the treatment was carried out rather than at the time they first could have been aware of the injury (and of those other elements prescribed by the 1991 Act). If discoverability is the fair test in general, and this is the principle underlying the 1991 Act, then it would be anomalous and injust that patients as a category of potential plaintiffs should uniquely be subjected to a far more stringent limitation period.

## CALCULATION OF LIMITATION PERIOD

If a plaintiff must issue proceedings within a specified period but the Central Office is closed for the last couple of days of that period, does the clock stop? In *Poole v O'Sullivan* [1993] ILRM 55, Morris J held that it does:

> [S]ince the plaintiff was unable to 'set the court in motion' on those days it appears to me that in the circumstances of this case the period envisaged by the Statute of Limitations should be construed as ending on the next day upon which the offices of the court are open and it becomes possible to do the act required.

Morris J thus favoured the same approach as had been adopted by Megarry and Karminski JJ in *Pritam Kaur v S. Russell & Sons Ltd* [1973] QB 336. He rightly rejected Lord Denning MR's spurious argument for consistency with the rule found in the Rules of Court — in Ireland, in O. 122,

r. 9 of the Rules of the Superior Courts 1986. In Morris J's view, the desideratum of consistency could not justify an extension of a period fixed by statute. Instead, the rationale should be that, if the period expired on a day when the offices of the court were closed, the plaintiff would not have the full period intended by the Oireachtas but rather a shorter period.

Some questions arise about the justice of a *universal* extension of time based on the closure of the court offices. It is to be noted that Morris J's rule was expressly grounded in the circumstances of the case before the court. It is one thing for a plaintiff who wishes to have access to the court offices and who is frustrated by their closure to be allowed an extension. It is surely a quite different proposition that similar indulgence be granted to a plaintiff who as a matter of fact was not thus frustrated because he or she simply was not seeking to initiate litigation during the period of closure. In *Poole*, the plaintiff's summons was in the post at the time the Central Office was closed, on its way back to his solicitors from the officials of the Central Office, who were not satisfied that the defendant had been accurately described in the summons. The plaintiff's solicitors received the summons on a Monday, the statutory time limit expiring on the previous Saturday, when the summons was on its way back to the plaintiff's solicitors from the Central Office. No doubt the plaintiff would have quickly lodged the summons a second time if he had received it on the Saturday rather than the Monday, but could it not be argued that his failure to initiate the proceedings within the statutory period was not directly attributable to his *inability to do so* on account of the fact that the Central Office was closed? Even if the Central Office had been open on the Saturday, the plaintiff would still not have been able to comply with the limitation period.

## DISCRETIONARY POWER OF DISMISSAL

In the recent past there has been a discernible increase in the courts' willingness to dismiss a case for want of prosecution. Few people could cavil at the removal from the litigation process of proceedings conducted with culpable delay or inanition, but it is an entirely different matter when courts dismiss actions prosecuted diligently by unimpeachable plaintiffs merely because the courts consider that the relevant limitation period could do with some shortening in the interest of balancing justice between the parties. Of course, the judiciary are entitled to have their own views about how limitation periods should be cast but it is equally necessary that they should recognise, and respect, that range of legislative choice which properly lies within the discretion of the Oireachtas. See our observations in the 1987 Review 250-3 and the 1990 Review, 394-8, as well as above.

Limitation periods are notoriously hard to formulate in a way that will be guaranteed to deliver anything approaching perfect justice. They have to operate blindly as to the guilt or innocence of particular defendants or as to the opportunism or legitimacy of particular plaintiffs' claims. Strict cut-off points can seem very stark in their application, yet judicial discretion is no panacea since it is unpredictable and uneven, yielding differing outcomes to similar factual situations.

In *Celtic Ceramics Ltd v Industrial Development Authority* [1993] ILRM 248, O'Hanlon J gave some important guidance on aspects of the problem that raise some of these broader questions as to the proper remit of the judiciary and the Oireachtas. The plaintiff sued the defendants for negligence and breach of contract arising from a failed industrial development going back to 1983. The plenary summons was issued in February 1988 but not served until the following October. The statement of claim emerged in August 1989. Silence greeted the defendants' notices for particulars, served in the latter part of 1989. The reply to these notices did not come until early 1992. A receiver had been appointed to the plaintiff company in February 1988. The company had been struck off the register in 1990 and dissolved later that year.

The defendants successfully sought dismissal for want of prosecution. O'Hanlon J was satisfied that the plaintiff had been guilty of inordinate and excusable delay. No reasons had been given by the plaintiff for the delay of nearly six years in commencing proceedings or for the apparent failure to give the defendants notice that these were contemplated so as to enable them to make the necessary preparation to defend the claim when it materialised. Moreover, the plaintiff had unsuccessfully defended proceedings brought by another party involved in the project in which issues of possible liability on the part of the defendants in the instant case could have been determined concurrently. The statement of claim put forward 'a claim of considerable obscurity and complexity', necessarily spawning very detailed notices for particulars, yet no replies had been received to them for nearly four years.

A further factor weighing against the continuance of the proceedings was that very serious charges of professional negligence, incompetence and breach of contract had been hanging over the defendants for several years. O'Hanlon J referred with approval to the English Court of Appeal decision of *Biss v Lambeth Southwark and Lewisham Health Authority* [1978] 2 All ER 125 and to Lord Griffiths's speech in *Department of Transport v Chris Smaller Ltd* [1989] 1 All ER 897, which recognised that concern for loss of professional or business reputation was a factor to be taken into account in deciding whether or not to dismiss proceedings for want of prosecution. O'Hanlon J sought to echo Henchy J's view, expressed in *Sheehan v Amond* [1982] IR 235, that it should be possible to invoke 'implied constitutional principles of basic fairness of procedures' to bring about the termination of the proceedings. O'Hanlon J also identified as an 'extraordinary feature' the fact that the plaintiff company had been struck off the Register of Companies and dissolved, without having been reinstated before the application for dismissal of proceedings had come before the Master. There was 'no evidence before the court to support the justice of the plaintiff['s] case, or even as to [its] firm belief in the justice of the case.' Nor was there any evidence to show why, if it believed in the justice of their case, it had failed to put it forward in correspondence or by commencing proceedings before the six-year limitation period had almost expired.

O'Hanlon J's judgment (which was affirmed by the Supreme Court in an *ex tempore* judgment on 4 February 1993) would appear to be an eminently reasonable one. It would be wrong to read it as laying down any general principle that it is necessary to commence one's action well within the limitation period unless there are good reasons for holding back or that a prospective plaintiff must notify a prospective defendant before initiating proceedings. These elements in the case were part of a broader picture of inactivity and were thus not ignored by O'Hanlon J, but they should not be inflated into general criteria which plaintiff's must fulfil under pain of dismissal.

In *Guerin v Guerin and McGrath* [1993] ILRM 243; [1992] 2 IR 287, the plaintiff, aged four, was injured in an accident when being driven by one of the defendants, his sister's fiancé. The accident occurred in 1964. The plaintiff's plenary summons was issued twenty years later. This was still within the limitation period, thanks to the legislative inertia that has followed the Supreme Court decision in *O'Brien v Keogh* [1972] IR 144. The defendants sought to have the case dismissed on the ground of delay.

Costello J declined to dismiss the proceedings. He acknowledged that the delay of over two decades was indeed an inordinate one but considered that it was not inexcusable, when the court had regard to the circumstances of the plaintiff and his family, who lived in poverty in the country, the plaintiff's father having died when the plaintiff was twelve years old. The plaintiff's mother had explained that she had not known of the possibility of making a claim on her son's behalf and the plaintiff learned of his possible entitlement only as a result of a casual conversation with a solicitor. Costello J stated:

> 'The plaintiff's family lived in one of the poorest sectors of the community, the permanently unemployed. With fourteen children to rear and dependant on welfare payments for their livelihood they must have lived most of their lives at or below subsistence level. Theirs was an economically and socially deprived world from which the world so familiar to lawyers in which people sue and are sued was remote and

> arcane. If, as I am sure was the case, they did not appreciate that their son might have had a cause of action to compensate him for the injury he had sustained, I do not think they should be blamed for this.

Nor did Costello J consider that the plaintiff should be blamed for the delay. He had left school at an early age and had accepted his misfortune with fortitude. It had not occurred to him that he might have a right of action until his chance discussion with the solicitor.

Even if the delay was inexcusable, Costello J was of the view that the balance of justice would strongly favour the maintenance of the proceedings. The plaintiff had 'a very strong, indeed almost unanswerable' case of negligence — the car had crashed into a ditch without any other vehicle being involved. (Costello J rejected the driver's evidence that the accident had been caused by brake failure.) If the plaintiff could establish that the condition of epilepsy from which he now suffered had been caused by the accident, his damages would be very considerable. No great injustice would be done to the defendants if the claim went ahead since the delay had not caused any significant prejudice either on the issue of liability or on the issue of damages. Accordingly Costello J declined to dismiss the proceedings.

It must be a rare case where the facts will be sufficiently clear for the court to come to such definite conclusions as to the absence of a likelihood of prejudice. Costello J's response to the social circumstances of the plaintiff's family is not perhaps surprising from the architect of *The Just Society*. If nonage and mental incapacity can stop the clock, why should not social deprivation leading to lack of awareness of one's rights also have this effect, or at least be the basis for rejecting an application for dismissal for want of prosecution?

A downstream difficulty may relate to the kind of case where ignorance of the right to sue is likely to be most frequent and most understandable. This where the plaintiff is injured when a passenger in a car driven by another member of the family, especially a spouse, parent, son or daughter. In such cases the personal incentive to contest actively the issue of liability is often weaker than in cases where strangers collide. Therefore there may be cases in the future where the liability issue, from the insurer's standpoint, will be hard to contest. In the United States, concern for such difficulties led many states to enact 'guest passenger' statutes requiring proof of gross negligence or wanton and reckless conduct as a condition of liability. This strategy was struck down on equal protection grounds in *Brown v Merlo* (1973) 8 Cal. 3d 855, 106 Cal Rptr. 388, 506 P. 2d 212. It is not impossible that these issues may yet surface in the Irish context when the courts attempt the delicate task of balancing social justice with the rights of individual defendants.

In the Practice and Procedure Chapter, below, 492-3, we analyse Barron

J's decision in *Prior v Independent Television News Ltd* [1993] 1 IR 405. The case involved an application under O. 8, r.1 of the Rules of the Superior Courts 1986 for liberty to renew a plenary summons for libel. Barron J. rejected the application on the basis that the defendant's capacity to mount a defence had been seriously compromised by the delay. Of present relevance is Barron J's disposition of the defendant's argument that, because the plaintiff had already succeeded in other libel actions arising out of the same facts, it would be wrong to let him continue with the instant proceedings. In Barron J's view, the fact of the plaintiff's success in these other proceedings was a question that went to the merits of the action but was not a matter affecting the ability of the defendant to defend the proceedings. Nevertheless it did 'largely counterbalance' the element which would normally exist in favour of the plaintiff that, if relief were refused, he would be deprived of damages. Such a factor clearly exercised Costello J in *Guerin v Guerin and McGrath*, above, 436-7.

## MALICIOUS DAMAGE

In the Chapter on Local Government, below, 446-7, we discuss the Supreme Court decision of *Cork County Council v Whillock*, 3 November 1992, on the duration period for compensation applications under the Malicious Injuries Act 1981.

# Local Government

## BUILDING CONTROL

**Bord Pleanála appeals** The Building Control Act 1990 (Appeals) Regulations 1992 (SI No. 111) provide for appeals to An Bord Pleanála against refusals of fire safety certificates under the Building Control Regulations 1991 and also in respect of compliance with the Building Regulations 1991: see the 1991 Review, 307-8. The Building Control Act 1990 (Fees) Regulations 1992 (SI No. 112) and the Building Control Act 1990 (Fees) (Amendment) Regulations 1992 (SI No. 182) lay down the relevant fees arising from such appeals.

**Building Regulations Advisory Body** The Building Regulations Advisory Body Order 1992 (SI No. 113) established the Advisory Body envisaged by the Building Control Act 1990. On the 1990 Act, see the 1990 Review, 404-6.

**Exemptions for local authority developments** The Local Government (Planning and Development) Regulations 1992 (SI No. 209) exempted certain local authority developments commenced before 1 July 1992 from the provisions of the Building Regulations 1991.

## CONTROL OF DOGS

The Control of Dogs (Amendment) Act 1992 substantially amended the Control of Dogs Act 1986 in order to introduce more effective measures to deal with the problems associated with attacks on humans by dangerous dogs. The 1992 Act had not come into force at the time of writing.

S. 2 of the 1992 Act amends s. 1 of the 1986 Act by introducing a new definition of 'general dog licence' to ensure that a licence relates to a location and thus prevents an organisation from obtaining a single licence for an unlimited number of dogs. S. 3 of the 1992 Act amends s. 7 of the 1986 Act by permitting the Minister for the Environment to provide by Regulations that dog licences may be valid for more than 12 months. S. 4 of the 1992 Act amends s. 8 of the 1986 Act by providing for increases in dog licences fees as well as providing that future increases may be made through Regulations made by the Minister. S. 5 of the 1992 Act amends s. 11 of the 1986 Act and requires a person, when claiming a stray dog, to make a declaration that he owns the dog or is authorised to claim the dog and produces a current dog licence. S. 6 of the 1992 Act amends s. 15 of the 1986 Act and dispenses with the need for a local authority to seek Ministerial consent to the policies it puts in place to implement the 1992 Act. This should be seen against the background of delegating modest powers to local authorities as envisaged by the Local Government Act 1991: see the 1991 Review, 310-13. S. 7 of the 1992 Act amends s. 16 of the 1986 Act by providing for increased powers of dog wardens to seize and detain dogs, to enter premises and to demand production of dog licences. S. 8 of the 1992 Act substitutes a new s. 19 of the 1986 Act and expands on the Minister's powers to make Regulations to control dogs. Existing Regulations are carried over by the 1992 Act: for examples of these, see the 1991 Review, 308-9. S. 9 of the 1992 Act amends the 1986 Act by providing for standard penalties for breaches of the Acts and Regulations made under them. Finally, s. 10 of the 1992 Act amends s. 28 of the 1986 Act to permit, *inter alia*, on-the-spot fines, a phrase which appears to have a uniquely eponymous ring in this context.

## DERELICT SITES

The Derelict Sites (Urban Areas) Regulations 1992 (SI No. 364) and the Derelict Sites (Urban Areas) (No. 2) Regulations 1992 (SI No. 408) prescribe certain areas to be urban areas for the purposes of the Derelict Sites Act 1990. On the Act, see the 1990 Review, 410-11 and the 1991 Review, 309.

## FORESHORE

The Foreshore (Amendment) Act 1992 amends the Foreshore Act 1933 by conferring additional licensing powers on the Minister for the Marine as well as other banning and control powers on local authorities to deal with the removal of material from beaches. The Act can thus be seen against the background of concern relating to the impact of activities involving the 'commercial' removal of material, of sand and gravel in particular, and the impact which this was having on the foreshore in general. Substantially increased penalties for contravention of the Foreshore Acts are also included in the 1992 Act. S. 6 of the 1992 Act also empowers the Minister, a local authority or an individual to apply for injunctive relief in the District, Circuit or High Court concerning any activity which is in breach of the Foreshore Acts. This section mirrors the 's. 27 relief' provided for in the planning code (see below, 449), though by conferring injunctive powers on the District Court, the 1992 Act is somewhat more extensive in scope.

## HOUSING

The Housing (Miscellaneous Provisions) Act 1992 constitutes a substantial addition to the housing authority legislative code, which is founded on the Housing Act 1966, as amended. It also provides for some significant changes in the landlord and tenant legislation. In addition, s. 22 of the Act seeks to reverse the precise holding of the Supreme Court in *Ward v McMaster* [1989] ILRM 400; [1988] IR 337 (see the 1988 Review, 428-33). A minor, but significant, change to the Building Societies Act 1989 was also effected by s. 30 of the Act: see the Commercial Law chapter, 32, 37, above.

For a detailed discussion of the 1992 Act, and its background in the Department of the Environment's 1991 White Paper *A Plan for Social Housing*, see Timothy Bird's comprehensive Annotation in *Irish Current Law Statutes Annotated.*

The Act, apart from s. 37, which concerns minimum standards for private accommodation, came into effect on 1 September 1992: Housing (Miscellaneous Provisions) Act 1992 (Commencement) Order 1992 (SI No. 223). S. 37 came into effect on 1 September 1993, when the new Regulations on standards in private accommodation came into effect: Housing (Miscellaneous Provisions) Act 1992 (Commencement) Order 1993 (SI No. 145). We outline the main provisions of the 1992 Act below in the order they appear in the Act.

**Shared Ownership** A major feature of the 1992 Act is that it sets out to extend the range of local authority housing which may be purchased by existing tenants. Ss. 2 to 4 of the Act place on a statutory footing the procedure known as 'shared ownership', introduced by local authorities in 1991 in anticipation of the 1992 Act, by which a tenant may purchase leased property by means of the equivalent of a lease-purchase agreement, and under which the tenant occupies the property as lessee with a view to eventual purchase of the property at the end of an agreed term. The 1992 Act also places on a statutory footing the subsidy scheme operated by the Department of the Environment to encourage such purchases. The 1992 Act also provides that this system can be applied to housing in the private sector.

**Improvement works** S. 5 of the 1992 Act authorises a housing authority to carry out improvement works on private housing as an alternative to building new local authority dwellings.

**Assistance by housing authority** S. 6 of the Act re-enacts with amendments s. 5 of the Housing Act 1988 relating to the assistance which may be provided by a housing authority to another housing authority or other 'approved body', such as a voluntary building agency, relating to the provision of housing needs. This now includes assistance in connection with the provision of halting sites for members of the travelling community. For the conditions attaching under the pre-1992 regime, see the Housing (Accommodation Provided by Approved Bodies) Regulations 1992 (SI No. 86).

**Rental subsidy** S. 7 of the Act provides for the payment of a subsidy by a local authority towards the rent payable in respect of house provided by an 'approved body' within s. 6 of the Act. This provision relates to what is generally described as the rental subsidy scheme.

**Policy on housing stock** S. 9 of the 1992 Act requires a housing authority to prepare a written statement of its policy concerning the effective performance of its functions under s.58 of the Housing Act 1966, which concerns the management and control of its housing stock. This statement of policy must be prepared within one year of the 1992 Act coming into force, i.e. by September 1993.

**Removal of temporary dwellings** S. 10 of the 1992 Act authorises a local authority to give notice to a person to remove any temporary dwelling, including caravans or tents, which are situated in a public place where that public place is within five miles of any halting site which has been provided by a local authority for members of the travelling community under s. 13 of the Housing Act 1988. Where such notice is not complied with, the local authority is authorised by s. 10 to remove the temporary dwelling in question onto the approved halting site or other place for storage. This extensive power can be seen against the background of a number of cases involving removal of temporary dwellings, such as *University of Limerick v Ryan*, High Court, 21 February 1991 (see the 1991 Review, 309-10). Clearly, of course, the power to remove under s. 10 of the 1992 Act can only arise where a suitable site exists within five miles of the temporary dwelling in question.

**Housing loans** S.11 of the 1992 Act re-enacts with substantial amendments the provisions of s. 39 of the Housing Act 1966 and s. 8 of the Housing (Miscellaneous Provisions) Act 1979 concerning the power of local authorities to make housing loans. S. 11 now authorises local authorities to make such loans not merely to individuals directly engaged in building or carrying out improvements on their dwellings but also to other persons, such as voluntary agencies. Regulations made by the Minister under the section may lay down conditions attaching to such loans. For the Regulations under the pre-1992 regime concerning house purchase, see the Housing Regulations 1980 (Amendment) Regulations 1992 (SI No. 30) which amend the 1980 Regulations of the same title.

**Securitisation** S. 13 of the 1992 act empowers the Minister for the Environment, with the consent of the Minister for Finance and after consultation with the Central Bank, to make Regulations for the control of the transfer, sale or assignment of mortgages, a process known as securitisation. This section re-enacts with amendments s. 18(6) of the Building Societies Act 1989, the most signifciant change being that the Minister may now make Regulations in relation to mortgages held by any body, not just building societies.

**Notice to quit** S. 16 of the 1992 Act provides that, in general, a notice to quit, whether from a landlord or tenant, must be in writing and must be served not later than four weeks before the date on which it is to take effect. This provision is without prejudice to greater periods of notice to quit required by contract, and certain categories of short-term tenancies and tenancies connected with employment are exempted.

**Rent books** S. 17 of the 1992 Act for the first time enables the Minister for the Environment to make Regulations requiring a landlord to provide a tenant with a rent book, a requirement confined until now under s. 25 of the Housing (Private Rented Dwellings) Act 1982 to the former rent-controlled sector. The 1992 Act applies to all lettings. On the detailed contents of such rent books, see the Housing (Rent Books) Regulations 1993 (SI No. 146 of 1993), which came into effect on 1 September 1993.

**Standards for rented houses** S. 18 of the 1992 Act extended another statutory requirement until now confined to the former rent-controlled sector, namely the power of the Minister to make Regulations concerning minimum standards for private rented houses. Some standards have also been laid down in housing authority bye-laws, but the 1992 Act provides for a uniform system for the entire State, in much the same way as the Building Regulations 1991 have done for construction standards (see the 1991 Review, 307-8). On the details of these standards, which came into effect on 1 January 1994 for private dwellings but will not come into effect until 1 January 1998 for local authority dwellings, see the Housing (Standards for Rented Houses) Regulations 1993 (SI No. 147 of 1993).

**Prohibition on distress for rent** S. 19 of the 1992 Act provides that a landlord shall not levy distress for any rent of any premises let solely as a dwelling. This section severely limits the common law power of distress, that is the power to seize the goods of another person without a court order.

**Effect of *Ward v McMaster* reversed** S. 22 of the 1992 Act provides that the granting of assistance by the Minister or of a housing authority in respect of a house shall not imply any warranty on the part of the Minister or the authority in relation to the state of repair or condition of the house or its fitness for human habitation. It will be recalled that the Supreme Court held, in *Ward v McMaster* [1989] ILRM 400; [1988] IR 337 (see the 1988 Review, 428-33), that where a housing authority had authorised a loan under s.39 of the Housing Act 1966 for the purchase of a house (s. 39 is now replaced by s. 11 of the 1992 Act) but had failed to ensure that the house was adequate security for the loan, it could be held to be in breach of statutory duty where the house in question was defective. S. 22 has the effect of precluding a claim such as occurred in *Ward v McMaster*. Of course, the general principles concerning the duty of care in negligence discussed in *Ward* (see the 1988 Review, 407-10) are not affected by s.22.

**Sale of houses by housing authority** S. 26 of the 1992 Act re-enacts with some amendments s. 90 of the Housing Act 1966 in relation to the power of housing authorities to sell their housing stock.

**Social segregation** S. 28 of the 1992 Act amends s.20 of the Housing Act 1988 by requiring housing authorities to draw up a written statement of their policy under s. 20 to counteract undue segregation in housing between people of different social backgrounds. This statement must, like that under s. 9 of the 1992 Act, be completed within one year of the act coming into force, i.e. by 1 September 1993.

## LOCAL AUTHORITY MEETINGS

**Estimates** The Public Bodies (Amendment) Order 1992 (SI No. 327) amended the Orders of 1946 to 1987 by specifying the period for preparation of the estimates of expenses and the holding of estimates meetings by local authorities.

## MALICIOUS INJURIES

Although the Malicious Injuries (Amendment) Act 1986 substantially amended the Malicious Injuries Act 1981 to limit the scope of such claims, it is a reflection of the current delays in the civil court system that three significant Supreme Court decisions were delivered in 1992 concerning the pre-1986 regime. Indeed, one of these decisions, the *Crown Chemical* case, concerns the pre-1981 Act malicious injuries code.

**Applicant having criminal record** In *Hutch v Dublin Corporation* [1992] ILRM 596, the applicant brought a claim under the Malicious Injuries Act 1981 arising from a fire which occurred in 1984 in the house in which he was tenant and which had resulted in the destruction of furniture in the house. It was agreed that the fire had been started maliciously. In the course of the Circuit Court hearing, the applicant was cross-examined as to whether he had a criminal record, and the applicant accepted that he had been convicted of a number of offences, including larceny. The applicant, who had been unemployed since 1977, produced receipts in respect of all items of furniture in respect of which claims were made and stated that the items had been paid for out of savings, loans from family members and also from part-time work. The Circuit Court judge (Judge Carroll) concluded that the furniture had been purchased from the proceeds of criminal activity and that, accordingly, he was disentitled to claim for malicious damage to the furniture under the 1981 Act. The case was referred on case stated to the High Court, which in turn stated a case for the Supreme Court. The Supreme Court (Finlay CJ, Hederman, McCarthy and Egan JJ; O'Flaherty J dissenting) held that the Circuit Court judge had erred, though the judgments delivered differed in certain points of detail on the reasons for this.

The Court first noted that while a witness was entitled, in general, to refuse to answer questions which might incriminate him, the applicant had agreed to answer the questions in the instant case and, in any event, questions as to convictions which had already been recorded were admissible.

On the substantive issue raised, the majority, which consisted of Finlay CJ, Hederman, McCarthy and Egan JJ, differed slightly in concluding that the applicant should not be precluded from claiming under the 1981 Act. Finlay CJ and McCarthy J pointed out simply that the conclusion of the Circuit Court judge that the furniture in the instant case had been purchased from the proceeds of crime was not warranted by the evidence proferred. Hederman and Egan JJ, on the other hand, took a more general approach in holding that there was no general public policy principle by which a person who suffered damage within the 1981 Act should not be compensated in full, where that person's criminal activity did not lead directly to the loss complained of. The judgments on this point sought to distinguish the instant case from *R. v National Insurance Commissioner, ex p Connor* [1981] 1 All ER 769.

Finally, to add to the complexity of the holdings in this case, O'Flaherty

J (who dissented on the conclusion of the majority) joined Finlay CJ and McCarthy J in stating an even more general proposition (clearly *obiter* in the instant case) that where it was established that proceeds of crime were destroyed maliciously, it would offend against common sense if the wrong-doer could also claim against the community for malicious damage in respect of the destruction of the proceeds of crime. It may be that this proposition will prove of some relevance in malicious injuries claims in the future, assuming that even the truncated code which survives after the Malicious Injuries (Amendment) Act 1986 will be allowed continue.

**Decree not carrying interest** *Crown Chemical Co. (Irl) Ltd v Cork County Council* [1993] ILRM 74 arose out of the pre-1981 malicious injuries code, but it deals with a point which remains of interest even in the post-1986 truncated regime. The Supreme Court decided that interest was not payable on a malicious injuries decree.

The company claimed that it was entitled to claim interest on a decree made in its favour under, *inter alia*, the Local Government (Ireland) Act 1898, arising from malicious injury to its property. The defendant Council argued that interest was not payable since the decree did not amount to a judgment debt. On a case stated the Supreme Court (Hederman, O'Flaherty and Egan JJ), as already indicated, upheld the Council's argument.

The Court held that the decree for compensation under the malicious injuries code cast an immediate duty on the responsible local authority to raise, levy and pay the sum, a duty enforceable by judicial review. However, applying the decision in *R.(Bennett) v King's County County Council* [1908] 2 IR 178, it concluded that the decree did not constitute a judgment debt within s. 26 of the Debtors (Ireland) Act 1840, and therefore interest was not payable on the decree.

**Extending time limit** In *Cork County Council v Whillock*, Supreme Court, 3 November 1992 the respondent claimed that a fire which occurred at his premises on 13 November 1983 was caused maliciously. On 14 November 1982, he served on the applicant Council a preliminary notice of intention to apply for compensation for malicious injuries under the 1981 Act. S. 23 of the Malicious Injuries Act 1981 sets out a three year limitation period from the date on which the cause of action accrues, which is the date of the service of the preliminary notice. No proceedings were instituted by the end of the limitation period, but the respondent applied to the Circuit Court for an order extending the time for making a claim under the 1981 Act. This was granted by the Circuit Court judge on the ground that s. 14 of the 1981 Act, which permits the Circuit Court to extend the time for any act or proceedings under the Act itself, allowed for such extension.

The applicant applied on judicial review for an order quashing the Circuit Court decision. In the High Court, Carroll J granted the order sought, but on further appeal the Supreme Court (O'Flaherty, Egan and Blayney JJ) reversed Carroll J and affirmed the Circuit Court's extension, overruling the High Court decision in *Dublin Corporation v Carroll* [1987] IR 410 in the process.

The Court held that there was no inconsistency between s. 23 of the 1981 Act, which provided for a three year time limit, and s. 14 of the 1981 Act, which permitted the Circuit Court to extend the time for any act or proceedings under the Act itself. Having regard to the obligation on a court to give effect to the literal meaning of the words of legislation and to avoid an interpretation which would render a provision inoperative, the Supreme Court concluded that the Circuit Court judge had the jurisdiction to make the order in the instant case.

## PLANNING

**Advertisement** In *Dooley v Galway County Council* [1992] 2 IR 136, the applicant successfully sought judicial review of a planning permission on the ground that the advertisement notifying the intention to apply for permission failed to comply with the Local Government (Planning and Development) Regulations 1977. The advertisement had stated that the application related to permission from Galway County Council to remove surface rock 'from lands at Cartron'. The Council indicated that its policy was that reference to a townland was sufficient compliance with Article 15 of the 1977 Regulations which requires that the 'location' be stated in the advertisement. But the applicant adduced evidence to indicate that there were at least 18 townlands in Galway with the name 'Cartron'.

Denham J agreed with the applicant that, in these particular circumstances, the policy of accepting advertisements with townlands only did not comply with Article 15 of the 1977 Regulations. She noted that in *Crodaun Homes Ltd v Kildare County Council* [1983] ILRM 1 Griffin J had repeated the point that the purpose of the advertisement was to give ready and easily identifiable notice to interested members of the public of the location of the lands involved. She concluded that the advertisement in the instant case did not meet this test. Finally, she rejected an argument by the Council that she should, in her discretion, refuse judicial review in light of the decision of the Supreme Court in *The State (Abenglen Properties Ltd) v Dublin Corporation* [1981] ILRM 54; [1984] IR 381. Denham J distinguished the instant case from that arising in *Abenglen* on the ground that the applicant had not been aware of the Council's decision until the time for bringing an appeal to An

Bord Pleanála had passed. Thus, the applicant's only remedy was judicial review, and the 'choice of remedy' issue which arose in *Abenglen* did not arise in the instant case. For a case involving the application of *Abenglen*, see *Cunningham v An Bord Pleanála*, High Court, 3 May 1990 (see the 1991 Review, 318-9).

**Appeals** The Local Government (Planning and Development) Act 1992 was intended to address the concerns of business interests in particular at delays in the planning process which it was felt was resulting in the potential loss of projects. The 1992 Act tackles this in two ways. First, it places a general four month time limit within which An Bord Pleanála must consider and determine appeals from planning authorities for planning permission, thus it is hoped leading to speedier decisions on planning applications. Second, the 1992 Act provides that challenges to planning decisions must in future be made by judicial review to the High Court, whose decisions will in most cases now be final. This second aspect of the Act is aimed at recent cases in which planning decisions have, in effect, been stayed pending appeals to the courts which, with present delays in the court system, have involved delays of years rather than months. Notable recent cases in this respect have included *Browne v An Bord Pleanála* [1989] ILRM 865 (see the 1989 Review, 202-4), a challenge which, although unsuccessful, was suggested to have influenced the decision of Merrell Dow not to proceed with the development involved in the case; and *Chambers v An Bord Pleanála* [1992] ILRM; [1992] 1 IR 134 (see the 1991 Review, 317-8), arising from which it would appear that the developer involved, Sandoz, did not decide to abandon its project.

S. 2 of the 1992 Act places a positive duty on An Bord Pleanála to ensure that there are no unavoidable delays in planning appeals, and lays down a general rule that appeals be decided within four months. S. 3 of the Act provides for a one month time limit within which a person other than the applicant can make an appeal to An Bord Pleanála. This in fact involves an extention over the previous 21 day period, and this was done to take account of s. 4 of the 1992 Act. S. 4 of the Act provides for a streamlined appeals procedure in which the appeal and all grounds for appeal are submitted in a single document at the outset to the Bord. Previously, the appeal and the grounds therefore could be contained in separate documents which produced some delays in the appeals system. S. 5 of the Act requires that planning authorities make available to the public any documentation in their possession relating to planning permissions where such permissions are appealed to An Bord Pleanála. Ss. 7 to 10 of the Act concern the power of the Bord to determine if parties are required to make submissions concerning an appeal, while s. 12 confers an absolute discretion on the Bord to decide in its absolute discretion whether an oral hearing of an appeal is required, replacing s. 15 of the Local Government (Planning and Development) Act 1983 in this respect.

The second aspect of the 1992 Act which concerns challenges to planning permissions, is contained largely in s. 19 of the Act, which is a somewhat convoluted and involved section, which in itself involves a number of substantial changes to a number of different statutory provisions in the planning legislation.

S. 19 of the Act first provides, by way of amendment to s. 82 of the Local Government (Planning and Development) Act 1963, that the validity of any planning permission may only be challenged by way of judicial review. The application must be made within two months of the planning decision, whereas the normal time limit for seeking judicial review is six months. Leave to apply for judicial review can only be granted where the High Court judge 'is satisfied that there are substantial grounds for contending that the decision is invalid or ought to be quashed'. This would appear to place a greater burden on applicants than in other applications for leave to seek judicial review. Decisions of the High Court on such applications are final unless the Court grants a certificate that a point of law of exceptional public importance is involved which requires an appeal to the Supreme Court. This is the formula used in relation to appeals from the Court of Criminal Appeal to the Supreme Court pursuant to s.29 of the Courts of Justice Act 1924, as to which see, for example, the 1991 Review, 152.

S. 19(4) of the 1992 Act provides for the insertion of a new s. 27 of the Local Government (Planning and Development) Act 1976, the provision allowing for, in effect a 'planning injunction' for the enforcement of planning permissions where there is unauthorised development. The new s. 27 inserted by the 1992 Act provides that such injunctions can now be obtained in the Circuit Court, in addition to the High Court which previously had exclusive jurisdiciton in this respect. In addition, a 'reinstatement' order can now be made under s. 27 in relation to a development being carried out without any planning permission or where an unauthorised use is being made of land. This 'reinstatement' order, new under s. 27, requires the developer to restore the land to its original state. However, reinstatements are not possible in relation to developments authorised by a permission but which are being carried on outside the conditions attaching to such permission. With effect from 1 January 1994 (see the discussion of commencement in the next paragraph), s.27(6)(b) of the 1976 Act now provides that applications under s. 27 of the 1976 Act can only be made within five years of the relevant contravention. For an early use of the 'new' s. 27, see *Dublin Corporation v McGowan* [1993] 1 IR 405, below, 460.

The Local Government (Planning and Development) Act 1992 (Commencement) Order 1992 (SI No. 221) brought ss. 5(2) and (3) of the 1992 Act into operation on 30 July 1992 and s. 5(1) into operation on 14 September 1992. The remaining sections, except one aspect of s. 19(4) of the Act, came into force on 19 October 1992. S. 19(4) of the Act (which inserted the new s. 27 of the 1976 Act) came into force on 1 January 1994 insofar as it relates to the five year time period referred to in the previous paragraph. The procedures to be followed under the 1992 Act are detailed in the Local Government (Planning and Development) (No. 2) Regulations 1992 (SI No. 222).

**Appeal: cheque payment** In *Maher v An Bord Pleanála* [1993] ILRM 359; [1993] 1 IR 439, the applicant sought judicial review of a refusal by the respondent Planning Board to grant planning permission to a proposed development. The main ground relied on was that the Board had entertained objections from representatives of local residents in the following circumstances.

The residents had lodged two notices of appeal to the Board on the last day for which appeals could be made under s. 26 of the Local Government (Planning and Development) Act 1963, as amended by s. 14 of the Local Government (Planning and Development) Act 1976. A blank cheque accompanied the two notices and a receipt was issued acknowledging the blank cheque. The fee for each appeal was £50. Subsequently, the blank cheque was filled in for £50 and the residents were informed by the Board that only one of their appeals would be heard by the Board, on the ground that s. 10 of the Local Government (Planning and Development) Act 1982 required that where a fee payable for an appeal is not received within the time allowed for lodging appeals 'the appeal shall be invalid.' The residents responded that their intention had been to put in two appeals and that this was evidenced by the receipt for the blank cheque received from the Board. The Board subsequently allowed the residents to lodge the two appeals, on payment of the other £50 fee. The applicant argued that the Board had acted *ultra vires* in hearing the residents' appeals. He argued that in relation to neither appeal had a fee been received by the Board within the time for appealing. In relation to the first blank cheque, he argued that payment to the Board could not be deemed to have been received by the Board until it had been transferred to the Board's bank account, and in relation to the second cheque he argued that this had been even more clearly received beyond the time limit. Blayney J rejected both arguments.

He concluded that, in relation to the first cheque, payment was deemed to be received under s. 10 of the 1982 Act on receipt of the cheque itself, rather than on its lodgment in the Board's bank account. He took this view on the basis that the applicant's argument would lead to unnecessary uncertainty in the operation of s. 10 of the 1982 Act, and that since payment by cheque was such a common practice in business relations it would take express language in the 1982 Act to exclude the use of payments by such method. As to the second cheque, Blayney J concluded that the date on which that cheque had been written was irrelevant in the instant case. He took the view that, when the Board had received the first blank cheque it was being given authority to fill it in for the appropriate amount, and that in accepting the cheque and giving a receipt for it, it was agreeing to act on that authority. On this basis, Blayney J concluded that the Board had received the appropriate fees for both appeals within the statutory time limit in s. 10 of the 1982 Act.

Blayney J also considered that there were grounds for supporting the actual decision of the Board in refusing the applicant's application for planning permission. Thus, on the authority of *O'Keeffe v An Bord Pleanála* [1992] ILRM 237; [1993] 1 IR 39 (see the 1991 Review, 16-8), he dismissed the application for judicial review.

**Compensation for refusal: exemptions** Two cases in 1992 concerned the question whether reasons given by a planning authority for refusing planning permission fell into the categories of reasons in respect of which no compensation is payable under the planning code. These were *Dublin County Council v Eighty Five Developments Ltd (No. 2)* [1993] 2 IR 392 and *Hoburn Homes Ltd v An Bord Pleanála* [1993] ILRM 368. The first case arose before the changes effected by the Local Government (Planning and Development) Act 1990: see the 1990 Review, 414-5.

In *Dublin County Council v Eighty Five Developments Ltd (No. 2)* [1993] 2 IR 392, the company had applied for planning permission for the erection of houses, a school and a shopping centre. The Council had refused permission on the ground, *inter alia*, that the development would not be desirable having regard to traffic density and the speed of vehicles which would be generated. On appeal, An Bord Pleanála also refused permission on the ground, *inter alia*, that the road on which it was proposed to site the buildings were 'substandard in width and . . . would give rise to traffic hazard by reason of the additional traffic turning movements it would generate'.

The Council sought a declaration that this ground for refusal came within the exemption to compensation contained in s. 56 of the Local Government (Planning and Development) Act 1963. S. 56 provides, *inter alia*, that no compensation for refusal shall be given where the ground for refusal was that the development would endanger public safety by reason of a traffic hazard. In the High Court in 1989, Gannon J held the ground given in the instant case did not come within s. 56 and that compensation was therefore payable. On appeal by the Council, the Supreme Court (Finlay CJ, Hederman, McCarthy and O'Flaherty JJ; Egan J dissenting) allowed the appeal and held that no compensation was payable.

Applying *dicta* of McCarthy J in *XJS Investments Ltd v Dun Laoghaire Corporation* [1987] ILRM 659, *sub nom In re XJS Investments Ltd* [1986] IR 750 (see the 1987 Review, 101) the Court held that a planning authority was not required to follow the precise words of s. 56 of the 1963 Act in order to bring the ground of refusal within the section. While acknowledging that great care should be taken to indicate with clarity the precise basis on which permission is refused, the Court stated that the ground given should be interpreted in an ordinary and common sense manner to ascertain whether it fell within s. 56 of the 1963 Act, and in the instant case, it concluded that the true interpretation was that the ground for refusal fell within s. 56 and that no compensation was payable under s. 55 of the Act.

We should note that, after Gannon J's decision in 1989 that compensation was payable, the matter was referred to a property arbitrator to determine the amount due to the company. This reference gave rise to a case stated to Carroll J in the High Court: see *Dublin County Council v Eighty Five Developments Ltd (No. 1)* [1993] 2 IR 378. Carroll J delivered her judgment in January 1992, two months before the Supreme Court's decision in *Eighty Five Developments (No. 2)*, above, had reversed Gannon J's 1989 decision. Carroll J's decision was appealed to the Supreme Court, but in light of its decision in *Eighty Five Developments (No. 2)*, the Court declined to address the issues raised in Carroll J's judgment as they had become moot. Nonetheless, we discuss Carroll J's judgment below, 453-5.

As we mentioned already, the *Eighty Five Developments* case arose from a development which preceded the enactment of the Local Government (Planning and Development) Act 1990, which further limited the grounds for which compensation for refusal can be claimed.

In the second case on this topic in 1992, *Hoburn Homes Ltd v An Bord Pleanála* [1993] ILRM 368, the 1990 Act was considered. In this case, three reasons had been given by An Bord Pleanála for refusing the applicants planning permission. Of these, only one was challenged on judicial review, namely that '[t]he development . . . would be premature by reference to the order of priority for development indicated in the Cork County Council Development Plan, which seeks to minimize population expansion in excess of targets in the area in which the proposed development is situated'. The net issue for Denham J was whether this reason for refusal fell within the terms of paragraph 3 of the Third Schedule to the Local Government (Planning and Development) Act 1990 which provides that no compensation would be payable where the ground for refusal is that '[d]evelopment of the kind proposed would be premature by reference to the order of priority, if any, for development indicated in the development plan'.

Clearly, the reason given in the instant case was intended to fall within the terms of the 1990 Act, but Denham J concluded that in the instant case the reason given was *ultra vires* An Bord Pleanála. This was because the Cork County Development Plan had designated the area in which the applicants had applied for planning permission to be an area of scenic landscape and that development be curtailed in this area. Other areas in the Plan were zoned for residential, commercial and industrial use. Denham J concluded that, since the area for which the applicants had sought planning permission simply had no development proposed in the existing Development Plan, the terms of paragraph 3 of the Third Schedule to the 1990 Act could not apply and it was thus *ultra vires* An Bord Pleanála to have given the challenged reason for refusing permission. She also made an important comment on the general nature of compensation for refusal. She stated:

> In coming to this conclusion, I am also influenced in construction [*sic*] by the fact that compensation is a statutory right, and it should only be removed in clear precise cases.

On these grounds, she quashed the particular reason given by An Bord Pleanála. It may be noted also that Denham J considered that this was an appropriate case to remit the matter to An Bord Pleanála pursuant to O.84, r. 26(4) of the Rules of the Superior Courts 1986, but not a full rehearing of the matter.

**Compensation for refusal: valuation** In *Dublin County Council v Eighty Five Developments Ltd (No. 1)* [1993] 2 IR 378, Carroll J considered two opposing approaches to the method of valuing land for the purposes of calculating compensation payable for refusal of planning permission under the Local Government (Planning and Development) Act 1963. As we have already noted above, Carroll J's judgment was rendered moot in light of the later Supreme Court decision in *Dublin County Council v Eighty Five Developments Ltd (No. 2)* [1993] 2 IR 392, in which the Court held that compensation was not payable in the instant case. Her comments may also have lost some impact arising from the restricted regime introduced by the Local Government (Planning and Development) Act 1990, which featured in argument before her.

As the summary already given in respect of the Supreme Court's decision indicates, the company had sought from the Council permission for the erection of houses, a school and a shopping centre. When permission was refused by the Council and, on appeal, by An Bord Pleanála, the company lodged a claim under s. 55 of the Local Government (Planning and Development) Act 1963 for compensation amounting to over £2 million. The

Council then instituted declaratory proceedings that the company was not entitled to any compensation.

In 1989, Gannon J held that compensation was payable under the 1963 Act. The case was then referred to a property arbitrator, who in turn stated a case for the High Court on two competing methods for calculating the compensation payable. This case stated was heard by Carroll J who delivered judgment in January 1992: [1992] ILRM 815. As already noted, her judgment seems moot in light of the Supreme Court's decision in April 1992 ([1992] ILRM 815) which reversed Gannon J's 1989 decision and found compensation was not payable, thus rendering redundant the calculation of compensation. However, in view of the extensive argument before Carroll J it seems proper to at least note the outline of the competing methods.

The Council had argued that any compensation should be on the basis of valuing the land on their open market value prior to the decision of An Bord Pleanála with such development potential including the possibility of obtaining planning permission (if any) as might be proved in evidence, less the open market value of the lands after the decision of An Bord Pleanála. The company, on the other hand, argued that the lands should be valued on their open market value as if the planning permission had in fact been granted, less the open market value of the lands after the refusal of permission.

The Council acknowledged that the traditional method of calculating compensation under s. 55 of the Local Government (Planning and Development) Act 1963 was the second method, but it argued that this was incorrect. The company pointed out that the calculation argued for by the Council had in fact been incorporated into the much more restrictive regime for compensation introduced by the Local Government (Planning and Development) Act 1990, whose provisions did not, however, apply to the development in the instant case. The company argued that, in light of the restrictive changes brought about by the 1990 Act, s. 55 of the 1963 Act could not have an identical restrictive meaning.

Carroll J ultimately rejected the Council's argument and reaffirmed the traditional method, which was of course much more favourable to developers. However, she did not accept that the 1990 Act could be relevant to interpreting the 1963 Act, as the company had suggested, relying on the general canon of construction that a statute cannot be interpreted by reference to subsequent amendments and citing *Cronin v Cork and County Property Co. Ltd* [1986] IR 559 in support. Nor did she consider that previous decisions such as *Owenabue Ltd v Dublin Corporation* [1982] ILRM 150 or *Byrne v Dublin County Council* [1983] ILRM 213 had definitively determined the matter in the company's favour. In the end, Carroll J concluded that, although s. 55 of the 1963 Act could have been more clearly worded and that the result did seem 'extraordinary', she commented:

> I can see no way of interpreting this section other than by holding that in determining the reduction in value, the calculation is to be made as if the permission had been granted.

It was on this basis that she found in favour of the company. As already stated, in the instant case this conclusion became moot after the Supreme Court later decided that compensation was not payable to the company under s. 55 of the 1963 Act. And the effect of the 1990 Act is, of course, to introduce a more restrictive regime for the future, as was conceded in the instant case. It is notable, however, that in *Hoburn Homes Ltd v An Bord Pleanála* [1993] ILRM 368 (discussed above), Denham J stated that since the right to compensation had been conferred by statute, it could only be removed in clear cases.

On the same day as she delivered judgment in the *Eighty Five Developments* case, Carroll J also delivered judgment in *Monastra Developments Ltd v Dublin County Council* [1992] 1 IR 468. This was also a case stated from the property arbitrator concerning an aspect of the assessment of compensation after a refusal of compensation. The area for which planning permission had been refused to the claimant company consisted of a plot of 3.37 acres in Foxrock County Dublin. In the Dublin County Development Plan 1983 part of this plot was zoned 'A' (to protect and improve residential amenity) and another part which was zoned 'F' (to preserve and provide for open space and recreational amenities. The zone 'F' area comprised a small part of the old Leopardstown racecourse.

Rule 11 of s. 2 of the Acquisition of Land (Assessment of Compensation) Act 1919 (inserted into the 1919 Act by the Fourth Schedule to the Local Government (Planning and Development) Act 1963) provides that, in assessing compensation regard shall not be had to any depreciation or increase in value attributable to 'the land, or any land in the vicinity thereof, being reserved for any particular purpose in a development plan'. The claimant company argued that since one part of the 3.37 acre plot was zoned 'A', this meant that the part zoned 'F' was reserved from that land and therefore ought to be valued as if it were zoned 'A'.

In her judgment in the case, Carroll J agreed with the claimant that, in general, the correct approach was that the designation of the 'reserved' land was, in effect to be disregarded under Rule 11, quoting with approval the judgment of McWilliam J to that effect in *Short v Dublin County Council* [1982] ILRM 117. However, she also accepted the Council's argument that this general approach was subject to the question of scale. She accepted that there must be cases where an area is large enough in its own right not to be considered as 'set apart' from other adjoining lands within Rule 11. She considered in this context that the old Leopardstown racecourse was sufficiently large to comprise an area in its own right and that, accordingly, it could not be considered as 'land set apart from other land in the area.' On this basis, she found against the claimant company.

**Default permission** In *O'Connor's Downtown Properties Ltd v Nenagh UDC* [1993] 1 IR 1, the issue arose as to whether a letter from the respondent Council seeking details concerning the applicant's application for planning permission amounted to a request for 'further information' under s. 26(4) of the Local Government (Planning and Development) Act 1963 and Regulations 26 and 27 of the Local Government (Planning and Development) Regulations 1977, as amended. If the Council's letter did come within s. 26(4) of the 1963 Act and the 1977 Regulations, then the two month time period laid down in s.26 for the making of a decision on the planning application would not be regarded as continuing to run. On the interpretation of s. 26 of the 1963 Act, O'Hanlon J applied the judgments of Butler J in *The State (Conlon Construction Ltd) v Cork County Council*, High Court, 31 July 1975 and of McMahon J in *The State (NCE Ltd) v Dublin County Council* [1979] ILRM 249. He held that a planning authority is not entitled to communicate to an applicant in a way that appears to fall within the terms of s. 26(4) by requesting information but where the Council in fact dislikes the application and wishes to have the applicant alter the specifications in certain ways. O'Hanlon J concluded that a Council was only empowered to request clarifying information under s. 26(4) of the 1963 Act. If the Council adopted a 'half-way' house approach to the application, by acknowledging the application but seeking 'clarification' as a means to change the nature of the application when the terms of the original application were clear, the result could be that the two month time period under s. 26 of the 1963 Act would expire. This is what occurred in the instant case. In the circumstances, the applicant obtained an order of mandamus that the Council was deemed to have granted planning permission under s. 26(4) of the 1963 Act.

**Exempted development** In *Dublin Corporation v Bentham* [1993] 2 IR 58, discussed below, 459, Morris J held that the installation of aluminium windows in a Georgian-style building was not an exempted development under s. 4(1) of the Local Government (Planning and Development) Act 1963.

**Fees** The Local Government (Planning and Development) (Fees) (Amendment) Regulations 1992 (SI No. 3) lay down revised fees for appeals to An Bord Pleanála.

**Mining ban** In *Glencar Explorations plc v Mayo County Council* [1993] 2 IR 237, Blayney J held that a ban on mining in the 1992 Mayo County Development Plan was *ultra vires* s. 19 of the Local Government (Planning and Development) Act 1963. The ban came against the background that the applicant company had, since 1986, held prospecting licences for the exploration of gold in the County Mayo area issued by the Minister for Energy under the Minerals Development Act 1940. It appeared that large gold deposits were to be found in the area being explored, but the mining ban in the 1992 Development Plan purported to preclude its development.

Blayney J found the ban invalid on a number of grounds. First, he considered that s. 19 of the 1963 Act required that a development plan must be in the nature of positive planning objectives for the area involved, and a mining ban did not fall within the positive nature indicated by s. 19. Second, he found that mineral exploration was, *prima facie*, exempted development under the Third Schedule to the Local Government (Planning and Development) Regulations 1977 and thus the Council was also precluded on this ground from imposing a ban on mining activity. Third, Blayney J found that the Council had failed to take account of government policy in this area, as required by s. 7 of the Local Government Act 1991. Of crucial importance in this respect was that the Assistant Secretary of the Department of Energy had written to the Council prior to the making of the ban explaining that a ban on mining would be contrary to government policy on mining and stating that the Minister's view was that the mining ban be deleted by the Council. For these reasons, Blayney J quashed that part of the Development Plan which included the ban on mining.

It is notable that Blayney J did not consider that he should declare the entire Development Plan *ultra vires*, this had the effect of retaining in the Development Plan certain restrictions on mining to take account of the environmental impact of such development. In addition, Blayney J did indicate, possibly *obiter*, that if the Council declared certain areas to be special amenity areas under the Development Plan, this would have the effect that mining would no longer be an exempted development under the Local Government (Planning and Development) Regulations 1977.

We should also note that the *Glencar* case was followed by a refusal by the Minister for Energy to renew the gold prospecting licence under the Mineral Developments Act 1940 for the Croagh Patrick area in Mayo, a well-known place of religious pilgrimage. In *Tara Prospecting Ltd v Minister for Energy*, High Court, 30 April 1993, Costello J rejected a challenge by the plaintiff company to the non-renewal of the licence. We will discuss this case in the 1993 Review.

**Penalties** S. 20 of the Local Government (Planning and Development) Act

1992 (the substantive contents of which are discussed above, 448-50) provides for the alteration and increase of certain penalties under the planning legislation.

**Section 4 motion** In *Kenny Homes & Co Ltd v Galway City and County Manager*, High Court, 3 April 1992, Blayney J upheld the decision of the Galway City and County Manager who had refused to implement a motion by Galway Corporation made under s. 4 of the City and County Management (Amendment) Act 1955 which had directed the Manager to grant a planning application to the applicant company.

It will be recalled that, in *P & F Sharpe Ltd v Dublin City and County Manager* [1989] ILRM 565; [1989] IR 701 (1988 Review, 296-301), the Supreme Court had held that a local authority was empowered under s.4 of the 1955 Act to direct the granting of planning permission as one of its executive functions as a local authority. However, the Court also stated that a motion under s. 4 of the 1955 Act must be approved in a judicial manner, and in particular must have regard to all relevant factors such as whether the application for permission is in accordance with the requirements of s. 26 of the Local Government (Planning and Development) Act 1963. S. 26 restricts a planning authority to considering an application for planning permission in accordance with the proper planning and development of the authority. S. 26 also provides that 'the [planning] authority may decide to grant the permission . . . subject to or without conditions or to refuse it. . . .' It was this latter requirement which Blayney J concluded that Galway Corporation had failed to consider in the instant case.

The applicant had initially been refused outline planning permission by Galway Corporation for a certain development. A motion under s. 4 of the 1955 Act was then tabled and passed which stated that 'Galway Corporation require the City and County Manager to grant outline planning to Kenny Homes' for the application in question. Although the s. 4 motion was considered in some detail by the Corporation, Blayney J concluded that its wording precluded the Corporation members from considering whether conditions would be attached to any permission ultimately granted. The members had, apparently, assumed that any conditions would be attached by the Manager, but Blayney J held that this was not sufficient to comply with the requirements of the *Sharpe* case that the application be considered in a judicial manner. On this basis, he held that the s. 4 resolution was invalid and that the Manager had thus acted correctly in declining to implement it. He thus refused the applicant's claim for judicial review of the Manager's decision.

It may be noted that the s.4 motion in this case took place on 24 May 1991, just before the new arrangements for such motions came into force on

7 June 1991 pursuant to Part VII of the Local Government Act 1991: see the 1991 Review, 310-3.

**Section 27 injunction** Two cases in 1992 concerned applications for injunctive relief under s. 27 of the Local Government (Planning and Development) Act 1976. The first, *Dublin Corporation v Bentham* [1993] 2 IR 58, dealt with the unamended version of s. 27, while the second, *Dublin Corporation v McGowan* [1993] 1 IR 405, although reported earlier dealt with s. 27 of the 1976 Act as inserted by s. 19(4) of the Local Government (Planning and Development) Act 1992: as to which see above, 449.

In *Dublin Corporation v Bentham* [1993] 2 IR 58, the respondents had purchased three adjoining Georgian houses in Belgrave Square, Dublin. The doors and windows of the houses were, in particular, in a dilapidated condition. During renovation, the respondents replaced the Georgian-style windows with aluminium windows. The respondents then began using the premises as a guesthouse. The applicant Corporation sought two main reliefs under s. 27 of the 1976 Act: the removal of the aluminium windows and their replacement by Georgian-style windows, and an order discontinuing use of the houses as a guesthouse. Morris J refused the first relief, but granted the second.

On the removal of the aluminium windows, Morris J cited with approval *dicta* of Gannon J in *Dublin County Council v Kirby* [1985] ILRM 325 and of Henchy J in *Morris v Garvey* [1983] IR 319 to the effect that s. 27 of the 1976 Act was not applicable to developments where there was a failure to comply with certain conditions of a planning permission, but was more appropriate to an entirely unauthorised development. He thus held that the court had no jurisdiction to deal with the windows under s. 27, thus reiterating the exceptional nature of the s. 27 remedy.

However, because Morris J was informed that the instant case was in the nature of a 'test' case for many other similar developments, he proceeded to deal with the question whether the installation of aluminium windows was in breach of the planning code. The respondents had argued that the windows only affected the interior appearance of the houses and thus was an exempted development under s. 4(1) of the Local Government (Planning and Development) Act 1963. Morris J rejected this argument, holding that the windows would not be exempted if they were inconsistent with the general character of the three houses themselves or with adjoining houses, citing with approval *dicta* of Finlay CJ in *Cairnduff v O'Connell* [1986] ILRM 465; [1986] IR 73 in this respect. He found that the windows were inconsistent with the general character of the three houses. It is also noteworthy, however, that he found that alterations done to other houses in Belgrave Square were also not in accord with their character and that the windows in the respondents' houses would have been exempted development if that was the sole factor to be taken into account. It must be said that these findings of Morris J could, strictly speaking, be regarded as *obiter* as he had already decided that the court had no jurisdiction to deal with the Corporation's application under s. 27 of the 1976 Act. Despite this, his comments are, of course, of importance as providing guidance on this area.

On the second relief sought by the Corporation, namely an order discontinuing use of the houses as a guesthouse, Morris J as already indicated granted the relief. On this aspect of the case, the question was whether the houses had been used as a hotel on the appointed day under the 1963 Act, that is, 1 October 1964. Although the Ordnance Survey maps for the period indicated that the houses were, at some time before, used as a hotel, there was evidence on affidavit to indicate that, during the late 1950s, the houses had been converted into bedsitters and that this use had continued well into the 1960s. On this evidence, therefore, Morris J concluded that the use of the houses as a guesthouse was an unauthorised development. Nor did he accept that conversion of the houses from use as bedsitters to guesthouse came within any of the categories of exempted change of user provided for in the Third Schedule to the Local Government (Planning and Development) Regulations 1977. He thus concluded that it was therefore appropriate to grant the Corporation injunctive relief under s.27 of the 1976 Act.

In the second case under s. 27, *Dublin Corporation v McGowan* [1993] 1 IR 405, Keane J declined to grant relief under the 'new' s. 27 of the Local Government (Planning and Development) Act 1976, as inserted by s. 19(4) of the Local Government (Planning and Development) Act 1992: as to which see above, 449. The background to the application was as follows.

In 1988, the respondents had purchased a house in Dublin which, at the time of purchase, was divided into seven self-contained bed sitters or flats. The first respondent made inquiries of Dublin Corporation planning department as to whether there was any planning permission affecting the house. He was informed there was not, but in fact a planning permission of 1979 did exist which required that the premises be 'maintained in a maximum of three residential units as existing'. The respondents upgraded the seven existing flats in the house and the applicant then sought an injunction under s. 27 of the 1976 Act, as substituted by the 1992 Act, to prevent use of the house other than in accordance with the 1979 planning conditions.

In refusing the relief sought, Keane J considered that it was not appropriate to use what he described as the draconian powers contained in s. 27 of the 1976 Act, as amended, in a case such as the present where the respondents had acted *bona fide*, albeit on the basis of a mistaken impression gained from a less than thorough inquiry as to planning conditions. He categorised s. 27 as in essence a 'fire brigade' section intended to deal with an urgent situation requiring immediate action rather than a situation where an unauthorised development was completed a number of years ago. In this respect he applied *dicta* of Gannon J in *Dublin County Council v Kirby* [1985] ILRM 325 (as Morris J had in the Bentham case, above) and *Dublin County Council v Browne*, High Court, 6 October 1987 (1987 Review, 269-70). These indicated that s. 27 should not be used as a mechanism for securing partial completion of a project or in any sense a usual part of the planning process.

Keane J went on, however, to point out that the refusal of relief under s. 27 did not confer any benediction on the present use of the premises, and he concluded his judgment by stating that the extent to which its use conformed to the planning laws remained a matter for the Corporation to consider.

**State bodies** The applicability of the planning code to State bodies was considered by Lynch J in *Byrne and Ors v Commissioners of Public Works in Ireland*, High Court, 27 November 1992 and by O'Hanlon J and Costello J, respectively, in *Howard v Commissioners of Public Works in Ireland*, High Court, 3 December 1992 and 12 February 1993. In the *Howard* case, Costello J held that the Commissioners of Public Works were required to seek planning permission for the development of an interpretive centre at Mullaghmore, Co Clare. The High Court decision in the *Howard* case was immediately followed by the enactment of the State Authorities (Development and Management) Act 1993, which purported to validate all developments entered into by State authorities prior to the *Howard* case. The *Byrne* and *Howard* cases were consolidated into one appeal for the Supreme Court. In May 1993, the Supreme Court upheld the decision of Costello J: *Howard v Commissioners of Public Works in Ireland* [1993] ILRM 665. In view of the substantial number of issues arising from these cases, we will deal with them in detail in the 1993 Review.

**Time limits** The Local Government (Planning and Development) Act 1992 (discussed above, 448-50) provides for numerous changes concerning time limits under the planning legislation, especially in relation to planning appeals.

**Urban renewal: challenge to designation** The validity of an urban renewal designation under the Urban Renewal Act 1986 as well as the constitutionality of the 1986 Act was upheld by Lynch J in *Ambiorix Ltd and Ors v Minister for the Environment and Ors (No. 2)* [1992] 2 IR 37.

The plaintiffs' companies, all engaged in property development in Dublin, instituted proceedings seeking a declaration that the Minister for the Environment had acted *ultra vires* the 1986 Act in determining that a site on George's Quay, Dublin, owned by the fifth defendant, Irish Life Assurance plc, was a designated area under the 1986 Act. The plaintiffs also sought a declaration that the 1986 Act, in authorising the Minister for the Environment and the Minister for Finance to approve urban renewal designations, was in breach of Article 15 of the Constitution on the ground that this delegation to the Ministers was more than a mere implementation of policies in the Act and amounted to an unconstitutional delegation of the power to legislate. For discussion of an important discovery motion in the proceedings, see *Ambiorix Ltd and Ors v Minister for the Environment and Ors* [1992] ILRM 209; [1992] 1 IR 277 (1991 Review, 338-9).

Under s. 6(2) of the 1986 Act, the Minister for the Environment may, with the consent of the Minister for Finance, by Order 'declare an area to be a designated area where he is satisfied that there is a special need to promote urban renewal therein'. The George's Quay site was given designated area status by the Urban Renewal Act 1986 (Designated Areas) Order 1990 (SI No. 204 of 1990).

The first issue addressed by Lynch J was whether the plaintiffs had *locus standi* to institute the proceedings. He concluded that they had on the ground that as they were developers competing for the same property market as Irish Life, they could be adversely affected by a wrongful designation under the 1986 Act.

On the substantive points raised in the case, Lynch J first examined the non-constitutional issues, in accordance with the existing case law on this topic. The plaintiffs had argued that a designation under the 1986 Act could only be made if there was, under s. 6 of the 1986 Act, a 'special need to promote urban renewal', but that all that had been demonstrated in the instant case was that there was at most a 'special need for urban renewal'. Lynch J did not accept that the distinction sought to be drawn by the plaintiffs between the phrase contained in s. 6 of the 1986 Act and the phrase 'special need for urban renewal' was a real distinction. In addition, having reveiwed in detail the evidence given by the various expert witnesses called by the plaintiffs and defendants in the case, Lynch J also concluded that there was ample material before the Minister for the Environment that the George's Quay site fell within the test laid down in s.6 of the 1986 Act. In addition, he rejected the suggestion that the Minister had taken into account irrelevant matters or that he failed to take into account other relevant matters; and indeed he emphasised that the issue had been considered in detail, that there were significant fiscal losses to the State arising from the designation and the consequent loss of rates from Irish Life as a result. He also rejected the suggestion in the pleadings (which admittedly had not been followed up in the trial of the action) that any improper motivations could have been attributed to either Minister involved in the designation. On these grounds, therefore, Lynch J rejected the *ultra vires* claim.

On the constitutional issue, Lynch J noted that the Urban Renewal Act 1986 must be read in conjunction with the terms of the Finance Act 1986, which laid down in particular the fiscal considerations to be taken into account in making a designation under the Urban Renewal Act 1986 itself. When the two Acts were read together in this way, Lynch J considered that there was no unconstitutional delegation of legislative power, within the meaning of Article 15, to the Ministers for the Environment and Finance. He considered that the scheme and policy of the two Acts were clear, thus leaving only the details to be filled in by the Ministers, and so it fell within the test of delegation laid down by the Supreme Court in *Cityview Press Ltd v AnCO* [1980] IR 381. He pointed out, of course, that this power was subject to judicial review in that it must be exercised *bona fide* for the purposes of the legislation, and he cited *Cassidy v Minister for Industry and Commerce* [1978] IR 297 in this respect. However, as already indicated, Lynch J dismissed the claim by the plaintiffs that the 1986 Acts were in breach of Article 15 of the Constitution. On Article 15, see also *McDaid v Sheehy* [1989] ILRM 342 (HC); [1991] ILRM 250 (SC); [1991] 1 IR 1 (HC & SC) (1989 Review, 111-4 and the 1990 Review, 464-5).

**Urban renewal: Custom House Docks area** The Urban Renewal (Amendment) Act 1987 (Transfer of Land) Order 1992 (SI No. 441) transferred land in the Custom House Docks area from Dublin Corporation to the Custom House Docks Development Authority.

**Urban renewal: designation** The Urban Renewal Act 1986 (Designated Areas) Order 1992 (SI No. 342), the Urban Renewal Act 1986 (Remission of Rates) Scheme 1992 (SI No. 343) and the Finance Act 1987 (Designation of Urban Renewal Areas) Order 1992 (SI No. 368) conferred urban renewal status, with the connected taxation reliefs associated with such status, on an area in Tallaght, Dublin. On the urban renewal regime generally, see the *Ambiorix* case, above.

**Urban renewal: Temple Bar** The Temple Bar Area Renewal and Development (Compulsory Acquisition) Regulations 1992 (SI No. 91) set out the procedures to be followed concerning compulsory acquisitions made under the Temple Bar Area Renewal and Development Act 1991 (see the 1991 Review, 322).

## VALUATION (RATING)

**Fees** The Local Government (Certificate of Rateable Value) (Amendment) Order 1992 (SI No. 85) amends the fees payable in respect of obtaining a certificate of rateable value.

**Minister or State body as occupier** In *Dublin County Council v Aer Rianta CPT*, High Court, 15 May 1992, the plaintiff had instituted proceedings in the District Court claiming that the defendant, as the entity listed in the Valuation List as being the occupier of certain parts of Dublin Airport, was liable to pay rates for such occupation. This arose against the historical background that, for many years, Dublin Airport had been listed as being in the occupation of the Minister for Tourism, Transport and Communications and his predecessors and that such occupation was for public purposes within the meaning of the second proviso to s. 63 of the Poor Law Relief (Ireland) Act 1838, and thus exempt from rating. However, in the 1990 Valuation List, some of the airport was listed as being in the occupation of the defendant and the plaintiff's proceedings followed this change.

On case stated to the High Court, the defendant, a company established under the Air Navigation and Transport Act 1936 as the national airports authority, argued that it was not in rateable occupation as all the revenue it collected as airports authority was the property of the Minister for Tourism, Transport and Communications and it was therefore merely an agent of the Minister. Barron J agreed with this interpretation of the position of what is a State company. He thus concluded it was irrelevent for rating and valuation purposes whether the Minister or Aer Rianta was listed as occupier. He also noted with regret that this did not dispose of the real issue between the plaintiff and defendant, namely whether the occupation of the relevant parts of Dublin Airport referred to in the Valuation List were for public purposes, in which case it would not be rateable pursuant to the second proviso to s. 63 of the Poor Law Relief (Ireland) Act 1838. He regretted this especially given that there would be little if any financial implications for the plaintiff one way or the other.

**Occupation under licence** In *Aer Rianta CPT v Commissioner of Valuation (Tedcastles Aviation Fuels Ltd, Notice Party)*, High Court, 13 July 1992, another case concerning rateable occupation in an airport arose. Here, Tedcastles Aviation Fuels Ltd entered into an agreement with the Minister for Transport to manage a fuel depot in Shannon Airport for the servicing of Aerflot planes. The net issue was whether, on foot of this agreement, Tedcastles was to be regarded as an independent contractor, in which case it would be regarded as being in rateable occupation of the fuel depot. Tedcastles argued that it was acting merely as a servant or agent of the Minister under the agreement and was thus not in rateable occupation. The Valuation Tribunal held that Tedcastles were not in rateable occupation. On a case stated Lavan J, having recited in full the arguments adduced by the parties to the appeal and the authorities on which they relied, held that the Tribunal had erred in law. He concluded that Tedcastles were independent contractors under the agreement with the Minister, that it was thus in rateable occupation and that the depot was thus not in the occupation of the State and thus not exempt from rating on the ground that it was being used for public purposes. In this respect, Lavan J approved the principles laid down in *Westminster City Council v Southern Railway Co.* [1936] AC 551, *Renfrewshire Assessor v Old Consort Car Co.* 1960 SC 226 and by Henchy J in *Carroll v Mayo County Council* [1967] IR 364.

**Rights of way and easements: phone booths in shopping centre** In *Telecom Éireann v Commissioner of Valuation*, High Court, 5 October 1992, Telecom Éireann had, at the invitation of the owners of the St Stephen's Green Shopping Centre in Dublin, installed a number of pay phones in the shopping centre. The pay phones continued in the ownership of Telecom Éireann and employees of Telecom would, with permission, enter the shopping centre for the purposes of maintenance and collection of monies in the machines. The question arose as to whether Telecom was in rateable occupation of the pay phones for the purposes of the Valuation Acts. The Valuation Tribunal made a finding that Telecom were in occupation, and on a case stated to the High Court, O'Hanlon J upheld this finding by the Valuation Tribunal. O'Hanlon J referred to the definitions of rateable hereditament and occupation contained in s. 63 of the Poor Law (Ireland) Act 1838 and the extension in s. 12 of the Valuation (Ireland) Act 1852 to include 'all Rights of Way and other Rights or Easements over Land. . . .' He noted that this latter general definition of rateable hereditament and occupation extended beyond the scope of comparable British legislation in this area. Nonetheless, he was able to call in aid some English case law which had dealt with rateable occupation in certain narrow categories of the British valuation code. Thus, he was prepared to follow and apply the decision of the Court of Appeal in *Lancashire Telephone Co. v Overseers of Manchester* (1884-5) 14 QBD 267, where the Court had held that a comparable situation to that in the instant case constituted rateable occupation for certain purposes. On the basis of that case in particular, O'Hanlon J upheld the decision of the Valuation Tribunal in the instant case that Telecom Éireann were in rateable occupation of the pay phones in question.

**Rights of way and easements: marina** In *Trustees of Kinsale Yacht Club v Commissioner of Valuation* [1993] ILRM 393, Barr J held that a marina could be regarded as rateable as an easement under s. 12 of the Valuation (Ireland) Act 1852. S. 12 of the 1852 Act is discussed in the judgment delivered by O'Hanlon J one week before in the *Telecom Éireann* case, above. In the instant case, Barr J held that the Valuation Tribunal had erred in law in holding that a marina was not 'lands developed for . . . sport' within the meaning of the Schedule to the 1852 Act, inserted by s. 3 of the Valuation Act 1986. Barr J concluded that the marina did fall within this category which was exempt from being rated. Indeed, Barr J found that the findings of the Tribunal on the nature of the marina were such that no reasonable tribunal would have made such findings. Thus, he held he was entitled to overturn the Tribunal's finding on the principles laid down by the Supreme Court in *Mara v Hummingbird Ltd* [1982] ILRM 421. However, as indicated, while Barr J held that the Tribunal had acted prematurely in valuing the marina, he remitted the matter to the Tribunal with a view to fixing a valuation on the marina on the basis that it constituted an easement under s. 12 of the 1852 Act.

**Passenger terminal** In *Iarnród Éireann v Commissioner of Valuation*, High Court, 27 November 1992, Barron J dealt with the question of the rateable valuation of the boat and rail passenger terminal in Rosslare Harbour, Wexford. The terminal had been erected by Iarnród Éireann. The first issue which arose was whether, since the terminal had been built on land reclaimed from the sea, it was exempt from rates under s. 14 of the Valuation (Ireland) Act 1852, which specifically refers to exemption in respect of reclaimed land. However, the text of s. 14 of the 1852 Act and its reference to the terms of the Landed Property (Ireland) Act 1847 made clear that such exemption only applied to permanent agricultural improvements and not to the type of development involved in the instant case. The second issue in the case was the extent of the valuation to be applied to the common concourse, ramps and escalators in the terminal and whether these should be valued separately. Barron J noted three essential ingredients of rateable occupation, based apparently on Mr Justice Ronan Keane's, *Law of Local Government in Ireland*, p. 283: (i) it must be exclusive; (ii) it must be of value or benefit to the occupier; and (iii) it must not be for too transient a period. In the instant case, Barron J held that Iarnrod Éireann satisfied these three criteria. Although the public had access to the areas in question, Iarnrod Éireann held the lease to the terminal and it exercised the right to close the terminal according to its own terms. As to whether the common areas actually had a value, Barron J held that this was a matter which remained to be determined, based on the normal test of valuation which was the rent which would be paid by a hypothetical tenant for the use of these common areas. He commented that whether such a hypothetical tenant existed was a matter of fact and only if a valuation could be placed on these areas based on that test could a rateable value be placed on them.

**Valuation List** Two Supreme Court decisions in 1992 upheld High Court judgments to the effect that, on appeal to the Circuit Court, errors in the

Valuation List may be corrected. The decisions also dealt with the meaning of 'machinery' for the purposes of the rating code.

In *Siúicre Éireann CPT v Commissioner of Valuation* [1992] ILRM 682, the essential legislative background was as follows. S. 7 of the Valuation (Ireland) Act 1860 provides that 'machinery' in a mill or manufactory is exempt from rating, unless the 'machinery' is used for production of motive power. The appellant company (now Greencore plc) was the occupier of a factory premises on which some oil tanks were situated. One of these, a diesel oil tank, was a holding tank for diesel oil to supply mobile equipment. The other tanks were heavy fuel oil tanks, which contained pumping and heating equipment. The diesel oil tank was erroneously entered into the Buildings column of the Valuation List by the Commissioner for Valuation. It was agreed that all the tanks would be rateable if entered into the Miscellaneous column of the List. The company argued that they were exempt from rates on the grounds that the courts could not alter the List on appeal from the Commissioner. In the High Court, Hamilton P (High Court, 5 October 1988) rejected this argument. On a case stated, the Supreme Court (Finlay CJ, Hederman and McCarthy JJ) also rejected the company's arguments.

Applying its decision in *Beamish & Crawford Ltd v Commissioner of Valuation* [1980] ILRM 149, the Court noted that the heavy fuel oil tanks were not involved in the manufacturing process of the company, and since they were essentially holding tanks and receptacles for oil they were thus not exempt 'machinery' within s. 7 of the Valuation (Ireland) Act 1860. The Court also pointed out that none of the tanks were buildings within s. 12 of the Valuation (Ireland) Act 1852, but that they would be rateable under the Miscellaneous column of the Annual List. The Court was thus required to consider whether the Annual List could be amended by the Court.

On this, the Court expressly approved the reasoning of Costello J in *Pfizer Chemical Corp v Commissioner of Valuation*, High Court, 9 May 1989 (see the 1989 Review, 337-8). It held that since an appeal against valuation under s.23 of the Valuation (Ireland) Act 1852 could involve correction of an error by the Commissioner, and since s. 11 of the Valuation (Ireland) Act 1860 allowed a Superior Court to make such order as it may seem fit, the court was empowered not simply to correct errors by the Commissioner in favour of the appellant but to make good any other error in the compilation of the List. Thus the court was empowered to alter the Annual List and to transfer a rateable hereditament from one column in the List to another column. Accordingly, the Court ordered that the tanks would be entered in the Miscellaneous column.

On the same day as its decision in the *Siúicre Éireann* case, the Supreme Court delivered judgment in *Pfizer Chemical Corp v Commissioner of Valuation*, Supreme Court, 7 April 1992 the appeal from the judgment of

Costello J which it had approved in the *Siúicre Éireann* case, above. Not surprisingly, perhaps, the decision of Costello J was upheld. However, it may be usfeul to outline the background to the *Pfizer* case itself.

The appellant company was the owner and occupier of a large factory premises in which it manufactured food chemicals and bulk pharmaceuticals. The company appealed against the Commissioner's valuation for rating purposes of certain installations on the factory site. These included tanks for the reception of crude beet molasses, tanks for the reception of sulphuric acid, a number of other tanks as well as pipelines (which were over 40 miles long) used to transmit the molasses and acid to the factory. In addition to claiming that the Commissioner should not have rated the installations, the company argued that the Commissioner had wrongly categorised them in the Annual Valuation List and that the Court had no power on appeal to amend the Annual List. As already indicated, in the High Court Costello J held that the Commissioner had erred in holding the installations were rateable as machinery, but concluded that, since they were not buildings, they could be rated under the Miscellaneous column of the Annual List; and that the court had power to amend the Annual List, and would do so in the instant case. The Supreme Court (Finlay CJ, Hederman and McCarthy JJ) upheld the reasoning and conclusions of Costello J, as it had done in the *Siúicre Éireann* case, above.

## WATER POLLUTION

Regulations concerning water pollution are referred to in the Safety and Health chapter, 534-6, below.

# Practice and Procedure

## ABUSE OF PROCESS

In *McKinnistry v Impac Ltd*, High Court, 14 May 1992, Budd J applied the decision of the Supreme Court in *Sun Fat Chan v Osseous Ltd* [1992] 1 IR 425 (see the 1991 Review, 325-6) in declining to dismiss a claim for being an abuse of the process of the courts under O.19, rr.27 and 28 of the Rules of the Superior Courts 1986, in circumstances where there were conflicts of fact to be resolved in the proceedings. In *D.K. v A.K. and Ors* [1993] ILRM 710, a similar approach was taken by Costello J.

In *Gannon v B & I Steampacket Co. Ltd and Ors* [1993] 2 IR 359 (discussed in the Conflict of Laws chapter, 127-8, above) the Supreme Court also considered whether an action could be dismissed as an abuse of process.

## APPELLATE COURT FUNCTION

**Appeal from Employment Appeals Tribunal** In *Bates and Ors v Model Bakery Ltd* [1993] ILRM 22; [1992] ELR 193; [1993] 1 IR 359 (discussed in the Labour Law chapter, 403-5, above), the Supreme Court held that, on an appeal on a point of law from the Employment Appeals Tribunal under the Redundancy Payments Act 1967, the parties were confined to the findings of fact made by the Tribunal and could only raise issues of law.

**Findings of fact** In *Trustees of Kinsale Yacht Club v Commissioner of Valuation* [1993] ILRM 393, Barr J held that certain findings of the Valuation Tribunal were such that no reasonable tribunal would have made them and held he was entitled to overturn them on the principles laid down by the Supreme Court in *Mara v Hummingbird Ltd* [1982] ILRM 421: see the Local Government chapter, 465-6, above.

**Fresh evidence** In *Smyth and Anor v Tunney and Ors (No. 3)*, Supreme Court, 26 June 1992, the Supreme Court declined to introduce fresh evidence in an appeal before the Court. For earlier decisions, see the 1989 Review, 341-3 and the 1991 Review, 327-8.

The plaintiff had brought proceedings against the defendant, which involved, *inter alia*, allegations of fraudulent conduct by the defendants. In the High Court, Murphy J dismissed the claim: *Smyth and Anor v Tunney and Ors*, High Court, 6 October 1989 (see the 1989 Review, 127-9 and 444-5). In the course of his judgment, Murphy J had suggested that one of the defendants had lied and that the plaintiff was the victim of self-delusion. In the course of his appeal to the Supreme Court, the plaintiff brought an application under O.58, r.8 of the Rules of the Superior Courts 1986 seeking to introduce additional evidence in the case. The first matter related to the fact that one of the plaintiff's witnesses had lied under oath but that this had not been challenged by the defendant at the time. In addition, the plaintiff sought to introduce evidence as to similar alleged fraudulent conduct by the defendants in other commercial transactions. As indicated, the Supreme Court (Hederman, Costello and McCarthy JJ) declined to allow in the evidence.

The Court, referring to *Attorney General v Hitchcock* (1847) 1 Exch 91, held that there was no authority for the proposition that a witness may ordinarily be permitted to give evidence on the hearing of an appeal from a decision on fact so that he may recant earlier evidence and support a different case. Citing its decision in *Murphy v Minister for Defence* [1991] 2 IR 161 (see the 1991 Review, 327-8), the Court opined that, in any event, it was doubtful if the amended evidence was material to the real issue as ultimately decided in the High Court.

Nor did the Court consider that there was any reason to believe that the trial judge's conclusions would have been different if there had been additional evidence concerning similar alleged fraudulent activities by the defendants in other commercial transactions. Referring to the leading House of Lords decision in *R. v Boardman* [1975] AC 442, the Supreme Court noted that, although such evidence concerning the defendants' character might be credible, it was relevant only to cases where mistake was to be negatived or to prove intent, and it was not relevant to the issues in the instant case.

**Review of trial court's findings** The well-established limitations in an appeal on a point of law were evident again in 1992 in the Supreme Court decision in *Hay v O'Grady* [1992] ILRM 689; [1992] 1 IR 210. Consistent with the general approach, however, the Court indicated in *Kennedy v Galway Vocational Education Committee*, Supreme Court, 1 July 1992 that there are some situations where conclusions of fact by a trial judge will be overturned. We will deal with these two decisions here and refer to other Supreme Court decisions which are discussed more fully in other Chapters in the Review.

In *Hay v O'Grady* [1992] ILRM 689; [1992] 1 IR 210, the plaintiff, a nurse, was employed as a community facilitator by a hospital, represented in the proceedings by the defendant. The plaintiff's work involved bringing patients with severe mental disability into the ordinary life of the community; in effect acting as house parent for the patient to ensure that the patient could fend for themselves. Patients were selected on the basis of a review of patients by a management group of the hospital. One patient, for which the plaintiff was community facilitator, was prone to moods in which she would catch a person's hair or bite somebody. On one outing to a hotel from the home in which she had been placed, the patient had snatched some food and was restrained; she also took a chair from under a hotel guest when he had stood up to lift something off the table. The plaintiff was with the patient at the time. After this incident, it was decided to allow the patient remain in the home under the care of the plaintiff rather than recall her to hospital. Shortly after this incident, the patient assaulted the plaintiff.

The plaintiff instituted proceedings for damages claiming that the hospital had been negligent in allowing the patient to continue under the plaintiff's sole control and that it should have recalled the patient to the hospital in the light of the patient's behaviour. In the High Court, Lynch J held that the hospital had acted in a reasonable manner and that it was entitled, even in light of the incident in the hotel, to allow the patient continue in the home under the sole control of the plaintiff. On appeal by the plaintiff the Supreme Court (Finlay CJ, Hederman, McCarthy, O'Flaherty and Egan JJ) declined to interfere with the High Court decision.

Delivering the leading judgment, McCarthy J pointed out that although O.58 of the Rules of the Superior Courts 1986 provides that appeals to the Supreme Court shall be by way of re-hearing, this was to be interpreted as involving a re-hearing of the legal issues arising in the court of trial and did not extend to a re-hearing of the oral evidence given at the trial court. He accepted that, by this interpretation, the Court had, in effect, limited its jurisdiction under Article 34.4.3 of the Constitution in the case law on this topic. He cited in this context the leading decisions in *Northern Bank Finance Corp. Ltd v Charlton* [1979] IR 149 and *Dunne v National Maternity Hospital* [1989] ILRM 735; [1989] IR 91 (see the 1989 Review, 421-5).

One might comment here that the normal rule of interpretation is that the Supreme Court will not ordinarily limit its own jurisdiction except where such limit appears obvious either from the Constitution or from some (constitutionally permissible) express statutory limitation: that is the test established in the leading case *The People v Conmey* [1975] IR 341. Thus, in *Minister for Justice (Clarke) v Wang Zhu Jie* [1991] ILRM 823 (1991 Review, 350-1) only the fact that a statutory provision expressly required leave to appeal from a High Court judge appeared to preclude the Supreme Court from hearing an appeal. The case law thus appears to favour a quite liberal view of the Supreme Court's own jurisdiction. A literal reading of O.58 of the 1986 Rules would appear to lean in favour of a full re-hearing in the Supreme Court. Of course, as *Hay v O'Grady* itself indicates the Supreme Court has clearly laid down that it will hear evidence only in the most exceptional circumstances (see the 1989 Review, 341-3 and the 1991 Review, 327-8). This view would appear to be dictated by pragmatic considerations rather than any realistic interpretation of O.58 of the 1986 Rules. Perhaps it is time for the 1986 Rules to reflect the reality of what happens in the Supreme Court in practice.

To revert to *Hay v O'Grady*, the Court picked up the pragmatic theme by noting that since the Supreme Court does not have the benefit of seeing and hearing the witnesses as a trial judge does, it was required to accept the findings of fact made by the trial judge where these are supported by credible evidence, even if there is evidence to support the contrary view. The Court would not interfere with conclusions of law made by a trial judge based on findings of primary fact where it was clear that, as in the instant case, the trial judge found that all relevant considerations had been taken into account by the hospital. McCarthy J stated that the Supreme Court would thus refrain from attempting to substitute its own view for that of the person or persons charged with making the decision in question unless the decision-maker failed to inform themselves or to apply appropriate standards.

In this context, it is of some interest to note that the decision in *Hay v O'Grady* differed in one respect from the decision in *Dunne*, though not from that in the *Northern Bank Finance* case. In *Dunne*, the Supreme Court was reviewing a jury verdict, while in the *Northern Bank Finance* and *Hay* cases, the Court was reviewing findings of fact made by a trial judge. In *Hay v O'Grady*, the Court held that it should apply the same approach to appeals from a trial judge as it had applied to appeals from juries prior to the enactment of the Courts Act 1988. As the *Northern Bank Finance* case indicates, of course, this approach was already being applied in appropriate cases prior to 1988, but *Hay v O'Grady* confirms this basic approach. While McCarthy J was correct to point out the continuity of approach, it is right to add, however, that review of trial judge's decisions differ in an important respect from jury decisions: namely, that a trial judge will usually set out the reasons for coming to a particular conclusion, whereas a jury is not required to do so. As has been noted in the past, the setting out of reasons by a trial judge will, in some cases, permit an appellant to present a case with more precision than where appealing against a jury decision: with a jury decision, the benefit of the doubt may be given to the jury by the appeal court, whereas a trial judge will have exposed the precise reasoning on which a conclusion is based. On this distinction, we should note the decision of the Supreme Court in *Dunne v Honeywell Control Systems Ltd*, Supreme Court, 1 July 1993, which we will discuss in the 1993 Review.

The approach in *Hay v O'Grady*, above, was expressly followed by the

Court in *A.S. v S.S.* [1992] ILRM 732. The same basic principle was applied by the Court, without overt reference to any line of authority, in *H.S. v J.S.*, Supreme Court, 3 April 1992 (also discussed in the Family Law chapter, 347-8, above). As already indicated, there are, however, situations in which the Court has been prepared to reverse findings of fact by trial judges: see the cases referred to in the 1991 Review, 328. A number of decisions in 1992 added to the list.

In this Chapter, we will discuss the decision in *Kennedy v Galway Vocational Education Committee*, Supreme Court, 1 July 1992. Here, the plaintiff had instituted proceedings claiming damages in respect of injuries alleged to have been sustained while she was a pupil in a vocational school under the control of the defendant VEC, at a time when she was 17 years. In evidence, the plaintiff stated that she fell in a pool of water in a kitchen in the school. She stated that she had been sent to the kitchen by a teacher, that she fell in the presence of another pupil, that she reported the accident immediately to a cleaner and that she attended a doctor concerning the accident. In evidence on the VEC's behalf, the plaintiff's teacher stated that pupils were not sent to the kitchen in the manner alleged by the plaintiff. The pupil stated by the plaintiff to have been in the kitchen denied being there and the cleaner to whom the plaintiff stated she reported the accident could not recollect the event. In the High Court, Egan J held that, although the plaintiff's evidence had been unsatisfactory in some respects, it could not be said that she had lied. He concluded that, as the plaintiff's evidence indicated that the pool of water had been in position for some time, the defendant was in breach of its duty of care to her and he awarded the plaintiff £20,762. On appeal by the defendant, the Supreme Court (Finlay CJ, Hederman and O'Flaherty JJ) unanimously allowed the appeal and dismissed the plaintiff's claim.

Without citing authority on the point, the Court noted that, while it would not normally interfere with findings of primary fact by a trial judge, there were exceptional cases where the evidence was so clearly one way as to require the intervention of the Supreme Court to say that the verdict entered by the trial judge could not stand. The Court stated that it would not have interfered with the findings in the instant case if the plaintiff's evidence had been contradicted on one item, albeit the plaintiff's account would then be rendered unsatisfactory. However, the Court concluded that the cumulative effect of the evidence on the defendant's behalf (which, the judges noted, had not been challenged as unreliable) was such that it was impossible to say that the plaintiff had made out her case, and on the contrary her case had been comprehensively disproved. In the circumstances, the Court held that the verdict in her favour would be set aside.

In keeping with the approach in the *Kennedy* case, the Court in *K. v K.*,

Supreme Court, 13 February 1992 (discussed in the Family Law chapter, 372-6, above) considered a matter not expressly dealt with in the High Court in a situation where the Supreme Court considered it was in as good a position to review the relevant evidence as the High Court judge had been. Similarly, in *Best v Wellcome Foundation Ltd and Ors* [1992] ILRM 609 (discussed in the Torts chapter, 610-11, below) the Court reversed a finding of primary fact by a trial judge in a situation where the Supreme Court considered it was in as good a position to evaluate the evidence given as the High Court judge had been.

## CASE STATED

**Service of case stated** In *Director of Public Prosecutions (Murphy) v Regan* [1993] ILRM 335, O'Hanlon J reluctantly declined to hear a case stated where the applicant prosecutor had failed to serve a notice in writing on the defendant as required by s. 2 of the Summary Jurisdiction Act 1857.

The defendant had been charged with an offence of driving with excess alcohol under s. 49 of the Road Traffic Act 1961, as amended. At the defendant's trial, the prosecution had established in evidence that the defendant had been arrested at 12.20 am on 18 December 1990 and had given a sample of his urine to a registered medical practitioner. The prosecution also tendered the form which had been duly completed by the registered medical practitioner, and this put the time of the taking of the specimen of urine as 12.50 am on 18 December 1990. However, oral evidence on this had not been tendered by the prosecution. The District Court judge had then dismissed the case on the ground that the prosecution had failed to prove that the specimen of urine had been taken from the defendant within three hours of the time when it was alleged the defendant was driving with an excess of alcohol.

The prosecutor then sought a case stated to the High Court as to whether the District Court decision was correct in law. However, two preliminary time limit issues arose in the appeal. First, the defendant argued that the appeal should not be heard because the prosecution had failed by one day to meet the three day period laid down in s. 2 of the Summary Jurisdiction Act 1857 for transmission of the case stated to the Central Office of the High Court after receipt of the case stated from the District Court judge. Second, the defendant also argued that the prosecution had also failed to meet the same three day period in the 1857 Act for the service of notice of the case stated on the other party to the appeal, in this case the defendant. On this point, the prosecution had been in communication with the solicitor who had acted for the defendant in the District Court in connection with the drafting of the case stated. During these communications, the solicitor stated to the prosecution that 'we have written to our client to enquire if we still have instructions to act for him' and that two letters seeking instructions for the appeal had elicited no reply from him. The case stated was served on the solicitor. In an affidavit for the case stated, the solicitor averred that at the time of service he had no instructions from his client.

S. 2 of the 1857 Act provides that the person seeking a case stated:

> shall, within three days after receiving such case, transmit the same to the Court named in his application, first giving notice in writing of such appeal, with a copy of the case so stated and signed, to the other party to the proceeding. . . .

As to transmission of the case stated to the High Court Central Office, O'Hanlon J was prepared, on the authorities, to extend the period for service by one day under the terms of the general discretion to dispense with procedural requirements conferred by O.122 of the Rules of the Superior Courts 1986. He relied in particular on the decision of the Supreme Court in *Attorney General v Shivnan* [1970] IR 66 in this respect.

However, on the second requirement, to serve notice of the case stated on the defendant, O'Hanlon J took a different view. He considered that the authorities did not support the view that the general discretion in O.122 of the 1986 Rules could be used to extend the time laid down in this part of s. 2 of the 1857 Act. He summarised the authorities as requiring service within the appointed time upon a person who could fairly be regarded as an agent for the respondent to the appeal and where diligent efforts had been made to effect personal service on the respondent. He cited the decision of Blayney J in *Crowley v McVeigh* [1990] ILRM 220 (see the 1989 Review, 154-5) as falling into this category where the requirements of s. 2 had been met. On this aspect of the case, he considered that since the solicitor who had acted for the defendant had indicated that he had no instructions from his client, the service on the solicitor of the case stated failed to meet the requirements of s. 2 of the 1857 Act. He also noted that no attempt had been made to effect personal service on the defendant, and in the circumstances to allow an extension of time would expand the scope of the existing authorities. As indicated, O'Hanlon J was reluctant to reach this conclusion as he had 'a strong impression that the decision in the case was not one which I would uphold'. He concluded by stating that:

> it would be desirable that rigid time limits prescribed by statute for procedural matters should be relaxed by giving more discretion to the courts to extend them where there are reasonable grounds for doing so.

While this is undoubtedly a general sentiment that many would applaud, it seems somewhat ironic in the particular context of this case. The authorities to which O'Hanlon J alluded in his judgment would appear to have taken an inconsistent line on s. 2 of the 1857 Act and thereby arrived at a self-imposed rigidity. As can be seen from the quotation given from s.2 of the 1857 Act, the two time limits laid down in s. 2 appear in the same sentence, yet in respect of one time limit the authorities are prepared to hold that there is a general jurisdiction to extend the time for service while with the other there appears to be the 'rigid' approach to which O'Hanlon J refers. Perhaps it is time for the courts to consider whether the authorities require reconsideration rather than for the legislation to be amended. There are many examples in recent years of the courts condemning the use of 'technicalities' to avoid a discussion of substantive issues. For an example, see the judgment of Lynch J in *Director of Public Prosecutions v Corbett (No. 2)* [1992] ILRM 674, discussed in the Criminal Law chapter, 248-50, above.

## CONSOLIDATION

In *Duffy v News Group Newspapers Ltd and Ors* [1992] ILRM 835; [1992] 2 IR 369, the plaintiff had instituted proceedings for defamation against the defendants arising from an article published by the defendants in a newspaper, 'The News of the World'. The article included descriptions of certain activities of paramilitary organisations, some of which were alleged to have occurred in the ground of Crossmaglen Gaelic Football Club. The plaintiff was, at the time, Chairman of Crossmaglen Gaelic Football Club and his statement of claim alleged that the article referred to him. A substantial number of other persons also instituted proceedings against the defendants arising from the article. The defendants' defence did not plead justification but stated that the article did not refer to the plaintiffs. The defendants sought to have the actions consolidated under O.49, r.6 of the Rules of the Superior Courts 1986. In the High Court, O'Hanlon J granted the application, but on appeal by the plaintiff the Supreme Court (Hederman, McCarthy and Costello JJ) reversed the High Court order.

Delivering the Court's decision, McCarthy J, in a helpful summary of the position, noted that the parties were agreed on the legal principle applicable to motions under O.49, r.6 of the 1986 Rules: (i) whether there is a common question of law or fact of sufficient importance at issue; (ii) whether there would be a substantial saving of expense or inconvenience; and (iii) whether there would be a likelihood of confusion or miscarriage of justice.

On the first point, McCarthy J pointed out that, in the absence of a plea of justification, the only issue for the court trying the action would be whether the article referred to the plaintiffs. In this context, he noted that although the actions arose out of the same article, they did not involve common issues of law or of fact, since the question of whether the article referred to the different plaintiffs would be a separate issue for each person involved. Citing the decision in *Horwood v Statesman Publishing Co. Ltd* (1929) 98 LJKB 450, McCarthy J stated that this would be a separate issue of law for the trial judge to determine and then to leave to the jury to decide as a matter of fact.

McCarthy J accepted that the wording of O.49, r.6 of the 1986 Rules was very wide, but added that this did not mean that the Court should apply that discretion widely or that there was not a heavy burden on the party seeking consolidation. Noting that the Supreme Court was in as good a position on this issue as the High Court, he concluded that consolidation should not be ordered. He stated, in connection with the other two issues identified as relevant under O.49, r.6, that there would be no substantial saving involved in a consolidation, and it was likely that some confusion and injustice would arise in relation to witnesses called for the different plaintiffs, carrying the risk that all plaintiffs might stand or fall together.

Although the Supreme Court considered that consolidation was not appropriate in the instant case, it did order that the actions be tried in succession and be presided over by the same judge. This conclusion is consistent with the decision arrived at by Blayney J in *O'Neill v Ryanair Ltd (No. 2)* [1992] 1 IR 160 (discussed in the 1990 Review, 429-30), which was referred to in argument.

## COSTS

**District Court** The District Court (Costs) Rules 1992 (SI No. 225), which came into effect on 10 August 1992, set out a new scale of solicitors' costs to take account of the changes in the District Court's jurisdiction contained in the Courts Act 1991: see the 1991 Review, 347.

**Indemnity against costs of appeal** In *In re Hibernian Transport Co. Ltd*, Supreme Court, 21 January 1992 was another Supreme Court judgment in a long-running liquidation. The named company, Hibernian Transport Co. Ltd, and a subsidiary, Palgrave Murphy Ltd, were put into liquidation in 1970. At the time, both companies were insolvent. However, as a result of complex legal issues which arose for determination in the course of the liquidation, it was not possible to pay the creditors until 1983, by which time a substantial sum stood in the company's bank account. The result was that after each of the creditors was paid in full, a surplus still remained and the question thus arose as to whether the creditors were entitled to interest on the sums owing.

Parties were nominated to represent the respective interests of the company's creditors and of the company's shareholders. The President of the High Court indicated that, although he would not make an order indemnifying these parties in relation to their legal costs, he would be prepared to make an order discharging their costs after the application was heard. In the application, Carroll J held that interest was payable on certain sums owing to the creditors: [1990] ILRM 42 (see the 1989 Review, 60-2). The representatives of the company's shareholders appealed this decision to the Supreme Court. On an application for an order indemnifying them in respect of the legal costs of the appeal, the Supreme Court (Finlay CJ, Hederman and McCarthy JJ) made the unusual decision of granting a declaration to that effect to the representatives of the shareholders, though not an order.

The Court pointed out that there was a general presumption against the making of orders for costs in advance of a hearing, whether by a court of first instance or a court of appeal, since an order for costs was largely a matter of discretion after the determination of the issue arising in the case. However, in the exceptional circumstances which arose in the instant case, where a difficult question of law arose which had not been addressed by Irish courts prior to the instant case, the Court accepted that it was appropriate that the Court indicate its intention to order the liquidator to discharge the parties' legal costs irrespective of the outcome of the appeal. The Court stated that no order would be made in relation to the priority of payment of costs because, having regard to the large surplus standing to the company, it was unlikely that any difficulty would arise as to payment of such costs. See also the Company Law chapter, 96-8, above.

## COURTHOUSES

The Civil Bill Courts (Ireland) Act 1851 (Adaptation) (No. 2) Order 1992 (SI No. 174) was made to enable the government to exercise the functions formerly exercisable by the Lord Lieutenant under s.31 of the 1851 Act. The Order was made by the Minister for Justice in purported exercise of the powers conferred on him by s. 22(4)(b) of the Courts (Supplemental Provisions) Act 1961. It is notable that the Civil Bill Courts (Ireland) Act 1851 (Adaptation) Order 1992 (SI No. 193) was made for precisely the same purpose as SI No. 174. However, SI No. 193 was made in purported exercise of the powers conferred on the government by s. 12 of the Adaptation of Enactments Act 1922 and s. 5 of the Constitution (Consequential Provisions) Act 1937.

The purpose of these Orders was to allow the government to determine that a particular courthouse was no longer required for sittings of the Circuit

Court. The validity of these Orders was successfully challenged in *Hoey v Minister for Justice* [1994] 1 ILRM 334. We will discuss this decision in the 1993 Review.

## DELAY

The case law on delay in civil proceedings is discussed in the Torts chapter, below. See also the case law in criminal proceedings discussed in the Criminal Law chapter, 246-7, above.

## DISCOVERY

**Discovery as substantive action** In the 1991 Review, 335-6, we discussed the Supreme Court decision in *Megaleasing UK Ltd and Ors. v Barrett and Ors* [1992] 1 IR 219, in which the Court had acknowledged the possibility that discovery could be sought as a substantive remedy. The Court did so in the context of granting a stay of execution on a High Court order allowing discovery as a substantive remedy. In *Megaleasing UK Ltd and Ors v Barrett and Ors (No. 2)* [1993] ILRM 497, the Supreme Court reversed the High Court order made in the instant case, but again acknowledged that a substantive discovery remedy could be given in appropriate circumstances.

The background to the case was, briefly, as follows. The plaintiffs (which we will describe as the companies) instituted plenary proceedings against the defendants in which the substantive relief was for orders of discovery concerning certain invoices which had been paid by the companies. Payment of the invoices had been authorised by certain of the defendants, who were employees of the companies, but the companies alleged that they had received no consideration or value for the payments made. The purpose of the discovery orders was stated by the companies to be to facilitate them in bringing proceedings against other parties whose tortious acts the companies claimed had caused them to suffer loss. As we already noted, in the High Court, Costello J had granted the plaintiffs the relief sought, and refused to grant a stay of execution upon the order, but the Supreme Court had granted the stay in its 1991 judgment: *Megaleasing UK Ltd and Ors v Barrett and Ors* [1992] 1 219. In the full appeal, the Supreme Court (Finlay CJ, Hederman, McCarthy, O'Flaherty and Egan JJ) reversed Costello J's order, allowing the defendants' appeal.

Referring to the decision in *Orr v Diaper* (1876) 4 Ch D 92, the Court pointed out that it was well established that the courts had jurisdiction to order discovery as a substantive remedy, in circumstances where a person who inadvertently became involved in tortious activity was in possession of information which would assist the victim to obtain justice. Citing the leading decision of the House of Lords in *Norwich Pharmacal Co and Ors v Customs and Excise Commissioners* [1974] AC 133 (as the Court had done in its 1991 judgment in the instant case), the Court held that this jurisdiction should be exercised sparingly and should be confined to cases where very clear proof of wrongdoing has been established, and to merely seeking the names and identities of wrongdoers rather than factual information concerning the commission of the wrong.

Applying this approach to the instant case, the Court noted that the companies had already established the names of the officers in their companies who were responsible for the issuing of the invoices in question and that, through the settlement of a number of claims with them, had obtained statements from them that they were unaware of the eventual beneficiaries. In these circumstances, the Court concluded that the further claim by the companies that they required discovery for the purposes of obtaining a satisfactory explanation for the payments fell far short of establishing a wrongdoing which would justify making an order for discovery as a substantive remedy. Like many leading decisions in the law, the *Megaleasing* case will be remembered for being the first which established the principle of discovery as a substantive remedy. Whether the narrow confines marked out for the remedy in the instant case will be followed in the future remains, of course, for future decisions. Certainly, the Supreme Court decision gives no cause for hope that discovery as a substantive relief will be a common armoury in civil claims alleging corporate fraud.

**Legal professional privilege** *Murphy v Kirwan*, High Court, 9 April 1992; [1994] ILRM 293 (SC) is a highly unusual case in that Costello J ordered discovery by the plaintiff of correspondence, notes and memoranda between the plaintiff and his legal advisers and between those legal advisers. The case thus constitutes an exception to the normal privilege attached to communications with legal advisers. The order arose in the following way.

The plaintiff had instituted the instant proceedings for specific performance claiming the existence of an enforceable agreement to assign certain shares in a company to the plaintiff. These shares related to ownership of a number of properties. The defendant at all times denied the existence of this alleged agreement and sought to have the claim dismissed by the High Court as vexatious and an abuse of the processes of the court. This application was refused, and the defendant then entered a full defence to the claim and also entered a counterclaim claiming damages on the ground that by the institution of the proceedings, the plaintiff had deliberately endeavoured to forestall the sale by the defendant to a third party of the properties connected with the shares involved in the litigation, and he claimed that the proceedings were frivolous, vexatious and brought without reasonable cause and were an abuse of the processes of the court.

On the hearing of the plaintiff's claim, the trial judge non-suited the plaintiff after hearing his evidence and dismissed his claim with costs. The defendant's counterclaim was then deferred and it was in this context that the defendant then sought discovery of the communications between the plaintiff and his legal advisers and between the plaintiff's legal advisers. The plaintiff sought to resist discovery on the basis of the usual privilege attaching to such matters. As already indicated, Costello J considered that the instant case fell within the narrow category of exceptional circumstances in which discovery should be ordered.

In this respect, Costello J noted that the general nature of legal professional privilege had been explained by Finlay CJ in his judgment in *Smurfit Paribas Bank Ltd v AAB Export Finance Ltd* [1990] ILRM 588; [1990] 1 IR 469 (see the 1990 Review, 435-6). He also noted that the Chief Justice had expressly stated that no argument had been addressed to the Supreme Court as to possible exceptions to the general rule. Costello J referred to *Williams v Quebrada Railway Land and Copper Co Ltd* [1895] 2 QB 751, *Crescent Farm (Sidcup) Sports Ltd v Sterling Offices Ltd* [1972] Ch 553 and *Gamlen Chemical Co. (UK) Ltd v Rochem Ltd* [1983] RPC 1 as indicating that the courts were prepared to refuse privilege in cases involving fraud and the somewhat wider category of circumstances which Costello J described as 'commercial dishonesty'. He noted that this involved a conflict between the proper administration of justice, which included the freedom to communicate with one's legal advisers in complete freedom and that such communications will remain secret, and the need for full disclosure of all relevant documents so that truth can be ascertained and justice done. He then asked, rhetorically, why the need for full disclosure should take priority over confidentiality. In answer to this, Costello J stated in an important passage:

> It seems to me that the basis for the exception must be the conclusion that in exceptional cases which may involve a degree of moral turpitude which is much greater than that which arise[s] in other causes of action it is in the public interest that no restriction be placed on the courts' capacity to ascertain the facts to ensure that a wrongdoer does not escape the consequences of his actions.

In the instant case, it was common case that the communications sought on discovery were relevant to the defendant's counterclaim, but this would obviously not be sufficient to warrant discovery. What was crucial in the case was Costello J's conclusion that the defendant's counterclaim involved a claim of moral turpitude on the part of the plaintiff which justified refusing to allow privilege attach to the legal communications. In particular, Costello J noted that what the counterclaim:

> alleged is that the plaintiff has abused the courts procedures and has deliberately maintained a baseless claim not for the purpose of redressing a wrong done but to obtain a commercial advantage by forcing the defendant to concede an unjustified claim so as to avoid the consequences of having to defend a High Court action.

Costello J concluded that the lack of honesty thus alleged fell into the categories of wrongdoing indicated in the case law referred to. He thus ordered discovery of the items sought by the defendant. We may note here that, in 1993, the Supreme Court upheld the decision of Costello J: [1994] ILRM 293. We will return to this decision in the 1993 Review.

While the instant case is of great importance in indicating circumstances in which discovery of communications with legal advisers which are clearly in contemplation of legal proceedings, it must be concluded that the general privilege remains intact. However, the courts have clearly indicated that this privilege will not be extended, a point noted in the 1990 Review, 435-6, and that it is not an automatic entitlement.

**Medical reports: previous litigation** In *Quinlivan v Touhy and Curtin*, High Court, 29 July 1992, the plaintiff had instituted proceedings in damages against the defendants arising from a road traffic accident. The plaintiff had been involved in a previous accident in which she had suffered similar injuries. Those previous proceedings had been settled, but medical reports had been prepared for the plaintiff in anticipation of those proceedings. The defendants in the instant case sought to discover those medical resports, and the plaintiff claimed privilege. Barron J agreed with the plaintiff that the privilege which had attached to those reports in the previous proceedings carried forward to the instant case. In this, he expressly approved the similar approach taken by Costello J in *Bord na Mona v J. Sisk & Son Ltd* [1990] 1 IR 85 (see the 1989 Review, 350). Barron J did hold out the possibility that the defendants might be able to obtain the reports in some other way. Some indication of how this could arise might be gleaned from another aspect of the application for discovery. Barron J was required to determine whether correspondence which led up to the settlement of the plaintiff's previous claim should have been discovered. He was prepared to hold that they could be discoverable, but only if what was in them was relevant to the issues in the present proceedings. However, he also stressed that a judge dealing with any such documents might wish to see them before making any order for discovery, since issues of privilege could again arise. In the circumstances, he merely made an order requiring the plaintiff to make discovery of any other documents relevant to the instant proceedings.

**Memoranda leading to legislation** In *An Blascaod Mór Teo and Ors v Commissioners of Public Works in Ireland and Ors*, High Court, 27 November 1992, Murphy J rejected an application for discovery of documents which had been used in the preparation of an Act of the Oireachtas: see the discussion in the Constitutional Law chapter, 139-41, above.

**Non-party discovery** In *Allied Irish Banks plc and Anor v Ernst & Whinney (Minister for Industry and Commerce, Notice Party)* [1993] 1 IR 375, the Supreme Court laid down important guidelines on the extent and scope of the procedure introduced by O.31, r.21 of the Rules of the Superior Courts 1986 by which discovery can be ordered against persons not party to proceedings. For previous decisions in this area, see the 1988 Review, 328-31.

The decision in the instant case arose in what had been heralded as one of the most complex civil actions in the history of the State, to involve claims totalling over £500 million, scheduled to begin its substantive phase in October 1993 and projected to last one year: see, for example, *Sunday Business Post*, 29 August 1993. However, it may be noted that the proceedings were subsequently settled in 1993.

The plaintiffs instituted proceedings in negligence against the defendant, a firm of accountants. The defendant had acted as statutory auditors for an insurance company, the Insurance Corporation of Ireland plc. The second plaintiff, a subsidiary of Allied Irish Banks plc, had purchased the entire equity in the Insurance Corporation. Subsequently, the Insurance Corporation suffered virtual financial collapse, and an administrator was appointed to the company under the Insurance (No. 2) Act 1983. The second plaintiff claimed that it invested in the Insurance Corporation in reliance on information provided by the defendant firm, that the defendant had been negligent in the putting up of that information, that it acted in breach of its duty of care to the plaintiffs, and that consequently the plaintiff suffered financial loss. The defendant firm denied all these claims.

In the course of the proceedings, the defendant firm sought discovery of certain documents from the Department of Industry and Commerce (the government department responsible for the overseeing of insurance companies and since merged into the Department of Enterprise and Employment), in particular documentation concerning the acquisition by the second plaintiff of its equity in the Insurance Corporation and of the events leading up to the appointment of the administrator to the Insurance Corporation. In the High Court, Costello J refused the order for discovery, on the ground that, although the defendant had established that the documents sought existed, it had not established that they must all be relevant to the proceedings between the parties, and that the Court had no jurisdiction to make an order which might uncover certain documents of relevance to proceedings.

After an appeal against this decision had been lodged by the defendant in the Supreme Court, a list was prepared of the precise issues in the case and of the categories of documents relevant to those issues. The Supreme Court thus had an opportunity to examine the application against a much more focused background than had Costello J. This was to prove influential in the decision by the Court (Finlay CJ, Hederman, McCarthy, O'Flaherty and Egan JJ) to reverse Costello J's decision and to order the discovery sought. As also indicated, the Court made some general observations on third party discovery.

Delivering the leading judgment, the Chief Justice (with whom Hederman and Egan JJ agreed) noted that, while the jurisdiction of the Court to order third party discovery under O.31, r.21 of the 1986 Rules differed in certain respects from that where discovery was directed at a party to proceedings under O.31, r.12, the essential purpose was the same, namely that justice be done on the basis of a full consideration of the evidence.

Finlay CJ stated that the differences in an application under O.31, r.21 were that the Court must be satisfied from evidence adduced by the application: (i) that the notice party is likely to have documents in its possession and that these documents are relevant to the issues in the case; (ii) that discovery will not be unduly oppressive to the notice party, although the applicant need not establish that specific documents are in the hands of the notice party; and (iii) that any order for discovery to the notice party should indicate in simple form the relevance to the case of the documents being sought by the applicant.

The Chief Justice stated that, taking account these particular factors, the High Court had taken the correct general approach in the instant case, except in relation to the onus on the defendant to establish the relevance of documents to the instant case, though he noted that the Supreme Court had been in a better position to assess the relevance of the documents sought to the issues in the proceedings having regard to the list prepared by the defendant for the appeal hearing. He also stated, for the benefit of practitioners in particular, that a similar list or schedule linking the issues in proceedings to the documents sought would appear an essential proof in an action involving multiple issues.

Finally, the Court concluded that although compliance with an order for discovery would involve the expenditure of considerable time by officials of the Department, this could not be regarded as being oppressive having regard to the contribution towards the administration of justice which discovery of documents made.

**Privilege: public interest** In *Attorney General v Mr Justice Hamilton* [1993] ILRM 81; [1993] 2 IR 250, the Supreme Court considered the application of the case law on public interest privilege in the context of evidence being given before a tribunal of inquiry having the powers conferred by the Tribunals of Inquiry (Evidence) Acts 1921 and 1979: see the discussion in the Constitutional Law chapter, 213, above.

## ENFORCEMENT OF COURT ORDERS

In *Berryman v Governor of Loughan House*, High Court, 16 November 1992, the extent of the discretion involved in determining whether a debtor may be committed to prison was discussed.

By an order of the District Court made in March 1991 under s. 5 of the Enforcement of Court Orders Act 1926, the applicant was committed to prison for two months for failure to pay instalments on foot of an instalment order in respect of a debt. On foot of the committal order, a warrant for the applicant's arrest was applied for and obtained in the District Court in May 1992 but this warrant was not executed until September 1992, when the applicant was lodged in Mountjoy Prison. He was later transferred to Loughan House. The applicant then applied for an inquiry under Article 40.4.2 of the Constitution into the legality of his detention. O'Hanlon J ultimately held that his detention was not lawful and ordered his release, the applicant having previously been granted bail.

O'Hanlon J rejected the applicant's first argument that the failure to issue a warrant for his detention within 6 months of the committal order made in March 1991 was in breach of the 6 month limit in r.68(5) of the District Court Rules 1948. Citing with approval the decision in *The State (McKeever) v Governor of Mountjoy Prison*, Supreme Court, 19 December 1966, O'Hanlon J concluded that r.68(5) was confined to criminal matters and did not apply to the *sui generis* powers exercisable under the 1926 Act.

However, O'Hanlon J went on to make some significant comments on the approach which should be taken in cases of this kind. He stated that where an application to commit a debtor to prison is made under s. 18 of the Enforcement of Court Orders Act 1926, as substituted by s. 6 of the Enforcement of Court Orders Act 1940, a District Judge has a considerable discretion to commit or not to commit or to vary any previous instalment order. He considered that this discretion could not properly be exercised unless the debtor is given notice of the making of an application to commit, and he held that failure to give such notice would invalidate a committal order made in the debtor's absence. However, he stated that this point did not determine the instant case since the applicant had challenged the validity of the arrest warrant.

On this, O'Hanlon J held that, having regard to the delay between March 1991, when the orginal committal order was made, and May 1992, when the warrant for arrest was applied for, and the further delay up to September 1992 when the arrest warrant was executed, it would have been more appropriate at that stage to apply *de novo* for a new committal order. This would have allowed the Distrrict Judge to reconsider the matter in the light of any evidence as to the debtor's financial circumstances in the intervening period and any other relevant evidence.

The *Berryman* case will undoubtedly prove of importance in the application of the 1926 and 1940 Acts in the future, assuming that the Acts remain in place in the future. We may briefly note here that the continued committal of debtors to prison (albeit only wilful defaulters within the 1926 and 1940 Acts) was subject to some criticism in 1993 by the UN Committee which examined the State's implementation of the UN Covenant on Civil and Political Rights. We will return to this in the 1993 Review.

## EVIDENCE

**Res ipsa loquitor** In *Lindsay v Mid Western Health Board and Ors* [1993] ILRM 550; [1993] 2 IR 147, the Supreme Court dealt with the doctrine of *res ipsa loquitor*: see the discussion of the case in the Torts chapter, 592-7, below.

**Similar fact** The circumstances in which similar fact evidence might be admissible were adverted to by the Supreme Court in *Smyth and Anor v Tunney and Ors (No. 3)*, Supreme Court, 26 June 1992 (discussed above, 469-70).

## INTEREST

In *Texaco (Irl) Ltd v Murphy (No. 3)*, Supreme Court, 15 May 1992, the question of ordering the payment of interest on an award was alluded to: see the discussion of the case in the Revenue chapter, 515-7, below.

## JUDICIAL INFLUENCE

In September 1992, Mr Justice Niall McCarthy and his wife Barbara McCarthy died in a car crash in Spain, while attending the annual conference of the International Association of Judges. His long and distinguished career at the Bar and on the Bench drew many tributes at the beginning of the Legal term in October 1992: see *Irish Times*, 6 October 1992. For a brief exegisis of his career, see the obituary in (1992) 14 DULJ.

## JUDICIAL AND COURT OFFICER PENSIONS

The Courts (Preservation of Superannuation) (Court Officers) Regulations 1992 (SI No. 10) make provision for pensions for the Master of the High Court, the Taxing Master and for County Registrars. The Regulations were made under the Courts (Supplemental Provisions) (Amendment) Act 1991 (see the 1991 Review, 346).

## JUDGMENT MORTGAGE

Certain aspects of the procedure for applying for a well-charging order on foot of a judgment mortgage were considered in *Irish Bank of Commerce v O'Hara*, Supreme Court, 7 April 1992 (see the discussion in the Land Law chapter, 410-3, above).

## LEGAL AID

**Civil Legal aid: family cases** In *M.F. v Legal Aid Board*, High Court, 4 November 1992; [1993] ILRM 797 (SC), O'Hanlon J in the High Court quashed a refusal by the Legal Aid Board to grant the applicant civil legal aid in connection with judicial separation proceedings instituted by her husband under the Judicial Separation and Family Law Reform Act 1989.

The Board had considered that the applicant did not come within the requirement of paragraph 3.2.3(4) of the non-statutory Scheme of Civil Legal Aid and Advice that she was 'reasonably likely to be successful in the proceedings'. O'Hanlon J held that this provision could not be applied directly to the context of judicial separation proceedings, where, he pointed out, there were no real winners or losers. Thus, such proceedings should not be approached on the same basis as ordinary civil litigation *inter partes*. O'Hanlon J concluded that the 'likelihood of success' test could only be applied in the context of family proceedings in wholly exceptional cases and, indeed, he felt unable to contemplate a particular example of such exceptional circumstances. He also pointed out that in the instant case the applicant's husband had, in fact, been granted a certificate of legal aid in connection with the proceedings instituted by him. He quashed the Board's refusal and ordered it to reconsider the applicant's application afresh in the light of the principles enunciated in his judgment.

The order made by O'Hanlon J was substantially upheld by the Supreme Court in a decision delivered in March 1993. While the Supreme Court varied the order of O'Hanlon J in minor respects, it also acknowledged that judicial separation proceedings were in a *sui generis* category. Thus, the Court held that the 'likelihood of success' test in the Civil Legal Aid Scheme should be interpreted as meaning that a person be granted legal aid if there was a reasonable likelihood that the point of view of the applicant for legal aid would be amongst the material to be taken into account in a decision concerning, for example, the welfare of the children of a marriage. The decision of the Supreme Court will be discussed in detail in the 1993 Review.

**Criminal legal aid** On this area, see the Criminal Law chapter, 274, above.

## LITIGANT IN PERSON

The extent to which a personal litigant may represent other parties involved in litigation was discussed by Budd J in his judgment in *P.M.L.B. v P.H.J. and Ors*, High Court, 5 May 1992.

## LODGMENT

*Brennan v Iarnród Éireann and Ors* [1993] ILRM 134; [1992] 2 IR 167 is an important judgment in which Barr J refused to allow a late lodgment in a personal injuries claim. The defendants sought leave to make the lodgment, after the time for so doing under the Rules of the Superior Courts 1986 had expired. The parties had entered into unsuccessful negotiations to settle the proceedings, in the course of which the plaintiff's solicitor furnished to the defendants all medical reports concerning the plaintiff's injuries. It was in those circumstances that Barr J felt that it would, in general, be undesirable to allow the defendants 'capitalise' on the plaintiff's full disclosure by making a late lodgment. However, he was prepared to acknowledge that, in exceptional circumstnaces, a late lodgment might be allowed even after such disclosure during settlement negotiations. However, this would only be where the injuries were more serious than pleaded by the plaintiff, and the instant case was not such a situation. The reporter's note in the Irish Reports indicates that, while the defendants appealed this judgment, the action was settled before the appeal was heard: [1992] 2 IR at 170.

## NON-SUIT

In *O'Toole v Heavey* [1993] ILRM 343; [1993] 2 IR 544, the Supreme Court took the opportunity to elaborate on its 1991 *ex tempore* decision in *Hetherington v Ultra Tyre Service Ltd and Ors* [1993] ILRM 353; [1993] 2 IR 535 (1991 Review, 334-5) on the principles to be applied in an application for a non-suit at the end of the evidence given by a plaintiff.

In *O'Toole*, the plaintiff instituted proceedings in negligence against the defendant, a dental surgeon, alleging that the defendant had failed to exercise reasonable care in extracting a tooth from the plaintiff, as a result of which the plaintiff's mandible had been fractured. It was agreed that the fracture had occurred in the course of the extraction. In evidence in the High Court, the plaintiff stated that the defendant had attempted to extract the tooth unsuccessfully, that part of the tooth came away, that the root had remained in her jaw and that the defendant had stated 'I knew this would happen'. A consultant dental surgeon called by the plaintiff stated in evidence that a fractured mandible could result from lack of due care but that it could also arise from a situation in which all proper procedures were followed. At the conclusion of this evidence for the plaintiff, the defendant applied for a non-suit. The trial judge granted the application on the ground that the plaintiff had not established negligence. The Supreme Court (Finlay CJ, Egan and Blayney JJ) allowed the plaintiff's appeal and ordered a new trial.

The Court held that, in the instant case, where the defendant had indicated that, if the application for a non-suit was refused, he would be going into evidence, the trial judge should have merely decided whether negligence could be inferred from the evidence, that is whether a *prima facie* case had been made out, rather than whether negligence had been established on the balance of probabilities. Since the Court considered that negligence could be inferred from the evidence given by the plaintiff, it ordered a new trial.

Dealing with the general approach in these cases, as indicated in the *Hetherington* case, the Supreme Court held that where, on an application for a non-suit, a defendant indicates that no evidence will be given on the question of liability, the trial judge is entitled to determine the question of liability on the balance of probabilities, provided that such a decision at that stage would not prejudice any other party where there is more than one defendant.

## PLEADING

**Amendment of claim** Two cases in 1992 dealt with applications to amend pleadings under O.28 of the Rules of the Superior Courts 1986.

In *Rubotham v M & B Bakeries Ltd and Irish National Insurance Co. plc* [1993] ILRM 219, the plaintiff was two years of age when, in December 1980, he suffered burns while in a van when it went on fire. The van was owned by the first defendant. Proceedings against the first defendant alleging negligence in the way the battery was fitted to the van were settled in 1986, when a sum of £150,000 damages was approved by the High Court, subject to a six month stay. The sum was never paid to the plaintiff and a provisional liquidator was appointed to the first defendant in June 1987. The plaintiff then instituted the instant proceedings against the two defendants. The principal relief sought was that the second defendant, who held insurance cover on the van in December 1980, was obliged to discharge the damages awarded in 1986 to the plaintiff, and was estopped from repudiating the policy by virtue of their conduct during settlement negotiations. The second defendant had, in fact, repudiated the motor insurance policy in May 1981 on the ground that the first defendant had failed to take all reasonable steps to maintain the van in proper condition. The first defendant had never contested this repudiation. The plaintiff then applied to have his statement of claim amended by introducing a new claim that it was a condition of the settlement agreement in the first action that the damages would be paid within six months by the two present defendants, that this was not done, that the plaintiff thereby suffered loss, that the settlement should be set aside and that damages should now be re-assessed. Morris J described this proposed amendment as 'fundamental and introduces into the action a claim for a relief which had not originally been made.' Morris J noted that whether the plaintiff would ultimately be successful in the claim being made in the amended pleadings was not a matter to be considered in an application under O.28 of the 1986 Rules. The only argument made against the proposed amendment concerned the delay in seeking the amendment. Morris J considered that the plaintiff's infancy was an answer to this, and noted that O.28(1) envisaged amendments 'for the purpose of determining the real questions in controversy between the parties.' On this basis, he allowed the amendment without expressing any view on whether the plaintiff's claim could succeed.

In the second judgment on this topic, *Shepperton Investment Co. Ltd v Concast (1975) Ltd and Ors*, High Court, 21 December 1992, Murphy J allowed certain amendments to the particulars in the plaintiff's statement of claim but disallowed others. The claim concerned various allegations of negligence against the defendants in connection with a building contract, and the work involved dated back to 1977 and 1978. In determining whether he would allow amendments to the particulars, Murphy J took account of the delays involved in the case, and compared the issues of justice which arose as comparable to those discussed in *Ó Domhnaill v Merrick* [1985] ILRM 40; [1984] IR 151 and *Toal v Duignan* [1991] ILRM 135. On the issue of delay, see the 1990 Review, 394-8, which also discusses the decision in *Toal v Duignan (No. 2)* [1991] ILRM 140.

**Failure to plead jurisdiction** In *Kelleher v Switzer & Co. Ltd*, High Court, 4 November 1992, the plaintiff had initiated a claim for unliquidated damages in the Circuit Court. The civil bill did not include any indication that the plaintiff was limiting his claim to the jurisdiction of the Circuit Court, this being £15,000 at the time the proceedings were begun. However, the President of the Circuit Court amended the civil bill to include the words 'and the plaintiff claims £15,000 and costs'. On appeal by the defendant, Lavan J upheld this amendment. The defendant had argued that the failure to refer to the jurisdictional limit rendered the civil bill a nullity and that the Circuit Court President lacked jurisdiction to amend the civil bill. Lavan J considered that the general jurisdiction to amend pleadings conferred by O.57 of the Rules of the Circuit Court 1950 was sufficient to answer the defendant's argument. He expressly approved the comments contained in the 1906 edition of *Wylie's Judicature Acts* on the the general power to amend conferred on the High Court by O.28 of the Rules of the Supreme Court (Ireland) 1905, in which a very broad discretion indeed was regarded as being the basis for that jurisdiction, and Lavan J was prepared to hold that that discretion was identical in all material respects to that contained in O.57 of the 1905 Rules. The equivalent to O.28 of the 1905 Rules is O.28 of the Rules of the Superior Courts 1986 discussed in the immediately preceding heading.

It is noteworthy that a similar view to that of Lavan J was taken by Blayney J in his exceptionally brief, *ex tempore*, judgment delivered earlier in 1992 in *Kearns and Clarke v Deery* [1993] ILRM 496. In the *Kearns* case, a mandatory injunction obtained in the Circuit Court had ordered the applicants to return certain cattle. The injunction had been granted on foot of an ordinary civil bill. When the applicants brought a motion in the Circuit Court seeking to set aside the injunction on the ground that the wrong procedure had been used, the respondent judge of the Circuit Court amended the ordinary civil bill to an equity civil bill under O.59 of the Rules of the Circuit Court 1950 and continued the injunction already granted. When the applicants applied to quash the respondent's order on judicial review, Blayney J went so far as to refuse leave to apply for judicial review, holding that the decision whether to amend the pleadings was entirely a matter for the respondent's discretion.

**Particulars** In *Behan v Medical Council* [1993] ILRM 240, the plaintiff sought an order of prohibition in respect of a proposed inquiry by the Medical Council into the plaintiff's conduct as a consultant psychiatrist. It was ordered that the judicial review proceedings be conducted by way of plenary hearing. The plaintiff entered a statement of claim and the defendant Council entered a defence traversing and denying the plaintiff's claim. The plaintiff then served a notice for particulars on the defendant Council, to which the Council replied. The plaintiff applied, however, for further and better particulars pursuant to O.19, r.7(1) of the Rules of the Superior Courts 1986. Morris J dismissed the plaintiff's claim for further particulars in the instant case, on the ground that since the defendant had traversed the plaintiff's claim in its defence, the plaintiff was fully informed of all matters arising out of the defendant's proposed defence and would not be taken by surprise by matters not fairly to be ascertained from the pleadings. In this respect, he cited with approval the decision of the Supreme Court in *Mahon v Celbridge Spinning Co. Ltd* [1967] IR 1 on the purpose of pleadings. The Surpeme Court dismissed the plaintiff's appeal from this finding in an *ex tempore* judgment delivered on 27 January 1993: see the Cases Appealed note in [1993] ILRM at 899.

**Renewal of proceedings** In *Prior v Independent Television News Ltd* [1993] ILRM 638; [1993] 1 IR 399, Barron J declined to renew a summons for libel issued by the plaintiff. In a 'News at Ten' programme broadcast by the defendant company in 1983, the plaintiff and another person had been falsely identified as kidnappers. In proceedings arising out of the same facts, the plaintiff had obtained substantial damages in libel against a number of parties. The plaintiff had instructed his solicitor to issues proceedings against the defendant at the same time as giving instructions to proceed against the other parties, but in fact no proceedings were issued until November 1988 and these proceedings had not been served on the defendant.

The plaintiff sought to have the summons renewed under O.8, r.1 of the Rules of the Superior Courts 1986. This requires that a renewal may be made where the court is satisfied that reasonable efforts were made to serve the defendant 'or for other good reason.' Barron J referred to the decisions of the Supreme Court in *Baulk v Irish National Insurance Co. Ltd* [1969] IR 66 and *McCooey v Minister for Finance* [1971] IR 159 on this question, summarising the principle behind them as being that 'where proceedings have not been heard on the merits it may be unjust that they should be barred by procedural difficulties'. Although he accepted that the results of the other proceedings indicated that the plaintiff appeared to have a good claim on the merits, Barron J also stated that this should be balanced against the fact that the defendant was unaware of any potential claim until the instant application for renewal had been notified to the defendant in January 1992 and that the defendant's staff now had no recollection of making the broadcast involving the plaintiff. In those circumstances, and bearing in mind that the plaintiff had received damages in the other proceedings, the delay involved in renewing the summons was such that the defendant in this instance would suffer an injustice from renewal of the summons, and so Barron J declined the plaintiff's application. It is notable that the reference to injustice in this context mirrors the issue of delay referred to by Barron J in his judgment delivered on the same date as the instant case in *Shepperton Investment Co. Ltd v Concast (1975) Ltd and Ors*, High Court, 21 December 1992: see above.

## PLENARY HEARING

In *Jackson-Soanes v Leisure Corp. International Ltd*, High Court, 18 December 1992, the plaintiff sought to enter judgment against the defendant for £40,000 sterling for monies alleged to be due to the plaintiff on foot of an agreement. The defendant sought to have the plaintiff's application adjourned for plenary hearing to enable the defendant enter a counterclaim for rescission of the agreement on foot of which the monies were said to be due and owing. After a review of the basis on which the defendant sought the adjournment, Geoghegan J declined to adjourn the plaintiff's application in the exercise of his discretion on the ground that he did not consider that the defendant would succeed in an action for rescission. He did, however, note that the defendant was entitled to initiate separate proceedings in damages against the plaintiff.

## RES JUDICATA

*Breathnach v Ireland and Ors (No. 4)*, High Court, 14 December 1992 was another preliminary application in long running litigation which has been considered in previous Reviews: see the 1989 Review, 358-61 and the 1991 Review, 341-2. The background, briefly, was as follows.

The plaintiff had instituted proceedings in damages against the defendants arising out of his prosecution, conviction in the Special Criminal Court and subsequent acquittal by the Court of Criminal Appeal on charges of armed robbery, a case which has become known as the Sallins Mail Train case. The instant proceedings largely concerned the circumstances in which the plaintiff confessed to involvement in the armed robbery in question. His confession was, ultimately, ruled inadmissible by the Court of Criminal Appeal on the grounds that the Judges' Rules had not been complied with: see *The People v McNally and Breathnach* (1981) 2 Frewen 43. Arising from a previous judgment of Lardner J in the instant proceedings, the plaintiff was held estopped on the basis of *res judicata* from alleging that his confession had been obtained through assault or battery, as these issues had been decided against him in the criminal prosecution: see *Breathnach v Ireland and Ors* [1989] IR 489 (discussed in the 1989 Review, 358-60).

Subsequently, the plaintiff obtained new scientific tests concerning speech patterns which, he alleged, indicated that he could not have made the confessions used in his prosecution. He then applied by motion to the High Court in the instant application to have the order of Lardner J set aside. Carroll J refused to grant the plaintiff the relief sought. In a short judgment, she held that the High Court had no jurisdiction to set aside the order of Lardner J since all relevant legal issues were fought out before him and had been decided against the plaintiff, and the defendants were thus entitled to rely on that judgment. She considered that the Supreme Court was the appropriate court to address if the plaintiff wanted to overturn the High Court order made by Lardner J. Although Carroll J did not use the phrase *res judicata* in her judgment, her conclusion mirrors very much the emphasis on finality of judgments inherent in the *res judicata* principle, which was ironically enough at the heart of the judgment of Lardner J himself in his judgment in *Breathnach v Ireland and Ors* [1989] IR 489. It may be said that never has one set of proceedings invoked so often the same basic principle in so many different contexts.

The judgment of Carroll J is likely to have been the last in these proceedings, as it was reported in 1993 that the proceedings had been settled by the plaintiff for a sum stated to be in the region of £500,000, thus bringing to an end the litigation over the *Sallins* case: see *Irish Times*, 17 July 1993. See also the reference to the Presidential pardon given to Nicky Kelly in the Constitutional Law chapter, 210, above.

## RULES OF COURT

The following Rules of Court were made in 1992.

**Costs: District Court** The District Court (Costs) Rules 1992 (SI No. 225) are referred to above, 477.

**Court Sittings: Circuit Court** The effect of the Civil Bill Courts (Ireland) Act 1851 (Adaptation) (No. 2) Order 1992 (SI No. 174) and the Civil Bill Courts (Ireland) Act 1851 (Adaptation) Order 1992 (SI No. 193) is discussed above, 478-9.

**Court Sittings: District Court** The District Court Areas (Alteration of Place) Order 1992 (SI No. 247) amends the 1961 Order of the same title by providing that Raphoe District hearings may be held in Convoy instead of Raphoe.

**Criminal damage** The District Court (Criminal Damage Act 1991) Rules 1992 (SI No. 53), which came into effect on 1 April 1992, deal with the making and adjustment of a compensation order and the issue of serach warrants under the 1991 Act: see the 1991 Review, 134-6.

**Limitation of costs** The Rules of the Superior Courts (No. 1) 1992 (SI No. 46) deleted O.99, rr.8 and 9 of the 1986 Rules concerning limitation of costs, with effect from 6 March 1992. See now s.14 of the Courts Act 1991, discussed in the 1991 Review, 347.

**Notice of trial: High Court personal injuries** The Rules of the Superior Courts (No. 2) 1992 (SI No. 260), which came into force on 1 October 1992, substitute a new O.36, r.2(b) into the 1986 Rules, and amend the list of towns where notice of trial may be served corresponding to the plaintiff's residence or the occurrence of the wrong in respect of which proceedings are taken under s.1 of the Courts Act 1988, that is, in personal injuries actions.

**Public works contracts: High Court** On the effect of the European Communities (Review Procedures for the Award of Public Supply and Public Works Contracts) Regulations 1992 (SI No. 38) see the Commercial Law chapter, 46, above.

**Service of summons by post** The District Court (Service of Summonses) Rules 1992 (SI No. 116), which came into force on 26 May 1992, set out the detailed provisions concerning serving of summonses by registered post, as envisaged by s.22 of the Courts Act 1991: see the 1991 Review, 149.

**Set-off or counterclaim: District Court** The District Court (Set-off or Counterclaim) Rules 1992 (SI No. 317), which came into effect on 10 November 1992, amended r.144 of the District Court Rules 1948 by providing that notice of set-off or counterclaim must be given by the defendant to the plaintiff and the District Court Clerk within one month of receipt of the Civil Process. It also provides for the method by which the Court may grant an extension of time for the giving of notice under r.144.

**Small claims procedure** The District Court (Small Claims Procedure) Rules 1992 (SI No. 119), which came into force on 29 May 1992, authorise affidavits and affirmations to be taken in evidence in the small claims procedure introduced under the 1991 Rules of the same title: see the 1991 Review, 343.

**Social welfare: District Court** The District Court (Social Welfare — Contributions Towards Benefit or Allowances) Rules 1992 (SI No. 47) lay down the procedure and forms in an application under s. 316(2) of the Social

Welfare (Consolidation) Act 1981, as amended by s. 21 of the Social Welfare Act 1992 (see the Social Welfare chapter, 541, below). S. 316 relates to contributions ordered to be paid to either a health board or the Department of Social Welfare. An application under s. 316 may be made by the Minister for Social Welfare or a health board, and an order made by the District Court has the same effect as an instalment order under the Enforcement of Court Orders Acts 1926 and 1940.

## SATISFACTION

In *Murphy v J. Donohoe Ltd and Ors* [1992] ILRM 378; [1993] 1 IR 527, the infant plaintiffs were seriously injured from burns sustained when the car they were in went on fire. The car was owned by their father, the fourth-named defendant. The plaintiffs' solicitors notified a number of parties, including the father (who had carried out some work on the car), of their intention to institute proceedings for damages arising from their injuries. The first-named defendant had sold the car to the father, the second-named defendant was the importer of the car and the third-named defendant had provided parts for the car which might have been involved in the fire.

Prior to the initiation of the proceedings against any of the defendants, the father's insurance company agreed to pay the sum of £815,000 into court to the credit of the plaintiffs in full discharge of the father's liability to the plaintiffs. This payment was approved by Hamilton P in February 1990, and was made a rule of court. The plaintiffs were also made wards of court. Hamilton P was informed at this hearing that proceedings would be started against all four defendants, including the father. None of the other three defendants were represented at this hearing, nor were they informed about the hearing. After the institution of proceedings, the second-named defendant pleaded in its defence that the payment made in February 1990 constituted satisfaction of the plaintiffs' claim against the defendants and that the proceedings should be discontinued on this ground under ss.16 and 17 of the Civil Liability Act 1961.

At a hearing on this point as a preliminary issue, Hamilton P rejected this argument. On appeal by the first and second defendants, the Supreme Court, by a 3-2 majority, (McCarthy, O'Flaherty and Egan JJ; Finlay CJ and Hederman J dissenting) upheld the President's decision.

The majority considered that the order of February 1990 did not constitute the 'satisfaction' of the plaintiffs' claim against the first and second defendants within the meaning of ss. 16 and 17 of the 1961 Act, since it was not made after any judgment of the Court on the issues between the parties and the payment was made on the basis of an express reservation that the plaintiffs would subsequently institute proceedings against the alleged joint tortfeasors involved in the matter. The majority thus held that the terms of the February 1990 order should be honoured in that the sum referred to should be incorporated in any order made in the proceedings. And the Court concluded that the proceedings should continue, without any limitation as to damages, against all four defendants.

## SERVICE OF PROCEEDINGS

**Vacation service** The service in the Vacation of notice of intention to claim relief was considered in *Slattery and Ors v An Taoiseach and Ors* [1993] 1 IR 286 (discussed in the Constitutional Law chapter, above, 137, 139, 218-9).

## SETTING ASIDE

In *Fitzpatrick v Garda Commissioner*, High Court, 19 June 1992, Murphy J declined to set aside a Supreme Court judgment involving the applicant. In so doing, he followed his own judgment in *Din and Arborfield Ltd v Banco Ambrosiano SPA*, High Court, 30 November 1990 (see the 1990 Review, 451-2) to the effect that only in exceptional circumstances, such as where a judgment is obtained by fraud, will a decision be set aside.

## SUPREME COURT

**Appellate court** Issues concerning the appellate nature of the Supreme Court's jurisdiction are dealt with above, 469-73.

**Stay of execution pending appeal** In *Emerald Meats Ltd v Minister for Agriculture and Ors* [1993] 2 IR 443, the Supreme Court removed a stay on a High Court award of damages pending an appeal of that award to the Supreme Court.

The plaintiff was a company engaged in the meat trade. The plaintiff claimed declaratory relief and damages in relation to the failure by the defendants to grant the plaintiff an import quota for 1990 under the terms of EC Council Regulation 4024/89, which concerns imports of meat from non-EC States coming within the terms of the GATT. In the High Court, Costello J granted the relief sought: *Emerald Meats Ltd v Minister for Agriculture and Ors*, High Court, 9 July 1991 (discussed in the 1991 Review, 199-200). The decree for damages was for £385,922 with interest. Without objection from the plaintiff, the defendants were granted in July 1991 a stay on the damages award pending an appeal to the Supreme Court. In July 1992, the plaintiff sought to have the stay removed. The Supreme Court (Hederman, McCarthy and Egan JJ) acceded to this request.

Applying the principles it established in *Redmond v Ireland* [1992] ILRM 291; [1992] 2 IR 362 (see the 1991 Review, 351-2), the Court accepted that although the plaintiff had not objected to the stay in 1991, circumstances had changed considerably since then, and it appeared that the plaintiff was in immediate danger of going out of business. Having regard to the issues raised in the appeal, the Court noted that it was possible that a reference to the Court of Justice under Article 177 of the EC Treaty might result, thus postponing final judgment for a further two years. Finally, in the light of the trial judge's findings, the prospects of success for the defendants seemed slight; and in those circumstances, even though the damages might become dissipated in the company's debts, the Court concluded that the justice of the case lay in removing the stay on the award.

## THIRD PARTY NOTICE

The decision of the Supreme Court in *Quirke v O'Shea and CRL Oil Ltd* [1992] ILRM 286 (1991 Review, 354-5) was applied by O'Hanlon J in *Hallahan v Keane and Harrington* [1992] ILRM 595. The plaintiff was an infant and the second named defendant sought to join the plaintiff's father (the plaintiff's next friend in the proceedings) as a third party in the event of the second defendant being held liable. In a short judgment, O'Hanlon J exhibited some sympathy for the application because he considered that there were reasonable grounds, not specified in his judgment, for the second defendant wishing to maintain a claim for contribution or indemnity against the plaintiff's father and that if this issue was heard together with the main proceedings this would ensure a cost-effective way of trying all issues. However, having regard to the *Quirke* case, above, O'Hanlon J refused the application to join on the ground of the plaintiff's father's limited means to defray High Court costs and any claim for contribution or indemnity that might be made against him. But he added that this refusal was without prejudice to the second defendant's entitlement to institute separate proceedings against the plaintiff's father for contribution or indemnity.

## TIME LIMITS

In *Director of Public Prosecutions (Murphy) v Regan* [1993] ILRM 335, O'Hanlon J reluctantly declined to hear a case stated where the applicant prosecutor had failed to serve a notice in writing on the defendant as required by s. 2 of the Summary Jurisdiction Act 1857: see the discussion, 474-6, above.

# Prisons

## INTERNATIONAL TRANSFER OF PRISONERS

In *Hutchinson v Minister for Justice* [1993] ILRM 602, Blayney J rejected the proposition that the government was in any way bound by its signature of the Council of Europe Convention on the Transfer of Sentenced Prisoners: see the Constitutional Law chapter, 148-9, above.

# Revenue Law

Dermot Kelly
Barrister-at-Law

This year the review of Revenue Law has been somewhat expanded to encompass a more detailed summary of the provisions of the Finance Acts for the year. 1992 was a bumper year for revenue legislation, there being a very lengthy Finance Act and the Finance (No. 2) Act 1992, a considerable portion of which involved amendments to provisions in the principal Finance Act.

In a work of this nature, it is not possible to examine, or even to refer to, all the provisions of the Finance Act. For a detailed examination of the provisions of the Finance Act see the Annotations in *Irish Current Law Statutes Annotated*. This work shall confine itself to a brief exegesis of some of the more important or novel provisions.

The Finance Act 1992 contained a considerable range of new provisions together with extensive amendments to existing legislation. The greater part of these new provisions and amendments were a consequence of the EC single market which compelled the removal of excise duty on motor vehicles manufactured within the community and imported into Ireland. The removal of excise duty was not, of course, a matter of such labyrinthian complexity as to require extensive legislation, rather was it the introduction of a new tax, called a Vehicle Registration Tax, designed to ensure that no reduction in tax revenue derived from motor vehicles, would result from the abolition of excise duty.

The impending single market was also responsible for changes in Value Added Tax and for provisions implementing two Council directives, No. 90/434/EEC and No. 92/1 2/EEC.

The usual range of adjustments and amendments to various taxes were made; but of the greatest significance in the long term, perhaps, was the extraordinary increase in the powers of the Revenue Commissioners, many of these powers appended to otherwise mundane provisions.

The more substantial matters shall be dealt with presently, but before moving on to those provisions, a summary of a number of the more important amendments and novations may prove useful.

S. 14 limits the interest relief available to individuals on loans applied in acquiring an interest in companies in which they have a material interest or have worked in the actual management or conduct of the business of a company or a connected company. The relief is limited to 70% of the interest paid in the first year following the specified date and 40% in the second year and no relief is given for any subsequent year. The 'specified date' is variable depending on when the loan is applied.

S. 14(4) inserts a new subs. (3) into s. 34 of the Finance Act 1974 which provides that relief shall not be given in respect of any payment of interest by an individual on a loan (under s. 34) applied on or after 24 April 1992 for any of the purposes specified in s. 34(1), 'unless the loan is applied for *bona fide* commercial purposes and not as part of a scheme or arrangement, the main purpose or one of the main purposes of which is the avoidance of tax'.

This much favoured formula essentially begs the question, since the main purpose or one of the main purposes of entering into the transactions to which s. 34 applies, is that the individual concerned obtains a tax advantage in relation to the interest payment and so requires a valuable asset at, in essence, a subsidised price.

## TAXATION OF SOCIAL WELFARE BENEFITS

S. 15 of the 1992 Act renders a number of Social Welfare benefits taxable under Schedule E of the Income Tax Act 1967. The tax chargeable is to be computed under s. 110(1) (inserted by the Finance Act 1991) of the Income Tax Act 1967.

The benefits which are so taxable are:

(a) Disability Benefit;

(b) Unemployment Benefit;

(c) Injury Benefit which is comprised in Occupational Injuries Benefit and

(d) Pay Related Benefit.

It is interesting to note that s. 15(2) provides that all amounts falling to be paid on foot of the benefits to which the section applies shall 'be deemed—

> (a) to be profits or gains arising or accruing from an employment and accordingly
>
> (i) tax under Schedule E shall be charged on every person to whom such benefit is payable'.

It may be instructive for those who complain of the artificiality of so called 'tax avoidance schemes' to consider the provision of s. 15 that Unemployment Benefit is deemed to be profits or gains arising or accruing from an employment, and to realise, that in dealing with the Tax Acts one enters into a realm not conceived in the wildest imaginings of the Brothers Grimm.

## GOLDEN HANDCUFFS

S. 18 substitutes a new s. 525 into the Income Tax Act 1967. The effect of this action is that an individual who holds or has held or is about to hold an office of employment gives an undertaking the tenor or effect of which is to restrict him as to his conduct or activities and any sum is paid either to him or to any other person in respect of the giving of the fulfilment, total or partial, of that undertaking, any such sum is deemed to be profits or gains arising or accruing from the office or employment and shall be taxable under Schedule E of the 1967 Act in the year of assessment in which said sum is paid.

## PATENT ROYALTIES

S. 19 provides for the phasing out of relief whereby the income derived by means of royalties or other sums paid in respect of the user of a patented invention in relation to which the research, planning, processing, experimenting, testing, devising, designing, developing or similar activity leading to the invention was carried out in the State, is disregarded for all purposes of the Income Tax Acts. S. 19 provides that only two thirds of the said income shall be disregarded for the period 24 April 1992 to 5 April 1993, one third of any income from a patent arising in the year of assessment 1993-4 shall be disregarded and for the year of assessment 1994-5, onwards the relief is discontinued and the entire income is liable to tax.

The full relief in respect of income from a qualifying patent continues where that income is saved by an individual who carried out either solely or jointly with another person, the research, planning, processing, experimenting, testing, devising, designing, developing or other similar activity leading to the invention which is the subject of the qualifying patent.

The purpose of the section is clearly to encourage the development of new inventions in the State, but to ensure that any tax benefit is derived only by the inventor and not by any individuals or companies which purchase the right to exploit the patented invention.

## SPECIAL SAVINGS ACCOUNT

S. 22 establishes the 'Special Savings Account' which needs little comment in this work. The salient features which are well known, are that an individual may hold only one such account but a married couple may maintain two such accounts in joint names; they may not, of course, hold any such account individually in such circumstances. An individual may not hold more than

£50,000 including accumulated interest, on such a deposit, a married couple may hold £100,000 jointly. A Special Savings Account may not be opened or held in the name of a minor. A tax rate of 10% applies to the interest earned on such deposits.

## LIMITED PARTNERSHIP

S. 23 limits the losses or interest payments allowable to a 'limited partner' to those arising from its participation in a trade and only against the profits or gains arising from the trade and only to the extent that such a loss does not exceed the amount of the limited partner's contribution to the trade.

## SUB-CONTRACTORS' TAX DEDUCTION

S. 28 extends the provisions of s. 17 of the Finance Act 1970, relating to the deduction of tax by main contractors or principals, which originally applied only to construction contracts, to forestry operations and to meat processing operations.

## URBAN RENEWAL; DESIGNATED AREAS

Ss. 29, 30 and 31 extended the various time limits for designated area urban renewal reliefs.

## CORPORATION TAX

Ss. 40-58 of the Act make many, and some quite complex adjustments to Corporation Tax; unfortunately, however, the limitations imposed by a work of this nature render it impossible to consider them as the nature of the provisions make cursory consideration not only impractical but dangerous.

## VEHICLE REGISTRATION TAX

The provisions relating to Vehicle Registration Tax (VRT) are contained in ss. 130-144 of the Finance Act 1992, and Finance (No. 2) Act 1992. (At the time of writing a number of amendments are contained in the Finance Act 1993). One of the major changes wrought by the Act is to transfer responsibility for vehicle registration from the local authority to the Revenue

Commissioners who by s. 131, are obliged to establish and maintain a register of all vehicles in the State.

The rate of VRT is to be calculated by reference to the open market selling price of the vehicle at the time of the charging of the tax thereon.

In relation to new vehicles on sale in the State, either the manufacturer or the wholesale distributor is required to declare to the Revenue Commissioners the price, inclusive of all taxes and duties, which, in the opinion of the manufacturer or distributor a vehicle of that model and specification, including any enhancement or accessories fitted or attached thereto, or supplied therewith or which would normally be expected to be fitted or attached thereto or sold therewith, might reasonably be expected to fetch on a first arms length sale thereof on the open market in the State by retail.

If the Revenue Commissioners form the opinion that the declared price is higher or lower than the open market selling price at which a vehicle at such time is being offered for the sale in the State at the time of such declaration, or if no such declaration is made, the open market selling price may be determined for the purpose of s. 113 (as amended by s. 9 of the Finance (No. 2) Act 1992) by the Commissioners.

'Open market selling price' is defined as, *inter alia*, the 'price' inclusive of all taxes and duties, which in the opinion of the Commissioners the vehicle including any enhancement or accessories fitted or attached thereto or sold therewith or which would normally be expected to be fitted or attached thereto or sold therewith, might reasonably be expected to fetch on a first arms length sale in the open market in the State by retail.

In the event that the person who has paid or who is liable to pay VRT being dissatisfied with the amount of tax charged, an appeal may be lodged with the Commissioners within 21 days of the date VRT become due (s. 138).

It is curious that the appeal brought against a determination by the Revenue Commissioners is to be brought to those self same commissioners and not to the Appeal Commissioners. It appears that the ordinary appeal procedures do not apply and that no Appeal lies to the Circuit Court and no case stated lies to the High Court. It would seem, *prima facie*, that there is a modicum of unfairness in this procedure in that the final determination on appeal is made by the same body which made the original determination against which the Appeal is brought. On its face, this appears to offend the principle of *nemo iudex in causa sua*. While much of the procedure in relation to the assessment and collection of taxes may be administrative rather than judicial (see the judgments of Murphy J in *Deighan v Hearne* [1986] IR 603 and *Kennedy v Hearne* [1987] 1R 120, Supreme Court [1988] IR 481; and Barron J in *The State (Calcul International Ltd and Soltrex Ltd) v Appeal Commissioners and Revenue Commissioners*, High Court, 18 December, 1989), the determination under s. 138 would seem to meet most of the characteristic features of the administration of justice, adumbrated by Kenny J in *McDonald v Bord na gCon* [1965] IR 217 at p. 231:

> 1. A dispute or controversy as to the existence of legal rights or a violation of the law;
> 2. The determination or ascertainment of the rights of parties of the imposition of liabilities or the infliction of a penalty;
> 3. The final determination (subject to appeal) of legal rights or liabilities or the imposition of penalties;
> 4. The enforcement of those rights or liabilities of the imposition of a penalty by the Court or by the executive power of the State which is called in by the Court to enforce its judgments;
> 5. The making of an Order by the Court which is a matter of history is an Order characteristic of Courts in this country.

The Revenue Commissioners may be found by a Court to be exercising a purely administrative function, as per the *Deighan v Hearne* and *Calcul International Ltd* cases *ante*, with no element whatsoever of a judicial or quasi judicial nature, although it would appear to satisfy the first three of the characteristics set out by Kenny J and approved by the Supreme Court, the power being exercised possibly does not satisfy the fourth and fifth characteristics. The commissioners, however, are exercising a statutory function and the statute appears to have conferred on that function, certain judicial characteristics by establishing a right to appeal on stated grounds; by conferring that appeal jurisdiction on the very body whose decision is being appealed it would, *prima facie* appear to make the decision of appeal vulnerable to judicial review under the *nemo iudex* rule.

S. 139 makes it an offence not to pay any Vehicle Registration Tax and states that in addition to any other penalty to which an offender may be liable, he shall, on summary conviction be liable to an excise penalty of £1,000 and the vehicle shall be liable to forfeiture.

S. 140 provides that in any proceedings for an offence under this chapter of the Finance Act 1992, in respect of failure to pay any amount of VRT, it shall be presumed until the contrary is shown, that VRT in respect of vehicle to which the charge relates has not been paid. A certificate purporting to be signed by an Officer of the Commissioners and to contain particulars extracted from any other records relating to vehicles shall, without proof of the signature of the said Officer, or that he was an Officer of the Commissioners, be evidence until the contrary be shown, of the particulars stated in the Certificate or documents. The Officers of the Commissioners are also given extensive powers of entry, search and seizure, these are dealt with under the Revenue Powers heading, post.

A number of exemptions from VRT are made by the Act including cars for use by the institution of the European Community, its officials and staff, diplomatic staff and vehicles given as a gift by a public authority or a public service body outside the State to a public body or service in the State, as well as a car imported by an individual transferring his permanent residence from outside the State to within the State. Among these exemptions is a particular curiosity contained in s. 134(5) which states:

> Whenever the Minister (for Finance) so thinks proper, he may authorise the Commissioners to register a vehicle, subject to such conditions, limitations or restrictions (if any) as they may impose, either without payment of VRT or on payment of the tax at less than the rate ordinarily chargeable or, where the tax has been paid, to repay the tax in all or in part.

Whether the Commissioners may refuse, when authorised by the Minister, to register a vehicle without payment of VRT is not clear. It is beyond the scope of this work to examine in detail the constitutional propriety of such a provision; suffice to say that the provision appears to give a Minister an absolute and unfettered discretion to remit, in whole or in part, a tax levied by the Oireachtas and there is no requirement to seek the sanction or approval of the Oireachtas. It is, perhaps, of particular interest that the Minister may direct a different rate of tax to apply than that which is established by the Oireachtas, a provision which, insofar as this author can determine, is unique in the Tax Acts. The provision essentially would appear to render this tax payable subject to ministerial whim; on its face this would seem to render its constitutional propriety somewhat suspect.

## REVENUE POWERS

A comprehensive extension of Revenue powers is contained in the 1992 Finance Act. The Revenue has been given powers in relation to the investigation of the tax affairs of citizens which, apparently, it has not been thought appropriate to give to the Garda Síochána in respect of the investigation of offences of murder, kidnapping, drug dealing, armed robbery and other serious crimes. These powers are extended by various sections of the Act.

In relation to the charge of excise duty on the brewing and importation of beer and the holding of such beer upon premises which, for the purposes of the Act are warehouses. s. 96 makes a number of provisions.

S. 96(1) requires a warehousekeeper to provide and maintain such appliances as the Revenue Commissioners shall deem necessary to enable a Revenue officer to obtain a true and accurate account of any materials or beer. The warehousekeeper must at any time allow an officer to use these or any other appliances in its possession and must provide all other facilities or assistance as may be necessary to enable the officer to take such account.

S. 96(2) permits an officer, at all reasonable times, to enter any premises in which brewing of beer is, or is reasonably believed to be, carried on or in which the officer reasonably believes beer to be held, stored or kept or in which any books, accounts or other documents or records relating or reasonably believed by the officer to relate to the brewing, importation, purchase, holding, storage, packaging, sale or disposal of beer are kept and may search, inspect, take samples, take copies of, or extracts from any books, accounts, records, or other documents and extract informations stored in non legible form, and may remove and retain any books, accounts, records, or other documents for such period as may be reasonable for further examination.

The warehousekeeper must provide all facilities and assistance necessary for the exercise of the power conferred on an officer by the section.

Anybody found on any premises by an officer entering under the Section must answer all questions asked of him and give all information required of him which is in his possession or procurement. Failure to comply is an offence and an offender is liable to a customs or excise penalty on summary conviction, of £1,000.

S. 116 makes almost identical provisions in respect of excisable products stored in any tax warehouse with the additional penalty of forfeiture of the goods on the premises in the event of the commission of an offence under the section, the forfeiture also applying to any goods which are backed with the goods liable to forfeiture.

S. 125 permits a similar entry and search in respect of any public place in which amusement machines are, or are believed by the officer, to be available for playing. The officer may make copies or take extracts from any documents or non documentary records, but, unlike ss. 96 and 116, the books, documents, records, etc. may not be removed from the premises. The officer is not given power under s. 25 to ask and require answers to questions; unlike ss. 96 and 116, the officer entering the premises under s. 125 is required to hold a belief as to the availability for play of amusement machines, this section does not require that belief to be 'reasonable'. This may, however, turn out to be a distinction without difference.

S. 152 permits an officer, duly authorised in that behalf by the Commissioners, at all reasonable times to enter premises in which manufacture, distribution, storage, repair, modification, importation, clearing, delivery or disposal of vehicles is reasonably believed to be carried on or in which books, accounts or other documents or records relating to such activities are reasonably believed by such officer to be stored or kept and may require any person to produce all books, accounts or other documents or records relating to such activities and may require the information, stored in non legible form, to be produced in a permanent legible form.

The officer may carry out such searches and investigations as he shall think proper.

The latter provision is very wide and while, presumably, to be read as restricted to the matters with which the rest of the section deals, admits of the possibility of a search into matters not related to motor vehicles. It is likely, however, that the Courts would restrict the right to search and make investigations into the matters with which the section above deals and would not allow an unlimited discretion to the Revenue officer. The right to inspect and take copies and books, accounts and other documents or records is specifically limited to those which are 'reasonably believed by the officer to relate to such activities as aforesaid'.

The officer may also, as in ss. 96 and 116, remove and retain any books, accounts, documents or records for such period as may be reasonable for further examination.

The officer may also require any person to provide all facilities and assistance necessary for the exercise by such officer of any power conferred on him by the subsection.

S. 142(2) requires that 'any person in charge of a moving vehicle shall, at the request of an officer of the Commissioners in uniform, stop the vehicle'. The person in charge of a vehicle shall allow the vehicle to be examined by the officer. What this 'examination' entails is not defined. The purpose of the provision is, presumably, to enable the vehicle to be identified so, it would seem, the examination should be restricted to inspecting those parts of the vehicle upon which it would be expected to find identifying marks and numbers. The provision does not authorise a 'search' of the vehicle but only its 'inspection' and so any search, it is suggested, would be *ultra vires* the powers of the officer under this section.

The officer may require any person to furnish to him any information or documentation relating to a vehicle which is in the possession, custody or procurement of such person referred to in the section. The officer may detain any vehicle which he reasonably suspects has not been registered, in respect of which a declaration of conversion required by s. 131 has not been made or in respect of which the registration tax has not been paid until such examination, inquiries or investigations as may be deemed necessary by the officer or another officer, has been made for the purpose of determining these matters to the satisfaction of the officer concerned. (s. 142(3)).

When a determination is made, or upon the expiry of one month from the date of detention, whichever is the earlier, the vehicle shall be seized as liable to forfeiture or released.

S. 233 makes provisions similar to ss. 96, 116, 152 in relation to any premises or place where an officer has reason to believe that an employer is or has been carrying on any activity as an employer, require any person who is or was either paying any emoluments or providing benefits in kind, or prerequisities or that any person is or was in receipt of any emoluments, benefits in kind or perquisites or that records are or may be kept.

All these sections have the common feature that the Revenue officer may require any person on the premises to produce any books, documents, records, or accounts whether maintained in written form or otherwise, and may require any such person to answer any questions and to give any assistance which the officer may deem relevant and the officer may search the premises and may examine, make copies of, take extracts from, remove and retain any records found thereon. In all of these cases, the entry and search is without a warrant. The person questioned must answer the questions and it would appear has no right to have a solicitor present and certainly has no right to silence unlike those who are questioned about crimes such as rape, murder, drug dealing, or breach of the peace. It is also clear that the Revenue officer does not have to caution the person questioned as to the possible use of his replies in criminal prosecution.

S. 181 amends s. 18 of the Value Added Tax Act 1972, by the addition of sub paragraph (ii), which provides that an authorised officer, if he has reason to believe that a person is carrying or has in his possession any records which may be required as evidence in criminal proceedings, in accordance with s. 94 (as amended by s. 243 of the Finance Act 1992) of the Finance Act 1983 in relation to the tax (Value Added Tax) request the person to produce any such records, and if that person should fail to do so, the authorised officer or member of the Garda Síochána may search that person.

The officer or the Garda conducting the search is required to ensure, as far as practicable, that the person understands the reason for the search; that the search must be conducted with due regard to the privacy of the person; the search must not be conducted by an officer or a Garda of the opposite sex to the persons searched; the person searched shall not be requested to remove any clothing other than headgear, a coat or jacket or gloves.

The powers conferred by this section on the Revenue official or the Garda in support of him, is very much more extensive than the power ordinarily reposed in a member of the Garda Síochána in the investigations of non tax related criminal offences.

S. 232 amends s. 34 of the Finance Act 1976, by the substitution of a new s. 34 which permits an authorised officer (defined as 'an officer of the Revenue Commissioners authorised by them in writing to exercise the powers conferred by this section') at all reasonable times to enter any premises or place where he has reason to believe that (i) any trade or profession or other activity, the profits or gains of which are charged with a tax, is or has been carried on, (ii) anything is or has been done in connection with any trade, profession or other activity, the profit or gains of which are chargeable to tax, (iii) any records relating to any trade, profession, other sources of profits or gains or chargeable gains, any tax liability or any repayments of tax in regard to any persons are or may be kept or any property is or has been located and he may require any person who is on those premises or in that place, other than a person there to purchase goods or to receive a service, to produce any records or properties. The officer may, if he has reason to believe that records or property have not been produced as required, search the premises or place where those records or properties are stored. He may examine any records or property and take copies of or extracts from records and may remove or retain any records for the purpose of examination or proceedings or criminal proceedings.

An authorised officer may require any person whom he has reason to believe has information relating to any tax liability to give all reasonable assistance, including providing information and explanation, furnishing documents and making available for inspection property as required by the authorised officer in relation to any tax liability or any repayment of tax in regard to any person. An exception, however, is made in relation to persons carrying on a profession or persons employed by them who can be required to produce only such documents as relate to their own tax affairs or such as may be required pursuant to s. 16 (insert by s. 101 of the Finance Act 1991) of the Stamp Act 1891. In particular, the section states that a person shall not be required to disclose any information or professional advice of a confidential nature given to a client.

The use of the word 'confidential' rather than 'privileged' is significant since most professional relationships involve an element of confidentiality but privilege usually attaches to legal advice. Confidential relationships include not only legal advisers but also accountants and other financial advisers. (See s. 227 Finance Act 1992 and the provisions regarding access to bank accounts in the Waiver of Certain Tax Interest and Penalties Act 1993, s. 13).

An authorised officer is not entitled without the consent of the occupier to enter a premises or part of a premises, occupied wholly and exclusively as a private residence, except on production of a warrant issued by a Judge of the District Court expressly authorising the officer to enter (s. 232(2)(e)) which warrant may issue if the district judge is satisfied by information on oath that it is proper for him to do so.

While relatively uncomplicated, this provision raises some curious possibilities. In a situation where a professional person or a person operates his business from his domestic residence, which parts are occupied wholly and exclusively as a private residence, presumably the bedrooms are private; the rooms set aside for use as an office or study in which the main business functions are performed, clearly would not be 'wholly and exclusively' private. If the study or office is used wholly and exclusively for business purposes, the revenue officer would have a right, at all reasonable times and without warrant, to enter such study or office; he does not, however, have a right to reach that room by passing through a hallway or other portion of the premises used exclusively for domestic purposes. The Act clearly states that the officer 'shall not enter', that he shall not 'search'.

A more difficult situation arises if the occupant occasionally or intermittently has clients consulting at home: does this mean that the premises is not 'wholly and exclusively' occupied as a 'private residence'?

On a literal interpretation the officer may enter without warrant and vouch and peruse all documents, letters and so on in any part of the premises upon which business or other non residential or domestic functions are performed. Does this mean that if a client walks through the hallway to reach the office or study that the hallway ceases to be occupied 'wholly and exclusively' as a private residence? On a literal interpretation the answer must be 'yes'. More complex still, perhaps, is the situation where a person entertains clients or other business associates in his private residence for the purposes of business profession or trade. Does this mixed social and business occasion remove those bounds of the house being used for the purpose of or in connection with such entertainment from the category of premises or parts of premises used wholly and exclusively as a private residence?

On a strict interpretation, any use even on an occasional basis of the domestic residence for the purposes of business, removes that premises or part of the premises. The Supreme Court ruled in *McGrath v McDermott* [1988] ILRM 647; [1988] IR 427 (1988 Review, 366-9), that taxing acts must be interpreted strictly. There is little direct authority available on the meaning of 'wholly and exclusively'. In *McNally v Ó Maoldomhnaigh* [1990] 2 IR 513, the Supreme Court held that a provision granting certain tax reliefs in respect of plant and machinery 'provided for use in a designated area' could not be interpreted as meaning that the plant and machinery must be 'exclusively' used in the designated areas: see the 1990 Review, 462.

While there are dangers in seeking to apply principles developed in one branch of the law to another, albeit a closely related branch, some assistance may be derived from the rather similar provisions in ratings cases.

In *Brennan v Commissioner of Valuation* [1969] IR 202, Henchy J held that a convent premises although used extensively for the purposes of education, but not used exclusively for such purposes as the convent was used for residential and other 'convential' purposes. It is clear from this decision that the word 'exclusive' is to be given its literal meaning.

The decision of Madden J in *McKenna v Commissioner of Valuation*

(1915) 49 ILTR 103, that a regular use of part of a premises for educational purposes did not cause it to cease being substantially the residence of the Christian Brothers would suggest that the business use would not prevent it being substantially a private residence that is insufficient to prevent the officer having the right to enter without warrant.

The dictum of the Chief Baron Palles in *O'Connell v Commissioner of Valuation* [1906] 2 IR 479 at 485, that he desired '. . . to be distinctly understood as not deciding that if the main purpose for which a building is used is a charitable one, as is that of a hospital for the gratuitous healing of the poor, the residents therein as part of their duty, of nurses or a a resident physician, would necessarily render the use not 'exclusively for charitable purposes', initially appears to support the contention that merely because there has been an occasional business use of the premises can remain exclusively a 'private residence'. Closer scrutiny, however, establishes that no such contention is sustainable. The residence therein referred to is clearly an element of the healing of the poor and while the nurses or doctor could derive a benefit, it was ancillary to and arose directly from the operation of the hospital and the provision of the care. The provision of the professional or other services could not credibly be described as arising directly from or being an ancillary part of the occupation and use of the premises as a private residence.

The position may be affected by Article 14 s. 5 of the Constitution which provides:

> The dwelling of every citizen in inviolable and shall not be entered save in accordance with law.

The word 'dwelling' received some definition by the Supreme Court in *People v O'Brien* [1965] IR 142. In the course of his judgment, Walsh J stated:

> In a case where members of a family live together in the family house, that house as a whole is for the purpose of Constitution, the dwelling of each member of the family.

This suggests that, unless there is a clear separation or partition of the occupation for the purposes of residence and business, the occupation of the premises as a 'residence' confers the status 'dwelling' within the meaning of the Constitution upon the entire premises. If this interpretation was to be accepted, then the entry without warrant of an office or business premises contained in a private residence, would be in breach of the constitutional protection and *ultra vires* and, insofar as s. 232 purported to permit such an entry, it would, it is submitted, be invalid. If such a matter was to arise for consideration, it is likely that a Court would characterise the section as having two possible interpretations, one purporting to authorise an unconstitutional entry, the other limiting such an entry into situations where a warrant is issued. In such a situation, a Court would prefer the constitutional interpretation. In order to achieve such a resolution, it is suggested that a Court would be compelled to ignore the wording of the Act and to hold that 'wholly and exclusively' means 'predominantly'. This would be a violation of the principle that taxing acts like acts creating criminal offences, must be strictly construed.

The phrase in the Constitution 'except in accordance with law' may be given the interpretation that because the provision is contained in an Act of the Oireachtas any action taken in reliance on that provision is therefore in accordance with law. This would accord with the somewhat circular argument adopted in the Supreme Court in *In re the Offences Against the State (Amendment) Bill 1940* [1940] IR 470. Sullivan CJ in his judgment, formulated the principle that an action is in accordance with law if it is done or taken in accordance with the provisions of a statute duly passed by the Oireachtas; subject always to the qualification that such provisions are not repugnant to the Constitution or to any provision thereof.

This appears to beg the question, the formulation adopted would appear to enable the constitutional rights to be delimited by statute to the point of extinction; it is difficult to accept that such a proposition accords with the will or intention of the people in adopting and enacting the Constitution.

A more reasonable interpretation, it is suggested, may be that, where constitutional rights may be delimited, they may not be extinguished by ordinary legislation; the Oireachtas in seeking to place limits on a constitutional right may not effectively abolish it.

To conclude, while there are a number of bases upon which a Court may uphold s. 232, it is equally the case that the provisions contained in the Section constitute a substantial, not to say gross, attack upon the constitutional inviolability of the dwelling which may persuade a Court that the constitutional inviolability of the dwelling is, in effect, being abolished by stealth under the guise of delimiting the right.

S. 227 imposes an obligation by amendment of s. 94 of the Income Tax Act 1967, by substitution of the new para. (d), on any agent who manages premises or is in receipt of rent or other payments arising from premises to prepare and deliver a return containing the full address of all such premises, that the name and address of every person to whom such addresses belong, statements of all rents and other such payments arising from such premises, and such other particulars relating to all such premises as may be specified in any notice.

## VALUE ADDED TAX

The changes in the Value Added Tax Acts, wrought by Part III of the Finance Act 1992, were necessitated by the impending single market. Essentially the effects of these amendments were to treat the supply of goods and services within the community in the same way as the supply of goods and services within the State.

Other technical amendments and adjustments to the Acts were made, little benefit would flow in a work of this nature in an extensive analysis of these matters.

We can, however, note some Regulations of general interest in this context.

The Value-Added Tax (Payment of Tax on Intra-Community Acquisitions of Means of Transport) Regulations 1992 (SI No. 412) lay down the regime for payment of VAT on the private purchase in another EC Member State of any means of transport, including of course, motor cars.

The European Communities (Value-Added Tax) Regulations 1992 (SI No. 413) are referred to above.

The Value-Added Tax (Exported Goods) Regulations 1992 (SI No. 438) revoked the Value-Added Tax (Exported Goods) Regulations 1984 and the Value-Added Tax (Goods Exported in Baggage) Regulations 1984 and lay down the new regime for relief from VAT on certain items, mainly connected with sales to visiting tourists.

The Value-Added Tax (Imported Goods) Regulations 1992 (SI No. 439) revoked the Value-Added Tax (Imported Goods) Regulations 1983 and set out the relief from VAT on the importation of raw materials and components by certain manufacturers. The Value-Added Tax (Imported Goods) (No. 2) Regulations 1992 (SI No. 440) revoked the Value-Added Tax (Imported Goods) Regulations 1982.

## EUROPEAN COMMUNITY IMPLEMENTATION PROVISIONS

Ss. 64-74 of the Finance Act 1992 implement Council Directive No. 90/434 EEC.

This directive sought to ensure that there was no tax advantage in relation to mergers, reconstructions and amalgamations where the relevant companies are registered in different member states.

Ss. 103-110 implement Council Directive No. 92/12/EEC.

The sections *inter alia* make the provisions necessary for the abolition of excise duty on excisable products acquired in other member states by an individual for his own use and not for commercial purposes. It also makes provisions in relation to excisable products in a 'tax warehouse' and such excisable products released for consumption in another member state.

The provisions of the 1992 Finance Acts were further amended in detailed ways by Ministerial Regulations in preparation for the coming into effect of the Single Market on 1 January 1993. The principal Regulations were as follows.

The European Communities (Value-Added Tax) Regulations 1992 (SI No. 413) amended the Value-Added Tax Act 1972 and the 1992 Acts in order to give effect to Directive 92/111/EEC on transitional arrangements for VAT collection.

The European Communities (Customs and Excise) Regulations 1992 (SI No. 394), the European Communities (Customs and Excise) (No. 2) Regulations 1992 (SI No. 431) and the Control of Exciseable Products Regulations 1992 (SI No. 430) amended, *inter alia*, the 1992 Acts in order to give effect to Directives 92/12/EEC, 92/78/EEC, 92/81/EEC and 92/83/EEC. These concern the harmonising of excise duty on alcohol, mineral oils and tobacco products in the internal market. The Beer (Deposit in Warehouses) (Amendment) Regulations 1992 (SI No. 429) were complementary Regulations which concern the need to update existing Regulations concerning the duty on beer to take account of SI No. 430 in particular.

The European Communities (Customs) Regulations 1992 (SI No. 207) amended s. 5 of the Customs Free Airport Act 1947, repealed s. 11 of the Finance (Miscellaneous Provisions) Act 1958 (as amended) and amended ss. 1 and 10 of the Free Ports Act 1986 in order to give effect to the following EC Regulations on Free Zones and Warehousing: 2503/88/EEC; 2504/88/EEC; 2561/90/EEC; 2562/90/EEC and 2485/91/EEC. The European Communities (Customs) (No. 2) Regulations 1992 (SI No. 431) amended, *inter alia*, the Customs Consolidation Act 1876 in order to give effect to Article 8a of the EC Treaty and to Council Regulations 3925/91/EEC and 1823/92/EEC. The European Communities (Customs) (No. 3) Regulations 1992 (SI No. 432) implemented Directive 90/504/EEC in order to simplify the procedure for releasing goods.

The precise effect of these Regulations can be seen in Judge, *Irish Income Tax Acts 1992-93* (Butterworth 1993).

## INTEREST ON OVERPAYMENT OF TAXES

After the Supreme Court had held, reversing the Appeal Commissioners and the High Court, that the expenditure of unsuccessful oil drilling in the years 1977 and 1979 was allowable in full in *Texaco (Ireland) v Murphy (Inspector of Taxes)* [1991] 2 IR 449; [1992] ILRM 304 (see the 1991 Review, 362-3), the Court was asked to rule upon whether interest should be paid by the respondent on the overpayment of taxes. The Supreme Court in an unanimous judgment held that the sums of improperly assessed tax paid by the appellants should be repaid to the appellants and that interest should be calculated and added to the sums to be repaid: *Texaco (Ireland) Ltd v Murphy (No. 2)* [1992] 1 IR 399. The rate of interest to be applied was considered in *Texaco (Ireland) Ltd v Murphy (Inspector of Taxes) (No. 3)* [1992] 2 IR 300.

The Supreme Court in an unanimous judgment, held that interest should be calculated pursuant to the Courts Act 1981, in that s. 428 (9)of the Income Tax Act 1967, left the calculation of interest, if any, on taxed determined to have been overpaid following the alteration by the Court of an assessment in the discretion of the Court.

S. 428(9) of the Income Tax Act 1967 provides:

> Notwithstanding that a case has been required to be stated or is pending, tax shall be paid in accordance with the determination of the Appeal Commissioners provided that, if the amount of the assessment is altered by the order of judgment of the Supreme Court or the High Court then—(a) that too much tax has been paid, the amount overpaid shall be refunded with such interest, If any, as the court may allow. . . .

This contrasts with the provisions of s. 550(1) of the Income Tax Act 1967, as amended, which provides:

> . . . Any cheques charged by any assessment to Income Tax shall carry interest at the rate of 1.25% for any month of part of a month.

This is applied to the revenue by s. 30(4) of the Finance Act 1976, which provides that overpayment of tax 'shall carry interest at the rate or rates enforced by virtue of s. 550(1)' of the Income Tax Act 1967.

It is also provided by s. 30 that such interest shall not be reckoned in computing interest for the purpose of the tax acts.

McCarthy J in the judgment with which the Chief Justice and Hederman J agreed, stated that he would not wish to shut out the possibility in an appropriate case of a tax payer proving and showing loss of interest sustained. As McCarthy J indicated, this approach could run the risk that an investigation might disclose that the relevant investment would itself have had an negative return. The court declined to express a view on the liability to tax in respect of the interest to which the appellant was entitled. It can be clearly seen from this decision that an appellant ultimately vindicated by appeal under s. 428 of the Income Tax Act 1967, could be doubly disadvantaged as compared with a taxpayer who can reclaim an over-payment of tax pursuant to s. 30 of the Finance Act 1976. This arises from the fact that a lower rate of interest applies under the Courts Act than that provided pursuant to s. 550 of the Income Tax Act 1967 as amended and to the additional factor that interest paid pursuant to s. 428 may also be subject to Income Tax whereas that paid under s. 30 is tax exempt.

In *Mooney v Ó Coindealbháin* [1992] 2 IR 23, in a case where the Revenue had been wrongly assessing the plaintiff taxpayer under Schedule E of the Income Tax Act 1967 rather than on Schedule D), and consequently substantial overpayments had been made (see *Ó Coindealbháin v Mooney* [1990] 1 IR 422: see the 1988 Review, 363-4), the plaintiff tax payer claimed interest on the overpaid sums pursuant to s. 30 of the Finance Act 1976. The Revenue resisted the claim on three grounds:

(a) It was claimed interest was not payable as the notices issued to the plaintiff were in respect of tax deducted at source and consequently showed a nil balance of tax payable, and since no tax was owing or claimed no appeal could arise and no interest could be payable.

(b) Tax, although deducted under Schedule E was payable under Schedule D and S 30 did not apply to refunds under that Schedule and consequently no interest was payable.

(c) No interest was payable for the period 1982/83 to 1987/88 as, by agreement between the parties to be bound for that period by the decision on the appeals for the years 1978/79 to 1981/82, no assessments were issued in respect of that period and accordingly there being no assessments, there was nothing to appeal and accordingly s. 30 did not apply.

Barr J rejected all these arguments holding that any relevant information regarding the amount or computation of tax paid or payable furnished to a taxpayer in a notice of assessment may be the subject matter of appeal. He held further that the tax charged by an assessment to tax is the total amount specified as being due and payable in any given year. It is not the nett amount of tax (if any) specified as unpaid at the date of assessment. It was, in addition, held that if the taxpayer is assessed to tax under the wrong schedule and has overpaid tax, then the taxpayer is entitled to a refund of all overpayments together with interest thereon under s. 30 of the Finance Act 1976.

Finally, Barr J held that the plaintiff was entitled to rely on the implied agreement that no assessments would formally issue but that the overpayments for the period 1982/83 to 1987/88 would be treated the same way as the appealed overpayments both as to repayment and as to interest.

## COSTS IN CIRCUIT COURT TAX APPEALS

*Inspector of Taxes v Arida Ltd* [1992] 2 IR 155, a case stated from the Circuit Court involved the issue of whether a Circuit Court Judge hearing an appeal from the Appeal Commissioners pursuant to s. 429 of the Income Tax Act

1967, has jurisdiction to award costs. The normal practice in such appeals is that costs are not awarded by the Circuit Court Judges. There is no specific legislative provision nor any rule of Court directly applicable to s. 429 Appeals.

O. 58 r. 1 of the Rules of the Circuit Court provides:

> Save as otherwise provided by statute or by these rules, the granting or withholding of the costs of any party to any proceedings in the court shall be at the discretion of the judge.

The respondent company appealed a determination of the Appeal Commissioners confirming assessments to tax to the Circuit Court. The Circuit Judge found in favour of the respondent which applied for and was granted the costs of the proceedings. The appellant appealed the awarded costs by way of case stated to the High Court. The question of law for determination by the High Court was whether a Circuit Court Judge hearing an appeal from the Appeal Commissioners pursuant to the provisions of the Income Tax Act 1967, has jurisdiction to award costs.

It was argued on behalf of the appellant, firstly that the Income Tax Acts provide a separate code for the determination of liability to tax, which conferred all necessary powers on the Appeal Commissioners and that under s. 429(2) it was those powers which vested in the Circuit Court Judge. Since those powers did not extend to the granting of costs to either party, the Circuit Court Judge had no jurisdiction to award costs. Secondly, it was argued that since s. 428(6) of the Income Tax Act 1967, expressly conferred power to award costs on the High Court hearing an appeal by way of case stated from the Appeal Commissioners, it was to be inferred on the basis of the *maxim expressio unius est exclusio alterius*, that the Circuit Court Judge had no such powers.

Murphy J, however, drew a distinction between granting of the power and the recognition of the authority of the High Court to award costs in such cases. It may well have been that the inclusion of the express power is a 'superfluous provision' but even if it was not, Murphy J ruled that a distinction would fall to be made between the awarding of costs on a case stated for the determination of a point of law and awarding costs on a re-hearing of matters of fact and law. Having regard to such distinctions, the inclusion of the power in one case and its absence in another, would not be a sound reason for concluding that the legislature intended by s. 429 of the Income Tax Act 1967, to curtail the extent of powers to award costs expressly conferred upon the Circuit Court by O. 58 r.1. Murphy J took the view that if an exception is to be created by something 'providing by statute' then the exception, if not expressly stated, must be implied with clarity.

Murphy J concluded that, while there was much to be gained by the adoption of the normal practice of Circuit Court judges not to award costs in s. 429 appeals, there is jurisdiction in the Circuit Court to award costs on appeals from the Appeal Commissioners; whether to do so is a matter for the discretion of the Circuit Court Judge.

## ADEQUACY OF EVIDENCE OF REVENUE OFFENCE: JUDICIAL REVIEW

In *Lennon v Clifford* [1992] 1 IR 382, the applicant appeared before the first named respondent in response to two summonses issued on foot of complaints made by the second respondent accused of failure to deliver returns in respect of the relevant chargeable periods. The only evidence which was tendered was a certificate pursuant to s. 10 of the Finance Act 1988, as amended which certified that the applicant was a chargeable person and had failed to deliver returns within the specified periods. The applicant offered no evidence but submitted that he was not 'a chargeable person' as alleged. The applicant was convicted in respect of each of the summonses.

The applicant seeking judicial review by way of *certiorari* quashing the orders of the District Court, contended that the proofs were inadequate to ground a conviction due, in particular, to an absence of formal proof of the existence of the nature of any prescribed form.

S. 10 of the Finance Act 1988, as amended by s. 46 of the Finance Act 1991, provides *inter alia*, that a certificate of an inspector shall be evidence until the contrary is proved that the person named is a chargeable person and that that person did not deliver a return and the certificate may be tendered in evidence without proof and the certificate may be deemed to have been signed by the Inspector.

O'Hanlon J refused to make the order sought on the grounds that relief by way of judicial review was confined to those cases where reliance could be placed on want or excess of jurisdiction or clear departure from fair and constitutional procedures, by fraud, perjury or error on the face of the record of the decision. O'Hanlon J made clear that judicial review was not available where the only matter being challenged was the adequacy of the evidence before the Inferior Tribunal.

In the course of his judgment, O'Hanlon J expressed his general impression that the evidence tendered in support of the prosecution was sufficient having regard to the very wide range of provisions of the relevant Finance Acts, but, he added that he did not consider it necessary to give a final decision on this point.

It is unlikely that the provision could be challenged successfully under the Constitution as an interference with the judicial process, since it does not make the certificate irrebuttable evidence of that which is therein contained.

## CUSTOMS AND EXCISE — POWER OF SEIZURE

*McCrystal Oil Co. Ltd v The Revenue Commissioners* [1993] ILRM 69, a case arising from the seizure in February, 1989, by the Revenue Commissioners, of a tanker containing a quantity of derv, kerosene and gas oil. The plaintiff's tanker was stopped by Officers of the Revenue Commissioners, who found gas oil marked in accordance with Hydrocarbon Oil (Rebated Oil) Regulations 1961 in one of its compartments. The driver was told by the Revenue Commissioners Official that the tanker was being seized because outlet of the compartment in question was not marked as required and was thereby in breach of the regulations. The case did not involve any challenge to the Revenue Commissioners' right in an appropriate case to seize goods pursuant to s. 202 of the Customs Law and Consolidation Act 1976 and s. 30 of the Inland Revenue Regulation Act 1890, and s. 21(12) of the Finance Act 1935, as amended by s. 18 of the Finance Act 1940 and s. 70 of the Finance Act 1983, but turned on whether any breach of the Hydrocarbon Oil (Rebated Oil) Regulations 1961 had been established, such that the Revenue Commissioners powers could properly be exercised in the instant case.

Article 8 provides:

> Except as may otherwise be permitted by the Commissioners, any vessel, delivery, pump or other container or outlet which contains any gas oil, marked in accordance with these regulations, shall be indelibly marked to the effect that such gas oil is not to be used for combustion in the engine of a motor vehicle or kept in the fuel tank of such vehicle.

The case for the Attorney General was that there was a breach of Article 8 of the 1961 Regulations, and this constituted an offence under s. 21 of the Finance Act 1935, which rendered the gas oil and the tanker, in which it was being conveyed, liable to be forfeited. This, of course, begged the question: had there been a breach of Article 8 of the Regulations?

At the hearing, the evidence before the court was that Revenue Officials tested the fuel in compartment 4, and found that it was marked 'gas oil'. They also found that none of the outlets on the back of the tanker was marked.

Blayney J held that if any breach of Article 8 were to constitute an offence under s. 21, the party alleged to be in breach was entitled to have it construed strictly and stated:

> In my opinion when this standard of construction is applied to the

> Article, it cannot be established that the particular breach alleged by the Attorney General occurred.

Blayney J based his finding on the phrase 'which contains any gas oil'. The requirement, as the learned judge indicated, is not that an outlet should be indelibly marked but that an outlet 'which contains any gas oil' must be indelibly marked. As there was no evidence as to the nature of the outlet, or whatever its nature, that it contained gas oil, Blayney J concluded that a breach of Article 8 had not been established. In the absence of a breach of Article 8, the provisions of s. 21 of the Finance Act 1935, as amended, did not apply and so there were no grounds for forfeiting the fuel in the tanker and, since the fuel could not be forfeited, the provisions of s. 30 of the Inland Revenue Regulation Act 1890, did not apply either and accordingly there was no entitlement to forfeit the tanker.

The plaintiff was entitled to the return of the tanker and of the fuel but, since the fuel had been sold, the plaintiff was entitled to the proceeds of sale.

Blayney J made it clear that the court was confined to dealing with the breach alleged and the fact that there was evidence that compartment 4 in the tanker contained gas oil and it appeared that it could be established that the compartment was not indelibly marked as required, was not relevant as the tanker and fuel were not seized on the basis that there had been a breach of Article 8 in respect of compartment 4 but on the basis of a breach of Article 8 in respect of outlet 4. It was not open to the Court to consider what the position would have been if the seizure had been made on other grounds.

## THE NATURE OF EXCISE PENALTY

In *Director of Public Prosecutions v Boyle* [1993] ILRM 128, the defendant a registered bookmaker, was prosecuted in the District Court for failing to pay excise duty on bets contrary to s. 24 (4) and s. 25 of the Finance Act 1926 as amended by s. 69(1) of the Finance Act 1982.

The defendant claimed that as the respective sections had not created criminal offences the complainant had no competence to prosecute the alleged breaches of those sections. The District Judge stated a consultative case stated pursuant to s. 52 of the Courts (Supplemental Provisions) Act 1961, to the High Court in the following terms:

> Is the recovery of an excise penalty under s. 25(2) of the Finance Act 1926, a criminal matter within the meaning of the Prosecution of Offences Act 1974?

In answering this question, Murphy J in the High Court referred to the Supreme Court decision in *Melling v Mathghamhna* [1962] IR 1, which considered the penalty provisions in the Customs Acts, and the High Court decisions in *McLoughlin v Tuite* [1986] ILRM 304 and *Downes v DPP* [1987] ILRM 665.

Kingsmill Moore J, in *Melling v Ó Mathghamhna*, posed the question; What is a crime? In answering the question, he quoted Lord Atkin's pithy encapsulation contained and unsurprisingly in the light of his Celtic origins, in the form of a question 'Is the act prohibited with penal consequences?' *Proprietary Articles Trade Association v Attorney General for Canada* [1931] AC 310 at 324.

Kingsmill Moore J also quoted the formulation in *Cross & Jones Textbook on Criminal Law* that 'A crime is a legal wrong the remedy for which is the punishment of the offender at the instance of the state'.

Kingsmill Moore J then identified the features which are regarded as indicia of crimes:

> (i) They are offences against the community at large and not against an individual;
> (ii) The sanction is punitive and not merely a matter of fiscal reparation;
> (iii) They require *mens rea* for the act must be done 'knowingly' and 'with intent to evade the prohibition or restriction'.

In the instant case, s. 24(4) provides:

> Every person who fails or neglects to pay any sum payable by him in respect of the duty imposed by this section shall be guilty of offence under this section and shall be liable on summary conviction therein to an excise penalty of £500.

The penalty was increased to £800 by the Finance Act 1982.

The sections of the Income Tax Acts with which the High Court were concerned in *McLoughlin v Tuite* [1986] ILRM 304, and *Downes v DPP* [1987] ILRM 665, posed penalties but did not use language appropriate to criminal matters such as 'offence', 'summary conviction', 'guilty', 'fine'.

Ss. 24 and 25 of the Finance Act 1926 are obligatory. Murphy J held that the excise penalties contained in the sections are punitive. Murphy J further held that the crucial factors in the present case were the presence of the words 'an offence' and 'on summary conviction', and that in the circumstances having regard to the express provisions of ss. 24 and 25 of the Finance Act 1926, that the wrongdoing or contravention referred to in those subsections constitutes a criminal matter and not a mere civil matter so that the Director of Public Prosecutions is entitled to institute proceedings in respect thereof.

## MARRIAGE GRATUITY; WHETHER TAXABLE

*Ó Síocháin (Inspector of Taxes) v Morrissey*, High Court, 9 July 1992, in the words of Murphy J, raises an interesting question as to whether a marriage gratuity constituted emoluments of Mrs Morrissey's employment and was taxable as such under s. 110 of the Income Tax Act 1967 or if not taxable under s. 110, whether it is taxable under s. 114 of the Income Tax Act 1967 as constituting a payment made directly or indirectly in consideration or in consequence of or in connection with the termination of her employment.

Murphy J referred the matter back to the Circuit Court for the Circuit Judge to make a specific finding under s. 110 but while reaching no final conclusion and in no way seeking to restrict or direct the discretion of the Circuit Judge in reviewing the matter, indicated that pension is itself a taxable subject matter distinct from the profit of an office so that a lump sum paid in commutation of pension rights even during the course of an employment was not and in principle would not be liable to tax as emolument of an office: see *Tilley v Wales* [1943] AC 386.

Murphy J further indicated that the finding that the marriage gratuity paid was a payment made to Mrs Morrissey in consequence of or otherwise in connection with the termination of her employment with the Bank within the meaning of s. 114 of the Income Tax Act 1967, could hardly be questioned. The real question, however, was whether the payment had already been captured by s. 110 and if that issue was only dealt with by implication by the Circuit Court Judge, the matter would be referred back to him to clarify the issue.

## COPYRIGHT ROYALTIES; VALUE ADDED TAX LIABILITY

In *Phonograghic Performance (Ireland) Ltd v Summers* [1992] ILRM 657, the appellant was a corporate body which had assembled a portfolio of copyrights in sound recordings for its members; it had vested in it the copyright in the recording, not the original copyright in the product itself. The corporate body (the appellant) then exploits the series of copyrights it holds. The respondent, the Inspector of Taxes, contended that in exploiting the copyright, the appellant was supplying a service within the meaning of s. 2 of the Value Added Tax Act 1972.

The appellant resisted the proposition arguing strenuously that it had no service to supply, and that less still did it supply one. The appellant argument turned on s. 17(4) para (b) of the Copyright Act 1963, which provides that the acts restricted by the copyright in any sound recording are:

> In the case of a published recording, causing the recording or any reproduction thereof to be heard in public, or to be broadcast or to be transmitted to subscribers to a diffusion service, without the payment of equitable remuneration to the owner of the copyright subsisting in the recording.

The appellant's submission can be distilled to the following proposition: That the appellant had nothing to give, that its only right is to receive equitable remuneration. The appellant could not prohibit anybody from making a record embodying any of its portfolio of copyright recordings, neither could it prohibit a third party from causing the recording to be heard in public; its sole right is to be remunerated by the payment to it of equitable remuneration.

Murphy J took the view that this argument ran counter to the appellant's own documentation. He referred in particular to clause 3 (b) of the Memorandum of Association of the appellant company which, *inter alia*, permitted the appellant 'to authorise others under licence or agreement or other arrangement . . . to broadcast . . . phonograms and videograms . . . and to collect and receive . . . all royalties, fees, and other monies payable under such licences. . . .' More embarrassing, he continued, was the document described as 'the information sheet' published by the appellant and dated 3 September 1990, which purported to explain the legal rights of the appellant in relation to persons wishing to perform in public recordings the sound recording copyright of which was vested in the appellant. The judge held that it was quite clear that the document — and every single paragraph of it — was based on the assumption or belief that a sound recording can be performed in public only with the permission of the person holding the copyright in the sound recording and on the terms to be agreed by him and that a licence from the person holding that copyright must be obtained.

It was contended by the appellant that no copyright vested in the appellants which would prevent the transmission to the public of published recordings. It was also contended that the public had the right to cause recordings to be heard by the public and the owner of the recording has nothing to give, only the right to receive.

Murphy J was of the view that it was unquestionable that one cannot, without restriction, cause to be heard by the public a recording. There is a restriction imposed, the nature of which is the payment of equitable remuneration; the essence is that there is a restriction and it is that restriction which defines the copyright. When one looks in that way at the agreement between the appellant and RTE, he continued, what one sees is that the right is being exploited. It is not just a question of agreeing what is reasonable remuneration.

In conclusion, Murphy J held that the appellant was supplying the right to RTE and that therefore, the appeal commissioner was correct in holding that the appellant supplied services to RTE in the relevant period within the meaning of s. 5 of the Value Added Tax Act 1972.

# Safety and Health

## DANGEROUS SUBSTANCES AND PREPARATIONS: CHEMICAL SAFETY

**Chemicals (single)** The European Communities (Dangerous Substances) (Classification, Packaging, Labelling and Notification) (Amendment) Regulations 1992 (SI No. 426), amending Regulations of the same title of 1979, implemented the 11th to 15th Adaptations to Technical Progress (ATPs) (90/517/EEC, 91/325/EEC, 91/326/EEC, 91/410/EEC, 91/632/EEC and 92/37/EEC) of the 1967 Directive on the Classification, Packaging and Labelling (CPL) of Dangerous Substances (67/548/EEC).

The 1967 Directive, as amended, deals with single chemicals (i.e. substances), and lays down detailed criteria as to the classification (toxic, corrosive, etc) of over 100,000 chemicals covered by its terms. It also lays down strict requirements as to the labelling of these substances in the familiar black on orange labels found on such items as domestic cleaning products as well as bulk industrial chemicals. Safety and risk information must also be included on the labels to be placed on containers of the substances covered by the 1967 Directive.

The 1992 Regulations also revoked a number of previous Regulations on CPL of Dangerous Substances (SI No. 34 of 1980; SI No. 27 of 1983; SI No. 335 of 1984; SI No. 224 of 1986; SI No. 47 of 1988; and SI No. 228 of 1989). These had become redundant with the updating resulting from the 1992 Regulations. We criticise the format of the 1992 Regulations below, after the discussion of the Dangerous Preparations Regulations 1992 (SI No. 393).

**Chemicals (mixtures)** The European Communities (Classification, Packaging and Labelling of Dangerous Preparations) Regulations 1992 (SI No. 393) implemented the 1988 Directive on the Classification, Packaging and Labelling (CPL) of Dangerous Preparations (88/379/EEC) as well as the amendments and the 1st and 2nd ATPs resulting from Directives 89/178/EEC, 90/35/EEC, 90/492/EEC, 91/155/EEC and 91/442/EEC.

The 1988 Directive established a similar regime for dangerous preparations (i.e. mixtures of chemicals) as the 1967 Directive on Dangerous Substances, referred to above, had established for single chemicals. One significant addition to the regime was that laid down in the 1991 Directive on Safety Data Sheets, 91/155/EEC, implemented by the 1992 Regulations.

The Safety Data Sheets Directive requires manufacturers and suppliers to provide industrial users of chemicals with information on the chemicals being supplied to them in a standard format laid down in the 1991 Directive and the 1992 Regulations. Such information may be circumscribed to the extent that it might result in the giving of trade secrets.

The 1992 Regulations revoked a number of previous Regulations on the CPL of Paints and Solvents (SI No. 365 of 1980, SI No. 189 of 1983, SI No. 170 of 1984, SI No. 205 of 1987 and SI No. 152 of 1991). These had become redundant with the implementation of the 1988 Directive.

One point of difference between SI No. 393 on Dangerous Preparations and SI No. 426 on Dangerous Substances may be noted. SI No. 393 is an extremely lengthy set of Regulations as it incorporates in the normal way the requirements of the 1988 Directive and the relevant amendments to the Directive. On the other hand, SI No. 426 runs to a mere few pages, stating baldly in effect that the relevant Directives on dangerous substances have been implemented in Irish law. SI No. 426 contains no text which would indicate the substance, as it were, of the legal changes effected by its terms; for this one would be required to consult the text of the Directives. This formula is in line with previous Regulations on this area, but it might be open to objection that it lacks transparency and, possibly, thereby validity. It is to be hoped that, in future, Regulations on dangerous substances will follow the more expressive, albeit expansive, approach taken in the 1992 Regulations on dangerous preparations.

**Cosmetic products** The European Communities (Cosmetic Products) (Amendment) Regulations 1992 (SI No. 400) amended the 1990 Regulations of the same title (1990 Review, 284) to give effect to Directives 92/8/EEC and 92/86/EEC, the 14th and 15th Commission Directives on Cosmetic Products. These Directives lay down the conditions concerning the substances which may be contained in cosmetic products in order to protect public health, taking account of the most recent advancements in scientific knowledge in cosmetology.

**Major accident hazards** The European Communities (Major Accident Hazards of Certain Industrial Activities) (Amendment) Regulations 1992 (SI No. 21) amended the 1986 Regulations of the same title in order to implement the 1988 Directive (88/610/EEC) which amended the 1982 Directive on the Major Accident Hazards of Certain Industrial Activities (the 'Seveso' Directive). The 1982 Directive, as amended, lays down detailed requirements aimed at limiting the effects of accidents arising from industrial activities which store large quantities of dangerous substances.

**Pesticides: inspection** The European Communities (Classification, Packaging and Labelling of Pesticides) (Amendment) Regulations 1992 (SI No. 416) amended Regulation 15 of the 1985 Regulations of the same title, making it an offence to obstruct an officer appointed under the Regulations from exercising the powers conferred by Regulation 13 of the 1985 Regulations. These Regulations were made after the decision of O'Hanlon J in *Minister for Agriculture and Food v Cahill*, High Court, 12 November 1992, discussed immediately below, in which another aspect of these powers was involved.

**Pesticides: sample taking** In *Minister for Agriculture and Food v Cahill*, High Court, 12 November 1992 O'Hanlon J dealt with procedural aspects of a prosecution under the Regulations on the control of pesticides. The defendant was charged by the prosecutor Minister in the District Court with offences alleging that he used on a product a pesticide containing a prohibited substance, contrary to the European Communities (Classification, Packaging and Labelling of Pesticides) Regulations 1981, as amended. The prosecution sought to introduce in evidence results from samples which had been taken from products under the control of the defendant. The statutory requirements concerning the taking of such samples, laid down in Regulation 13 of the European Communities (Classification, Packaging and Labelling of Pesticides) (Amendment) Regulations 1985, as amended by the European Communities (Classification, Packaging and Labelling of Pesticides) (Amendment) Regulations 1987, had not been complied with and the results were therefore deemed inadmissible by the District Judge (for the 1992 Regulations further amending the 1985 Regulations, see above). Other evidence given for the prosecution was to the effect that the defendant had admitted that he had used a pesticide containing a prohibited substance. The District Judge concluded that, as the product sample had been taken in breach of the 1985 Regulations, the case should be dismissed. On a case stated, O'Hanlon J held that the District Judge had erred in dismissing the case.

O'Hanlon J concluded that the 1981 Regulations, as amended, did not lay down as a condition precedent to a conviction that any samples taken must be proved in the manner prescribed by the Regulations, and there was thus the possibility that, even where the sample evidence is rejected the defendant may be convicted on other evidence. He considered that, in the instant case, the District Judge had been correct to rule out evidence of the samples, but added that he should have proceeded to consider whether on the remaining evidence it was open to convict the defendant on the charges brought. Accordingly, O'Hanlon J remitted the case to the District Court to consider further the charges in the light of his judgment.

**Transport of dangerous goods** The European Communities (Vocational Training for Drivers of Vehicles Carrying Dangerous Goods) Regulations 1992 (SI No. 204) are referred to below, 540.

## ENVIRONMENTAL PROTECTION AGENCY ACT 1992

**Introduction** The Environmental Protection Agency Act 1992 comprises two essential elements. First, the 1992 Act envisages some substantial amendments to existing legislation on pollution control as well as providing for the implementation of a further number of EC-based requirements in this area. In the process, it is likely that a more satisfactory integrated picture will be produced on a topic which had previously been scattered through numerous Acts and Regulations concerning planning and development, air pollution, water pollution and waste management. Second, the 1992 Act envisages a substantial shift from local authority control over environmental safety to centralised control under the aegis of the eponymous Environmental Protection Agency (EPA). Overall, as the Act's title suggests, the intention would appear to be to move from pollution control to protection of the environment. In light of the detailed and complex nature of the 1992 Act's provisions, we will provide here a discussion of its more significant elements only. For a comprehensive analysis, including a valuable overview of the impact of the 1992 Act on existing legislation on environmental safety, see Richard Humphreys' Annotation, *Irish Current Law Statutes Annotated.*

**Commencement** By virtue of s. 2(1) of the 1992 Act, some of the 1992 Act, which is divided into six Parts, came into force immediately on its promulgation by the President on 23 April 1992. The provisions brought into force immediately by s.2(1) were: Part I (other than s.18(1)), Part II (other than s. 43), Part III, Part IV (other than s. 93) and Part VI. However, although the bulk of the Act became nominally operational in April 1992, many of its provisions require Ministerial Regulations or Orders to become fully operational. One of the most significant events which was subject to such an Order was the establishment of the EPA itself. This occurred on 26 July 1993: Environmental Protection Agency (Establishment) Order 1993 (SI No. 213 of 1993). Further powers were conferred on the EPA in early 1994: see below. Of course, the effectiveness of the EPA will be dependent on the extent to which resources are made available to put into effect the ambitious intentions of the 1992 Act, which will become evident even from the outline of its provisions given here.

**General provisions concerning EPA** The establishment of the EPA in 1993 had the effect of breathing some life into Parts I, II and III of the 1992 Act, which had nominally been brought into force by s. 2(1) of the 1992 Act (that is, apart from s.18 of the 1992 Act, which will repeal s. 51 of the Local Government (Planning and Development) Act 1963 concerning noise pollution, and s. 43 of the 1992 Act, which relates to regional environmental units). Part I of the 1992 Act (ss. 1 to 18), as well as providing for the usual preliminary matters of definition, provides in s.11 that summary prosecutions may be taken by the EPA in respect of a contravention of the Act. It also provides for an immunity from suit for the EPA along the lines as those contained in the Safety, Health and Welfare at Work Act 1989 (see the query raised on such immunity in the 1989 Review, 384).

Part II of the 1992 Act (ss. 19 to 51) relates primarily to the administrative side of the EPA. This included the appointment of the Director General of the EPA through an unusually complex procedure under s. 21, by which a number of different organisations were represented in the selection process. For the detailed arrangements, see the Environmental Protection Agency (Selection Procedures) Regulations 1992 (SI No. 215). Ss. 27 and 28 of the Act concern the functions of the Advisory Committee to the EPA. For the details of membership selection see the Environmental Protection Agency (Advisory Committee) Regulations 1993 (SI No. 43 of 1993).

The remainder of Part II consists of relatively common provisions concerning meetings, transfer of staff to the EPA, confidentiality of information, charging for services and the making of annual reports to the Minister for the Environment. Similar provisions were included in the Safety, Health and Welfare at Work Act 1989. S. 32 of the 1992 Act envisaged the dissolution of An Foras Forbatha Teo, the National Institute for Physical Planning and Construction Research Ltd, and a transfer of its staff to the EPA. This was effected on 1 August 1993 in the wake of the establishment of the EPA itself: see the Environmental Protection Agency Act 1992 (Dissolution of An Foras Forbatha Teoranta) Order 1993 (SI No. 215 of 1993).

**Monitoring functions of the EPA** Part III of the 1992 Act (ss. 52 to 81) concerns the functions of the EPA. S. 52 of the Act provides that the EPA immediately becomes a monitoring agency for compliance with existing pollution control legislation. It is empowered to conduct research on the environment, and thus the link with the, now dissolved, An Foras Forbatha is clear. S. 71 of the Act also specifies in further detail the EPA's environmental research brief.

In a clear mandatory tone, s. 64 of the Act requires the EPA to collect hydrometric data, that is, water flow information, throughout the State.

Similarly, s. 65 requires the EPA to prepare programmes for monitoring the quality of the environment and to ensure their implementation by the relevant authorities. Technical specifications for the gathering of data are laid down in s. 66, which provides for an accreditation scheme for laboratories involved. S. 70 requires the EPA to prepare every five years a report on the quality and condition of the environment in the State.

The EPA is also authorised by s.74 to encourage the carrying out of environmental audits. S.76 authorises the EPA to publish Codes of Practice which would provide practical guidance as to compliance with relevant statutory provisions. However such Codes have no legal status as such, unlike the Codes of Practice provided for under ss. 30 and 31 of the Safety, Health and Welfare at Work Act 1989 (see the 1989 Review, 390-1). S. 78 empowers the EPA to introduce a labelling system to conform to, for example, the ECO-labelling system envisaged under EC law. Such a system would be backed by criminal sanction.

**Integrated pollution control (IPC) and BATNEEC** S. 52 of the 1992 Act envisages a potential future role for the EPA as the central agency for a system of integrated pollution control (IPC), through a licensing system monitored by the EPA itself. This would not apply to all industrial installations, but to those which were above certain thresholds to be laid out in Regulations under the 1992 Act. Prior to the 1992 Act, licensing systems were operated and controlled by local authorities. While local authorities will continue to have a role after the introduction of IPC, they will deal only with industrial installations below the thresholds for IPC. The IPC system is dealt with in Part IV of the Act (ss. 82 to 99).

S. 83 provides that the essential legal standard on which such a licensing system would be based is that referred to in s. 5 of the 1992 Act, namely 'the use of the best available technology not entailing excessive cost'. This is usually known by the acronym BATNEEC. S. 5 of the Act provides a detailed description of the factors to be taken into account in determining whether particular measures meet the standard set by its terms. It is envisaged that the BATNEEC test will replace existing standards, such as those contained in the Air Pollution Act 1987. The EPA is empowered by s. 5 to lay down detailed specifications for particular activities in order to meet the BATNEEC standard. 'Regard must be had to' such specifications in the administration of the 1992 Act.

Part IV (other than s. 93, which concerns charges in relation to emissions) had been nominally brought into force in 1992 by virtue of s. 1(2) of the Act. However, the IPC system contained in it only became operational in early 1994 when a number of Orders and Regulations were made which set out, in effect, commencement dates for certain aspects of the new IPC system.

These were: the Environmental Protection Agency Act 1992 (Commencement) Order 1994 (SI No. 82 of 1994); the Environmental Protection Agency Act 1992 (Established Activities) Order 1994 (SI No. 83 of 1994); the European Communities (Environmental Impact Assessment) (Amendment) Regulations 1994 (SI No. 84 of 1994); and the Environmental Protection Agency (Licensing) Regulations 1994 (SI No. 85 of 1994).

S. 53 of the 1992 Act also envisages additional functions being assigned to the EPA, while s. 54 provides that functions under Regulations specified in the Second Schedule could be transferred to the EPA. Both these provisions require a Ministerial Order or Regulations before such new arrangements could become effective.

**EPA link with local authorities** S. 56 of the 1992 Act provides that the EPA may provide information or advice to local authorities or make recommendations on environmental protection to local authorities. The authorities are required to 'have regard to' any such advice or recommendations. S. 58 empowers the EPA to require a sanitary authority to submit information as to whether drinking water complies with the European Communities (Quality of Water Intended for Human Consumption) Regulations 1988 or similar legislation concerning drinking water. S. 59 of the Act provides that the Minister for the Environment may make Regulations for the purposes of giving effect to Council Directive 91/271/EEC on the treatment of sewage and other effluents, while s. 60 empowers the EPA to specify criteria for local authorities concerning drinking water or sewage treatment and s. 62 authorises the EPA to specify criteria concerning landfill sites. As with s. 56, local authorities must have regard to such criteria or specifications. In addition, s. 63 authorises the EPA to request from a local authority a report as to how the authority is performing its functions concerning environmental protection generally.

**Environmental impact assessment** S. 72 of the 1992 Act empowers the EPA to prepare guidelines on the information to be contained in environmental impact statements where these are required as part of a planning application under the Local Government (Planning and Development) Acts 1963 to 1992, as amended by the European Communities (Environmental Impact Assessment) Regulations 1989 (in relation to road developments, see now ss. 50 and 51 of the Roads Act 1993). When the IPC system was introduced in early 1994 (see above), the provisions on Environmental Impact Assessment, including the 1992 Act itself, were amended by the European Communities (Environmental Impact Assessment) (Amendment) Regulations 1994 (SI No. 84 of 1994).

**General pollution control** Part V of the 1992 Act (ss. 100 to 105), which was not brought into effect in 1992, concerns the possible transfer of responsibilities to the EPA under existing environmental legislation, such as the Air Pollution Act 1987. It is also envisaged that the EPA could be give additional recommendation powers concerning emission levels for various pollutants.

**Reports and inquiries** S. 104 of the Act empowers the EPA to conduct reports and investigations into the causes of any incident causing environmental pollution. This power was brought into force on 10 August 1993: Environmental Protection Agency Act 1992 (Commencement) Order 1993 (SI No. 235 of 1993). This occurred in the immediate wake of incidents in the Ringaskiddy area of Cork which led to calls for an investigation by the EPA, and the s. 104 power was brought into force for that purpose (the Commencement Order itself was signed on 10 August 1993, thus indicating the immediacy of its introduction). The more formal power to conduct an inquiry pursuant to s. 105 of the 1992 Act had not been brought into force at the time of writing.

**Noise control** Ss.106 to 108 concern the power to control noise as an environmental nuisance. When these provisions become operational, s. 18 of the 1992 Act will repeal s. 51 of the Local Government (Planning and Development) Act 1963 which is the current legislative provision concerning environmental noise pollution.

S. 109 provides that ss. 106 to 108 are expressly without prejudice to the powers contained in the Safety, Health and Welfare at Work Act 1989. The 1989 Act authorises the Minister for Enterprise and Employment to make Regulations concerning noise levels at work. The European Communities (Protection of Workers) (Exposure to Noise) Regulations 1990 (see the 1990 Review, 474-5) contain the current provisions on this topic, though they were made under the general powers in s. 3 of the European Communities Act 1972, rather than under the 1989 Act.

**Public access to information** S. 110 of the 1992 Act required, in mandatory language, that the Minister for the Environment make Regulations requiring public authorities to make available to the public information concerning the environment. This was expressly stated to be for the purpose of giving effect to Council Directive 90/313/EEC. The relevant Regulations are the Access to Information on the Environment Regulations 1993 (SI No. 133 of 1993).

**Genetically modified organisms** S. 111 of the 1992 Act empowers the

Minister for the Environment to make Regulations on the control of activities concerning genetically modified organisms (GMOs) with the express purpose of implementing Directives 90/219/EEC and 90/220/EEC on this topic.

**Civil liability for air pollution** S. 18(2) of the 1992 Act, and the connected provisions in the Third Schedule to the Act, provide for certain amendments to the Air Pollution Act 1987. The main changes provide for a civil remedy for damage arising from air pollution, by the insertion of new ss. 28A and 28B into the 1987 Act. These came into force on 23 April 1992 by virtue of s. 1(2) of the 1992 Act.

## ENVIRONMENTAL SAFETY

**Air pollution: civil liability** We note the effect of s. 18(2) of the Environmental Protection Agency Act 1992 above.

**Air pollution: limit values** The Air Pollution Act 1987 (Combustion Plant) Regulations 1992 (SI No. 273), in implementing Directive 88/609/EEC, lay down emission limit values for sulphur dioxide, nitrogen oxide and dust emissions from combustion plant. The 1992 Regulations also provide directions on the best practicable means for limiting and monitoring emissions.

**Bathing Water** The European Communities (Quality of Bathing Water) (Revocation) Regulations 1992 (SI No. 154) revoked the European Communities (Quality of Bathing Water) Regulations 1988 and 1989. These have been replaced by the Quality of Bathing Water Regulations 1992 (SI No. 155), which implement the Directive on Bathing Water, 76/160/EEC. The 1992 Regulations were made under the Local Government (Water Pollution) Acts 1977 and 1990. On the 1990 Act, see the 1990 Review, 470-3.

**Coal** The Air Pollution Act 1987 (Marketing, Sale and Distribution of Fuels) Regulations 1992 (SI No. 274) amended the 1990 Regulations of the same title (1990 Review, 470) by increasing the permitted sulphur content of coal for sale in Dublin from 1.5% to 2%.

**Environmental Protection Agency** The Environmental Protection Agency Act 1992 is examined under a separate heading, above.

**Inland water pollution: Bord Pleanála appeals** The Local Government (Water Pollution) Regulations 1992 (SI No. 271) amend the procedure concerning appeals to An Bord Pleanála in water pollution matters. In light of the 1992 Regulations, the Local Government (Water Pollution) Act 1977 (Transfer of Appeals) Order 1977 was revoked by the Local Government (Water Pollution) (Transfer of Appeals) (Revocation) Order 1992 (SI No. 272).

**Inland water pollution: commencement of Act** The Local Government (Water Pollution) (Amendment) Act 1990 (Commencement) Order 1992 (SI No. 270) brought ss. 4, 5, 6, 13, 14, 15 and 16 of the 1990 Act into effect from 1 November 1992. This completed the implementation of the 1990 Act, its other provisions having come into effect on its signing on 8 July 1990. On the 1990 Act, see the 1990 Review, 470-3.

**Inland water pollution: groundwater** The Local Government (Water Pollution) Regulations 1992 (SI No. 271), implementing Directive 80/68/EEC, concern the protection of groundwater against pollution caused by dangerous substances. The 1992 Regulations were made under the Local Government (Water Pollution) Acts 1977 and 1990. On the 1990 Act, see the 1990 Review, 470-3.

**Sea pollution: International Liability and Compensation Conventions** The Oil Pollution of the Sea (Civil Liability and Compensation) Act 1988 (Commencement) Order 1992 (SI No. 381) brought the 1988 Act into force on 20 November 1992, the date the Commencement Order itself was signed. It may be noted that the original, stencilled, A4 version of the Commencement Order had erroneously indicated that the Act was being brought into force with retrospective effect from 18 May 1992. This was not, apparently, the date specified in the Order actually signed by the Minister for the Marine, and the correct commencement date of 20 November 1992 appeared on the later A5 printed text of the Commencement Order (correction confirmed in communication between authors and Department of the Marine). On the 1988 Act, see the 1988 Review, 437-9. The Oil Pollution of the Sea (Annual Returns and Contributions in Respect of Compensation Fund) Regulations 1992 (SI No. 402) require that annual returns to the Minister for the Marine be made by persons who receive more than 150,000 tonnes of crude oil, and that they must also pay pro-rata annual contributions to the International Fund Convention incorporated into Irish law by the 1988 Act. The Oil Pollution of the Sea (Civil Liability and Compensation) Act 1988 (Insurance of Ships) Regulations 1992 (SI No. 403) provide that a ship carrying 2,000 tonnes or more of crude or fuel oil must have insurance against pollution damages which satisfies the criteria laid down by the Minister for the Marine under the 1988 Act. The Oil Pollution of the Sea (Civil Liability and

Compensation) (Convention Countries) Order 1992 (SI No. 404) lists the countries which have variously accepted the Liability and Compensation Fund Conventions, both of which were incorporated into Irish law by the 1988 Act.

**Sea pollution: national measures** The Sea Pollution Act 1991 (Commencement) Order 1992 (SI No. 380) brought the 1991 Act, except s. 8, into force on 20 November 1992. The choice of 20 November 1992 would appear to have been intended to coincide with the bringing into effect of the Oil Pollution of the Sea (Civil Liability and Compensation) Act 1988, the Commencement Order for which (SI No. 381) was also signed on 20 November 1992: see above. On the 1991 Act, see the 1991 Review, 366. It may be noted that, like with the Commencement Order for the 1988 Act, the original, stencilled, A4 version of the Commencement Order for the 1991 Act had erroneously indicated that the Act was being brought into force with retrospective effect from 18 May 1992. This was not, apparently, the date specified in the Order actually signed by the Minister for the Marine, and the correct commencement date of 20 November 1992 appeared on the later A5 printed text of the Commencement Order (this correction was confirmed in a telephone communication between the authors and the Department of the Marine).

**Waste oil** The European Communities (Waste Oils) Regulations 1992 (SI No. 399) give effect to Directive 87/101/EEC, which requires a permit system be introduced by local authorities in connection with the disposal of waste oils. The 1992 Regulations revoked 1984 Regulations of the same title.

## FOOD SAFETY

**Additives** The European Communities (Labelling of Additives for Use in Foodstuffs) Regulations 1992 (SI No. 23) gave effect to the Directive on Additives, 89/107/EEC.

**Emulsifiers etc.** The Health (Emulsifiers, Stabilisers, Thickening and Gelling Agents in Food) Regulations 1992 (SI No. 24) amended the 1980 Regulations of the same title in order to give effect to Directive 90/612/EEC.

**Flavourings** The European Communities (Flavourings for Use in Foodstuffs for Human Consumption) Regulations 1992 (SI No. 22) gave effect to the Directive on Flavourings, 88/388/EEC, as amended by Directive 91/71/EEC.

**Foodstuff Lot** The European Communities (Identification of Foodstuff Lot) Regulations 1992 (SI No. 110) implemented Directive 89/396/EEC, as amended by Directives 91/238/EEC and 92/11/EEC. They require that the foodstuffs covered by the Regulations contain a visible indication of the lot from which the particular foodstuff was made.

**Fruit Juices** The Food Standards (Fruit Juices and Fruit Nectars) (European Communities) (Amendment) Regulations 1992 (SI No. 27) amend the 1978 Regulations of the same title to implement Directive 89/394/EEC, which had revised the requirements of the Principal Directive, 75/726/EEC.

**Inspection** In the 1991 Review, 367, we noted that the Health (Official Control of Food) Regulations 1991 had implemented Directive 89/397/EEC on the Official Control of Foodstuffs and that, consequently, the Health (Sampling of Foods) Regulations 1970 had been revoked. A number of references in pre-1991 Regulations on food safety had referred to the inspection provisions of the now-revoked 1970 Regulations. In 1992, a series of Regulations, SI Nos. 65 to 73, were made to replace the obsolete references to the 1970 Regulations with references to the 1991 Regulations.

Since these Regulations are largely identical in effect, we will note the import of one only and then list the remainder. Thus, the Health (Vinyl Chloride in Food) (Amendment) Regulations 1992 (SI No. 65) amended the 1984 Regulations of the same title by replacing the reference in the 1984 Regulations to the Health (Sampling of Foods) Regulations 1970 with a reference to the Health (Official Control of Food) Regulations 1991. The other Regulations having the same effect are: the Health (Preservatives in Food) (Amendment) Regulations 1992 (SI No. 66) (amending 1981 Regulations of the same title), the Health (Erucic Acid in Food) (Amendment) Regulations 1992 (SI No. 67) (amending 1978 Regulations of the same title), the Health (Colouring Agents in Food) (Amendment) Regulations 1992 (SI No. 68) (amending 1973 Regulations of the same title), the Health (Antioxidant in Food) (Amendment) Regulations 1992 (SI No. 69) (amending 1973 Regulations of the same title), the Health (Solvents in Food) (Amendment) Regulations 1992 (SI No. 70) (amending 1972 Regulations of the same title), the Health (Mineral Hydrocarbons in Food) (Amendment) Regulations 1992 (SI No. 71) (amending 1972 Regulations of the same title), the Health (Arsenic and Lead in Food) (Amendment) Regulations 1992 (SI No. 72) (amending 1972 Regulations of the same title) and the Health (Cyclamate in Food) (Amendment) Regulations 1992 (SI No. 73). (amending 1970 Regulations of the same title).

**Purity Criteria** The European Communities (Antioxidant in Food) (Purity

Criteria) (Amendment) Regulations 1992 (SI No. 63) (amending 1985 Regulations of the same title) and the European Communities (Preservatives in Food) (Purity Criteria) (Amendment) Regulations 1992 (SI No. 64) (amending 1984 Regulations of the same title) were made to take account of the requirements of Directive 89/397/EEC on the Official Control of Foodstuffs (see the 1991 Review, 367).

**Quick-frozen foodstuffs** The European Communities (Quick-frozen Foodstuffs) Regulations 1992 (SI No. 290) give effect to Directive 89/108/EEC.

## MANUFACTURING STANDARDS IN THE EC

In the 1991 Review, 368, we noted the increased number of EC 'New Approach' or 'Approximation' Directives which establish minimum safety and health criteria for various products and which are linked to detailed technical standards, or European Norms (EN), developed by the European Standards bodies such as CEN and CENELEC.

Relevant Regulations implementing such Directives in 1992 were as follows, of which we might single out the European Communities (Machinery) Regulations 1992 (SI No. 246) as particularly significant.

**Appliances Burning Gaseous Fuels** The European Communities (Appliances Burning Gaseous Fuels) Regulations 1992 (SI No. 101) implemented the 1990 Directive on Appliances Burning Gaseous Fuels (90/396/EEC). The 1992 Regulations become fully operational on 1 January 1996, from which date the Industrial Research and Standards (Section 44) (Gas-operated Ovens) Order 1983 will be revoked.

**Construction Products** The European Communities (Construction Products) Regulations 1992 (SI No. 198) implemented the 1988 Directive on Construction Products (89/106/EEC), which lays down extensive requirements for materials intended to be used in buildings. The 1992 Regulations should thus be read in conjunction with the Building Regulations 1991 (see the 1991 Review, 307-8). The Department of the Environment published a Guidance Booklet on the 1992 Regulations at the time of their promulgation.

**Low Voltage Electrical Equipment** The European Communities (Low Voltage Electrical Equipment) Regulations 1992 (SI No. 428) implement the 1973 Principal Directive on Low Voltage Electrical Equipment, 73/23/EEC, as amended. It may be noted that the 1973 Directive was one of the first

Directives in this area, arising from the Franco-German dispute of the 1960s concerning importation of TVs. The 1992 Regulations revoked Regulations of 1975, 1976 and 1979 of the same title.

**Machinery** Possibly the most significant and wide-ranging Regulations to have been made in this area in recent years are the European Communities (Machinery) Regulations 1992 (SI No. 246). The 1992 Regulations implemented the 1989 Principal Directive on Machinery, 89/392/EEC, as amended by Directive 91/368/EEC, which incorporated requirements on mobile machinery. Prior to the 1989 Directive, only a very limited number of Directives on industrial machinery had been adopted at EC level.

The 1989 Directive is extremely wide-ranging in scope, and partly for this reason the 1992 Regulations implementing it will not become fully operational until 1996. This is to allow the phasing-in the onerous standards to be imposed on manufacturers of machinery covered by the 1989 Directive, as well as to allow CEN to formulate relevant technical standards to back up the 1989 Directive. When the 1992 Regulations become fully operational in 1996, previous Directives and their implementing Regulations will be revoked. The Regulations in question are the European Communities (Wire-Ropes, Chains and Hooks) Regulations 1979 (will be revoked on 1 January 1995), the European Communities (Roll Over and Falling Object Protective Structures) Regulations 1990 (will be revoked on 1 January 1996) and the European Communities (Self-Propelled Industrial Trucks) Regulations 1991 (will be revoked on 1 January 1996).

**Motor vehicles** The Regulations governing the type approval for motor vehilces are referred to in the Transport chapter, 627, below.

## OCCUPATIONAL SAFETY (GENERAL)

**Dangerous substances and preparations** We discuss the important Regulations concerning the control of dangerous substances and preparations above, 526-9.

**Employer's liability** The case law from 1992 on employer's liability is discussed in the Torts chapter, 568-70, below.

**Harbours** Aspects of the procedure for granting a ship's piloting licence were considered in *Heavey v Pilotage Committee of the Dublin Pilotage Authority*, High Court, 7 May 1992: see the Transport chapter, 621-3, below.

**Factories Act: 'machine'** In *Hetherington v Ultra Tyre Services Ltd* [1993] ILRM 353; [1993] 2 IR 535 (considered on a different point in the 1991 Review, 334-5), the Supreme Court held that a fork lift truck, which fell on the plaintiff when he was replacing one of the truck's tyres, did not constitute a 'machine' for the purposes of s. 32 of the Factories Act 1955. This was because the fork lift truck was 'dormant' at the time of the accident and was thus not 'in use' for the purposes of s. 32.

**Major accident hazards** We also discuss the Regulations concerning the precautions to be taken connected with the storage of large quantities of dangerous substances and preparations above, 526-8.

**Merchant shipping** The Merchant Shipping Act 1992 is discussed in the Transport chapter, 625-6, below. We also refer there to the Regulations made in 1992 under the Merchant Shipping Acts.

**Radiation** The Radiological Protection Institute of Ireland, which replaced and took over the powers and functions of the Nuclear Energy Board, was established on 1 April 1992, pursuant to the Radiological Protection Act 1991 (Establishment Day) Order 1992 (SI No. 48). The effect of that Order was that the Nuclear Energy Board stood dissolved on 1 April 1992, and the Nuclear Energy Act 1971 was also repealed and replaced by the Radiological Protection Act 1991. On the 1991 Act, see the 1991 Review, 372-5.

**Transport of dangerous goods** The European Communities (Vocational Training for Drivers of Vehicles Carrying Dangerous Goods) Regulations 1992 (SI No. 204) implemented Directive 89/684/EEC. The 1992 Regulations require that drivers of vehicles carrying prescribed quantities of dangerous goods within the meaning of the UN-based ADR Agreement on the Carriage of Dangerous Goods must pass an approved course related to the precautions to be taken in the conveyance of such goods. The Regulations overlap to some extent with similar requirements contained in the Dangerous Substances (Conveyance of Scheduled Substances by Road) (Trade or Business) Regulations 1980 and 1986, although the 1992 Regulations do not explicitly refer to the terms of the 1980 or 1986 Regulations. The overlap may be due to the fact that the 1992 Regulations emanated from the Department of Transport, whereas the 1980 and 1986 Regulations were promulgated by the Department of Labour under the Dangerous Substances Act 1972.

# Social Welfare

## 1992 ACT AND REGULATIONS

For a detailed analysis of the Social Welfare Act 1992, see Robert Clark's Annotation, *Irish Current Law Statutes Annotated.* As well as giving effect to the changes in benefits announced in the 1992 Budget, the 1992 Act also involved a significant element of substantive changes to the social welfare code. Thus, s. 6 of the Act attempts to improve the take up of the Family Income Supplement (FIS) by increasing the weekly income ceiling below which families are entitled to FIS. S. 19 of the 1992 Act deals with maternity allowance and, as Robert Clark points out, is designed to increase the primary importance of the 14 week maternity leave scheme operated by the Department of Enterprise and Employment under the Maternity Protection of Employees Act 1981. Ss. 20 to 23 of the 1992 Act are intended to improve the mechanisms for ensuring that relatives do not default on their obligations under the Family Law (Maintenance of Spouses and Children) Act 1976, which default can oblige spouses and children to claim social welfare benefits or allowances. It remains to be seen whether these new provisions, which aim to strengthen those introduced in the Social Welfare Act 1989, will prove effective. For the associated court rules, see the Practice and Procedure chapter, 495-6, above. S. 34 of the Act discontinues the payment of pay-related benefit to persons who are already in receipt of disability benefit or occupational injury benefit. Part X of the 1992 Act (ss. 53 to 63) amend a number of provisions of the Pensions Act 1990.

In addition to the 1992 Act, the following Statutory Instruments were made in 1992 in relation to social welfare.

Social Welfare Act 1992 (Section 19) (Commencement) Order 1992 (SI No. 81).

Social Welfare Act 1992 (Section 19) (Commencement) Order 1992 (SI No. 447).

Social Welfare Act 1992 (Sections 25 and 26) (Commencement) Order 1992 (SI No. 263).

Social Welfare Act 1992 (Section 27) (Commencement) Order 1992 (SI No. 239).

Social Welfare Act 1992 (Section 28) (Commencement) Order 1992 (SI No. 446).

Social Welfare Act 1992 (Section 29) (Commencement) Order 1992 (SI No. 188).

Social Welfare Act 1992 (Section 32) (Commencement) Order 1992 (SI No. 162).

Social Welfare Act 1992 (Section 34) (Commencement) Order 1992 (SI No. 99).

Social Welfare Act 1992 (Section 37) (Commencement) Order 1992 (SI No. 320).

Social Welfare (Agreement with Australia on Social Security) Order 1992 (SI No. 84).

Social Welfare (Amendment of Miscellaneous Social Insurance Provisions) Regulations 1992 (SI No. 218).

Social Welfare (Child Benefit) Regulations 1992 (SI No. 309).

Social Welfare (Child Benefit) (Normal Residence) Rules 1992 (SI No. 310).

Social Welfare (Deserted Wife's Benefit) Regulations 1992 (SI No. 237).

Social Welfare (Disability Benefit) Regulations 1992 (SI No. 163).

Social Welfare (Insurable (Occupational Injuries) Employment) Regulations 1992 (SI No. 83).

Social Welfare (Maternity Allowance) Regulations 1992 (SI No. 87).

Social Welfare (Miscellaneous Control Provisions) Regulations 1992 (SI No. 311).

Social Welfare (Miscellaneous Social Insurance Provisions) Regulations 1992 (SI No. 211).

Social Welfare (Miscellaneous Social Insurance Provisions) (No. 2) Regulations 1992 (SI No. 448).

Social Welfare (Occupational Injuries) (Amendment) Regulations 1992 (SI No. 82).

Social Welfare (Pre-Retirement Allowance) (Amendment) Regulations 1992 (SI No. 164).

Social Welfare (Preservation of Rights) (Amendment) Regulations 1992 (SI No. 43).

Social Welfare (Rent Allowance) (Amendment) Regulations 1992 (SI No. 219).

Social Welfare (Rent Allowance) (Amendment) (No. 2) Regulations 1992 (SI No. 267).

Social Welfare (Supplementary Welfare Allowances) (Amendment) Regulations 1992 (SI No. 220).

Social Welfare (Temporary Provisions) Regulations 1992 (SI No. 389).

Social Welfare (Treatment Benefit) (Amendment) Regulations 1992 (SI No. 187).

Social Welfare (Treatment Benefit) (Amendment) (No. 2) Regulations 1992 (SI No. 405).
Social Welfare (Unemployment Assistance) Regulations 1992 (SI No. 238).
Social Welfare (Unemployment Benefit) Regulations 1992 (SI No. 189).
Social Welfare (Unemployment Benefit) (No. 2) Regulations 1992 (SI No. 449).

See also the Disabled Persons (Maintenance Allowance) Regulations 1992 (SI No. 212) and the Infectious Diseases (Maintenance) Regulations 1992 (SI No. 213), made under the Health Act 1970 and Health Act 1947 respectively.

## EQUALITY OF TREATMENT

The European Communities (Social Welfare) Regulations 1992 (SI No. 152) represent part of the legislative response to the recent litigation in the Court of Justice on the failure of the State to implement in good time the 1979 Directive on equality between men and women in social welfare payments, 79/7/EEC.

It will be recalled that the Social Welfare (No. 2) Act 1985 had purported to implement the 1979 Directive after the deadline of December 1984 contained in the Directive itself: see the discussion in the 1988 Review, 381-4. In *McDermott and Cotter v Minister for Social Welfare* [1987] ILRM 324, the Court of Justice had held that 1979 Directive had direct legal effect in Ireland as from December 1984. Subsequently, two apparently inconsistent High Court decisions had dealt with whether the Court of Justice decision was fully retrospective: see *Cotter v Minister for Social Welfare (No. 2)*, High Court, 10 June 1988 (1988 Review, 382) and *Carberry v Minister for Social Welfare*, High Court, 28 April 1989 (1989 Review, 395-6), the latter arguing for full retrospection.

The position was finally clarified by the 1991 Court of Justice decisions in *McDermott and Cotter v Minister for Social Welfare (No. 2)* and in *Emmott v Minister for Social Welfare* which favoured the full retrospection approach taken in *Carberry*. The 1992 Regulations represent part of the Irish response to the *McDermott* and *Emmott* cases. However, further litigation against the State was initiated in 1993 concerning the failure of the 1992 Regulations to respect fully the retrospection element of the Court of Justice decisions, and we will return to this matter in the 1993 Review.

## INSPECTORS' POWERS

In *Minister for Social Welfare v Bracken*, High Court, 29 July 1992, the defendant had been prosecuted by the Minister for offences under s. 114 of the Social Welfare (Consolidation) Act 1981 and s. 143A of the 1981 Act as inserted by s. 13 of the Social Welfare Act 1985. These offences concerned alleged obstruction of social welfare inspectors when the inspectors were on the defendant's premises. The inspectors had entered the defendant's premises without seeking his permission. On being approached by the defendant, they had produced their identity cards, and they had been told by the defendant to leave his property. The judge of the District Court before whom the defendant was tried stated a case for the High Court concerning the charges. The issues raised were as follows: first, were the inspectors acting within their powers under the 1981 and 1985 Acts in entering the defendant's premises without seeking his permission; second, were the inspectors' identity cards sufficient proof of their identity as inspectors under the Acts; and third, were the inspectors required to caution the defendant as a condition precedent to any evidence being given of what the defendant said and did during the encounter leading to the prosecution.

In his judgment, Lavan J examined the first issue as a matter of interpreting the range of powers conferred on inspectors by ss. 114 and 143A of the 1981 Act. He noted that both s. 114(2) and s. 143A(3) of the 1981 Act empowered inspectors to enter premises 'at all reasonable times' and that s. 114(5) and s. 143A(6) referred to inspectors 'applying for admission' to premises. These provisions indicated in his view a limitation on the extent of an inspector's powers under the 1981 Act. Lavan J applied the principles laid down by the Supreme Court in Director of Public Prosecutions v McCreesh [1992] 2 IR 239 (see the 1991 Review, 131-2) as indicating that the common law rights of the defendant concerning his property must only be affected by the clearest language. In particular, Lavan J considered that the language of the 1981 Act was not clear enough as to indicate that the inspectors had a right of entry onto the defendant's property without first seeking an invitation to enter. In the instant case, it was clear that the inspectors had not sought any permission or received any invitation to enter from the defendant, and thus their entry was unlawful under the 1981 Act.

However, it is worth noting on this issue that Lavan J went on to say that under the two sections providing for entry onto premises, the owner of premises was under an obligation not unreasonably to refuse permission to an inspector who seeks permission to enter for the purposes of ensuring that the terms of the Act are being applied. Once the owner is satisfied by appropriate means of identification that the inspectors are authorised inspectors under the 1981 Act, Lavan J stated that an unreasonable refusal to enter would leave the owner of property open to 'the full rigours' of ss. 114 and 143A of the 1981 Act.

On the issue of identification, Lavan J noted that this form of authorisation from the Minister was dealt with in s. 114 of the 1981 Act as well as s.

264(7). In determining what was appropriate identification, Lavan J followed the approach laid down by Lynch J in *Minister for Agriculture v Cleary* [1988] ILRM 299 (see the 1987 Review, 125-6) that the proferring of a certificate of authorisation given to inspectors under the 1981 Act was sufficient to provide a property owner with the information necessary to satisfy the requirements of the law, provided that the property owner has reasonable time to satisfy himself that the authorisations are valid.

Finally, on the issue of cautioning the defendant as to the consequences of refusing to allow the inspectors carry out their statutory functions, Lavan J noted that s. 114(4) and s. 143(5) of the 1981 Act provided that, in answering questions put by an inspector, no person was required 'to answer any question or to give any evidence tending to incriminate himself'. However, as he had already determined that the inspectors were trespassers on the defendant's property, he concluded that the defendant could not be successfully charged with any offence under the 1981 Act, and in the circumstances he did not consider that he was required to deal with this third issue. Nonetheless, it must be said that the language of both sections gave a clear indication that the privilege against self-incrimination is being expressly preserved by the sections and that the power to require persons to answer questions is somewhat limited.

## OVERLAPPING BENEFITS

*McHugh v A.B. (Deciding Officer) and Ors,* High Court, 23 November 1990; Supreme Court, 11 March 1992 is an important decision on the Regulations concerning payment of overlapping benefits, that is, those Regulations under which a person is entitled to more than one social welfare allowance or benefit.

The case arose against the following background. The applicant gave birth in December 1987 and she applied for and received an unmarried mother's allowance for her child. In September 1988, she ceased working and she obtained unemployment benefit but, under the Social Welfare (Overlapping Benefits) Regulations 1974, as amended by the Social Welfare (Overlapping Benefits) (Amendment) Regulations 1987, the benefit was paid at half-rate only as she was already receiving the unmarried mother's allowance. The applicant suffered from epilepsy and from September 1989 she suffered an increase in attacks to such an extent that she was advised not to go out. She then ceased signing on for unemployment benefit as she was unavailable for work. She applied for disability benefit, for which she had sufficient social insurance contributions, but was refused under Article 4 of the 1974 Regulations, as amended by Article 5 of the 1987 Regulations, which provided that a recipient of an unmarried mother's allowance was disentitled to any disability benefit. Arising from changes to the 1974 Regulations which came into effect in April 1990, the applicant became entitled to the disability benefit and the unmarried mother's allowance. She applied, however, for judicial review on the ground that the 1987 Regulations had been *ultra vires* the Social Welfare (Consolidation) Act 1981 and that she had been entitled to both benefits prior to the changes effected in 1990.

In the High Court, Lavan J granted the relief sought on the ground that the 1987 Regulations were *ultra vires* s. 130 of the Social Welfare (Consolidation) Act 1981. We may note that the effect of Lavan J's decision would have had a far-reaching effect on the *vires* of much of the Overlapping Benefits Regulations. For this reason (as we noted in the 1991 Review, 378), s. 43 of the Social Welfare Act 1991 amended s. 130 of the 1981 Act to provide that double payments were, in general, prohibited except where the Minister allowed them in Regulations, thus reversing the effect of Lavan J's decision. The defendants had also appealed Lavan J's decision, and although the Supreme Court (Finlay CJ, Hederman, McCarthy and O'Flaherty JJ; Egan J dissenting) upheld Lavan J's verdict, it did so on different grounds which left the Minister for Social Welfare to consider different factors in the context of overlapping benefits.

Delivering the leading judgment in the Supreme Court, McCarthy J noted that the Minister was empowered, under s. 130 of the 1981 Act, to disallow in whole or in part the payment of any social welfare allowance or benefit to any person who would otherwise be entitled to claim two or more benefits or allowances. Differing in a crucial respect from Lavan J, however, McCarthy J went on to hold that since s. 18 of the 1981 Act had provided that entitlement to the disability benefit was subject to the provisions of the Act itself, this must be taken to include s. 130. It is relevant to note that, in a concurring judgment in *McHugh*, Finlay CJ disowned certain *dicta* of his own in *Harvey v Minister for Social Welfare* [1990] ILRM 185; [1990] 2 IR 232 (discussed in the 1989 Review, 394-5), one interpretation of which might have led to the conclusion that the Overlapping Benefits Regulations were *ultra vires* the 1981 Act. The Chief Justice considered that the relevant *dicta* in *Harvey* should not be regarded as correctly stating the law.

Despite this narrowing of the breadth of the *Harvey* decision, the actual basis on which the Supreme Court upheld the decision of the High Court in *McHugh* is of some importance. The Supreme Court in *McHugh* considered that the prohibition in the 1987 Regulations on payment of a disability benefit to a person already in receipt of unmarried mother's allowance was *ultra vires* the 1981 Act for unreasonableness. Applying the reasonableness test set out in *Cassidy v Minister for Industry and Commerce* [1978] IR 297, McCarthy J held that the prohibition lacked any logical basis bearing in mind that the same Regulations provided for the payment of unemployment benefit — albeit at half rate — to a person (such as the applicant had been between September 1988 and September 1989) who was in receipt of an unmarried mother's allowance. On this basis, therefore, the Court upheld the plaintiff's claim.

In an insightful comment on the *Harvey* and *McHugh* decisions, (1992) 14 DULJ 193, Mel Cousins suggests that future challenges to the Overlapping Benefits Regulations based on unreasonableness may prove somewhat difficult, particularly in the light of the amended s. 130 of the 1981 Act introduced by s. 43 of the 1991 Act in response to Lavan J's decision in *McHugh.* He also raises the compatibility of the amended s. 130 with the Constitution, bearing in mind the almost unbridled delegation of Regulation-making power it confers on the Minister for Social Welfare. This was, of course, the precise basis on which the decision in *Harvey* rested, a basis not affected by the doubts expressed by the Chief Justice in *McHugh* on his own *dicta* in *Harvey*.

## SHARE FISHING AND SOCIAL INSURANCE

In *Minister for Social Welfare v Griffiths* [1992] ILRM 667; [1992] 1 IR 103, Blayney J held that fishermen operating on a 'share basis' did not come within the social welfare code for employment contributions purposes. In the instant case, the defendant was the owner of a fishing vessel in respect of which a particular member of the crew, Eugene Pepper, was not paid any salary or wages but was paid a share from the proceeds of catches. The defendant had been prosecuted by the Minister for failing to pay employment contributions for Eugene Pepper under s.10 of the Social Welfare (Consolidation) Act 1991 and the Social Welfare (Collection of Employment Contributions for Special Contributors) Regulations 1989. The 1989 Regulations related specifically to crews of a fishing vessel.

The question for decision by Blayney J was whether the requirement to pay employment contributions necessarily presupposed the existence of a relationship of employer and employee. Blayney J held that it did. He considered that the 1981 Act did not indicate any intention to depart from this traditional meaning of the term 'employment'. And this was not, in his view, affected by the provision in paragraph 6 of Part I of the First Schedule to the 1981 Act which stated that 'employment' included 'employment as a member of the crew of a fishing vessel where the employed person is wholly remunerated by a share in the profits or the gross earnings of the working of the vessel'. Blayney J pointed out that the use of the words 'employed person' still envisaged the employer-employee relationship and did not encompass the instant case in which Mr Pepper was, in effect, a partner of the defendant. Thus, he was not an 'employed contributor' within the meaning of the 1981 Act and thus the defendant was not required to make any contribution under the 1981 Act in respect of him.

It may be noted that a contribution system for share fishing was subsequently introduced by the Social Welfare (No. 2) Act 1993. This will be discussed in the 1993 Review.

## ROTATING WORK AND UNEMPLOYMENT BENEFIT

In *Louth and Ors v Minister for Social Welfare* [1992] ILRM 586; [1993] 1 IR 339, the plaintiffs were 27 dockers working in Drogheda port. The procedure under which they worked was that, when a ship arrived in the port, the stevedore in charge of the unloading would contact the first plaintiff who would select the dockers from amongst the other 26 plaintiffs on a rotating basis for the unloading work required. Where one of the plaintiffs was not selected for unloading, they would sign on at the local employment exchange as being unemployed on that day and thus claim unemployment benefit.

Because of the uncertainty attaching to the rotation system, the dockers agreed between themselves to pool all earnings from their work and to divide all income equally between themselves. This arrangement was approved for tax purposes by the Revenue Commissioners. The Department of Social Welfare considered that this pooling of incomes meant that the plaintiffs were at all times employed and that the existing arrangement by which dockers who were not selected through the rotation system were not entitled to sign on as being unemployed for the purposes of the Social Welfare code. The instant proceedings were initiated to determine this issue. Barron J held that the crucial factor was whether the plaintiffs were employed from time to time by the stevedore under contracts of service or whether, as the Department argued, the 'pooling' arrangement in effect indicated that they were involved in continuous contracts for services. Barron J held that the pooling arrangement between the dockers *inter se* did not in any way affect the stevedore, and thus it could not affect the overriding fact that they entered into contracts of service with the stevedore. On this basis, he distinguished the instant case from that in *Construction Industry Training Board v Labour Force Ltd* [1970] 3 All ER 220, the basis for which he had approved in his own judgment in *Minister for Labour v PMPA Insurance Co. Ltd*, High Court, 16 April 1986. On this basis, he therefore found in favour of the plaintiffs.

# Solicitors

## APPRENTICESHIP

**Arrangements** The Solicitors Acts 1954 and 1960 (Apprenticeship and Education) (Amendment) Regulations 1992 (SI No. 359) and the Solicitors Acts 1954 and 1960 (Apprenticeship and Education) (Amendment) (No. 2) Regulations 1992 (SI No. 360) amend the 1991 Regulations (1991 Review, 381) and revise the arrangements for obtaining apprenticeships as well as the requirements concerning the Law Society's School in Blackhall Place, Dublin.

**Fees** The Solicitors Acts 1954 and 1960 (Apprentices' Fees) (Amendment) (No. 2) Regulations 1992 (SI No. 361), which revoked the Solicitors Acts 1954 and 1960 (Apprentices' Fees) (Amendment) 1992 (SI No. 20), prescribe the examination fees at the Law Society's School in Blackhall Place, Dublin.

## NEGLIGENCE

Cases involving solicitors' liability in negligence are discussed in the Torts chapter, 553-5, below.

## PRACTISING CERTIFICATES

The Solicitors Acts 1954 and 1960 (Fees) Regulations 1992 (SI No. 2) set out the revised fees for obtaining practising certificates.

# Statutory Interpretation

**Commencement Order** In *Masterfoods Ltd (t/a Mars Ireland) v HB Ice Cream Ltd* [1993] ILRM 145 (the substantive arguments in which are discussed in the Commercial Law chapter, 27-30, above), Keane J rejected an argument that a Minister had acted *ultra vires* in the making of a Commencement Order under the Competition Act 1991. The Competition Act 1991 (Commencement) Order 1991 (SI No. 249 of 1991) had repealed the Restrictive Practices Acts 1972 and 1987, but left intact the Restrictive Practices (Groceries Order) 1987 which had been made under the 1972 and 1987 Acts. Keane J held that the Order-making power conferred on the Minister by s. 2(1) of the 1991 Act was drafted in sufficiently broad terms to allow the Minister to repeal the 1972 and 1987 Acts except in so far as this involved the 1987 Order. This is of some importance as such Order-making powers are common in many Acts of recent years.

**Expressio unius** The maxim *expressio unius est exclusio alterius* was applied by Murphy J in *Inspector of Taxes v Arida Ltd* [1992] 2 IR 155: see the Revenue Law chapter, 517-9, above.

**Interpretation Act: duplicity of charges** The prohibition in s. 14 of the Interpretation Act 1937 against punishment twice over for the same offence was considered by O'Hanlon J in *O'Brien v Patwell* [1993] ILRM 614 (discussed in the Criminal Law chapter, 292-3, above) and, less than a week later, in *Doolan v Director of Public Prosecutions* [1993] ILRM 387 (also discussed in the Criminal Law chapter, 286-7, above).

**Later amendment** In *Dublin County Council v Eighty Five Developments Ltd (No. 1)* [1993] 2 IR 378 (discussed in the Local Government chapter, 451-3, above), Carroll J rejected the suggestion that she could take account of any amendments to a statutory provision in order to interpret that provision, expressly followed the decision of the Supreme Court in *Cronin v Cork and County Properties Ltd* [1986] IR 559 in this respect.

**'May' as discretionary** In *Jennings Truck Centre (Tullamore) Ltd v Offaly County Council*, High Court, 14 June 1990, Murphy J declined to interpret the word 'may' as having a mandatory meaning: see the Transport chapter, 631, below.

**Overall purpose** In *Deane v Voluntary Health Insurance Board* [1992] 2 IR 319, the Supreme Court considered the overall purpose of the Competition Act 1991 in interpreting s. 3 of the 1991 Act: see the discussion in the Commercial Law chapter, 30-2 above.

**Retrospection** In *Chestvale Properties Ltd v Glackin* [1992] ILRM 221; [1993] 3 IR 35, Murphy J upheld the retrospective effect of the Companies Act 1990: see the discussion in the Company Law chapter, 68-73, above.

# Torts

## THE DUTY OF CARE

**Economic Loss** In *John C. Doherty Timber Ltd v Drogheda Harbour Commissioners* [1993] ILRM 401; [1993] 1 IR 315, the plaintiffs, who were timber importers, received a consignment of timber at Drogheda harbour. Having paid the appropriate tonnage dues and cargo dues levied by the defendant harbour authority, the plaintiffs left the consignment on the quayside with the permission of the defendant. It could have lain there for at least a fortnight without incurring any charge or rental. The defendant provided no security of any type in relation to the timber. The day after it was placed on the quayside, it was set on fire by children and destroyed.

The plaintiff's action rested on negligence, breach of duty as bailee and breach of statutory duty. Flood J held that the defendant was *not* a bailee since it lacked the minimum degree of control in the circumstances. We discuss the issue of breach of statutory duty later in this chapter, below, 603-4.

On the question of negligence, Flood J approached the matter from the standpoint of Lord Wilberforce's 'two-step' test in respect of the duty of care, in the House of Lords decision of *Anns v Merton London Borough Council* [1978] AC 728, at 751-2, as modified by Lord Keith's 'just and reasonable' addendum, expressed in *Peabody Donation Fund (Governors) v Parkinson (Sir Lindsay) & Co.* [1985] AC 210, at 241. Flood J also noted that, in *Ward v McMaster* [1988] IR 377, McCarthy J had considered that the duty of care arose from the proximity of the parties, the foreseeability of the damage and the absence of any compelling exemption based on public policy.

Applying these considerations to the facts of the instant case, Flood J considered that the foreseeability of damage must have been just as apparent to the plaintiff as to the defendant:

> It seems to me that the reality of the relationship was a bare permission which carried no further obligations of care on the part of the defendant for the very simple reason that it would be virtually impossible to effectively implement. In my opinion the inference to be drawn from the relationship of the parties is that each party knew that the goods were placed and retained on the quayside at the consignee's risk. Further, the consignee being the person primarily involved, it was for him to

> evaluate and assess the risk of damage to his goods. If damage flowed from his failure to take steps to eliminate or mitigate such risk the proximate cause of the damage would be his failure to act rationally, and reasonably, and in my opinion, in the circumstances, would negative and override any duty of care on the part of the defendant alleged to arise from any proximity or neighbourhood of the parties. It follows that I am of opinion that in this instance there was no common law duty of care imposed on the defendant. . . .

This holding seems eminently sensible. The idea that the Harbour Commissioners should be required to take care for the plaintiff's property, under pain of civil liability, seems quite misplaced.

There has been much discussion in legal circles in Ireland as to whether the Irish courts will join the British courts in the retreat from *Anns* and in the effective denial of compensation for negligently caused pure economic loss. *Doherty Timber* affords no weight to the argument of those who contend that such a retreat will occur. Flood J was clearly content to apply Lord Wilberforce's 'two step' test. Moreover the court was being asked to impose a duty of care well beyond what the case law in either Ireland or Britain had previously upheld, even in decisions most favourable to recovery for pure economic loss.

## PROFESSIONAL NEGLIGENCE

**Solicitors** The main features of the law relating to the negligence of solicitors have been spelt out by the courts over the past twenty five years. Previously there had been little enthusiasm to recognise a tortious right of action in negligence, as a supplement to the client's contractual action. In *Deignan v Greene*, Supreme Court, 21 October 1954, Ó Dálaigh J observed that:

> [i]t may indeed be that the categories of negligence are never closed; but it does not necessarily follow that all the rejected claims of other branches of the law can there find a sanctuary. . . . I much doubt if refuge can be found for claims which must flee the inconvenience of the doctrine of consideration.

Subsequent decisions, notably *Finlay v Murtagh* [1979] IR 249 and *Roche v Peilow* [1985] IR 232, have made it clear that solicitors may indeed be sued in tort and that they may be found liable in negligence if the practices of their profession, even those receiving universal endorsement, have inherent defects which ought to be obvious to any person giving the matter due consideration: see further McMahon & Binchy, *Irish Law of Torts* (2nd ed., 1990), 258-60, 275-81.

In *McMullen v Farrell* [1993] 1 IR 123 (High Court, 1992), affirmed by Supreme Court, 9 February 1994, the plaintiff sued three firms of solicitors for negligence. His action succeeded at trial against the second and third firms but failed against the first firm; the Supreme Court affirmed.

The essence of the plaintiff's case was that, having leased a castle just outside the town of Tullamore in 1972 (and thus unable to benefit from the Landlord and Tenant Act 1931), he had not been fully informed by the second and third firms of the effect of the Landlord and Tenant (Amendment) Act 1980. He had been informed that it provided that a landlord's consent to an *assignment of the premises* could not be unreasonably withheld; but he had not been advised that a similar provision applied to *change of user of the premises*. This was of some importance as the plaintiff, who was required to use the premises as a private residence, realised that the prospects of selling his interest would be enhanced if the castle could be used as a hotel or put to some other commercial use.

Barron J set out in some detail what he considered a solicitor's duty to be, in a manner that Finlay CJ, on appeal, considered to be 'entirely correct'. It is worth recording what Barron J had to say, in view of its general application:

> A solicitor cannot in my view fulfil his obligations to his client merely by carrying out what he is instructed to do. This is to ignore the essential element of any contract involving professional care or advice. The professional person is consulted by the client for the very reason that he has specialist or professional skill and knowledge. He cannot abrogate his duty to use that skill or knowledge. To follow instructions blindly is to turn himself into a machine. In my view a solicitor when consulted by a client has an obligation to consider not only what the client wishes him to do, but also the legal implications of the facts which the client brings to his attention. If necessary, he must follow up these facts to ensure that he appreciates the real problem with which he is being asked to deal. When he is sure that he is clear as to the way forward, then he advises his client accordingly. In most cases, perhaps, this will involve doing what the client wants. Where a client has been involved in a road traffic accident, he wants to know whether he can recover damages. It is sufficient for a solicitor, having been given the facts and being satisfied that it is an appropriate case to sue, to indicate to his client that he will issue proceedings. Even in such a case, where the cause of action is weak, for example, and the client is a person of means, he cannot just

> issue proceedings. His client is entitled to advice as to the wisdom of so proceeding.
>
> In more complicated cases, the duties of the solicitor are also more complex. If his opinion corresponds with what he is asked to do, then there is no problem. When it does not, he must advise his client of his views and all reasonable approaches to the problem. The solicitor then acts on the basis of the instructions which he receives in the light of these advices. It is probably better that the solicitor's advice should be in writing, but that is a matter for him. In other words, as part of his duty to his client, a solicitor is obliged to exercise his professional skill and judgment in the interests of his client. The extent of this particular obligation is dependent on the nature of the case presented to him.

Barron J provided a clear analysis of the nature and purpose of evidence that a solicitor can give as a witness in proceedings for professional negligence against a solicitor. Such a witness could give evidence as to an accepted practice, or standard of conduct laid down by a professional institute or sanctioned by common usage; but he or she could *not* simply give evidence as to how he or she would have acted in the circumstances of the case. Barron J drew a distinction between allegations of negligence *in the conduct of litigation* and similar allegations in respect of *other aspects of a solicitor's practice*:

> [I]n the case of a solicitor, the court is in a different position from cases of other professional negligence because the court has of itself its own factual knowledge of how litigation is conducted. Nevertheless, the practice of solicitors is something of which a court is not necessarily aware. For that reason I have considered the evidence which has been adduced although, as here, where no real practice has been put forward it seems to me that I must make up my own mind as to what a reasonably competent solicitor exercising proper care ought to have done in the particular circumstances of the case.

This passage suggests that the court should take judicial notice of how litigation is conducted. It would also seem to imply that the court is in the position, on its own, to assess good and bad practice of judicial notice. Precisely how great an area of potential negligence is possible here is hard to discern in view of the immunity attaching not only to barristers (*Rondel v Worsley* [1969] 1 AC 191) but also (it appears) to solicitors in the exercise of their advocacy functions: *Somasundram v M. Julius Melchior & Co.* [1988] 1 WLR 1394. See further *Jackson & Powell on Professional Negligence* (3rd ed., 1992), para. 4-62, McMahon & Binchy, op. cit., 272-5..

## Medical malpractice

*Surgeons* In *Dunleavy v McDevitt and North Western Health Board*, Supreme Court, 19 February 1992, some interesting issues of general importance arose for consideration. The plaintiff was referred to the first defendant, a consultant surgeon, with regard to a lump on the parotid gland behind his jaw, near to his left ear, which had not responded to treatment. The first defendant, who suspected malignancy, performed an operation, during which the lump was removed. This resulted in damage to the plaintiffs facial nerve. The lump proved not to have been malignant in fact.

The plaintiff sued for assault and battery and for negligence, arguing first that he had not given an informed consent to the treatment performed on him and secondly that the first defendant (for whose torts the second defendant could be vicariously liable) had been guilty of negligence in the manner in which he carried out the operation. MacKenzie J dismissed the case on both grounds and the appeal to the Supreme Court was restricted to the latter ground.

The second issue in *Dunleavy* presented its own complexities. The surgeon had performed one of two types of operation that could have been chosen: what was known as the limited rather than the wider option. The wider option would involve exposing the facial nerve by excision of the surrounding tissues, which would make it easier to avoid coming in contact with it. The limited option did not involve such exposure but consisted of identifying a plain of cleavage between the tumour capsule and the surrounding tissue and excising the tumour from its capsule leaving an area of surrounding tissue between the line of excision and the facial nerve. The evidence made it clear that the wider operation was one requiring 'very extensive experience', in the words of Finlay CJ. Significant evidence supported the general contention that, for surgeons working in hospitals supplying a relatively small community, whose experience of removing tumours from the parotid gland might occur on a limited number of occasions in each year, it was safer for them to be trained in, and choose, the limited option rather than the wider option.

The plaintiff argued that, where malignancy was strongly suspected, it would be quite wrong to carry out a limited operation, since this could leave behind tissue which could generate a recurrence of the malignancy. If the surgeon had performed the wider operation, the plaintiff contended, he would not have suffered the injury to the facial nerve. Expert medical evidence was adduced on behalf of the defendants to the effect that the limited option was a legitimate choice even in cases of suspected malignancy but the Chief Justice was disposed to hold against the plaintiff even if that expert evidence had not been convincing. He was:

> satisfied that the existence of a reasonable precaution . . . for the purpose of avoiding one potential, though eventually non-existent, problem cannot properly be a ground for holding that there was negligence on the part of a surgeon, causative of a totally different danger.

What seems at issue here is essentially a question of foreseeability. If we assume (contrary to the expert evidence) that it was negligent to adopt the limited option then, in the view of the Chief Justice, the only injury for which a patient might successfully sue would be injury resulting from a *recurrence of the malignancy*, not injury in respect of the facial nerve. This seems difficult to reconcile with the medical evidence in the case, not contested by the defendant, that the wider option, involving the exposure of the facial nerve, would have reduced the risk of contact with it. The fact that the reason for choosing the wider option was entirely unconnected with the question of relative risks of contact with the facial nerve does not affect the objective fact that a failure to choose the wider option did expose the patient to an enhanced risk of contact with the facial nerve.

Finlay CJ proceeded to reject, on the evidence, the plaintiff's assertion that the particular immobility and hardness of the tumour amounted to a contra-indication to carrying out the limited operation. He also held that the surgeon, having found an unusual difficulty in identifying the plain of cleavage, should *not*, as the plaintiff argued, have stopped the operation, closed the operating wound and sent the plaintiff to another surgeon. Expert medical evidence was to the effect that such a course would be negligent since it should render the subsequent operation very difficult and would very greatly increase the risk of the spread of malignancy.

In *Maitland v. Swan and Sligo County Council*, High Court, 6 April 1992, Barr J held that the first defendant, a general surgeon, had been negligent in his treatment of the plaintiff, who was aged thirteen at the time of the treatment. The plaintiff had been admitted to hospital with a condition of pain and tenderness in her right side. The defendant diagnosed appendicitis or a ruptured ovarian cyst. He operated on the plaintiff two days after admission. He removed the right ovary, on which there was a large benign cyst. Several years later, the plaintiff discovered that she had no left ovary either.

Barr J held that the defendant had been negligent in a number of respects. He had proceeded to surgery without having previously sought gynaecological advice and assistance; he had negligently failed to conserve functional ovarian tissue; and he had impliedly represented to the plaintiff that he had the gynaecological skills and experience necessary to deal competently with the ovarian cyst when he lacked these qualities.

*Informed consent* In *Walsh v Family Planning Services* [1992] 1 IR 486, the Supreme Court confronted the issue of informed consent to medical treatment for the first time since its decision, three decades ago, in *Daniels v Heskin* [1954] IR 73; 86 ILTR 41(1952). It cannot be said that *Walsh* has left the law in a clear or satisfactory state.

The plaintiff, aged forty-four, married with five children, sought to have a vasectomy performed at the first defendant's clinic. He and his wife had an interview with one of the doctors associated with his clinic, in which aspects of the proposed operation were discussed. On the day scheduled for the operation, the plaintiff met another doctor who enquired whether he had changed his mind; he said that he had not. At that point a third doctor came into the room. The operation was conducted by the third doctor. The plaintiff claimed that the third doctor had to be given instructions by the second doctor as to the correct procedure.

The operation turned out very unfortunately for the plaintiff who developed a condition of orchialgia, involving impotence and constant nagging pain, which required surgical treatment.

The plaintiff's action was for trespass to the person and battery. He argued that he had never consented to the third doctor's participation in the operation; that it had been carried out without due care; and that he had not been given a sufficient warning of the risks attached to an operation of this kind.

MacKenzie J held in his favour. He considered that there had been 'a technical assault and battery' in that the plaintiff had never consented to the third doctor's participation:

> He was confronted with a situation which, having regard to the nature of the position, made him powerless to do anything but submit to [this doctor]'s assistance.

MacKenzie J went on to hold that the plaintiff had not proved his case in negligence. All the evidence was that the operation had been performed properly. The first doctor had given sufficient warning. MacKenzie J added:

> The plaintiff must have known this to be a consequence of the operation, otherwise he would have followed the direction in the circular to report immediately if anything unusual should have happened to him. Why he did not do this is a mystery, but in my view his constitutional right, that is an unspecified constitutional right to bodily integrity, has been violated. It is to be noted that it is conceded by some of the witnesses for the defence . . . that all the plaintiff's troubles stem from the operation. . . .

MacKenzie J awarded the plaintiff £30,000 damages for violation of his constitutional rights as well as special damages.

A mystery as to MacKenzie J's judgment is the precise basis of the award for interference with the plaintiff's constitutional right to bodily integrity. The judges in the Supreme Court, notably McCarthy and O'Flaherty JJ, considered that the unconstitutional violation consisted of the 'technical assault and battery' resulting from the third doctor's participation. There is, however, reason to believe that MacKenzie J sought to compensate the plaintiff for what might be called a 'strict liability' violation of his right to bodily integrity. Certainly the passage from the judgment quoted above suggests that the compensation related to a violation of this type. MacKenzie J makes no reference to the technical tort in this context nor does he seek to explain why compensation should be for such high sum for such a small tort, nor, indeed, why the characterisation of the wrong should, quite gratuitously, be changed from that of tort to violation of a constitutional right. The more plausible explanation, therefore, is that MacKenzie J considered that a physical contact with the plaintiff's body which resulted so miserably should entitle him to compensation for violation of his constitutional right to bodily integrity, without proof of fault on the part of any of the defendants.

Is there anything to be said in favour of such an interpretation of the view that the entitlement of an individual to sue for compensation for violation of his or her constitutional rights, recognised in *Meskell v CIE* [1973] IR 121, should not be conditional on proof of fault, whether intentional or negligent, on the part of the violator? The answer is that such a view cannot be dismissed *in limine*. Just as, within the system of tort law, there are some cases where a defendant may be strictly liable, without any fault, so, it might be argued, the violation or infringement of certain constitutional rights generates an entitlement to compensation, even in the absence of fault on the part the violator or infringer.

There are, however, huge difficulties in a regime of compensation for innocent infringement of the constitutional right to bodily integrity. If a doctor is obliged under the Constitution to compensate a patient for an unhappy outcome of a medical intervention, for which the doctor is in no way to blame, it might be thought that there would be a rapid exodus from the profession, which would have crippling insurance costs. Doctors are already complaining about insurance premiums. A strict liability system, rooted in the Constitution, might be considered to be totally counterproductive (apart altogether from the issues of justice it would raise) since it could destroy the medical profession.

To this it might be replied that it all depends on how a system of strict liability is operated. It will be recalled that in *Hegarty v O'Loughran* [1990] ILRM 403; [1990] 1 IR 148, McCarthy J observed that '[t]he case for a no-fault system of compensation for those who suffer injury as a result of medical treatment seems so strong as to be virtually unanswerable.' Of course a no-fault system of compensation is different from one of strict liability. In a no-fault system the fund that pays out does not usually do so as agent for a strictly liable defendant. The New Zealand scheme, for example, does not involve the imposition of liability on any doctor. MacKenzie J's observations thus raise the possible response that the right to bodily integrity may perhaps be more effectively vindicated through a no-fault scheme rather than by the imposition of strict liability.

In *Walsh*, the defendants' appeal to the Supreme Court against MacKenzie J's judgment was successful and the Supreme Court dismissed the plaintiff's cross-appeal. The Court divided three to two: Finlay CJ, Hederman and O'Flaherty JJ for the majority with McCarthy and Egan JJ dissenting. Several issues arose, on which there was a wide variety of judicial views. It seems best, therefore, to examine each of these issues separately rather than to review the judgments *seriatim.*

(i) *Identity of the doctor essential to validity of consent?* Four of the judges, Finlay CJ, Hederman, O'Flaherty and Egan JJ, held that MacKenzie J had been mistaken in holding that there had been a technical assault and battery on account of the participation by the third doctor. O'Flaherty J observed that it seemed to him that 'what the plaintiff was agreeing to was that the operation should be carried out by a person or persons with the requisite skill and that it should be competently done'. McCarthy J, dissenting, considered that it was open to MacKenzie J to have come to the conclusion that the plaintiff's consent had not been validly obtained: '[a]t a time when [the plaintiff] was in some state of anxiety yet ready for the operation a third party was introduced'.

The issue arising here is essentially one of evidence rather than of complicated legal principle. There can be no objection *in principle* to a patient's providing his or her consent to being operated upon by any of a team of doctors even where the identity of the person who will perform that operation is not known to the patient at the time of providing the consent.

(ii) *Treatment without informed consent a trespass or negligence?* Courts throughout the common law would have had to resolve the question of the nature of the tort committed where a doctor performs treatment on a patient without having properly explained to the patient the nature of the treatment. Is it *battery*, a species of trespass to the person, or is it negligence? Decisions in Canada (*Reibl v Hughes* (1980) 114 DLR (3d) 1 (Sup St Can) and England (*Sidaway v Bethlem Royal Hospital Governors* [1985] AC 871) favour the negligence characterisation. Courts in the United States formerly favoured battery but have since generally transferred their allegiance to negligence.

In *Walsh*, the members of the Supreme Court were agreed that negligence was the appropriate pigeon-hole. (The issue was strictly *obiter*, since the majority found that the warning had in fact been adequate.) O'Flaherty J, expressed the view that:

> If there had been such a failure to give a warning as to possible future risks that would not involve the artificial concept of an assault, but, rather, a possible breach of a duty of care giving rise to a claim in negligence. A claim of assault should be confined to cases where there is no consent to the particular procedure and where it is feasible to look for a consent.

O'Flaherty J placed much reliance on Laskin CJ's analysis of the issue in *Reibl v Hughes* (114 DLR (3rd), at 10):

> I can appreciate the temptation to say that the genuineness of consent to medical treatment depends on proper disclosure of the risks which it entails, but in my view, unless there has been misrepresentation or fraud to secure consent to the treatment, a failure to disclose the attendant risks, however serious, should go to negligence rather than to battery. Although such a failure relates to an informed choice of submitting to or refusing recommended and appropriate treatment, it arises as the breach of an anterior duty of care, comparable in legal obligation to the duty of due care in carrying out the particular treatment to which the patient has consented. It is not a test of the validity of the consent.

(iii) *The duty of disclosure* If the duty of disclosure is to be determined by reference to negligence rather than battery, what is the proper test for deciding whether the doctor has given sufficient information to the patient? Three principal solutions have received support.

The *first* resolves the question by reference to the generally accepted practice in the medical profession. This approach stresses the fact that the decision of what to tell the patient has traditionally been regarded as primarily a matter of medical judgment and discretion. In the House of Lords decision of *Sidaway v Governors of Bethlem Royal Hospital* [1985] AC 871, Lord Diplock favoured this approach. He noted that this was the test in England for determining whether a doctor's decision relating to diagnosis and treatment were negligent: *Bolam v Friern Hospital* [1957] 2 All ER 118. He considered that it was appropriate to extend it to decisions as to disclosure, which were integrally related to treatment which the doctor considered desirable.

The *second* approach favours the *Bolam* test in all cases save where disclosure of a particular risk 'was so obviously necessary to an informed choice on the part of the patient that no reasonably prudent medical man would fail to make it'. These are the words of Lord Bridge in *Sidaway* ([1985] AC at 900). They represent the dominant view in English law today.

The *third* approach springs from a radically different philosophical source. It concentrates on the patient's right of self determination in regard to what is to be done to his or her body. It requires full disclosure of all material risks incident to the proposed treatment, so that the patient, rather than the doctor, makes the real choice as to whether treatment is to be carried out. As was observed in *Miller v Kennedy*, 530 P. 2d 334 (Wash. Court. App., 1974):

> The patient has the right to chart his own destiny, and the doctor must supply the patient with the material facts the patient will need in order to intelligently chart that destiny with dignity.

The third approach finds favour in Canada (*Reibl v Hughes* above), Australia (*F. v R.*, (1983) 33 SASR 189, *Ellis v Wallsend District Hospital* (1989) 17 NSW LR 553), and in Lord Scarman's speech in *Sidaway*.

It is agreed by proponents of all these approaches that doctors have a 'therapeutic privilege', if not, indeed, an obligation in some instances, to keep from a patient certain information about proposed treatment where disclosure would be positively injurious or even fatal. Clearly, a doctor would be entitled not to mention a particular risk to a vulnerable patient who is likely to have a heart attack if he or she is told. While it is accepted unanimously that some information may be withheld for this reason, there is considerably less agreement as to the scope of this exception.

In *Walsh*, the members of the Court were divided as to which approach should be adopted. Finlay CJ considered that the same standard of care should govern medical treatment, advice and the giving of a warning of the consequences of proposed surgical treatment and that this standard was that which the Supreme Court (in his own judgment) had spelt out in *Dunne v National Maternity Hospital* [1989] 1 LRM 735; [1989] IR 91, which we discussed in the 1989 Review, 421-5. That test protects conduct that adheres to a general and approved practice, save where the particular practice has inherent defects which ought to be obvious to any person giving the matter due consideration. The *Dunne* test, when applied to the context of informed consent, is essentially the same as that favoured by Lord Bridge in *Sidaway*. Interestingly, Finlay CJ's desire to have a unified test for the several aspects of medical practice echoes that of Lord Diplock in *Sidaway*; the Chief Justice differs from Lord Diplock in that the *Dunne* test, in contrast to that of *Bolam*, makes it clear that the court is not required to give its benediction to practices with inherent defects, even if they have general or universal endorsement from the medical profession.

Whilst declaring an unambiguous preference for the application of the *Dunne* test to the informed consent context, Finlay CJ made the following observations, which merit extensive quotation:

> I am satisfied that there is, of course, where it is possible to do so, a clear obligation on a medical practitioner carrying out or arranging for the carrying out of an operation, to inform the patient of any possible harmful consequence arising from the operation, so as to permit the patient to give an informed consent to subjecting himself to the operation concerned. I am also satisfied that the extent of this obligation must, as a matter of common sense, vary with what might be described as the elective nature of the surgery concerned. Quite obviously, and apart even from cases of emergency surgery which has to be carried out to persons who are unconscious or incapable of giving or refusing consent, or young children, there may be instances where as a matter of medical knowledge, notwithstanding substantial risks of harmful consequence, the carrying out of a particular surgical procedure is so necessary to maintain the life or health of the patient and the consequences of failing to carry it out are so clearly disadvantageous that limited discussion or warning concerning possible harmful side-effects may be appropriate and proper. On the other hand, the obligation to give warning of the possible harmful consequences of a surgical procedure which could be said to be at the other end of the scale to the extent to which it is elective, such as would undoubtedly be the operation of vasectomy, may be more stringent and more onerous.

Finlay CJ made it clear that these observations were subject to the *Dunne* test. He went on to express the view that, in response to a defence of general practice,

> it may be, certainly in relation to very clearly elective surgery, that the court might more readily reach a conclusion that the extent of warning given or omitted contained inherent defects which ought to have been obvious to any person giving the matter due consideration than it could do in a case of complicated medical or surgical procedures, and an allegation that, although generally adopted, they were inherently unsafe.

These passages from Finlay CJ's judgment are of particular interest since they reveal a willingness on the part of the Chief Justice to articulate broad principles as to the requirement of disclosure in particular contexts which are hard to reconcile with the 'long-stop' strategy of *Dunne*. Under the *Dunne* test, a court should look first to generally approved practices and only if a particular practice can be stigmatised as obviously containing inherent defects should the court depart from it. *Dunne* thus does not involve the court in the process of lying down general rules as to what constitutes negligence, yet this is what Finlay CJ does in the first of the two passages quoted above. The second passage formally subjects the first to the language of *Dunne* but nonetheless the tenor of the Chief Justice's analysis is to favour a significant dimension of judicial control over the principles of what must be disclosed. This indicates a sensitivity to the fact that disclosure of risk to patients involves issues ranging beyond matters of medical judgment.

O'Flaherty J stated unambiguously that he did not accept that *Dunne* governed the question of disclosure. Rather he thought that it was:

> a matter for the trial judge, in the first instance, to find whether there has been a breach of the duty of care owed by the defendants to a person such as the plaintiff. That is to be resolved on the established principles of negligence. This was the approach of the Supreme Court of Canada in *Reibl v Hughes*.

This amounts to an acceptance of the position endorsed by Lord Scarman in *Sidaway*.

O'Flaherty J went on to express 'no hesitation' in subscribing to the view that, in cases of *elective* surgery,

> if there is a risk — however exceptional or remote — of grave consequences involving severe pain stretching for an appreciable time into the future and involving the possibility of further operative procedures, the exercise of the duty of care owed by the defendants requires that such possible consequences should be explained in the clearest language to the plaintiff.

Hederman J concurred with O'Flaherty J's judgment. It is necessary to examine the respective approaches of McCarthy and Egan JJ since their dissents related essentially to the application of the relevant legal principles to the facts of the particular case. Their position on whether the *Dunne* test applied to disclosure was not entirely clear.

McCarthy J quoted a passage from McMahon & Binchy's *Irish Law of Torts* (2nd ed., 1990), 268 which refers to the differing approaches of Lords Bridge and Scarman in *Sidaway*. He considered that these two solutions 'in a case such as the present' were:

> essentially the same. In determining whether or not to have an operation in which sexual capacity is concerned, it seems to me that to supply the patient with the material facts is so obviously necessary to an informed choice on the part of the patient that no reasonably prudent medical doctor would fail to make it. What then is material? Apart from the success ratio of the operation, what could be more material than sexual capacity after the operation and its immediate sequelae?

While the Bridge and Scarman formulae may sometimes yield the same outcome to legal proceedings, they are not of course 'essentially the same' in their definition. Is it possible to discern how McCarthy J would approach a case which was not 'such as the present'? We suggest that the most reasonable answer is that McCarthy J was essentially a proponent of the Bridge test, which is consistent with that favoured in *Dunne*. McCarthy J quoted with approval the *Dunne* criteria, including the passage from Finlay CJ's judgment to the effect that a doctor who adheres to a customary practice will be held negligent if the practice has inherent defects which ought to be obvious to any person giving the matter due consideration. McCarthy J considered that his task was to consider 'the application of th[is] principle, adapted, as needs be, to the special circumstances of what is called elective surgery'. These special circumstances made it clear to him that failure to disclose material risks would render the doctor liable on account of his or her adherence to a practice with inherent defects. Thus, McCarthy J joined Finlay CJ in *Walsh* in adopting *Dunne* as the appropriate test for informed consent issues.

With O'Flaherty and Hederman JJ rejecting *Dunne's* application in favour of a straightforward negligence test involving the requirement to disclose material risks, Egan J's judgment assumed a decisive role. It is difficult to discern precisely where Egan J stands on this issue. He referred to the opposing judgments of McCarthy and O'Flaherty JJ and noted that they were agreed in the view that, 'if there is a risk, however exceptional or remote, of grave consequences involving severe pain stretching for an appreciable time into the future and involving further operative procedures, the exercise of the duty of care owed by the defendants requires that such possible consequences should be explained in the clearest language to the prospective patient'. This passage does not give any inkling as to Egan J's opinion on whether the formulation of such a duty depends of *Dunne* or an unencumbered negligence criterion. Perhaps it is best to read Egan J's judgment as affording no real support for *Dunne*, since he made no reference to the *Dunne* test and did not refer at all to Finlay CJ's judgment, which had given *Dunne* a clear endorsement.

It is curious that the Supreme Court should have placed such little emphasis on British decisions. *Sidaway* received only a passing reference and *Gold v Haringey Health Authority* [1988] 1 QB 481 was not deemed worthy of mention. Nor did the court address wider, and more controversial, issues, on which see the helpful analysis by Clive Symmons (1987) *Professional Negligence*, 56.

(iv) *The causation issue* The next issue confronting the Court was that of causation. The general principle on which the law proceeds is that a plaintiff will not succeed against a defendant who has been guilty of negligence unless that negligence has caused the injuries of which the plaintiff complains, as a foreseeable consequence: see McMahon & Binchy, op. cit., chapter 3. (We need not here consider the exceptional extension relating to 'egg shell skull' plaintiffs: cf. *id.*, 69-73).

If a doctor fails to give a patient the requisite degree of disclosure, and is thus negligent, and the patient suffers an injury which falls within the risks that were not disclosed, does this mean that the doctor should have to compensate the patient in *all* cases or must the patient prove something more? Two principal approaches have found favour in the decisions. The first permits recovery where the patient establishes that he or she would not in fact have undergone the proposed treatment if the doctor had made the appropriate disclosure. This approach is entirely consistent with the general principles of causation but has been criticised by some judges as being unrealistic in practice since almost every patient will be so affected by hindsight as to deny that he or she would have undergone the treatment if proper disclosure had been made.

The second approach, conscious of the frailties of human recollection and hindsight, applies what is known as the 'prudent patient' test, whereby liability will be imposed if a prudent patient, in the position of the plaintiff, would not have undergone the treatment if the proper degree of disclosure had been made. This approach can perhaps be criticised on the basis that it suspends the general requirements of proof of causation on the basis of a concern that may have no application in particular cases. It raises an interesting question as to whether, in conjunction with the Scarman test, which requires disclosure of material risks, it *completely* dispenses with a causal enquiry. The answer to this question depends on whether there are *some* risks which ought to be disclosed under the Scarman test but which nevertheless are not such that a reasonable patient, on learning of them, would inevitably decline to go through with the proposed treatment. There surely are risks of this category. In *Walsh*, there was general agreement among the judges in the Supreme Court that, with elective treatment, the doctor is required to disclose risks that are remote and not necessarily serious. Even though a patient is entitled to be told of all these risks, it can hardly be considered that such disclosure would necessarily have resulted in his or her declining to go through with the proposed treatment in *every* case.

In *Walsh* the judges gave clear guidance on what test should be applied to the causal question. The only judge to address the general issue unambiguously was Egan J, who did not consider it necessary that the plaintiff should have to prove that, had a proper warning been given to him, he would not have submitted to the original operation:

> If he never, in fact, received a proper warning, his answer to a question asking how it would have affected his attitude would necessarily be hypothetical and, unless it was by any unlikely chance in the negative, the court would be entitled to come to the conclusion that the failure to give the advice was negligent and actionable.

The complicating factor in *Walsh* was that the plaintiff had alleged that he received *no* warning from the first doctor whereas MacKenzie J held that he had received *some* warning from this doctor. O'Flaherty J derived 'no assistance' from the plaintiff's assertion that, if he had received the correct warning from this doctor, he would not have undergone the operation:

> This is because he must now be taken to speak with the wisdom of hindsight and, naturally, no rational human being who has undergone what the plaintiff has, undoubtedly, undergone would say that he would go through it all again for the sake of what was to be achieved by the operation. The plaintiff is bound by the primary finding of fact made by [MacKenzie J] in his regard, *viz.* that the warning was given to the plaintiff and, in those circumstances, it seems to me that I am precluded from engaging in any examination of whether if a more powerful warning was given the plaintiff would have acted on it in the light of his flat contradiction that any warning at all was given.

This passage merges two quite separate issues. The first is that of causation; the second that of some species of estoppel, whereby a plaintiff who alleges that no warning was given is denied the entitlement to argue, as a matter of law, that the scope of the warning which the trial judge found was given was inadequate. Egan J was surely correct to reject the proposition that the court was in these circumstances precluded from engaging in an examination of whether the warning was adequate. It should be noted that the hypothetical quality of the answer to the question whether the plaintiff would have undergone the treatment if a proper disclosure had been given is exactly the same regardless of whether *no* disclosure or *partial* disclosure had occurred. This does not appear to have been fully appreciated by O'Flaherty J. Nor, it seems, did the Chief Justice: cf. [1992] IR, at 512.

(v) *Application of the legal principles of the facts* Against this background of differing views as to what legal principles should govern, it is not surprising that difficulties also arose in the application of the legal principles of the facts of the case. Finlay CJ, applying the *Dunne* test, upheld the holding at trial that the first doctor's warning had been adequate. McCarthy J, also applying the *Dunne* test, held that the defendants were negligent in failing to have identified the risk of impotence, however remote, to the plaintiff and his wife. O'Flaherty J, applying the unencumbered negligence test, held that the plaintiff, having contended that no warning was given, could not argue in the alternative that if a warning was given it was insufficient. If he had been permitted so to argue, O'Flaherty J considered that his case 'would have been difficult to refute', in view of the lack of emphasis in the warning on the possibility of lasting complications. Confusingly, O'Flaherty J went on later to express the belief that the warning given by the first doctor *was* 'sufficient in the light of the prevailing medical knowledge and experience'. How can one explain this seeming contradiction? Perhaps the answer lies in O'Flaherty J's view that what happened to the plaintiff after the operation was so unusual that it *could not have been foreseen* by the doctors. In other words, liability should not be imposed, not because the warning was inadequate, but because what happened to the plaintiff fell outside the scope of what the plaintiff would have been told if the warning had been adequate. This appears to be a classic instance of a case failing on account of remoteness of damage under the *Wagon Mound (No. 1)* test.

Finally Egan J, as we have seen, did not clarify whether he favoured the *Dunne* test. He was not satisfied that the first doctor had given an adequate warning of the possible consequences of a vasectomy operation, 'however remote such consequences might be'. Moreover, the literature supplied to the plaintiff had been equally defective in this regard. Accordingly, '[i]n the end result' he agreed with McCarthy J's judgment.

The overall effect of the several judgments was that, by a three to two majority, the defendant's appeal was successful. McKenzie J's finding of no negligence in the conduct of the operation or in regard to disclosure was upheld. His findings of a technical assault and battery and of a violation of the plaintiff's constitutional right to bodily integrity were reversed.

## EMPLOYERS' LIABILITY

**Safe plant** In the 1990 Review, 505-7, we discussed *Connolly v Dundalk Urban District Council and Mahon & McPhillips* [1990] 2 IR 1, where O'Hanlon J imposed liability on the first defendant, the plaintiff's employers, for negligence in exposing the plaintiff to the risk of injury from inhaling chlorine gas escaping from a pipe that had become disconnected. He also imposed liability on the second defendants, who had supplied the pipe and were under a contractual duty to maintain it in proper repair. O'Hanlon J apportioned liability equally.

The first defendant successfully appealed against this apportionment to the Supreme Court which reduced its proportion of liability to 20%.

Of particular interest is O'Flaherty J's statement of the principles relating to an employer's liability for the negligence of an independent contractor:

> The common law duties to take reasonable steps to provide safe plant and a safe place of work — I speak of the place of work as being part of the employer's property . . . — are such they cannot be delegated to independent contractors so as to avoid the primary liability that devolves on employers to make sure that these duties are carried out. These are responsibilities which cannot be put to one side; they must remain with the employer. They are owed to each individual employee. That is not to say, of course, but that the employer on occasion is entitled to and very often should get the best expert help that he can from an independent contractor to perform those duties. If he does so and the contractor is negligent causing injury to an employee, the employer retains a primary liability for the damage suffered though if he is not himself negligent he may obtain from the contractor a contribution to the damages and costs which he has to pay which will amount to all indemnity.

This statement goes further than that of O'Hanlon J, in including 'safe plant' as well as 'a safe place of work' when articulating what is in effect a principle of *vicarious* liability applying to employers: see our observations in the 1990 Review, 506-7. If plant includes equipment supplied by an employer to an employee for use in the course of the employee's employment, then O'Flaherty J's approach is inconsistent with the earlier Supreme Court decision of *Keenan v Bergin* [1971] IR 192: cf. McMahon & Binchy, op. cit., 328.

**The Army** In the 1989 Review, 410-18, we analysed with some misgivings the decision of *Ryan v Ireland, the Attorney General and Minister for Defence* [1989] IR 177, in which the Supreme Court took upon itself to define the obligations of the defence forces to their members, even in situations of combat, in terms of the duty of care in negligence. The Court appeared to conflate the separate issues of whether there was a constitutionally-based immunity on the part of the State, on the one hand, and whether, accepting that there was no such immunity, it would be right to impose a duty of care.

If a duty arose in such a case, it is easy to see why the same question could be perceived as beyond argument in *Rohan v Minister for Finance, the Minister for Defence, Ireland and Attorney General*, High Court, 19 June 1992. In *Rohan*, the plaintiff, an army captain, sought compensation for back injuries he sustained when organising the training for members of the army taking part in military pentathlon championships. The plaintiff had acted as organiser and instructor. He engaged in a great deal of practice runs over an obstacle course which he had helped to construct. The pain did not become serious until two years had elapsed. In the meantime, the plaintiff, had participated in SAS-type training with the Ranger Unit of the army, as well as parachute jump training and a diploma course in physical training and outdoor education, which involved canoeing, hill walking, orienteering, wind-surfing, rockclimbing and rope descents. He failed to complete this course because of pains and growing doubts about his physical condition.

The plaintiff's allegation of negligence extended only to his activities in relation to the pentathlon. O'Hanlon J imposed liability because the defendants should have sought expert advice as to the physical hazards for participants and as to the ways in which the risks could be minimised for participants and their instructors. The use of landing mats during practice periods would have been a sensible precaution. The plaintiff should not have been left to work matters out on a trial and error basis.

O'Hanlon J, however, found the plaintiff guilty of contributory negligence for his failure to have taken all the precautions that a reasonably prudent person would have taken for his own safety and for his failure to mitigate the damage flowing from the defendants' negligence. The plaintiff was a person of considerable experience. Much of what had been suggested by the plaintiff's expert witness as constituting due care could have occurred to the plaintiff himself by the exercise of ordinary commonsense. The plaintiff's over-eagerness to embark on all kinds of punishing physical activities once he had become aware that his body was beginning to complain of the treatment that was being meted out to it constituted a culpable failure to mitigate the damage. O'Hanlon J accordingly reduced the plaintiff's compensation by 20%.

In computing the quantum of damages, O'Hanlon came to the conclusion that the plaintiff's injuries had been brought about by a multiplicity of causes. The pentathlon activities were not a major cause; his participation in the Ranger courses, parachute jumping and rock climbing was also causally implicated.

O'Hanlon J, stated:

> I cannot accept that the sudden end to a promising career in the Army

> at an early age can be attributed to the wear and tear produced by the obstacle course some ten years ago and I think the plaintiff was simply unlucky in his constitutional make-up and in being unable to withstand the many demands he made on himself throughout his years in the Army. . . .

This reference to the fact that the plaintiff 'was simply unlucky in his constitutional make-up' should not be understood as modifying in any way the 'egg-shell skull' rule, which was not affected by the demise of *In re Polemis* in *The Wagon Mound (No 1)*. (For discussion of the rule, see McMahon & Binchy, op. cit., 69-72, Rowe, 'The Demise of the Thin Skull Rule?' (1977) 40 Modern L Rev 347). Nowhere in his judgment did O'Hanlon J suggest that the plaintiff's injuries were in any sense attributable to a weak constitution. Instead, he made it plain that these injuries sprang from multiple external causes. If in this case the plaintiff's participation in the pentathlon training had resulted in injuries more extensive than ought to have reasonably been foreseen, but the kind of foreseeable injury was such as, in the context of its occurrence, involved negligence on the part of the defendants, then the plaintiff would have been entitled to recover damages for *all* his injuries: see *Burke v John Paul & Co. Ltd* [1967] IR 277.

In *Dowdall v Minister for Defence, Ireland and the Attorney General*, High Court, 23 July 1992, the plaintiff, a corporal in the army, was injured during a training exercise with the FCA. The plaintiff was acting as 'the enemy' in a training sectional attack. He had to hide from the FCA men; when they located his position, their function was to overrun it with their guns in the firing position. The captain in charge of the FCA stumbled as he was overrunning the plaintiff's position and his gun was accidentally discharged. Particles of several blanks hit the plaintiff's face and the noise damaged his ears.

Denham J held on the evidence that the captain's finger had been on the trigger at the time when it should have been outside the trigger guard lying alongside the barrel. If the correct position had been adopted, then, even if the captain had stumbled, there could have been no discharge.

Denham J imposed liability in negligence, fortified by expert evidence and the existence of army regulations that the firing finger must lie outside the trigger guard, alongside the barrel. It was only on this basis that she was disposed to countenance liability. She did not consider it negligent for the defence forces to have a training exercise where men (especially those who had previous training) were being trained in locating and overrunning an enemy site with guns ready for firing. It was not necessary for the guns to be placed in a safety position before overrunning 'the enemy':

> The object of the exercise is to teach the trainees how to deal with the situation. If the FCA were to put their guns out of use before overrunning the site, then the training would be of less value: the procedures would be different to that which would be used in an actual situation and therefore they would be of a reduced worth in training.

Nor was it necessary for the captain to have pointed his weapon in the air. The model — a Gustaf submachine-gun — made this a very awkward movement.

In recognising that certain practices necessarily invoke risk if they are to achieve the purpose for which they are established, Denham J has much support from earlier Irish cases. See, e.g., *Callaghan v Killarney Race Co.* [1958] IR 366, *Donaldson v Irish Motor Racing Club*, Supreme Court, 1 February 1957, *Muldoon v Ireland* [1988] ILRM 367 (1987 Review, 326). More generally, see McMahon & Binchy, op. cit., 115-9.

Particular difficulties may arise in the employment context, since some jobs cannot be done without risk, but to pose the problem in this way disguises complex policy issues relating to the appropriate level of protection of an employee's life and bodily integrity and the related question as to whether the action for damages for employer's liability is the best way of securing that protection. Courts in the past were content to identify certain types of employment as inherently risky. Thus, in the Supreme Court decision of *Depuis v Haulbowline Industries Ltd*, 14 February 1962, Lavery J observed that shipbreaking was employment 'of a sort that admittedly has a certain degree of risk'. It would seem fair to say that today the courts are a good deal less fatalistic about dangerous jobs. If the risk of injury can be removed or reduced, even at high expense, employers will now be called on to pay that price, even if this may involve downstream social effects, such as the reduction of access to socially beneficial service or in the discharge of employees from employment: see, e.g., *Heeney v Dublin Corporation*, High Court, 16 May 1991, analysed in the 1991 Review, 389-9. It may be predicted that no judge today would state, as Henchy J did in *Bradley v CIE* [1976] IR 217, at 223, that 'even where a certain precaution is obviously wanted in the interests of the safety of the workman, there may be countervailing factors which would justify the employer in not taking that precaution'.

It seems, therefore, that, in assessing traditionally dangerous modes of employment, the courts today will require employers to remove all risks save for the dangers inherent in the process, which cannot be avoided by good management or the expenditure of money. Inevitably, any manoeuvres such as arose in *Dowdall* will involve *some* such dangers. Denham J's judgment differentiates well between the two categories of danger.

**Concurrent liability** In *Hollywood v Cork Harbour Commissioners and Ronayne Shipping Ltd* [1992] 2 IR 457, O'Hanlon J addressed the question of concurrent liability on the part of an employer and a third party where the negligence of the employer consisted of exposing the employee to the risk of the third party's negligence and the negligence of the third party consisted in exposing the employee to the risk of the employer's negligence. The case was a fatal accident claim brought by the dependants of an employee of the defendant. When working on top of a container on the deck of a vessel, he had been swept off it by another container, suspended from a crane, which was in the process of being brought ashore by an employee of the defendant.

O'Hanlon J had little hesitation in imposing liability on the third party, whose crane-driver had been negligent in failing to have taken the 'obvious and simple' precaution of raising the container above a height that could strike any person if unobserved by the crane-driver. But the deceased's employer was also liable in requiring its employees to engage in such work at a time when suspended loads were being brought over their heads. Although this had been a regular practice for many years, it was inherently dangerous and could have been avoided easily by adopting a different and equally efficient unloading procedure. Moreover, the deceased's employer should have established a regular means of communication with the crane-driver so as to give him warning in good time when the operation of the crane threatened danger to any of the employees assisting in the discharge of the cargo. No banksman had been employed to watch out for their safety at all times. (O'Hanlon J noted the ambiguous evidence of a fellow-employee of the deceased to the effect that 'a banksman in practice doesn't be there, but is employed'). O'Hanlon J apportioned fault on the basis of 60% or against the deceased's employer and 40% against the Cork Harbour Commissioners.

**The risks of the road** In *Coyle v An Post* [1993] ILRM 508, the Supreme Court, by a majority, declined to make a very radical extension of employer's liability, which would have had further reverberations in a wide range of social relationships. The plaintiff, the sub-postmaster of Raphoe, Co. Donegal, had been injured when driving his car on an icy road. The incentive for his journey was to collect cash from Lifford Post Office. A critical issue of fact was whether he had been *ordered* by his superior to make the journey. The essence of the plaintiff's case was that he should not have been subjected to the risks of such a hazardous journey, in view of the icy conditions. The essence of the defendant's response was that he had made the journey of his own free will, in order to facilitate a number of social welfare and social insurance claimants who came to his premises that morning.

Johnson J held in favour of the plaintiff but the Supreme Court reversed. The majority (Finlay CJ, Hederman, Egan and Blayney JJ) held that the evidence did not support a finding of negligence, since it did not establish that the plaintiff had been ordered to make the journey.

Hederman J delivered the leading judgment, which examined the evidence in considerable detail. He was of the view that the plaintiff had simply forgotten the likelihood of extra people coming to his sub-Post Office on the day in question, which was at a time when a bonus payment was made before Christmas. He was satisfied that the plaintiff's superior, far from ordering him to go to Lifford, had merely given him an indication that if he wanted money that day, he could obtain it only by going to Lifford.

Hederman J observed:

> It is one thing for an employer to order an employee to engage in dangerous work when a safe alternative is readily available. It is quite another thing for an employer not to prevent an employee from engaging in a dangerous activity at the employee's option in circumstances where, by deviating from the established procedures, the likelihood of the employee so acting could be reduced or removed. In the first instance it would usually be relatively easy for an employee to succeed in an action for negligence. In the second instance the court cannot rush to the conclusion that the defendant had breached a duty of care, but . . . must instead examine closely the evidence and seek to determine whether, in all the circumstances, liability should be imposed. . . .
>
> The law of negligence is not a system whose primary purpose is to ensure that injured persons will receive monetary compensation. It is a system premised on the establishment of fault on the part of the defendant. The present case has no precedent; certainly none was cited to us in argument. If the court were to impose liability in relation to the circumstances that arose in this case, it is hard to see why it would not follow that every employer, whose employees journey in frosty weather, which journey would be avoided by the employer taking other steps, is under a duty of care, under pain of being found liable in negligence, to arrange to have the journey called off. This is a bold proposition which goes well beyond what the law of negligence should demand. In my view the court cannot slip into a strict liability regime.
>
> The essence of the concept of negligence is that the defendant should have acted as a reasonable person would have acted. While negligence is not determined by reference simply to how people in fact act, nevertheless the courts are entitled to have regard to common experience when determining the scope of negligent conduct. What the plaintiff avers to be negligent conduct has never been stigmatised as such by any court. Indeed the plaintiff's case is a particularly weak instance of the principle since it is far from clear that [he] was under

> any obligation, legal or moral, to make the journey on that particular morning.

O'Flaherty J, dissenting, construed the conversation between the plaintiff and his superior as involving an instruction to the plaintiff to come to Lifford for the money. The superior could, in O'Flaherty J's view, have permitted the plaintiff to use the facilities of a local bank, whose services had been dispensed with by An Post some time previously.

In O'Flaherty J's view, the plaintiff was under a legal obligation as sub-postmaster to do all in his power to make sure that he had the money to pay those who were expecting their social welfare payments and who could look to An Post's legal obligation to supply the payments to them. In this context O'Flaherty J instanced the earlier decisions of the Court in *Purtill v Athlone UDC* [1968] IR 205, *Moynihan v Moynihan* [1975] IR 192, *Ward v McMaster* [1988] IR 357 and *Sunderland v Louth County Council* [1990] ILRM 678, which he considered, established that:

> the answer to the question whether negligence had been made out is best achieved not so much by seeking out a prior authority which may resemble the case in debate on the facts but rather to enquire whether such a finding is justified in principle.

This endorsement (albeit indirectly) of Lord Wilberforce's 'two-step' test in *Anns* is similar to that of Flood J, in *John C. Doherty Timber Ltd v Drogheda Harbour Commissioners* [1993] 1 IR 315, which we examined, above, 552-3.

O'Flaherty J sought to put the issue in *Coyle* in starker relief by the illustration of a sub-postmaster on the island of Aranmore, Co. Donegal, who was confronted with a shortage of money for social welfare payments. In this hypothetical scenario, there was someone on the island who was in a position to facilitate the sub-postmaster with a loan of cash for some days, the other options being to send the potential recipients away or for the sub-postmaster to make a hazardous journey on a dangerous sea four miles or so to the mainland. If the sub-postmaster made a call to his head office looking for guidance, would there be any doubt as to what the supervisor should have told the sub-postmaster? O'Flaherty J continued:

> Is there any difference, except one is more vivid and immediate, between a dangerous sea and a dangerously icy road? The standard of care required in this case, as in other cases of negligence where a duty is owed, is denominated by having regard to two factors, *viz.* the magnitude of the risk to which the plaintiff is exposed (involving the

gravity and likelihood of injury which he might sustain) and the importance of the object to be attained.

He quoted in support a passage from Salmond & Heuston's *Law of Torts* (20th ed., 1992), p. 234, to the effect that '[t]o expose others to a risk of harm for a disproportionate object is unreasonable, whereas an equal risk for a better cause may be lawfully run without negligence'.

O'Flaherty J's invocation of these elements of the formula that determine the standard of care in negligence raises once more the question of the role of the duty of care in negligence. There is no doubt that the standard of care formula is capable of yielding an answer to all negligence issues, including the one arising in *Coyle*. Rightly or wrongly, however, the courts have considered it desirable to render the question of the standard of care secondary to consideration of the *duty of care* requirement. If a court holds that there is no duty of care, this determines the issue of law more definitively for the future than does a calibration of the elements of the standard of care formula in any particular case.

**Underlying social policies** The Supreme Court decision of *Hay v O'Grady* on 4 February 1992 raises troublesome issues of social policy in relation to employer's liability. The facts were straightforward. The plaintiff was employed as a community facilitator, working as a house-parent at a hospital where severely mentally handicapped patients were being brought into the ordinary life of the community. The plaintiff's role was to help these patients to fend for themselves and to keep themselves and the house clean. Patients were selected for this house from time to time by a board consisting of a psychologist, social workers, staff nurses and coordinators, with the house-parent sometimes being involved.

In the spring of 1988 the plaintiff became house-parent at a house where there were four patients, one of whom was Margaret. Margaret was thirty one years old, small in stature and of light weight. Her behaviour was changeable, ranging from lethargic to times when she would throw things, catch people's hair and try to bite people. After a series of such disturbances in May and June, Margaret was returned for a six week period to the hospital during the day, while spending the nights in the house supervised by the plaintiff. Thereafter she was gradually phased back into the house. A further incident took place on 10 August, when Margaret was on a day's outing. This involved snatching food and removing a chair when a person was about to sit down, but not any act of violence. She was restrained and brought home to the house but she was not returned to the hospital. Eight days later, Margaret assaulted the plaintiff and injured her.

The plaintiff's case was that, having regard to Margaret's history of aggression, she should not have been returned to the house after the six-week stay in the hospital or that, if this was not itself negligent, that she should have been returned to hospital after the further incident on 10 August or the plaintiff should have been given a colleague to share the burden of controlling Margaret.

Lynch J found that the defendants were not guilty of negligence. He concluded that those concerned with management had not failed to give due consideration to all relevant incidents and that there had been no obvious need to transfer management back to the hospital after the incident of 10 August. He described the case as 'a very difficult' one; he considered the defendants' scheme of rehabilitation to be 'a most laudable' and 'very good' one, which 'accorded with state policy that those fit for community living should not, as far as is possible, be locked away in large institutions for the rest of their lives'. It was inevitable that there would be some failure with persons referred to the houses. This did not mean that such a scheme should be abandoned, because it was a good one, nor did it mean that 'if an individual falls from grace, so to speak, because of some tantrum or other . . . he or she must immediately be treated as forfeiting the benefit which has been offered to him [or her], without giving him [or her] the opportunity to be retrained'.

The Supreme Court appeal, affirming Lynch J, is somewhat disappointing. Only one judgment was delivered: by McCarthy J (Finlay CJ, Hederman, O'Flaherty and Egan JJ concurring). McCarthy J spent much of his judgment in setting out the principles on which the Supreme Court acts on appeal from High Court proceedings involving a judge sitting alone. (We discuss this aspect of the case in the chapter on Practice and Procedure, above 470-4.) It is somewhat curious that McCarthy J should have chosen this case for such an exercise, since it was one in which there was no significant dispute as to the nature or quality of the evidence or as to what inferences of fact should properly be drawn from the evidence. The issue was quintessentially in the realm of values and one of how social policy should operate in such a sensitive area.

All that McCarthy offered by way of analysis was the view that Lynch J's conclusion had been wholly supported by the evidence, followed by the observation that:

> [i]t is not a strict analogy, but, in my view, as in cases of alleged malpractice, a court should ordinarily refrain from substituting its own view of appropriate decision for that of those charged with making such decision and apparently qualified to do so. This is not to say that, where appropriate, a court might not conclude that the decision-maker had failed adequately to inform himself or to apply appropriate standards. In the present case, for what one may assume to be lack of such evidence,

> there was no evidence whatever from any expert source to the effect that the management of Margaret fell short of any reasonable standard of care.

Let us try to unravel the issues that truly underlie the facts in *Hay v Grady*. They bear some comparison with *Mulcare v Southern Health Board* [1988] ILRM 689 (High Court, 1987, Murphy J), which we analysed in the 1988 Review, 422-4. There a home help employed by the defendant injured her ankle on an uneven floor in a somewhat dilapidated house of an elderly woman whom she was visiting in the course of her employment. She sued her employer unsuccessfully, claiming that the house should have been surveyed before she was permitted to visit it. In our analysis, we pointed out that the case involved three innocent parties: the plaintiff, the defendant and the elderly woman. To impose liability the health board would almost inevitably have harsh consequences for the elderly and infirm who need the services of home helps. On the other hand, to relieve the health board of liability has the effect of letting the loss fall on the unfortunate employee. So unsatisfactory is either course that we tentatively suggested the establishment of a state-supported compensation scheme to deal with such cases.

In *Hay v O'Grady* the parallels are clear. Again, there are three innocent parties, again the implications of imposing liability are unpalatable since the economic costs could be perceived by decision-makers as so prohibitive that they would conclude that the better course would be to restrict the present policy of encouraging mentally handicapped patients to live in the community. Conversely, leaving house-parents uncompensated makes them carry the burden of subsidising a desirable social policy by sacrificing the right to compensation.

We do not here address the question of the merits of the policy of encouraging mentally handicapped adults to live in the community. What seems clear is that such a policy will fail if it is not adequately funded: cf. Kirk & Therrien, 'Community Mental Health Myths and the Fate of Former Hospitalized Patients' (1975) 38 Psychiatry 209, at 214-5.

It would be a mistake to treat the legal issue of negligence in such cases as involving merely micro-decisions by persons within the system. However much the courts would wish it to be otherwise, the issue is a large one, going to the root of social policy. It may be that, if the court were to have imposed liability in the instant case, the effect would effectively have been to increase the restraint on mentally handicapped adults.

Having said that, it must also be observed that McCarthy J was surely right in giving decision-making in such cases a margin of appreciation akin to that applying in medical malpractice litigation. It seems arguable that the decision-makers here fell within the remit of the professional negligence laid down in *O'Donovan v Cork County Council* [1967] IR 173, *Dunne v National Maternity Hospital* [1989] ILRM 735; [1989] IR 91 and *Roche v Peilow* [1986] ILRM 189; [1985] IR 232. Cf. McMahon & Binchy, op. cit., 258-60. The process of deciding when, and by what means, a mentally disabled adult should be brought into the ordinary life of the community has a significant component of medical expertise, albeit tempered by other considerations. No one should discount the formidable difficulty of predicting where the courts will set the frontiers of professional negligence, however. In *Kelly v St Laurence's Hospital* [1989] ILRM 437; [1988] IR 402, nurses were held to fall outside the professional net; in *Hughes v J.J. Power Ltd*, High Court, 11 May 1988, a mechanic fell within it. See our observations in the 1988 Review, 413.

## SCHOOLS' NEGLIGENCE

In *Dolan v. Keohane and Cunningham*, Supreme Court, 8 February 1994, affirming High Court, 14 February 1992, the plaintiff, a nine-year-old pupil at a primary school was injured when swinging on the entrance gate of the defendants' secondary school which was across the road from the primary school at a distance of thirty yards. The accident happened at about 3 pm when the primary school pupils were going home. Children who lived near to the school walked or cycled home. Those who lived at a further distance were either collected by car or went home by bus under a private arrangement between their parents and the bus operator. The bus drivers had formerly collected the pupils at a pre-arranged spot which had formerly been at the entrance to the primary school but, after consultation with the Gardaí, had recently moved to a point close to the entrance to the secondary school.

On the day of the accident the pupils, including the plaintiff, had left their satchels at this collection point and gone to swing on the gate. It appeared from the evidence that, although the plaintiff and his friends had been swinging on the gate every day, no teacher from the defendants' school had been aware of this practice.

The plaintiff's case rested on two main planks. The first was that the defendants' duty of supervision did not end at the school gate and that the 'pre-ordained system of collection' necessarily involved a continuing duty on the defendants' part to take reasonable care for the safety of the pupils until such time as they boarded the bus. Keane J rejected this argument. The degree of supervision required of school authorities obviously varied with the circumstances, including the age of the child. This duty, in the case of very young children, might include the obligation to ensure that they did not escape from the school on to a street where there was any significant volume of traffic, but no such considerations arose in the instant case. In Keane J's view, it would be unreasonable to treat the teachers in the primary school as being under any obligation to supervise the plaintiff at a stage when he had crossed to the other side of the road and walked an appreciable distance to the gates of the secondary school. Manifestly, children of the plaintiff's age could get into 'mischief of various sorts' between the time they left the school grounds and arriving at their home. In Keane J's opinion, the plaintiff was 'well outside the ambit of any possible duty of supervision' on the part of the primary school teachers by the time he reached the gate. It was wholly immaterial that he was there because of an arrangement between the parents and the bus drivers that the boys would be collected at that particular point, since the uncontested evidence was that the defendants had not been involved in any way in making those arrangements. Equally, the teachers in the *secondary* school had not been under any duty to supervise the plaintiff at that point, their duty being confined to the secondary school pupils under their care.

The second basis of liability asserted by the plaintiff related to the defendants' duty, as owners and occupiers, to take reasonable care for the safety of children climbing on to a gate which they knew, or ought to have known, would be a source of danger to them. The defendants pleaded that the plaintiff was a trespasser but their counsel approached the case on the basis that, if the defendants had failed to take reasonable care for the plaintiff's safety in the circumstances where they were under a duty to do so, he would be entitled to succeed in his action. Keane J held that the defendants should not be held liable. None of the teachers in either school had known of the children's practice of swinging on the gate; therefore, the only conceivable basis on which they could be found liable was that they ought to have foreseen that the absence of a stopping device of the type referred to by an expert witness of the plaintiff would be likely to cause injury to children who might be attracted to swinging on the gate. Keane J thought that it would be 'entirely unreasonable' to impose such a duty at the time the gate was installed. He preferred the evidence of one to the defendants' expert witnesses, which was that the stop would not have been effectual since the gate could swing inwards and it would not have been good practice for the contractor to have placed a metal obstruction in a part of the pavement over which members of the public paced on foot; furthermore, such an alleged safety device was not incorporated in the standard details for gates approved of by the Greater London Council which were, he said, the standards accepted in Ireland.

Whichever view one took of the expert evidence, Keane J considered that it would not be reasonable to say of an owner of property who installed a gate of standard design that he should have anticipated that the absence of a particular safety feature, on the merits of which experienced engineers had differed, would have prevented at some time in the future a child who happened to be swinging on the gate, unknown to the defendants, from catching his hand as the plaintiff had done in the instant case.

The Supreme Court dismissed the plaintiff's appeal. O'Flaherty J was unable to identify any distinction in principle between the respective positions of pupils from the town and those who were awaiting the arrival of the buses. While there were clearly cases where the duty to supervise did not end at the school gate, the present case was not one of them.

O'Flaherty J also rejected the claim based on the defendants' status as occupiers. It seemed to him that the only basis on which the defendants could be liable 'would be if one were to introduce the concept of absolute liability with the law in regard to teachers (as occupiers of premises) and pupils. This extension of the law cannot be justified on any basis'.

In her concurring judgment, with which Finlay CJ agreed, Denham J echoed this concern. She commented that:

> [t]hese cases must be decided with a modicum of common sense. To hold to the contrary would be to establish an unreal situation or, as O'Flaherty J stated, to introduce absolute liability.

The decision is to be welcomed. It is important that schools should not be driven by judicial favouritism for injured children into a draconian regime which would stultify one of the most important goals of education, which is to encourage self-reliance.

In *Kennedy v Galway Vocational Educational Committee*, Supreme Court, 1 July 1992, a finding by Egan J in the High Court in favour of the plaintiff in negligence proceedings was reversed on appeal. The plaintiff, a seventeen-year-old pupil at the defendant's vocational school, claimed that she had slipped on some water in the school's kitchen when preparing trays of tea and snacks for some visitors, at the request of a teacher. Her evidence was challenged in several aspects by the defendant's witnesses. The school roll indicated that she had not attended on the day she alleged the accident had occurred; her teacher denied that she ever sent pupils to the kitchen on such an errand; another teacher gave evidence that she was holding a home economics class in the kitchen at the relevant time; two other students gave evidence that was inconsistent with the plaintiff's account. O'Flaherty J, for the Court, while acknowledging that the Court had repeatedly said it would not interfere with the findings of primary fact made by a trial judge (cf. the 1991 Review, 405-6), considered that this was an exceptional case where the evidence was so clearly the one way as to require the Supreme Court's intervention.

## ROAD TRAFFIC

*McEleney v McCarron* [1993] 1 IR 132 concerned a traffic road accident. The plaintiff was returning home from a disco by bus in a comatose state of drunkenness. He was helped off the bus and propped against a wall. Two young women who knew him tried to get him home but he kept falling, eventually lying with his feet on the path and his torso and head on the road. The women pulled him further in from the road but had not completed this operation when the defendant's car approached. One of the young women signalled to the defendant, who interpreted this as a attempt to thumb a lift, which he was not willing to provide. He then caught a half glimpse like a shadow adjacent to the young women. This was the plaintiff; the defendant's car came in contact with his head almost immediately and injured him severely.

Carney J imposed liability in negligence, stating:

> The case comes down to whether the . . . defendant kept a proper look-out. On the . . . defendant's own evidence he did not, for presumably by reason of concentration on the girls he never saw the plaintiff's torso and head on the road until after he had run over it. Accordingly I find the ... defendant guilty of negligence. . . .

The Supreme Court reversed. Finlay CJ (Hederman and O'Flaherty JJ concurring) stated:

> It seems to me that the manner in which the conclusion of the learned trial judge is stated would appear to assume that the mere fact that the defendant failed to see, in the very short space which was available and in the short space of time which was available, the torso of the plaintiff lying on the road, of itself, must establish a negligent failure to keep a proper look out.
>
> I do not think that this is so, and I am satisfied that it would be placing upon the defendant an absolute duty and not what is required by law, namely a duty to take reasonable care.

The Chief Justice considered that the defendant's 'major obligation' was to keep an eye on the two women whom he understandably understood to be trying to thumb a lift. The road was 19 feet wide; the defendant's car was over 5 feet wide. There was probably only about 2 feet between the side of the car and the footpath. The defendant owed a duty by keeping them under his observation, to ensure that neither of the young women stepped forward to further their apparent intention of trying to get a lift. The defendant's concentration on them 'was the proper reasonable care which he should have exercised on that occasion'. Once the trial judge concluded that this was the explanation for the defendant's failure to see the part of the plaintiff's body on the road, 'it would be a wholly artificial standard of care to hold him guilty of negligence. . . .'

The Supreme Court's decision is a convincing one. It is worth considering how an appeal would have fared if a jury rather than a judge had found in favour of the plaintiff. We suspect that it would have been far more difficult for the Supreme Court to reverse the verdict. In contrast to the opaque verdict of a jury, a trial judge has to explain the process of legal reasoning whereby he or she arrives at his or her holding in the case. This exposes to the scrutiny of the Supreme Court all the elements — whether assumptions, influences or other legal or evidential conjunctions — which generated the conclusion. In *McEleney* this exposure appears to have been the reason for the outcome of the appeal.

## NEGLIGENT MISSTATEMENT

In *Potterton Ltd v Northern Bank Ltd* [1993] ILRM 225, O'Hanlon J gave an important decision on negligent misstatement. The plaintiff, whose business was in auctioneering and livestock sales, had sold cattle at its mart to a farmer for many years. The purchases were paid by means of cheques drawn on the farmer's company account with the defendant bank. At one sale the farmer bought cattle to the value of just under £40,000 and paid with a post-dated cheque. When the cheque was sent on for clearance, the defendant bank returned it with the words marked on it 'refer to drawer present again alteration req's drawer's conf.' — shorthand for 'alteration requires drawer's confirmation'. It was re-presented for clearance without alteration and without seeking the drawer's confirmation of any part of the writing on the cheque; the defendant once more returned it with the same message, save that the words 'present again' were struck out. In the meantime the farmer had bought more cattle with a separate post-dated cheque for over £13,000 which when presented was returned marked 'refer to drawer'. The plaintiff never received payment on either cheque as the farmer's company went into liquidation.

It transpired that the query raised by the defendant regarding the 'alteration' on the cheque had been merely a device invented to extricate the defendant bank from an awkward situation where more cheques were coming in for payment than the account could meet in circumstances where the bank was unwilling to dishonour the farmer's cheques became of its belief, based on previous experience, that it was likely to be put in funds if more time was given for the purpose. O'Hanlon J was satisfied that there had been no justification for returning the cheque uncashed on the basis that the word 'nine' had been written in block letters and the other words in ordinary script. It had 'all the appearance of having been written at the same time, and with the same writing instrument, and by the same hand as all the rest of the writing on the cheque; moreover, the bank had previously cleared without question cheques similarly written by the farmer.

In O'Hanlon J's opinion:

> the words written in when returning the cheque unpaid were calculated to, and did, lull the payee into a false sense of security and led the plaintiff to believe that payment was only being withheld for some technical reason having to do with the manner in which the cheque had been written. If this were, in fact, a cause of concern to the bank, they could have cleared it up immediately by means of a simple one minute telephone call to their own customer.

O'Hanlon J considered that, while a bank generally does not owe any duty to one who is not its customer when a cheque is presented for payment, this rule 'must be subject to qualification if the bank deliberately embarks on a course of conduct for its own purposes which is calculated to deceive the payee of the cheque in a manner which may result in financial loss to such payee, and where there is no lawful justification for such action on the part of the bank'. In contrast to the facts of *Dublin Port & Docks Board v Bank of Ireland* [1976] IR 118, which concerned the obligation of a bank on which a cheque was drawn to make payment on foot of it, the issue in the instant case related to the *message communicated by the defendant bank* to the plaintiff's bank, and thus to the plaintiff also, when declining to make payment on foot of the cheque. The plaintiff's case was that this message giving the alleged reason for dishonouring the cheque amounted to a negligent misrepresentation of the true situation which induced the plaintiff to act to its detriment or to forbear from taking steps for its own protection which it would have taken had the true position been made known. O'Hanlon J reviewed the *obiter* utterances of Kenny J in *Bank of Ireland v Smith* [1966] IR 646 to the effect that *Hedley Byrne* liability arose only where the relationship between the parties was such that 'but for the absence of consideration, there would be a contract'. Kenny J had found some support for this very narrow formulation of the principle in Lord Devlin's phrase, 'equivalent to contract', in *Hedley Byrne*. But, as O'Hanlon J pointed out, the scope of liability had been stated in a more ample manner in Lord Reid's speech. He returned to what Lord Morris Borth-y-Gest had said. He noted that significant developments in the law of negligence had taken place since

*Hedley Byrne* and *Bank of Ireland v Smith* had been decided, 'not least in the area of negligent misrepresentation and negligent misstatement'.

In the instant case, the defendant was under the ordinary banker's obligation either to pay the cheque forthwith if there were sufficient funds or otherwise to refuse payment at once. Had it done so in an unqualified manner, no liability could have attached to it and the plaintiff would have been alerted to take whatever steps were then open to it to secure payment or otherwise protect its interests. But, said O'Hanlon J,

> [t]he defendant elected to go further . . . and took it upon itself to communicate to the plaintiff its reason for refusing to honour the cheque at that point in time. In doing this I consider that it assumed an obligation to act honestly and carefully and not to deceive the plaintiff by putting forward a reason which was not the true reason, but was a spurious reason (as alleged in the statement of claim in this case, and as supported by the evidence adduced on behalf of the plaintiff).

This brought the case, 'assuming that it is still necessary to do so', within the scope of the situation envisaged by Lord Reid in *Hedley Byrne*, where a reasonable man knows that he is being trusted or that his skill and judgment are being relied on. Lord Reid had identified *three* courses open to him:

> He could keep silent or decline to give the information or advice sought; or he could give an answer with a clear qualification that he accepted no responsibility for it or that it was given without that reflection or inquiry which a careful answer would require; or he could simply answer without any such qualification. If he chooses to adopt the last course he must, I think, be held to have accepted some responsibility for his answer being given carefully, or to have accepted a relationship with the inquirer which requires him to exercise such care as the circumstances require.

In the instant case, the defendant had taken the third course and had breached its obligation to reply in a careful and honest manner once it indicated its reason for refusing payment on foot of the cheque. This had caused the plaintiff economic loss.

Quantifying that loss was a task 'fraught with difficulty'. O'Hanlon J considered that, if the cheque had been bounced, the plaintiff would have immediately applied the maximum pressure on the farmer to pay up, either by apportioning some of whatever moneys were still available to him to the plaintiff's claim or by returning any of the plaintiff's stock which still remained in his possession. O'Hanlon J assessed this figure at £20,000.

## OCCUPIERS' LIABILITY

**Invitees** In *Redmond v Equipment Company of Ireland Ltd*, High Court, 28 July 1992, the plaintiff, a security guard employed by the second defendant, was injured when working on the first defendant's premises by a tyre which was blown off a stack of tyres of at least seven feet in height, which had been constructed in what Budd J found to have been a 'higgledy-piggledy' manner. The winds that day were force six on the Beaufort scale. (Budd J was proud to record Admiral Beaufort's Louth origins.)

Budd J imposed liability on the first defendant, 'who was obviously an invitee on the premises and a person in respect of whom the [first defendant] owed a duty of care'. The first defendant had been negligent as it was foreseeable by a reasonably prudent warehouseman that, if the tyres were stacked too high and higgledy-piggledy, they would be blown down in a strong wind and would be likely to become a danger to persons lawfully in the compound.

In coming to his conclusion Budd J was not assisted by the *res ipsa loquitur* doctrine, invoked by counsel for the plaintiff. We discuss the aspects of the case below, 600.

*Redmond* is yet another instance of the reluctance of Irish courts over the past two decades to insist on the full requirements prescribed by Willes J in *Indermaur v Dames* (1866) LR 1 CP 274, at 287, in relation to the occupier's duty to an invitee. Willes J had defined the occupier's duty as being to take due care to protect the invitee from injury from unusual damages of which the occupier is, or ought to be, aware. The notion of an *unusual danger* is notoriously difficult to pin down: it connotes not simply an infrequent danger, but rather a danger which the invitee has a right not to expect. See McMahon & Binchy, op. cit., 283-43 (1st ed., 1981). Courts throughout the common law world have expended too much time and effort in puzzling whether particular dangers are or are not 'unusual'. There is very little point in such a waste of judicial energy, which elevates Willes J's language to the status of a legislative provision.

Budd J wisely did not ask the question whether the pile of tyres was an 'unusual' danger. To pose such a question frankly defies rational analysis.

In *Timbs v Templeogue Taverns Ltd*, High Court, 18 December 1992, the plaintiff, an elderly woman, slipped and fell on a tiled floor when leaving the defendants' premises. She claimed that the defendant had failed to take reasonable care to protect her from an unusual danger in the premises, which consisted of unsafe tiles. The case thus resolved itself into a question on which expert evidence was of great significance.

It transpired that the tiles were 'anti-slip' rather than fully 'non-slip' as they did not have a carborundium dust finish and were not ridged or ribbed.

The plaintiff's expert witness, an architect, said that, whereas the ideal tiles would be of the 'non-slip' category, the tiles in question could be faulted only if one was looking for complete 100% safety and, while they were not ideal, they were reasonably suitable for the circumstances and conditions in which they were laid and to be used. He explained that he was not saying that the tiles constitituted a danger in either wet or dry conditions and he agreed with the defendant's engineer that they were a good and suitable surface for the hallway in question.

The defendant's engineer gave evidence that the respective coefficients of friction when the tiles were wet and dry fell within the British standard definition of 'good' and within the 'generally satisfactory' category for normal use. His tests had shown that, from a practical point of view, they were satisfactory and safe.

Not surprisingly Morris J dismissed the plaintiff's action. There is, however, an interesting issue raised by this seemingly simple case. To what extent do expert or professional criteria of safety dictate the outcome of negligence litigation? Of course there is necessarily a close relationship between scientific and legal norms in this context, coupled with a general judicial willingness to respect the customary practice of architects and builders. But in the last analysis the resolution of the negligence issue does not reduce itself simply to a consultation with expert witnesses. In deciding whether or not to stigmatise acts or omissions as negligent the court must weigh the potentially competing considerations of the *likelihood* of injury, the *gravity* of the threatened harm, the *social utility or inutility* of the defendant's conduct and the *cost of preventing the injury*: see McMahon & Binchy, op. cit., 110-19. No doubt the scientific notion of safety encompasses these four considerations to some degree but there is no reason why its calibration should necessarily be identical to that of the courts. This is demonstrated by the famous decision of *Latimer v AEC Ltd* [1953] AC 643, where the House of Lords held that keeping a factory in operation after a flood did not constitute negligence, even though the floor surface was very slippery, because the employers had done what they could, albeit unsuccessfully, to make the floor safe.

In the instant case the converse argument was perhaps worthy of consideration. In a generation where sensitivity to the consumerist philosophy has greatly increased, could it be contended that proprietors of premises thrown open to the public for commercial gain should be stigmatised as having acted unreasonably if they choose tiles less than the safest on the market? The judgment throws no light on questions of cost differential but, even if there were substantial extra costs, this would not *necessarily* silence an argument on these lines.

It is interesting that the notion of 'unusual danger', specifically invoked by the plaintiff, presented no obstacle to the court, which proceeded on the basis that, if the tiles were unsafe, the plaintiff would succeed in her action. Thus, 'unusual danger' was stripped of its technicalities to mean simply an unreasonable danger.

In the section on *res ipsa loquitur*, below, 598-600, we discuss *Foley v Quinnsworth*, High Court, 10 April 1992, a Circuit Appeal, where Carroll J dismissed the plaintiff's proceedings arising from a slip and fall injury in the defendant's supermarket. The judgment proceeded on the basis that, if liability were to be established, it would be in negligence. Carroll J made no reference to any distinctive legal principles attaching to the plaintiff's status as an invitee. In following this course, she had good authority at the Supreme Court level: see *Foley v Musgrave Cash & Carry Ltd*, Supreme Court, 20 December 1985, *Mullen v Quinnsworth t/a Crazy Prices (No. 1)* [1991] IR 59.

**Liability for dogs** In *Duggan v Armstrong and Tighe* [1993] ILRM 222, the plaintiff, a seven-year-old child, when using the leisure facilities of the first defendant's hotel, was attacked by a mongrel alsatian dog owned by the second defendant, the manager of the hotel. At trial, Egan J had granted a non-suit in regard to both defendants. The Supreme Court set aside this order unanimously and remitted the care by consent to the Circuit Court.

McCarthy J (Hederman and Costello JJ concurring) dealt first with the question of *scienter*. Evidence had been adduced that the dog 'was always growling', that it used to run at a child and that it would attempt to climb up on children. McCarthy J considered that this constituted evidence to support the conclusion that the dog had a mischievous or vicious propensity:

> One does not have to wait for the growling and frightening dog to bite someone in order to know that it may do so; the requirement of *scienter* is not that the dog *will* bite somebody but that, having displayed a vicious propensity, it *may* do so.

As to the question of the dog owner's knowledge of this propensity, McCarthy J relied on what Judge Davitt had said in *Brennan v Walsh*, 70 ILTR 252 (Circuit Court, 1936). In *Bennett* as in *Duggan*, the knowledge of a nine-year-old child of the dog-owner of complaints being made about the dog was held imputable to the father.

McCarthy J noted that no submission had been made to the Court as to whether or not the *scienter* doctrine had survived into modern times and, in particular, had survived the guarantees contained in the constitutional framework, but added, surely significantly, that in his judgment:

> it goes against commonsense that the family of the owner can have an intimate knowledge of a dog's vicious propensities but the owner himself can escape liability unless one can prove direct communication to him.

This passage is of particular interest because it raises again the possibility that specific principles in the general body of tort law should be rigorously scrutinised to ensure that they comply with constitutional requirements. It is useful to contrast McCarthy J's approach with the more passive stance of Henchy J in *Hanrahan v Merck Sharp & Dohme (Ireland) Ltd* [1988] ILRM 629 at 636 and Barron J in *Sweeney v Duggan* [1991] 2 IR 274. See our observations in the 1988 Review, 462-6 and the 1991 Review, 458-60.

One might question whether it 'goes against commonsense' in every case that the family of the owner can have an intimate knowledge of a dog's vicious propensities but the dog owner 'can escape liability unless someone can prove direct communication to him'. If the suggestion is that commonsense dictates the conclusion that, *as a matter of fact*, such communication should be inferred, this might perhaps be sensible in cases of actual bites or other serious attacks, but one could hardly expect that every manifestation of a vicious propensity would be retailed by family members to the owner. There is, moreover, a legal difficulty in establishing an unqualified principle of liability on the basis of a factual hypothesis that may be incorrect in some instances. A rebuttable presumption might perhaps be acceptable but not an absolute rule: cf. *O'Leary v Attorney General* [1991] ILRM 454 and our observations in the 1990 Review, 178-82.

McCarthy J went on to address the question of 'the liability of the occupier of the hotel premises to a guest on the premises'. (He did not specifically identify the owner or the manager as the occupier of the hotel but, since he held that the knowledge of the manager was the knowledge of the owner and that there was 'clear evidence of a breach of the duty owed to the plaintiff as a result', it would appear that he regarded the owner as the occupier. The judgment is silent on the question of what level of control the occupier had over the day-to-day running of the hotel. A general lack of clarity is also apparent as to whether liability in *scienter* was envisaged as arguable against the manager of the hotel alone or also against the owner on the basis of vicarious liability. If the latter was the case, one might have expected some discussion on the question whether the manager's tort (if it was such) had been committed in the course of his employment.)

McCarthy J disposed of the occupier's liability issue summarily:

> No niceties of distinction between licensee and invitee arise here, if they could arise at all everywhere. It is not in issue that the plaintiff was on

> the premises as a hotel guest. In an area where a large number of people, including children, tended to congregate, a fairly large dog with a known propensity to jump on children, if not to growl and chase them, was permitted to run free. What some might think inevitable happened — a child got bitten. The knowledge of the manager . . . is the knowledge of the owner. There was clear evidence of a breach of the duty owed to the plaintiff as a guest.

A few points about this disposition of the question may be noted. First, McCarthy J was in the forefront of those seeking to apply a single test of negligence in occupier's liability cases, regardless of the status of the entrant. He had signalled this view as early as in *Daly v Avonmore Creameries Ltd* [1984] IR 131, at 138. Secondly, it is hard to see how a hotel guest could be owed anything less than a full duty of care in negligence by the proprietor since the guest is a contractual entrant to whom, in the absence of an express term to the contrary, an implied duty of due care is owed: see McMahon & Binchy, op. cit., 211-12. There is no prospect of any contractual constriction of that duty, since s. 4(1) of the Hotel Proprietors Act 1963 imposed on the proprietor a duty 'to take reasonable care of the person of the guest and to ensure that, for the purpose of personal use by the guest, the premises are as safe as reasonable care and skill can make them'. (S. 4(2) provides that this duty is independent of any liability of the proprietor or occupier of the premises.)

McCarthy J did not consider that s. 4 imposed a duty on the proprietor *additional* to his duty arising at common law; he was content to support a finding of a breach of statutory duty as well as common law liability.

A further feature of note in relation to McCarthy's J analysis of the occupier's liability issue is that it would enable a court to find negligence in relation to the control of a dog in a case where the employee for whose negligence the owner of the hotel would be vicariously liable was not in fact aware of the dangerous qualities of the dog and was not necessarily culpably ignorant in failing to be so aware. One may question whether classical principles of negligence would permit such an extension of liability. What appears to have happened is that the robust attribution of knowledge to the dog owner which *scienter* permits had been spirited into the negligence action. This is hard to justify since a *scienter* action differs from an action for negligence in that it does not require the dog owner to have been aware the incident wherein the plaintiff sustains his or her injuries.

Finally we may enquire what would have been the position, on McCarthy J's analysis, if the plaintiff had been a trespasser. Under s. 21(3) of the Control of Dogs Act 1986, the owner owes a trespasser *only* a duty of care in negligence; *scienter* liability appears to be completely excluded: see

McMahon & Binchy, op. cit., 514. In such circumstances, why should the knowledge of the manager, the owner of the dog, be attributed to the owner of the hotel so as to render the proprietor liable?

**Occupiers and independent contractors** In *Power v. Crowley and Reddy Enterprises Ltd*, High Court, 29 October 1992 Blayney J imposed liability on an occupier in circumstances that are likely to generate some discussion. The second defendant was a company which owned a licensed premises where the plaintiff, a carpenter, was working as employee of the first defendant who had been engaged by the second defendant to carry on work on a scheme for refurbishment of the premises. Part of the work involved the destruction of two internal walls of almost ten feet in height. Scaffolding was used for the first wall but not for the second as apparently it could not be found when work on the second wall was beginning. Because he could not therefore start demolishing the second wall from the top, a labourer employed by the second defendant thought it appropriate to remove a line of blocks from the second wall at a height of almost three feet from the ground, creating an open slit in the wall. The plaintiff decided to test the stability of the wall by giving it several bangs with a sledgehammer. After he had done this, one of the directors of the second defendant company allegedly said 'That's not going to stir' and walked away. The plaintiff and the labourer then took up their jackhammers and started to take the wall away from the gap up. It fell down immediately and the plaintiff was struck by some of the falling blocks.

Blayney J held the second defendant liable. It was clear from the director's evidence that he had seen the slit in the wall. Although he had denied that he considered it dangerous, he had gone on to say that his attitude was: 'Someone must know what they are doing'. Blayney J considered that, by qualifying his answer in this way, he showed that he must have been having doubts about the security of the wall. Blayney J found support for this inference in the concession by the manager of the premises that he thought the wall 'a little bit dangerous'. Blayney J reasoned that, if the manager could have come to that conclusion, it was 'very likely that [the director] did also, or at least that he ought to have done'.

In these circumstances, Blayney J considered that the defendant company, through its director, owed a duty of care to the plaintiff. The wall with the line of blocks taken out of it constituted an unusual danger of which the director was, or ought to have been, aware:

> [A]dmittedly it had not been created by him, or by any servant or agent of the defendant company, but it was present on the defendant company's premises, a potential risk to persons coming on to the premises and a particularly imminent risk to anyone who might continue to work

> at it. . . . [T]he plaintiff's engineer said that if he had seen the wall he would have been horrified. [The director] obviously could not be expected to have had his expertise, but there is no reason why he could not have had as good an appreciation of the situation as the plaintiff, who was a carpenter, and not a stonemason, and he considered that the wall was dangerous.

Blayney J was of opinion that the director was not entitled to assume that the plaintiff and the labourer knew what they were doing. Once he had doubts about the security of the wall, he had a duty as the agent of the company, the occupier of the premises, to take steps to ensure that the wall did not cause injury or damage to anyone. This could easily have been done: all that was required was a direction to the plaintiff and the labourer to stop working on the wall, and a general warning to keep away from it until the first defendant or the architect engaged by the second defendant had been consulted about the position. Such direction and warning would have been effective in preventing the accident.

This omission was compounded by the fact that the director had expressed the opinion that the wall was not going to stir. It was partly in reliance on this that the plaintiff resumed working on the wall. But, even if the director had expressed no opinion, Blayney J considered that he would still have been negligent 'as he had a duty to avoid injury being caused by the wall'.

Blayney J held that the plaintiff was guilty of 50% contributory negligence. We discuss this issue below, 601-3.

It has to be said that the finding of liability against the occupier seems harsh. The director was clearly not in charge of the job; that was the function of the independent contractor who presumably charged the appropriate price for taking that responsibility. The idea that a casual remark could generate liability in these circumstances is difficult to accept. The notion that the director would have been liable even if he had given no such encouragement is even harder to support. It is well established law that an occupier is not liable for the torts of an independent contractor who has been selected with due care. The effect of this decision is to impose an affirmative obligation on an occupier to prevent the commission of a tort by an independent contractor where he or she becomes aware of such a risk.

## RES IPSA LOQUITUR

In the 1991 Review, 415-7, we analysed Morris J's decision in *Lindsay v Mid-Western Health Board* [1993] 2 IR 147. We noted that the Supreme Court had reversed Morris J and we indicated that we would discuss the

Supreme Court decision in this year's Review. It will be recalled that the case concerned a girl who, at the age of eight, in 1982, was admitted to the defendant's hospital with suspected appendicitis. An alternative diagnosis of mesenteric adonitis was also considered by the medical staff. The plaintiff was operated on; she appeared initially to be recovering consciousness after the operation but had a sudden epileptic form attack and regressed into a deep coma from which she had not regained consciousness at the time of the litigation nine years later. It was not disputed that the hospital would be vicariously liable for any tort committed by any member of the hospital staff in the course of his or her duty.

The plaintiff's action for negligence against the hospital involved the invocation of *res ipsa loquitur* doctrine. The expert witness on her behalf, a highly qualified and experienced anaesthetist, identified three possible causes for the plaintiff's condition: sub-arachnoid haemorrhage, hypoxic insult and 'miscellaneous possibilities'.

Morris J approached the matter on the basis that the *res ipsa loquitur* principle applied since the defendant was 'in total control of the event' giving rise to the occurrence and the accident was such as did not happen in the ordinary circumstances if those in control of the procedures used proper care. The result, in his view, was that the defendant had 'the onus of proving that there [was] a reasonable explanation for what occurred to [the plaintiff] and . . . that this occurred without negligence on [its] part'. He considered that it would be quite wrong for the court to adopt 'a theory based on pure speculation' as a reasonable explanation for what had occurred. He regarded the defendant's hypothesis of a viral explanation was having this speculative quality, and accordingly held that the defendant had not discharged the onus cast upon it.

The Supreme Court, as we noted, reversed: [1993] ILRM 550; [1993] 2 IR 147. O'Flaherty J (Finlay CJ and Egan J concurring) agreed with Morris J that the *res ipsa loquitur* doctrine applied:

> It is true that a precise circumstance of negligence cannot be pointed to — such as in the classical cases of bags of sugar falling on a passing pedestrian (*Scott v London & St Katherine Docks Co.* (1865) 3 H&C 596) or a motor car driven onto a footpath (*Murray v Gilmore*, unreported, Supreme Court, 20 December 1973) — but it seems to me that if a person goes in for a routine medical procedure, is subject to an anaesthetic without any special features, and there is a failure to return the patient to consciousness, to say that that does not call for an explanation from defendants would be in defiance of reason and justice.

This passage raises some interesting issues as to the application of *res ipsa loquitur* in particular cases. It may be argued that in neither *Scott* nor *Murray* could the plaintiff point to 'a precise circumstance of negligence', if by that concept is envisaged the precise identification of the particular mode of negligent conduct of which the defendant was guilty. What both plaintiffs could do was to raise a commonsense inference that the defendant was negligent, how precisely it did not matter. Of course it is possible to describe the defendant's conduct in both cases by a formula that points the finger of negligence at the defendant: the defendants in *Scott* were (inferentially) guilty of negligent control of the bags of sugar on their premises and the defendant in *Murray* was (inferentially) negligent in the manner in which he drove his car. But what do these formulae really tell us about what happened? Nothing very much, it would seem. Equally, in *Lindsay*, the plaintiff could not point precisely to a specific act of negligence on behalf of the defendants but she was entitled to say that the facts raised an inference of negligent treatment. Far from being an embarrassment in the invocation the *res ipsa loquitur* doctrine, this lack of specificity is in fact a frequent characteristic of a case based on *res ipsa loquitor*.

It is interesting that O'Flaherty J did not refer to Henchy J's rationale for the *res ipsa loquitur* doctrine in *Hanrahan v Merck Sharp & Dohme (Ireland) Ltd* [1988] ILRM 629, only four years previously, which based the doctrine on the defendant's superior capacity of proof. Undoubtedly in the context of medical operations, where the patient is rendered unconscious, the defendant will almost invariably have just such a superior capacity of proof. Indeed, this superior capacity so tilts the balance in favour of the defendant that the California Supreme Court fifty years ago, in *Ybarra v Spangard*, 25 Cal 2d 486, 154 P 2d 687 (1944) extended the principles of vicarious liability, under the guise of the *res ipsa loquitur* doctrine, to ensure that a plaintiff who is injured when under anaesthetic will not find himself or herself in the situation of knowing that *someone* of those involved in his or her treatment must have been guilty of negligence, without being able to find out who that person was.

O'Flaherty J went on to express the view that, in the instant case, the most that the defendant should be required to do was to show that it had exercised all reasonable care and that it should not be required to take the further step of proving, on a balance of probabilities, what had caused the plaintiff's brain damage. He observed that '[t]he distinction between a negligent act and causation requires to be emphasised'.

O'Flaherty J adopted as 'an apt description of the scope of the [*res ipsa loquitur*] maxim' the following passage from John Fleming's *Law of Torts* (7th ed., p. 291):

> In some circumstances, the mere fact that an accident has occurred raises

> an inference of negligence against the defendant. A plaintiff is never obliged to prove his case by direct evidence. Circumstantial evidence is just as probative, if from proof of certain facts other facts may reasonably be inferred. *Res ipsa loquitur* is no more that a convenient label to describe situations where, notwithstanding the plaintiff's inability to establish the exact cause of the accident, the fact of the accident by itself is sufficient in the absence of an explanation to justify the conclusion that most probably the defendant was negligent and that his negligence caused the injury. The maxim contains nothing new; it is based on common sense, since it is a matter of ordinary observation and experience in life that sometimes a thing tells its own story. Unfortunately, the use of a Latin phrase to describe this simple notion has become a source of confusion by giving the impression that it represents a special rule of substantive law instead of being only an aid in the evaluation of evidence, an application merely of 'the general method of inferring one or more facts in issue from circumstances proved in evidence': *Davis v Bunn* (1936) 56 CLR 246, at 268.

Fleming advocates that *res ipsa loquitur* should be understood as no more and no less than a convenient label for a case based on circumstantial evidence which (in the days of a jury) was sufficiently strong to get to the jury, without a non-suit. It does *not* shift the onus onto the defendant to disprove negligence on his or her part. Nor does it *require* the defendant to adduce exculpatory evidence: on Fleming's approach a jury would be quite entitled to find in favour of a defendant in some cases where the doctrine applied and the defendant elected not to adduce any evidence. All that the doctrine involves is the process of identifying the case as being of sufficient strength to ensure that the trial judge will not withdraw it from the jury. There always was a certain range within which a reasonable jury could find negligence or the absence of negligence. Obviously, at the higher range of the register, there were and are cases where a verdict for the defendant would be perverse, but there are many *res ipsa loquitur* situations falling well short of such a coercively strong case for the plaintiff. It is curious that Fleming should be quoted with apparent approval when no member of the court in *Lindsay* appears to have interpreted the *res ipsa loquitur* doctrine as Fleming does.

O'Flaherty J adopted the reasoning of Andrews J, in the British Columbia decision of *Girard v Royal Columbian Hospital* (1976) 66 DLR (3rd) 676, at 691, that medical science had not yet reached the stage where the law ought to presume that a plaintiff must come out of an operation as well as or better than he or she went into it. In that case, the evidence indicated that the kind of injury the plaintiff suffered could have occurred without negligence on anyone's part. Andrews J had concluded that, since he could not infer that there had been negligence on the part of the doctors, the maxim of *res ipsa loquitur* did not apply.

O'Flaherty J accepted that in the circumstances of the instant case an answer was clearly required from the defendant:

> That answer could be provided in two ways. [It] could have proved, on the balance of probabilities, that the plaintiff met her injuries in a particular manner that caused her condition but which was not connected with the administration of the anaesthetic. This [it] failed to do. The furthest the defendan[t] got was to suggest as possibilities other means by which the plaintiff sustained her injuries. I believe this evidence is not, however, to be regarded as totally inadmissible. It was legitimate, I believe, for the defendan[t] to adduce evidence of possibilities, remote though they might be, as an explanation; in contradistinction to saying that [it] could not offer *any* explanation of any description whatsoever. It went to provide some corroboration, as well, that there was no negligence on [its] part in the administration of the anaesthetic. The other course was for the defendan[t] to establish that from beginning to end of this anaesthetic procedure there was no negligence on [its] part. This [it] did decisively and, in those circumstances, it appears to me that [it] rebutted the burden of proof that rested on [it] to displace the maxim *res ipsa loquitur* and so the case returned to the plaintiff's bailiwick to prove negligence.

O'Flaherty concluded as follows:

> I believe that it is necessary to ensure that the rule embodied in the maxim does not put a burden on defendants which is so onerous as to produce an unjust result. Each case must, of course, be dealt with in accordance with its own particular facts but, as I have said, I believe that in the circumstances here the defendan[t] ha[s] met the *prima facie* case made against [it] as fully as could be expected. It would be an unjustifiable extension of the law to say that in the absence of an explanation that could be proved, on the balance of probabilities, negligence on the part of the defendant must be inferred. It has often been said that medical science is not an exact one and it is safe to prophesy that medical science and its technology will advance past frontiers which are not within anyone's contemplation at this time and so matters at present not amenable to explanation will be capable of resolution.

It is hard to categorise O'Flahery J's approach. His conclusion that the *res ipsa loquitur* doctrine no longer applies where a defendant establishes that he or she acted without negligence must be correct. What is less clear about this approach is whether there is an actual *onus* on a defendant to disprove negligence, whether the defendant is required merely to offer an alternative explanation for the plaintiff's injuries, or whether (as seems unlikely) the characterisation of a case as one to which the *res ipsa loquitur* doctrine applies is no more than a graphic way of saying that the plaintiff has established a *prima facie* case but not one that must succeed if the defendant fails to adduce evidence.

In *Maitland v Swan and Sligo County Council*, High Court, 6 April 1992, which we analyse in greater detail in the section on professional negligence, above, 557, the *res ipsa loquitur* doctrine fell for consideration. Briefly, the case involved the removal by the defendant surgeon of the plaintiff's right ovary in circumstances where this ultimately resulted in interference with the plaintiff's procreative capacity on account of the failure of her left ovary. Barr J held that the surgeon was negligent in failing to have prior recourse to a gynaecologist for assistance and advice. He did so without reference to the *res ipsa loquitur* doctrine, rejecting the plaintiff's contention that it applied to the facts of the case. The plaintiff invoked the judgments of Henchy J (for the Court) in *Hanrahan v Merck Sharp and Dohmne (Ireland) Ltd* [1988] ILRM 629, at 634 and Morris J in *Lindsay v Mid-Western Health Board* [1993] 2 IR 147 (reversed by the Supreme Court subsequent to Barr J's judgment in *Maitland v Swan and Sligo County Council*). It will be recalled (cf. 1988 Review, 447-50) that in *Hanrahan* Henchy J had identified the defendant's pre-eminent access to the explanation of the mystery of the case as the reason for placing onus of disproof on the defendant:

> The rationale behind the shifting of the onus of proof to the defendant in such cases would appear to lie in the fact that it would be palpably unfair to require a plaintiff to prove something which is beyond his reach and which is peculiarly within the range of the defendant's capacity of proof.

In *Lindsay*, Morris J had relied on this passage and had also quoted with approval the following passage from Denning LJ's judgment in *Cassidy v Minister for Health* [1951] 2 KB 343, at 356:

> If the plaintiff had to prove that some particular doctor or nurse was negligent, he would not be able to do it. But he was not put to that impossible task: he says, 'I went into the hospital to be cured of two still fingers. I have come out with four still fingers and my hand is useless. That should not have happened if due care had been used. Explain it, if you can'.

Barr J perceived crucial differences between the facts of *Lindsay* and *Cassidy* on the one hand and the instant case on the other. In *Lindsay* the plaintiff patient had failed to recover consciousness after routine surgery. These circumstances seemed to Barr J to be precisely within the ambit of Henchy J's *dictum* in *Hanrahan* that 'it would be palpably unfair to require a plaintiff to prove something which is beyond his reach and which is particularly within the range of the defendant's capacity of proof'. In contrast, in the instant case there was no immediate unexplained damage arising out of or contemporaneously with the operation performed by the surgeon on the plaintiff. The plaintiff's case was not that the surgeon had been negligent *per se* in removing the plaintiff's right ovary but rather that in a wider context of professional responsibility the removal constituted negligence. In making the case of negligence in this wider context the plaintiff had all the information that was known to the defendant, who had no recollection of the operation and was forced to rely on his documentation made shortly after the operation. In these circumstances, the plaintiff was not required to prove something which was 'beyond [her] reach and which [was] within the defendant's capacity of proof'. Furthermore, the defendant's removal of the right ovary was not in itself evidence of negligence on his part; it would be so only if the cyst affecting the plaintiff's right ovary had not destroyed all functional ovarian tissue. If it had done so, then the removal of the ovary would not have caused the plaintiff further harm.

Barr J's conclusion is convincing. He was of course bound to follow the Supreme Court decision in *Hanrahan* and was thus obliged to address *res ipsa loquitur* in terms of the defendant's superior access to knowledge of how the injury occurred. As we argued in the 1988 Review, 448-9, this is not the best way of formulating the *res ipsa loquitur* doctrine.

**Occupier's liability** In *Foley v Quinnsworth*, High Court, 10 April 1992 (Circuit Appeal), the plaintiff, a customer in the defendant's store, suddenly slipped and fell backwards when wheeling a trolley, with her infant daughter sitting in it, along the home baking/soup aisle. Why she fell was a mystery. Neither the plaintiff nor her mother saw anything untoward on the ground. The trainee manager for the store and a cleaner whose responsibility lay in this area examined the floor and found nothing. The defendant's system of operations was that for every aisle an employee had responsibility to pack the shelves and keep an eye on it. If the employee saw a spillage, he or she was required to stand beside it until some other member of staff came to clean it up. The cleaner spent her time sweeping the aisles and cleaning up spillages.

The plaintiff claimed that the doctrine of *res ipsa loquitur* applied, arguing that, as she was doing nothing wrong and fell for no known cause, there should be 'a *prima facie* assumption of negligence' and the onus should shift to the defendant to disprove negligence. Carroll J rejected this contention, and granted the defendant's application for a non-suit. The instant case fell well short of *Mullen v Quinnsworth t/a Crazy Prices (No. 1)* [1991] IR 59, which applied the doctrine *where there was a slippery substance on the floor*. The doctrine could not apply, said Carroll J, where there was no known cause or reason for the accident:

> It would be tantamount to imposing absolute liability on a defendant. How could a defendant prove there was no negligence, if the cause of the accident is not known?

Carroll J's rejection of the application of the *res ipsa loquitur* doctrine seems undoubtedly correct; her reasoning leading to that conclusion gives pause for thought. The essential flaw in the plaintiff's case was the absence of any coherent evidence linking her injury to any act or omission of the defendant. Perhaps the reference to 'absolute liability', which echoes the argument of defence counsel in *Mullen v Quinnsworth t/a Crazy Prices (No. 1)*, might with advantage have been omitted. It is one thing to impose liability on a defendant for an act or omission causing injury to the plaintiff, where the defendant is guilty of no fault. This type of liability may properly be characterised as absolute. It is quite another thing to impose liability on a defendant whose act or omission is not shown to have caused the plaintiff the injury of which he or she complains. For the Court to hold against a defendant in such circumstances is to breach, or dispense with, the requirement of proof of causal implication rather than merely to dispense with the requirement of proof of fault.

There is no universal rule that *res ipsa loquitur* has no application in cases where the cause of the accident is not known. There are *some* instances where it does indeed apply even though the cause of the accident cannot be specifically determined. These cases occur where the plaintiff can establish that the injury was caused by an instrumentality under the defendant's control. In such circumstances, if accidents such as the one that occurred do not usually happen when those who have control take due care, then the doctrine of *res ipsa loquitur* applies. At this point, the court becomes interested in determining what was the *precise* cause of the injury. Often this can never be established, either because the defendant does not choose to disclose the true explanation or because the precise cause of the accident is as much a mystery to the defendant as it is to the plaintiff. An air crash can lead to the application of the *res ipsa loquitur* doctrine because air crashes do not usually occur without negligence on the part of the airline. If the 'black box' is not recovered the airline will have to compensate the relatives of those killed in the crash, even though the cause of the accident is unknown to it. Another way a defendant can escape liability in circumstances where the court has applied the *res ipsa loquitur* doctrine is to establish that he or she could not have been negligent in the circumstances of the case. If this can be done, the plaintiff will lose, even though the actual cause of the injury has not been identified. See our discussion of *Lindsay v Mid-Western Health Board* [1993] ILRM 550; [1993] 2 IR 147, above, 492-8.

In the 1988 Review, 447-50, we criticised the Supreme Court's restatement of the *res ipsa loquitur* doctrine in *Hanrahan v Merck, Sharp & Dohme (Ireland) Ltd* [1988] ILRM 629. One of the reasons for our concern was that the doctrine can have application only where the plaintiff has shown that the instrumentality which caused him or her damage was under the control of the defendant, and this was the very issue that required resolution in *Hanrahan*. It simply is not possible to invoke the doctrine until that issue has been determined in the affirmative.

A number of commentators have expressed dissatisfaction with the requirement that the *res ipsa loquitur* doctrine should require that injury be caused by an *instrumentality* under the defendant's *control*. Both concepts create unnecessary artificialities. In a supermarket slip-and-fall injury, what is the instrumentality? The spilled cooking oil or yoghurt on the floor? The floor? Or the entire shop premises? In some cases it may be very hard to point to any instrumentality that caused the injury and far easier to identify a *process* or *system*. The notion of control is equally a source of anomalies. If a gas central heating system explodes two hours after it had been installed, there may be strong circumstantial evidence that the installer was negligent, yet it can not be credibly argued that the installer was still in control of the system at the time of the explosion. Courts have therefore engaged in unconvincing characterisations of control in order to ensure that the case benefits from the *res ipsa loquitur* doctrine. Cf. McMahon & Binchy, op. cit., 135-6.

In *Redmond v Equipment Company of Ireland Ltd*, High Court, 28 July 1992, the plaintiff, a security guard, was injured by a tyre which was blown off a stack of tyres by a high wind. Budd J imposed liability on the occupier: we discuss this aspect of the case above 586-8. He did not rely on the doctrine of *res ipsa loquitur*, invoked by the counsel for the plaintiff, who had argued that four tyres would not roll off the pile unless they had been stacked negligently. Budd J considered that the evidence of the plaintiff provided an explanation of what had occurred: that the tyres had indeed been stacked so haphazardly and at such a height that they were reasonably susceptible to being blown down by a wind of the force that was blowing that day.

## BREACH OF STATUTORY DUTY

**Health and Safety legislation** In *Power v Crowley and Reddy Enterprises Ltd*, High Court, 29 October 1992, Blayney J imposed liability on the second defendant, under the rubric of occupier's liability, for failing to order the plaintiff not to demolish a wall after another worker had made a hole in it. We examine this aspect of the case above, 591-2. Here we are concerned with the plaintiff's allegation of breach of statutory duty against both defendants.

Against the first defendant, his employer, the plaintiff successfully contended that he had failed to comply with certain of the Construction (Safety, Health and Welfare) Regulations 1975 (SI No. 282 of 1975). Against the second defendant, he argued that it should be deemed the occupier of a factory, under s. 43(1) of the Safety in Industry Act 1980, for the purposes of the application of s. 88 of the Factories Act 1955 to the building works being carried out by the first defendant.

As to the first defendant's statutory liability, the first defendant came within the definition of 'contractor' in paragraph 3 of the 1975 Regulations and under paragraph 5(3) it was his duty to comply with the requirements of Regulations 43 to 46 'insofar as they relate to the falling of materials and articles'. The work of taking down the two walls on the day in question constituted 'demolition operations' under Regulation 43, which defines the term as meaning 'the demolition of the whole or any substantial part of a building or other structure. . . .' The first defendant thus fell under a duty to comply with the provisions of Regulation 44(1), which requires contractors undertaking demolition operations to appoint a competent person experienced in such operations to supervise the work. He was required, moreover, to comply with Regulation 46(2), which made it necessary to have the supervision or direction of a competent foreman or chargehand when demolishing any building, or structure or part of it. The first defendant was in breach of these regulations since he had not appointed anyone to supervise the work and the work had not been carried out under the supervision or direction of a competent foreman or chargehand. Blayney J went so far as to express the tentative view, *obiter*, that he was probably also guilty of negligence at common law.

Turning to the allegation of breach of statutory duty against the second defendant, Blayney J first examined the question whether it came within the provisions of s. 43 of the Safety in Industry Act 1980. This section provides that where a person undertakes building operations or works of engineering construction to which, by virtue of s. 88 or 89 of the Factories Act 1955, the provisions of the 1955 Act apply, then:

> any person, other than the first mentioned person or any employee of the first mentioned person, who designs and controls or directs the operations or works, or supervises the manner in which or the method by which the operations or works are carried out, shall be deemed for the purposes of the said provisions, in their application to the operations or works, to be the occupier of a factory.

The architectural technician, practising as an architect, who designed and put out the tender for the refurbishment scheme in relation to the premises, on the instructions of the second defendant, and who supervised the first defendant's building operations should, in Blayney J's view, be deemed the occupier for the purpose of s. 88. But he had not designed or supervised the works *on his own behalf*; he had done so *solely as agent for the second defendant*. The question at issue, therefore, was whether the second defendant also came within the section on the principle, *qui facit per alium facit per se*.

Blayney J, adopting a literal rather than teleological approach, held that the section should *not* be construed as bringing the second defendant within its scope. One had to construe the actual words listed in the section without making any addition to them. On this basis the section applied only to *the actual person* who designed and controlled or directed the operations or works. For the section to apply to that person's principal, additional words would have had to be inserted so as to read 'any person who, personally or by his agent. . . .' In the absence of such, or similar, words, the section did not apply to the second defendant.

Blayney J's preference for a literal approach is of interest. Of course there are many Supreme Court precedents where a literal interpretation was adopted by the Court which laid emphasis upon the absence of qualification in statutory language, when interpreting provisions as involving strict or absolute liability rather than incorporating the requirement of fault on the part of factory proprietors or owners of mines and quarries see, e.g., *Doherty v Bowaters Irish Wallboard Mills Ltd* [1986] IR 277; *Gallagher v Mogul of Ireland Ltd* [1975] IR 205; cf. McMahon & Binchy, op. cit., 388-90. One suspects that, in adopting this course, the Supreme Court was not unmindful of the policy implications of doing so. The purpose of the Factories Acts and related litigation was undoubtedly to protect workers from injury and to force onto employers, under pain of criminal and civil sanctions, the task of introducing an adequate regime of safety on their premises.

It is an entirely different policy, however, to force people who are not employers to assume the burden of heavy safety precautions appropriate to those of employers of factories merely because they engage the services of independent contractors who in turn employ persons to work for them on the premises of those who have engaged those services. A teleological approach to s. 43(1) would have yielded the same result as that attained by Blayney J's journey via the literal route.

Finally, it should be noted that Blayney J rejected, on the evidence, the plaintiff's contention that the second defendant's director came within s. 43 because he had supervised the manner in which the wall was being demolished. While the director was undoubtedly from time to time in the area where the work was going on, Blayney J was satisfied that he had not in fact supervised it:

> He had retained [the architect] to do this. While he saw what was being done, and was obviously interested in the progress of the work, he did nothing which could be described as amounting to supervision of the work.

This holding seems eminently reasonable but its good sense may to some degree be contrasted with the imposition of liability in *negligence* on the second defendant by reference, in part, to the reliance reposed by the plaintiff on the director's comment about the safety of the wall: see above. If, as seems reasonable to hold. the director was in no way supervising the demolition, why should the plaintiff have given any heed to his view as to the wall's safety?

**Harbours legislation** In *John C. Doherty Timber Ltd v Drogheda Harbour Commissioners* [1993] ILRM 401; [1993] 1 IR 315, which we have analysed earlier in the chapter, above 552-3 in relation to the duty of care, Flood J addressed the question whether the plaintiffs could succeed in an action for breach of statutory duty where a consignment of timber which the defendant harbour authority permitted them to leave on the quayside was destroyed by fire caused by young children. S. 47 of the Harbours Act 1946 provides as follows:

> (1) A harbour authority shall take all proper measures for the management, control and operation of their harbour and shall provide reasonable facilities and accommodation therein for vessels, goods and passengers.
>
> (2) A harbour authority shall take all proper measures for the maintenance and operation of all works, structures, bridges, equipment and facilities under their control.

The plaintiff argued that the proper management of the harbour, using the phrase in an extended sense of the facilities in the harbour area, required reasonable provision of security or security services in respect of goods deposited in the harbour area.

Flood J held that the defendants were not in breach of the section. Undoubtedly their duties under it were very wide but they had to be related to the physical reality presented by the quayside in question:

> This quay has been used as an open quay virtually since the founding of the harbour back in the seventeenth century. It is in fact part of a public thoroughfare and to impose a duty of safe custody or something akin to safe custody on the harbour authority in relation to goods permitted to be placed on the quayside and placed by the owners thereof in the full knowledge that the quayside was open to all and sundry, would be an excessively wide interpretation of the duties imposed by this section and would be unrealistic. In my opinion no such duty can be inferred from this section.

This conclusion seems eminently sensible. The courts would be well advised to avoid giving artificially broad interpretations of statutory provisions simply to find a crock of gold for plaintiffs. This is especially so where (as here) the plaintiff's case in common law negligence has been defeated by a judicial finding that the defendant did not owe the plaintiff a duty of care to prevent the loss that occurred.

## CONTRIBUTORY NEGLIGENCE

In *Power v Crowley and Reddy Enterprises Ltd*, High Court, 29 October 1992, Blayney J imposed liability, on occupier's liability principles, on the second defendant for the failure of its director to order the plaintiff, a carpenter, to stop demolishing a ten-foot high internal wall where a labourer working with the plaintiff had removed a line of blocks at a height of three feet. In our analysis of this aspect of the case, above, 601-3, we express the view the disposition of liability on this basis was at variance with established case law.

On the issue of the plaintiff's contributory negligence in proceeding to attempt to knock down the wall, Blayney J observed that it was clear that the plaintiff considered that the wall was dangerous and that he had no experience of demolishing walls. As between the plaintiff and the labourer working with him, it appeared that the plaintiff had been in charge and thus had to consider the labourer's safety as well as his own. While the plaintiff had undoubtedly been influenced by the director's remark that the wall was not going to stir, 'he ought to have realised that [the director] was not an expert, and so his opinion carried no greater weight than his own, and further that his opinion could have been influenced by his desire to see the work progress'. Blayney J reduced the plaintiff's damages by 50% on account of his contributory negligence.

## VICARIOUS LIABILITY

**Motor vehicles** S. 118 of the Road Traffic Act 1961, continuing a policy that goes back to the Road Traffic Act 1934, has enabled our courts to do overtly what courts in other jurisdictions have been required to resort to legal fictions to achieve: ensuring that those injured in traffic accidents will have maximum access to an insurance fund in cases where the negligent driver is uninsured. In *Buckley v Johnson & Perrott Ltd and Woods*, High Court, 29 July 1992 (Circuit Appeal), Lavan J rightly observed that s. 118 was 'intended to affect a radical extension of the principles of . . . vicarious liability in order to ensure that the victim of a traffic accident was not confined by common law principles in his remedy to damages in an action against a driver who might be uninsured'.

In *Buckley*, the second defendant, who had rented a car from the first defendant, failed to return it within the agreed rental period and was involved in an accident a few hours later. Clearly he was in breach of his rental contract, the sanction for which was an extra charge; but could it be said that he was driving *without the consent* of the first defendant?

Lavan J concluded that the answer was in the negative. The first defendant had taken no steps to repudiate its consent to the second defendant's continuing to drive the vehicle after 5.20 pm. The fact that the first defendant had the practice of making an extra charge for tardiness, part of which was attributable to insurance cover, encouraged this conclusion. Once it was established that a consent within the meaning of s. 118 could be implied, it was not material that the first defendant had not consented to the driving of the vehicle where the driver was not insured.

In *Guerin v Guerin and McGrath* [1993] ILRM 243; [1992] 2 IR 287, Costello J had to resolve what was essentially a question of fact, as a preliminary issue, in relation to s. 118 of the Road Traffic Act 1961. The plaintiff had been injured by a car owned by the first defendant, his brother, and driven by the second defendant. The first defendant had previously gone to live in England, leaving his car behind him. No other member of the family was able to drive. When he was leaving, the first defendant arranged with a neighbour of the family that the neighbour would drive them to Mass. He left the keys of the car with his father. On the day of the accident, the father suggested that the second defendant should take the car and drive to the post office and he gave him the keys.

There was no doubt, therefore, that the second defendant was driving with the consent of the father of the first defendant but it was argued on behalf of the first defendant that he had restricted his permission to the neighbour. Costello J rejected this recollection as mistaken. The father was, in the words of his wife, 'a hard man to deal with'. He had a drink problem. Costello J thought it 'inherently improbable' that the first defendant, who was twenty years old when he left for England, would have directed his father that only the neighbour was permitted to drive the vehicle:

> He left the car in his father's custody knowing that neither he nor anyone else in his family could drive it, but he had no objection to the car being used for the convenience of the family. In the absence of specific restriction I think that there was an implied consent that the car could be used for family purposes by persons allowed to drive by [the father]. I must hold therefore that [the second defendant] was driving with the implied consent of [the first defendant] on the occasion of the accident, and was his servant or agent.

**Control as the basis of liability** In *Phelan v Coilte Teoranta, Ireland, Attorney General and Minister for Fisheries and Forestry*, High Court, 12 October 1992, the question of vicarious liability arose in the context of an act of negligence by a welder/fitter who carried out work for the first defendant, a company owned by the State which manages all State forests on behalf of the Minister for Fisheries and Forestry, the fourth defendant. The welder/fitter worked full-time for Coilte. His job took him to forests all over the State wherever machinery required his attention. He was paid an agreed hourly rate, which was negotiated each year, together with a mileage allowance for his own vehicle. He provided his own tools and equipment. He was not entitled to holiday pay and had no pension rights, nor were PAYE tax or PRSI contributions deducted by Coilte. As regards instructions for work, on some occasions he met a Coilte engineer who gave him instructions on what was to be done but in most cases an engineer or supervisor would make contact and ask him to attend to a machine that had broken down or had been damaged in a particular forest. He did not provide any labour for Coilte other than his own. 99% of his time was spent working for Coilte. From time to time, Coilte directed one of their employees to assist him, as happened in the instant case.

Barr J approached the question on the basis that the predominant thread running through most of the authorities was that of *control* of the employee by the employer:

> Although control is not invariably a crucial factor (e.g. it is not so where the [alleged] employee is a specialist having a professional qualification such as a surgeon or physician on the staff of a hospital), in cases where the employer's right to direct the worker as to how he shall perform his task is the norm, it is of major significance. . . . The *raison d'être* for th[e] distinction [between contracts of service and contracts for services] is simply that (subject to exceptions which are irrelevant to this case) there is no justification in law for holding an employer vicariously liable for the negligence of a person over whom he has no control.

Barr J went on to note that, within the confines of contracts of service, the degree of control exercised by the employer in practice would vary enormously. A new inexperienced apprentice might well require detailed instructions on how he should perform the task in hand, whereas an experienced tradesman would rarely require any instruction on how he should do his work.

Barr J considered that, in reviewing the nature and degree of control exercised or exercisable by the putative employer in a given case, it was useful to compare that situation under review with what one would expect to find if the relationship was one arising under a normal contract of service. Here the person in question was a skilled tradesman. Such a person, whether employed under a contract of service or otherwise, rarely if ever required instruction from his employer as to *how* to do his work. He was told what to do but, in general, the employer did not interfere with the tradesman in the exercise of his skills and the tradesman decided how the work should be performed.

In the instant case, the evidence indicated that the welder/fitter's work was no different from what one would have expected if his employment by Coilte had been on foot of a normal contract of service. It seemed probable to Barr J that the nature and extent of control over him as exercised by engineers and supervisors would have been no different in the latter case. In terms of his day to day working life there were also other significant factors indicative of a contract of service: he was employed on a full-time basis by Coilte, he occasionally received specific instructions from the engineer on the site about particular jobs, he did not provide labour other than his own and was given assistance when necessary by Coilte and he was paid a mileage allowance for use of his own car.

Barr J acknowledged that there were other factors which might at first indicate that the relationship was one arising out of a contract for services, but the fact that he provided his own tools and equipment was not one of these:

> Many tradesmen, such as motor mechanics and carpenters, traditionally provide their own tools. It may well be that the rates of remuneration negotiated between the parties included an element of 'tool money'.

Barr J considered that the factors pointing in favour of an independent contractor status were 'essentially financial in nature' and did not in any way affect the working aspect of the relationship. These related to the mode of remuneration and the absence of a pension and holiday pay.

It seemed to Barr J that, where an employer and full-time employee decided to structure their relationship in such a way that it was most cost effective for both, but in so doing did not interfere with the work aspect of the agreement which had the hallmark of a contract of service, it would be 'quite unreal and also unjust' for a court to hold that the rights of an injured third party against the employer would thereby be fundamentally altered to such an extent as to render the employer free from vicarious liability which otherwise he would have had for the negligence of his employee:

> The Court ought not to ignore the realities of the relationship, in particular the control exercisable by the employer over the employee and his work is unaffected by the financial aspects of the context between them.

In Barr J's view, the proper course was to examine the work aspect of the employment contract under review in all its facets and decide whether it was indicative of a contract of service or one for services. In the instant case, the work aspect of the agreement indicated a contract of service and therefore Coilte was vicariously liable for the welder/fitter's negligence.

Barr J was willing to go further. He was satisfied that, in a case such as the present, where the degree of control that was exercisable by the party sought to be made vicariously liable was 'the same as one would expect a master to have over a tradesman servant', then that party should be vicariously liable *even if the person under such control was found to be an independent contractor.*

This emphasis on *control* reflects the thrust of judicial thought in the past couple of decades in tort litigation, most notably in the controversial Supreme Court decision on *Moynihan v Moynihan* [1975] IR 192. The willingness of courts in this context to look beyond contractual form to empirical reality may be contrasted with the somewhat acquiescent attitude in relation to tax avoidance schemes: cf. *McGrath v McDermott (Inspector of Taxes)* [1988] 647; [1988] IR 258, analysed in the 1988 Review, 356-8 and *O'Grady v Laragan Quarries Ltd*, High Court, 27 June 1990, analysed in the 1990 Review, 184-6.

**Extra-hazardous activities** In the realm of vicarious liability, courts have required that a person be liable for the tort of an independent contractor where the independent contractor has been engaged to perform an 'extra-hazardous' activity: see McMahon & Bincy, op. cit., 761-2. In such circumstances the person may not be relieved of liability simply by asking another to perform the task.

In *Power v Crowley and Reddy Enterprises Ltd*, High Court, Blayney J, 29 October 1991, the plaintiff, a carpenter, was injured when demolishing a ten-foot high wall on the second defendant's premises. A labourer working with the plaintiff had rendered the wall highly unsafe by knocking out blocks from it at a height of three feet, leaving a gaping hole in the wall. We examine the plaintiff's successful claim against the second defendant, his employer, above, 601-3. Here we are concerned with the plaintiff's suggestion that the demolition of the wall was an extra-hazardous operation which imposed a duty on the second defendant to see that care was taken.

Blayney J rejected this argument. He considered that the law was correctly stated by *Salmond & Heuston on the Law of Torts* (19th ed.), p. 545, as follows:

> The real question is whether the defendant is, in the circumstances of the particular case, in breach of a duty which he owes to the plaintiff. If the plaintiff proves such a breach it is no defence to say that another has been asked to perform it. The performance of the duties, but not the responsibility for that performance, can be delegated to another. This seems to be all that is meant by talk of 'non-delegable duties'.
>
> The main difficulty in this branch of the law is to discover when the law will impose such a duty. One thing can, however, be said with confidence: the mere fact that the work entrusted to the contractor is of a character which may cause damage to others unless precautions are taken is not sufficient to impose liability on the employer. There are few operations entrusted to an agent which are not capable, if due precautions are not observed, of being sources of danger and mischief to others; and if the principal was responsible for this reason alone, the distinction between servants and independent contractors would be practically eliminated from the law.

Blayney J considered that the job in question could have been performed perfectly safely if carried out with reasonable care. Had scaffolding been used, as it had on another wall before it went missing during lunchtime, Blayney J had no doubt that the second wall would have also been taken down without incident. The demolition of the wall was thus not an extra-hazardous operation in respect of which the second defendant could be held vicariously liable for the negligence of the independent contractor.

In this context we should note the decision of the Supreme Court in *Connolly v Dundalk Urban District Council and Mahon & McPhillips* [1990] 2 IR 1, which we discuss above, 568-9. There the court held that an employer's duty to take reasonable steps to provide employees with a safe plant and a safe place of work is, in essence, non-delegable. This may not be easy to harmonise with Blayney J's approach.

## PRODUCT LIABILITY

In the 1991 Review, 434, we noted that in *Best v Wellcome Foundation Ltd*, High Court, 11 June 1991 Hamilton P had held that the defendant manufacturer had been negligent in releasing a particular batch of whooping cough vaccine but that this had not caused the plaintiff's injuries. We also noted that the Supreme Court on 3 June 1992 had reversed this finding as to causation: [1992] ILRM 609.

The proceedings raised an important issue of general public importance: whether the pertussis (whooping cough) component of the DTP (diphtheria, tetanus and pertussis) vaccine could cause encephalopathy. The plaintiff had developed this condition shortly after having received the vaccine. There was evidence that the particular batch from which the plaintiff had been injected had not complied wiht the accepted standards with regard to potency and toxicity but that the defendant manufacturer had nevertheless released the batch for commercial distribution.

Much of the case was concerned with what was a crucial question of evidence relating to the time when the plaintiff first manifested the condition of encephalopathy. If this was not shortly after the time he was vaccinated there was *no* possibility that the vaccination was the cause; if it was shortly afterwards, then the issue of the vaccine's possible causal role would have to be investigated and determined.

Hamilton P held that the condition first manifested itself so long after the vaccination as to exclude its possible causal role. He did, however, hold that the defendant manufacturer had been negligent in releasing the batch in view of its failure to comply with the accepted standards. On the general scientific question whether encephalopathy could result (albeit in rare cases) from the vaccine when it *complied* with the accepted standards, Hamilton P received a great deal of conflicting evidence. He expressed the conclusion that 'there was a possibility that the pertussis component in the vaccine could in some rare cases cause encephalopathy'. It is not clear whether he envisaged that these 'rare cases' were limited to cases where the accepted standards had not been complied with. The point is of great significance, since important and difficult questions concerning the possibilities of negligence liability would arise if *properly tested* whooping cough vaccine is capable of causing encephalopathy.

The Supreme Court, as we have mentioned, reversed Hamilton P on the evidential question relating to the time of the occurrence of the plaintiff's first convulsion. It upheld his holding on the link between the vaccine distributed by the defendant manufacturer and the onset of the plaintiff's condition. Accordingly it held that the plaintiff was entitled to succeed against the defendant manufacturer.

In an important passage in his judgment, Finlay CJ said that he was:

> satisfied that it is not possible either for a judge of trial or for an appellate court to take upon itself the role of a determining, scientific authority resolving disputes between distinguished scientists in any particular line of technical expertise. The function which a court can and must perform in the trial of a case, in order to acquire a just result, is to apply common sense and a careful understanding of the logic and likelihood of events to conflicting opinions and conflicting theories concerning a matter of this kind.

With respect, the task of the judiciary on some occasions cannot be sidestepped so easily. This case raised the clear question as to whether or not the vaccine, when complying with accepted standards, could cause encephalopathy. No doubt the court would not wish to have to decide such a controversial question especially when an affirmative answer would have such important downstream effects, but this does not mean that the court can avoid the responsibility on the entirely unconvincing basis that it is not its function to determine a scientific issue on which the scientific community is divided. The court does this every day in medical malpractice litigation. What was distinctive about the *Best* case was not that the court had to determine a scientific controversy but rather that the particular scientific controversy had such a significant political dimension, with major consequences for public health policy.

In his concurring judgment, O'Flaherty J interpreted Hamilton P's judgment as involving a finding that post-pertussis vaccine encephalopathy exists. O'Flaherty J's observations give no clear indication that he considered this finding to be limited to cases where the accepted standards had not been complied with, but the tenor of his remarks does not appear to provide clear support for that limitation.

## FATAL INJURIES

In *Hollywood v Cork Harbour Commissioners* [1992] 2 IR 457, which we discuss above, 573, on the issue of employers' liability, the deceased was killed as a result of the defendants' negligence. At the time of his death he was fifty eight years old. He had married at the age of twenty-one; his wife had left him two years later. Within the next six years he set up house with a woman. The couple lived together for the remainder of his life and the woman bore him five children. She was initially named as one of the dependants of the deceased but did not ultimately press her claim. Nonetheless, O'Hanlon J thought it desirable to express a view, *obiter*, on the entitlement of a person in her place to sue under part of the Civil Liability Act 1961.

O'Hanlon J held that the woman was a person in respect of whom the deceased had been *in loco parentis*, and thus fell within the definition of 'dependant' in s. 47 of the Act. He observed:

> While it may seem bizarre to suggest that someone should be regarded as standing *in loco parentis* to a partner in a relationship which has all the characteristics of a marital relationship save the blessing of the law, the phrase can, in my opinion, be construed as referring to any situation where one person assumes the moral responsibility, not binding in law, to provide for the material needs of another.

O'Hanlon J ruled that it had been accepted in a series of decisions culminating in *In re Ashton, Ingram v Papillon* [1897] 2 Ch 574 that the term *in loco parentis* referred to the single circumstance that a person had assumed a moral obligation to provide for another's material needs and welfare and did not refer to any other of the functions and duties that devolved on a parent in the relationship of parent and child. Viewed in this light, it appeared to O'Hanlon J that the dependent party need not be a child but might be an adult and that the relationship between the parties need not be a broad relationship of the kind that would in ordinary circumstances subsist between their 'members of family' referred to in s. 47(1) of the Act.

O'Hanlon J expressed the view that it would be preferable if the matter could be clarified at some stage by legislation 'to give effect to what already appears to be the intention of the Act, namely, to establish a claim in favour of those who were really and genuinely financially dependent on the deceased at the time of his death'. It is doubtful, however, whether this was in fact the true intent of the Oireachtas. The idea that the expression *in loco parentis* should extend as far as O'Hanlon J was willing to press it would unquestionably have surprised the legislators.

## LOSS OF CONSORTIUM

In the 1989 Review, 441-3, we analysed Johnson J's decision in *McKinley v Minister for Defence*, High Court, 15 November 1989, Irish Times Law Report, 14 May 1990, refusing to strike out an action brought by the plaintiff for loss of her husband's consortium. The husband had been severely injured in an explosion allegedly caused by the defendants' negligence, which resulted in a condition of sterility and impotence.

On appeal, the Supreme Court, by a three-two majority (Hederman, McCarthy and O'Flaherty JJ; Finlay CJ and Egan J dissenting) upheld Johnson J: [1992] 2 IR 333. The analysis and resolution of the issue range widely from one judgment to another and are worthy of close examination. The most straight-forward conflict may be perceived in the judgments of O'Flaherty J and Finlay CJ since they proceed on essentially the same premises and differ only in their conclusion.

O'Flaherty J conceded that the action for loss of *consortium* was of 'discredited and anomalous ancestry and one . . . clearly discriminatory of wives. . . .' Nevertheless, he considered that the better approach was to extend the action to wives rather than remove the anomaly by holding that the cause of action had not survived the enactment of the Constitution:

> If the history of the law is not only logic but experience, that experience goes to show that many matters that started out as anomalies in the course of time and by a process of refinement were brought into alignment so as to ensure that a just solution was evolved. The history of the development of the equitable jurisdiction of the courts is replete with such examples. So, too, is the history of the development of the law relating to employers and employees. The law originally regarded the master as having a property in his servant. A random glance through any law digest of the last thirty years or so will show how far 'ownership' has come around to providing extensively instead for the duties that an employer owes to his employees.

O'Flaherty J considered that an analogy might be drawn with the shift in judicial thinking in another domestic area. Formerly, courts had taken the view that a husband, wife, parent or child should not be entitled to compensation for looking after an injured relative, since they thought that these services should be rendered gratuitously. This had meant that the wrongdoer was saved the obligation to make due compensation. Nowadays, O'Flaherty J thought, courts would regard such persons as being 'entitled to be justly compensated in their endeavours in regard to the injured party *but as part of the injured party's claim for damages*'.

O'Flaherty J went on to express the view that it was noteworthy that in certain decisions in the United States the extension of the remedy for loss of *consortium* to wives had been based as a matter of equal protection under constitutional provisions. He cited Prosser & Keeton's *Handbook of the Law of Torts* (5th ed. by W. Page Keeton, 1984), pp. 931-2 in this context.

O'Flaherty J based his conclusion that the right of action should be extended to wives, not only on the equality provisions of the Constitution but also on the fact that the Constitution gives marriage a special recognition and lays down that no law is to be enacted providing for the dissolution of marriage. This highlighted the need to afford equal rights to both spouses. O'Flaherty J's approval on this aspect of the case is similar to that adopted by Barr J in *C.M. v T.M.* [1988] ILRM 456 and in *C.M. v T.M. (No. 2)*, 30 November 1989: see the 1989 Review, 88-90.

Finlay CJ's dissent proceeded as follows. He had no doubt that the common law right of action for loss of *consortium* and *servitium*, confined as it had been to the husband, offended against Article 40.1 of the Constitution and therefore, in that form, could not have been carried forward by Article 50. The nature of that right and the principles on which it was based at the time of the enactment of the Constitution in 1937 were not such as to make it possible to view the right of action as containing two constituents which were severable: first the right to damages for loss of *consortium* and *servitium* and, secondly, a restriction of that right to the husband:

> The whole basis of the right to damages and its origin makes it an inevitable and a constituent part of it that it must be confined to the husband. It is by reason of the particular *quasi*-proprietary right of the husband to the services of the wife that the right to claim damages for loss of them has been recognised in the common law.

The Chief Justice acknowledged it to be 'very clear' that the consequences of serious injuries to either spouse must necessarily inflict on the other spouse very considerable trauma, distress and anxiety. The provisions of the Constitution protecting, in particular, the institution of the family and the marriage on which it was founded 'could be attractively urged in support of an extension of the right', as the plaintiff had asserted. But the Chief Justice could:

> not accept . . . that such a development of the law not taking place on the basis of any extension of foreseeability, or the persons within the ambit of those entitled to claim damages for injury to another, such as has been considered in the case of *McLoughlin v O'Brian* [1983] 1 AC 410, but rather, as is urged in this case, as a 'development' of the

> common law right of the husband to damages for loss of or impairment of *consortium* and *servitium* of his wife, could possibly be correct. To establish such a 'development' would logically be to remove from the doctrine of the right to damages for loss of *consortium* and *servitium* the entire reasoning upon which it was originally based, and upon which it was based at the time of the enactment of the Constitution in 1937.

Which of these two opposing perceptions of the nature of the action is to be preferred? We suggest that O'Flaherty J's is the more convincing, for a number of reasons. First, because the most rewarding way of approaching a right of action would seem to be not simply to examine the sources from which it is derived historically, but also to seek to discover the contemporary values which it is capable of serving and which it perhaps already serves, even only partially. The notion of *consortium*, far from involving social and personal distance between spouses in fact connotes its precise opposite. The intimacy it envisages and which the right of action seeks to protect is of a type which, as Walsh J observed in *McGee v Attorney General* [1974] IR 284, at 312 is 'by its nature an area of particular privacy'. That intimacy inheres in the joint decision-making process in which spouses engage and which, the Supreme Court recognised in *In re Article 26 and the Matrimonial Home Bill 1993* [1994] 1 ILRM 241, is protected by Article 41. Courts now accept that damage to one member of a family is particularly likely to cause further injury to other members of that family. The decision of the House of Lords in *McLoughlin v O'Brian* above and of Denham J in *Mullaly v Bus Éireann* [1992] ILRM 722 are rightly regarded as progressive rather than retrospective; in contrast, Judge O'Connor's dismissal of the plaintiff's actions in *Mulholland v Murphy & Co. Ltd* (1943) 77 ILTR 212 and in *Marx v Attorney General* [1974] 1 NZLR 164 seem to us today to be quite misguided: cf. Binchy (1975) 38 Modern L Rev 468.

So far as the element of *servitium* is concerned, again it may be argued that, although it originally connoted the kind of *quasi*-proprietal relationship which has no place in contemporary culture, the law today recognises that injury to one person may cause another economic loss by depriving that other of the benefit of the injured person's labour. If a bread-winner — husband or wife — is killed through negligence, the negligent party has to compensate the spouse and children of the deceased. The task of awarding damages in such cases may involve the court in the difficult and politically controversial task of placing a value on housework and childcare, yet there has been no indication from Irish judges that they should decline to engage in this process: see, e.g., *Byrne v Houlihan* [1966] IR 274 (Supreme Court), *Fitzsimons v Bord Telecom Éireann and ESB* [1991] ILRM 276 (High Court, Barron J, 1990), *Cooper v Egan*, High Court, Barr J, 20 December 1990, *Ward v Walsh*,

Supreme Court, 31 July 1991, *McDonagh v McDonagh* [1992] ILRM 841; [1992] 1 IR 119. See our discussion in the 1990 Review, 568-74 and the 1991 Review, 443-6.

Let us now consider the two other majority judgments in *McKinley*. Hederman J regarded as 'surreal' the Attorney General's argument that the Court should hold that the action for *consortium* should be denied to a husband on the basis of the principle of equality:

> This argument is made in the context of a Constitution which gives special protection to marriage, to the family and to children and prohibits divorce. The logical extension of this argument of the Attorney General would be to believe that the framers of the Constitution had more advanced ideas about the procreation of children than was scientifically possible in 1937.

Hederman J noted that, even in common law countries with no written constitution, the increasing tempo of social change had resulted in a progressively more urgent challenge to the law:

> It has been said that it is almost certain that the common law would no longer exist if judges had not from time to time accepted the challenge and boldly laid down new principles to meet new social problems.
>
> It is perhaps even more important in countries such as Ireland with a written Constitution that we face the problems of the role of the courts in the evolution of the law.

Turning to the Constitution, Hederman J noted that the particular status which Article 41 gave to marriage 'attached to the women by virtue of Article 41.2, perhaps even to a greater extent than it attaches to the men'. The instant case, therefore, was based, not on a question of a discrimination in favour of men pre-dating the Constitution but rather on the status which the Constitution gave to marriage and to married women in particular. Articles 40 and 41 should be construed accordance with the objective, in the Preamble, that 'the dignity and freedom of the individual might be assured'. The plaintiff's dignity and freedom were assured only by a dismissal of the appeal.

McCarthy J adopted a somewhat different approach. In his opinion, where a common law rule offended against the principle of equality in a marriage relationship the solution was 'to identify and declare the equality by positive rather than negative action'. Whatever the origin of a particular common law right, however artificial its base as viewed from a modern standpoint, if, as in the instant case, such a right was so firmly established as part of the common law, equality among equals required a Court declaration to that effect, 'rather from what would be judicial legislation' by denying such a claim to the husband. The historical inequality should be dealt with by extension of the right of action to wives, 'to make the common law of Ireland conform to constitutional requirements'.

McCarthy J considered that this was 'the simpler solution'. In ruling in this fashion:

> the Court would not be legislating in matters of social policy; it would be removing discrimination. If it were to declare that the husband's right ... did not survive the enactment [of the Constitution] in 1937, the Court would be legislating in a matter of social policy. The origin of the right of action is of historical interest only; the right was so well established that, as quoted by Maguire CJ in *Spaight v Dundon* [1961] IR 201], it could only be removed by legislation.

McCarthy J's analysis may be questioned. His contention that the Constitution *requires* extension of a common law rule that offends against the principle of equality in a marriage relationship is far from self-evident. Whether such extension should be made surely cannot be resolved by some *a priori* formula but only after an investigation of the values underlying the common law rule and of the respective implications of extension and abolition. Gerard Hogan provides a detailed, convincing argument that McCarthy J's approach would yield perverse results: (1992) 14 DULJ 115, at 117-20. Perhaps McCarthy J's approach can be maintained if it is severely restricted to legal *rights of action*; thus there would be no question of extending the domicile of dependency of married women or the presumption of marital coercion. So, for example, the Family Law (Maintenance of Spouses and Children) Act 1976 might be considered to have obeyed McCarthy J's criteria in extending the right of action for maintenance to husbands as well as wives. But even in that context a right of action generating compensation on a non-discretionary basis might be thought incapable of extension to both sexes where the premise of that right is that all members of one sex are at a discernible disadvantage relative to members of the other sex. The maintenance legislation is acceptable because it does not presume that *all wives* or *all spouses* are entitled to a maintenance order for the asking. The Court must engage in an individuated enquiry in each case.

In *McKinley*, the majority was able to surmount the embarrassment of s. 35(2)(b) of the Civil Liability Act 1961, which is premised by the assumption that only a husband has a right of action for loss of *consortium*. Gerard Hogan (op. cit. at 121) points out that it would be a great deal harder to cure a statutory discrimination where the discrimination was actually *created or entombed* by legislation, as opposed to receiving passing recognition as an existing course of action. His discussion (*id.* at 122) of Keane J's decision in *Somjee v Minister for Justice* [1981] ILRM 324 is particularly enlightening.

## CONCURRENT WRONGDOERS

In the Chapter on Practice and Procedure, above, 496-7, we discuss the Supreme Court decision of *Murphy v J. Donohoe Ltd* [1993] 1 IR 527, on the question whether a settlement between the infant plaintiffs and one of four defendants, which was approved by Hamilton P, discharged the other defendants. The words of McCarthy J, in response to the complex and uncertain factual elements of the case, are worth recording by way of guidance for future litigation invoking multiple defendants:

> There is nothing wrong or inappropriate in settling an action on behalf of a person under disability before the issue of proceedings and then issuing such proceedings in order to bring the matter before the court for ruling; there is nothing improper in arriving at a settlement on the maximum amount of contribution to a plaintiff by one of a number of defendants; it might well be improper to conceal that event from the other defendants. Where, however, a settlement has been effected, there should be some permanent record of the material that was brought before the court so that a ruling might be made on the settlement. Where an action is to be tried, important issues should only be determined upon pleadings raising those issues, as amended or not. Where such an issue arises, it is not desirable that its nature be formally identified and that it be tried upon appropriate admissible evidence, including, if necessary, discovery of documents and other procedures.

## DAMAGES

**Loss of earnings** In *Power v Crowley and Reddy Enterprises Ltd*, High Court, 29 October 1992, the plaintiff, a carpenter born in 1959, was severely injured in an accident in 1987, caused by the defendant's negligence. It was clear that the plaintiff could never work again as a carpenter and Blayney J was satisfied, on the balance of probabilities, that he would never be able to find other gainful employment.

The actuarial multiplier for a loss of £1 per week up to the age of 65 was £1,036. If one multiplied the plaintiffs projected earnings in 1992, had he not been injured, by the actuarial figure, the result was £230,499. Blayney J commented:

> That is the maximum to which the plaintiff could be entitled [under this head of damages]. But a reduction has to be made on the *Reddy v Bates* [1984] ILRM 197; [1983] IR 131 principle, and I must also take into account that the figure which I allow should not be such as to make the overall figure for damages excessive.

Allowing for both these factors, Blayney J assessed damages for future loss of earnings at £150,000.

In *Phelan v Coilte Teoranta, Ireland, the Attorney General and Minister for Fisheries and Forestry*, High Court, 12 October 1992, the plaintiff, a heavy machinery operator was injured in an accident caused by the defendant's negligence. (See above 606-8). This rendered him incapable of engaging in heavy labour but still capable of light work. His orthopaedic surgeon gave evidence that the kinds of work for which the plaintiff was fit included driving a car or truck. No evidence was adduced on behalf of the plaintiff as to what he might earn as a trained commercial vehicle driver or taximan.

Barr J considered that the groundwork had not been sufficiently prepared for the introduction of actuarial evidence and that future loss of earnings ought not to be taken into account save 'in the general sense' that his job prospects had been significantly diminished and that time for re-training and 'waiting time' for employment should be taken into account.

**Evidential aspects** In *Furlong v Waterford Co-operative Society Ltd*, High Court, 31 July 1992, Budd J had to determine where the truth lay in a case involving a 'ferocious conflict' between the medical experts. One of the witnesses called for the defence, described the plaintiff as that 'rare bird, the true malingerer'. Counsel of the defendant framed the issue as being that the Judge was driven to decide whether the plaintiff was genuine when certain of the eminent medical experts said he was a malingerer.

Budd J accepted the plaintiff's evidence as truthful. Having observed the plaintiff closely over five days in court, he was convinced of the genuineness of his complaints. He did not believe that the plaintiff's general practitioner, who had known him on his home ground over the years, and an eminent and experienced consultant could have been deceived. Moreover, objective evidence relating *inter alia* to muscle wasting and nerve damage supported the finding of the plaintiff's veracity.

# Transport

## AIR TRANSPORT

**Air Cargo** The European Communities (Operation of Air Cargo Services) Regulations 1992 (SI No. 11) implemented the requirements of Council Regulation 294/91. The 1992 Regulations amended the Air Services Authorisation Order 1966 for this purpose.

**Competition** The European Communities (Application of the Rules on Competition to Air Transport) Regulations 1992 (SI No. 379) implemented the requirements of Council Regulation 3975/87 concerning competititon between air carriers.

**Rules of the Air** The Air Navigation (Rules of the Air) Order 1992 (SI No. 52) consolidates with amendments the 1973, 1974 and 1975 Orders of the same title in order to give effect to new standards contained in the Chicago Convention. The Order was made under the Air Navigation and Transport Acts 1946, 1950 and 1988.

**Sanctions** The Air Services (Authorisation) (Amendment) Order 1992 (SI No. 92) amends the 1966 Order of the same title to take account of the 1992 UN Security Council Resolution 748 concerning sanctions against Libyan civil aviation. The Air Services (Authorisation) (Amendment) (No. 2) Order 1992 (SI No. 159) amended the 1966 Order to give effect to EC Council Regulation 1432/92 on prohibiting trade with the Republics of Serbia and Montenegro, the rump of former Yugoslavia, insofar as this applied to civil aviation.

## INTERNATIONAL CARRIAGE OF GOODS BY ROAD

**Hungary** The International Carriage of Goods by Road Act 1990 (CMR Contracting Party) Order 1992 (SI No. 39) adds Hungary to the list of CMR Contracting Parties specified in the International Carriage of Goods by Road Act 1990 (CMR Contracting Parties) Order 1991. See also the Road Transport (International Carriage of Goods by Road) Order 1992 (SI No. 190) and the Road Transport Act 1978 (Section 5) Order 1992 (SI No. 191), which give effect to a road transport agreement between Ireland and Hungary by allowing Hungarian transport authorities to issue permits on behalf of this State to facilitate access by Hungarian hauliers to Ireland.

## HARBOURS

**Piloting** *Heavey v Pilotage Committee of the Dublin Pilotage Authority*, High Court, 7 May 1992 concerned the procedure for the issuing of a licence to a ship's harbour pilot. The pilot is the person who guides a ship initially from a port but will disembark shortly after the ship has left its moorings. The legislative background to the case was as follows. Pursuant to the Pilotage Act 1913, the Dublin Pilotage Order 1925 designated the Dublin Port and Docks Board as the Pilotage Authority for Dublin Port. Under Article 5 of the 1925 Order, the Board in turn delegated its functions as Pilotage Authority to a Pilotage Committee, such functions including the power to grant a pilot's licence to an applicant. The day-to-day control of ship's pilots in Dublin port was in the hands of the Pilotage Superintendent. Article 8 of the Dublin Pilotage Bye-Laws 1987 provided that, on being granted a pilot's licence for the first time the pilot would be a Pilot Class 2, and that after completion of two years service a person could apply to the Committee for indorsement as a Pilot Class 1. It continued that the Committee 'may, on the recommendation of the Pilotage Superintendent, accede to the application'.

The applicant in the *Heavey* case had been a Pilot Class 2 in Dublin port for two years and he applied under the 1987 Bye-Laws for a licence to act as Pilot Class 1 in the normal way, which was to request the Pilotage Superintendent to recommend him to the Pilotage Committee. The Superintendent told the applicant that he would do this, and had intended to raise the applicant's case at the Committee's regular monthly meeting in November 1991 but had inadvertently omitted to do so. Before the next meeting of the Committee occurred, there was a collision in Dublin port between two motor vessels, MV Hasselwerder and MV Kilkenny, with the loss of three lives on the MV Kilkenny.

The Pilotage Superintendent was required to investigate the collision under the 1987 Bye-Laws. The applicant had piloted the MV Hasselwerder out of Dublin port but had disembarked before the collision in question, and the Pilotage Superintendent informed the the applicant that he considered him to be in breach of the 1987 Bye-Laws for failing to make a written report to him concerning his piloting of the MV Hasselwerder. When the applicant raised his application for a Pilot Class 1 licence, the Superintendent indicated that he would look foolish recommending his name to the Pilotage Committee when the applicant was in breach of the 1987 Bye-Laws for not making a report and that the applicant 'should keep his head down for the moment' because of this. The applicant decided to have his application raised by a member of the Pilotage Committee at its next meeting. When the Chairman asked the Pilotage Superintendent for his views, he indicated that he could not recommend the applicant in view of his failure to compile a satisfactory report of his piloting of the MV Hasselwerder, but did not in any way wish this to be taken as being a reflection on the applicant's piloting on the date of the collision. The Pilotage Committee decided that, in the absence of a recommendation from the Pilotage Superintendent, it could not accede to the applicant's request for a Pilot Class 1 licence.

The applicant unsuccessfully sought judicial review to quash the Committee's decision.

Blayney J dealt firstly with the approach of the Committee that it could not act without a recommendation from the Pilotage Superintendent. Blayney J agreed that the Committee had correctly interpreted Article 8 of the 1987 Pilotage Bye-Laws in requiring a positive opinion from the Pilotage Superintendent before it could proceed to grant a Class 1 licence. He commented that the Committee may refuse to accept the recommendation but added: 'They are not bound to act on foot of the recommendation, but they are not free to act without it'. Although he acknowledged that the 1987 Bye-Laws need not have required the Superintendent's positive opinion on this, Blayney J considered that such a requirement was not unreasonable in view of the Superintendent's day-to-day control of pilots.

As to whether the Superintendent had acted reasonably in withholding his recommendation, Blayney J agreed that he had. In particular, he agreed that the applicant was required to furnish a full report of his piloting of the MV Hasselwerder and that this had not been forthcoming at the time of the Pilotage Committee's meeting which the applicant sought to quash. Blayney J went on to note that the applicant had since furnished a full report on this question and that his position had therefore changed. Blayney J made two comments on this. First, applying *dicta* of O'Higgins CJ in *The State (Abenglen Properties Ltd) v Dublin Corporation* [1982] ILRM 590; [1984] IR 381, he considered that since the applicant would now be entitled to renew his application and that, even if there were some grounds to quash the Committee's decision, certiorari should be refused on the ground that to grant it would not avail the applicant anything. He therefore dismissed the applicant's claim for relief. The second comment of Blayney J on the applciant's changed position was to express the hope that, in light of the applicant having furnished his report to the Superintendent, his renewed application would be successful as this seemed to the sole ground on which the initial application had been unsuccessful.

For another case in this area, see *Turner v Pilotage Committee of the Dublin Pilotage Authority*, High Court, 14 June 1988 (1988 Review, 12-14).

## MERCHANT SHIPPING

**Merchant Shipping Act 1992** Because of its significance, the Merchant Shipping Act 1992 is discussed separately below.

**Dangerous goods** The Merchant Shipping (Dangerous Goods) Rules 1992 (SI No. 391) revoke the 1983 Rules of the same title to give effect to amendments to the SOLAS Convention on the shipment of dangerous goods.

**Emergency information** The Merchant Shipping (Emergency Information for Passengers) Rules 1992 (SI No. 392) require a public address sytem be installed in ships entitled to carry more than 20 passengers.

**Fees** The Merchant Shipping (Fees) Order 1992 (SI No. 156) revised the fees payable under the Merchant Shipping Acts for certification and surveys of ships. The relevant fees for passenger boats are contained in the Merchant Shipping (Fees) (Passenger Boats) Order 1992 (SI No. 295).

**Light dues** The Merchant Shipping (Light Dues) Order 1992 (SI No. 60) revised the light dues payable to the Commissioners of Irish Lights by ships using Irish navigation facilities, such as lighthouses.

**Navigational warnings** The Merchant Shipping (Navigational Warnings) (Amendment) Rules 1992 (SI No. 444) amend the 1983 Rules of the same title so that references to Greenwich Mean Time are replaced by references to Universal Co-ordinated Time.

**Radio installations** The Merchant Shipping (Radio Installations) Rules 1992 (SI No. 28) consolidate with amendments the 1983 Rules of the same title and give effect to certain requirements of the Global Maritime Distress and Safety System (GMDSS), under the general terms of the IMO 1974 Convention for the Safety of Lives at Sea (SOLAS), as to which see below. To the same general effect, see the Merchant Shipping (Radio) Rules 1992 (SI No. 224).

**SOLAS Countries** Many recent Regulations concerning merchant shipping implement standards laid down by the International Maritime Organisation (IMO) under the 1974 Convention for the Safety of Lives at Sea (SOLAS), whose essential requirements were incorporated into Irish law by the Merchant Shipping Act 1981. The Merchant Shipping (Safety Convention) (Countries of Acceptance) Order 1992 (SI No. 307), which replaces the 1983 Order of the same title, contains a list of those countries which have accepted SOLAS.

**Tonnage measurement** In *Eurocontainer Shipping plc v Minister for the Marine*, High Court, 11 December 1992, the applicant company operated the largest merchant fleet on the Irish Register of Shipping through its subsidiary the Bell Shipping Line. In 1989, the applicant purchased a new container ship, the 'Bell Pioneer'. The ship was of a particular design, the first of its kind in the world and it differed significantly from the traditional container ship. In order to determine, *inter alia*, the shipping dues to be paid to harbour authorities all container ships must be given a tonnage measurement pursuant to the Conventions agreed by the International Maritime Organisation (IMO), of which Ireland is a member, and whose Conventions are incorporated into Irish law by the Merchant Shipping Acts 1894 to 1992, in particular the Merchant Shipping Act 1955. The Regulations on tonnage measurement are the Merchant Shipping (Tonnage) Regulations 1984.

Regulation 4(2) of the 1984 Regulations provides that in the case of 'novel types of craft with constructional features which render the application of the [measurement] provisions of these Regulations unreasonable or impracticable, the gross and net tonnage shall be determined as required by the Minister'. Because of its particular design, the applicant company considered that the 'Bell Pioneer' should be measured by the Minister in accordance with Regulation 4(2) of the 1984 Regulations and not by means of the method used for traditional container ships. The company made clear its views on this point in a meeting with the respondent Minister's Chief Surveyor and in the subsequent transmission of counsel's opinion that the 'Bell Pioneer' was a novel craft within the 1984 Regulations. In declining to accede to the company's request and in proceeding to have a tonnage survey conducted in accordance with the general terms of the 1984 Regulations, the Chief Surveyor had regard to a Memorandum of 1990 from the IMO Maritime Safety Safety Committee in which certain recommendations on the measurement of ships such as the 'Bell Pioneer' should be conducted. It was common case that these recommendations were not binding on Member States, though the Chief Surveyor appeared to act on the basis that he should follow the recommendations contained in the Memorandum. The company applied for judicial review in which they sought an order of mandamus requiring the Minister to consider the tonnage measurement of the 'Bell Pioneer' in accordance with Regulation 4(2) of the 1984 Regulations. Barr J granted the applicant the relief sought.

Noting that the Minister was required to act reasonably and fairly in connection with Regulation 4(2), he accepted that the Minister was, of course, entitled to act on the basis of advice from his officials. However, once the company had made clear its view on the application of Regulation 4(2), Barr J held that the Minister was required to deal with this, and it was accepted in this context that this was a matter which could not be delegated by the Minister under the 1984 Regulations. Of course, as Barr J pointed out, the granting of the order of mandamus did not in any way involve a determination as to whether the ship would meet the requirements of Regulation 4(2) as to novelty.

Finally, Barr J rejected the Minister's argument that relief should be refused on the ground of delay. The company's application for judicial review was made just one day short of six months after the tonnage certificate had been issued for the 'Bell Pioneer', in other words, one day within the six month time limit specified in O.84, r.21 of the Rules of the Superior Courts 1986. The company averred that it was only after some months of operating the 'Bell Pioneer' that it became fully aware of the commercial disadvantage resulting from the tonnage certificate and consequent high level of harbour dues payable. Barr J accepted that this was an acceptable explanation for the delay in applying for judicial review, applying the test laid down by McCarthy J in *The State (Furey) v Minister for Justice* [1988] ILRM 89 (on which point generally, see the 1988 Review, 33-5, and the 1991 Review, 15).

## MERCHANT SHIPPING ACT 1992

The Merchant Shipping Act 1992 is the latest in a series of over 30 Acts which have amended and updated the provisions of the monumental Merchant Shipping Act 1894. Numerous and substantial Regulations have also been made under the Merchant Shipping Acts with a view to setting out in detail the standards required. In recent years, many such Regulations implement standards laid down by the International Maritime Organisation (IMO) under the 1974 Convention for the Safety of Lives at Sea (SOLAS): see above. The fatalities associated with the sinking of the pleasure craft The Bowbelle on the London Thames and of the Irish fishery patrol vessel off Ballycotton (on the latter see the 1991 Review, 461-2) have also led to calls for increased standards for such craft. The Merchant Shipping Acts aim to protect the safety and health both of crews and, where relevant, passengers on the various types of vessels covered by their provisions.

Brian Hutchinson's Annotation, *Irish Current Law Statuts Annotated*, contains a detailed analysis of the impact of the 1992 Act on existing Merchant Shipping Acts. We provide here a brief description of main features of the 1992 Act. The Act, except for Part II, came into effect on 1 August 1992: Merchant Shipping Act 1992 (Commencement) Order 1992 (SI No. 205).

Part II of the 1992 Act (ss. 6 to 13) envisages a State-wide set of standards for passenger ships, that is vessels carrying more than 12 passengers. Part II of the 1992 Act will, when implemented, replace the requirements of Part III of the Merchant Shipping Act 1894 (ss. 271 to 286) and create a much more rigorous regime for such vessels. In particular, it increases the penalties for overcrowding in breach of the annual survey and passenger ship's certificate required by ss.6 and 8 of the 1992 Act. As indicated, Part II has not yet been brought into force. Fees under the existing 1894 Act are prescribed in the Merchant Shipping (Fees) Order 1992 (SI No. 156).

Part III of the 1992 Act (ss. 14 to 18) deals with passenger boats, that is vessels carrying not more than 12 passengers. Until the 1992 Act, these vessels were outside the scope of the Merchant Shipping Acts, and were only regulated, if at all, by requirements imposed by local authorities. The Department of the Marine is now the central authority for licensing and supervision of such passenger boats. The relevant fees for surveys and certificates, prescribed pursuant to s. 31 of the 1992 Act, are contained in the Merchant Shipping (Fees) (Passenger Boats) Order 1992 (SI No. 295).

Part IV of the 1992 Act (ss. 19 to 32) deals with a number of matters. S.19 empowers the Minister for the Marine to make Regulations concerning safety of fishing vessels and their crews. It seems likely from this specific power that Regulations to implement EC Directives on safety of fishing vessels will be made under the 1992 Act rather than under the general power of the Minister for Enterprise and Employment under the Safety, Health and Welfare at Work Act 1989 (on the 1989 Act, see the 1989 Review, 379-93). S. 20 of the 1992 Act empowers the Minister for the Marine to make Regulations concerning safety on pleasure craft, which would include pleasure craft on hire to persons on holiday who crew such a boat themselves and power boats used for water skiing or jet skiing purposes. The Merchant Shipping (Jet Skis and Fast Power Boats) Regulations 1992 (SI No. 387), made under s. 20 of the 1992 Act, provide that certain bodies, such as local authorities and harbour authorities, may make proposals to the Minister for the Marine setting out why jet skis and fast power boats should be restricted in their operation.

S. 23 creates offences and prescribes penalties concerning acts or omissions by a master or seaman which would endanger the safety of a vessel or of any person on the vessel. S. 24 authorises the master of a vessel to refuse permission to board a vessel any person who, because of being under the influence of alcohol or other reason, would be likely to cause injury or annoyance to persons on the vessel or to obstruct a crew member. Ss. 25 and 26 concern powers of entry, inspection and detention of authorised officers of the Minister for the Marine.

## ROAD TRAFFIC

**Construction Standards** The European Communities (Motor Vehicles Type Approval) Regulations 1992 (SI No. 178) and the European Communities (Motor Vehicles Type Approval) (No. 2) Regulations 1992 (SI No. 345) further amended the Principal Regulations of 1978 to take account of EC Directives laying down technical specifications for the construction of motor vehicles. SI No. 345 in effect superceded SI No. 178 by substituting a new Schedule to the 1978 Regulations listing the Directives implemented in Irish law. In particular, now implemented is Council Directive 92/53/EEC, the Framework Directive on this area, which introduces the European Whole Vehicle Type Approval (ECWVTA) system for motor vehicles, currently only applicable to passenger vehicles. This becomes fully operational on 1 January 1996. Also implemented is Directive 92/61/EEC, the Framework Directive for two three wheeled vehicles.

The Road Traffic (Construction, Equipment and Use of Vehicles) (Amendment) Regulations 1992 (SI No. 325) amend the 1963 Regulations of the same title to implement Directive 92/7/EEC on the maximum weights of certain heavy goods vehicles.

**Community transit** The European Communities (Community Transit) Regulations 1992 (SI No. 433) implemented Council Regulation 2726/90 on the Community Transit procedure and Commission Regulation 1214/92 on the implementation and simplification of the transit procedure.

**Co-ordination of roadworks** The Road Traffic (Co-ordination of Roadworks) Regulations 1992 (SI No. 323) authorised named local authorities to exercise the roadworks co-ordination powers conferred by s.101D of the Road Traffic Act 1961, as inserted by s.9 of the Dublin Transport Authority (Dissolution) Act 1987. Previous Regulations of the same title of 1988 had confined this power to Dublin Corporation.

**Dangerous Goods** The European Communities (Vocational Training for Drivers of Vehicles Carrying Dangerous Goods) Regulations 1992 (SI No. 204) are discussed in the Safety and Health chapter, 000, above.

**Emission levels** The European Communities (Mechanically Propelled Vehicle Emission Control) Regulations 1992 (SI No. 363) provide that, from 1 January 1993, new vehicles must comply with the emission levels specified in Directive 91/441/EEC, subject to the exemptions contained in Directive 92/53/EEC for certain end of series vehicles.

**Insurance** The Road Traffic (Compulsory Insurance) (Amendment) Regulations 1992 (SI No. 346) amend the 1962 Regulations of the same title in order to implement certain provisions of Directive 90/232/EEC, the Third EC Directive on Motor Insurance. It provides that the coverage required now extends to front seat passengers on goods vehicles (as from 31 December 1995) and to pillion passengers and side car passengers of motor cycles (from 31 December 1998). Coverage is not included for passengers on agricultural tractors or trailers or passengers in the rear of goods vehicles. In addition, the Regulations provide that non-resident insured persons are required to display a disc in the form required by Irish law: this gives effect to the terms of Directive 90/618/EEC, the EC Non-Life (Motor) Services Directive. The European Communities (Road Traffic) (Compulsory Insurance) (Amendment) Regulations 1992 (SI No. 347) amend the 1975 to 1987 Regulations of the same title in order to implement other elements of the two EC Directives implemented by SI No. 346, above. They extend third party cover to travel in the EC Member States as well as to certain other 'designated territories', namely, Austria, the Czech Republic, the Slovak Republic, Finland, Hungary, Norway, Sweden and Switzerland. Finally, the Mechanically Propelled Vehicles (International Circulation) Order 1992 (SI No. 384), which revoked Orders of the same title of 1961 to 1987, concern the licensing of visiting drivers; the recognition of 'green card' insurance; and that vehicles registered in the EC Member States or in the 'designated territories' referred to in SI No. 347 are deemed to be insured under the European Communities (Road Traffic) (Compulsory Insurance) Regulations 1975, as amended most recently by SI No. 347, above.

**International carriage of passengers** The European Communities (International Carriage of Passengers) Regulations 1992 (SI No. 341) revoke 1974 and 1985 Regulations of the same title and implement EC Directives concerning carriage of passengers by coach and bus.

**Licence plates** *Ní Cheallaigh v Minister for the Environment*, High Court, 4 May 1992 was an unsuccessful challenge to the constitutional validity of the licence plates requirements introduced by the Road Vehicles (Registration and Licensing) (Amendment) Regulations 1986: see the discussion in the Constitutional Law chapter, 149-51, above. However, see now the Registration and Licensing heading, below, on the Regulations made in 1992 in this regard.

**Motor car** The meaning of words 'motor car' was considered by Blayney J in *King v Cornhill Insurance Co. Ltd* [1993] 2 IR 43. The plaintiff's insurance policy with the defendant indemnified him in respect of accidents in a 'motor car' owned by another person but driven by the plaintiff. The plaintiff was involved in an accident while driving a Mitsubishi 'Shogun' owned by his father. This was a jeep-like vehicle and had no back passenger seat. At the time of the accident, the plaintiff was carrying one person in the front passenger seat and three others in the back of the vehicle. The defendant company claimed that this was not a 'motor car' within the meaning of its insurance policy and was thus not required to indemnify the plaintiff arising from the injuries sustained in the accident. In this connection, the defendant referred to the Road Traffic Act 1961, as amended, for some assistance in defining 'motor car'. The term 'motor car' is not defined in the 1961, as amended, but the defendant argued that it should be defined as a 'vehicle constructed primarily for the carriage of one or more passengers', which is one of the categories of vehicles for which compulsory insurance is required under s. 65(1)(a) of the 1961 Act and Article 6(1)(b) of the Road Traffic (Compulsory Insurance) Regulations 1962. The expert evidence tendered to the Court indicated that the practice in the insurance industry was to refuse passenger cover for a vehicle that had no seat behind the driver. The defendant thus argued that, since the 'Shogun' had no seat behind the driver, it was not a 'vehicle constructed primarily for the carriage of one or more passengers', and was thus not a motor car for the purposes of the insurance policy. Evidence for the plaintiff, however, was that many insurance companies, including the defendant, categorised the 'Shogun' as a 'private motor car.'

It was this latter evidence that led Blayney J to conclude that the 'Shogun' was a 'motor car' within the meaning of the defendant's policy. He considered also that the true test of its meaning was whether an ordinary person would understand the 'Shogun' to be a motor car, and he was satisfied that on this test the 'Shogun' was a motor car. It was thus irrelevant whether the vehicle had no back passenger seat and equally irrelevent whether the insurance company would not have given passenger cover if it had been insuring the vehicle itself. He thus concluded that the company was required to indemnify the plaintiff in respect of the injuries incurred.

**Public service vehicles** The Road Traffic (Public Service Vehicles) (Amendment) Regulations 1992 (SI No. 32) transferred the fixing of fares for public service vehicles under the 1991 Regulations of the same title from the Minister for Industry and Commerce to the Minister for the Environment. The Road Traffic (Public Service Vehicles) (Amendment) (No. 2) Regulations 1992 (SI No. 172) removed the restrictions on the creation of new licences contained in the 1991 Regulations. The Road Traffic (Public Service Vehicles) (Amendment) (No. 3) Regulations 1992 (SI No. 308) concerns taxi signs.

**Registration and licensing** The Vehicle Registration and Taxation Regulations 1992 (SI No. 318) and the Vehicle Registration and Taxation (No. 2) Regulations 1992 (SI No. 437) introduced a new method of motor vehicle registration and collection, in which the Revenue Commissioners became the central registration agency for vehicles. This was provided for in the Finance Act 1992, as amended by the Finance (No. 2) Act 1992: see the Revenue Law chapter, 503, 515, below. The Regulations also introduced a revised format for licence plates for motor vehicles, which includes the use of the Irish language version of the licensing area with which a vehicle is registered. On the use of the Irish language, see *Ní Cheallaigh v Minister for the Environment*, High Court, 4 May 1992, discussed in the Constitutional Law chapter, 149-51, above.

The Road Vehicles (Registration and Licensing) (Amendment) Regulations 1992 (SI No. 385) introduced a new change of ownership regime for motor vehicles, taking into account the role of the Revenue Commissioners became the central registration agency for vehicles. The system deals with vehicles first licensed after 1 January 1993. The Regulations also revoked a number of previous Regulations on this area.

The Road Vehicles (Registration and Licensing) (Amendment) (No. 2) Regulations 1992 (SI No. 409) laid down a new system of trade licences and plates for motor traders.

**Signs** The Road Traffic (Signs) (Amendment) Regulations 1992 (SI No. 183) provide for the relevant signs for the following: parking bays for drivers with a disability; cycle tracks; and prohibiting stopping outside school entrances.

**Speed limit: general** The Road Traffic (General and Ordinary Speed Limit) Regulations 1992 (SI No. 194) laid down a general speed limit of 60 m.p.h. for cars on main roads. The Regulations exempt ambulances, fire brigades and Garda Síochána vehicles from these limits.

**Taxi** The Road Traffic (Public Service Vehicles) (Amendment) (No. 4) Regulations 1992 (SI No. 358) reduce the maximum dimensions of wheelchairs which a vehicle must be capable of accommodating in order to be licensed as a wheelchair accessible taxi.

**Testing** The European Communities (Vehicle Testing) (Amendment) Regulations 1992 (SI No. 324) made a minor amendment to the 1991 Regulations of the same title in order to implement the requirements of Directive 88/449/EEC, requiring the production of a certificate of roadworthiness for imported used vehicles which are subject to the compulsory testing contained in the 1991 Regulations.

**Testing centre appointment** In *Jennings Truck Centre (Tullamore) Ltd v Offaly County Council*, High Court, 14 June 1990, the applicant company had been refused an authorisation to act as an authorised tester to carry out appropriate tests of roadworthiness for various vehicles pursuant to the European Communities (Vehicle Testing) Regulations 1983. The company applied for judicial review of this refusal. Rejecting the claim, Murphy J held that the provisions of the 1983 Regulations, under which a local authority 'may' appoint authorised testers clearly imposed a discretion on the local authority. Provided, as in this case, the authority had applied proper procedures, its decision could not be challenged. While he accepted that, in certain circumstances, the word 'may' could have a mandatory meaning, he held that the burden was on the plaintiff in this respect and noted that the word 'may' occurred more than once in the 1983 Regulations. He therefore declined to regard 'may' as indicating a mandatory obligation to issue an authorisation even where, as here, the applicant company appeared to meet all the requirements indicated in the Regulations as to staffing and equipment in such an authorised testing centre. In this respect, Murphy J cited with approval the decision of Carroll J in *O'Connell v South Western Fishery Board*, High Court, 15 April 1986. Since the judgment in the *Jennings* case, the 1983 Regulations have since been replaced by the European Communities (Vehicle Testing) Regulations 1991 and 1992: see the 1991 Review, 464, and immediately above.

## ROAD TRANSPORT LICENCE

**Merchandise licence** The European Communities (Merchandise Road Transport) (Amendment) Regulations 1992 (SI No. 217) amended the 1991 Regulations of the same title (1991 Review, 465) in order to allow existing operators until 30 September 1992 to comply with the provisions of the 1991 Regulations.

**Passenger licence** The European Communities (Road Passenger Transport) (Amendment) Regulations 1992 (SI No. 216) amended the 1991 Regulations of the same title (1991 Review, 465) in order to allow existing operators until 30 June 1992 to comply with the provisions of the 1991 Regulations.

## SHANNON NAVIGATION

The Shannon Navigation (Construction of Vessels) Bye-Laws 1992 (SI No. 79) and the Shannon Navigation Bye-Laws 1992 (SI No. 80) were made pursuant to the Shannon Navigation Act 1990 (see the 1990 Review, 585-6). They lay down the limits of size of vessels as well as the general rules of navigation on the Shannon, respectively.

## TOUR OPERATORS AND TRAVEL AGENTS

The Travel Agents (Licensing) (Amendment) Regulations 1992 (SI No. 175) and the Tour Operators (Licensing) (Amendment) Regulations 1992 (SI No. 176) revised the application forms and fees for travel agents and tour operators licences, respectively, which are required under the Transport (Tour Operators and Travel Agents) Act 1982. On the 1982 Act, see the 1987 Review, 242. The 1992 Regulations amended the Regulations of 1983 to 1989 of the same respective titles.

# Law Reform

In 1992, the Law Reform Commission published reports on the international sale of goods, offences of dishonesty and conveyancing. In the Conflict of Laws chapter, above, 132-3, we examine the Commission's *Report on the United Nations (Vienna) Convention on Contracts for the International Sale of Goods 1990* (LRC 42–1992). In the Criminal Law chapter, above, 275-6, we consider the Commission's *Report on the Law Relating to Dishonesty* (LRC 43–1992). In the Land Law chapter, above, 406-9, we discuss the Commission's *Report on Land Law and Conveyancing Law (5) General Proposals* (LRC 44–1992).

# Subject Index

compiled by Julitta Clancy